AUSTRIA.

VIENNA, PRAGUE, HUNGARY,

BOHEMIA, AND THE DANUBE;

GALICIA, STYRIA, MORAVIA, BUKOVINA,

AND

THE MILITARY FRONTIER.

BY J. G. KOHL

LONDON:
CHAPMAN AND HALL, 186, STRAND.
1843.

This scarce antiquarian book is included in our special *Legacy Reprint Series*. In the interest of creating a more extensive selection of rare historical book reprints, we have chosen to reproduce this title even though it may possibly have occasional imperfections such as missing and blurred pages, missing text, poor pictures, markings, dark backgrounds and other reproduction issues beyond our control. Because this work is culturally important, we have made it available as a part of our commitment to protecting, preserving and promoting the world's literature. Thank you for your understanding.

PREFACE.

The following pages consist chiefly of a condensed translation of a work in five volumes, published by Mr. Kohl last year, under the title of "A Hundred Days in Austria," comprising an account of a tour through Bohemia, Austria, Hungary, and the Military Frontier. To this has been added the concluding volume of that gentleman's work on Russia, containing his remarks on the Bukovina, Galicia, and Moravia; which, as not referring in any way to Russia, were omitted in the two first parts of the *Foreign Library;* but which, on account of their intrinsic value, have been deemed a fitting sequel to the Austrian tour.

CONTENTS.

BOHEMIA.

	PAGE
From Dresden to Teplitz	1
From Teplitz to Prague	11
Prague.—The Vissehrad	14
The Metropolitan Church on the Hradshin	22
Public Institutions and Convents	34
The Jews' Quarter	46
Popular Scenes in Prague	56
The National Movement among the Bohemians	61
The Book of Life on the Moldau	68
From Prague to Budweis	72
The Castles and Estates of Schwarzenberg	75
From Budweis to Linz	85

UPPER AUSTRIA.

Linz.—The Carpet Manufactory	88
The Madhouse	91
Jesuit School	93
Provincial Museum	96
Monastery of St. Florian	97
Visit to the House of an Austrian Peasant	102
Public Library	105
The Picture Gallery between Linz and Vienna	106

LOWER AUSTRIA.

Vienna, or Betsch	125
Visit to St. Stephen's Tower	127
The Menagerie at Schönbrun	132
The Fratschelweiber — Fishmongers and Dealers in Game	139
Summer-nights' Dreams and Flower Festivals	145
The Projected New Quarter	149
The Quarter of the Nobility and that of the Manufacturers	151
The Shops of Vienna	153
Railroads	156
Sunday Walks	160
Klosterneuburg	164

HUNGARY.

	PAGE
Oedenburg, Zinzendorf, Esterhazy, and the Neusiedler Lake	171
The Morass of Hansag and the Gulyas	179
The Raabau and Raab	185
The Abbey of Martinsburg	191
The Danube from Raab to Pesth	198
Buda.—Pesth	206
The Fair at Pesth	208
The Congregation of Nobles	215
The Bridge at Pesth	220
The Rascian Town —Turkish Baths and Oriental Pilgrims	224
Hotels and Casino at Pesth	229
The Hungarian Literary Society, and the Hungarian language	235
Ofen, or Buda	238
Public Collections	243
The Jews of Pesth	245
Hospital of St. Roche	247
The Danube in the Central Plains of Hungary	251
The Batschka and its German Colonists	256
Syrmia and Peterwardein	257
The Mouth of the Save	260
Steamboat Life	261
Cataracts of the Danube	263
A Night in the Military Frontier	265
Political Importance of the Military Frontier	269
The Lower Clissura	272
Visit to a Turkish Pasha	273
Austrian Orsova	277
The Hercules Baths at Mehadia	279
Upper Valley of the Tsherna, and Life of the Borderers	284
The Keys of Teregova and Slatina	293
Karansebes	298
Lugos, Temesva, and the Banat Fever	301
First Shower	308
First Interval of Sunshine	309
Second Shower	310
Second Sunshine	310
Third Shower	312

CONTENTS.

	PAGE
The Colonies and Lowlands of the Banat	313
Thoughts on the Peaceful Migrations of European Nations	317
The Slavonians	319
The Greeks	320
The Italians and French	321
The Germanic Nations	321
The Subordinate and Dependant Races	323
The Banat	327
Szegedin and the Italian Prisoners	333
The Pusten and their Inhabitants	341
The Kumanen, Yazygen, and Haiducken	346
Heaths of Ketskemet	349
Stuhlweissenburg.—Vesprim	354
Convent of Tihany, and the Platten lake	365
Bakony Forest; its Poets, Castles, and Robbers	373

STYRIA.

Fürstenfeld to Grätz	386
Grätz	387
From Grätz to Leoben	394
Eisenärzt and the Eisenberg	397
The Styrian Rocks	401
The Abbey of Admont	404
The Upper Valley of the Enns	407
The Salt District of Styria	408
The Austrian Salt District	413
The Gaisberg	415

	PAGE
Salzburg	419
Farewell to Austria	424
BUKOVINA	425

GALICIA.

From Tshernovitze to Lemberg	432
Sniatyn and Stanislavov	436
From Stanislavov to Stry	440
Stry	445
From Stry to Lemberg	446
Lemberg	449
The Polish Jews	458
The Germanization of Galicia	463
The Galician Nobles	467
Grudek, Moshiska, and Yaroslav	469
Lanzut	477
Rzeszov, Pilsno, and Tarnov	480
The Salt-works of Vieliczka	489
Cracow	498
Podgorze	507
Landskorona and Biala	510
Austrian Silesia	512

MORAVIA.

The Kuhländl	515
Olmütz	517
The Hanna	520
Austerlitz	522
Brünn	523
The Castles of the Great Austrian Nobility	527

BOHEMIA.

FROM DRESDEN TO TEPLITZ.

To travel or not to travel, was once more the question. To wander, to stroll through the world, or to remain and shoot out roots like a tree. Whether 'twas nobler in a man to tend his own little garden, or to arm himself against a sea of troubles, and plough his way round our terrestrial planet? A house, or a tent? A warm room, or a windy seat in a post-coach? A shady tree, or a budless staff? One friend, or a thousand friendly faces?

I must own I had heard in a quiet little farm on the banks of the Elbe, the cackling of hens and the crowing of cocks; I had visited the peaceful chambers, and the cozy garden with its circling wall; had seen the contented cattle fattening in their stalls, and the tempter had said to me, " Might not all this be thine? and mightst thou not find here all that thou seekest in the wide world, and bearest thou not in thy own breast a world that cannot come to a birth for want of repose?"—" Yes, if a wish could command repose, who would fardels bear, and groan and sweat beneath a load of travelling troubles?" I replied to my advising friend, whispered many other things into his ear that were not intended for the crowd, and concluded with these words: " Look, my dear friend, thus it is that necessity makes brave men of us, and enterprises that seem full of great pith and moment, with this respect lose much of the merit ascribed to them." So saying, I once more took leave of him, and stepped into the Saxon *Postwagen* that had been standing for some time ready harnessed in the courtyard of the Diligence office at Dresden. I was about to start for Teplitz, there to consign myself to the keeping of a Bohemian vehicle, by the aid of which I hoped to reach the deep-rolling Danube, where I fully intended to embark on a steamer that should convey me to Vienna. After that I contemplated intrusting my person to a Hungarian *Bauerwagen*, and alternately by land and by water, sometimes with the aid of a living steed, and sometimes by that of the many-horsed power of the unquiet steam-engine, to press forward to the confines of Turkey, and when I had done all this, my purpose was to return quietly to my native land.

Such was my plan, but in the execution of it I was delayed for full five minutes, by a countryman of the gallant Falconbridge. " A proper man's picture," as Portia says; *i. e.* an Englishman, came rushing into the courtyard, just as the horses were starting. His appearance was striking enough. His collar, I believe, had been bought in Italy, his trousers in

France, his cap in Germany, and his manners had been picked up everywhere. It did not rain, nevertheless he carried a huge umbrella to shield him against the sun. He was out of breath, placed himself right before the horses, and having slightly adjusted his cravat and dusted his coat, he began a series of pantomimic demonstrations, addressed by turns to the horses, the postilion, and the conductor. The horses whom he had grasped by the bridle, were the only part of his audience who seemed to understand him; for he spoke neither Latin, French, nor Italian, and not one mortal word of German. We made him out to be a passenger who had overstaid his time, and the diligence was stopped. He ran immediately into the office, where he paid the remainder of his fare, and then again, in mute despair, he rushed through the crowd of spectators, to gaze out into the street. The conductors took him by the arm to lead him back to the carriage, but he broke from them and ran into the street again, where he stood gazing to the right and to the left, in evident anxiety. No one could guess the meaning of all this, and in a little time we should have left him alone with his despair, if at the critical moment a valet-de-place, who came panting into the yard, with a hatbox in his hand, had not afforded a solution to the enigma. My Englishman now took his place by my side, and related to me that he was setting out with a determination to visit and inspect all the provinces of the Austrian empire. He appeared to me like one who had gone forth to till a field, but had forgotten his plough at home. Even in English he was not very talkative. "Who can converse with a dumb show?" as Portia says; so I found I had abundant time to meditate further on the theme with which I started—to travel or not to travel.

All the charming vineyards, and all the comfortable country-boxes that smiled over to us from the other side of the Elbe; all the cheerful Saxon villages of the Dresden plain; all the 80,000 peaceful townsfolk of Dresden, whom we were leaving behind us—all seemed to be reproaching me for leaving them; and every time that a labourer by the roadside looked up at our wandering vehicle, he looked as though he would say to me, "Friend, stay at home, and earn thy bread like an honest man." Perhaps when Napoleon retreated over the same ground, after the battle of Culm, the Saxon villages may have spoken to him in the same strain. He might still be reigning in France, had he known better how to stay at home.

After passing Pirna, indeed all the way from Dresden to Teplitz, you pass over a succession of fields of battle. The War of Liberation, the Seven Years' War, the Thirty Years' War, and the Hussite War, have all contributed to make memorable the mountain passes of Bohemia; at Culm, at Pirna, at Maxen, again and again at Culm, up to that battle of Culm which the German king Lothair lost to the Bohemian, Sobieslav, in 1126, when Albert the Bear was taken prisoner by the Bohemians, much in the same way in which Vandamme was taken 700 years later by the Cossacks.

At Peterswalde, we come to the Austrian frontier. This frontier runs, for the most part, along the highest summit of the Erzgebirge; but, strange as it may seem on a frontier of such ancient standing as that between Saxony and Bohemia, there exists to this day a boundary dispute, the existence of which, by the by, was only recently discovered, in consequence of the surveys rendered necessary for the magnificent map of Saxony lately executed. The Saxon surveyors came to a frontier village, which they took to belong to their own country, but the inhabitants declared they were Austrians, and drove the strangers away. In the same way these villagers are said constantly to have repelled the visit of the Austrian tax-collector, by declaring themselves Saxons. Upon the Saxon map the village has, in consequence, been marked by a white spot, and will continue so till the labours of diplomatists have determined under what royal wings these mountaineers are to have a shelter assigned them.

The Erzgebirge must not be supposed to be a series of mountain pyramids placed side by side. It is rather a huge extended mound, sloping away to the north into Saxony, but rising abruptly on the Bohemian side. Seen from Saxony the chain presents nothing very striking, but from the Bohemian side it looks like a huge wall girting the land. In the same way, the views from the summit are tame, looking towards Saxony, but magnificent when the eye wanders over the Eger and Bila valleys of Bohemia.

"Heavens! what beautiful country is that?" exclaimed one of our lady passengers, as we reached the summit; "only look, deep precipices and mountain ravines; a wide plain, with towns and villages scattered over it, while in the distance again, mountains rise to close in the horizon!"—"This portion of our resplendent planet," we replied, "presents itself to the astronomers of the moon as a bright square enclosed by a dark rim, and may be known to those learned personages as the territory of Alpha, or the land of Psi. Perhaps they may inform their students that the said territory is an island, and that the dark frame by which it is bounded is a mass of light absorbing water. Here upon earth we call the tract Bohemia, and if we knew how to impart it to them we might inform the sages of the moon that the dark circling mass is caused by light absorbing forests, and by yawning ravines. No doubt, in the same way in which we terrestrials often talk of the man in the moon, do the learned there speak of the virgin of the earth. The square piece of surface which we call Bohemia, as it corresponds very nearly with the virgin's girdle, may pass for her buckle; and when the country, covered with clouds and mist, seems darker than on those days when the sunbeams are immediately reflected from the surface, the mooners perhaps say, 'The virgin's buckle looks dull to-day;' or, in the contrary case, 'The virgin has brightened up her buckle this morning.'" Be this as it may, upon one point the Bohemians may fully rely—namely, that the boundaries of their country must be apparent to the very schoolboys in the moon, to whom the limits of Saxony, Prussia, and of other merely politically-bounded countries, must be utterly unknown.

The piece of Bohemia which first becomes visible to the enraptured eye of the traveller, from the heights of Nollendorf, is the valley of the Bila, and so lovely is the view that there presents itself, that every one who sees it for the first time, however he may have been prepared beforehand, will be likely to exclaim with our fair companion, "Heavens! what beautiful country is that?"

Along winding roads the diligence descends gradually into the valley, accompanied the whole way by a troop of children, who, in exchange for raspberries and strawberries, levy a little frontier-tribute on the traveller, and greet him on his entrance into a new country with the pious salutation, "Blessed be Jesus Christ." The three eagles, whose wings upon these heights fluttered so fatally around the French legions, have erected three monuments upon the field of battle, and weather-beaten veterans are stationed there as sentinels. English travellers, on passing the place, are wont to note down very conscientiously how many hundredweight of metal have gone to the composition of each monument. Our Englishman wrote among his memoranda that the Austrian was large and solid, the Prussian very small, and the Russian remarkable for its elegance.

In Teplitz, not only the inns and public-houses, but even private buildings have each a distinguishing sign. Thus one house is called the Lyre, another the Angel, and a third the Golden Ring. It is, if not more convenient, at all events a much prettier and more picturesque way of marking the houses, than our fashion of numbering them, and prevails through the greater part of Bohemia, and even in some of the adjoining countries.

To become well acquainted with Teplitz, one should endeavour to wander about the place with one of the regular annual visiters. There are certain sufferers from the gout who arrive there at fixed seasons, and may be looked for as confidently as a stork at her last year's nest, or as certain human fixtures may be reckoned on in their accustomed coffee-rooms. Such people gradually conceive for Teplitz almost as much interest as for their own homes, and when they arrive, can have no rest till they have satisfied themselves that Clary Castle stands where it did, and that all the public walks are in due order. They hasten to the bath-rooms to receive the obsequious salute of each well-remembered attendant, and enter the glass magazines to admire the new colours and fashions; for every year is as certain to bring its new colours into the Bohemian glass manufactories, as to usher in its old ones to the Bohemian meadows.

The invalid who visits the baths of Teplitz passes the first few days at an inn; and, during this time, he abandons himself to the delights of reviewing the old scenes, till he is able to find a private lodging at the Three Cossacks, or at the Paradise, or at the Palm-tree, or at the Prince of Ligne. Then he calls in his physician, and delivers himself over to the prescriptions of the place, rises early, and drinks most scrupulously his allotted portion of sulphur water, which glides through his lips to the enchanting accompaniment of a band of music; he is careful not to miss the promenade at noon in the garden of the Castle of Clary, even though he should not be able to participate in its pleasures otherwise than in a rolling chair; and eats, drinks, sleeps, and reposes, accordingly as his doctor directs him, in whose hands he is even as a watch—wound up, regulated, and made to go.

From the castle hill the view is most beautiful and comprehensive, extending over nearly the whole valley to the sources of the tributary streams. I made a pilgrimage to the summit, in company with some Poles. In a small village, on our way, we met with some Polish Jews, who are frequently to be seen in Bohemia. They carried in their boxes a variety of little ornaments for sale among the peasants; needles, pins, beads, &c. They called such an assortment of merchandise *Spindliki*, a word half Polish and half German; and they told us they had been to Riga, Brody, Warsaw, and Cracow. They spoke Bohemian, Polish, German, and Russian, and were a fair sample of the jew pedlars that generally wander about the Slavonian countries of Eastern Europe. In Russian Poland, they told us, they used formerly to gain most money, but the government did not allow them to go there any longer.

Like the whole country round Teplitz, the castle hill is evidently of volcanic origin. It is a tolerably regular cone, rising 1600 feet in height from the surrounding plain. A girdle of beautiful oaks encircles the middle, and the summit, an extinct crater, is crowned by the ruins of the castle which was destroyed by fire. From among the oaks may be discovered the most beautiful landscapes, charmingly framed by the spreading branches of the stately trees; but all that the pen can do to convey an idea of pictures such as these is idle and impertinent, and even the pencil may timidly shrink from the task. On fine days the hill is swarming with visiters, who form for themselves a temporary settlement, in the corners, under the porches, and on the terraces of the ruins, and watch the sun as he describes his marvellous course, till he vanishes behind the Carlsbad mountains.

The wondrous effects of the light at sunset, with the endless gradations of its colours, and all the glories of the evening we had spent together, had excited our Poles to such a degree, that, as we passed through the girdle of oaks, the place was made to ring again with the national songs of *Jescze Polska nezginala* (yet is Poland not forsaken), and *Gdy na wybrzezech*. The latter is one of the most beautiful of all the patriotic melodies of Poland. The words run nearly as follows:—

" When thou seest a ship by the sea-shore, tost about by the storm, and cast upon a treacherous shoal, less by the fury of the waves than by the fault of the pilot; oh, then, deign to shed a tear for that poor ship, for it will remind thee of the fate of unhappy Poland.

" When thou beholdest a volcano, a giant among mountains, pouring forth lava, and emitting smoke, while in its bosom is burning an eternal fire: oh, then, remember, that such is the love of his country that burns in the bosom of the Pole."

The Milleschauer, three thousand feet high, is the loftiest among the Central mountains, the whole of which may be seen at ease from its summit. These central mountains are all extinct volcanoes, and all of a tolerably regular conical form. The Elbe breaks here in quick succession through two chains of mountains; the Central mountains and the Erzgebirge, and it is remarkable that just at this point, where the water forced its way through the hills, the violence of the fire should likewise have been so great. When Bohemia was still a lake, these central mountains must have borne some resemblance to the Lipari islands, a group of volcanoes crowded together, and surrounded by water. The Milleschauer is also called the Donnersberg, or Hill of Thunder. May not this name refer to a remote period, when loud detonations were yet heard within the mountain's womb? Are not many hills that bear the name of Donnersberg extinct volcanoes?

It is difficult to imagine a more delightful prospect than that from the summit of the Milleschauer. The distant blue lines that bound the horizon, belong on one side to the Riesengebirge, or Giant Mountains; on the other, to the nearest hills of the Bohemian forest, while towards the south the plains of central Bohemia lay spread out before you, so that you may yield to the flattering belief of having more than half the kingdom at your feet, and of contemplating at one glance, the scene of the joys and sorrows of several millions of human beings. You behold the vessels that dot the surface of the Elbe, but of whose presence the dwellers by the Eger, whom you comprehend in the same glance, have no suspicion. You see the carriages that roll forth from the little town of Lobositz, unknown to those that dwell in the valley of the Bila. The weather was remarkably favourable when we reached the summit of the Milleschauer, the air was clear and transparent, and the eye roamed unconstrained over the most distant objects. A few clouds indeed were flying about, and a thunder-storm was expending its fury on a distant portion of the landscape. The whole dukedom of Schlan and Munzifay, for instance, was overcast for a while with grey clouds that menaced with thunder and hail. . The fowls there were scudding with ruffled feathers before the storm, the dogs were creeping into their holes, and the men as they barred their doors, and made their houses fast, seemed to say:—" Heaven be merciful to us! Is the last day come?" —" Ye fools of Munzifay," thought we on our Olympian thrones, "be warned by this of the shortness of earthly sufferings!" and then we looked into the county of Teplitz, and into the circles of Leitmeritz and Bunzlau, smiling in the tranquil light of sunshine, and enjoying themselves in the cheerfulness of the atmosphere. Seven thousand human beings dwell there upon every square mile,* and from every square mile seven thousand voices rise in praise of the beautiful weather. Without umbrellas they walk forth, and in uncovered carriages do they take their diversion! Short-sighted mortals that they are! Oh that they could but see the clouds that are gathering behind the Krkonorski hills, as the Bohemians call the Giant mountains. That mischievous wight Rübezahl† is preparing to blow over towards them a mass of vapour that will spoil their diversion, by pouring down some millions of drops of rain.

On the summit of the most elevated peak of the Donnersberg stands a wooden chair under a roof, said to have been erected for his own convenience by the late King of Prussia. Here he was wont to abandon himself for hours together to the enjoyment of the glorious landscape. It is a throne fit for a king, nay for a god, and I am surprised that the ancient Kings of Bohemia should not have chosen this spot for their coronation instead of the Vissehrad, on the banks of the Moldau. Here on the Donnersberg, within sight of the whole kingdom, while invested with crown and sceptre, they might have received the homage of all their subjects at once. The eye ranges to the eastern mountain frontier, from behind which rises the Bohemian sun, and follows the glorious orb in his course till he sinks again behind the western rampart of the kingdom. Here the nobles, while uttering the oath of allegiance, might have been impressed with the vastness of their fatherland, and the littleness of its minute parts. As Socrates once said to Alcibiades, though he, like the Prince of Schwarzenberg, had his ninety-nine lordships—even so the King of Bohemia, before receiving the homage of his magnates, might have taken them each by the arm, and have said to them:—" Look, magnate, what you see before you is our common fatherland Bohemia, but that little misty point which you see yonder, marks the extent of dirt with the possession of which Heaven has blessed you, and of which you are so immoderately proud. You, Duke of Friedland, will find your dukedom hidden in the valley behind yon hill; and you, Imperial Prince, by the grace of God, of Schlan and Munzifay,

---

* Whenever a mile is spoken of in the course of the present work, a German mile is understood. The German mile is equal to about 4 3-7th English miles, and consequently a German square mile is equal to rather more than 21 English square miles, or to about 13,680 acres.

† Rübezahl is the name of a goblin supposed to inhabit the Riesengebirge. The legendary lore of Germany is full of tales, in which Rübezahl plays a part.

we must wait a little before we can find out your principality, for a passing cloud conceals it for the moment. As to you, combative gentlemen of the Beraunerthal, there is your home, a small clear streak beyond the cloud; cut the streak up into little pieces, and each piece will be the territory of one of you, save only two of the pieces that belong to the high wise councilmen of Beraun and Rakonitz. Be advised, gentlemen, and live peaceably together, like good neighbours, instead of cutting each other's throats for a fragment of the streak. And now, honourable gentlemen and councillors, look round upon the whole. Look at the spires of Raubnitz, of Lobositz, of Trebnitz, of Brozan, and of Anscha; and there on those of Bilin, Brux, and Dux; see how cozily the smoke curls up from among yonder cottages, or from among those, or those, or those. See how life nestles in every corner, and how the mountains girdle the whole picture, and how the rivers run sparkling through the landscape. All this is our great and beautiful fatherland. The whole is great, the fragments trivial. Let us then stand faithfully and firmly for the whole, and now, gentlemen, come and set me my crown upon my head."

Should the King of Bohemia then have had the wit to select for the moment of his coronation, the period of a rainbow such as we had the pleasure of greeting, the splendour of the solemnity would be complete. A group of clouds, that seemed to have detached itself from the main army which had been moving over the country the whole day, and that now poured down its abundance close before the summit of the mountain, afforded us the glorious spectacle. The golden pearls were dropping down almost within reach of us, and as the sun had almost set, the rainbow was stretched out right above our heads. Gradually, however, we became more nearly acquainted with the damp materials whereof the bow was constructed, and, moistened by the liquid seven-coloured gems, we were glad to find a shelter among the mossy huts of the Donnersberg, that form about as curious an hotel as a traveller might wish to see. A number of small, low huts, built of stone and draperied with moss, form a close circle around a small open space. In the centre is a kind of orchestra for Bohemian musicians, who play every day during the Teplitz season. Some of these mossy huts are refreshment rooms, others are fitted up as sleeping apartments, and in one there is even a museum to illustrate the natural curiosities of the mountain. Each door is decorated by some metrical inscription, from the pen of the poetical host, whose daughter presents to each guest on his departure, a neat little nosegay composed of flowers of the mountain.

It had rained heavily while we were sheltered in the mossy cabinets on the mountain, and when we issued forth on our downward journey, our guides told us the peasants near Trzeblitz would be certain to find great quantities of garnets; not that the garnets came down from heaven in the rain, but because, after a rain, they were more easily detected when turned up by the plough. Trzeblitz is a village at the foot of the Central Mountains, where garnets are not merely found thus by accident, but are likewise carefully dug for. "The corn, however, will have suffered from the rain," added my guide.—" Why so?"—" Because it fell through a rainbow. The rain that falls through a rainbow always breeds a mildew, and if it falls on a newly sown field, it burns the corn away."—" Why this is downright witchcraft," said I.—" Ay, ay," resumed the guide, " we have witches and devils enough here. On yonder hill, where you see the ruins, there's a cave called the Devil's Cave, that is full of them." I had to translate this to my French companion, who philosophically exclaimed, "*Partout on parle plus des démons que des anges. En France c'est la même chose.*" And to say truth, it is strange, that throughout Christian Europe, so many beautiful and picturesque objects should be pointed out to us as Devil's Caves and Devil's Bridges, Devil's Rocks and Devil's Leaps. Why does not fancy sometimes attribute the workmanship to angels? The Greeks would at least have talked to us of Bacchus' Caves and Diana's Bridges; and how much more pleasing and cheerful are the images called forth by such names, than by constant allusions to a dirty, ugly, black, lanky-tailed devil! And then, how abominable a superstition must that be, which announces woe to the land over which the lovely Iris has swept with her many-coloured train! From what perverse imagination can such a notion have sprung? Is it that there is something peculiarly gloomy in our northern blood? Does not the Bible itself teach us to hail the rainbow as a heavenly messenger of peace?

Amid such discourse, my Frenchman and I had lost sight of our party, and suddenly found ourselves alone. He became all at once afraid he should have to pass the night on the mountain, and commenced a series of lamentations on the shortness of German beds, and the scanty dimensions of German quilts; on the bad teeth of the German ladies, and on the incapacity of the Germans to prepare so simple an article of food as a *lait au poulet*, which insipid decoction, it seems, is to be had nowhere, save in the "Capital of Civilisation." In proportion as the night grew darker, he became more and more eloquent on German superstitions, and on the absurd tales of ghosts and goblins, in which the people believed so firmly. I consoled my companion, however, by assuring him I would lead him the right way; nor did we miss it, but arrived safely at the little village where we had left our carriage prior to our ascent, and where we now found the rest of our party awaiting our arrival.

The following morning was again bright and cheerful, and we omitted not to avail ourselves of it for another excursion to the environs of Teplitz. In addition to that of an esteemed friend, I had the company of two Bohemians from Prague, who told us much of the national efforts now making in Bohemia, of the learned societies at Prague, and of the patriotic balls that had been given there during the preceding winter, when the ball rooms were each time decorated with white and red, the national colours of Bohemia. No German, nothing but Bohemian, was allowed to be spoken at these balls, and the guests were saluted, on their entrance, by the stewards, in the Bohemian dialect, which, not many years ago, was universally looked upon as a mere peasant's patois. The public announcement of the balls was to have been also made in Bohemian; but to this the police refused their consent, permitting, however, by way of compromise, that the balls should be announced at once in both languages; a plan very generally adopted for other announcements, besides those of patriotic balls.

Our first visit was to the convent of Osseg, one of the most ancient in Bohemia, several portions of the building dating back as far as the year 1196. In the passages and corridors of convents, you may generally meet with a number of pictures, illustrative of the history of the religious order to which the convent belongs. Sometimes a pedigree of all the convents of the order, sometimes pictures of miracles performed by former monks and abbots, and sometimes portraits of the popes that have been members of the order. Here at Osseg, accordingly, I made the acquaintance of the six popes who had belonged to the Cistertian order.

Among the large paintings in this monastery, there were three that particularly interested us. One represented a learned Frenchman, of the name of Alanus, sitting as a shepherd among his sheep, in a solitary part of the wood. This worthy Parisian, the quintessence of all learning and science, had discovered that it was only in the simplest occupations that a man enjoyed real happiness, and impressed with this belief, he had laid aside his doctor's cap and gown, to take up the crook of a philosophical keeper of sheep. The second represented the Abbot Erro of Armentaria, wandering away into the forest, to reflect upon what appeared to him an unintelligible verse in the Bible, that "before the Lord years pass away like moments, and centuries like thoughts." Coming into the wood, a bird rises, and so charms the abbot with its song, that he follows deeper and deeper into the recesses of the forest. When the bird ceases, the abbot, regretting the shortness of the melody, turns again homeward, but is surprised to find his convent in ruins, and a new one erected by its side. The monks, however, who dwell there, are all strangers; and, on inquiry, he learns that he is now in the year 1367, whereas it was in 1167 that he started on his walk, so that he has been listening to a bird for 200 years. Satisfied now of the truth of holy writ, he prays God to take him up into Heaven. On a third picture was another Cistertian of the name of Daniel, who studied and read so indefatigably in his solitude, that the flames of his holy zeal issued forth at his fingers' ends, so that he could hold them, at night, like so many little tallow candles before his book. This allegory is a beautiful one; for no doubt there is within the human breast a self-illuminating power, that enables the possessor to read the mysteries of God without the aid of a teacher; but in the way the painter has placed his subject before us, it loses all dignity, and looks rather as if the artist had designed to turn the matter into ridicule.

In the picture gallery, in the upper rooms of the convent, we were much interested by two portraits of Luther and Melancthon. They are painted on wood, and marked with the initial of Albrecht Dürer. Luther gave them to his sister, a nun in a Lusatian convent, who remained true to Rome to her end. The Lusatian nunnery was, and still is, a dependency of Osseg, and thus it was that the pictures came hither.

In the beautiful park of the Cistertians we enjoyed magnificent views of the Bila valley, and, on going to the carp ponds in the garden, a few crumbs of bread brought hundreds of lusty carp to the surface in a minute. The monk who showed us over the place, told us these were only the small reservoirs, to furnish the daily supply; the large fishponds, he said, were farther away. He told us also, that the convent possessed twenty-four villages, besides a separate estate of six villages for the abbot's private use. As soon as we pass the Erzgebirge we find things of which the name only is known farther north. With us these wealthy almsgiving convents are mere things of romance, but here in Bohemia you see them and feel them. The present abbot of Osseg, Mr. Salesius Krüger, is spoken of as a highly distinguished and amiable man. We were sorry not to be able to make any nearer acquaintance with him, than was afforded us by his portrait, painted by Professor Vogel.

The convent of Osseg lies immediately at the foot of the Erzgebirge, whence you drive down into the plain to the Castle of Waldstein, and the small dependant town of Dux. The artistical treasures of this castle are of the highest interest, and may be enjoyed with the greater satisfaction, as they are not arranged with any view to system or completeness like the collections of a German university. The paintings decorate the customary sitting-rooms of the owner of the castle, and sofas and ottomans seem to indicate the leisure and comfort with which the pictorial representations are daily enjoyed. The museum of natural history is chiefly illustrative of the natural peculiarities of Bohemia. The salle d'armes is connected with the castle, and the library adjoins the owner's cabinet. A beautiful picture in most of our public collections has to me an abandoned and orphanlike look, while the statues and antiques are crowded together without harmony or connexion. In a private mansion, on the contrary, everything seems to have found its own place, and to harmonize with the building, with the men that dwell there, and with the scenes by which they are surrounded.

It is to the portraits of the celebrated Duke of Friedland, by Van Dyk, that our attention is naturally first directed, and should even the host of Netschers, and Dows, and Rubenses, by which they are surrounded, be confounded in the traveller's mind with the Netschers, Dows, and Rubenses, which he has had elsewhere to pass in review, yet never, I am satisfied, will the features of Wallenstein be effaced from his recollection—features which he will nowhere be able to look upon as here. There are two portraits here of the duke. In the one he is painted as a young man; and in the other, as a gray-headed warrior. The comparison between the two pictures is highly interesting. There the youth stands before you, with his light curly hair, of which a lock falls coquettishly upon the forehead, while a small neat moustache is carefully turned up at the end, with an evident view to effect. The face is a lengthened oval; the nose is handsomely formed, and the eyes, beautifully expressive, are, if I remember rightly, blue. An azure cloudless sky forms the back ground. The same noble features, but hardened and stern, mark the second portrait. The smooth skin is furrowed by innumerable lines that seem to bear testimony to violent passions and chequered fortunes. The hair of the head has grown thin, while the moustache, having lost its graceful curl, is changed into a wilderness of bristles, many of them standing stiffly out, like those with which Retzsch has often known how to give such expressive effect to his outlines. The old weather-beaten countenance looks angrily and imperiously down upon us, like the wrinkled bark of a sturdy old oak. The sword is half drawn, as about to give the signal for battle. Gloomy scattered clouds are sweeping over the back ground remnants of a recent storm, or tokens of fresh levies that are to expend their electricity in new battles. The azure sky of peace that smiled upon the youth never returned for the duke, as it has often done for the aged and retiring warrior when his battles are over; it was among the gloomy agitations of his career that Wallenstein fell. A portion of his skull is preserved at the Castle of Dux, and has been duly examined by phrenologists. The protuberances discovered there have been carefully numbered and ticketed. Among them may be seen No. 6, Firmness; No. 7, Cunning; No. 18, Boldness; No. 19, Reflection; No. 20, Vanity; No. 21, Pride and Love of Glory. The partizan with which he was stabbed is likewise shown, and his embroidered collar, stained with the blood that flowed from the deadly wound. Also a letter written by his own hand, commanding the execution of some citizens who had served against the emperor.

The picture of his first wife hangs by the side of that of the youthful duke. The expression of her face is beautiful. So much so, that the beholder finds it difficult to tear himself from the painting. It is quite a type of Bohemian beauty, and as such ought to be studied and got by heart by every ethnologist. As he advances farther into the country, he will constantly meet with similar large dark eyes, a similar oval head, black hair, and melancholy cast of countenance.

Among the family portraits, our guide called upon us to notice some scenes in the Spanish War of *Sections*, as he very innocently characterised the War of Succession. A remarkably pretty picture was pointed out by him as that of the Princess of Something, who, he said, had " lost herself very much" since it was painted, in saying which, he simply meant to inform us, in his Bohemian-German, that Time had not failed to leave his traces upon the lady's countenance. As we were taking leave, we were advised to seek another opportunity of paying our respects to the present owner of the castle, our guide assuring us that the Count was very " forward" to strangers.

FROM TEPLITZ TO PRAGUE.

On leaving Teplitz you have to pass the Mittelgebirge, or Central Mountains. A Bohemian bird takes three minutes to do this, a Bohemian coachman three hours. From these hills you descend into the marshy country, in which the Elbe and the Eger unite their waters. Even as the waters mingle here, so also do the elements of population; for there are here three famous Bohemian towns lying close together: Lobositz, Leitmeritz, and Theresienstadt. The first, through which the traveller passes, is a comfortless city of Jews; the second, seen only at a distance, has the appearance of a thriving manufacturing place; the third, examined at greater leisure, is the most important fortress of Bohemia, and the usual breakfasting station for those who start from Teplitz at an early hour.

The building of Theresienstadt was completed, not by Maria Theresa, but by Joseph, in honour of her memory. It is a strong fortress, surrounded by marshes, and still a virgin, though more than sixty years old. She was courted by Napoleon in 1813, and his bridal envoy Vandamme was, it must be admitted, received within the coy lady's walls. It was not, however, as a conqueror, but simply as a prisoner of war. The ancient maiden's wardrobe must have cost a pretty penny in her time, and her maintenance must still be expensive, for every thing about her is of the smartest and the best ; and so indeed it ought to be, for at her girdle she carries the key of the whole of northern Bohemia, and the suitor that conquers her scruples, may have all her land along with her. Her collection of pearls is of inestimable value. We saw them in huge piles in the public squares, where they looked for all the world like so many bombs and cannon balls.

Among the prisoners or convicts at Theresienstadt, I remarked the considerate care that had been taken to lighten the weight of their fetters. The thick iron rings which hang loose on the leg, were supported by a broad band of leather strapped round the thigh, so that the iron did not press with its full weight upon the flesh. The arrangement is one that deserves to be imitated, wherever it is felt that a criminal is laden with chains for security's sake, and not merely for the infliction of incessant torture. There are cases enough still in Europe, where no one inquires whether the fetters, resting on the ancles, eat their way into the flesh or not.

The valley of the Eger is the most beautiful part of Bohemia, and also the part best known to the rest of Europe. The population is chiefly German, and our proverb respecting Bohemian villages has no application here, where there are many villages which no one must be ignorant of if he would pass for a travelled man. These are the villages of the circles of Leitmeritz, Saatz, and Elnbogen, bordering on Saxony, and only projecting at their southern extremities into the country of the genuine Bohemians, or *Stockböhmen*. The whole of Bohemia is divided into sixteen circles, of which three border on Saxony, three on Silesia, three on Bavaria, and three on Moravia. Three are central, and border on nobody, and one, the circle of Budweis, borders on Austria. It is only the three central circles, the core of the kingdom, that are *Stockböhmisch*, or thoroughly Bohemian, in all the other circles a large portion of the population is German. The most populous are the three that border on Silesia. In that of Koenigingrätz, there are as many as 6900 inhabitants to the (German) square mile. The least populous is that of Budweis, where there are only 2800 inhabitants to the square mile. The circles in the valley of the Eger have from 4000 to 5000.

The different parts of Bohemia differ quite as much in the quality as in the quantity of their population. In the north and north-east, the Saxon and Silesian circles, the people are industrious, and the country is full of manufactories and commercial establishments of every kind. In the south and south-west there is more of grazing and tillage. How great the difference must be, is shown by the difference in the rate of wages. In the north, in the circle of Leitmeritz, a common labourer earns from five to seven *groschen* a day; in the south, in the circle of Tabor, only from two to four *groschen*.* These were the current wages when I was there, and people assured me they might be looked on as a fair average of ordinary times.

My coachman was a genuine Bohemian. As we were passing through the gate of Theresienstadt, he told me that we should find no more Germans between that and Prague. "At Koenigingrätz, however, you come to the Germans again, and so you do at Budweis and Pilsen. All round our country the Germans are everywhere peeping over the border." Hereupon I began to turn it over in my own mind, that this land belonged to the Germanic Confederation, and then I began to speculate upon what the people themselves might think of the said confederation. I found it impossible, however, in any language, to make the people understand what I meant, and I believe there are very few of them that have any notion of what sort of thing the Germanic Confederation may be, of which they, nevertheless, form a part. Probably not one Bohemian in a hundred has ever heard the confederation spoken of. I once saw a Bohemian most immoderately angry on reading in a German book this sentence: "Prague is one of the handsomest cities in Germany."

---

* A *grosch* is rather more than an English penny.

I need not attempt a description of the Bohemian villages through which we passed after leaving Theresienstadt, for though we Germans profess to know so little about them,* yet we are all familiar with the lamentations of those who have made a nearer acquaintance with them. I will not, however, repeat these melancholy ditties about dirt and disorder, for I know of places in Germany, ay of large districts, where the population live in quite as much dirt as the Bohemians do. What attracted my attention most in these villages were the characteristic little booths that we saw erected in every market place, with their German-Slavonic wares and inscriptions. A booth of this sort is called a *Kramek*, from the German word *Kram*, and in it are usually displayed for sale a pile or two of tasteless pears, a plate of sour cherries, and some wheaten rolls of various forms, among which the *bandoor* and the *rokhlitshek* seem to be most popular. A few pots of flowers, by way of decoration, are seldom wanting, and in the dark background may usually be seen the guardian spirit of the place, in the shape of a little old man sitting silently, like a contemplative philosopher, waiting for customers.

Passing through a dreary and badly cultivated country, in comparison with the neighbourhood of Leitmeritz, we arrived at Weltrus, situated on the Moldau, the chief river of Bohemia. Melnik, at the mouth of the Moldau, we saw only at a distance. Melnik is celebrated for its wine and its hops, but the latter part of its celebrity is probably of the earlier date, for *mel* is the Bohemian word for hops, and the name of Melnik may be translated into the *City of Hops*. The Emperor Charles IV. (the Bohemians call him Charles I.,) is said to have first planted the vine here, but this is scarcely credible, for in that case the vine must have been naturalised on the Rhine and Danube, a thousand years before it was known on the Elbe. The red wine of Melnik is the best of all the Elbe wines, but all the wines of the Elbe, in quality as well as in quantity, stand to those of the Rhine and Danube in about the relation of one to ten.

Charles IV. ushered not only Bacchus but the Muses also into Bohemia, for he it was that planted the ancient university in Prague, where the venerable tree still flourishes. " Under him," say the Bohemian historians, "the Tshekhs laid aside their rude manners. They had among them the most learned scholars and the greatest statesmen, and were, in a word, the predominant nation of Europe, so much so, that to have been born a Bohemian was everywhere held to be an honour." If this was so, times have altered strangely since then. For, be it prejudice or not, few people nowadays will make it matter of boast, unless perhaps in Austria, that they are genuine Bohemians; not only in France and England, but even in many parts of Germany, the name is held synonymous with that of gipsy, and even now, our peasants when they hear the gipsy dialect spoken, are very apt to turn away with disgust, and tell you, " the creatures are talking Bohemian."

The lordship of Weltrus belongs to the Count of Chotek, a member of whose family occupies at present the highest post in Bohemia. There was a bridge here formerly, but many years ago it was destroyed by a flood, since when the good people appear to have contented themselves with a ferry or " flying bridge," made fast by a cable fixed to one of the ruined

---

* The Germans have a saying : " *Diess ist mir so unbekannt wie die böhmischen Dörfer*" (I know no more about it than I do of the Bohemian villages).

piles of the former stationary one. This transition from standing to flying is any thing but "progressive," and it is really a marvel that on so frequented a road no measure should yet have been taken to repair the defect.

It is no shortening of the road to cross the Moldau at Weltrus; but, on the contrary, a great round. It so happens, however, that more than one-fourth of all the roads to Prague, including that from Dresden, unite at the north-eastern gate, at which there enter more travellers and merchandise, than at all the other seven gates taken together. The reason is, that Prague is of easier access at this than at any other point, and the consequence has been that the quarter of the town which has been most modernised and improved of late years, is that which lies in the vicinity of the Porzizer Thor, or north-eastern gate.

Attended, accordingly, by all the persons and things that happened to stream together at that point, exactly at 7 p.m., on the 23d of July, 1841, from northern and eastern Bohemia, from Saxony, Prussia, and Scandinavia, from Siberia, Poland, Russia, and Asia, did we, precisely at the time stated, hold our entry into Prague New Town, which having done, and having duly placed ourselves under the protection of the Burgomaster of the Old Town, we consigned ourselves for that night to the welcome repose of bed.

THE VISSEHRAD.

Every part of Prague is still verdant and blooming with the ruins and monuments of remote countries. The streets, the churches, and the burying grounds are full of eloquent appeals to the history of the land and the people. Palaces and countless steeples are trying to overtop each other in their zeal to talk to you of times gone by. Even on the walls of their taverns, the townsmen may read the names of the first dukes of Bohemia, and thus familiarise themselves with their ancient annals. On the outside of one large house of public entertainment, near the Vissehrad, on the place where formerly the dukes were interred, there may yet be seen six grotesque fresco paintings of the six first Bohemian dukes, with their names very legibly inscribed:—Przemislus,—Nezamislus,—Mnata,—Vogen,—Vratislav,—Venzislaus. The features of these redoubtable potentates have even been repaired and beautified within the last few years. Where, I would ask now, is there a place in all Germany, in which the ancient history of the land is made palpable to hand and eye as here? Where is there a town where so much has been done for German, as here for Tshekhian history? Where the Germans do as much for their mighty emperors, as is here done for petty dukes?

Bohemia is a piece of land wonderfully separated by nature from the rest of the world. The magic circle which surrounds it, consists of stupendous hieroglyphics, traced by the hands of the primeval Titans, and from this mighty wreath depart a multitude of concentrating rays that join together in a vast central knot. These are the streams that flow from the east, the west, and the south, the life-sustaining arteries of the land. In the middle of this magic circle rise the hills of Prague, where every great event by which the country has been agitated has set its mark, either in the shape of new edifices and enduring monuments, or of gloomy ruins and wide-spread desolation. The central point of a country sharply cut off from the rest of the world, and witness constantly to new modifications of its political life, Prague has become full of ruins and palaces, that will secure to the city an enduring interest for centuries to come; and while the hills are singing sweetly to us the traditions of past ages, let it not be supposed that the whispers of futurity are not likewise murmuring mysteriously around them.

The hill first spoken of in Bohemian chronicles, and upon which resided the first dukes of Bohemia, is the Vissehrad, whence the Prophetess Libussa announced to Prague her future glory, declaring that the city would one day become a sun among cities. The old chroniclers hence call their city often the daughter of Libussa, exclaiming in their rapture: *O ter magna triurbs, triurbs teringens, o orbis caput, et decus Bohemiae! Pulchrae filia pulchrior Libussae!* Such were the words with which the venerable Hammerschmidt apostrophized the glorious city on her thousandth anniversary, in 1723, in his *Prodromus Gloriae Pragenae*, the city of which Charles IV. was so enamoured, that he declared her *hortum deliciarum, in qua reges deliciarentur.*

The Vissehrad is a hill, abrupt on every side, but flat on the summit, presenting a plateau of some extent, convenient to build on, and easy of defence. The Hradshin is indeed more elevated, and has a more picturesque situation, but is commanded by other hills near it, and offered, on many accounts, fewer inducements to the early rulers than the Vissehrad, to choose it as their place of residence. The steepest side of the Vissehrad is towards the river Moldau, which seems to be compressed between the hill and the opposite meadows, rushing over its bed with greater rapidity here than in any other part of its course. Here, probably, were the rapids or *poragi*, to which the city is supposed to have been indebted for its name. If we may believe what the historians and chroniclers of Bohemia relate to us of the former condition of the Vissehrad, the pomp and magnificence that once dwelt there offer a strange contrast to the dust and rubbish that have usurped their place. This, once the centre of a bustling city, is now the most remote point of the town; and the most wretched quarters are grouped about the humbled Vissehrad, whose chief glories now live only in the imagination of the Bohemian antiquary.

On the northern side of this Acropolis—for such the Vissehrad may well be called—flows the little brook Botitz, now a dirty piece of water, but memorable in the songs of ancient bards, and witness to numberless bold deeds and hard-fought battles. On the extreme point of the little peninsula formed by the Botitz and Moldau, whence the finest view may be obtained of Prague, of the valley of the Moldau, and of its enclosing the hills, there we may suppose the bard to have stood, as he composed the favourite old national ditty, *Kde domof mug*, of which the following is nearly a literal translation:

> Where is my house? where is my home?
> Streams among the meadows creeping,
> Brooks from rock to rock are leaping,
> Everywhere bloom spring and flowers,
> Within this paradise of ours;
> There, 'tis there, the beauteous land!
> Bohemia, my fatherland!
> Where is my house? where is my home?
> Know'st thou the country lov'd of God,

Where noble souls in well-shap'd forms reside?
Where the free glance crushes the foeman's pride?
There wilt thou find of Tshekhs the honour'd race,
Among the Tshekhs be, ay, my dwelling place.

For my own part I was twice on the Acropolis of Prague. Once with an honoured friend, a professor at the university, whose antiquarian lore enabled him to point out to me every fragment of the ruins, to which any historical associations attached. The second time I was there in the company of a couple of humble originals, who, equally learned in their way, found means, by the mingled simplicity and zeal of their narrative, to breathe life into every bush and stone about the place. These were old Joseph Tshak, who has been for 52 years attached to the service of the church on the Vissehrad, and his daughter, herself past the meridian of life. I had made a kind of acquaintance with this pair of living curiosities, on the occasion of my first visit, when I promised them if they would stop at home the following Sunday I would visit them again. Now, though I must own that I derived myself quite as much pleasure from the society of my esteemed and learned friend, yet I am inclined to believe that my reader may prefer seeing me in the company of old Joseph and his daughter, and, to say truth, they were certainly the most original guides by whom it has ever been my fate to be attended.

Joseph Tshak was originally *pullesant, i. e.* bell-ringer, to the church on the Vissehrad. In course of time he obtained preferment to some more exalted office on the ecclesiastical establishment, and since then, somewhat about the close of the last century, he has been invested, as a mark of his present dignity, with a red coat, now faded and almost as gray as his once auburn locks. His daughter, since her mother's death, has succeeded to the appointment of laundress to the eight venerable canons of the church, in addition to which she washes, starches, and irons the lace and linen of the altar, and of all the "blessed saints" that dwell within the holy edifice. The father and daughter live together in a little house perched upon the summit of the hill, where they have ample elbow room, dwelling in complete solitude on a spot which, 500 years ago, was animated by the bustle of a populous city. Here, amid relics of the olden time, the daughter was born and has grown old; while the father has for more than half a century been the attendant cicerone of all the great and little people, from emperors and kings downward, who in the meantime have honoured the Vissehrad with their visits. The ruins of the place are the only objects with which the worthy pair have ever occupied themselves, and with these they have so completely identified themselves, that they have become in their own persons almost as interesting to a stranger, as the scenes among which they dwell. The "Bohemian Chronicle" of Hajek, Hammerschmidt's "Glory of Prague," and a few other books of the same character, they may almost be said to have learned by heart. In addition to the learning thus acquired, they have caught up and treasured in their minds every little tradition or anecdote about the Vissehrad that they happen to have heard from the priests of the church, or from the strangers that visit it, and all this they have embellished and connected here and there by the helping hand of their own imagination. In short, they have pursued the course usually followed by our own professors of history, and have retailed their medley tales to all the numerous listeners they have had around them during the last half-century. Their lectures have not indeed been taken down in shorthand, yet have their instructions extended far and wide, and not only the citizens of Prague, but simples and gentles from the farthest lands have carried away with them the tales and legends of old Tshak, and would be ready on occasion to stake their own honour on the old sexton's veracity.

"Gracious me, your honour, and there you are indeed!" exclaimed Joseph's daughter, as I presented myself at their little dwelling on the promised Sunday. The day happened to be the festival of St. Anne, and all Prague was making merry in the taverns, at the public dancing-houses, and on the islands of the Moldau. The Vissehrad, as was its wont, lay solitary and forgotten. Upon its naked and desolate brow, sported a moist breeze, and scattered clouds were sweeping over it, attended by sundry flights of ravens, who were winging their flight towards the city; for even they have abandoned the old hill, and fixed their quarters in less elevated regions.

"And there you are indeed, sir! Father and I were just sitting together, and this being St. Anne's day, we were thinking of my mother, whose name was also Anne. I was weeping a tear or two, and looking out of the window. There father's eye caught the steeple of St. Jacob's, and said, 'Thou shalt go down to St. Jacob's to-morrow, and have a mass read for Mother, Anne.' 'Ay,' said I, and then I thought to myself, 'Mother is dead; father and she lived 45 years up here together; Father, too, is old now. Friends we have none in the world. If he dies thou'lt be alone.' So, thought I, I'll have a prayer read for father too, and I'll pray God to spare him to me for many years. Not true, your honour, 'twill be well so? And look, just as I was thinking so, you come and climb up all this weary way to us. Gracious! you must be tired; pray sit down."

I did so with pleasure, for I was struck by the little domestic arrangements of the venerable sexton. The furniture was all of great antiquity, and the walls were hung with maps and pictures, one of which represented the Vissehrad, as it may be supposed to have looked in the days of its glory, when it must have had somewhat of the same appearance as the Kremlin at Moscow. A bible was lying on the table, and I expressed my pleasure at seeing the book there. "Ay, ay," said the daughter, "we set great store by the book. A Jew once offered us two florins for it, but father said he would not give it him. Henry, my brother's son, has children, they may use it one day, when we can read it no more. Is it not so, father?"—"Ay, ay," answered the old man, "I wouldn't part with the book." I commended them for their good resolution, and we proceeded, all three, to go over the curiosities of the Vissehrad, which I longed to see, not only in its own form, but as modified through the medium of the fancy of my guides.

"There is but little left of what was once here," began the old man, "and of that little there is much of which we know the meaning no longer. Even old Hammerschmidt, in his time, could only tell us, that this was *supposed* to be, and that was *said* to be, and we are not likely to know as much now as was known then; but we will show your honour nothing but what is certain. First of all then we come to the church itself, formerly consecrated to St. Vitus, and afterwards to St. Peter. The warriors that broke down the rest of the brickwork had some respect for God's house I suppose, and so it has remained standing somewhat longer."

The trembling hands of the old man, as the keys clattered in his grasp, worked away for a few moments at the crazy gates, before we obtained access to the interior of the church. The place has been sacred to religion from a very remote antiquity. Before the introduction of Christendom, there stood on the same spot a temple dedicated to Svantovid, the God of War of the Slavonians. The emblem of this heathen divinity was a cock, and this bird was likewise the chosen bird of St. Vitus. This similarity of taste, and perhaps the similarity of their names (Svantovid and Sanct Vit) may have facilitated the transfer of the property from the heathen to the saint. The church was built by Vratislav, the first king of Bohemia, and was finished in 1088. It was afterwards rebuilt, having been destroyed by the Hussites, who seem to have dealt even more hardly by the sacred edifice than the devil himself, for his Satanic majesty, in his rage, contented himself with knocking a hole in the roof, which it was long found impossible to repair. The memorable tale was told me in the following words, by my conductress:

"Once upon a time a poor man went into the forest. There he met a smart, jovial-looking huntsman; at least so he supposed, but in truth it was no huntsman, but the devil in disguise. Now the huntsman spoke to the sorrowful man, and said, 'Art poor, old boy?'—'Ay, miserably poor, sir, and full of care,' replied the other.—'How many children hast thou?'—'Six, noble sir,' answered the poor man.—'Give me for ever that child of thine that thou hast never seen, and I'll give thee thy fill of money.'—'Willingly, sir,' was the silly father's reply.—'Then come, and we'll sign and seal on the bargain!'—The old man did so, and received countless heaps of money. When he got home, however, to his own house, to his surprise he found that he had seven children, for his wife had in the mean time brought the seventh into the world. Hereupon, the father began to feel very uncomfortable, and to suspect that the devil had talked him out of his child. In his anxiety, he called his newborn son, Peter, and dedicated him to the apostle; praying St. Peter to take the boy under his protection, and shield him against the devil's arts. Peter, who appeared to the old man in a dream, promised to do what he was asked, provided the boy were brought up to the church; so, of course, the lad was given to God's service, that he might be a priest when he grew up. Peter turned out a good, pious, and learned young man. When he was twenty-four years old, and had been installed as a priest at the church on the Vissehrad, the devil came one day to put in his claim to his reverence; but the holy apostle St. Peter interfered, and declared the deed which the devil produced was a forgery. The devil and the saint came to high words at this; while the poor priest, frightened out of his wits, ran into the church, and betook himself to reading the mass. Now, as they could no way come to an understanding, St. Peter, by way of a compromise, proposed a new bargain. 'Do you fly to Rome!' said he to the devil, 'and bring me one of the twelve columns of St. Peter's church, and if you're back with it before my priest has read to the end of the mass, he shall be yours; but else mine!' The devil, who thought he should have plenty of time, accepted the proposal with pleasure; and in a few seconds, Peter saw him flying up full speed with one of the columns. The devil would have won, there's no doubt, if St. Peter had not quickly gone to meet him, and begun to belabour him with a horsewhip. The devil, in his fright, dropped the huge pillar, which fell plump to the bottom of the Mediterranean sea. He lost but little time in diving for it, and bringing it up again; but he lost quite enough, for when he arrived at the church, the priest had just said his *Ita missa est*, and so his mass was at an end. St. Peter laughed heartily; and the devil was so vexed, that in his rage, he flung down the big column, which went through the roof of the church, and fell upon the floor, where it was broken into three pieces. Many attempts were made to repair the hole in the roof, but they could never make the work hold, for it always fell in, and so at last they gave it up; and there the hole remained for many hundred years, leaving a free way for rain and wind. The Emperor Joseph, however, insisted upon having the roof repaired, so they carved the two keys of St. Peter in the centre stone of the vault, and since then the work has held."

The cross-keys still remain, but I am inclined to think it was the priests and not the emperor, who ordered them to be placed there, and that they did so to save appearances. If they are now asked how the masonry comes to hold, they have their answer ready, attributing every thing to the virtue of Peter's keys.

As long as the hole continued in the roof, the fragments of the broken column remained on the floor of the church; but, according to the old sexton's account, " the Emperor Joseph said, people should pray to God in the church, and not gossip about the devil and his wicked works. Those were his very words," continued the old man, " for I heard them from his majesty's own mouth, as I was showing him about the place, when he was here and looked closely at every thing. And for my own part, I don't know that it would be a serious sin, if a man should not happen to believe the story."

Since Joseph's time, a large painting representing St. Peter horsewhipping the Prince of Darkness, and the Mediterranean rolling its waves beneath them, has, I am sorry to say, found its way back into the church. The broken column, in three fragments, lies on the grass in front of the church. " The stone," said my old guide's daughter, " is put together out of seven sorts of stones. One is very precious, one very hard, and one stinks detestably. When his majesty the blessed Emperor Francis was here, and my father told him the story, his majesty Francis said, ' the stone stinks, I suppose the devil has left something sticking to it.' Down below, you may see the stone is somewhat worn away, for that's where father knocks off bits for strangers to carry away as a remembrance. The soldiers also grind bits of the stone into powder, and have found it good for all sorts of complaints."

In addition to the painted and belaboured devil, I found a little miniature of his Satanic majesty, neatly cut in wood, and led by a chain, which was held by a St. Procopius, likewise carved in wood. Two celebrated men of this name figure in the history of Bohemia; one a distinguished leader of the Hussites, the other the first herald of Christianity in the country. The latter of these was the saint, and wherever he is represented in a Bohemian church, he never fails to have a few devils in chains, like so many greyhounds in a leash. He was a great exorciser of devils, and there is still a hole in the mountains near Prague, into which he fastened a vast number of them, where they fly about by hundreds to the present day.

There is in this church another relic of great celebrity in Bohemian christendom, namely the stone coffin of St. Longinus. This man, according to the legend, was a Roman centurion, and was present at the Crucifixion. He was blind, but some of our Saviour's blood having fallen upon him, he recovered his sight, and immediately began praising the Redeemer, crying out, " This is Christ the Anointed !" The soldiers seized him and stoned him, and put him into a stone coffin, which they threw into the sea. The coffin, however, would not sink, but floated on the surface till it arrived at some Christian city, and in due time found its way to Bohemia. The Hussites threw him again into the water, namely, into the river Moldau, and for a long time nobody knew where to look for the saint. One day, however, when the Hussite disturbances were at an end, some fishermen saw a flame burning on the surface of the water. They tried to extinguish the flame, but they could not, and it always continued precisely at the same spot. A miracle was immediately presumed to be on the eve of birth. An ecclesiastical commission was appointed, and lo, before their eyes, the stone coffin of St. Longinus rose up from among the waves, and was carried back with due honours to the Vissehrad.

"Who knows whether it's all quite true or not ?" observed my talkative conductress ; " but one thing's certain. An arm of St. Longinus lies still in the coffin. When their majesties the blessed Emperor Francis, the Russian emperor Alexander, and the Prussian king Frederick William, were up here, they were all alone with father and me. Only one soldier-like servant had they with them. Well, they made us show them this coffin most particularly, and we had to take two candlesticks from the altar, that they might see the better. The Russian emperor's majesty was most anxious of all to know about it, and he crept in as far as he could, to feel after the saint's arm, and when the emperor's majesty came out again, he was all covered with cobwebs and dust. ' Oh, your majesty,' said I, you've made yourself quite dirty,' and with that I knocked the dust off his back with my hand. ' That'll do, child, that'll do,' says he to me, and I was quite surprised to hear him speak such good German."

In the year 1187 there lived in Bohemia a duke of the name of Frederick, who involved himself in a quarrel with the clergy, in consequence of having applied to his own use the revenues of the village of Czernovitz, then the property of some convent or chapter. The priests imposed heavy penance upon him for this offence, and one of them seems to have had the audacity to subject the duke to a scourging. Gregory VII., who kept a German emperor waiting like a beggar in a courtyard, had not yet been dead a hundred years. The memory of this scourging, the priests sought to preserve by a picture, in which the duke is represented receiving punishment from the hand of St. Peter. This picture, which still hangs in the church, bears the inscription, *Flagellatus Fredericus, Dux Bohemiae, a S. Petro ob Pagum nomine Czernovitz abalienatum,* 1187. Frederick, who died in 1190, was reconciled to the clergy before his death, for, it seems, he authorized the canons of the church on the Vissehrad, to adopt the said flagellation as their coat of arms, and the reverend gentlemen still preserve it, representing the saint belabouring the duke with a cat-o'-nine-tails of most awful dimensions.

" When we showed this picture to his majesty Joseph the Second," my old sexton continued,—" I believe it was in '84, and the emperor was up here with Laudon, Lascy, and other great gentlemen,—I was a young *pullesant* then, and had to stand modestly aside, but I saw and heard every thing for all that. The fine Hungarian guard was drawn up on the Vissehrad, and the carriages and servants waited below. Now when we showed his majesty the picture, he looked vexed, and shook his head, saying, 'It was not civil for Peter to scourge a prince in that way, no, it was very uncivil.' Then he looked down for a moment, as if he was considering to himself, and after that he said, 'but the thing is old, so it may stop there.' Laudon was standing by, and smiled."

Another object that interested me in the church, was the tomb of a Utraquist or Calixtine. The ruling idea with those people was the wine-cup. They bore it as an emblem on their banners, and after death had it carved on their tombs. Before these wild zealots drove Sigismund's troops from the Vissehrad, no less than thirteen churches stood there. Only one now remains, and the fragment of what was once the wall of another, and which seemed to me like a few odd lines of a lost poem. "Oh! it must have been sad work here," said my old sexton; "the Hussites had no mercy at all, but brought dogs and eagles with them, to fight against Christian men."

Behind the church lies a newly-erected arsenal, and several barracks for soldiers, for the Vissehrad still preserves its character as a kind of citadel. On the edge of the rock, that overhangs the Moldau, may be traced some ruined walls of great antiquity. These, according to tradition, belonged to the fortress of Libussa, and one part of the ruin is still pointed out as having been Libussa's bath-room. "But all that is mere vulgar talk," resumed my conductress, "for nothing is known for certain. That Queen Libussa did once live up here in a fine palace, among these rocks and shrubs,—oh, that's certain enough. She was a heathen to be sure, but she was Queen of Bohemia, and a very good woman for all that. She had two sisters, Kasha and Theka. Kasha helped her to govern the land, but Theka was an apothecary, and knew all about plants, and the nobles came from far and wide to be cured by her. She also used to give medicines to the sick peasants, and she could prophesy, and gave good advice to her sisters. Of course things changed when Libussa married Przemysl, who as king had a right to have his own way. Now, Libussa had a waiting-woman called Vlasta, a very beautiful maiden; and when the queen was dead, Vlasta thought Przemysl would marry *her*, and make her Queen of Bohemia. He did not do so, however, which so enraged Vlasta, that she vowed vengeance, and resolved to make herself Queen of Bohemia without his aid. She went over the Moldau,—there was a bridge here then,—and she set up her kingdom right opposite the Vissehrad. She got together four hundred Bohemian maids and wives, who were at feud with their husbands and lovers. There, beyond the meadow, in the corner between the hills, your honour may still see the spot where Vlasta's castle stood. It was called Divin, and thence she used to sally with her maidens, and wage a cruel war against all the Bohemian men. She cut the right thumb off of all the boys that fell into her hands, that they might not be able to draw a bow, and from all girls she cut off the right breast, that it might not hinder their archery. She might not herself have been able to do what she did, but she had a sorceress in her service, who used to say to her, 'My gentle lady, when you go into battle, I will fly on before you. Observe my flight and my signals. I'll show you the ambush of your enemies, and advise you what you must do.' So, when she sallied forth, the old witch always flew before her, and all the Amazons rushed on, crying, 'Yaya, yaya! baba, baba!' Not true, father, that was their cry?" "Ay, ay, child, that was their cry."—" And then they lured the knights into their power, and cut off their noses and ears, or threw them from the rocks, and captured all their castles hereabout. Up there, on that high hill, lay the castle of the Knight Modol, a true friend of Przemysl's. That they captured too. Vlasta, with her own hand, cut Modol's head off, and then (mad wench that she was) she got upon the wall, and blew her trumpet, that Przemysl might hear her triumph here on the Vissehrad. She had her silver armour on, and her beautiful hair fell down to her elbows, and in her left hand she carried her banner. When Przemysl saw her and heard her trumpet, I warrant you he was vexed enough to think he had not made her his wife at once, and spared all this turmoil. He made one more trial, however, and sent out his general Prostirad, who went over with a countless number of knights, and took back Modol's castle, and killed Vlasta, and brought back her beautiful round head. The rest of her women fled to Divin Castle, and defended themselves for a while, but they were all taken at last, and all their heads were cut off. Not true, father?"—"Ay, girl, all their heads were cut off."

Amid these and many other legends of the same kind, evening crept on, and I could no longer distinguish the distant objects to which my talkative conductress directed my attention. Her eloquence and animation invested her in the sober twilight, almost with the air of an ancient sibyl, or Druid prophetess, nor did her flow of words cease when I prepared to take my departure. On the contrary, still conversing of the antiquities of the place, she accompanied me down the hill to the French Gate, where the countrywomen and the *Devi Slovanski* (Slavonian maidens) were entering heavily laden with vegetables and other provisions for the market, at which they meditated to display their wares at an early hour on the following morning. For more than a thousand years has such been the accustomed evening-scene at that gate, and for a thousand years perhaps have the same old Tshekhian ditties been nightly sung by the fair rustics that have meanwhile provided for the pantries of the townspeople.

THE METROPOLITAN CHURCH ON THE HRADSHIN.

Even in the time of the last dukes, much of the glory of the Vissehrad was transferred to the rival hill, the Hradshin, which became the residence of the sovereign in time of peace, while the Vissehrad was only an occasional retreat, in summer, or when the city was pressed by an enemy. At present, much of the Vissehrad, that was once covered with houses, has been converted into arable land, or pasturage for cattle, while at the foot of the hill dwell the most wretched portion of the population of Prague. "They are poorer even than those behind the Hradshin," said a Prague friend to me one day. Thus to each of the castle crags has poverty clung, to shame the luxury of wealth by the contrast of misery.

High upon the Hradshin stands the glorious cathedral, the metropolitan church of Prague, dedicated to St. Vitus, and which, during the wars by which Bohemia has successively been desolated, has alternately suffered from the sacrilegious violations of Hussites, Catholics, and Protestants, Swedes, Germans, and Hungarians. The Hussites, on one occasion, stripped the church of nearly every thing in the shape of ornament. The Swedes, who, towards the close of the Thirty Years' War, made themselves masters of the Hradshin by stratagem, plundered the church to such a degree, that they were able to send whole shiploads of valuables down the Elbe to Stockholm, where they may still be seen among the public collections. Frederick the Great, too, when he besieged Prague, in 1757, seems to have set his heart on the destruction of the cathedral, against which the fire of his artillery was peculiarly directed. What his motive was, it would be difficult to say. He could scarcely think that the garrison of 50,000 men would surrender to him, for the sake of saving the cathedral. It could not be zeal for Protestantism that impelled Frederick to vow the destruction of an ancient Catholic church, without regard to its beauty, its antiquity, and the numberless objects of art which it contained. I should like to know whether Frederick, in any of his works, has attempted to justify himself for this barbarous treatment of the Hradshin church, or whether any one has ever cited him before the tribunal of public opinion on account of it. The impartial Bohemian historian, Pelzel, gives a very detailed enumeration of all the balls, bombs, and shells, that were hurled against this admirable specimen of ancient architecture, by the merciless order of Frederick. On the 5th of June the building served as a target for 537 bombs, 989 cannonballs, and 17 *carcasses*, of which, however, it must not be supposed, that all, or indeed any thing like half of them, hit the mark they were fired at. On the 6th, 7th, 8th, and 9th, the town was complimented with 7144 bombs, 14,821 balls, and 111 *carcasses*, of which the majority were aimed at the cathedral. During those four days the building was thirty times on fire, and each time it was saved from entire destruction by the vigilance and exertions of the canon, John Kaiser. The roof was perforated by no less than 215 balls, and when, after the cannonade, the church was cleared of the rubbish that had meanwhile accumulated there, no less than 770 balls were collected from different parts of the edifice. Napoleon, when he entered Moscow, sent a guard to protect the children in the great Foundling Hospital. Why did not Frederick, when he fired his first gun against Prague, grant a similar protection to the cathedral on the Hradshin, by ordering his artillerymen rather to fire on any object than that? Perhaps it was fortunate for Frederick that he did not succeed in entering the city. He, the friend and patron of the arts, would have grieved in very bitterness of soul, had he witnessed the destruction his own artillery had effected. The Gothic ornaments cast down, the graceful columns shattered, and the beautiful statues mutilated in every imaginable way.

Scarcely one of the many splendid tombs remained uninjured. Neither the beautiful marble monument, executed by Kolin of Nuremberg, and erected in 1589, by Rudolph II., to the memory of Maximilian II., Ferdinand I., and Anne, his wife; nor the venerable statues, stretched on their sarcophagi, of the old Bohemian dukes Spitignev and Brzetislav; nor the chapel of the tombs of the archbishops; nor the other chapel that contains the monuments of twenty-four of the noblest families of Bohemia; indeed the monument of Vratislaus von Bärenstein, the Chancellor of Maximilian II., is almost the only one that escaped unscathed.

Few churches in Germany surpass this cathedral in beauty, richness, and in the interest of its historical associations. There is none to which it seems to bear more affinity than to the metropolitan church of Cracow, in which reposes the dust of all the Polish kings. In both may be traced a similarity of architecture, and a similarity of fortunes. It is astonishing how much there is about each to remind one of the other. Even the legend of Nepomuk has its companion at Cracow, so closely resembling it in all its details, that one cannot help wondering at the occurrence at places so remote from each other, of two series of events so perfectly alike.

Nothing is there that a stranger in Bohemia is doomed to have more frequently related to him than the history of St. Nepomuk, and next in importance and frequency of repetition come the adventures of the two imperial counsellors, Slavata and Martinitz, to whom it happened, in 1618, to be one day tossed out of a window. These two narratives may literally be said to persecute a stranger from the day of his arrival till that of his departure. However well you may have prepared yourself by historical studies with a knowledge of all the details of the Thirty Years' War, whose commencement, as your professors at Bonn or Gottingen will have told you, is to be dated from the day on which the two above-named personages were tumbled upon the dunghill under the Hradshin; yet rest assured that in the first diligence you travel in, there will be some learned gentleman or other who will find or make an occasion to tell the story over again for your especial benefit. And by the time your learned gentleman has got to the end of his first story, it will go hard, but at the next bridge you cross there will be a chapel, or an image dedicated to St. Nepomucene, and, if so, you may rest equally assured that you will have related to you, with all its accompanying incidents, the whole legend of the saint, which, it is odds but you have heard and forgotten again sundry times before you set foot on Bohemian ground. By the time the story is at an end, you are probably at the next bridge, where, of course, your attention is called to another effigy of the bridge-protecting saint, when your charitable informant will be likely to open again with "There, look there, sir; there you have the holy Nepomuk again; he is the same as the one I was telling you of, whom King Venzeslaus, &c.," and how far the et cætera may extend will depend on your patience under the infliction. Well, in due time the hills of Prague present themselves to your view, the Hradshin towering proudly above the rest. Immediately your travelling companion will open again upon you with "There, look there, sir; there you may see the castle from the windows of which the two imperial counsellors, Slavata and Martinitz, &c." The next morning you are tempted to walk abroad, but if you come to the Prague bridge, beware how you stop to look at five golden stars that are erected there. If you neglect my caution, rely upon it your quality of stranger will be discovered, and some kind self-elected cicerone will approach and tell you, "This, sir, is the very spot from which St. Nepomuk was thrown into the water. He was a pious man, but King Venzeslaus, &c." Animated, no doubt, by this time, with a salutary dread of the saint, you probably cut your interlocutor short, by praying him not to inflict upon you a legend which you have learned by heart during the few days you have been in the country. You fly to a neighbouring coffee-house, the windows of which, to your sorrow, look upon the Hradshin. You order a cup of bouillon perhaps, and while you sit sipping it, your host comes simpering up to you. In your unguarded innocence you may allow some such question to escape you, as "What's the news?" If so, you have sealed your fate. "Your honour *were* looking out of the window. Have your honour already had the condescension to go to the top of the hill? But you have from here a very good view of the two windows—

look, your honour, there they are, at which many years ago a very remarkable event occurred."—"What, some romantic love-story?"—"No, sir; from those windows it was that the two counsellors of the Emperor Matthias—their names were Slavata and Martinitz——" "Oh, heavens!" you exclaim. Your very bouillon turns to bitterness, and you snatch up hat and stick, and run to St. Vitus's church, in the hope that if any volunteer informant take you in hand again, he may make the patron of the edifice the topic of his discourse. Idle hope! Of St. Vitus no one deems it necessary to say a word, but one of the attendants of the church will be sure to come up to you, with a face all radiant with the hope of a *douceur*, and thus his oration will begin: "The most remarkable object in our church, is this rich monument of silver, which contains no less than twenty-seven hundredweight of that metal. It was erected in honour of St. Nepomuk, whom the Emperor Venceslaus, &c." My poor stranger! this is one of the discomforts of travel that thou must not hope to escape, and the sanctity of the place forbids thee the relief of a good set oath. Nay, wouldst thou even save thyself by sudden flight, the chances are that thy retreat is cut off by some venerable priest, who takes up the story at the point that thy humbler attendant had just reached. In that case, patience is thy only resource. Listen with resignation, and thou hast a chance that the story will come all the sooner to an end. So, now having prepared thee for the infliction, hear and attend.

Nepomuk, or more properly, Johanko von Nepomuk, was born about the middle of the fourteenth century, in the little Bohemian town of Nepomuk. At his birth, it is said, bright rays of glory were seen to shine around his mother's house. He became a preacher in the ancient city of Prague, where his fame spread so rapidly, that he was raised to the office of almoner to the king, and became the queen's confessor. Now the king (Venzeslaus IV., the celebrated German emperor, the son of Charles IV., who had also in his time been King of Bohemia and Emperor of Germany), —the king, I say, was desirous of knowing what the queen, who had often manifested great dejection of spirits, might have confided to her confessor. Venceslaus wished to know whether she made his own rude behaviour the subject of complaint, or whether perhaps her melancholy were occasioned by a secret love-affair. Johanko, however, could never be prevailed on to betray a syllable of what he had learned in the confessional. Sometime afterward it so chanced that there was brought up to the royal table a very fine capon, but which, on being carved, was found to be very much underdone. The king was hereupon in such a rage that he ordered the cook to be spitted alive and roasted to death. Nepomuk did not fail to rate his majesty roundly for so atrocious an act of barbarism, but the holy man took nothing by his motion but a few days' solitary confinement, where he would probably have been permitted to indulge for some time longer in his pious meditations, had not the king still hoped to draw from him some of the queen's secrets. Nepomuk remained firm, though he appears to have had some foreboding of what the consequence would be, for he prophesied one day that he would shortly die a violent death, and so saying took an affectionate leave of his friends. The following morning, as he was passing by the castle, the king called him in, and renewed his former solicitations. Johanko was inflexible, whereupon the king had him seized, bound hand and foot, and had him thrown that very evening from the bridge into the Moldau. The king thought nobody would have known any thing about the matter, but there he was mistaken, for not only were bright rays of glory seen to shine over the spot where the body lay, but for three whole days the bed of the river was dry, no water flowing over it. Miracles without number were performed at the saint's grave, and people observed that if any man happened to express a doubt of the holy man's beatitude, or to step slightingly or scornfully upon his tomb, the day never passed over without some disgrace or calamity to the sceptic. In due time the saint was beatified by Pope Clement XI., and canonized by Benedict XIII.

Since then, the veneration for St. Nepomucene has spread with marvellous rapidity through Bohemia, Moravia, and a part of Poland and Austria. In all these countries he is esteemed the patron saint of bridges, and the usual oraison addressed to him by his devotees is this, " O holy St. Nepomucene, grant that no such misfortune befall us on this bridge as once befell thee."

By the side of the silver monument of the saint, over which sundry silver angels are seen to hover, there hangs a golden lamp of immense value. This lamp has been stolen on three several occasions, and now, to protect this and the other valuables of the church, a large fierce dog is nightly shut up there as a guard to the gems and relics of the holy place. It is well that the Turks but seldom visit the Hradshin, or this dog in charge of a churchful of saints would be added to the already formidable catalogue of atrocities laid to the charge of the Christians. So unclean is this animal in the eyes of a Mahometan, that I believe he would greatly prefer to have a whole legion of devils shut up in his mosque.

With the varying versions that have obtained currency of the saint's adventures, I will not now detain the reader, that I may the sooner have done with the other great national bore of Bohemia, which, as he is now accompanying me through the country, he is bound to endure, as I have done many a time before him. So here goes for Slavata and Martinitz, and if we are to have the story, we could have it nowhere more opportunely than in this very church, in which we may at the same time admire the monument erected to the memory of Counsellor Martinitz himself. *Allons! Courage!*

Frightened by the daily increasing spread of Protestantism in Bohemia, a Catholic nobleman and a Catholic abbot had found means, in 1618, to shut up and destroy two newly-erected Protestant churches, alleging that they did so by order of the Emperor Matthias. All the Protestants and Utraquists of Bohemia, among whom were many of the first men in the country, were greatly excited, and held meetings, at which it was logically demonstrated that such treatment was in direct violation of the royal Letters of Grace that had been granted them. A deputation was sent to Vienna to remonstrate. The emperor, meanwhile, had taken serious offence at the stormy meetings of the Protestants and Utraquists, to whom he sent a menacing epistle, which the states of the kingdom were summoned to the Hradshin to hear read. They assembled, listened to the formidable threats of the emperor, and promised to return an answer on the following day. They assembled again, accordingly, at the time appointed, attended by bodies of armed men, when they found the royal governors, Slavata, Martinitz, Adam von Sternberg, and Diepold von Lobkowitz, waiting to receive them. Of these four men, the two last were generally popular; but the two first, bigoted Catholics, and tyrannical rulers, were universally detested, and there were many among the states who were of opinion, that religious freedom could never be firmly established in Bohemia, so long as those men continued in power, and that therefore the best thing they could do, would be to get rid of them as soon as possible. Some opposed these violent counsels, but the majority applauded them, and crowded from the Green Chamber, where they had been consulting together, into the Government Hall, where they addressed bitter reproaches to the governors, for attempting to deprive the Utraquists of their Letters of Grace. The *Oberstburggraf,* Adam von Sternberg, addressed the tumultuous assembly in a conciliatory tone, and warned them against the commission of any act of violence. Kolon von Fels thereupon stepped forward, and said that they meant no harm to the Oberstburggraf, nor to his Lordship of Lobkowitz, with whom they were well contented, but that they were in no way satisfied with Messrs. Slavata and Martinitz, who were always seeking occasion to oppress the Utraquists.* Venzeslaus von Rapowa exclaimed, that the best thing they could do, would be to throw them out of the window, according to the good old Bohemian fashion (*po starotshesku*). Some of the party now went up to Sternberg and Lobkowitz, took them by the arm, and led them civilly out of the room. Slavata and Martinitz began to be seriously frightened, made great protestations of their innocence, and demanded, if they had done any thing wrong, that they might be allowed a fair trial. The incensed feelings of the assembly could not, however, be appeased. William von Lobkowitz stepped up to Martinitz, and seized him by both his hands. This may be said to have been the first revolutionary act of the Bohemian insurrection. Could William of Lobkowitz have foreseen the unspeakable misery that was about to overtake his country, he would probably have shrunk back and have cried, " I will not be the man to raise the first stone to that frightful avalanche." Not that it can be shown that the horrors of the Thirty Years' War would have been averted if William of Lobkowitz had kept his hands off Martinitz, or if the Calixtine States had been more moderate, and had tried to gain their ends by fair means, for great events are like streams fed by hundreds of sources, and the historian who argues that if this or that incident had not occurred, some great political development would not have followed, is like a certain Austrian, who fancied if he could

---

* To some of our English readers it may not be superfluous to explain that the Utraquists or Calixtines received their name in consequence of their demand that the calix or wine-cup should be given to laymen as well as priests in the communion. Their demands were complied with by the Council of Basil in 1433, and after their victory at Böhmischbrod, in 1434, over the Emperor Sigismund, they obtained liberty of conscience, and after the Reformation manifested on various occasions their sympathy for the Protestants. Their refusal to serve against the Protestants in the Smalkaldic war, drew upon them, at first, severe persecutions, but after 1556, Ferdinand I., who was not ill-disposed towards them, allowed them to share in the advantages conceded to his evangelical subjects. Maximilian II. granted to the Utraquists a complete freedom of religious exercise. Under Rudolph II., their situation was less favourable, and they had considerable difficulty in obtaining from him the *Majestätsbrief*, or Letter of Grace, alluded to above, which was granted on the 9th of July, 1609, and by which the Bohemian confession, handed in conjointly by the Utraquists, the Bohemian brethren, and the Evangelicals, was publicly recognised, and their ecclesiastical ordinances, by which their schools and churches were regulated, and by virtue of which they had had their own Consistorium at Prague, were confirmed. The repeated violations of the *Majestätsbrief* by Matthias, led to the tumultuous scenes at the Hradshin, which are described in the text, and which are generally looked on as forming the outbreak of the Thirty Years' War.—*Tr.*

stop the source of the Danube with his foot, he should be able to prevent the Danube itself from reaching Vienna.

Be this, however, as it may, William of Lobkowitz, did not stop to make any such reflections. He seized Martinitz by both his hands. Four other nobles lifted the trembling governor from the ground, bore him to the nearest window, and without ceremony pitched him out. It is said, that the assembly stood for several moments in dead silence, terrified apparently by what they had themselves done. A similar interval of silence is said to have occurred in the Roman capitol, after the conspirators had struck Cæsar to the ground.

The first to interrupt this silence was the Count of Thurn. " Gentlemen," he exclaimed, "there's another of them," pointing at the same time to Slavata; who was immediately seized, and dealt with in the same way as his colleague. Master Philip Platter, the private secretary, was also ejected in the same unceremonious way as his masters. No record is left us of what was said after the outrage, by those who remained in the room; nor how they looked at one another. They soon appear to have found the air of the place too close for them. In a little while we see them, particularly the Count of Thurn, riding down into the city, to appease the fears of the people, whom they told to be under no uneasiness, for that the entire responsibility of what had been done, would rest upon those who had done it. It was not till the third day after the scene of violence at the Hradshin, that the states met again. They then entered into a covenant, and elected thirty men, who, on the resignation of the royal governors, were to take upon themselves the administration of public affairs. The Bohemian revolution was now proclaimed, that was to terminate, only two years later, by a counter-revolution, terrible in its consequences, and carried through with a cruel consistency. It was the last time that the Bohemians can be said to have manifested a consciousness of their old Tshekhian political usages, for never since then have they again had an opportunity of exercising the *po starotshesku.*

Not the least remarkable part of this little political drama was the fact, that not one of the three gentlemen, who so unwillingly showed their agility, suffered any serious inconvenience from the compulsory leap, though the window through which they made their exit, was at least sixty feet from the ground. Master Philip was the first to get upon his legs again; whence it may be inferred, that the occupation of a secretary tends less to the promotion of obesity than that of a royal governor, and the inference will generally be found to apply to the secretaries and governors of other countries as well as to those of Bohemia. Platter, as soon as he had scrambled out of the castle-ditch, into which he had fallen, ran as fast as he could to Vienna, where he told the emperor what had taken place. How happy Platter must have felt, to have thus the first telling of a story, in the repetition of which so many thousands continue, even to this day, to take such unspeakable delight!

Martinitz and Slavata found some kind Samaritans in the street, who helped them into the house of the Chancellor Zdenik von Lobkowitz, where they found succour and protection. Count Thurn, indeed, at the head of a riotous multitude, appeared before the house, and demanded the delivery of the two obnoxious governors, but the lady of the mansion, Polyxena von Lobkowitz, pacified the count with fair words, and assured him that both her guests were lying in bed in a miserable condition. Slavata had indeed a wound on his head, that obliged him to remain her guest for some time, longer, but Martinitz was able to leave the city in disguise. He went to Munich, where he died about six years afterwards.

I trust the reader will not have forgotten, while we have been thus discoursing of tales of the olden time, that we are still in the metropolitan church of the Hradshin, where we have a multitude of curiosities to pass in review. In the chapel of Venzeslaus I was curious to know the precise spot where the Bohemian regalia were preserved. My guide told me he dared not give me the required information, the place where they were kept being a profound secret. The entrance, he added, was by an iron door secured by three separate locks, to each of which there was a separate key, and these three keys were committed to the keeping of three of the first officers of state. I pressed him not the less to let me into the secret; telling him that I took especial delight in knowing myself to be in the vicinity of any object of historical interest, because I felt within myself a particular susceptibility for the electrifying impressions emanating from such objects. This, I added, was particularly the case with respect to crowns and sceptres, in whose poetical atmosphere I loved to bathe myself, and of whose influence, I felt assured, I should become conscious, even through the intervening impediment of a wall. Moreover, I told him, no crown could have more interest in my eyes than one that had been worn by so many Bohemian kings and German emperors, a crown for whose sake so many a bloody battle had been fought, a crown which Joseph II. had carried away with him to Vienna, and which Frederick of the Palatinate (the winter king, as he is called in Bohemia) had carefully packed up when about to take his departure, but which, owing to the precipitancy of his flight, was left standing with various other valuables, in the public market-place of Prague.

It had meanwhile struck one o'clock. A heavy rain was falling without, and detaining me a prisoner within the church. I was alone with my attendant, who imboldened by this circumstance, or moved by my eloquent appeals, manifested symptoms of relenting. He opened the Venzeslaus chapel, and told me that, though he dared not on any account point out the spot to me, yet if I would keep my eye on him, he would slightly nod his head when he came to the picture behind which was concealed the iron door of the shrine where the regalia were kept. We proceeded accordingly to inspect all the curiosities of the chapel. Firstly, the beautiful agates and jaspers with which the walls of the chapel are inlaid. Then the tombs of the first dukes of Bohemia, and lastly, the ring which Duke Venzeslaus grasped when he fell to the ground wounded by his brother. This brother, whose name was Boleslav, coveted the crown, and placed himself at the head of a conspiracy of malcontents, in whose eyes Venzeslaus was too pious, too credulous, and too fond of the priests. Venzeslaus carried his piety so far, that he planted and tended with his own hand the grapes and the corn of which was prepared the bread and the wine used for the communion, cutting, thrashing, and grinding the corn, baking the bread, and pressing the wine. What with these pious exercises, and his constant attention to the churches he was planning and building, he left himself no time to attend to state affairs. One day, having repaired to Bunzlau, to attend the consecration of a church, he became his brother's guest, and this opportunity was looked on by the conspirators as favourable to the execution of their design. On the following morning, the 28th of September,

936, Venzeslaus hastened, as was his custom, to church, in obedience to the matin's chime. At the church-door he met his brother, whom he praised for his hospitable entertainment of the preceding day. Boleslav then said, in a bantering tone, "I will entertain thee better to-day," and with that drew his sword and dealt the duke a heavy blow over the head. He did not wound him mortally, and Venzeslaus had strength enough left to disarm his assassin and fling him to the ground. "May God forgive you for this, brother," he cried. Boleslav, meanwhile, having fallen, roared out for help as though he had not been the assailer but the assailed. His servants and several of the conspirators came to his assistance and attacked the duke, who defended himself stoutly while retreating to the church-door, where he fell, pierced by the swords of his enemies. In dying he grasped convulsively the iron ring of the door, and when his body was brought to the Hradshin, to be buried in St. Vitus's church, which he had built there, the ring, also, was brought thither, and has been preserved there ever since, where every traveller may have the pleasure of grasping it in his turn, even though he should feel no avocation to earn the glory of martyrdom and canonization, after the fashion of Duke Venzeslaus.

We came next to the tomb of Duke Brzetislav II., then viewed some pictures of saints, including those of St. Ludmilla, St. Christopher, and sundry others. I kept a sharp eye on my guide, and did not fail to notice at which picture it was that he nodded, however slight the gesture was. My reader and I are both in the secret as to the meaning of that nod; but at which picture was it? That is a secret, gentle reader, in which I must not let thee participate, lest thou betray it to some designing revolutionist, from whom the crown and sceptre of Bohemia might be exposed to serious peril.

Every Bohemian loves to wander among these monuments of the ancient dukes and saints of the land, rich with a thousand associations with names and things, the memory of which he has learned from infancy to love and venerate; but the cathedral of the Hradshin has also its reverse, for at the opposite side of the church is a series of votive tablets, paintings, and carvings in wood, intended to commemorate the victory on the White Mountain, a victory which, even at the present day, is an object of sorrow to the Bohemians, and which certainly exercised a more permanent influence over the fortunes of the country, than was ever exercised by any other victory in Bohemia, either before or since, for it may be said to have decided the fate of the kingdom for the 220 years that have since elapsed. Rudely carved in wood may be seen a complete representation of the battle; of the entrance of the Duke of Bavaria, the Emperor Ferdinand's general, into Prague; of the poor Winter King's flight; of the tribunal that Ferdinand established. No German, no Austrian, no lover of his kind can withhold his pity when he sees a Bohemian moving mournfully through this gallery. Who, in fact, can withhold a tear when he thinks with what fearful throes Utraquism and the Reformation came into life in Bohemia, and with what frightful reactions, after so painful a birth, they were again annihilated?

Truly gratifying are the pictures presented to us by Bohemian historians of the condition of the country under the mild emperors and kings towards the close of the sixteenth century. The arts and sciences flourished. The churches were adorned with paintings of rare merit; picture-galleries were collected; Tycho Brahe, Kepler, and other eminent spirits of the age, studied, wrote, and taught in the capital of Bohemia. The schools, both in town and country were excellent, and even among the women of the land, there were many distinguished for their learning and information. Poets and orators rose and flourished, and the works then written still serve as classical models of language. The several religious parties, the Utraquists, the Hussites, the Bohemian Brethren, the Catholics, and the Protestants, all lived in harmony with one another, and such was the spirit of toleration, that often in one and the same village, three religious parties, with their three several pastors, lived in peace and friendship together.

The angels in heaven must have rejoiced over such a state of things, but the Jesuits were grieved and offended by it. They held the hearts of the princes in their hands, and never rested till they had hurled the firebrand into the peaceful house, and when they had succeeded in setting it in a blaze, they sent princes and armies in to quench it, and utterly to destroy the burning edifice. The battle of the White Mountain, where the insurgents under the Winter King, Frederick of the Palatinate, were defeated by Maximilian of Bavaria, decided every thing. The imperial troops occupied Prague, whence they commanded the whole land, and held it like a victim bound to the stake, while Ferdinand II., in obedience to the suggestions of his Jesuists, subjected the country to a series of operations that bore a striking similitude to the ordinances with which Philip II. had afflicted Belgium.

A scaffold was erected at Prague, upon which the leaders of the insurrection suffered in quick succession. The sentence pronounced and executed upon those declared guilty of high treason, was a masterpiece of elaborate criminal adjudication. It was therein minutely determined, who should be executed with the axe and who with the sword, who should lose his right hand *before* and who *after* the execution, and who was to have his tongue torn out. It was also specified how the bodies of such as were already dead were to be disposed of; who were to be cut into four, who into eight pieces, and on what gates these several pieces were to be exposed to the public gaze.

The establishment of this tribunal was followed by the commencement of a systematic counter-revolution. In every house of every Bohemian town, not only the heads of families, but their wives, workpeople, and servants, in short all the inmates of each house, were called on to return a categorical answer to these questions:

Are you by birth a Catholic?
Have you been converted to the Catholic faith?
Do you promise to become a Catholic?

Whoever refused to embrace Catholicism, was declared incompetent to exercise any corporate trade, and was generally deprived of his property into the bargain, and expelled from the country. So far was the system of persecution carried, that the Protestant poor and sick were turned out of the hospitals, and orders were given that none but Catholics should in future be admitted there.

After this state of things, the details of which are frightful and revolting, had continued for seven years, the emperor came to Prague with his family, and, having summoned a diet, had his son Ferdinand III.

crowned as king. A few years before, the question had been gravely discussed by the states, whether it would not be better to erect Bohemia into a republic, like Switzerland or Holland, than to elect Frederick of the Palatinate to the throne; in this new diet, no one even ventured to raise the question whether the crown was elective or hereditary. Ferdinand annulled the Letter of Grace, and all the privileges of the states, commanding at the same time, that the Bohemian language should no longer be used in any of the law tribunals. The nobles readily adopted the German language, and the townspeople were obliged to learn it, for the monks preached only in German. The burghers in the cities began to be ashamed of speaking Bohemian, though, not long before, even the nobles had prided themselves on their national language, and had not hesitated to speak it at the court of the German emperors. The peasant only continued to speak as his ancestors had spoken, and what had been the language of a nation, came to be considered the dialect of the vulgar. Distinguished as Bohemia had been, under the preceding emperors, for the cultivation of science and art, she now sank rapidly into ignorance and barbarism. That the people might be more easily ruled by being kept in ignorance, the Jesuits went from house to house, as missionaries, and took away what books they could find, and burnt them. So effectually do they appear to have performed their mission, that to speak of a "Bohemian" book, or a "scarce" book, is now esteemed the same. Even the costume of the people was changed, and gradually superseded by that of the conquerors.

"I must remind my hearers," says the historian Pelzel, at the close of his reflections on the consequences of the battle on the White Mountain, "that here the history of Bohemia closes, and the history of other nations in Bohemia commences."

Bohemia now stands like its metropolitan church, incomplete, weather-beaten, and covered with scars, but like its church, also restored to peace and order. We must read the resolutions of the Bohemian diet if we wish to know, to what extent, and according to what plans, the Bohemians meant to have constructed their state edifice; but the original plan of St. Vitus's church may more easily be studied, for all the drawings are still preserved in a small room over the vault of one of the chapels. In its present condition the church is evidently a mere commencement of the architect's design; if completed, the building would have been more than three times its present size.

The treasury of the church is rich in a multitude of curious and valuable objects. In one cabinet I counted no less than 32 golden mitres. I took several of them in my hand, and observed to my guide that I thought them heavy. "And yet, sir," said the man, archly, "our gentlemen are so very fond of wearing them!" In various drawers are preserved no less than 368 priestly vestments for the service of the mass, many of them of astonishing richness and splendour. One of them was of a material that might have furnished a mantle, either for a beggar or a prince; it was of common straw, but plaited and worked with such surprising art, that the whole looked like elaborate embroidery. Most of these vestments are gifts from Bohemian nobles, and the history of some of these presents may contribute to illustrate the character of the country. Thus, one vestment has been made up from the bridal dress of a Countess Tshernin, another of the coronation robes of Maria Theresa. One of the richest of all, and which is only displayed on occasions of great solemnity, has been decorated by the Prince of Schwartzenburg, with a number of golden bunches of grapes and vine-leaves, and with all the buttons worn on his wedding coat. Each of these buttons is a jewel of considerable value, fashioned into the form of an animal, and set in gold. What wasteful profusion! and what a strange whim, to dedicate the wedding dresses of lords and ladies to the service of the church!

One of the vestments was embroidered by the hand of Maria Theresa, but of all the embroideries, the most wonderful is one made in the beginning of the fourteenth century by Anne Queen of Bohemia (*Anna Karolevna Tsheska*). She and her sister Elizabeth were the two last descendants of the ancient princely line of Przemysl, whom Libussa called to the throne from the village of Staditz near Teplitz. Some of our young ladies who think they have attained no mean proficiency in the art of embroidering, ought to come to Prague for the sake of looking at the work of the last princess of the house of Przemysl. It is a piece of white linen upon which are worked, with threads of gold, the most beautiful and delicate flowers and arabesques. The pattern is precisely the same on each side, and withal, so accurate and yet so fanciful, that one is never tired of admiring it. The pattern, moreover, is constantly varied by the invention of new figures and forms, though the whole piece is thirty-three ells in length. The length of way which the little needle and the dainty finger of the queen must have traced over the linen with golden thread, is estimated at about ten leagues, and to me it seems as if the labour of half a life must have been devoted to the work, which was executed in exile, and sent to the Hradshin, as the parting gift of the last scion of a long race of kings.

Of religious relics the church has also an abundant supply. Among others, a neatly ornamented little hand, said to have belonged to one of the little children killed at Bethlehem, on the occasion of the massacre of the innocents; a piece of the tablecloth that served our Saviour and his disciples on the occasion of the last supper; and a nail taken from the real cross, and now shown in a splendid setting of pure gold. A piece of the sponge with which our Saviour's lips were moistened when on the cross, and a thorn from the real crown of thorns, are set in a crucifix, which crucifix, the kings of Bohemia respectfully kiss on the occasion of their coronation. In addition to these, there are several relics brought by Godfrey de Bouillon from the graves of Abraham, Isaac, and Jacob.

In addition to the crown and sceptre, concealed in the secret cabinet of which mention was made several pages back, there are other parts of the regalia respecting which less mystery is made, and upon which, accordingly, I was allowed to feast my eyes. There were, for instance, the four golden statues of the four ancient Bohemian saints: Adalbert, Venzeslaus, Vitus, and Ludmilla. These four statues are always carried in procession before the kings on the occasion of their coronation. I was also shown the sword of state, with which the newly-crowned monarch always imposes the honour of knighthood upon the shoulders of a select number of his subjects. This sword is remarkably light. Some time ago, a little rust was discovered about half way down the blade. That it might not, however, be said, Bohemia's sword of state had grown rusty, the offending spot was cut or filed away, and the form of a cross was given to the hole thus formed. The said hole I saw with my own eyes; its cause and origin I can only give upon the authority of my informant.

PUBLIC INSTITUTIONS AND CONVENTS.

The royal library is contained in the Great College Building (*Collegiumsgebäude*) as it is called. My visit to the 100,000 volumes happened on a noiseless holiday afternoon. The reading-rooms that in the morning had been occupied by the studious, were now still and untenanted, like a deserted beehive. It was an unaccustomed time for a visit to the library, but the goodnatured librarian made an exception on my account, and did not grudge the trouble to which I put him. When the last heavy lock closed behind us, and I was able to let my eye wander through the long halls, I experienced that feeling of mingled awe and enjoyment, which I always experience on entering a large library, where the boards are so richly decked with the produce of human intellect. Thick walls and stout bolts shut out the rest of the world from us, and we wandered like hermits in a solitude, but a solitude where nearly all the fruits of mental speculation hung invitingly around us. I thought of Ulysses in the Cyclops' cave, examining the bright bowls full of rich milk, and the packages of cheese and butter, and the casks of honey, all filled to the brim. The difference was, that Ulysses had been locked *in* by his Cyclops, whereas we had just locked *out* our Cyclops, the great, noisy, busy, bustling world.

At a time when, according to the exaggerated accounts of some, 60,000 students were assembled in Prague from all parts of Germany,* these rooms must have literally swarmed like a beehive, but if those times were to return again, the halls and reading-rooms of the library would still be found sufficiently spacious. Of the sixty-six deans, who were then at the head of what was called the nations, only twelve were Bohemians. The Germans were by far the most numerous. Even then there appears to have existed something of the jealousy that still prevails between German and Bohemian. Huss was a zealous adherent to the Bohemian party. To destroy the influence exercised by the Germans, he recommended that in all university affairs the Bohemian nation should have two votes, and all the other nations together only one. This measure led, in 1409, to the departure of the German students, and to the rapid decline of the university. Thus did the people of Prague strike a severe blow at the prosperity of their city, and even in Bohemia there was at the time no lack of ridicule cast upon the Bohemian party; but the incensed German students and professors, it is still believed in Prague, addressed bitter remonstrances to the emperor and clergy, and the vindictive charges thus brought against Huss, are supposed to have done more in exciting the pope and the emperor against the reformer, and to have contributed more to bring about his melancholy fate, than any apprehension that was ever entertained on account of his doctrines.

---

* The most moderate accounts say 20,000, a number still abundantly large, when we consider that even at the present day, all the German universities together do not contain a larger number. And yet there were then other universities in Germany, and many German students went to Italy. Besides Germany is at present much more populous, and must contain a great many more people than it did then, who occupy themselves with learned pursuits.

Unless the University of Prague had at that time more books than it has now, the whole library must have been exhausted if only each student occupied one work at a time. On the 26th of July, 1841, the number of volumes was 99,888, and the catalogues are so arranged, that the sum total may every day be known with the greatest precision.

Although much that was interesting has been removed to Vienna, there are still books in the Prague library quite as well deserving of description as any other curiosity, either in the town or its vicinity. One of the most curious is, perhaps, a Hussite hymn-book, which is written and illuminated with singular splendour. The book, which must have cost many thousands of florins, was the joint production of a large portion of the inhabitants of Prague. Every guild and corporation of the city had a few hymns written, and pictures painted to accompany them, and several noble families did the same, each family or corporation placing its arms or crest before its own portion of the book. In most of the other cities of Bohemia similar hymn-books were composed during the ascendancy of Utraquism, and I doubt whether of all the Christian sects that have at various times protested against the pope, there ever was one that produced hymn-books of such surpassing splendour. All the pictures in that of Prague are of a superior order, and executed in a masterly style. Most of them represent incidents from biblical history, or from the life of Huss, as for instance, his dispute with a popish priest, and his death at the stake. Bloated priests and monks, pope and emperor, are represented grouped around the funeral pile of Huss, whom angels are comforting in his agony.

Poor Huss raised a flame in which he himself was burnt, as well as many that came after him, but from that flame posterity has derived neither light nor warmth. The history of the Calixtines of Bohemia is a sadder one than that of any other religious sect, for no doctrine ever made its way amid acts of greater violence, and none was ever annihilated by a more ruthless reaction. Lutheranism was also cradled amid fearful storms, but the tempests have spent themselves, and millions have become peaceful participators in the blessings at which Lutheranism aimed. The Hussites raised a mighty conflagration, of which the Austrians succeeded in treading out the last spark; the Lutherans lighted a roaring fire on their own hearths, and their homes, in spite of pope and emperor, have been warmed by its genial influence ever since. Yet Huss, despite of his heresy, lives in the affections of his countrymen. I have often observed in them a strange struggle, on this score, between religion and nationality. As Bohemians they love to take credit for all the great things that the Hussites did, though as Catholics they cannot, of course, approve of them.

Utraquism preceded the art of printing; hence the profuse adornment of the hymn-books I have described. The Hussites afterwards caused a multitude of books to be printed in Bohemia, and when this could no longer be done in the country itself, their bibles were printed abroad, in Venice, for instance, whose printing-presses in the sixteenth and seventeenth centuries, were at the disposal of almost every religious sect. In the Prague library are several bibles in the Bohemian language, that were printed at Venice. In one of the year 1506, is a picture of hell, in which the devil is treading down a whole host of monks and popes; to this some zealous commentator has affixed a manuscript annotation, to inform us that the picture represents " Pope Julius II. in Hell."

The best bible, however, in the Tshekhian language was of a much later date (1579—1593) when a Moravian nobleman called together a number of learned Bohemians to his castle of Kralitz, where the sacred volume was translated anew from the original text. This translation is said to be the best: the Bohemians even maintain its superiority to any translation that has ever appeared in any language, a point which very few scholars are in a condition to dispute. This translation is known under the title of *Biblia Czeska Braterska* (*i. e.* the Tshekhian Brother Bible), and is still occasionally printed at Berlin for the use of the Moravian brethren.

In the Prague library I found a copy of the first book ever printed in Bohemia. It's date is 1462. These old Bohemian books are well printed, and upon solid lasting paper, like our old German and Dutch editions, which look nothing the worse for the three or four centuries that have passed over their heads. Our modern paper is mere tinder in comparison. I took up a new book that had come from the binder's only a few days before, and while I was turning over the leaves several of the corners broke off. If we go on *improving* the manufacture of our paper, as we have done of late years, there will be nothing left in our public libraries, five hundred years hence, but the solid old incunabulæ and parchment manuscripts.

In the halls of the library may be seen the portraits of several Jesuits of Prague, and of other distinguished men. Among them are Campianus, the Jesuit, who was executed in England under Elizabeth, and Collin, the friend of the last Palälogus, who was burnt in Rome by order of the inquisition. There is also a picture of Georg Plachy, who, at the head of the students of Prague, defended the city bridge so gloriously against the Swedes. The most interesting of all these worthies, to me, was a marble bust of Mozart, the greatest musical genius that Germany ever produced. This bust stands in a room, the shelves of which are filled only with the works of the great master.

Mozart is one of the very few Germans for whom even the Bohemian patriots express their respect without any *arrière pensée;* but then they usually remind you, that though Mozart was born in Germany, they consider him to have been a Bohemian in all but the place of his birth. In the first place, they will tell you, he wrote all his best works, his "Don Juan," "Figaro," and a few others, in Prague, in the atmosphere of Bohemian song. Then they will add, that nowhere out of Bohemia is Mozart properly understood. In Vienna the people were at first quite unable to estimate him, and Mozart himself, they will assure you, would often say, that he had nowhere been comprehended but in Prague. "My father," said a Bohemian once to me, "was one day looking for Mozart's grave in the cemetery at Vienna, but the gravedigger was a long time before he could make out whom my father meant by the divine Mozart. At length the man suddenly cried out, 'Oh, perhaps your honour means the musician that was drowned!'" I thought the anecdote much more characteristic of the place where it was told me, than of that to which it referred.

The Bohemians in thus claiming Mozart because he lived among them, reverse the conduct of the Poles, who would rob us even of Copernicus, because he was born in a city subject to Poland, though his parents were Germans, though he received a German education, and resided the greater part of his life in Germany. The Slavonians are apt to appropriate every German who comes among them, and assimilates himself to their spirit. On the other hand, however, we are often disposed to look upon many a Slavonian author as a German, merely because he has chosen the German language as the vehicle for giving his ideas to the world, in the same way that many a German, because he happened to write in French, is always set down in France for a Frenchman. We often look upon all the Western Slavonians as so many Germans, perhaps because we consider that those countries owe their education and enlightenment to Germany, but the Slavonians themselves are much more exact in these matters. For instance, before I came to Bohemia, I never dreamt of looking on Huss but as a German. In Bohemia I was soon corrected on this point, and learnt that Huss (the h must be pronounced with a strong gutteral intonation) is a genuine Tshekhian plebeian patronymic, and means neither more nor less than *goose*. Huss himself was born in a Tshekhian village, and was the son of Slavonian peasants, and in proportion as I became acquainted more intimately with his history, among his native hills, I was made gradually aware that the Hussite wars were not merely religious wars, but were in reality, a struggle on the part of the Bohemians to shake off the domination of the Germans; the emperor and his priests were hateful rather as foreign rulers than on account of their theological errors.

If I am not mistaken, I have heard it asserted at Prague that the first inventor of gunpowder was likewise a Bohemian; that we owe the art of printing, not to a German, but to a Slavonian of Bohemia, has lately been repeatedly maintained, and many imagine they have demonstrated it in the most incontrovertible manner. The Bohemian version of the story is this. There lived in the early part of the fifteenth century, in a Bohemian town called Guttenberg, or Kuttenberg, a man of the name of Joseph Tshastni. He was a learned man, and after the fashion of the learned men of his time, he translated his Bohemian name into Latin, and called himself Faustus, for *tshastni* is the Tshekhian word for *happy*. At the same time, according to a practice that also then prevailed among learned men, he added to his own name that of the place of his birth, and called himself Joannes Faustus Kuttenbergensis. In 1421, about the commencement of the Hussite wars, he was driven from his country, and arrived as a fugitive at Strasburg, where he dropped the name of Faustus, and called himself simply Johann Guttenberg. There is an ancient manuscript to which reference is made in support of this claim, and in which the following sentence occurs:—" *Posteaquam artem librorum imprimendorum isdem Joannes Kuttenbergensis Boëmus, patria Kuttenbergensis, prius Joannes Faustus nominatus, qui circa annum* 1421, *bella Hussitica fugiens in Germaniam abiit Strassburgi se Kuttenbergium a patria (ex more ejus temporis et simul ut patriam suam ab inventione Typographiae commendaret) appellavit.*"

The house is still shown in Prague in which this Mr. Faustus is said to have lived. He must have been in comfortable circumstances, for the house is a large one, and has since been fitted up for the reception of a public institution, that of the Deaf and Dumb School, which I visited, partly for Faustus's sake, and partly for the sake of the pupils instructed there. There were forty-one pupils residing in the house, besides twelve children who came merely as day scholars. Very few among them, I found, were completely deaf. The sound of the German *u* (like the English *oo* in proof) they could always distinguish, and when we spoke very slowly and distinctly, the children could understand the greater part of what we said, by closely observing the movement of our lips; but, of course, they understand their own language of signs much more fluently. Many of their signs were of their own invention. The sign for God and heaven was always accompanied by a pious look upward. I tried to tell them something about a *tower*, and in doing so, endeavoured to imitate the sign which the teacher had taught me as representing the word; but I saw evidently that they misunderstood me, and when the teacher came to my assistance, it turned out that they had imagined I was telling them something about the pope, whom they picture to themselves as a kind of moral tower rising far above the rest of human kind.

One of the most important public institutions of Prague is the lunatic asylum, which, though it may not "fulfil all that, at the present day, is expected from such an establishment," as one of the physicians belonging to the house expresses himself, must yet be considered among the best of its kind, as I think my readers will themselves be ready to infer from the particulars I am about to relate of it.

The average number of patients yearly received into the house is 100, of whom about one half are dismissed cured. The number of patients usually in the hospital is 190. The gardens are handsome and spacious, and distributed into different sections for the several gradations of madness. Those who are not considered dangerous meet every Sunday in the principal garden, on which occasion a band of music is always provided. The labour in the kitchen gardens is always performed by the patients, and beyond these gardens there are some fields of considerable extent, which are ploughed, sown, and reaped by the inmates of the house. A piece of hop-ground even is attached to the establishment, that those patients who come from the circle of Bunzlau, where this species of cultivation prevails to a great extent, may find themselves engaged in their accustomed occupation. Constant occupation is looked upon as contributing more than any other means to a cure. We saw no less than forty or fifty poor lunatics engaged in mowing, digging, weeding, watering, planting, &c.

With the exception of the straight-jacket, no species of corporal punishment is ever resorted to. Nearly all the work in the interior of the house is likewise performed by the patients,—such as cleaning the rooms, making the beds, chopping wood, cooking, carrying water, and the like. For my own part, I experienced sincere satisfaction, as I wandered about among the busy multitude, and thought of the principles by which such institutions were governed only 30 or 40 years ago, of the scenes which were then daily witnessed there, of human beings laden with chains, or strapped to benches, and frequently scourged with revolting cruelty. A lunatic asylum in those days was a place in which madmen were shut up that they might not inconvenience the rest of the world, now the object kept in view is to restore them to society.

It is characteristic of music-loving Bohemia, that in the lunatic asylum of its capital, music should be considered one of the chief instruments for the improvement of the patients. In addition to the garden concerts, in which all assist who can, there are quartettos every morning and evening in the wards, and a musical director is appointed for the express purpose of superintending this part of the domestic arrangements.

Among the patients there was none who excited my interest more than a gentleman of the name of Sieber, an accomplished scholar, who had spent some time in the East, had written several works of acknowledged merit, and had, at one time, been looked upon as a man of great natural abilities, as well as of varied acquirements. On first entering the house, he continued for some time to devote himself to his accustomed avocations, but gradually he fell into a brooding melancholy, and thence into a state of sullen madness whence no man had been able to rouse him. I saw him lying in his bed, quite motionless, with his eyes closed, and his arms crossed over his breast, more like a statue on a tomb than a human being. In this position, I was told, he lay almost always, no word ever issuing from his lips. His friends occasionally visit him and weep around his bed, but he seems unconscious of their presence. I was afterwards sorry to hear that this gentleman's presence in the madhouse stood in some connexion with his political opinions, which he had, perhaps, had the imprudence to proclaim somewhat too freely.*

I was allowed to see the lists of the patients treated during several preceding years, from which I deduced two or three statistical inferences that may not be without value when compared with the results obtained at other establishments of a similar character. Among 517 patients, I found there had been 206 women and 311 men; so that the men were in the proportion to the women of more than three to two. Wedlock seemed in some measure to be a preservative against madness, for of the 517 patients, 293 had been unmarried, and 224 had been in the holy estate; the proportion, therefore, of the single to the wedded patients had been as 4 to 3. The middle stage of life would appear to be most liable to attacks of insanity,

---

* This expression might lead Mr. Kohl's readers to suppose the orientalist Sieber, to have been a political victim of the Austrian government, whereas, in point of fact, during his stay in Paris, in 1830, he manifested such evident symptoms of insanity, as left his friends little hope of being able to preserve him to society much longer. Francis William Sieber was born at Prague, in 1785. At his own expense he travelled, in 1817, by the way of Vienna and Trieste, to the Archipelago, where he made the island of Candia the immediate object of his researches, and collected materials for a work which he published in 1822, under the title of *Reise nach der Insel Kreta*, which is accompanied by a number of valuable engravings executed from his own drawings. In 1818 he visited Egypt, ascended the Nile to Thebes, and afterwards travelled through Palestine and Syria, and during this journey his collections were so extensive and valuable, that, when on his return they were exhibited in Vienna, the public refused for a long time to believe that one man could have collected so much in, so short a time. His collection of Egyptian antiquities was afterwards purchased by the Academy of Sciences in Munich. In 1822, Sieber sailed from Marseilles on a voyage round the world, during which he visited the Isle of France, the Cape of Good Hope, New Holland, New Zealand, Cape Horn, and arrived in London in July, 1824. His collections in the department of natural history, during this voyage, were astonishingly extensive, and were exhibited to the public in Dresden in 1824. Here already symptoms of insanity began to manifest themselves. He was haunted by a belief that an eminent Austrian statesman aimed at his life, and this notion continued to engross him more and more. He imagined he had discovered an arcanum for the cure of hydrophobia, and offered to sell his secret to the Emperor of Austria for a large sum of money. Neither the Austrian, however, nor any other government manifested a willingness to pay Sieber's price, which induced him to go to Paris, where in 1830 he published a *Prospectus d'un nouveau système de la nature*, a work which betrays in every page sufficient proof of the melancholy condition into which its author had sunk, to say nothing of the remarkable signature affixed to the book: "*François Guillaume Sieber, le plus grand sot du monde, la bête de l'Apocalypse.*" Among his other works may be mentioned the following: On the Radical Cure of Hydrophobia, Munich, 1820; On the Mummies of Egypt, their Origin, Object, &c., Vienna, 1820; A Journey from Cairo to Jerusalem and back, Prague, 1823.—*Tr.*

for of the 517 inmates there were 156 in whom mental alienation had manifested itself between the ages of 30 and 40.

Of the 311 men, 148 had been servants and day labourers. Of agricultural labourers and gardeners there were only 4. Among the 206 women there had been 11 sempstresses. Among the men, I also observed, as a remarkable fact, that there had been 8 schoolmasters, or 2⅔ per cent of the whole.

The blind-school is, comparatively speaking, unimportant, affording accommodation to only sixteen children, and remarkable only on account of the religious ladies (the Grey Sisters) under whose superintendence the house is placed. For this purpose four young ladies were sent from Prague to Nancy, to pass their noviciate in the house of the Sœurs Grises, and prepare themselves for the charitable office of tending the sick. These four ladies on their return, with a French abbess at their head, founded the institution, to which has already been added, an asylum for the sick blind, in which I found twenty-eight patients. It is generally said that the sick are much better tended by these ladies, who devote themselves to the cause from a motive of religious zeal, than by hired nurses who can seldom be influenced except by the fear of losing their places. We visited the French abbess, and found in her a stirring, bustling lady. She was writing at her table when we entered, and left her papers and account books to receive us. She told us we must look upon the institution as only in its infancy, but that it would gradually grow and become more extensive. I asked her whether she felt herself comfortable in a foreign country. At first, she answered, she had pined after home, and one day, as she was sitting alone in her room, brooding over the many inconveniences of a foreign residence, somebody knocked at her door. An elderly gentleman came in, who introduced himself as a landed proprietor, and began to inquire after the circumstances and prospects of the institution. "Ma chère mère," he said, "you are a stranger here, and must have many difficulties to contend with. Your undertaking is still a young one, but it deserves universal sympathy. Allow me to hand you this parcel as a trifling contribution to the comforts of those under your charge." Before she could thank him, the stranger was gone, and had left a package containing a considerable sum of money in her hands. About three years afterwards she received a letter from a Prince L., who expressed a wish to establish a branch institution for the poor blind at Melnik. After some preliminary correspondence, she proceeded to Melnik, to superintend the formation of the new asylum, when in Prince L. she discovered the benevolent stranger, who had contributed so much by his benevolence, to dissipate the melancholy of the early part of her residence in Prague.

She told me she often received visits from Protestants, like myself, out of Northern Germany, on which occasions she always enjoyed, in secret, the timid embarrassment, with which they entered a conventual house, their minds evidently full of prejudice and wicked thoughts. She never allowed herself, she said, to be at all put out of her way by this, but spoke with them unreservedly, and seldom failed to have the pleasure of observing that her guests were gradually inspired with confidence, and departed with better thoughts than those with which they came. And I must own, it went so, in some measure, with me. Some of the Protestant scales fell from my eyes, when two of the sisters entered the room and presented themselves to me, not as pale, withered, hollow-eyed nuns, but active, healthy, busy housekeepers. One of them, in particular, was full of life and bustle, as she stirred about in the kitchen among the helpless inmates of the house. She could hardly be said to have retired from the world, she said, for she rose early, and was hard at work all day long.

The order of the Sisters and Brothers of Mercy—the grey, the brown, the black, the green, the blue, and the red—fill so important a blank in the system of public charity in Catholic countries, that every one must wish for their continuance until a better organisation is substituted. In striking contrast, however, with these, is an order that has not known so well how to combine the *labora* with the *ora*, and was therefore abolished by Joseph II. as useless, but has been restored since his death : I allude to the order of Carmelite nuns, who claim for their sisterhood the distinction of being more ancient than any other in Christendom, Mary, Anne, Magdalen, and all the other holy women of the New Testament having belonged to it. The Carmelite monks assert that their order was originally founded by the Prophet Elias on Mount Carmel, in Palestine, and that all the prophets and holy men, from Elias to Christ, had belonged to the order. In the proud feeling of a piety ennobled by such unsurpassed antiquity, and by their connexion with so many saints and prophets, the Carmelites seclude themselves with greater strictness than any other order from the profane world ; subject themselves to severer rules, and hold themselves to be entirely dispensed from the duty of doing any thing for the benefit of the rest of their fellow creatures. Joseph II. closed the convents belonging to this order in Prague and in other parts of his dominions, and sent the Carmelite nuns back into the world. The nuns, however, even after leaving their convents, continued, as well as they could, to observe the rules of their order, lodged generally two or three together, held little or no intercourse with the world, and lived on alms and on the work of their hands. When the Emperor Leopold heard this, he was moved by the tale, and made over to them the Barnabite convent on the Hradshin, where the Carmelite nuns have immured themselves, and shut out the rest of the world according to their ancient fashion.

These Carmelite nuns never allow any but the meagrest food to pass their lips ; they pray night and day, and sleep but little. They never sleep on any other bed but naked boards, and their only pillow is a stone. They wear a hair-cloth garment next the skin, and sometimes an iron chain, by way of girdle, with sharp prongs that run into their flesh. Into the interior of their convent no living creature of the male sex is allowed to penetrate, and yet there are among them many delicate and young girls. Such was the account I generally heard of them at Prague, together with a multitude of marvellous and mysterious particulars. My curiosity was, therefore, excited, and I determined to penetrate, as far as I could, into the mysterious recesses of the community, and to obtain for myself some authentic information on the subject. It was a monk of the convent of Strahoff who lent me his aid and advice. He described to me a door of the nunnery where I might knock, and to the woman who came to inquire what I wanted, he bade me say, I was a stranger who wished to see the holy Mary Electa. This holy Mary Electa, it seems, is the weak point of the Carmelites, who are very proud of having her among them, and seldom refuse a stranger the favour of paying his devotions to her. "But, reverend father," I replied, "I am a Protestant, so I hope I shall not be called on to kiss the hands or feet of the saint, or to affect to pray at her shrine." "You will be asked no questions about your religion; but as I tell you, there is no other way by which you can obtain admittance."

I went accordingly, found the door to which I had been directed, and knocked. The door was opened, and in a small vestibule I saw an elderly woman, who belonged to the domestic attendants of the convent, and who asked me what it was I wanted. I replied, as I had been taught, that I was a stranger, and wished to see the Holy Mother, Maria Electa.

In the wall, opposite to the door, was a small opening, and in this opening was a kind of perpendicular valve, that turned round, and through which small matters might be passed in and out of the convent. Here the attendant knocked, and shortly afterwards, a low voice was heard to inquire what was wanted. "It is a stranger, venerable sister, who wishes to see our Holy Mother, Maria Electa, and requests the keys of the chapel." "Yes, yes," was the reply, and in a few minutes a heavy bunch of keys fell into one of the compartments of the perpendicular valve, the old woman who acted as my guide, took the keys, and we proceeded to the chapel. I saw nothing very remarkable in the chapel on entering, except an iron railing near the altar, behind which railing some black object appeared to be moving about. "What is that?" I asked. "Behind that railing," answered my guide, "sits our Mother, Maria Electa, and one of our venerable sisters is now opening the shrine, that you may see it the better. Wait here a moment, and—" But I did not wait. On the contrary, I hastened up to the railing, which consisted of thick iron bars, and in the gloom behind them, I saw a nun closely veiled, who was kneeling before an old, brown, dried up mummy, kissing its hands and feet, and repeating one prayer after another. The mummy was the Maria Electa whom I was supposed to have come in search of. She sat upon a richly ornamented throne, and was adorned with a profusion of lace and tinsel. She was surrounded by a glass case, which the nun had opened, that I might see the better. The holy sister had been somewhat long over her work, or I had been somewhat quick, but at all events I found, in spite of the severe rules of the Carmelite order, that it was very possible for a young man to find himself tête-à-tête with a nun, and to converse with her with even less reserve than is often imposed by the etiquette of the great world.

"Excuse me, venerable sister," said I, addressing her; "Is that the Maria Electa?"

"Praise be to Jesus Christ!" she replied, after a few moments, and after she had completed her prescribed number of kisses and prayers; "Yes, this is our dear, holy, revered Mother, Maria Electa!"

The nun was now standing upright before me, and though she was wrapped in a thick woollen garment, and her face was covered with a close black woollen veil, yet her form appeared to me handsome and graceful. Her voice was remarkably soft; indeed, she seemed to breathe and lisp, rather than to speak. This was at first pleasing, till I afterwards observed that all the Carmelites have the same soft, lisping, melting voice, with a kind of sentimental whine while speaking, the effect of a habit acquired from their constant praying.

In this softly breathing voice the nun told me the whole history of Maria Electa. "She was the principal of our order two hundred years ago, and her pious and holy life will never allow us to forget her. Heaven has miraculously preserved for us her cherished frame, which continues uncorrupted. She is just as she was when living. Her hands, arms, and fingers are still quite pliant. Our holy father the Pope will therefore probably canonize her, which has not yet been done."

"You wish that he should do so, I suppose?"

"Oh certainly, we wish it very much; and indeed the business has already been taken in hand. Should we succeed, it would be to the honour and to the profit of our convent. We have printed the history of Maria, and I will give you a copy of the book."

With that she handed me a little book, which I squeezed with some difficulty between the bars, and observed at the same time that her hand was exquisitely white and delicate. My imagination immediately pictured to me a countenance equally pleasing, and in harmony with the softness and melody of her voice. I began to relate of the other saints and churches that I had seen, and of my own erratic manner of life. She listened to me with evident interest, and I indulged her the more willingly, that I might have a right, in my turn, to question her a little about her customary way of living.

"Oh, our life," said she, "is glorious, for it is devoted to praying to God. I have been here now for five years. I was born in Styria, and when I declared my determination to enter a convent, my parents wished me to choose one of the less severe orders. But I preferred the Carmelites to every other, for only those who renounce the world altogether, can belong altogether to Heaven. I readily submitted to the strict noviciate of three years, to which all must submit who wish to be received as sisters of our order. During this time we must pass through several ordeals, one of which is to abstain for a whole year from all speech, save to God and his saints. Even our sisters, during this year, speak to us only by signs, and that as seldom as possible. Those who, during these three years, have not constantly manifested a joyful devotion to their severe task, are not received into the order. Those who, before the expiration of the time, feel their resolution fail them, may retire, for we wish to have none for our sisters but such as freely and zealously long to renounce the world, that they may devote themselves to prayer, and to a communion with the saints. Nor is any allowed to take the vows before her 24th year, for when the vows have once been taken, all return to the world is impossible."

From these premises, I calculated the age of my informant to be under thirty. A pretty age! thought I, and a marvellously long way off from that total benumbing of the flesh, which I observed in the third personage to our interview, the Mother Electa, who sat enthroned in her glass case. I inquired whether there were any novices at present in the house.

"Yes, four; and there are sixteen sisters of us."

Sixteen marvellous, romantic, and very melancholy perversions of mind, thought I; a state of things, of whose existence, at this time of day, many of our cold Northerns will find it hard to form a very clear conception.

"As sisters too," she resumed, "we lead a life of constant self-denial, such as to you, no doubt, will seem very hard. Seven hours a day we invariably spend in prayer, besides which, on certain holidays, we have prayers and masses to chaunt at midnight. During the day we seldom speak to one another, and only in the morning and evening we have one hour of recreation. During these two hours we visit each other, and converse together. We make and mend our own clothes, and attend to other work in the convent, endeavouring to do as much of it as possible with our own hands."

"Is it true," I asked, "that you wear nothing but this coarse garment of wool or hair?"

"This is the only garment we wear, and our food is equally simple. Meat we never touch, but only vegetables, and fish, dressed either with oil or butter, and water is our only drink; but we are cheerful and contented, and it never occurs to us to covet any thing beyond that. We sleep on straw, and a sack of straw serves us for a pillow. Some of us, however, impose, at times, additional hardships on themselves. They will sleep, for instance, on the naked boards, or will save a portion of their scanty meals, and send it out to the poor in the world, or they will pass whole nights in prayer. In these exercises we often emulate each other, and think we cannot carry them too far; for, indeed, how can we ever hope sufficiently to chastise and mortify our sinful flesh?"

Good God! thought I; and these sacrifices, these ordeals, are imposed in a house surrounded by sumptuous palaces, and in the very centre of a populous luxurious city. Almost unconsciously I exclaimed—"But why do you not rather choose to live in some remote solitude, in some gloomy forest, or on some bleak heath?"

"It would indeed be better," resumed my nun, with her accustomed sweetness of voice, "and we would much prefer it, but we cannot remove the convent that has been assigned to us, and are not rich enough to build one in a more suitable place. Besides, we may live here as elsewhere, free from all commerce with the world, happy and cheerful, in perfect concord, and devoted to God, and to friendship for each other." At this moment there arose before my mind's eye, one of those crooked little black things that ask questions, and I began to think, that before my informant persuaded me of the cheerfulness and perfect concord of her little community, it would be necessary for her to admit me a little more behind the curtain. "And you were right in your doubts," said a friend to me afterwards; "the concord, I am sorry to say, is not such as might be expected to prevail among beings devoted to such constant exercises of piety. Intrigues and cabals are of constant occurrence in this little state within the state, particularly on the occasion of electing their principal, who is chosen anew every third year."

My gentle Carmelite, however, unconscious of my doubts, continued in the same strain. "Oh, you cannot imagine how happily, how blissfully, we live here, without a wish or a want to gratify. It is only rules so severe as ours that make it possible to enjoy heaven already upon earth." Thus saying, she closed the glass case of Maria Electa, after she had once more kissed the hand of the withered mummy, and praying God to have me in his keeping, she withdrew into the interior of the convent. Through the open door I discerned a long passage, and at the end of it a small piece of ground planted with trees, the only place whence these poor creatures are ever able to gaze upon God's heaven. God be with thee, poor girl, thought I, as the end of her garment vanished round the corner, how grievous makest thou life to thyself! and yet has not the Lord himself said—"My yoke is soft and my burden is light?" and then I thought of the many faithful, pious mothers that I had known without the convent walls, living a life of godliness, and of daily usefulness to their fellow-creatures.

The great charm which convents, particularly nunneries, have for us, lies in the nature of the vows taken by those who retire there, and partly in the unusualness of character and fortune which we presume in the inmates. Another cause of the great interest we take in these institutions, is the mystery which surrounds them. This charm, so irresistible to a sober Protestant, attracted me once more to the Carmelites, but this time in company with a lady of rank of Prague, who went to pay a visit to the principal or *Oberin* Aloysia. We were received in the parlour, which is separated into two divisions by a double grating, such as is placed in all Carmelite convents before every window or opening through which the profane world might look into the dwelling of the holy sisters. Behind this grating hung a dark curtain which was rolled up, and presented to us the principal, and another nun, who had preceded her in office. Both were closely veiled, and my imagination was left at liberty to embellish them with endless charms, of the existence of which I was not allowed to obtain any more satisfactory evidence. My companion offered indeed to ask the principal to unveil, and expressed a conviction that the request would be complied with; but I prayed her, on no account to do so, for I feared, I scarce know why, the dissipation of those agreeable illusions in which I had been indulging.

My two visits convinced me, at all events, that the Carmelites did not live in such complete seclusion from the world as I had been told. The principal keeps up friendly relations with many ladies in Prague, receives visits from them, and accepts trifling presents. Nor do I believe, in spite of the assurances of my first informant, that they would at all like to remove into a wilderness. They do not see the world, indeed, but it is something to know that the world is about them, and though they imagine they have renounced every feeling of vanity, still it is necessary to them to know themselves admired for their self-denial. They place their solitude among the princely palaces of the Hradshin, as Diogenes placed his tub opposite to the palaces of the Athenians. The palaces that he despised were as necessary to his self-importance as to the pomp of Pericles and Alcibiades. Had the Athenians all taken to living in tubs, Diogenes would have soon found his way back into a decent house; and in the same way, I am convinced, the Carmelites would not be long in knocking away their gratings, if they were to hear one fine morning that all the fine ladies in Prague had immured themselves.

In Vienna the Carmelite nuns have not been able to re-establish themselves since the days of Joseph, any more than the Jesuits. The latter, however, are tolerated in several of the provincial cities of Austria. Prague has, indeed, far more convents and religious orders than Vienna, or than any other city in the Emperor's dominions. It would be much more easy to enumerate the orders that are not to be found in the Bohemian capital, than to count all the varieties of religious habits and uniforms that one encounters in every street.

It would be an interesting thing perhaps to observe all these monks in their cells, but we satisfied ourselves with a visit to the most important of them, the white Premonstrants of the monastery of Strahof, which contains one of the most celebrated libraries in Bohemia. This convent, whose real name is Strasha, which the Germans have corrupted into Strahof, was founded in 1140, or only twenty years after an angel had shown to St. Norbert, near Coucy in France, the field on which he was to build the first convent of the order. In the thirteenth and fourteenth centuries, the order possessed two thousand monasteries. At present the number does not exceed one hundred, of which that of Strahof is probably by far the the most wealthy.

Like all the *Prachtklöster* or convents on a large scale in Austria, Strahof is only partially finished. The church is in a ruinous condition, and offers a painful contrast to the magnificence of the interior of the library. The beneficial effects of this library must be inestimable, if all the pious texts and moral precepts with which its walls and columns are so liberally inscribed, have not only served as architectonic decorations, but have, at the same time, been duly impressed upon the hearts of the monks.

The library contains fifty thousand volumes, arranged with exemplary order and elegance, which would be the more gratifying if there were not so few bees to collect the honey from so fair a garden. The thirty monks of the convent can enjoy but a small portion of the rich sweets consigned to their keeping, and the channels through which their fertilizing influence might be made to flow over a wider space, require the bold hand of another Joseph to open them. Zisca, who preached in the name of Huss, and baptised with fire where Huss had come armed only with water,—Ziska whose name next to that of Joseph II., is oftenest heard in Bohemian monasteries, instead of setting the garnered sweets free for the benefit of mankind, would have stopped them up altogether, for he destroyed the monastery of Strahof as he had destroyed many others before. At present, however, his wild one-eyed countenance hangs in the picture gallery at Strahof, along with a multitude of other historical portraits; indeed I have found the picture of this puller down of castles and convents, occupying a prominent and honorable place in the collections of the many Bohemian convents and castles that I have had occasion to visit; and those who, if he were still living, would move heaven and earth to bring him to the gallows, now that he is not likely to do them any more mischief, appear to be not a little proud of the privilege of counting such a dare-devil among their compatriots.

THE JEWS' QUARTER.

The Jewish community of Prague, boasts of being the most numerous and most ancient of the Austrian monarchy, and indeed of all Germany. It consists of 10,000 individuals, so that it comprises about one-tenth of the whole population of the city. In the Galician cities only are the Jews sometimes found in a greater proportion. In Vienna, on the contrary, they amount only to one-fifth of the number resident in Prague, and if the greater population of Vienna is taken into account, the Jews of the Bohemian stand in numerical proportion to those of the Austrian capital, as twenty to one. All Bohemia is said to contain about 70,000 Jews; one-seventh of the whole, therefore, have their domiciles in Prague. All Bohemia contains four millions of inhabitants; consequently, every sixtieth man in Bohemia is a Jew, and in the capital every tenth. There are Austrian provinces in which no Jews are to be met with. These are Austria above the Ens, Styria, Carinthia, and Carniola. In the last-named province, within a few years, ten Jews have established themselves. In Styria one solitary Israelite is said to hold his residence.

In the whole of the Austrian states there are at present 652,000 Jews; more than one-third of the whole, 265,000, being included within Austrian Poland, and nearly as many, 260,000, in Hungary. About one-sixth, or 110,000, inhabit Bohemia and Moravia, and the remainder are distributed in small portions, over the remaining provinces of the empire. Thus, in Transylvania there are 3,500; in Tyrol, 1,900; in Dalmatia, 500; in Lombardy, 2,000; in Venetian Lombardy, 4,000; in the Military Frontier, 400, &c. Hence it would seem, that in ancient times, the Slavonians and Magyars must have been most tolerant to the Israelites, while the Germans and Italians must always have been less willing to admit them as residents. The purely German provinces of Austria contain only 5,000 Jews, the purely Italian only 7,000; whereas in those provinces in which the Slavonian and Magyar elements of population preponderate, the Jews number no less than 620,000. Moreover, in the German and Italian provinces, the Jews are yearly decreasing in numbers, although the population generally is increasing; in Hungary, on the other hand, the Jews are increasing at a far more rapid ratio than any other class of the population.

The other question, that which refers to the antiquity of the Hebrew community at Prague, will be less easy to solve; indeed, so wide a range is there between different authorities, that there is a difference of no less than a thousand years between the date assigned by one party, and that contended for by those of an opposite opinion. The Jews maintain that their settlement at Prague dates back at least to the year 632 of the Christian era, that date being inscribed upon the most ancient tombstone of their cemetery, while several tombstones are still to be found inscribed with various dates from the 8th century. The Bohemians, however, refuse to recognise the claim of the Jews, and deny the authenticity of the stone altogether. The Jews, they say, have occupied their present quarter only for a few centuries, having been removed to it, from the opposite side of the river, by the express command of one of the kings of Bohemia, who assigned to them the locality now known under the name of *Judenstadt*, or Jews' Town. One Bohemian antiquary told me that the inscription in question referred probably to the year 1632, and not to 632, it being still usual in many parts of Austria to abridge dates by leaving out the first figure, and to say for instance, 841, in speaking of the year 1841.

If the Jews are correct in their chronology, their community must have existed as early as the reign of the celebrated Slavonian king, Samo, who united Bohemia and Moravia into a powerful Slavonian empire; nor would there be any thing very marvellous in supposing that this mighty sovereign, under whom commerce is known to have been actively carried on, should already have had Jews among his subjects. It is not, however, known in what part of his dominions King Samo held his residence, and it is only his successors Krok and Libussa to whom credit is given for having founded Prague. Nevertheless, according to Ptolomæus, there is very little doubt that Marobudum, the ancient capital of the mighty Marbod and his Markomans, stood on the same spot on which Prague was afterwards built, in which case it is very likely that Samo ruled over the whole land from the banks of the Moldau. There would be nothing absurd therefore in supposing that the Jews may have dwelt for 1200 years where Prague now stands, even though we may not feel disposed to receive their tombstones as authentic evidence of the fact. Nay, it is quite possible, that Marbod himself, the cotemporary of Augustus, as he adopted so many things from the Romans, may, among other importations from Italy, have received a consignment of Jews for the supply of his city of Marobudum. A Hebrew colony may even have existed here at a still earlier period, when, previously to the Christian era, and before the invasion of the country by the Markomans, the Celtic sovereigns held their court in their antique capital Bubienum, which must also have been situated very near to where Prague now stands, and probably on the spot now occupied by the village of Bubenetz. In this way the Jews may have dwelt in the country even before it was ruled either by Germans or Slavonians.

Whether or no there be any foundation for these speculations, it is not the less certain that the said Jewish cemetery has all the outward appearance of great antiquity, and belongs, as well as several of the synagogues, to the most interesting objects that a traveller can expect to look upon.

The cemetery lies in the very heart of the *Judenstadt*, where it is encircled by buildings and narrow lanes. Its form is very irregular, winding, now broad and then narrow, amid the houses that overtop its lofty wall. This very irregularity of form seems to speak in favour of the high antiquity of the place, to which, through succeeding centuries, a fragment seems now to have been added here, and now there. In the central part of the enclosed space, the tombstones are crowded together in a manner I never saw equalled anywhere else. Close to the wall, on the inside, is a footpath, and a man must walk tolerably fast to be able to make the round in a quarter of an hour. The Jews do not, as we do, inter fresh corpses in graves whose former tenants have mouldered into dust, but always place their dead either over or by the side of each other. This practice occasions the astonishing accumulation of tombstones, of which I am sure there are several hundred thousand in this cemetery. They have all a family resemblance, being four-cornered tablets with neatly-executed inscriptions. They stand literally as closely together as ears in a cornfield. All are carefully preserved, though some have sunk more or less into the ground, so much so, that here and there you see a stone, of which only a small portion is still visible. The whole is overgrown with elder bushes, that stretch their knotty and confused branches from stone to stone. These elders are the only trees that grow there, and some of them seem to be nearly as old as the stones which they overshadow. The presence of the elder tree in burying-grounds is not, however, peculiar to this place, but prevails very generally throughout Bohemia.

Here and there a small path winds among the thicket of tombstones and elder trees, and on following it you come to small elevated spaces of ground, that have been left unoccupied, and are now overgrown with grass. If I were a painter, and wished to paint a picture of the Resurrection, I must confess, I should choose one of these little grass-grown knolls in the Jewish cemetery of Prague for the scene, in preference to any other. I can imagine no more picturesque spot from which to contemplate so vast a spectacle, and I wonder, when we have so many pictures of the celebrated burying-ground at Constantinople, that our artists should not also have taken that of the Jews at Prague as a subject for their pencils.

The inscriptions are nearly all in Hebrew. Nowhere did I see a Bohemian inscription, and only here and there, on a stone of comparatively modern date, has the German language been used. The year is always at the top. The tombs of those of Aaron's race are distinguished by two hands graven into the stone, and those of the Levites by a pitcher, to mark the office of the latter to pour water on the hands of the former, when performing their ablutions in the temple.

The descendants of Aaron never visit the cemetery during their lives. Any contact with, or even a near approach to, a dead body, is a pollution for them. They may not, therefore, remain in a house in which a dead body is lying. There is but one exception made to this law, namely, when the father of an Aaronite dies, in which case the son may come within three ells of the body, and follow it to the burying-ground, till within three ells of a grave. The Jewish laws even prescribe the distance at which an Aaronite must keep when passing a burying-ground, which distance, however, is not calculated from the outer wall, but from the nearest grave. Now, in Prague, it happens that one street passes close to this wall, and that just in this spot the graves not only reach up to the very wall, but that some are even supposed to lie under the pavement of the street. This would, consequently, be a forbidden road to every Aaronite, had not particular arrangements been made to provide a remedy. This has been done by undermining that part of the street, and the empty vaulted space thus obtained, protects the Aaronite against pollution, for, according to the law, one hundred ells of vaulted space, are deemed equal to one thousand filled with solid earth.

Here, as in every other Jewish cemetery, a piece of ground has been set apart for the interment of children stillborn, or of premature birth. In the course of time, this portion of the cemetery has grown into a hill or mound, eighty paces long, ten paces broad, and twelve feet high. *Ephel* is the Hebrew word for a child whose life does not extend beyond the fourth week, and *Ephel* is the name given by the Jews to this mound formed of infantine remains. Close to this *Ephel* are situated some old houses that seem to be on the point of falling in. They are propped up by beams resting on the Ephel; thus the mouldering bones of deceased infants lend their support, perhaps, to the tottering dwelling-places of their living parents.

When some sixty years ago, the Emperor Joseph prohibited all future interments within the walls of the city, the Jews had purchased a small piece of land, and consecrated it as an addition to their cemetery. Having once been consecrated, though not one body has been interred there, the ground has become holy, and may not be sold again; but though it may not be sold, it may be let for hire, and accordingly a dealer in wood has become the tenant, and uses the place as a depot for his merchandise. The whole cemetery, since Joseph's time, has been only an interesting piece of antiquity, still no portion of it can be sold or built upon.

The Hebrew community of Prague enjoys a high reputation among all the Jews of Central Europe, and many celebrated Hebrew scholars, many distinguished women, and many eminent merchants and bankers, rest within its cemetery. The community of Prague may even be looked on as the parent hive, whence many an enterprising swarm departed for the colonization of Poland and Hungary, and I had subsequent opportunities of satisfying myself of the influence which a Jew from Prague is able, even at the present day, to exercise among his co-religionaries of Hungary.

In the cemetery of Prague, many a grave is pointed out to the stranger as that of a man high in renown among those of his own nation. Among others, I was called on to admire the beautifully-sculptured monument of a fair Jewess, who had risen to be a lady of high rank, the wife of a wealthy

Polish Count. There were several tombs which, I was told, belonged to Levites and Rabbis of high fame and distinction, and to one my attention was directed, as that of a youth who died some centuries ago, at the early age of eighteen. This youth had been, even in childhood, they told me, a miracle of learning, wisdom, beauty, and virtue. God had endowed him with the most pleasing qualities, and Jehovah's spirit hovered unceasingly over the boy's head. He was too virtuous, however, for this world, and his Creator therefore called him away in his eighteenth year. At his death there were signs and miracles, and the heavens were obscured. The King of Bohemia who then reigned, observing this, sent over to the other side of the river to demand of the wise men among the Jews, the cause of this sudden darkness, and was informed, in reply to his interrogatories, that an angelic soul had just departed from the earth.

One tomb, erected early in the last century, was pointed out to me as that of a wealthy and benevolent Israelite of the name of Meissel. He had inherited nothing from his father, and continued, till death, to be a dealer in old iron. He lived in the same modest and parsimonious manner as the majority of his nation; but with the money that he was thus able to save, he built the Jewish council-house at Prague, and four synagogues. Six streets were paved at his expense, and sixty poor people were weekly fed by him. No one knew whence his money came, or where he concealed it, but it was supposed that he had found a quantity of gold among some old iron that he had accidentally purchased.

At present, the Jewish cemetery, like most old ruins or deserted places, serves as a refuge to a number of thieves and deserters, who are often able to conceal themselves for a long time among the bushes and tombs. Among the immediately adjacent houses are an asylum for young children, an infirmary, and an hospital. For the accommodation of the children a doorway has been broken through the wall, and a small unoccupied space of the cemetery has been assigned to them as a playground, where a shed with benches and tables has been erected for their use. I own, when I saw the little creatures sporting about in their little corner of a churchyard, and frolicking among the closely-crowded gravestones, I could not help asking myself what influence such a playground was likely to exercise over the future development of their minds. They were plucking wild flowers from the graves, and wreathing them into garlands. There were many pale, meager, helpless little creatures among them; and, as I looked on them, I could not but think of the different fate of the little favourites of fortune, whose first tottering steps are made among flowery parterres, or over the lawn of a park. A singular contrast to this scene presented itself when I visited the infirmary, where I found a number of aged creatures of both sexes, who had completely sunk into the helplessness of a second infancy. Among them was a Jewess more than a hundred years old, who had been bedridden for years. She lay crooked, blind, and almost motionless, more like a vegetable than an animated being, and the only sign of life manifested by her, was an occasional whining sound. About forty old men and women were coughing, hobbling, and groaning around us. I was accompanied by a man of some consideration in the community. He was saluted by the inmates of the house in a completely oriental style. They came tottering up to him, kissed his garment, addressed him over and over again by the title of "Gracious Master," and wished him long life, health, and the blessing of God. Many of these poor people had nothing in this institution but a rude couch in a very uninviting corner of a room; yet they were unceasing in their professions of gratitude for the mercies vouchsafed to them, though there seemed to me to be little about the house deserving of commendation except the fact of its existence. I shuddered when I thought how wretched must be the dens, to be rescued from which, was calculated to call forth such warm expressions of thankfulness. In fact, I believe, that in the Jews' quarter of Prague, many a human being breathes forth his spirit among scenes of such heart-rending wretchedness that even an infirmary, such as that I was now visiting, may still deserve to be deemed a beneficent institution, entitling its founders and supporters to the thanks and esteem of every truly benevolent mind. Would that they were more powerfully seconded in their humane endeavours, that they might redeem a larger share from the floods of misery with which the Judenstadt of Prague is at present overflowing!

What a vast extent of moral desolation there must still exist in this city, was made evident to me by the case of a human being whom I saw in this infirmary. He was a boy that had been found wandering about the streets of Prague. He appeared to me to be between ten and twelve years old. He was taken up by the police in the streets, a wild little creature, and unable to speak or understand any language. He was handed over to the Jewish magistrates, who placed him in the infirmary, after having vainly endeavoured to obtain a clue to the child's family. The name of Lebel Kremsier was given him. We found him crouching in a corner between a window and a large chest. "He is wild and ungovernable," said the superintendent of the house, "and though I have beaten him for it repeatedly, he will sometimes jump like a cat out of the window, and go hiding among the bushes and gravestones yonder. His delight is to hunt the cats, and if he catches them he kills them. His limbs are powerful, and his teeth remarkably strong and sharp." So saying, the man pulled open the boy's mouth, and showed us his teeth, much in the same way that a showman at a fair would have exposed the tusks of some wild animal. "He will eat as much as two grown men," continued the superintendent, "but he is not at all dainty, swallowing indifferently every kind of food offered him. Sometimes he is more than usually wild, and then he is dangerous, biting and scratching all who come near him; me, however, he never ventures to attack. He says nothing, and if any one speaks to him, he merely repeats the words like an indistinct echo." The countenance of the child was regularly formed, and his eyes were full of animation. I said to him, "What is your name?" and he replied only by imperfectly articulating the two last words, "your name." "Why have you no trousers on?" said I. "No—trow—on," was the echo that answered to my interrogatory. "Lebel Kremsier, are you not cold?" "Old" was the sound with which he replied. While he was thus repeating my words, his face was distorted by a kind of smile or grin that seemed to tremble over his features. I attributed this to embarrassment, but my guide told me it was the effect of mere terror, and then, for the first time, I observed that the whole body of the child was trembling. After I had passed on, I looked back, and saw that he still sat cowering, trembling, and grinning.

In desolate places, among forests or marshes, such wild abandoned beings have sometimes been found; but how it was possible for a wretched creature like Lebel Kremsier to grow up in a populous city, is a riddle I am unable to solve.

There are no less than twenty Jewish *Bessa Mederesh,* or houses of instruction, besides eight temples, the greater part of which are in the immediate vicinity of the cemetery. The oldest and most interesting is that called the *Altneuschule,* whose internal arrangements interested me the more, as the ancient style of the architecture, and the order of divine service still observed there, afforded me an opportunity of instituting a comparison with the reformed system of worship which is making rapid way among the modern Jews, and has already taken firm root at Prague, where it threatens to drive the old synagogues and the old schools completely out of the field. I scarcely believe that there is any thing like the *Altneuschule* of Prague to be found, at the present day, in any other part of Germany.

The outside of this synagogue looks like one of those old warehouses that may still be seen in some of our German cities, that have undergone but little change since the middle ages. Within, the dust, dirt, gloom, and smokiness of the whole place, remind one of a catacomb. From the ceiling hangs a large flag, so large indeed that it extends the whole length of the synagogue. This flag was given to the Jews by Ferdinand III., after the termination of the thirty years' war, for the patriotism and gallantry they had displayed when Prague was besieged by the Swedes in the last year of the war. During this siege, all the citizens of Prague, even the students, the Jesuits, and the monks, had fought bravely on the walls, and had even made several sorties to attack the besiegers. In reward for their gallant behaviour, the emperor conferred the honour of knighthood on a number of the citizens, including all the city councillors, in addition to which, various honours and immunities were conferred on several of the corporations and convents.

The *Esoras Nashim* (that portion of the synagogue set apart for the women) is partitioned off from the body of the temple by a wall a foot and a half in thickness. A narrow staircase, such as may be seen behind the scenes of a low theatre, serves as the only means of access for the women. In the narrow passages surrounded by walls, they have their chairs. At regular intervals there are in the wall certain rents or apertures, about an ell in length and an inch in breadth, and through these narrow holes comes all that the female members of the congregation are allowed to hear of the word of God. Here they crowd together, looking and listening down into the temple, through an opening that would be abundantly small for one of them, if she had it all to herself. "They will hear but little there," I observed to the Israelite who conducted me down the stairs. "Oh, quite enough for women," was his ungallant reply.

On the tribune, in the centre of the synagogue, stood an old Rabbi and preached. His listeners crowded around the tribune, and some had even intruded upon the tribune itself. Close before the preacher sat a white-haired old man, who appeared to be hard of hearing, and stretched forth his ear in the effort to catch the words of the speaker. Near him was a crowd of boys. The preacher was not, as with us, confined within the limited space of a pulpit, but moved freely about from one side of his stage to the other. There was much in this that would have been highly indecorous to our Protestant notions. As far as grouping and outward form are concerned, a highly interesting daguerreotype picture might have been furnished by the assembled congregation; but, however loudly the preacher vociferated, the spirit that should have given warmth and life to his discourse was altogether wanting. His discourse was the strangest medley of German and Hebrew that I had ever heard. Every text from the Bible was first given in Hebrew, and then translated into German. At one moment the speaker would be commenting upon Nebuchadnezzar, then upon the destruction of Jerusalem by Titus, then again he would enlarge upon the false lights of modern times, to elucidate which he would skip up the whole ladder of history to the days of Adam.

The changes introduced into their temples of late years by the more enlightened Israelites, have altered none of the essential parts of divine service, which, in spirit and form, remains precisely such as it is prescribed by the ancient law. It is only the innovations, that had crept in during the course of time, that have been reformed; and in complying with the letter of the law, they have endeavoured to avoid, as much as possible, whatever is calculated to offend the enlightenment of modern times. Thus, in the reformed Jewish temples, the women still continue to be separated from the men; but by open railings, and not by thick walls. The ancient hymns have been retained; but they are more carefully performed, and a suitable choir of singers is maintained for the purpose. The doctrine of the sermon may be also little altered; but some oratorical ability is looked for in the preacher, who is expected to cultivate a purer style, and to refrain from a perpetual repetition of Hebrew quotations.

It was in Berlin and Hamburg that the first associations were formed among the Jews, with a view to bring about these reforms, and the example was soon followed in every part of Germany. In Prague, about a hundred men joined together, built a new synagogue, and sent a deputation to Berlin and Hamburg, to obtain more complete information respecting the reformed mode of worship, and to select a preacher of learning, piety, and oratorical ability. The first selection was not a fortunate one; for the new teacher obtained but little favour in the eyes of his flock. The second, Mr. Sax, who, like his predecessor, came from Berlin, has, however, become so popular, that even Protestants and Catholics will often go to hear him preach. I went to hear him on the day kept in commemoration of the destruction of Jerusalem by Titus; but, unfortunately, I arrived too late, the sermon being just over. The women, like the men, were sitting in the lower space of the temple, with this difference only, that the men occupied the centre, and the women the side aisles. The choir was composed of a number of young men and boys, in a black costume, with small black velvet caps. As they sung, they were accompanied by a small organ, and the psalms had been rendered into a pure and well-written German version.

The reform in the Jewish temple took root in Vienna somewhat sooner than in Prague, and is now extending its influence from those two centres to all the Hebrew communities of the Austrian empire. Schools, hospitals, and other institutions connected more or less with religion will not fail to be beneficially affected by the movement; which, indeed, they already feel, as I had subsequently more than once occasion to remark. The Austrian government has tolerated and even encouraged these reforms; the more readily, as they have not hitherto led to any religious cabals and dissensions. These indeed, the friends of reform and progress, are sedulous to avoid, and for that very reason they always protest against their being called or treated as a separate party. Nevertheless, something like a feeling of aversion shows itself between those of the old faith and the new. The Old Jews look upon their innovating brethren, however cautious these may be, as violators of the law, and murmur at their proceedings accordingly; but if the reformers continue to observe the same moderation, they will carry their whole nation with them in time. " Our chief rabbi, Rappoport, is an enlightened man," said one of the reformers to me, " and in his heart he is certainly on our side; but he must not quarrel with either side, and therefore does not choose to pronounce himself too openly against the old ones."

This Mr. Rappoport is at present one of the most eminent and most highly-considered men in the whole community of Prague, though it is but lately that he arrived there, and that from Poland, a country in which no one can say that enlightenment has as yet made any great progress among the Jews. He resided formerly at Tornopol, in Galicia, but his reputation for learning and liberality spread far and wide, and caused him, a few years ago, to be promoted to the post which he now holds. I went to pay my respects to him, and found him surrounded by a circle of learned scribes.

The rabbis in this part of the world—I mean in Bohemia, Poland, and Hungary—continue to live after the fashion of the wise men of the East. They allow the light of their wisdom to shine upon the world in a very different way from our learned philosophers of Europe, who, unless when addressing a respectfully listening auditory from the rostrum, are seldom accessible to the multitude that stand so much in need of their instructions. Here the rabbis sit upon the open market-place, like the kings and judges in eastern lands, and in their houses they sit with open doors, ready to receive and answer all who come for consolation or advice. This is particularly the case on the solemn festivals, when the rabbis receive all who come to them, their dwellings being looked upon, apparently, on those occasions, less as private houses, than as places of assembly for the whole congregation. The wife and daughters are generally found in an anteroom, where they receive the guest, and usher him into the inner apartment, into the presence of the rabbi, who, arrayed in his pontificals, generally sits at the end of a long table, encircled by a numerous assemblage of visiters, strangers, and friends.

It was thus that I found the chief rabbi, Rappoport, whose acquaintance I was desirous to make. He had not yet laid aside the costume of the Jews of Eastern Europe, and sat in his arm-chair in a black silk caftan and a high furred cap. Israelites from Magdeburg, from Hamburg, from Warsaw, and from Amsterdam, were sitting around him, and other visiters were constantly arriving and departing. Mr. Rappoport is an Aaronite, a distinction that carries with it privileges far more burdensome than profitable. Of one of these I have already spoken. Another is, that every newly-born child is brought to an Aaronite that he may bless it. There are also some Levites at Prague, but they are less numerous than the Aaronites. The same is observed to be the case in all the other Jewish communities of Europe; and this, I was told, was because Cyrus, when he re-established Jerusalem, brought back to Palestine a greater number of Aaronites than of Levites.

Mr. Rappoport told us that the Jewish Caraïtes of the Crimea and Turkey, had lately found a stone, from the inscriptions on which they sought to show the very remote antiquity of their sect; but that he had lately written an epistle to them to show that the stone could not be genuine, as it professed to be dated from the creation of the world, at a time when that was not the era by which the Israelites reckoned. In his letter he said, he had proved to the Caraïtes, that the era from which the Jews originally reckoned was the flight from Egypt, with which their political history commenced. This system of chronology they retained for about one thousand years, when they adopted the era of the Seleucidæ, which prevailed among the Chaldeans, the Syrians, the Persians, and among most of the oriental nations. This system of computation was retained by the Jews till about five hundred years ago, when the creation of the world was adopted.

Religion among the Jews forms naturally a subject of constant and familiar conversation, as having been the element in which their political and moral relations have at all times been developed. We were led to speak of the subject by an allusion to the cherub wings lately placed by the Israelites of Prague, over the holy shrine of the tablets of the law. I observed that these wings appeared to me very incomplete without the bodies of the angels. This they told me, one and all, was a remark that none but a Christian would have thought of making; that to them such figures of angels would be an abomination, and that whenever they entered a Christian church, with its pictures and statues, they felt much as their forefathers must have felt when they entered the temples of the heathens.

From the rabbi's house my Jewish friends conducted me to their council-house, erected by the Israelite Meissel, of whom I have already spoken. In this building is preserved the ancient charter of the community, which has been signed and confirmed by each of the emperors and empresses of Austria. This charter is preserved as an invaluable treasure, and yet I believe the only privileges granted by it are such as peaceful subjects ought to enjoy, without requiring the security of the sign manual of their sovereigns—namely, the toleration of their religion, and the permission to exist. From the turret of this council-house the whole *Judenstadt* may be surveyed, bounded on one side by water, and on the other by a row of Christian churches. From this turret may be seen all the Jewish streets, swarming with beggars, and all the wretched roofs under which so many forms of wretchedness creep for shelter. As I gazed on what I knew to be the scene of so much suffering, the words of the prophet Baruch came into my mind:

1 Therefore the Lord hath made good his word, which he pronounced against us, and against our judges that judged Israel, and against our kings, and against our princes, and against the men of Israel and Judah,

2 To bring upon us great plagues, such as never happened under the whole heaven, as it came to pass in Jerusalem, according to the things that were written in the law of Moses;

3 That a man should eat the flesh of his own son, and the flesh of his own daughter.

4 Moreover he hath delivered them to be in subjection to all the kingdoms that are round about us, to be as a reproach and desolation among all the people round about, where the Lord hath scattered them.

5 Thus we were cast down, and not exalted, because we have sinned against the Lord our God, and have not been obedient unto his voice.

BARUCH, chap. ii.

It is melancholy to think that this description has continued true through centuries, and applies even at the present day to the condition of the Israelites in every hemisphere and in every land.

POPULAR SCENES IN PRAGUE.

The Austrians say of the Bohemians (that is to say, of the genuine Tshekhs), that they are incapable of abandoning themselves to any thing like a frank, cheerful gaiety, their temper being naturally gloomy and reserved, with a tendency towards melancholy. This judgment respecting the Bohemians is so universally adopted by the Austrians, that there must be some foundation for it, for there is always some truth in the sentence which one nation passes on another. We will not at present inquire how the Austrians came to adopt such an opinion, for our business is at present rather with facts than speculations; and as far as the city of Prague is concerned, the manners of the people have been so decidedly Germanized, or rather Austrianized, that the provincial distinctions at which I have hinted are not likely to appear very evident to a stranger. A German arriving at Prague feels himself in an Austrian city; he hears everywhere the Austro-German dialect; meets at every turn some specimen of Austrian goodhumour; and in the popular scenes that present themselves to his notice, he will recognise the characteristic gaiety of the humbler classes of Vienna; nor will he, for some time, even detect the modifications which the manners of Vienna have undergone in their transplantation to Prague.

I was one day passing through the streets of the latter city, and saw a house-door standing open. Music and song were sounding from within. I stopped, and saw in the courtyard a boy with a barrel-organ, playing a Bohemian Polka, and two pretty girls were waltzing along the hall and around the courtyard to the accompaniment which chance had thus provided. Their dance was graceful and spirited, and I continued for some time to look at and enjoy the scene. As I went away, I endeavoured in vain to remember having ever seen the like, from the street, in any other great city.

Another day I went to the *Färberinsel* (Dyers' Island), to close the day agreeably by listening for a while to the evening music of the grenadiers. I came unfortunately, too late, for before I reached the *Sperl* garden, I met the band on their return. They marched along the broad road of the island, playing a lively air. This already pleased me. I had elsewhere seen military bands break up, but they went home singly; here they were marching homeward in military order, and giving one tune more for the benefit of the public. This made an agreeable impression on me. But now for the manner of their march. By their side went some five or six boys with torches, and in front of the band, along the broad level path of the promenade, some ten or twelve merry couples were dancing away lustily. The band were playing one of Strauss's waltzes. These dancers were not merely children, but grown people were among them, whirling and tripping, in frolicsome mood, around the stiffly marching soldiers, like flowery garlands wreathing themselves around the huge trunk of some time-honoured monarch of the forest. The bearded grenadiers, meanwhile, seemed to enjoy the gaiety of their youthful attendants, and the more merrily these danced, the more lustily the others blew away. The young girls seemed indefatigable, for if one pair gave in, another was sure to issue from the accompanying crowd, and join the dancers. Thus the march proceeded along the whole promenade of the *Färberinsel*, and over the bridge which connects the island with the mainland, where the roughness of the pavement put an end to the ball. Here was another popular scene that I thought well worthy of being engraven on my memory, and I would fain have had a painter at hand, to preserve a copy of what afforded me so much pleasure to look on. "This is really a remarkable scene," said I to my companion. "It is an every-day one here," was his reply.

That the Bohemians are passionately fond of music, dance, and song, is undoubtedly true. So far as music is concerned, the world has long been aware of the fact, for Bohemian musicians are to be met with, not only in all parts of Europe, but some have even wandered with the Russians into Siberia, to the very confines of the Chinese empire; others have of late years accompanied the French to Algiers; and even in Syria and Egypt Bohemian bands are listened to with pleasure. Of their fondness for dance and song I had daily opportunities of convincing myself while at Prague. I met with dancers where I could never have expected them, and where I should not have met with them in any other country; and song—ay, and well executed—I was daily hearing from cellars, from servants' halls, and upon the public street. As to music, not the lowest alehouse in the city is without it.

These low alehouses again have quite a different air from those of the large cities that border on Bohemia,—such as Dresden, Munich, Breslau, &c. Those of Prague have something more poetical about them. Let us enter for instance, one of the many beerhouses about the cattle-market of Prague. They consist mostly of large rooms or halls on the ground floor, and are nightly filled with merry guests. The entrance is generally tastefully adorned with branches of fir or other evergreens, and the walls of the room are often tapestried in the same way. Here and there you may see some neat arbours fitted up in the courtyards, which are illuminated at night. Saturdays, Sundays, and Mondays there is music in all these houses, and in many of them on the other days also, and music of so superior an order, that I often wondered where so much musical talent could come from. These itinerant orchestras of Bohemia, I was told, had much improved of late years, in consequence of the revolution effected at Vienna by Strauss, Lanner, Libitzki, and the other composers, so popular among the dancing world. The compositions of these gentlemen require to be played with remarkable firmness and precision; and though in some respects their influence may have operated very unfortunately, yet I believe it has had the effect, by exciting emulation among the inferior class of musicians in Bohemia, of rousing them to increased efforts to improve themselves.

Nor is it an uncommon thing, in the beerhouses of Prague, to find singers who accompany themselves on the harp. They have in general a very varied collection of songs and melodies, and a musical collector might discover many that would be new to the world at large. Their songs are sometimes German and sometimes Bohemian, and many that I heard were evidently popular favourites, for I could see that the waiters and the guests knew the words by heart, and frequently joined in chorus. Sometimes, the whole assembly would suddenly interrupt their conversation, and accompany the singer with a sort of wild enthusiasm. The singer had generally a table before him in the centre of the room, and on this table the little piles of copper *kreuzers* accumulated fast, for almost every guest, as he left the room, deposited his offering unasked. These are trifles, no doubt, but I believe them to be peculiar to Prague, and they afford an insight into that love of song and music which pervades all classes in Bohemia.

It seems strange to me, that after Teniers and Ostade have immortalized the boorish dances, the broken bottles, the black eyes, the torn hair, and the red Bardolph noses of the Dutch gin-shops, and that so delightfully, that princes think themselves happy in having one or two of these coarse bacchanalian pictures in their drawing-rooms,—it seems strange to me, I say, that none of our modern painters should have attempted the far more poetical and characteristic scenes that are of daily occurrence in one of these beerhouses of Prague. Imagine the crowded room transferred to canvass, the singer forming the central figure, the guests joining in chorus, the waiters with their mugs of beer snatching up a fragment of the song as they hasten from one customer to another; the jolly well-fed host moving with dignity through his little world; nor must we forget the stalls at the door for the sale of bread and sausages, for the vender of beer supplies not these, he ministers only to the thirst of his visiters, and those who would satisfy their hunger must bring their viands with them.

Even the coffee-houses, which are numberless in Prague, whereas in Dresden there are none, have many peculiarities; but they are all fashioned after Austrian models, of which I shall have occasion to speak hereafter. I, coming from the north, was struck by the brilliant manner in which these places were lighted. I could not at first persuade myself that the rooms were not illuminated with gas. The fact is, the people here understand the management of oil lamps better than in any other part of Germany. Something of this, I believe, is owing to the superior quality of the oil.

"So, now we're to be bored about lamp-trimming!" methinks I hear some of my fair readers exclaim. "Pretty company you take us into! First you introduce us to girls that go dancing about the streets, heaven knows why; then to the beer-bibbers of the cattle-market, to the tobacco fumes of the coffee-houses, and—" No farther, my fair censor, pray. Does your name happen to be Anna, or Annette, or Annchen, or Annerl, Nancy, Nannette, Nannerl, or Nettchen? for so far as the Austrian eagle stretches its wings over the fair sex, these names all pass for one and the same. If any one of these names then belong to you, I congratulate you, for in that case you are most pressingly and kindly invited to the festival of St. Anne, celebrated this day in the charming Moldauinsel, and there it will be my agreeable duty to introduce you into very well-bred and agreeable company, in which you will find all the pretty Annes of Prague, a crowd worthy of all admiration, and where you will find the popular manners of Prague presented to you in a totally different point of view.

St. Anne's day is one of the most distinguished popular festivals in all parts of the Austrian dominions, but nowhere are the Annes made more of than in Prague. This holiday falls on the 26th of July, and on the preceding evening every street-corner is tapestried with urgent invitations to festivities of every description. The tavern-keepers and other masters of the revels are emulous in their descriptions of the brilliant preparations made by them for the entertainment of all the pretty Annes in Prague. One addresses himself simply to the "beautiful Annes," another to the "charming Annes of the Bohemian capital," a third heads his placard with an invocation to the "highly respected Nannettes." Accordingly, when, on the all-important day, the rising sun sheds his illuminating rays on the corners of the streets of Prague, those pretty maidens for whom their godmothers have taken the necessary care, may behold their fêted name made glorious in yellow, blue, and red letters, in Latin, Gothic, and German characters, and may see themselves invited to such a countless number of dinners, suppers, breakfasts, rural excursions, balls, and illuminations, that it must sadly puzzle them to determine to which of so many kindly soliciting admirers they will extend their approving smiles.

The beautiful *Färberinsel* is always the chief point of attraction on this day. This island, perhaps one of the most beautiful places of public resort in all Germany, is not large, of an oval form, about 150 fathoms long, and 100 fathoms broad, is surrounded by the rapid waters of the Moldau, and presents its visiters with a complete Panorama of Prague and its hills. To the right you see from the *Färberinsel* the old city, to the left the Hradshin and the *Kleinseite*, behind rises the Vissehrad, and in front lies the old Moldau bridge. In the centre of the island are some elegant buildings, which stand open all day long for the entertainment of strangers. In the rear of these buildings, he who feels himself disposed for sedentary enjoyment, will find abundance of benches and tables laid out under the canopy of huge spreading trees, and a tribune erected for the accommodation of an orchestra will seldom be found unoccupied. On both sides are paths, which wind off among grassplots and bushes, and on St. Anne's day, every place is hung with wreaths and garlands, with here and there triumphant arches, illuminated at night, and decorated with colossal A's and N's.

Early in the morning the host who farms the bridge that leads to this charming little island, has already taken a more considerable toll than is received during the whole twenty-four hours on any other day in the year; for the music, on St. Anne's day, begins at sunrise, and closes not till the moon has vanished on the following night. The greatest throng is between five and seven in the afternoon, but the more aristocratic of the Annes generally retire on the first appearance of the moon and lamplight.

The afternoon on which I found myself in the *Färberinsel*, in honour of the distinguished day, was favoured by the most delightful weather. The fair sex were in a majority of two to one, owing, no doubt, to the great number of Annes with whom Prague has from time immemorial been blessed. The place was small and the crowd great, so great that the visiters could do little else than move in slow procession along the broad walk which encircles the island.

"I can confidently say that I am not what is generally called an enthusiast," said a friend who accompanied me, as we plunged from the little bridge over the Moldau, into this stream of life and beauty, " but it does seem to me as if in the whole course of my life I had never been surrounded by so many angels' heads, by so many graceful forms, or by so many beautiful faces."—" It is truly a bewitching spectacle," was my answer. We now proceeded to stem the current, that we might admire the fair promenaders at greater leisure, and without making use of the slightest hyperbole, I was obliged to own that never in my life had I seen so magnificent a display of beauty. One lovely face followed another in quick succession, and even I, dull and unexcitable as I have often been obliged to deem myself, could not resist the influence of the scene, and the enthusiasm with which I felt myself inspired, was to me the best proof that the spectacle was one of unusual beauty. Like Xerxes at the Hellespont, when contemplating his numerous array of soldiers, I could have shed a tear at the thought, that all the loveliness before me was destined to be the prey of Time and Death.

That the little ugly, squalling, red-faced creatures (for all newly-born babies are alike) should grow up in Prague into such remarkably beautiful girls, is one of those phenomena of nature which I cannot take upon myself to explain. Some have attributed the fact to the mingling of German with Slavonian blood, but this the Slavonians protest against most loudly, telling you that in the villages of the interior, where no such mixture of the races has taken place, much finer specimens of female beauty are to be found, than in any of the frontier districts. The members of the Bohemian Patriotic Association boast, moreover, that by far the richest display of beauty is to be seen at their balls, where nothing but Bohemian is ever spoken, and where, consequently, the bulk of the company must be genuine Slavonian; nay, even the far-famed beauty of the Hungarian ladies is attributed by these zealous patriots to the mixture of Slavonian blood with that of the original races. The theory is not one that I would at once reject as absurd. On the contrary, I often fancied, in the course of my subsequent wanderings, that I saw reason to believe there was some ground for it. Be this, however, as it may, Prague is decidedly a very garden of beauty. For the young ladies of 1841, I am ready to give my testimony most unreservedly, and many an enraptured traveller has left us his books as living witnesses to the loveliness of the grandmothers and great grandmothers of the present generation. The old chronicler, Hammerschmidt, and his contemporaries, dwell with equal pleasure on the sweet faces that smiled upon them in their days, and the picture gallery of many a Bohemian castle is there to testify to the truth of their statements. One witness there is to the fact, whose right few will question to decide on such a point. Titian, who studied the faces of lovely women for ninety-six years, and who, while at the court of Charles V., spent five years in Germany, tells us, it was among the ladies of Prague, that he found his *idéal* of a beautiful female head. If we go back beyond the times of Titian, we have the declaration of Charles IV. that Prague was a *hortus deliciarum*, and whoever has read the life of that emperor, will scarcely doubt that beautiful women must have been included in the delights of a capital so apostrophized. Nay, the time-honoured nobility of the beauty of Prague, may be said to go back even to the earliest tradition, where we find it celebrated in the legends of Libussa and Vlasta, and the countless songs composed in honour of the *Deviy Slavanske* or Tshekhian damsels.

I own I am still at a loss to conceive how it was possible for Przemysl to reject the overtures of his fair Bohemians, and how he could find it in his heart to wage against them the barbarous war that has since become so famous in history. I am not at all surprised that his first enterprises against them should have been marked by such singular failure. I am sure that if the two thousand Nancies and Nannettes whom I saw assembled on the *Färberinsel* had taken it suddenly into their heads to get up an insurrection, and intrench themselves within their little island, any army that the Emperor could have sent against them, would have been much more likely to surrender at discretion to the besieged, than to turn their murderous artillery against such a garden of loveliness, or to flesh their bright swords among the Vienna shawls and French silks that were paraded so bewitchingly before 'my eyes.

By the time that, stemming this tide of beauty, we had made the round of the island some three or four times, night had stolen upon us, though to do him justice, Helios was in no hurry to run away from so fair a scene, but seemed to linger long, unwilling to depart, before he could make up his mind to consign himself to the accustomed embraces of Thetis. The fireworks had to wait long before it was sufficiently dark for the proper display of the rockets and Chinese fire that were intended to blaze in honour of the day, and when they were let off, they turned out to be very little worthy of being waited for ; but the music of the Bohemian *polkas* and *redovaks* compensated for the failure of the fireworks. The whole festivity closed with a " splendid supper," at which I found it impossible, either for money or fair words, to obtain the slightest particle of any thing to eat or drink.

From the delightful promenade of the *Färberinsel*, I went to one of the popular balls, given at the twelve dancing-rooms at Prague. These rooms are never closed on Sundays or holidays, but on this day they had recommended themselves to public favour with even more than wonted assiduity, I extended my patronage to an establishment of which the host recommended himself by a feeling of "Veneration for all Nannettes." The classes represented in this ball-room belonged to the humbler section of the middle orders, and I am sorry to be obliged to own that I found neither the Bohemian beauty nor the Austrian merriment that I had looked for. There is something repulsive in the impression produced by an assemblage in which we find the costume of the cultivated classes copied with great precision, but from which the manners and conversation of refined life are entirely excluded. In proportion as the fashions and habits of the great are imitated by the little world, will all originality, cheerfulness, and fun, be extirpated from among us.

THE NATIONAL MOVEMENT AMONG THE BOHEMIANS.

One of my first walks in Prague was to a Tshekhian bookshop, and to the Museum of the Patriotic Association. I was anxious to see what new blossoms the Bohemian tree had shot forth, and what ancient fruits it had garnered up. The shop in which the literary novelties of Bohemia are offered to a patronizing public, is situated in a narrow gloomy lane, and the man who owns the shop, and is the chief publisher of modern Bohemian literature, is a German. His shop is small, but is often visited by the young patriots,—the advocates, the students, and the literati,—who go there to turn over his Bohemian, Illyrian, Polish, and Russian books, and sometimes to buy them. All these Slavonian languages are at present studied with great zeal by the Bohemian patriots ; and it is a singular coincidence, that in Russia, also, there is at present quite a rage for the study of Bohemian, Polish, and Illyrian. For Russian books, I was told, there was a frequent demand, but they were difficult to obtain. It has long been customary among the young men at Prague to study Russian, which they acquire with little trouble, and which many find of great advantage, numbers of young Bohemian physicians emigrating yearly to Russia, where their familiarity with the Slavonian languages facilitates their advancement.*

Bohemian literature works for the enlightenment of four countries: Bohemia, Moravia, a part of Silesia, and the country of the Slovaks in Hungary. For this reason the Bohemian journals (the *Vlastimil* for instance) point to the four corners of the world, or more properly to the four corners of the paper, with the four words: *Slezan,—Czech,—Slovak,—Moravan,*—(the Silesian,—the Bohemian,—the Slovak,—and the Moravian).

Among the new publications of 1841, I was shown the *Semski Sud*, or the Old Law of Bohemia. The Austrian censors were long before they could be induced to accord the *Imprimatur* to this work, on account of some severe articles which it contains against the Germans, but the censorship is becoming more indulgent now, and, with a few omissions, the book has been allowed to walk forth into the world. The Bohemians, therefore, may again sing in the words of the famous old poem, the Judgment of Libussa:—

> Shameful 'twere from Germans' laws to borrow,
> Laws we have ourselves of holy statute
> Brought in days of yore by our good fathers
> To this land of blessing.†

Twenty years ago, nay, fifteen years ago, the literature, that is the *living* literature of Bohemia, was perfectly insignificant. At that time little was spoken or heard of the Slavonians living under German domination. Some of our travellers of the last century carried their simplicity so far, as to express surprise in their printed books, at finding the country people of Bohemia speaking a dialect altogether unintelligible to a German. Some very learned people had only an indistinct notion, that in some parts of Germany the population was of Slavonian origin. Bohemian literature, in the mean time, had sunk to a level about as low as that of the Lettes and Esthonians in the Baltic provinces of Russia, and was confined almost exclusively to popular ballads. Things have changed since then, and the Bohemians go so far now as to take it very much amiss when they read in a German book, that "Prague is one of the most interesting towns in Germany." The cuckoo, they say, might just as well call the nest his own, from which he has just expelled the linnet, as the Germans call Prague a German city, seeing it was built by the Tshekhs; but here I would humbly remark, that the cuckoo would play a less odious part in our books on natural history, if after taking possession of another bird's nest, he were to embellish and beautify it as the Germans have done

---

* The various Slavonian dialects (Russian, Polish, Bohemian, Illyrian, &c.) bear so strong a resemblance to each other, that the peasants of one of these countries can usually make himself understood to those of all the rest. The grammatical acquirement of the Russian language must, therefore, be an easy task to a well-educated Bohemian.—*Tr.*

† Bohemian poetry, like that of most of the Slavonian languages, is destitute of rhyme, a deficiency the less felt on account of the distinct measure of time which prevails in the Bohemian words, and which makes it more easy to adapt the Roman and Greek rhythm to the versification of this than of any other modern language.—*Tr.*

by Prague. The fact is, the whole of Bohemia is still a disputed territory between the Germans and the Slavonians. The Germans maintain it was originally a German land, or, at least, that it was inhabited by the Germans four hundred years before the Tshekhs came into the country; but the Tshekhs (see Palazky's History of Bohemia,) say—"You Germans took the country from the Boyers, and held it by no other right than that of the sword. By the sword you won it, and by the sword you lost it again, and for eight hundred years we held it against you." To this we Germans may reply:—"But we have again won the mastery of the land from you with the sword, and we have triumphed over you yet more by the energy of our civilization. Here are two swords for one, and as ancient and modern lords we have the most perfect right on our side; so we shall continue to call Bohemia a German land, in right of our sword, our civilization, and our industry,—a German land, in which the intruding Tshekhs are condemned to plough our fields."*

Till very lately, there had existed no good Bohemian dictionary; but this want has now been supplied by Mr. Jungmann, who, though a German by name, is said to be a very zealous Bohemian patriot. His dictionary was the work of several years, and has been published at his own expense. He is even said to have sold a vineyard, to defray the cost of his undertaking. The publication commenced in 1836, and is now complete. I was not so much surprised at the sacrifices made by the patriot scholar, as at the backwardness of other patriots, to assist him in his undertaking. One might almost be led from this to believe what a Bohemian once said to me, in speaking of the great movement and excitement among the Bohemian patriots.

"It is a kind of luxury," said he, "in which a few idle young men indulge, and in which they are encouraged by the professors and antiquaries; but it is no movement originating in the wants, or emanating from the wishes, of the people. All that is eminent with us is German. Our men of education read Schiller and Goethe in preference to any other writers; every official man, down to the humblest clerk, writes and speaks German; and as every Bohemian feels that he cannot get on in the world without a knowledge of German, he seeks to learn it himself, and teach it to his children, and has no time to trouble himself about the fantastic visions of the Tshekhian patriots. Besides, the German language is taught, *ex-officio*, in every school, and many of our gentry do not even understand the patois of the country. With all these mighty agents at work, what avail the efforts of a few enthusiasts? The government, meanwhile, feels itself strong enough to let the Tshekhian party go their own way. Foreigners, moreover, are deceived, if they attribute to politics all that is done here in the way of Slavonian investigation. The inquiring spirit of the time, the revived fondness of every thing that tends to the illustration of antiquity, has led to similar efforts in other countries, as well as in those inhabited by Slavonians. Every province in Europe has been burnishing up its recollections; every city has been turning over the leaves of

---

* Bohemia can scarcely be said to owe much civilization to Germany. When the country passed under the domination of the house of Austria, there was no other country that stood higher in point of civilization. If the Bohemians have since fallen into the rear of the "march of improvement," Austrian oppression, and particularly the unrelenting barbarity with which the Protestant religion was extirpated, must bear the blame.—*Tr.*

its chronicles, and repairing its cathedral or its town-house. Not only the Slavonian provinces, but all the provinces of Austria, have been collecting their antiquities, dusting their records, and new binding their chronicles. The same has been done in the provinces of Prussia, and indeed in the provinces of almost every European country. We have seen Ossian's literature rescued from its tomb in Scotland, and in Germany we have seen Voss writing poems in *Platt Deutsch;* we have seen Westphalian, Saxon, and Brandenburg Associations, not to speak of hundreds of other provincial societies; and thus the fashion has reached Bohemia at last. It is not any inclination on the part of the Western Slavonians to accept the fraternization offered them from the East, that has led to all these Slavonian journals, grammars, dictionaries, and poetical anthologies. In England, and even in France, books and newspapers have been printed in the local dialects, and so in Russia have works been of late published in Lettish and Esthonian, languages of which, some years ago, no cultivated man made use, unless perhaps in the pulpit. It is not to be denied that the provincial, literary, and patriotic movements in the Slavonian provinces of Austria, acquire a peculiar character from the spirit of Panslavismus, of which so much has been heard of late years. No nation, while yet a breath of life is in it, becomes reconciled to the loss of its independence; and though the Bohemians, the Slovaks, and the other Slavonians, would do better to attach themselves more and more to the mild sceptre of Austria, than to stretch out their hands after the questionable independence which seems to be offered them from the East, yet nations, like individuals, are not exempt from acts of folly, prejudicial to others as to themselves; and for their own sake, therefore, as well as for Austria's, the Bohemians must be watched. The classes, however, which have most influence in the country, are the least disposed to sympathize with Russia. The clergy and the nobility know how little they would be likely to gain by exchanging the sovereignty of Austria for that of Russia. Recent events in Poland have likewise much contributed to cool the enthusiasm formerly manifested for Russia. The less instructed Bohemians, indeed, look upon much that they hear of Russia as mere German calumnies; but those among us who stand higher, have had opportunities, many of them, of seeing with their own eyes. In short, should it ever come to a struggle between the Slavonian and German elements, the Tshekhs, in spite of their sympathies and antipathies, will be found fighting on the side of the Germans, and it will be for their own advantage to do so."

In the museum of the Bohemian Patriotic Association, on the Hradshin, whither I went in company with a learned and highly esteemed Bohemian, nothing interested me more than the collection of coins. Though not so complete as the Bohemian antiquaries wish, it is by far the richest Bohemian collection in existence, and consists exclusively of national coins, those merely put into circulation by the Boyers, the Markomans, and the Romans, being excluded. There are old Tshekhian coins of a period far antecedent to the Christian era;—these are rudely fashioned pieces of gold, somewhat in the form of modern buttons. In the early period of Christianity, when it was still uncertain whether Bohemia would be brought within the influence of Byzantine or Roman civilization; the coins of the country seem to have had a decidedly Byzantine character. At a later period, when the Hungarian invasions had cut Bohemia off from the Byzantine world, the coinage assumed an Italian or rather a Florentine character. On the Florentine ducats coined in Bohemia, may be seen the Florentine St. John, with a small Bohemian St. John by his side, in the same way as during their revolution of 1831, the Poles coined Dutch ducats, on which a diminutive Polish eagle appears by the side of the Batavian knight.

As we reach less remote ages we may observe alternate advances and retrogressions in the arts. The cultivated age of Charles IV., and the fanatic century of the art-destroying Hussites, may be distinctly traced in the little glittering denarii and ducats, dollars and bracteati. Coins may likewise be seen here of all the great Bohemian families that, at various times, have enjoyed the privilege. Among these families the most distinguished are the Schlicks, the Rosenbergs, and the Waldsteins, or Wallensteins, as Schiller, for the convenience of his rhythm, has thought proper to call them. Of the Waldstein family, however, none have exercised the right of coinage since the days of their great ancestor, of whom some very beautiful gold coins still exist. The Counts of Schlick exercised the privilege longer than any other of the old Bohemian families. Coins of a very recent date may be seen with their effigy. Their celebrated silver mines at Joachimsberg were so productive, that in the beginning of the 16th century, they coined what were called *Joachimsthaler*, which weighed a full ounce, and which may still be found in circulation in Russia, where they are known sometimes by the name of *Thaleri*, and sometimes by that of *Yefimki*.

A peculiar kind of Bohemian coinage are the royal *Rechenpfennige*, or counters. Among the various public departments of the Bohemian government, it seems to have been usual from the earliest period to have employed, for balancing public accounts, a certain coin which may be looked on in the light of a copper representative of a certain amount of gold or silver. These arbitrary coins circulated only from one public department to another. The noble families in Bohemia appear to have adopted this custom, and coined similar copper counters for the convenience of the various departments of government on their estates. The collection of the Patriotic Association is richly provided with various specimens of these royal and lordly counters.

The Bohemian lion, with a crown on his head, with his two tails, and walking erect on his hinder feet, is to be seen on all Bohemian coins, even on most of those struck by the sovereigns of the house of Habsburg. Under Maria Theresa the lion becomes less omnipresent. The latest ducats that bear the effigy of the royal beast are those of 1780. It was on the large silver money that he first resigned his crown. On the smaller silver coins he continued to hold his state throughout the whole of Joseph II.'s reign, but since then the whole coinage has been purely Austrian.

Of all joyful and deplorable events in Bohemian history, there seems to have been a desire to preserve the recollection by means of silver and gold medals. Thus we have medals of Huss, who, as the inscriptions inform us, was burnt at Constance in violation of public faith. Frederick of the Palatinate has also not failed to leave golden and silver monuments of his brief and disastrous sojourn in Bohemia. Close to these, and adorned with ominous inscriptions lie the medals struck by Ferdinand on the occasion of his sanguinary victory on the White Mountain. In honour of the victory, Ferdinand erected on the mountain a church, which he dedicated to the Virgin, and under the foundation-stone a very large gold medal was deposited. At a subsequent period, Joseph demolished this church, and the medal, being found, was sent to Prague, and came, in due time, to the museum of the Patriotic Association. On one side is a view of the conquered city of Prague, over which is seen hovering the image of *Maria de Victoria in albo Monte*, with the inscription *Reddite ergo quae sunt Caesaris Caesari, et quae sunt Dei Deo*. Christ little thought, when he pronounced those words, that they would become one day in the mouth of an imperious victor, a symbol of terror to millions of human beings. Ferdinand, as we are told, saw a vision the night before the battle. Our Saviour, it is said, appeared to him in a dream, and said to him, " Ferdinand, I will not forsake thee." To this vision allusion is made on the reverse of the medal on which is represented a crucifix, whence rays of light shine on the emperor, who kneels before it, and underneath are the words, " *Ferdinande, ego te non deseram*." It seems strange that after he had made so unchristianlike a use of his victory, our Lord did not again appear to him in a vision, and say to him, *Sed tu, Ferdinande, me et meos deseruisti*.

After the Battle on the White Mountain, Germanism became so impressed on Bohemia, that many Bohemian families Germanized the Slavonian names they had borne till then. Thus the family from which had issued the celebrated St. John of Nepomuk or Nepomucenus, bore originally the Slavonian name Hassil. Nepomuk is a small town in Bohemia, and the bishop, according to the fashion of his day, was called John Hassil of Nepomuk, and sometimes, for greater brevity, John Nepomuk. After the battle of the White Mountain, the Hassils translated their name into German, and called themselves Loeschner. Many of the nobles, however, had Germanized their names long before the catastrophe of the White Mountain. Instances of the kind occurred during the reigns of Charles IV. and his son Venzeslaus. During their reigns, many castles were built on mountains and rocks, according to the German fashion, whereas the ancient Bohemians had been accustomed to build for greater strength among marshes or on the banks of rivers. These castles, built after German fashion, received also German names, ending generally in *berg* or *burg*, and the families began to be called after their castles. In this way the family of Vitkovy came to be the family of Rosenberg, the house of Dipolditz changed into the house of Riesenburg, Ransko was metamorphosed into Waldstein, and Divishovzi into Sternberg, and all these families became much more famous under their German than they had ever been under their Slavonian *firmas*. The Bohemian patriots claim all these families as genuine Slavonians; maintaining that a Slavonian is no more a German because he has taken to speaking German, than the Russian nobles can be said to be Frenchmen because they speak habitually French.

The largest Austrian gold coins have the weight of twenty ducats. Ten ducat pieces, I am told, are still coined, and are occasionally found in circulation. As my readers are all honest people, there can be no harm in my telling them that fifty of these seductive looking lumps of gold are to be seen in the collection at Prague. The largest gold medal in the museum weighs no less than one hundred ducats. The most modern medal is one struck a few years ago, in honour of a visit paid by the Emperor Nicholas to Prague. The inscription is: *Nicholaus I., Cesarsch Russki, &c.* (Nicholas I., Russian Emperor, the Illustrious Guest in Prague.)

I also found much that interested me in the library of the Bohemian

Association, though I was not so fortunate as to have the learned and esteemed librarian, Professor Hanka, for my guide. The department of Bohemian literature is by no means complete, much having been taken by the Royal Library where a section is set apart for it. The collection on the Hradshin is rich chiefly in Natural History. On the other hand, however, the kindred Slavonian literatures of Russia, Poland, Illyria, Servia, and Carinthia, have each its department. I was told that a Russian grammar for the use of Bohemians would shortly be published, and could not but feel surprised that the relations between the great Russia and the little Bohemia should already have become so active, that the want of such a work should have been felt. It is not many years that Germany has been in possession of a usable Russian grammar.

Of Bohemian Bibles many are to be seen here, as well the faithful Utraquist version from the original languages, as that arranged for the Catholics from the Vulgate of Hieronymus. At present, Bohemia can be supplied with Tshekhian bibles only by contraband. There is not indeed any prohibition against their sale, but they are not allowed to be either printed or imported. The smugglers on the Saxon frontier, however, are very active, and keep the market supplied, though perhaps rather sparingly. The bibles are supposed to come from Berlin and from England. The Bible Society of Dresden, I was assured by the president himself, did not themselves send a single copy into Bohemia, but the free traders of the frontier, in the same way in which they receive orders for coffee and sugar, receive orders probably from time to time for bibles. Two years ago, I was told, several waggon-loads of bibles fell into the hands of the Bohemian custom-house officers, by whom they are kept to the present day under lock and key.

Autographs of men celebrated in the history of Bohemia are likewise to be seen at this museum; among many others, those of Huss and Zizka. The latter usually added the place of his nativity to his signature, and signed—Zizka von Trotznow. Some of his letters, however, are signed— Jan Zizka z'Kalichu, from a castle which he had built and to which he had given the name of Kalich or the Chalice.

In the cabinet of natural history on the Hradshin is shown what strangers are told was the last bear that ever existed in a state of nature in Bohemia. This animal is said to have been shot in 1817, but I had subsequently an opportunity of satisfying myself that the race of wild bears is not yet extinct in the country, for on the Schwarzenberg estates, near Budweis, I saw at least a dozen of them. Lynxes and wild cats are also to be found in the mountains, and beavers along the banks of the Moldau, and sometimes even in the immediate vicinity of Prague. Their unsuspected presence near the capital led, not long ago, to a singular lawsuit. A farmer who owned a field near the river, observed that some trees and shrubs had several times been cut down and carried away during the night. He brought an action, in consequence, against one of his neighbours. The court appointed persons to visit the place and inspect the stumps that remained. These persons, on viewing the ground, declared immediately that the property had been carried away by fourfooted thieves, and after a close search, a little colony of beavers was discovered, supposed to have come down the river from the neighbourhood of Budweis.

In the mineralogical collection the most celebrated piece is the "accursed burgrave," a meteoric stone weighing upwards of two hundred pounds, to which popular tradition has attached a legend of a tyrannical noble, who, when his soul was taken away to hell, left this black metallic lump behind in the place of his body. Not as a natural curiosity, but as a visible proof of the devil's potency, the stone was for many years preserved at the council-house of Elnbogen, where miraculous powers were even attributed to it. Whoever lifted the "accursed burgrave," it was said, would be cured of sundry complaints, and many peasants frequently came to Elnbogen to test the healing powers of the stone. I have no doubt its effects were frequently very satisfactory, for a sick man who retained strength enough to lift such a weight, was not likely to be in a desperate condition, and might at the same time hope to derive benefit from a few gymnastic feats. In later times, when science encroached more and more upon the domains of superstition, the Museum at Vienna laid claim to so rare a specimen of aerial mineralogy. The counsellors of Elnbogen fought lustily for their treasure, and at last a compromise was agreed to: the burgrave was sawn in two, and one half went to Vienna, while the other half remained at Elnbogen. The Bohemian Patriotic Association possesses only a model of the whole as it appeared before the ruthless partition was carried into effect.

THE BOOK OF LIFE ON THE MOLDAU.

To those who have read the history of Bohemia, it will be no matter of wonder to be informed, that even at the present day there continues to be so much talk at Prague of the *Herren Stände* (My Lords the States), of whom you will one day hear that they have been establishing an agricultural institution, on another that they have directed a suspension-bridge to be built over the Moldau, or that they have advanced money for the construction or repair of some public building. There is as much attributed in Prague to My Lords the States, as there is in Rome to the Pope. In ancient times they elected kings, and regulated the articles of public faith; at present their activity is limited to the less important sphere which I have just indicated. Formerly the cities of Bohemia, particularly Prague and Guttenberg, had considerable weight in the assemblies of the States; at present the few deputies for the towns that are still admitted, are consigned to a single bench—a sort of stool of repentance—in an extreme corner of the hall, where the burgesses are effectually separated from the remainder of the deputies, and that in such a way, that no civic representative, unless of more than ordinary boldness, will be likely to have the assurance to intrude his opinions upon his august colleagues. "My Lords the States," in Bohemia, are at present neither more nor less than the highest order of nobility—namely, "the reigning" counts, princes, and barons. The head of the family being in possession of the estate of the family, is always described as the "reigning" count, &c.

The Bohemian nobility, owing to their great wealth, to the good education most of them receive, and to the distinguished abilities of some among them, occupy a highly important position in the Austrian monarchy, and exercise a far greater influence upon the administration of the empire, than do the nobles of any other province. The highest office in Bohemia, after the king, is that of *Oberstburggraf,* a Bohemian dignity of very remote antiquity. He is assisted by fourteen counsellors of government or *Gubernialräthe,* and by a vice-president, besides which the country is divided into sixteen circles, each circle having a captain and three commissaries to superintend its affairs. This graduated list of public officers, from the *Oberstburggraf* to the *Kreiscommissär*, or commissary of the circle, is called the government of the country (*die böhmische Landesregierung*), and nearly all these offices are filled by members of the old noble families of Bohemia.

This Bohemian government, like that of Galicia, Moravia, Austria, &c., stands under the control of what is called the United Court Chancery at Vienna. At the head of this central department is a Superior Chancellor, assisted by a Chancellor of the Court, two Vice-Chancellors, and as many Aulic Councillors as there are provinces or governments subject to this court chancery. Hungary and Transylvania have separate chanceries for the control of their affairs. A singular circumstance connected with this court chancery is, that it enjoys the title of Majesty, being addressed "Your Majesty the Chancery of the Court." This is in some measure characteristic of Austria, where it is a common saying, that it is not the emperor who reigns, but his officers.

Not only over the administration of their own country, but over the whole empire, the Bohemians exercise great influence, owing to the important posts to which they have raised themselves by their ability and official aptitude. In every office in Vienna you are sure to find Bohemians, and they are mostly the favourites of their superiors. In the Polish and Italian provinces it is the same, so that while the Bohemians are grumbling about the state of dependance in which their country is kept on Austria, the other provinces might with more justice complain in their turn that they are subject to Bohemians. Two of the most distinguished members of the Austrian government are at present Bohemians—namely, Count Kolowrat and Count Mitrowski.

To give an account of the picture-galleries, libraries, and museums, collected at the various castles of the Bohemian nobles would, no doubt, be a highly interesting occupation, but would at the same time be found an herculean labour. At Prague, there are many private palaces well deserving the attention of a traveller, but I am sorry to say I was able to visit but few of them. The only private picture-gallery I was myself able to inspect was that of the Nostitzi palace, but the palaces of the families of Wallenstein, Czerni, Lobkowitz, Schwarzenberg, and others, are all deserving of attention. What particularly interested me at the Nostitzi palace, was the model of a marble monument intended to be erected at Teplitz. It represents the Knight Przemysl labouring at the plough, at the moment when the envoys of Libussa arrive to offer him the crown. On another side is a group in which he is seen as King of Bohemia holding his entrance into the palace of his consort. The Bohemians show quite a passion just now for illustrating the early periods of their history by monuments, and many a name is brought to light, and becomes more famous perhaps in these days, than it ever was during the life of its owner. There is in the same gallery, a beautiful group by Canova, of Cupid and Psyche. Schidone's Woman taken in Adultery is a charming picture, but there is one by Eyk that is most revolting. Christ is represented under a press, with blood spouting from different parts of his body. A stream of blood gushes from his breast, and is caught by priests, who distribute it among the people. There is an exquisite picture by Von Schalken, of a girl eating a peach. The peach is such a soft, juicy, delicate, velvet-clad fruit, that a painter can choose no more suitable viand on which to make a lovely maiden feast. To bite into an apple, she must make an effort that distorts her features, but a peach may be enjoyed with a kiss.

I spent but little time, however, in the Nostitzi Gallery, for there were other objects in Prague that I was more anxious to see. Among others I went to visit the Tein Church, once the chief temple of the Hussites. In their time the pictures and images were all destroyed, but at present the building is again amply provided with them. This church contains a multitude of monuments, but those that most attracted my notice were one of Tycho de Brahe, with a Latin inscription to the effect that neither wealth nor power, but only the works of science are immortal; and secondly, the tomb of a Jewish boy, on which was a Latin inscription, of which the following is a translation: "A little Hebrew boy (Hebraeolus) being inspired by God, fled, in the year 1693, to the Clementinum, the College of the Jesuits, that he might be baptized. After a few days he was treacherously taken away from his place of refuge. He was tortured by his parents, who assailed him with caresses, menaces, blows, hunger, and other torments; nevertheless, he remained steadfast in the true faith, till on the 12th of February, 1694, he died, in consequence of the treatment he had received. His body was privately buried, but on the sixth day was dug up again, and, on being inspected by the magistrates, was found free from all offensive smell, of its natural colour, and floating in rosy blood (*roseo sanguine*), whereupon it was carried from the townhouse in solemn procession, followed by an immense multitude of pious people, and was brought to this spot."

It is strange what different answers you will receive in Prague, if you inquire whether there are still any Hussites in the place. Some say positively "yes," and others are quite as positive in saying "no." Several persons assured me there was a Hussite house of prayer in Prague, but one, likely to be well informed, said there had been such a place, but it had since been converted into a warehouse. Most people will tell you, "Oh, in the mountains there are Hussites enough," but then the people of Prague dispose of a multitude of things by turning them over to the mountains. "Yes there are Hussites," another will add, "but they pretend to be Protestants." In point of fact, there are no Hussites officially recognised as such, but it is probable that many in secret still sympathize with their doctrines. Of Protestants, according to the official census, there were 81,000 in 1839, or about $2\frac{1}{4}$ per cent. of the entire population. In Moravia they are more numerous, amounting to 110,000 souls, or 6 per cent. of the population. Moravia excepted, however, the Protestants form a larger proportion of the population in Bohemia than in any other Austrian province.

Among the princely gardens of Prague, I visited those of Count Salm, and Prince Kinsky. In the count's garden I found twenty gardeners and assistant gardeners employed, with a court gardener (*Hofgärtner*) to superintend them. They told me they had no less than 350 kinds of ericas; and of these, as of the fine collection of Australian plants, there were many that had been brought into Bohemia for the first time that year. A great trade in plants is carried on with the interior of Austria from Prague, where they can be had from England and Holland with tolerable facility over Hamburg. In the Kinsky garden, I was too much taken up with the beauty of the place, to make many inquiries about its statistical details. The garden is arranged on a succession of terraces, that rise from the Moldau up the side of a hill, from the summit of which the eye revels in a panoramic view of Prague and its environs; one of those views on which one dwells with lingering fondness, but of which the pen is powerless to convey a description, and of which all we can say is, that it is *beautiful.*

At my feet lay the isles of the Moldau, and the suspension-bridge. When this bridge and its approaches are finished, the aspect of Prague will be materially improved. There was formerly no quay along the side of the river. This want will now be supplied, a number of old and ill-looking houses having been bought up and pulled down, with a view to the construction of a quay and of some handsome buildings calculated to form a more suitable frame to the stream. Numerous *Schinakels* (an Austrian word for boats) animated the water, along whose banks lay stretched a botanical and several private gardens. On the other side the deserted Vissehrad seemed to mourn his departed glories; and on tracing the upward course of the river, the eye rested at length on the Brannik rock, from whose entrails had been torn the materials that had gone to the making up of the many houses that lay at my feet. The stone obtained from this rock is remarkably fine, and, in the time of Charles IV., was known to his Italian architects under the name of *pasta di Praga.* The rock itself has its legend. A valiant knight of the name of Brannik is said to have dwelt there, and to lie buried there with his brave companions. In one of the caverns of the rock, the double-tailed Bohemian lion is said to hold his residence, and watch over the graves of its former tenants. Once a year he comes out and salutes the Moldau valley with a roar, and then, having received no answer, he creeps into his hole again, to take another twelvemonth's repose. Should he, however, one day receive an answer, there will be a mighty struggle in Bohemia, for the ghosts of the deceased heroes rise from their graves, and are to secure the victory to their countrymen. This legend seems to live still in the full confidence of the people; but then in Bohemia there is no end to legends. You fall in with them at the corners of the streets and in the depths of forests; they abound and thrive amid the crowded thoroughfares of Prague, as in the silent solitudes of the country.

Among the manufactures of Prague we must not forget to speak of the warehouses of glass goods. The workshops are generally at some distance in the country; but the warehouses in Prague, for the greater part, are the property of the manufacturers. These have chemists and artists in their pay, who are constantly tasking their invention to extend the domains of glass, by discovering new articles that may admit of being formed of so brittle a material, and to give new colours and forms to those articles which the glass-cutters have long looked upon as belonging to their legitimate sphere. Of each new discovery or modification a drawing is made, and a copy sent to the manufactory. The drawing and the copy bear corresponding marks and numbers, so that if a sudden demand comes to the warehouse for any particular article, all that is necessary probably is to send an order down to the country, to make up immediately so many dozens of B 288, or whatever else the number may be. I was allowed to look over a number of these drawings, which were neatly bound up in folio volumes, and I was astonished at the immense variety of designs and inventions for coffee, tea, and milk pots; at the endless modifications of form which so simple an article as a glass stopper was made to undergo; and at the prodigality of ingenuity that had been expended on varying the conformation of a thing so unimportant as a lady's smelling-bottle. In the different shades of colour there was almost as much variety as in the form; yet the prevailing taste appears to be always, in the long-run, in favour of that which is most simple. The plain, pure, colourless, crystalline glass has always been in favour, and will maintain its supremacy in the end, however taste may sport for a while among the brilliant colours and variegated forms which science has found the means of imparting to this beautiful manufacture. All the bright "Leonore greens" and "Chrysopras" of 1840, and the "Anne green," the "gold glass," the "dead glass," and the "alabaster" of 1841, may hold their place in public favour for a time; but they will have passed away when the pure crystal will be prized as much as ever. Even so man may surrender himself awhile to a chaos of absurdities and fancies; but the pure crystal of good taste, morality, and justice will, ere long, make its worth be felt, and carry away the prize of public favour from all its competitors.

FROM PRAGUE TO BUDWEIS.

Various as are the means by which a traveller may cause himself to be conveyed from Prague to Budweis,—by diligence, by mail post, by *Stellwagen*, or with a *Lohnkutscher*, or hired carriage and horses,—yet none of these means of locomotion can be called excellent in their kind.* The Bohemian diligences are very inferior to those of northern Germany, and the *Lohnkutschers* are quite as slow in their movements as in any other part of our country. The *Stellwagen* had one powerful recommendation for me, and that was that I had never travelled in one of them before. They are to be met with in all parts of the Austrian dominions, and serve as a means of communication between the several provincial towns, for those who make but few pretensions to gentility. The *Stellwagen*, in consequence, is rarely favoured by foreigners, and therefore all the more to be recommended to those who are desirous of making acquaintance with provincial peculiarities. Accordingly, one morning, as the watchmen of Prague had just announced the important fact that it had struck four o'clock, I was rolling, in one of these humble vehicles, through the Rossthor, and out upon the Budweis road, in company with a goldsmith of Prague, an engraver, a forester, a farmer, and a young mother with her little boy upon her lap.

I had an excellent opportunity here of studying the peculiarities of the Bohemian-German dialect, and I was not a little surprised at the systematic and consistent manner in which the good people modify our grammar and pronunciation to suit their own views. Sometimes Slavonian words are Germanized, and sometimes German words effectually disguised by Slavonian terminations, and at other times the strangest gibberish is produced by the least cultivated classes, who frequently mix up their

---

* The railroad at present making from Vienna to Prague, and from Prague to Dresden, and which will probably be finished in 1844 or 1845, will effect a complete revolution in Bohemian travelling. At the time Mr. Kohl's work was published, the arrangements between the Austrian and Saxon governments, relative to this railroad, had not yet been completed.—*Tr.*

German and Slavonian in so indiscriminate a manner, as to make their meaning unintelligible to any one not familiar with both languages. These remarks do not, of course, apply to the more educated classes, who claim for themselves the honour of speaking the Austrian-German better and more correctly than the Austrians themselves; a similar claim is set up by the gentry of Hungary, Croatia, and Slavonia, in the same way that the Courlanders and Livonians maintain,—and not without reason,—that they speak the North German dialect more purely and correctly than the North Germans themselves.

I spent the whole morning in the study of the various systems of torture to which my mother-tongue was subjected by the Bohemian mouths of my fellow-travellers. We dined at Miltschin, and shortly afterwards we arrived at Tabor, the celebrated stronghold of the Hussites in the fifteenth century. Many have supposed that the Hussites named the town and the hill on which it stands after Mount Tabor in Palestine, but Tabor is a genuine Slavonian word, that occurs in all the Slavonian dialects, and signifies a piece of ground surrounded by a paling, whence it is figuratively used for an intrenched camp.

The usual road passes not through Tabor, but close by the side of it, so that few travellers ever see the inside of the town; we, on our part, however, ventured to deviate from the general rule, and proceeded to take a nearer inspection of so interesting a locality.

The Lusnitza, a tributary of the Moldau, by describing nearly a circle, has isolated an oblong hill from the surrounding country. On three sides this hill is steep, and surrounded by water; on the fourth side art has come to the aid of nature, to strengthen the place. On this hill, at an early period of the religious disturbances, some of the Hussites were wont to assemble, and to receive the chalice in the communion; but when the royalists began to raise the cry of "heretic, heretic" against the Bohemians, and to burn all that fell into their hands, and when the Hussites, by way of retaliation, clapped their German prisoners into tarred beer-barrels, and set fire to these in the public market-places; in a word, when the Hussite wars broke out, the persecuted race endeavoured to obtain possession of strong places; and as those in royalist hands could not always be had for the asking, it became necessary to build fresh ones. Zizka,* not the less sharp-sighted for having but one eye, soon saw how well this mountain was suited to be the site of a strong fortress, which he lost no time in erecting there; and from the fortress of Tabor he made his devastating excursions against convents and castles, his adherents, from the place of their residence, being generally called Taborites.

The little city is still most curious to see, bearing even now the most complete stamp of the age in which it was erected. The gates are narrow, and the double walls and bastions, which remain from the days of Zizka, present a striking contrast to the peaceful Catholic cloth-weavers that now shelter behind those formidable works. The streets, as in most of the old Bohemian towns, radiate from an open space in the centre which serves as a market, and many houses of an antique castellated shape, continue standing. In front of one of these, at the corner of the market-place, stands an antique balcony, which is still called Zizka's pulpit, from which

---

* The name should be pronounced Shishka, or rather more softly, the Bohemian z having a sound like the French j in jardin.

he is said frequently to have harangued his warlike scholars. The townhouse is the most ancient of all the buildings. Within it are still preserved Zizka's shirt of mail, his arms, and a quantity of old books, but we were unable to obtain a sight of these curiosities, in consequence of the Burgomaster, who had charge of the keys, being from home. Cannon-balls may be seen in the walls of many of the houses, but can hardly belong to the times of the religious wars. In front of the church is a bust in stone of Zizka, and the grim features of the one-eyed hero may likewise be seen on the façade of a private house. Zizka was of a middling stature, rather bulky in shape, with broad shoulders, and a high chest. His head was large, round, and inclining forwards; his beard black and bushy, his mouth large, his nose thick, and his complexion brown. So indelibly have these features impressed themselves upon the Bohemians, that even now, after an interval of four hundred years, the people of Tabor continue to cut portraits of Zizka in wood, as knobs for walkingsticks. I, too, bought one of these Zizka sticks, upon which the Hussite chief is represented with a plain helmet on his head, and a bandage over his right eye, which he had lost early in life. His left eye he lost at the siege of Rabi castle, where, a javelin striking a tree near him, a splinter flew aside and completely blinded him. Nevertheless, he retained his command as general, though he had to be led into battle by a guide; and it was, in fact, after his blindness, that he attained the zenith of his power, when he gained his victory over the people of Prague, who, though Hussites themselves, had gotten into a quarrel with the devastator of their country. Hereupon, he concluded a treaty of friendship and alliance with them, and their elective king, Korybut, and so great was at this time the power of the blind chief, that the Emperor Sigismund offered him the government of the kingdom and the command of its army, if he would consent to recognise the imperial authority. During the negotiations that followed, Zizka, at the height of his power, died suddenly of the plague.

Every thing about the man, even from his birth, appears to have been extraordinary. His mother was suddenly attacked by the pains of childbirth while in a forest, and Zizka was born with no shelter but that of a tree. In his character he was savage and cruel, as much as he was valiant and eloquent. Bohemian writers say that the peculiarities of his style are as difficult to render into German, as are the refinements of Cæsar's eloquence. He rose from a comparatively humble station, to supreme power in his native land, and gained thirteen pitched battles, several of which were fought after the loss of his second eye. The manner of his death was also remarkable, and so is the memory preserved of him to this day by his countrymen. The place of his birth is still pointed out as an unblessed spot, and the ground where stood the tent under which he breathed his last, remains uncultivated to the present day. Just as the history of Napoleon is known to all Europe, so is that of Zizka, in all its details, familiar to every Bohemian, and there is scarcely a castle or a convent in the land, in which his portrait is not to be found.

After the death of Zizka, his soldiers called themselves his orphan children, and divided themselves into four parties: the Orphans, the Taborites, the Orebites, and the Praguers. Bohemia was denominated the Promised Land, and the surrounding German provinces were declared to be the lands of the Philistines, the Moabites, and the Idumeans. It was at this time, no doubt, that the large lake near Tabor received the name of Jordan, and the hill behind Tabor, that of Horel. As Tabor was the chief city of the Hussites, so it now became the scene of their worst excesses, which attained their culminating point in the wild extravagance of the Hussite sect of the Adamites. At Tabor too, where the Hussite wars had commenced, they were likewise brought to a close, for it was the last city that submitted to the Royal States. It is said, that a remnant of the Adamite sect still exists in Bohemia, and that other Hussite sects have maintained themselves under such denominations, as the "Red Brothers," and the "Brothers of the Lamb."

From the foregoing it will be seen, that we had turned our time to good account during our short stay at Tabor. At the next stage, the name of which I have forgotten, I had an opportunity to see a Bohemian pheasant-preserve. The rearing of pheasants in Bohemia is carried on upon an enormous scale, as may be judged from an advertisement which I saw, and in which a certain Count Schlick offered three thousand pair of living birds for sale in one lot. In these preserves the pheasants are divided into wild and tame; the wild are kept in large woods, the tame under roof or in enclosed yards.

The night was already far advanced when we reached Budweis, but in that city, for the consolation of travellers be it known, the sun never ceases to shed his light upon the benighted stranger, for the inn so named has a large lamp burning conspicuously, from evening till morning in front of the chief entrance.

THE CASTLES AND ESTATES OF SCHWARZENBERG.

The southern extremity of Bohemia, the country round Budweis, is distinguished, even in a land so rich in stately mansions and princely estates, for the magnificence of its castles, and for the extent of territory held by individuals. Here it was that formerly dwelt the family of the Rosenbergs, a race so powerful, that several of the Bohemian monarchs wooed the daughters for their brides. The Lords of Rosenberg frequently contracted matrimonial alliances with the sovereign houses of Germany, and on one occasion we find the name of Rosenberg among the candidates for the Polish crown. At present the family is extinct, a circumstance that cannot but seriously have afflicted Charlemagne, the Trojan heroes, Noah, and sundry others of the ancestors of so illustrious a line. It is certainly a singular coincidence, that the branch of the Rosenberg family which had been planted and had taken root in Courland, should have died away much about the same time as the main family-tree in Bohemia. Similar coincidences, however, are on record respecting other families, of which different branches established in distant countries have all become extinct nearly at the same time.

In the cellar of the Senate at Bremen there is a wine that by its great age has acquired such an odour (so exquisite a bouquet as the connoisseurs of wine express it) that you need only pour a few drops upon your pocket-handkerchief, and you will have no occasion for eau de Cologne for several days afterwards. Nobility seems to be like this wine—the older it grows the more it is prized, and if its origin is lost in the dark ages it becomes quite inestimable. The last of the Rosenbergs, according to all the things that are related of him, seems to have thought his nobility just such a jewel of priceless value, but dear as it was to him, he was unable to bequeath it to a successor; for nobility, like genius, virtue, and learning, is not to be disposed of in a man's last will and testament. Unblessed with an heir to what he most esteemed, the last of the Rosenbergs went to his grave, but his sublunary possessions, his broad lands and stately castles found an heir soon enough in the family of the Schwarzenbergs, who are now the undisputed lords of all the lands in which the Moldau and its tributaries take their rise.

The most important of their castles and estates are called Krummau, Wittingau, and Frauenberg, and all that I had heard of the charms of these castles excited too much curiosity in me to allow me to neglect an opportunity of paying them a visit. What I saw far exceeded what I had expected to see.

I paid my first visit to the one that passed for the least important, and drove with an hospitable friend, a resident of Budweis, down the verdant banks of the Moldau to Schloss Frauenberg, which stands on a rock by the river-side, where it forms a conspicuous object to all the surrounding country.

Upon the said rock there stands an old castle, and a new one of much greater splendour is rising by the side of it. Over the entrance to the old one stands the inscription, *Fructus Belli*, referring, I believe, to the gift which one of the Austrian emperors, Ferdinand II., if I am not mistaken, made of this castle and lordship, to one of his Spanish generals, Don Balthasar Maradas, Count of Salento. Under the gateway of the castle may still be seen a tablet, on which this Don Balthasar is styled Comes, Dominus in Frauenberg. At present, however, the gateway is surmounted by a Turk's head, from which a raven is picking out the eyes. This is the crest of the Schwarzenbergs, who, like many Austrian families, carry Turkish emblems and spoils in their shields. The view from the castle is unspeakably beautiful. The fields and meadows of the Moldau lie at your feet, and farther on lies a plain, from the midst of which rise the steeples of Budweis. The whole is bounded by branches of the mountain range of the Bohemian Forest, and over the landscape lie scattered a number of villages, all of which belong to the lordship of Schwarzenberg. Towards the east the eye travels on towards Wittingau, another Schwarzenberg lordship.

When the French Marshal, Bernadotte, visited the castle in 1805, (by the by, the French must have carried away more agreeable recollections from this southern extremity of Bohemia, which they visited leisurely as visiters, than they did from the northen part of which they obtained only a few hasty glances through the sulphurous smoke of Culm;) but when the marshal visited the castle, as I was saying, and the intendant pointed out the magnificent prospect to him, and then asked him what he thought of it, the marshal answered, " What strikes me as most wonderful is, that your prince should be lord and master over all I see." And, in fact, without being a French marshal of the days of the empire, whose fingers would naturally be itching at the sight, it is difficult for any one to let his eyes roam from village to village, and from field to field, without some little sensation of envy, without some slight approximation to a wish that he were able to step into the Schwarzenberg's place. All the while I was there, I was thinking of the old fairy tale of "Puss in Boots," where, as the king and his son-in-law are driving through the country, the cat keeps saying, "Every thing you see belongs to our lord and master the prince, your majesty's son-in-law."

I am not aware that the old castle is yet in so ruinous a condition, that it might not have stood, and kept out the wind and rain for many years longer; but when a man has 4,000,000 florins (£400,000) a year, as Prince Schwarzenberg is said to have, he is not expected to take as much care of his pennies as might beseem a thrifty cobbler; and as the prince is passionately fond of Gothic architecture, it is very excusable in him to have set aside 500,000 florins to build himself a new house according to his favourite fashion. When this new building is finished, Frauenberg will be one of the handsomest castles in Bohemia. The sandstone for the Gothic ornaments comes all the way from Vienna. We saw standing in the courtyard a quantity of these stones, packed up in chests with as much care as if they had been so many loaves of sugar.

Frauenberg is celebrated throughout Bohemia for its wild-boar hunts, which are carried on here, probably, on a grander scale than in any other place in Europe, and are, indeed, unique in their kind, like the Esterhazy stag-hunts on the Platten Lake in Hungary. The menagerie or *Thiergarten*, in which the wild boars are kept, covers a space of a (German) square mile and a half; and even of late years, as many as 300 boars (a kind of game growing every day more scarce in Europe) have been killed at one of these hunting-festivals. The sport is carried on with extraordinary pomp, and something after the following fashion:

Near the park in which the animals are kept, is a small reedy lake, bounded on three sides by gently-rising heights. On the fourth side the bank is low and swampy. This lake is the scene of the yearly slaughterings. On the swampy side of the lake, a high and hollow dike has been erected, resting upon vaults, in which are confined the animals intended to be hunted. By the side of the dike projecting into the water, are small tribunes or balconies, in which the lords of the chase take their places. On the dike, ready, if wanted to afford assistance, stand the foresters and huntsmen of the prince; all, from the head forester to the whippers-in, in splendid uniforms. There are not less than twenty of the prince's foresters, and 150 of his huntsmen present on one of these occasions. The animals are let out of their vaulted prison about fifty at a time, and, driven by a crowd of peasants collected for the purpose, they immediately take to the water, to conceal themselves in the reeds, or to swim towards the opposite hills, where they hope to find shelter in the forest. On the way thither they seldom fail to find their death from the constant fire poured in upon them by the gentlemen stationed in the balconies.

I observed to my companions that this kind of sport seemed to me mere butchering, and must be very insipid and monotonous; but they assured me it was full of pleasure and excitement, on account of the pomp with which the whole was conducted. In the centre of the dike there was always a full orchestra, and behind it an amphitheatre for spectators, of whom numbers came from all parts of the surrounding country. The moment, they told me, when the sport was about to begin, when the trumpets sounded, and the gates were opened to set the wild boars free, was one of great suspense. Then the situations in which the creatures presented themselves to the fire of the hunters, were very varied. Sometimes the game would hide itself among the reeds, whence it would have to be driven by the rifles; sometimes it would swim as a mere black speck upon the water. Now one would swim directly toward a balcony filled with its foes, and often a few would gain the opposite shore, and put the best marksman to the proof to prevent their escape. Then, an old established law among German hunters requires that the creature's head should remain uninjured, and the hunters are often put to it, to avoid the penalties which an infraction of this law draws after it.

In the plain below Schloss Frauenberg, and not far from the lake I have just described, lies an old castle erected for the express purpose of bear-baiting. Such castles existed formerly in many parts of Germany, but have all disappeared now, with few exceptions. The building I am now speaking of is an extensive one, with apartments below for the huntsmen and keepers, with dens for bears and kennels for dogs, and large suites of rooms above for the prince and his guests. A balcony, for the accommodation of spectators, projects into the courtyard, which is surrounded by high walls, and in which beasts of all kinds were formerly baited. The last great bear-baiting that took place there, occurred only sixty years ago.

The principal saloon of this castle is hung all round with beautiful pictures by the celebrated animal-painter, Hamilton, and I believe the collection contains the best paintings he ever made. Hamilton spent the years 1710 and 1711 with a Schwarzenberg, who arranged sundry bear-baitings, deer-stalkings, and boar-hunts, for the painter's sake, and the latter had thus an opportunity, under peculiarly favourable circumstances, of painting these beautiful pictures, which may now be said to waste their sweetness on the wilderness, being but rarely seen by an eye capable of estimating their worth. The pictures are all of the natural size, and the subjects mostly—a stag overpowered by dogs, a bear battling it with his assailants, wild boars surprised in a thicket by hunters, and other scenes of a similar kind; and all so full of truth, that as formerly Hamilton became for a while a recluse here to study the physiognomy of the huge beasts of the chase, so a modern painter, profiting by the labours of his predecessor, might shut himself up in the castle for a while, and pursue a similar course of study with infinitely more ease and convenience. The dogs in these pictures are all portraits of animals famous in their day, and deserving even greater fame now that they have been transferred to the canvass. When the French were here, in 1742, they would fain have carried away the whole collection, but for some reason or other contented themselves with cutting the best head—that of a wild boar—out of the best picture. The damage was repaired as well as it could be, but the scar is evident at the first glance, and so is the inferior workmanship of the modern artist.

After leaving Frauenberg, our next visit was to Schloss Gratzen, another *fructus belli*. The battle of the White Mountain, which gave Bohemia back to Ferdinand, and which lost Frauenberg for the house of Malowitz, deprived the Protestant Lords of Schwamberg of their castle of Gratzen, which they defended valiantly for a while against the imperial troops. With the castle went also their seven (German) square miles of territory. The confiscated estate was conferred on a Frenchman, Charles Bonaventura Longueval, Count of Bucquoi, and Baron de Vaux, whose descendants still possess it. The estate is entirely unincumbered, and is said to bring in an annual revenue of 700,000 florins, or 70,000*l*.

There are three castles at Gratzen. One is the old fortress that was so stoutly defended by the old Baron von Schwamberg, another is the summer residence of the Count de Bucquoi, and the third is intended for the accommodation of the Count's officers of state, in whose hands is the administration of the lordship. This central government of the estate is called the "princely court chancery," at the head of which are four "princely court counsellors." These Bohemian nobles exercise in fact a multitude of rights, which in other countries we are accustomed to look on as the exclusive attributes of sovereignty. They confer the dignity of court counsellors, grant privileges to their cities, and compose coats of arms for them. The magistrates, however, whom they appoint, are obliged to go through the same studies, and submit to the same examination as those appointed by the state.

We found the officers of the Bucquoi household paying compliments to one another at the entrance to a concert-room. Here, as on many of the large estates of music-loving Bohemia, a private band is kept, to give occasional concerts, and on the fêtes of the lord or lady of the castle to accompany the organ in the church. Several pieces from Norma and other modern operas were performed, and were executed with tolerable brilliancy, the gentlemen of the household were loud in their applause, and resolved that the concert should be repeated on the following Sunday, the birthday of the young heir, when the money taken at the doors was to be applied to the relief of the poor.

We supped at the castle, where the conversation turned chiefly on two subjects, partly on the Austro-Bohemian frontier, and partly on the great fishponds, the most interesting feature in an economical point of view, of the large plain between Wittingau and Gratzen.

In Northern Germany, we understand under the name of Austrian every one who comes from any part of the great Austrian conglomeration of lands, provided he speaks German; but every well-educated Bohemian, Hungarian, Croatian, or Slovak, speaks our language quite as well as do the people of Vienna or Styria. Here on the mountain border, however, the contrast between the Bohemian and Austrian, and their mutual antipathies were forced upon my attention. Of *sym*pathies between neighbouring nations there is seldom much to be said. In Paris or Berlin indeed, a Bohemian and an Austrian may sympathize with each other, but at home they know of no such feeling. Not merely the common people in Bohemia, but even the higher classes, participate more or less in this aversion to the Austrians, and even the German part of the population agree with the Slavonians in this, with whom in other respects they are little in the habit of singing in unison. Our evening party at Gratzen consisted almost entirely of Bohemian-Germans, yet I observed upon the countenances of all of them a certain half-suppressed sarcastic smile, when I undertook the defence of the Austrians. "Ay, ay," said one of them at last, "honest enough they are, no canting hypocrites like the Italians, and hardworking enough too; but good God!" and here he shook his head with a smile of evident satisfaction, "what unlicked cubs they are! How awkward, stupid, and helpless in every thing! In short," added he, "it is a perverse and wrongheaded people."

On their part, the Austrians reproach the Bohemians with insincerity. "A false Bohemian," is a common expression, and the Austrian generally describes the Bohemian as a gloomy, melancholy, uncomfortable creature. The antipathy felt by the Bohemian, however, is decidedly marked by more bitterness.

A fat carp, served in black sauce, composed according to a national recipe, of grated gingerbread, blood, and onions, led our conversation naturally to the great fishponds of the neighbourhood. Gratzen has sixty ponds, the Dukedom of Krummau seventy, Frauenberg one hundred and forty-five, and Wittingau two hundred and seventy. Among these is the celebrated Rosenberg pond, which occupies nearly twelve hundred yoke of land, from which and the other Wittingau ponds, no less than four thousand cwt. of carp are yearly taken, and sent chiefly to Vienna.

I cannot say I ever made myself so familiar with the complicated system of management to which the Bohemian fishponds are subjected, as I did with the manner in which the fish were usually brought to table, still, as I am not aware that any of the travellers who have preceded me have spoken at all upon the subject, I will endeavour to give a concise account of what I learned about it.

The main point, it seems, is to take care that at different ages and at different seasons, the fish be provided with the depth of water suitable to them, and also that the kinds of fish that do not suit each other should not be put together in the same pond. Now, as it is impossible that one pond can satisfy all these demands, the Bohemian landowners have brought the ponds on their estates into a sort of connected system, and have given to each class of ponds its separate destination.

Firstly there are the brood ponds, (*Brut*, or *Satz-teiche*,) in which the young fish receive the rudiments of their education. These ponds are small, and contain but little food, that the rising generation may not injure themselves by gluttonous indulgence. In proportion, however, as the finny babes improve in size, they are removed to the *Streck-teiche*, or stretching ponds, where the interesting little ones are to begin to stretch themselves. Thence the creatures are removed into the large reservoirs called *Kammer* or *Haupt-teiche*. In winter the water is warmest at the bottom, in summer at the top; young fish, therefore, who require warmth, must often be put into deeper ponds in winter.

It would of course be as absurd to put old pike and young carp into the same pond, as to shut up wolves and lambs in one stable. Accordingly there are separate ponds for each. When the carp, however, grow older, they are apt to grow lazy, and bury themselves in the mud, which prevents their proper development; and then, by way of making them more lively, a few young pike are put into the pond, for the purpose of keeping the young republic in a state of healthful excitement, like opposition men in a representative assembly.

It may easily be supposed that all these removals and minglings necessitate a great variety of occupations. Usually the work is performed in spring or autumn, and great care and caution are necessary. If, for instance, snow were to fall on a fish, he must on no account be put back into the pond, but must be sent to market and sold for what he will bring. If a sudden frost covers the ponds with ice, great mischief is done to the fish, if air-holes are not immediately opened. If this is not done, the fish swarm to the surface, and even if they are not suffocated, they "burn" their fins against the ice. A scarcity of water, also, in case of a dry summer, causes great destruction in the ponds.

The intendants of the ponds require, of course, at all times, to know how much water there may be, and poles marked with feet and inches are therefore fixed in each pond. A few inches too much may easily occasion inundations to the neighbouring fields, and then the damage must be made good by the owner of the pond.

Immense swarms of herons, wild ducks, and other waterfowl frequent these ponds, and the consequence is, that all the surrounding peasantry become practised marksmen. The birds are particularly watchful for the time when the water is to be let out of a pond, on which occasion they fail not to feast upon the frogs and upon such fish as may happen to have remained in the mud. These, however, they are not left in undisturbed possession of, for it is customary, when the owner of the pond has secured the main tribute by means of nets, to abandon what is left to the peasants. The pond inspectors give the signal for the scramble as soon as the noble's boxes are thought to be sufficiently filled. The signal is for the inspectors to cry out *Horzi horzi* (It burns, it burns); whereupon the crowd rush with loud cries into the mud, and drive the geese and herons from their prey. The peasants obtain a good deal of fish in this way, and preserve a considerable quantity for the winter, by smoking them.

The geese and herons are by no means the only plunderers of these ponds, in which otters and beavers likewise abound, though less now than formerly.

On the following morning we started for Krummau, the most famous of all the castles in the neighbouring country, and certainly one of the most interesting of all the princely mansions of the Austrian monarchy, with a dependant lordship of fifteen German square miles, and fifty thousand inhabitants. The dukedom of Krummau is one of those half-sovereignties of which there have at all times been several in Bohemia, as the dukedom of Friedland, which was given to Wallenstein; the dukedom of Reichstadt, with which Napoleon's son was invested; and the dukedom of Raudnitz, which belongs to the Prince of Lobkowitz.

You enter the first courtyard by crossing a drawbridge, and passing through a massive stone gateway. The castle ditch was formerly occupied by a number of bears, but these have of late years disappeared. In the second courtyard stands the guard house of the Schwarzenberg grenadiers of the body-guard, a corps of forty men in splendid uniforms, all in the prince's pay, and commanded by an officer who holds the rank of captain. In this courtyard I paid my respects to one of the officers of the castle, and told him I wished to see as much as possible of the place. He asked me, with a smile, how many weeks I intended to devote to the inspection, and I soon found, particularly after I had had a glance at the archives, that the question implied by no means an exaggeration. From the second I passed into a third, a fourth, a fifth, and a sixth courtyard.

The castle looks as if no part had ever been pulled down during the whole time that it has been successively held by the Rosenbergs, the Eggenbergs, and the Schwarzenbergs. The whole summit of the hill on which it stands is covered by a labyrinth of turrets, walls, and other buildings, in every imaginable style of architecture, with noble suites of rooms, such as we are accustomed to look for only in imperial palaces, and little poking holes, fit only for the rock-built nest to some robber chief of the feudal times. That the oldest part of the old buildings must be very old indeed, may be inferred from the simple fact, that the most modern portion, the New Castle as it is called, is mentioned under that name in the archives, as much as three hundred and fifty years ago.

Our first visit in the interior was to the picture-gallery, in which are preserved the numberless portraits of the various members of the three noble families to whom the castle has successively belonged. What a family party they would make, if they could all step from their canvass and join in a merry festival! There would be ample room in the castle for all of them; but there is only one of them to whom it is still given to wander through the old halls and corridors, and this is Bertha von Rosenberg, the celebrated White Lady of Neuhaus, of whom a portrait may here be seen as large as life.

This Bertha, or Brichta, was married to a Lichtenstein, a family with which the Rosenbergs, like their successors the Schwarzenbergs, often arranged matrimonial alliances, even before the bride and bridegroom had been fairly emancipated from the cradle. There are still such things as family sympathies and antipathies among the great houses in Austria, as there were in the earliest times of which a record has been preserved, and some of the family feuds that have been retained to the present day trace their origin to the middle ages. Now this Lichtenstein, the husband of Bertha, was a monster, and treated his gentle wife little better than Bluebeard did his. Often in the morning, it is said, Bertha's pillow was found soaked with her tears, and sometimes even with her blood. Before her marriage she is supposed to have been as fond of the pleasures of the world as most young ladies, but when it pleased Heaven to release her from her tyrant, she retired to the castle of her brother the Lord of Rosenberg, who about the same time had lost his wife, and with whom she lived thenceforth as a pious widow and a notable housekeeper. Her chief delight was to do acts of kindness to the poor, whom she was in the habit of calling together on certain days, for the purpose of entertaining them with a sweet dish (*dulce mus* it is called in the archives of the castle), and which still continues to be distributed. Attempts have more than once been made to substitute a money distribution, but the peasants have always stoutly resisted such an innovation, which they are afraid " Bertha might take amiss."

It is only in more recent times that black has been adopted in Bohemia, from France and Germany, as a mark of mourning. Bertha, like all widows of her time, wore white, which she continued to wear till death, when she was buried in her white widow's weeds. To this she owed her name of the White Lady, by which she was known during her life, and under which she is now almost worshipped as a saint. The people of the surrounding country firmly believe that she continues to wander through the castles then belonging to the house of Rosenberg, that she looks about to see whether the houses are kept in good order, and whether the poor receive their *dulce mus* regularly. In general, in these her wanderings, she is invisible to every eye, but sometimes she is seen, a circumstance always supposed to announce some great calamity to the family. On such occasions the country-people whisper timidly into each other's ears—*Brichta z' Rosemberka khodi* (Bertha von Rosenberg is wandering about), and a death in the family is then confidently looked for. At Schloss Wittingau there is a corridor, and at Neuhaus another, which Bertha is supposed to have particularly selected for her nocturnal promenade; and few of the inmates are hardy enough to visit either of these haunted passages, except under good escort, and with a sufficient illumination. To be sure, by daylight, they most of them speak of the whole story in a very rational manner, as a popular fable; but I have my doubts whether even the heads of the family remain altogether unaffected when the whisper flies about that Bertha has shown herself again to mortal eyes.

There are three portraits of the White Lady, one at each of the three castles of Neuhaus, Wittingau, and Krummau, and the three pictures are so exactly alike that two of them are evidently copies, but at each castle the people maintain that they possess the original. Her countenance is pale and meager, and her features full of melancholy, but with a remarkably sweet expression. Her whole person is enveloped in a white garment.

My guide was the captain of the body-guard, who, as we passed from one suite of rooms to another, apologized for his imperfect knowledge of the great labyrinth of masonry, by telling me he had only been a year in the house. The present head of the house of Schwarzenberg is a young man,* who has abandoned all these stately chambers of a bygone time, and has had a set of rooms fitted up for him with modern simplicity and comfort, in a corner of the great house. Then why, will you say, is not the rest of the place turned to account, and made habitable for those, of whom there are so many, to whom the shelter of a roof would be a blessing? Why, you see, my good friend, a large useless house is indispensable to the proper dignity of a great family, and the terms of the entailment do not allow a single corner of the mansion to be neglected.

If you wish to have a proper notion of the importance of the lords of the castle in former days, you must go and have a look at the armory, where you will find the whole rows of trumpets and kettle-drums that were wont to mingle with the family revelry when a Rosenberg was married. There you will see a collection of the coins and medals struck at various times by the family. My companion assured me that the Rosenbergs were accustomed to keep ready at all times arms for twenty thousand men, and that the arms now in the armory would suffice for the equipment of nearly that number, provided the greater part would content themselves with halberds, partisans, and battle-axes.

The subterranean dungeons of the castle have been carved out of the rock with an immense expenditure of labour. We descended with torches as if we had been going down into a mine, and came to the main shaft, which was nothing else but a deep broad well, cut into the solid rock, down which the prisoners were let by means of ropes. We threw stones into the dark abyss, and heard them strike the bottom after a few seconds. We threw down some whisps of burning straw; but, even by these means, we were unable to obtain a view of the bottom. There are other dungeons, less horrible than the one described, but quite ugly enough in their way; yet one of them served at one time as a lodging to the German emperor Venzeslaus, who was locked up there, in 1402, by Henry IV. of Rosenberg. The Henrys of Rosenberg seem, indeed, to have been sad fellows; for about one hundred years afterwards, another Henry of Rosenberg put three magistrates into one of these dungeons, for coming, in the name of the supreme tribunal of the country, to lay claim to a portion of his estate for the Lord of Schwamberg. The claim was founded on the will of Henry's predecessor; but Henry denied the validity of the will, and made the magistrates eat the documents with which they had come armed. Every particle—seals, signatures, and all—were they obliged to devour;

---

* He was born in 1799, and is, consequently, about 44 years of age.—*Tr.*

and when they had finished their meal, they were set free, and, by way of accelerating their retreat, the dogs were let loose upon them.

The castle contains a theatre, with a wardrobe sufficient for a dozen theatres; a riding-school; and an agricultural institution, which, every three years, turns out about thirty practical and scientific farmers, who are mostly appointed to offices about the Schwarzenberg estates. Then there are collections of natural history, a chemical laboratory, the castle church, &c. English castles may be more comfortable to live in; but they have little of the interest that pertains to one of these ancient Austrian piles, where remote antiquity is seen connected with modern times by an uninterrupted chain. At Krummau alone, with its legends and reminiscences, a moderately fertile writer might find materials for twenty romances.

The steep rock on which the castle stands is separated by a deep ravine from the remainder of the rocky plateau. Over this ravine runs a covered bridge, at the end of which you come suddenly upon a beautiful garden terrace, whence the view is ravishingly beautiful; the bold position of the castle, as it looks down upon the little town of Krummau at the foot of the hill, producing a most peculiar effect. The Moldau forms almost a circle in the landscape; rushing, with great rapidity, by the foot of the rock, and nearly surrounding the little town, in which the chief buildings all date from the time of the Rosenbergs; at whose cost the churches and convents were erected, as well as an old arsenal and an hospital, and a house which served as a retreat for the widowed lady of the castle, whenever a new lord entered into possession.

Towards evening, after having enjoyed the beauties of the garden, we retired into the castle to partake of the hospitality of the civil and accommodating officers of the establishment—the directors, foresters, stewards, &c. To those who know how well these gentlemen live upon the possessions of the Austrian nobles, it will be less matter of surprise to hear of the handsome suites of rooms occupied upon this castellated rock by such functionaries as the director of the castle, or the captain of the bodyguard. There are no less than fifty small gardens (or *deputatgärten*) dependant on the park, and understood to belong to the officers of the castle. These are so numerous, that they have a coffee-house within the walls for their own accommodation; indeed, so numerous are the *employés*, of one sort or another, on the estates of the Schwarzenberg, that the printed list of them forms a tolerably thick octavo volume.

A wood near Krummau is the only place in Bohemia where bears are yet to be found in a state of nature. They are preserved with some care, defended against poachers, and occasionally fed with horseflesh, though in general they require no other food than the berries and roots which they find in the forest. They are mostly harmless, and no one now living remembers the time when a human creature or tame animal was torn to pieces by them. The last man in the neighbourhood who had come into collision with the bears died lately. He was passing through the forest, and seeing a young cub tumbling about on a grassy glade, he took it into his head to carry the creature home. Soon, however, he saw to his horror that the mother had seen him, and was coming after him in full pursuit. He set his prize down immediately; but the mother, after having smelt and caressed her little one, for a few instants, resumed the chase. The poor fellow ran for his life, and was just in time to reach the entrance to a neighbouring farm, where he fell down senseless ; and when the servants came out to his assistance, it was found that the anguish and terror of those few moments had been sufficient to whiten his hair.

FROM BUDWEIS TO LINZ.

Budweis is completely a German city, though in Bohemia, and has the advantage of being the highest point to which any of the tributaries of the Elbe is navigable. Within twelve German miles of this point lies Linz on the Danube, and the approximation of two such important navigable rivers has at all times caused a very active commerce to be carried on between the two cities. This commerce has of late years been promoted by many improvements in the navigation of the Moldau; improvements for which the country stands mainly indebted to the exertions of Mr. Lanna, a shipbuilder, whose timber-yard at Budweis no stranger ought to leave unvisited. It was he who built the suspension-bridge at Prague, and it is owing to him that no less than seventy vessels so constructed as to suit the navigation of the Elbe and Moldau, arrive now every year at Budweis, and that there is even a regular river communication kept up between the latter place and Hamburg.

One of the consequences of the favourable geographical position of Budweis was, that one morning early, at five o'clock, I repaired to the office of the railroad, with the view of embarking my person in a train about to start for Linz.

The Linz-Budweis railroad is the grandmother of all the railroads on the European continent; and, taking this into consideration, we must not deem it matter of surprise to find it manifesting occasionally some symptoms of the debility of old age. It was the *coup d'essai* of Baron von Gerstner, who afterwards laid down rails in Russia, and died in America. He had great natural difficulties to contend with in the mountainous region over which his road had to be carried. To overcome these difficulties he was obliged to make his railroad take so circuitous a route, that though the distance between the two towns, in a straight line, is not more than ten (German) miles, the railroad has a length of seventeen. After arriving at Linz, the railroad is carried ten miles further to Gmünden, for the convenience of the government salt-works at that place.

The railroad from Budweis to Linz cost 1,700,000 florins. It consists of a single pair of rails, with arrangements at intermediate stations to enable two trains to pass each other. The rails are partly of Styrian, but chiefly of Bohemian, iron ; partly cast and partly wrought. In many places they seem sadly in want of repair. Some have been completely worn away, others have lost their nails, and stand up from the wooden sleepers to which they were originally fastened. Sometimes a very sensible jolt of the carriages reminds the passengers of a striking difference between the respective altitudes of two succeeding rails ; at other times a drag must be put upon the wheels, to prevent the train from rattling down the hill at too rapid a pace. My journey was performed immediately after rainy weather, which had made the rails extremely dirty and slippery; and I find, from a memorandum in my journal, that our wheels occasionally sunk into the soft earth. It is evident from all this, that this railroad must have been left in a very neglected condition; but its importance to the commerce of the Danube is so great, that the government will be obliged, before long, to step in, and, by a timely treatment, endeavour to save this grandmother railroad from an untimely fate.

The trains on this railroad are drawn by horses, and owing to the inequalities of the ground over which it passes, there is little likelihood that steam locomotives can ever be introduced there. One horse generally draws two or three carriages; but sometimes two or three horses are yoked on, in which case the train consists of six, seven, or even eight carriages. On an average, a horse is able to draw from seventy to a hundred cwt., at a slow walk; the trains for passengers travel at a smart trot. On the common road, in this mountainous district, a horse cannot well draw more than twelve cwt.

The rich kingdom of Bohemia has been sadly neglected by Nature with respect to salt, one of the necessaries of life. Every particle consumed within the kingdom comes from beyond the Danube; and this salt trade, one of the chief supports of the railroad, has likewise led to an active commerce in other goods. Merchandise of various descriptions finds its way from Trieste and Southern Italy to Gmünden, to be forwarded by railroad to Bohemia.

The terminus at Budweis is in the centre of the town close to the imperial salt-magazines, and to these magazines the travellers and the salt-bags must alike repair. It was, as I said, five o'clock in the morning when I made my appearance there, and I found our little one-horse trains ready to start, as they did almost immediately, at an easy trot, each having about fifty passengers in charge. The coachmen sat on their boxes smoking their pipes, and the draught was evidently so easy, that had the horses been in the habit of indulging in the poisonous weed, they too might have amused their leisure by "blowing a cloud" as they went along.

On a railroad where the trains are drawn by horses you travel with less noise than you do either on one where you are hurried along by steam engines, or on a common road. I was, therefore, soon engaged in an agreeable conversation with my fellow-travellers, and we were able to discuss undisturbed every object that presented itself within the reach of our constantly varying horizon. At Leopoldschlag we reached the highest level of the road, and were there two thousand feet over the sea, and one thousand over the plain of Budweis. At this point likewise we quitted Bohemia to enter Austria, and soon perceived symptoms of our having arrived among a more industrious population than that we had left, though this part of the archduchy of Austria is far from being its most populous or best cultivated district. Detached farmhouses become more numerous, and though the estates are still large, you see no longer so striking and painful a contrast, as in Bohemia, between the castle of the prince and the peasant's hut. Many of the peasants, on the contrary, have houses quite as comfortable as castles, and most of them have a well-to-do look about them.

The family of which one hears as much on the Austrian side, as one does of the Rosenbergs and Schwarzenbergs on the Bohemian side of the hills, is the family of the Starhembergs who, from time immemorial, have been men of might on the Danube, and, in the middle ages, were often involved in sanguinary feuds with the Rosenbergs. At present, three rich

Starhembergs dwell close together,—a prince, a general, and a count,—whose castles we had an opportunity of admiring as we passed along.

Many interesting and picturesque views present themselves on the road, though upon the whole it is much shut in by woods. Just before reaching Linz, however, as we were rolling down a zigzag line into the plain, a magnificent prospect opened suddenly upon us. The plain of Linz, the picturesque banks of the Danube, and the distant Alps in the background, combined to form a glorious picture, and while we were yet descanting on its beauties, we rolled onwards through the gates of Linz to the imperial salt-magazines, here, as at Budweis, the terminus of the road.

UPPER AUSTRIA.

LINZ.—THE CARPET MANUFACTORY.

WHEN, in the middle ages, an individual presented himself before the eyes of his fellow-men, it was known immediately, by the colour and cut of his garments, to what rank he belonged, and what was his vocation; but in our times, when superficially, that is, as far as the dress is concerned, all are more or less equal,—although the real distinction of persons, according to position, dignity, and wealth, are as sharply defined as ever,—a traveller in a simple brown frock-coat, entering a Linz manufactory, may be taken for,—what may he not be taken for? particularly if his German accent sound somewhat foreign to an Austrian ear. He may be a Dr., a Professor, a Privy Councillor, or a military officer of high rank in civil costume—or an "Excellency"—or perhaps, what would perhaps not be among the least welcome, he may be a traveller for a great mercantile house, come to make large purchases. "Assuredly," thought I, as a crowd of obsequious persons met me on my entrance into a noted carpet-manufactory, greeted me most courteously and expectingly, and hastened to display their wares,— "assuredly some such fancies are passing through their heads." I held it therefore to be my duty to explain to them, that in leaving my home, I had left behind neither kingdom, nor nabobship, nor lands containing 10,000 souls, nor a capital of 250,000 fr. rentes; but that I stood there simply a curious traveller, or, if they would have it so, a traveller desirous of information, without any design whatever of purchasing, or carrying off any thing more than could be conveyed by the eye and ear; whereupon, to my admiration, these people seemed to hold it no less their duty not to abate a particle of their hospitable Austrian obligingness, but rather to assist me the more zealously in viewing their labours and productions. I was the more curious about them, as I knew how considerable a part the Linz fabrics play in the Austrian manufactories, and to what importance they have lately risen.

As late as the year 1783, or 4, the Linz woollen-manufactures were nearly the only ones of the kind in the Austrian states. They were founded, I believe, at the end of the seventeenth or the beginning of the eighteenth century, by a citizen of Linz, and are the oldest in Austria. This citizen made them over subsequently to the so-called Oriental Company, which had a privilege for the preparation of woollen stuffs of all kinds.

The bad economy which reigned in the affairs of the company, and the profuse expenditure in the erection of superb and unnecessarily large buildings, threatened the undertaking with ruin. To prevent the injury which the stoppage must have caused to the many individuals interested, the government took the business under their own management, reserving to themselves the privileges before granted to private persons. The interval between 1740 and the total abolition of these privileges, may be considered to have been the period of the greatest splendour of the establishment: there were employed at times more than 20,000 workmen, spinners and weavers, in Bohemia; and in Linz alone not less than 2000. The great mind from which nearly all the new life in the Austrian body politic emanated, Joseph, abolished the privileges by which these 20,000 men profited, at the cost of many millions; and since that time, the workmen, scattered over all parts of the monarchy, have founded manufactories in Brünn, Vienna, and other cities, and have laid the foundation of the now considerable woollen-factories of Lower Austria and Moravia.

Since then, the Linz factories have declined, and their great barrack-like buildings, stand partially empty and seem awaiting another destination. Two branches alone of the woollen manufactory have again struck root and prosper: that of carpets, and the printing of woollen table-covers. So much taste is here displayed in these articles, the colours are so lively and so lasting, that the productions of the Linz manufactories have obtained considerable celebrity in the shop and the drawing-room. They have warehouses in Leipzig, Prague, Milan, Vienna, Pesth, &c., and exports have even been made to France and England. Their extraordinary cheapness will no doubt lead to a further demand for these goods. For five or six florins* a most artistical and magnificent bouquet of flowers may be purchased; while one of the quickly-fading productions of the garden would cost double the money. Establishments for woollen printing are still rare in the world, and it is therefore the more cheering to learn that the art has already been brought to such perfection here. It seems to me, however, that they have been partly indebted for their progress to the influence of France; the designers, at least, are in part French, and the newest drawings are made from designs received from Paris, which city, in the invention of new shades, and in the arrangement of tasteful wreaths and groups of flowers, is certainly not to be excelled. The person, too, at the head of the carpet printing, is of French descent.

The name of this man is Dufresne. He took the trouble to show me over the table-cover department and, as I visit such establishments much more on account of the men than of their productions, he became to me, in a short time, an object of much interest and respect. He halted in his gait, and in speaking of his infirm limb, related the history of his life. His father, a French emigrant, had sought refuge in Vienna, and there endeavoured to gain a livelihood by the establishment of a small cotton-printing factory. An Austrian nobleman, Count X., a great friend to the French, lent him a small capital, and a corner of his house. The business turned out well, the father hoped for the re-establishment of his worldly prosperity, and the son, who had been born subsequently to the flight of

---

* The Austrian florin is equal to about two shillings sterling. The Rhenish florin is worth rather less. Ten Austrian florins are equal to one pound, or to twelve Rhenish florins.

his parents from France, was destined for the military service; but Heaven willed it otherwise; his horse fell with him, his leg was broken, and thenceforward he made up his mind to follow his father's pursuit. Soon afterwards, his father died, less wealthy than he had hoped to be, and the son found the business necessary to the maintenance of his mother. He studied how to improve it, and having one day met with some English woollen printing, he never rested till he had not only imitated, but surpassed it. Having thus grown up in adversity, and being endowed with an active spirit, he had made himself what he was when I saw him, "Imperial and Royal Inspector of woollen printing," with a good salary.

The manufactory which I inspected in M. Dufresne's company was exceedingly well arranged, clean, light, and in good order. In the large room where the colour setters were busied, I read on a board conspicuously placed these words written in chalk: "With God's aid." "You are surprised?" observed M. Dufresne, "but you will see this is the chief point. Our business is very laborious and difficult, and requires not only clever and thoughtful, but also diligent and conscientious workpeople. When I give a pattern to a colour setter, I give him also some direction how to proceed. He must listen and apply this cheerfully, but he must also consider well with what colour it will be best to begin and end, and give to these matters zeal and attention, as a painter would do; for I cannot attend to the detail, and must trust much to the conscientiousness of the workmen, who by a single careless step might occasion great damage. On their side they must have full confidence in me, and apply to me in all difficult points. All this is best obtained when a man keeps in mind the words you see written there. It is said that the inmost soul of all art is religion and the fear of God, and our work is a kind of art. I take no workman of whose character I am not certain; I pay far more heed to this than to their skill. And when I have taken one into my employ I observe him closely, and note whether he works in a pious spirit. Many a one have I dismissed solely on account of his want of conscientiousness, and I believe the chest of the imperial and royal manufactory has been the gainer by this policy. We begin in the morning with a short prayer, and those words are never effaced from the board. I have a design of inscribing on a tablet over the door, those fine lines from Schiller's Song of the Bell:

'And when with good discourse attended,
The course of labour cheerful flows,' &c.*

and I believe money so laid out will yield a good interest. Now you see, sir, you know my way of thinking," added M. Dufresne, smiling and clapping me on the shoulder in a friendly manner, as I applauded what he had said, and he further entreated me to write my name in his pocket-book as a memorial.

The manipulation of the wool is one of the prettiest operations that can be seen, and I think there must be more pleasure in working at carpets in a manufactory animated by so good a spirit than in wearing out the finished product in dull company. The workman has the large white woollen fabric spread out before him, and by it the design, the coloured drawing. The different tints are set singly with wooden types, and the workman has

---

* "Wenn gute Reden sie begleiten,
So fliesst die Arbeit munter fort," &c.

soon the satisfaction of seeing the picture unfold itself with tolerable rapidity before him. There are about two hundred and forty different designs for covers in this establishment. This number may at first appear small, but the difficulty of working a new pattern is very great. A peculiar plan must be pursued with every one, and of course for every one a new set of wooden types made. Some of the colours are set abruptly one by the other, and some are partially covered and gently shaded into each other. In this manner, with ten pots of colour, twenty or thirty tints are produced on the wool. It is particularly difficult to judge where the single colours may be best placed, in order to prepare the wooden types accordingly. The true life, spirit, tone and softness are given to the colours by the hot vapour to which the fabric is afterwards exposed for a time.

THE MADHOUSE.

Near the woollen manufactory, and like it, by the side of the Danube, stands this edifice, which was erected long since, although the city has but twenty-five thousand inhabitants. I was accompanied by the obliging overseer of the house, which, at the period of my visit, contained about eighty simply insane patients. Among these were some that especially awakened my sympathy.

One was a painter, a Tyrolese, who had distinguished himself in the war of freedom, and had received, in consequence, a small sum of money from the government. As he had shown from his youth taste and talent for drawing, and had already studied it in some degree in Vienna, he appropriated this money to the expenses of a journey to Italy. In Rome, however, on comparing himself with the great living, and greater dead, masters, he became aware of the little he was likely to accomplish with the greatest exertion. His anxious labours, unsupported as it appeared by true genius, induced a degree of morbid excitement; his efforts could not satisfy him, and the masterpieces of art, which he saw daily before him, appeared in his eyes so many reproofs of his own incapacity. He was not a bad draughtsman, and had he stuck to the pencil, he might have become a good mathematical or architectural artist. Unfortunately he did not possess the prudence so many want, that of contenting himself with his own modest portion of talent, as God had given it him, and putting it to usury in the prescribed direction. In the exertion to become a distinguished painter, and reach a height unattainable to him, he destroyed himself. In despair he fled from Rome, and returned to his friends—a madman. He now fancies that oil-colours are baneful to him and full of poison. The sight of an oil-painting causes him the greatest suffering, and every thing that tends to remind him of brush or palette must be carefully kept out of his sight. He takes a pleasure in the use of the crayon and blacklead-pencil, and several of the patients have had their portraits sketched by him, very good likenesses, hanging up over their beds. I found him occupied in drawing a pretty little landscape, and he himself assured me, with a friendly smile, that it was his peculiar misfortune to suffer so much from oil-colours that he should die on the spot if he only smelt them. Rome, Raphael, and Correggio he had quite forgotten. In madness itself there is a kind of happiness and tranquillity; the condition that precedes it, the struggle between reason and frenzy, must be infinitely more terrible. What chambers of torture must the studios and galleries of Rome have been for this man! *The becoming mad* must be like an active conflagration, but the being mad must resemble the condition of the burnt-out edifice, more fearful, perhaps, to the spectator, but far less frightful to the sufferer than the former convulsion.

In another room a poor lunatic was busily rubbing a brass ring. He told us with great glee, that it was becoming brighter and brighter, and that the gold would soon appear. The director told us, he had been rubbing that ring for weeks together, and every day asserting the same thing; a prize in the lottery had been the original cause of his calamity. He had wasted his money in idle extravagance, and in a short time all was gone but a few hundred florins. These he made use of to purchase fifty more shares. They came up all blanks, and the gulf of ruin he saw yawning before him deprived him of his reason. Since that time he has employed himself in polishing brass rings in the expectation of their turning to gold.

In all the Austrian lunatic asylums, we hear wonders of the Douche or cold water cure, and, in Linz, accordingly, we were told of a striking cure performed by the help of this remedy in the course of the preceding summer. A man labouring long under the deepest melancholy, and a prey to monomania of all kinds, which ended in periodical fits of perfect frenzy, was completely cured in the course of three weeks by the Douche, and dismissed to his fellows as a reasonable being.

Here also, behind an iron grating, we saw some poor wretches whose madness had already cost the lives of several fellow-creatures. Among them were some of whom it was doubtful whether their deeds should be atoned for on the scaffold, or their correction sought for in the madhouse. The story of one was particularly horrible. This person was a citizen of Linz, noted some ten years before for an unconquerable dread of spectres and witches. In every strange noise, and every unusual appearance, he fancied the presence of supernatural influences; even his own wife, if she appeared unexpectedly before him, was sometimes taken for a spectre. His wife was accustomed to laugh at and ridicule her husband for these puerile terrors. On one wild and stormy evening, when all the vanes and window shutters shook and rattled fearfully, she said to him, "There you foolish man, some of your witches will certainly come to fetch you to-night." The night came on, and the unhappy man became more silent and terror-stricken. At a late hour one of the children awoke, and the mother, unable to still it cried at last, "Sleep you witch's brat, or I'll kill you." These thoughtless words acted like an electric spark on the dark fancies that lay brooding in the troubled brain of the miserable man. Armed with a hatchet, he sprang to the cradle of the child, crying, "Yes, yes, witch's child! Kill it! Witches are all around us and about us! I'll kill ye all." His weeping wife and shrieking children were all murdered one after the other, and then a poor maid-servant. He then barred all the doors and windows to keep out the evil spirits that might be without, and watched the whole night through, armed with his hatchet, by the bodies of the supposed witches. The sun was standing high in the heavens, when the neighbours saw him crossing the street bearing the corses of his children, dripping with their gore. He called out that they were witch's children, whom he was going to throw into the water. He was immediately seized as a furious and mischievous maniac, and has been ever since confined in the grated cell where we beheld him crouching before us in the straw.

JESUIT SCHOOL.

If the object of the Lunatic Asylum be the restoration of the crazed to reason, the Jesuit school may be held in some respects as one for rendering crazy those whom nature has made rational, at least if we share the opinions of many of the enlightened of our times with regard to the Jesuits. Linz possesses one of their schools, oddly enough installed in one of those celebrated towers or citadels which surround the city with their strong girdles. The Archduke Maximilian, who planned and built these towers, gave the Jesuits one of those first built, for an experiment, and at his own cost, on the Freiberg. The Maximilian towers are large, round buildings, with thick walls, as great a portion of them being sunk under ground as appears above it. Below the level of the soil they contain several stories, while above it they rise but a few feet, and these are partly covered with turf, so that from without, by the additional shelter of a gradually elevated wall, they are scarcely to be seen. The balls of the enemy must for the most part fly harmlessly over them, while their own, discharged from cannon rising but a few inches from the sod of the bulwark, and hidden besides in deep hollows in the walls, must burst quite unexpectedly out of the grass. All the towers, to the number of seventeen or twenty, stand in a certain regular connexion with one another, yet each is susceptible of individual defence, if the chain were broken, and could pour its fire on an advancing enemy as well from one side as the other. Really, if the illustrious and deeply experienced inventor were not known, one might fancy this defensive system the invention of the Jesuits themselves.

In these fortresses the fathers are now firmly established, after making such changes as their own wants and taste dictated. On the thick bomb-proof ground-walls they have reared two additional stories; the interior of the fortress is laid out cheerfully, the exterior washed over with an agreeable red colour; every door bears the initials J. H. S., and every niche of the walls, where formerly cannon were lodged, is changed into a sleeping and sitting room for the accommodation of the pupils or the superiors, attainable by elegant winding staircases running round the interior of the building. In addition to the towers a garden was bestowed on them, which is most diligently cultivated, and a second piece of ground on the foremost point of the Freiberg, where they have built an elegant small church in the Gothic style.

The most striking piece of furniture in this church is a magnificent throne-like seat with a canopy, both so bedizened with gold, that one can scarcely believe it destined for a place of prayer, and for those who should set a conspicuous example to the flock, of humble devotion to God. But so it is. "It is the throne of the superior," answered the Jesuit lay-brother, who was in the church, and of whom I had inquired if this were destined for the emperor or any other illustrious person occasionally visiting them. The church is further decorated with several new pictures, representing scenes from the life of a newly-canonized Jesuit of the name of Hieronymus; one, representing him with the sacramental chalice in his hand on the seashore, and obtaining for the Neapolitan fishermen a miraculous draught;

another depicting him, cross in hand, checking the fiery eruption of Vesuvius. These and other pictures were lighted, not by side windows, but from the roof, according to the new fashion. When such objects are found covered with dust in an ancient half-ruined cloister, or in a picture-gallery, from a long mouldered pencil, one finds nothing amiss in it; but I cannot deny that it made a most disagreeable impression on me, to find them decorating the walls of a modern temple, and purporting to be the events of our own day.

I do not think, however, that the Jesuits have made any great progress of late in Austria. Complaints are certainly heard that the nobles are too much devoted to them, but that they should ever obtain their former position is almost impossible. All enlightened persons, of whom there are undoubtedly many in Austria, have decided against them; even the lower classes make zealous opposition. Nevertheless the Jesuits have begun to spin their strong yet subtle nets. They are most numerous in Galicia. In Hungary there are none at all; in the German provinces there are three "houses," one in Gratz, one in Linz, and one at Inspruck. They have acquired most influence in the latter city. Not long ago the Gymnasium there was given up to them, and teachers supplied from their body, and since that time many complaints have been heard, that it is no longer the ability of the pupils, but the rank and credit of their parents which decide their advancement.

Each of the " houses" has a superior, a " minister," the superior's deputy and assistant, several priests (seculars), and some lay-brothers to cultivate the garden, attend to household affairs, and be serviceable in many other ways. The superior of the Linz house was absent on a " journey of business" at the time of my visit. The minister was in the confessional chair, where I saw him with his features concealed, listening to a kneeling penitent. I went afterwards, accompanied by a priest, who obligingly offered his services, to see the interior of the building. We passed through the schoolrooms and others appropriated to the pupils of the institution. They live two and two together, (in some of the rooms there were three,) agreeably to the principles of the Jesuits, that no member of their order shall be left without the company and assistance of another. No brother of the order ever receives permission to visit the city alone, he must always have another brother, his " Socius," with him. According to this regulation no Jesuit can ever be entangled in a dispute or struggle of any kind without being sure of help. Hence, wherever there is a Jesuit he is double-headed and four-armed, and beyond a doubt this is one of the most politic laws in their code. Even the lay-brothers have also each of them his " Socius." They remind us of the Spartan legion, which was so unconquerable, principally because it consisted entirely of pairs of fraternal friends linked together for life and death. Two men so bound to each other, yield a much greater amount of *power* than two separate individuals; as two cannon-balls linked together by a chain produce a much more terrible effect than when fired singly. At present there are thirty Jesuits in the Linz house, nine of whom are priests, nine lay-brethren, and the rest novices. They are nearly all Germans.

" We are recruited principally from German Bohemia," said my attendant priest, as we stepped out on the broad and beautiful platform of the tower to enjoy the magnificent prospect; "thence come the greater number of our pupils. We have reason to rejoice so far, but this is not to be compared with our progress in Belgium. There not less than eighty-four young, and several elderly men, entered our order in the course of last year. We have few or no Slavonians in our house. In Linz we have made no great progress, hitherto; indeed we possess nothing here but this house provisionally. The Florians have still the Gymnasium. We are therefore here only provisionally, and *ad interim*, and educate our pupils *ad interim*," (is there no roguery concealed behind this *ad interim?* thought I,) "in the hope that in time a wider sphere of influence will be opened to us. We employ ourselves *ad interim* with the sciences, yet we think that if we form useful subjects, they must in time be made use of. The houses of our order in Austria do not form as yet an organized and individual *province*, but we *hope* it will soon take that form. In Vienna we have not yet received permission to establish ourselves; the cause may be the old prejudices against us, and a lurking remnant of a belief in the disorders attributed to our order: but we *hope* that in the constantly increasing enlightenment of the times, these prejudices will die away. I have read all the books which have been written for and against the Jesuits; for the order was always an object of great interest to me; and since I have myself belonged to it, I have been amazed at the unfounded accusations and bitter persecutions to which it has been exposed. God be praised, we have fallen on better times, and people have already begun to acknowledge their earlier injustice. When our order was dissolved, at the close of the last century, the canonization of not less than eighty distinguished Jesuits then in progress was interrupted. In later times, seven of these causes have been taken up again, and brought to an end. By the two last popes (the present and his predecessor), seven Jesuits have been canonized, or pronounced blessed. Among these was the celebrated Canisius, whose services in Germany have been so great. At this moment another is about to be pronounced blessed, who suffered martyrdom on his mission to Poland. He was slain there by the barbarians in the middle of the eighteenth century. The cause has been long in hand; but as such matters are proceeded in with great circumspection, their progress is necessarily slow. The documents proving his purity of life, and his blessed and worthy end, are all forthcoming; but exact and authentic intelligence of the death of his "Socius," who accompanied him on his mission and suffered with him, are yet wanting; and these, according to our laws, are absolutely necessary to the canonization of a Jesuit. We *hope*, however, that these supplementary points will speedily be cleared up, when the Holy Father may follow the impulse of his heart, and bestow the crown of martyrdom upon this excellent man."

My Jesuit friend had pronounced the word *hope*, at least, four or five times, whence I should conclude that the Jesuits of our day are very full of this agreeable feeling. Often, however, as the Jesuit appeared, I had no fault to find with my companion; but as I looked on the turf-covered, bomb-proof, and cannon-bristling towers of Linz, and compared them with the smiling, decorated building, in holiday attire, of which the Jesuits have taken possession, I thought also how quickly such a smooth, friendly, and courteous man of peace might be metamorphosed into a rude, hostile antagonist in times of strife and trouble, and how certainly we two friendly interlocutors would then find ourselves opposed to each other.

From our lofty stand, we commanded an extensive view over the Austria so rich in *hope* for the Jesuits. The city of Linz, with its black roofs, lay at our feet; and in the distance, on the magnificent plains of Lower

Austria, gleamed the cloister of St. Florian. The noble Danube flowed, in its winding course, through this beautiful land to Vienna, attended, no doubt, by many a longing sigh of the Jesuits, wafted towards the stately "*Residenz.*" Towards the south, the plains swelled, by degrees, into hills and eminences, which lay like shadows in the foreground, backed by the sharply-defined and majestic Alpine chain of Rhœtia and Noricum.

PROVINCIAL MUSEUM.

Among the many national museums and collections of provincial rarities, which have arisen within the last ten years in all parts of the Austrian monarchy, in Prague, Pesth, Gratz, Laybach, &c., one has taken root in Linz, whose object it is to collect and preserve in a separate museum all that can have reference to the history and natural productions of Austria. Formerly, all such things found in any of the provinces of the monarchy were sent without exception to Vienna. The provinces considered themselves as the lawful possessors of such curiosities, and looked upon their removal as little better than robbery. No doubt jealousy of the all-grasping capital caused the neglect of much that might have been collected. In fact, objects of this kind can only be properly estimated in the place of their nativity. Many have provincial value and significance alone, and are quite worthless and unnoted in an extensive general museum. Few citizens embrace the whole state in their patriotic sympathies; the interest of the greater part is limited to the narrow circle of their homes.

The Linz museum has now six rooms filled with antiquities, coins, petrifactions, fossils, stuffed animals, minerals, books, and industrial productions, and in the treatise published every year a light has been thrown on many a dark corner of Austrian history, which would probably not have been done if the bureau for the advancement of such purposes had remained at Vienna.

None of the antiquities I saw here interested me more than the shield of a Roman warrior, and a Roman brick. The shield was from the celebrated shield manufactory which the Romans had at the mouth of the Ens, and from which the greater part of the legions on the Danube were supplied with arms. The Austrians have at present for the supply of their Danube army, a similar manufactory in the city of Steyer, not far from the Ens, where pikes, guns, and pistols are the weapons now made instead of spears and shields. The brick attracted my attention from the traces of dust and of straw, and the mark of the workman's fingers, which were still visible on its surface. An accidental puff of wind probably scattered the broken straw upon the brick while it was yet soft, the workman kneaded it in, and thus the memorial of the unheeded motion of a careless hand has remained undestroyed for centuries. In the invisible physical laboratory of the human world trifles are often perpetuated from analogous causes.

The Romans had their principal station on the Danube, at Linz (Lentium); and in fact it is a position that will continue to be occupied so long as the land is inhabited. The Danube here issues from a narrow mountain-pass, into a rich and beautiful plain, in which roads branch off in every direction, and traverse the broad valley of the Traim, joining that of the Danube, in the neighbourhood of Linz. The division even of the country into the province above, and that below the Ens, is old and of Roman origin. The whole land was called Noricum ripense ; all that lay below the Ens, the Romans called the lower towns and castles, and those above, the towns and castles of Noricum ripense.

THE MONASTERY OF ST. FLORIAN.

One morning, in company with a new acquaintance, I stepped into a *stellwagen* bound for Ebelsberg, a small market-town at the mouth of the Ens. A thick morning vapour covered the whole valley. My companion had justly calculated the movement of the foggy particles, and said to me after a time, " We shall have a most beautiful day ;" and in fact, as we approached the more elevated neighbourhood of Ebelsberg, we left the fog behind us, and had as he had prophesied, the finest weather we could have desired.

These public carriages (*stellwagen*) have been introduced in Linz within the last ten years, and now run in every direction from that city. Ten years ago, if a person wished to go from Linz to Steyer, and was at all in haste, he must have paid five florins, and given abundance of good words besides. Now he can go for about forty pence, and the vehicle makes the journey twice a day.

My object was to visit the renowned convent of St. Florian, and also some of its peasants so well known for their opulence. I left Ebelsberg, therefore, on foot, and, striking into a by-road, proceeded deeper into the country. A little countryman who had bought a nook of land from the lords spiritual, and had therefore some business to settle with them, went with me, and we soon came in sight of the stately abbey which stands on a hill. The fields and meadows, the orchards, and all around announced a system of careful cultivation. A storehouse, an apothecary's shop, a tavern, and an hospital, all attached to the abbey, lay at the foot of the hill. I praised the arrangement of all these to my peasant companion. "Ah," said he, " yes, yes, the holy fathers, they are clever fellows, they look after their affairs, and keep things under their own eye." In the village stood two waggons with four horses, each laden with six-and-twenty calves. The poor creatures lay with their legs bound, and their heads hanging down in a most painful position. Some had wounded themselves against the ironwork of the high wheels, by the constant convulsive twitching of the mouth. I suppose there was no society in the abbey for the prevention of cruelty to animals. I looked from the poor calves to the picture of the Madonna, which hung from the corner of the abbey tavern, and read beneath these words : " Blessed is the holy and immaculate conception of the Virgin Mary."

I had heard much beforehand of the grandeur of the Austrian abbeys, standing like a magnificent chain of palaces, mostly on the right side of the Danube as far as Vienna ; but I must confess that when I trod the interior courtyards and chambers of St. Florian's cloistered palace, my expectations were far exceeded by the reality. The principal part is built in a most superb style, from a plan of the time of Charles the Sixth, and is *almost* finished. To be *almost finished* has been the destiny of almost all the stately erections of that ruler, who died ten years too soon, as the zeal for building in the Gothic style did by a hundred. However, in St. Florian's abbey, it is but little that is wanting.

H

Few monarchs in Europe can boast of being so grandly lodged, whether in reference to the form or material of their dwellings, as the "regular Augustine chapter of St. Florian in Upper Austria." On either side of the lofty entrance, broad marble steps lead to the principal floor, and corridors above a hundred feet in breadth run round the various wings of the buildings that surround the four quadrangular inner courts. The corridors, as well as the outer passages, and the floor of the great hall, are elegantly paved with black and white marble, and everywhere the cleanliness is so perfect, that every atom of dust must be remorselessly pursued with brush and broom. As I paced these corridors, the water splashing in the midst of the courts, the rays of the sun playing through the countless arched passages, casting rich lights and shades upon the polished marble beneath, I thought if the pleasure of a stranger in wandering here was so great, what must be that of the owners, the fathers of St. Florian? In the corridors are the—little doors they should be, but they are lofty portals, leading to the monks' cells, to the apartments of the prelate, to the emperor's hall, the library, the cardinal's chambers, and others.

I was really somewhat embarrassed which door to attack first, for I was afraid of disturbing some personage of importance turn whither I would. At last, wiping the dust carefully from my feet, I chose a cell at random, and found, in the person of the father and professor Kurz, so celebrated throughout Austria, for his learning and historical works, the very best guide to lead me through this labyrinth that my good angel could have led me to.

The great convents and abbeys in Austria have been, at all times, the nurses and cherishers of science and of art; in every one is to be found a museum of natural history, a noble library, and, generally, a picture-gallery; and each boasts its celebrated names, either of those who have long departed from this world, and live only in the affection and respect of posterity, or of those still living, and actively engaged in the service of their order. Of the latter class is the reverend Father Kurz, a kind and venerable old man of seventy-two, who now advanced to meet the intrusive stranger. He was for a long time professor of history in the Gymnasium of Linz, and has written some learned works on Austrian history. At present, borne down by years and feeble health, he has retired to his cell where he busies himself with lighter literary labours, and the affairs of the convent. I found with him a couple of peasants, who had come to request his advice respecting a lawsuit, and a peasant-girl asking him for some medicine for her sick mother.

I know not whether we North German protestants entertain very just notions respecting the influence, the sphere of operation, or the business and manner of life of the monks of the great Austrian Augustine and Benedictine convents; nor whether our opinion of them may not be too unfavourable; and I shall therefore permit myself a few remarks on the subject. It would be highly unjust to consider such establishments, simply as the retreats of lazy monks, whose sole employments are praying and eating. On the contrary, the manifold relations in which such a convent stands to the external world, and the great sphere of activity connecting it, with nearly every phase of life, have opened the way for the cares, the business, and the vexations of humanity, and paved for them an easy entrance to the cells of these monks; these, consequently, are busy men of the world, rather than feasting and praying anchorites; and if they are worried somewhat more at their ease than other people, they have to bend like other Christians under the common burden. It is only a small minority of the members of such a house that are commonly resident within its walls. In St. Florian only twenty-one out of its ninety-two fathers were dwellers there at the time of my visit. The rest were almost constantly absent on different employments and missions, some as parish priests in their respective parishes, some as instructors in schools, professors at the Gymnasia, or as stewards and overseers of the lands of the abbey, which must all be administered and overlooked.

As teachers and professors, they must submit to examinations like other people, and as agriculturists they are as responsible as others in similar employments. Those who remain in the convent are either the old and feeble, or those who have their employments in the abbey itself. One is master of the household, and has the kitchen, the stable, &c., under his direction, another is master of the forest, a third, librarian and director of the museum. Some of the convents which possess observatories, have also their own astronomers, who, as professors of astronomy, teach the science in the convent. The observatory of Kremsminster has long been celebrated, and almost every person here can tell which father is now at the head of it. Even the old and feeble find much in their cells to interest them in the sayings and doings of the world without. They are the friends and patrons of many far and near, who visit them frequently to ask counsel and assistance. The prelates,—so are styled the heads of the great convents,—the prelates, if not princes by birth, live like princes, and have the usual allotment of business and influence, cares and crosses, that fall to the share of princes. They have their banquet-halls like them, but also their halls of audience and rooms for business, whence they overlook and direct the affairs of the convent. They are also frequently members of the provincial states, and hence, although monks, are entangled in some measure in the contest of politics. The whole range of great abbeys in the valley of the Danube may be looked upon as among the most distinguished pillars of the Austrian state edifice; and not only its supporting pillars, but also the foundation and corner-stones of that edifice. These religious foundations, founded in the earliest ages of the Austrian sovereignty, were the very strongest elements in the formation of the future archduchy. In the middle ages, the abbots of those convents often furnished the most considerable reinforcements to the Austrian armies, and at a later period, one of them contributed as large a sum as eighty or a hundred thousand florins to the expenses of a war. At the commencement of the reign of Maria Theresa, she could obtain from the bank of Genoa the three millions she required, only on condition, that the Austrian abbeys would be her security.

On almost every house-wall in Austria a St. Florian is painted, emptying a pail of water over a burning house, as its protecting saint; pious verses are sometimes inscribed beneath, recommending the house to his guardianship, and sometimes verses any thing but pious, as the following:

> "House and home trust I to Florian's name;
> If he protect it not, his be the shame."

But of late, the signs and tokens of the Vienna and Trieste Fire Assurance Companies have made their appearance by the side of St. Florian, whose credit appears to sink as theirs rises. St. Florian was a heathen, and a

Roman centurion in the time of Olim. Here in the camp by the Danube, his mind, bent on serious matters, and withdrawn from the frivolities of Rome, may have been duly prepared for the seed of the Christian religion; but *how* it fell, and how it germinated, the legend says not. Enough Florian became a zealous Christian, confessed and preached the new doctrine, and was in consequence condemned as a rebellious and frantic innovator by his general, Aquilius, and beaten to death with clubs on the shores of the Danube. His body was thrown into the water, where it remained till the princess Valeria, the daughter of the emperor Dioclesian, withdrew from the embraces of the river nymphs the remains of a saint known and honoured as far as the Turkish frontier, and in the year 304, buried them in the place where now the abbey stands. His long acquaintance with the water nymphs of the Danube, it may be, which has rendered him so peculiarly fit for a fire extinguisher.

"You may believe what you please of this story" said my guide to me, "but you will find it not only in black and white in our old chronicles, but also in bright colours in our picture-gallery, where we have the whole history represented in a series of twenty paintings."

In the library of the convent there are forty thousand volumes. The hall is large and beautiful, a hall worthy of the muses, as is always the case in the Austrian convents of the first rank. Except Gottingen, I know no German university which has so splendid an apartment for this purpose as St. Florian's. With respect to the collection itself, it is naturally somewhat different. The chief part, of course, is composed of theology. The fathers are in full force, some of them in the splendid Paris editions. Other branches of knowledge have not, however, been neglected. The censorship of the press affects this convent but little. For them there is no forbidden fruit, and the convents are exactly the fittest asylums for writings persecuted by the censor; works, which in any other library, or in a bookseller's shop, would be seized by the police, are frequently to be found in cloisters where such unquiet productions are held to be in the quietest place. The monks know how to arrange these matters, only taking the precaution sometimes of placing such writings on the second row, behind others, or on the topmost shelves. The influence of these fine collections cannot be great, as they are the private property of the convents, and the books are never lent out. Nevertheless, they are interesting with a view to the future; it is well to know where such literary materials are to be looked for; doubtless, the day will come when another Joseph will throw these noble halls open to the public, and declare their contents the property of the state. On this account I was glad to find everywhere a goodly assemblage of our German historians, down to Luden, Menzel, and Pfister. The Monumenta Germanorum are also not wanting. An historical-geographical work on Lower Austria, in thirty volumes, put me in a terrible fright. If this work, like Meidinger's Grammar, should arrive at a twentieth edition, one might cover a good portion of the three hundred (German) square miles of Lower Austria with the paper. If we were to use all the waste paper of this kind in Germany we might cover the whole surface of the globe, and perhaps paper up the sun besides.

The Florian convent owns not less than seven hundred and eighty-seven houses and farms, or, as they express it here, so many "numbers," and yet it is only a "three-quarters" cloister. The greater number of the convents are only "half" or "quarter." Kremsminster is one of the few "entire, cloisters." I never could learn from what measure these expressions of half and whole, &c., which are in constant use among the people, are taken, nor could the fathers themselves give me any information. Perhaps it may be a mode of speech, remaining from the times when the convents were rated for military contributions; Florian must then have paid fifty thousand florins, where Kremsminster paid eighty thousand. In those times, an archduke of Austria sometimes resided as a guest at St. Florian's, with four hundred and fifty horsemen and horses; the present emperors come much more modestly attended. The convent is in constant readiness for such visits. Here, and in all other Austrian convents, there is a suite of rooms called "the imperial apartments." The number of illustrious guests that have visited the Augustine lords spriritual, from the emperor Arnulph the child, downwards, is countless—among them was Prince Eugene, the high-hearted conqueror of the Turks. He slept here, during his stay, on a splendid bedstead, at each of whose four corners a Turkish prisoner was chained in effigy. Pictures of the battles of Zenta, Mohacs, and Belgrade, adorned the walls, and every wax light in the antechamber, was borne by the figure of a Moor, carved in wood. All these are preserved as memorials to the present day. Pope Pius VI., on his memorable journey to Vienna, was entertained at St. Florian's Abbey, and from the balcony of his chamber, bestowed his blessing on not less than thirty thousand people.

Emperors, princes, and popes, are not the only visiters: travelling students usually halt here in the vacations; some may always be found in the rooms below, appropriated to their service. In one of them I found an enigmatical-looking piece of furniture, whose use I was at a loss to divine. My companion directed my attention to an inscription on the front, which displayed the following spiritual reference to a stove : "Hoc in tumulo hiems arida æstatis ossa consumit."

In almost all the conventual churches I found multitudes of redbreasts as regular inhabitants. In the splendid church of St. Florian, their pleasant chirpings were the only praises to God I heard during my visit. The church servitor told me that, in the brooding season, their numbers were so great, that the preacher's voice was often overpowered by their song. The sparrows keep to the outside of the roof; swallows come sometimes for years together, and then disappear again.

Carlo Carlone was the architect of this church. This man's ear must have been well opened to the harmonies that lie in numbers, and grand proportions, for the height, breadth, and length of the church, the place and proportions of the windows, the stalls, corridors, and choir, the arches and pillars, form a whole so exquisitely symmetrical, that the musical impression, received on entering the place, is irresistible. The principal lines of the building are covered with the most solid, rich, and tasteful stuccoes. Round all the galleries, cornices, and ceilings, hundreds of angels are wreathed and grouped. Curtains, executed in the most masterly manner in plaster, hang in rich profusion over every door and passage; and the most beautiful garlands, wreaths of flowers, and arabesques, wind and droop in lavish abundance, and in the most graceful forms throughout. I must confess that I learnt, for the first time, here to know what stucco was, and what might be made of it.

The church has three organs; the largest is in the background, opposite the high altar, and two smaller ones are in the choir. The largest, the masterwork of an Austrian of the name of Christmann, has 5230 pipes, and the strongest of these, cast in the finest English tin, is thirty-two feet high, four feet and a half in circumference, and weighs five hundred-weight. The "organ-basket," which supports the seat of the organist and the singers, displays the most beautiful and inimitable workmanship in carved wood. It has the figure of a giant basket, or balcony, formed of the thickest bush of acanthus-leaves. Below, the woodwork of this balcony is intermingled with that of the stalls and prayer-desks. The pillows of those seats and their canopy, consist partly of black fretted woods, and partly of speckled beech-wood, of which the massive blocks are in themselves curiosities. The whole range of stalls for the chapter exhibit the finest architectural drawing, and the greatest solidity of construction, and yet the minutiæ are executed with a neatness and elegance such as are usually bestowed only on boxes destined for the reception of ladies' jewels or gentlemen's snuff. On a closer examination, every little knot and edge is found to be most artistically and laboriously put together, and exquisitely polished.

In one word, present arms and show honour due to the Austrian monks, all ye who so often contemn, without even knowing them. I must confess, that I desired nothing more than that Father Kurz and the other gentlemen might accept my farewell pressure of the hand as it was meant, as a token of the most sincere goodwill and esteem.

VISIT TO THE HOUSE OF AN AUSTRIAN PEASANT.

The peasants of Upper and Lower Austria have, with the exception of some of the peasants of Lombardy, certainly reached a higher degree of wealth and freedom than any other peasants in the Austrian empire. Those of Galicia, Bohemia, and Hungary, are, on the whole, still serfs; the inhabitant of Illyria and the Tyrol is poor. There are *parts*, indeed, of all these provinces where the land is better cultivated, and the peasants more free and opulent. Hanna, in Moravia, is celebrated for this, so is Zips, in Hungary; Saxonland, in Transylvania; Egerthal, in Bohemia; and many rich Alpine valleys, are also remarkable exceptions. Neither ought we to pity or despise the peasants of other parts of the monarchy as mere slaves, without duly estimating many alleviating circumstances. To take them all in all, however, it is not less certain that the peasants of the Danube, in reference to mental cultivation, solidity of character, firmness of position, and a recognition of their rights as men, surpass the majority of their fellow-subjects, as far as they do in agricultural knowledge and opulence. Among the richest and best known are those in the neighbourhood of St. Florian's Abbey. Some of them, indeed, are so distinguished, as to have had the honour, more than once, of receiving their emperor, and one of these is the much-talked-of "Meier in der Tann." Accompanied by a guide from the Abbey, I made my way, by a narrow footpath, through beautiful woods, over luxuriant meadows, and through well-cultivated fields and orchards to the farms of this wealthy peasant.

The Florian and Austrian peasants in general, although more those above than below the Ens, live more frequently in solitary farm-houses in the midst of their lands, than in villages. The peasants have all a double name; in the first place, a family name which is inherited by their children, and secondly, one as possessor of the farm, which passes to their successors only. These official names are no doubt extremely old, as old perhaps as the farms themselves. " Lehner, in Fohrenbach." " Meier im leeren Busch." " Zehnter, near Gommering." " Meier in der Tann." " The Schildhuber." " The Dindelhuber," and the entire name of such a peasant sounds quite long and stately; for example, " John Plass, Meier in der Tann," " Joseph Fimberger, the Schildhuber." In ordinary life the designation from the land is much more usual than the family name. It is more usual to say " the Schildhuber was here to-day," than " Joseph Fimberger was here." The women are generally called by the family name, but in a manner differing from ours. A feminine termination is attached, as Maria Fimberger*in*, the Moser*in*, instead of Frau Fimberger, Frau Moser, as *we* should say. " Meier in der Tann, ah, he has a house like a castle," said every one to me, and in fact the majority of these great farmhouses are built like castles with four wings forming a quadrangle. The foot-passenger enters the dwelling-house in one wing by a narrow doorway, and the loaded waggons enter at another through a wider gate, and drive into the inner court. The stabling, cartsheds, granaries, barns, &c., are in the other wings. The building has two stories and has a stately exterior. The house is well furnished with pious sentences over the doors, both within and without, and all the household utensils down to the plates, are garnished with verses and passages from the Bible. At the house of " Meier in der Tann," I found a flour-sack, speaking in the first person, and where we less poetical North Germans would have placed simply a stamp, or have contented ourselves with the name, Fritz Meier, the flour-sack had it :

" Be it known to every man
I belong to Meier in the Tann."

The principal chamber in the house is called " Meier's room." It is the usual place of assembly of the members of the family, and also the eating-room; here the women sit at their spinning in the winter, or at any other of the minor domestic occupations. Near it are the bedchambers of the heads of the family and their children, and opposite, on the other side of the passage those of the maids and the men. " Meier in der Tann" has, moreover, his private room of business.

On the second story were the best rooms for guests, and the store-rooms. In these " Sunday rooms" many have the portraits of their progenitors. Those of " Meier in der Tann," were all clothed from head to foot in raven-black, and looked like so many Venetian nobles. Here are always a number of beds with magnificent mountains of feathers and gay-coloured quilts, for any visitors who may happen to come. In these " Sunday rooms," in presses, chests, and drawers, the bridal finery, the treasures of linen, metal, and the holiday clothes of the wife, a black spencer, a black silk *kittel* (so they call the best gown), and a pretty cap of otter-skin, surmounted by a star of pearls, are stowed away, all things which in form and material remind us of Bavaria, whence there is little doubt this part of Austria was colonised. Then there is the *kastl* (room) for fruit, in which are kept whole chests full of dried apples, pears, and plums; and a harness-room, where the abundance, order, and simple ornament, please more than all the brilliant show and rigid accuracy of a suite of royal stables. In many peasants' houses in this part of the country, there are not less than forty rooms.

The most celebrated race of horses in all the countries between Munich and Vienna, south of the Danube, is the Pinzgauer. These are large, magnificent animals, brought here as colts, and reared on the fine meadows of the Danube. They are used awhile for agricultural labours, and then sent to Vienna, where these huge animals are met with in the service of the butchers and brewers.

The stock of horned cattle on the Danube is constantly supplied from the mountain pastures, where the breeding of cattle is often the only possible occupation. From Pinzgau, Pongau, and the Styrian Alps, the cattle descend to the plains to fill up the gaps made by death and the butcher, and which the smaller cattle production of the plains cannot sufficiently supply. The most remarkable of the arrangements for stall-fed animals are the pigsties. The lodgings for swine in Austria are lofty spaces filled with long rows of chests, shut in on all sides and left open at the top. Each of these chests is the dwelling-place of a pig. In general they are made of thick beams, but some of the richer farmers have them of solid smooth hewn blocks of freestone. Every pig has his food in his own stall. In this manner each animal enjoys constantly fresh air, and yet is closely enough shut up to grow fat at his leisure. This system of solitary confinement protects them from each other, and the greatest cleanliness is preserved among these unclean brutes. More perfect swinish accommodations are not, I believe, to be found in Europe. Circe could have had no better for Ulysses and his companions.

The cider presses in an Austrian farmhouse are also worth seeing. The vine is not cultivated in Upper Austria, but cider is made on a very large scale, and an intoxicating drink is prepared from pears as well as apples. The fruit is first crushed under a large stone, put in motion by a horse, and is then put into the presses to complete the operation. In a large household there are sometimes ten or twelve such presses. Little as we esteem this acid beverage, it is here an absolute necessity, and "Zehnter im Gommering," or "Meier im leeren Busch" would lose all his men-servants to-morrow, if they did not get their due portion of "apple wine." Further up the Danube, in the land of beer-drinking Bavarians, the use of cider declines. Lower down the river the sour Austrian wine comes into use, and further on the sweet Hungarian.

"Meier in der Tann," including his children, has not less than forty people in his house. He related to me many anecdotes of the emperor Francis and the archduke Maximilian, who had often stopped at his house. His wife and children, in the mean time, were making dumplings for the morrow's holiday. Strict order and discipline were kept in the house, and behind the picture of the Saviour, on the wall, I saw stuck up that educational auxiliary which we generally hide behind the piece of furniture that repeats to us daily and hourly, the most agreeable, or disagreeable, truths.

As "Meier in der Tann" accompanied me over his farmyard, and showed me his abundance of good things, I said to him, "You sell this rich produce in the city no doubt?" "Nay," was his answer, "why should I sell it in the city? I can eat it myself; it is better so." I afterwards learnt that this was a usual answer of the wealthy Austrian peasants to such questions. "I can use it myself, it's better so."

Two blooming, goodhumoured children accompanied us, and gave me a friendly "God be with you, God be with you," when we reached the great trees surrounding the yard (every one of the yards, as usual, was surrounded with old trees); which I acknowledged in the same style, and returned to Edelsberg through all the rich lowlands, on which the rude, bleak mountain range casts down such black and envious looks. The richest peasant in Upper Austria is supposed to be Stedinger. I had occasion to visit him also, subsequently; but all these farms are as like each other as so many eggs.

The personal service which the peasants are held to render to their superior lord, is trifling in real amount. It is, for the most part, commuted for money. But the tithes, which are levied by the lords of the soil, the billeting of soldiers, the military conscription, to which the nobles are not subject, and the many imperial and seigneurial taxes, press heavily on the peasants. As the land, however, is, on the whole, fertile, the people sober and diligent, and the law, despite its oppressive enactments, is administered in a spirit so favourable to the subject, that the emperor Francis sometimes complained he could not obtain justice in his suits against his own peasants, agriculture, with all its disadvantages, is in the flourishing condition I have above described.

An odd law prevails in this class—namely, that the farm descends to the *youngest* son instead of the *eldest*, on the death of the father. It is supposed that by that time the elder sons are otherwise provided for, while the youngest may often need an inheritance. With us the more rational notion prevails that the eldest son, as the ablest and most natural guardian of the younger branches, must first be enabled to supply effectually the place of the parent.

PUBLIC LIBRARY.

The water of the Danube is of the colour of aqua marine, that of the Rhine emerald green. The waters of the Danube are thick, those of the Rhine transparent; the colour of the former may probably be affected by the slime it brings with it, and which is of a milky green as if a quantity of serpentine stone dust were mingled with the quartz sand. This slime is deposited in the cold baths which are erected along the banks of the river. The waters of the Danube seemed to me much colder than those of the other great rivers of Germany, and a bath in its green waters is certainly one of the most refreshing enjoyments that can be offered to the wearied body.

I had just come out of such a one, and was taking my last walk through the streets of Linz, when I came upon the Bibliotheca publica of the Lyceum, whereon stands the beautiful Greek inscription, ψυχῆς ιατρεῖον (the house for the healing and refreshment of the soul). What could be more opportune? I entered; the first name I heard here, as in nearly every public institution in Austria, was that of Joseph the Second. He was the founder of this and many other libraries. He induced or compelled the wealthy convents to furnish books, and thus formed in the principal cities of the monarchy, collections accessible to all, from treasures that had before been hidden.

I found here, as in all other Austrian libraries, Rotteck's History of the World, and the "*Semplice Verita opposta alle menzogne di Enrico Misley,*" a work written by an Italian, in answer to a book published by the Englishman, in condemnation of the Austrian system of government in Italy.

In many Austrian libraries the forbidden fruit is enthroned high above the vellum-bound volumes of theology; it is placed there purposely, lest the grown children should over-eat themselves: the same arrangement I observed here; and moreover, the ladder by which it was to be reached, was so short, that it was at the risk of my life, standing on the topmost step, that I succeeded in obtaining a glance into these regions. I remarked there, "The Triumph of Philosophy," Moser's "Patriotic Fantasies," his "Political Truths," and similar works. A second dive which I ventured upon, placed two volumes of Buffon's Natural History in my hand. I could look on this with tolerable indifference; but to the Austrian student, how costly must appear this forbidden, and, therefore, doubly sweet fruit! Doubtless as the finest cherries on the tree's topmost branch to the eyes of the boy who is unable to reach the unsteady crown.

The most remarkable part of the collection, was a copy of Luther's complete works, and moreover, the oldest edition. They were extremely dusty, and I asked the attendant whether they were much used. "No," said he; "in the thirty years I have been here, I have never taken them down." Perhaps they were procured at a time when some hopes of refuting Luther's heresies were still cherished, and they have never been looked at since. Perhaps the time may not be far distant, when Austria will allow the ladders in her libraries to be made a little longer, or bring the spirits now abandoned to the dust and the spiders, a little lower down; the library may then in a loftier sense than now become the $\psi v\chi\hat{\eta}s$ $\iota\alpha\tau\rho\epsilon\hat{\iota}\alpha$, and the soul may then luxuriate here in as refreshing a bath, as the body enjoys in the quickening waters of the Danube. In this, perhaps, approaching epoch, such old Gothic laws and prohibitions will not be renewed, as we now see carved in stone, on the Town-house of Linz. This singular inscription runs thus:

"His Roman and Imperial Majesty, King of Hungary and Bohemia, our most gracious lord wills and commands, that no one, be he who he may, presume in or before this free land house to carry arms, or to wrestle, or fight, or *make any riot whatever.* Whoever act in any wise contrary to this prohibition, will be punished with all severity in life and limb. Renewed 1568, 1679, 1745, 1825."

I thought at first that this singular and harshly-sounding prohibition had only been renewed for the sake of its historical curiosity; but a native of Linz assured me that it was seriously meant to infuse terror, and was deemed one of the privileges and immunities of the Town-house.

THE PICTURE-GALLERY BETWEEN LINZ AND VIENNA.

The portion of the Danube lying between Linz and Vienna, is certainly the finest part of the great river, for here nature and art have united to adorn its shores, as they have done nowhere else along the whole sixteen hundred miles of its course. In one half-day to see all these beautiful, great, graceful, and interesting objects, with all their historical monuments and natural beauties, pass before one's eyes, seems an enchanted dream, and keeps the susceptible mind in a constant state of intoxication.

The Romans, while they held these lands, seem, however, to have felt no such intoxication; to them an abode by the shores of the Danube was rather a dream of a heavy and oppressive kind, yet it was exactly this beautiful part of its banks as far as Vindobona, that was the site of their most important battles with the Germans. The left bank they called the forehead of Germany (*Frons Germaniæ*), and the eyebrows of the Danube (*Supercilia Isthri*). The wrinkles, excrescences, jagged rocks, and horns of Germany's rude front, may have figured strangely in the letters to their friends in Italy from these cold northern boundaries of their beautiful land. Here, if anywhere on earth, the mutability of matter and the course of events may be admired. The eyebrows of the Danube are now smoothed beneath the hatchet and the plough; the fields are smiling under the fairest and richest cultivation, and of the forests only so much remains as the painter would desire to preserve, in order to enrich and elevate the softer expression of the meadow and the cornfield. The forehead of Germany and what was its extreme frontier, are now the core of a great monarchy; the rejected stone is become the foundation and corner-stone of the building, for here lies the cradle of the Austrian monarchy.

Strangers from all lands now come to gaze on the cities that have arisen round the Roman camp-station on the now smooth *Frons Germaniæ*, and the subdued back of the wild Isther. Years ago, the English and North Germans heeded not the inconveniences of the Danube navigation; but now, that the establishment of steamboats has increased the facilities ten or twenty fold, the river is visited even by those that dwell near it. Monks now wander from their cloister and gaze on these new wonders. Students throng from all parts, for now even their slender purses suffice for a voyage down the Danube; *employés*, whose short leave of absence did not formerly permit such excursions, now take their places, with their wives and children, in the handsome cabins, and float up and down the Danube under the protection of the public at large. In these days of steamboats, people have found feet who had none before, some have got seven-league boots who possessed before but ordinary shoes, purses have become fuller, and days longer.

At six o'clock in the morning, on the fifth of August, the bell of the steamboat the *Archduke Stephen*, summoned its passengers, specimens of all the above-mentioned classes of society, crowded together. There were Englishmen who spoke not one word of German; monks with shaven crowns, ladies with children, whiskered Hungarians, Vienna dandies with eye-glasses instead of eyes in their heads, Berlin travellers with *Donnerwetter* in their mouths, and many others laden with cloaks and wraps, hats and bandboxes, parasols and umbrellas, sticks, pipes, chests, and trunks. It was just such weather as according to the imagination of the Romans must generally have prevailed in "*nebulosa Germania.*" A thick fog hung like an impenetrable veil over the Alpine chain, and hid the black and gold arabesque borders of the towers of Linz. From out the fog distilled a fine rain, which gradually increased, till we were threatened with a day to enchant all the snails and ducks in the country. We poor passengers who thronged the decks of the *Archduke Stephen* as thickly as the wild ducks did the reedy inlets of the Danube, crept like snails in sunshine under our mantles and umbrellas, while those who could find a place, took shelter in the cabins.

The beautiful changes of scenery afforded by the city of Linz and its environs, round which the Danube sweeps almost in a semicircle, passed unnoticed by; indeed, as far as I was personally concerned, I could discern objects only so far as the circumference of my umbrella reached, from whose extremity fell a heavy shower of drops, and my companions were more anxious about the light of their cigars, than the light of travelling inspiration. We were all deplorably dull and out of tune; and foresaw not what was preparing for us overhead, nor what a day was before us.

At the very beginning of our journey, as I stepped from the bridge that led to the vessel, I had the good fortune to get such a thrust in the side from the trunk of one of the passengers, that I thanked God in silence for the elastic strength of my ribs. I say the good fortune, because the punch was such a hearty one, that the man was not content with the usual *excusez* or *pardon, Monsieur*, with which we usually satisfy ourselves on such occasions, but came to me again after he had stowed away his box, seized my hand, begged my pardon a thousand times, and inquired most anxiously whether I was hurt. Thus, among so many strangers, I suddenly found a friend, whom I might not have acquired for hours by the observance of the conventional ceremonies which condemn us so long to silence, until some unexpected occurrence brings us nearer to each other.

My new acquaintance was a man of business; he had followed the Danube in all its windings, and had lived from his youth upon its banks. While he sat by me I allowed the useful to take precedence of the beautiful for a time, and took a lesson from him on the constitution of the bed of the Danube, and the course of traffic on its waters, and so long as the rain continues I will share with the reader the information I acquired.

The Danube, hemmed in by mountains, flows by Linz in an unbroken stream. Below the city it begins to expand, embracing many large and smaller islands, and dividing into many arms, one of which may be considered the main artery. Thus it continues till it reaches the celebrated whirlpool near Grein, where all its waters, uniting in one channel, flow on majestically for forty miles, till they have worked their way through the mountains and narrow passes near the city of Krems, and coming to level ground again, divide, forming arms and islands beyond Vienna. The condition of the water in this varying and sometimes obstructed course, and its consequent practicability for trade and navigation is very various, and hence many peculiar words descriptive of it have been invented, which are not known on other rivers.

The main stream, which must offer the principal course of navigation, is called the "*Naufahrt,*" and the steersmen, who must know it accurately, and some of whom are always on board of the steamboats, are named *Nauförch,* or *Nau* guides. The Nau channel undergoes little or no change in the narrow passes, but in the neighbourhood of the islands, the furious rapidity of the current changes it very often; sometimes an arm of the stream, navigable before, will close, and another open that was formerly quite impracticable. The larger branches are called arms, but the smaller ones are denominated "*Runze,*" and they are distinguished again as great or little "*Runze.*" The little creeks and broader expanses, which are often found shut in between the sandbanks and the islands, or peninsulas, are called lakes. Among these lakes a constant change is taking place; sometimes they burst their boundary, the stagnant water becomes current, and the lake is again a "*Runze.*" The subsiding matter contained in the Danube, is called "*Bachgries,*" "*Stromgries,*" or "*Schutt.*" The sandbanks formed by this "*gries*" are not called sandbanks, but "*Haufen,*" or heaps. If these banks are formed not of sand, but of rock, and remain under the surface of the water, they are named in the Danube language *Kugeln*, or bullets, perhaps from the rounded forms of all these rocks.

If these "*Haufen*" rise high out of the water, and are overgrown with wood, they are called *Auen*, or meadows. These meadows, when covered with aspens, alders, poplars, maples, willows, and shrubs of all kinds, afford cover for innumerable game; even stags are found there, while the lakes and *Runze* are thronged with waterfowl, wild ducks and geese, herons, cranes, plovers, and especially a bird called "fisher" by the people of the country.

These meadows are often inundated in the course of the year. When the land has obtained such a height that it can be subjected to regular cultivation, the formation of the Danube island is completed. But all these formations are subject to constant change. Now a sandbank is formed where before it was deep water; now the stream is gnawing at an island it slowly raised centuries before. Here a *haufe* is raised to an "Au" or meadow, and overgrown with bush, which, in the course of time, changes to a wood, there man is turning to profit the first turf, which he hopes will one day become arable land. Promontories, peninsulas, and natural dikes are thrown together by the waves on one side, while, on the other, they are wearing away and destroying others, and thus the wild river-god tosses about in his procrustean bed, which he finds now too narrow, and now too spacious.

Such places, where the water is undermining the shore, are called *Bruchgestätte*, or break-banks, and here the beavers of the Danube have their especial dwelling. By the shore, (*am Ufer*) means a narrower part of the river where the banks approach, and there is a ferry.

The passage down the Danube is the "*Nabfahrt*," that against the stream is the "*Naufahrt.*"* The expressions mountain and valley passage, which are in use on the Rhine, are not known here. An Austrian sailor whom I questioned about it, answered—"Mountain and valley passage! nay we know nothing about such things here. How is that possible? How can we get over mountains and through valleys."

For the "*Nabfahrt*" the beforenamed *Nau* pilots are required; but when they are going against the stream, several vessels are usually fastened together. We often see two or three large and several smaller vessels so chained together, and such a flotilla, with the necessary team, is called a *Gegenfuhr*, or countercourse. These countercourses often require from thirty to forty horses, and sometimes more. On every horse a man is mounted, and the whole squadron is commanded by an old experienced outrider, called the *Waghals* or *Stangenreiter* (daredevil or pole-rider), because his baton of office is a long pole, with which he makes signals, and sounds the river. The other riders are called the "*Yodels.*" The commands issued by the pole-rider, or which are issued to him from the ship, are immediately repeated by the whole corps of "*Yodels*," in a wild cry. The words of command are generally shortened to mere interjections, as "Ho! ho!" (Halt, halt,) or "*Lasse ha!*" (Let them go on.) Scarcely has the pole-rider, or steersman from the ship, sent the sound slowly through the air, than it is taken up by forty throats, and forty whips, and four times forty hoofs, are arrested or set in motion.

The horses ridden by the "*Yodels*" are generally Pinzgauer horses, but

---

* Evident corruptions of *hinab* and *hinauf*.

are all called Traun horses along this part of the Danube, perhaps because the greater number of the articles exported from Pinzgau, find their way to the Danube through Traun valley.

The roads on the banks of the Danube are often very bad; the great meadows and reedy islands are mostly swampy, hence artificial towing-paths for the horses are very necessary. The roads are named "*Leinpfad*" by the Rhine, and here, the "*Huffschlag*" or "*Treppelweg.*" These "*Treppelwegs*" are sometimes on one side of the river, and sometimes on the other, and then a frequent halting, and shipping over of the horses becomes unavoidable. For the long tracts of passage where the banks are not passable, or where the "*Naufahrt*" is very distant from them, the horses must go into the water, and it may therefore be easily imagined how dangerous a service they and their "Yodels" have to perform.

The large vessels that navigate this part of the Danube, are called "*Hohenauer.*" They carry two thousand hundredweight of goods. Next to them in importance, are the *Kehlheimers.* The *Hohenauers* go only down the river, and though larger, are worse built than the *Kehlheimers,* which pass both up and down. Then again there are the *Gamsels* and *Platten,* and the *Zillen* (boats). The latter, which are attached to the larger *Hohenauer* and *Kehlheimer,* are called supplements (*nebenbei*). Again those vessels used to convey the "Yodels" and their horses to the other side, have their peculiar name, "*Schwemmer.*"

A complete reform, at present, awaits the whole of the Danube shipping; in fact, it has already begun. The introduction of steam-vessels compels all manner of improvement. I shall have occasion, hereafter, to mention how even the ordinary vessels for the navigation of the river have begun to be constructed on a better plan than formerly.

The Danube boatmen have a peculiar terminology for all natural appearances, objects, and accidents. A calm is the wind's holiday (*windfeier*). The ship is "*gewappt,*" they say, when the waves strike the sides and fill it with water, if it be too heavily laden, or when it is too strongly impelled by the "Yodels." But a book might be filled with these things. Enough for the useful; turn we now to the agreeable.

The rain, which, in the bottomless depths of our despair, we had expected was about to spoil our pleasure entirely, had already ceased. On the wings of steam, we were rapidly borne through the region of rain, and came to a part where all looked cheerful again. A bright sun descended on our dewy fields of cloaks, and drank up the moisture tha. trested on them and on the ringlets of the ladies. Steyeregg, the castle of old Khuenringer; Lichtenberg, the seat of the Starhembergs and Schallenbergs; Tillysburg, the old fortress bestowed on his veteran general, Tilly, by the emperor Ferdinand; and Spielberg, the seat of the knights of Spielberg, and afterwards of the lords of Weissenwolf, with many other beautiful castles and villages, were lost to us; only thus much the rain had allowed us to observe, that the site of many of these was admirably adapted for pillage on the river. Spielberg, for instance, lies, like a beaver-village, behind the bushy meadows in the middle of the islands, close to the interior harbour of a "Runze," and had, by means of it, two water-passages to the Danube, so that many a stratagem of the lords of Spielberg may have been suggested by the position. The Rhine, which in that portion of it flowing between Mainz and Bonn, is so often compared to this part of the Danube, has nothing of this wild island-meadow scenery. Many admire the Rhine the more for this want; but, I must confess, their presence lent an additional charm to the Danube in my eyes. These castles, hidden in the reeds—these islands, tenanted by a solitary fisherman—these widely-spreading river-veins, losing themselves a while in the wilderness, and then again emerging, bright and clear, from the woods, to unite once more with the great stream (an island has, in itself, something poetical, and is an object that can scarcely be repeated too often)—in a word, all this vehement motion, and the almost antediluvian events recorded of the Danube, opposed to the rich cultivation, the historical associations, and the picturesque views on its banks, form a contrast wholly wanting to the Rhine. There the cultivation is more striking, almost too striking; on the Danube, Nature is wilder—many will add, *too* wild.

St. Peter's, in the meadows, Abelsberg, and Pulgarn, were lost to us by the rain. At the mouth of the Ens, on the frontier line between the two Archduchies, where the fine-weather region began, that picture-gallery first became visible, to which the "Naufahrt" of the Danube represented the corridor, and the deck of the steamboat the rolling chair.

The first piece which presented itself was Mauthausen, opposite the mouth of the Ens. The place is extremely old, and lies close to the shore, with a ruinous, tower-like castle in its vicinity. The antique houses crowded together in a few narrow streets, give us double pleasure : first, as affording picturesque objects, and then on account of the pleasant reflection, that we are not obliged to live in them. Behind the town rise the hills containing the celebrated stone-quarries, from which a beautiful kind of granite has been long obtained, though at the cost of much labour, for the use of the capital. An old German church (St. Nicholas's) rears its head in the midst, and a flying bridge in the foreground conveys passengers in the old, troublesome fashion, over the animated stream. The steamboat stopped just long enough to catch these scanty features of the landscape, and to put a beautiful Hungarian countess, and her yet fairer daughters into a boat. I had been long rejoicing in the sunshine of their aspect, when they vanished with the view of Mauthausen, whose foreground they so much embellished. They were going to pay a visit of some days at Thurheim, as they informed me.

At the mouth of the Ens, opposite Mauthausen, there is not much to be seen, as the stream itself flows through a low foreland, its own formation, into the Danube. But there is the more to be thought about; for, considered either in an historical or geographical point of view, it is certainly the most important and interesting spot between Linz and Vienna. I had often reflected on the importance of this Ens-embouchure, and asked myself why the Austrians had made their lands to lie on either side of the Ens, rather than on either side of the Danube. With my map of the Danube country before me, I pondered on the subject, and came to this conclusion.

The Danube, this mighty navigable river has been the great electric conductor for all those nations whom the course of events brought within its territory. They clung to it as the main artery of their life, and spread themselves from its shores on either side, as their various relations permitted. Thus Hungary formed itself on both sides of the Danube, so did Austria, Bavaria, and Swabia, like pearls on one string. Above and below the stream also, the various tribes settled on its tributaries, the Iller, the Inn, the Ens, the Leitha, and March, the Drave, and Save. These rivers cut up the land connected longitudinally by the Danube, into many portions; the tribes made these streams their boundaries, and enclosed their territory as these natural divisions prescribed. Thus the Iller separates the states of Wirtemberg and Bavaria; the Lech, some of the Swabian nations from Bavaria; the Inn runs between Bavaria and the Archduchy of Austria; the March and the Leitha between Austria and Hungary; the Drave between Hungary and Slavonia; the Save between Slavonia and Turkey. But between the Inn and the March, there is no considerable incision in the land except the Traun and the Ens. The Ens being near the middle of this strip of land, was particularly adapted for a subdivision, the more so, because its course is exactly rectangular to the main stream of the Danube.

It has been before mentioned that the Romans recognised the importance of these separating valleys, and therefore partitioned their *Noricum ripense* into nearly the same sections that are now called above and below the Ens. At the mouth of the Ens they had their largest settlement in this neighbourhood. Laureacum afterwards Lorch, where a legion had its stationary camp, a Dux limitis his abode, and a fleet its harbour. After the time of the Romans, on the site of Lorch, arose the present Ens, celebrated in the Nibelungenlied, and important on account of its commerce. The empire of Charlemagne extended at first only as far as the Ens; and when, in the year 791, he had resolved on his great campaign against the Avares, it was opened on the banks of this river, from which he drove them back to the next arm of the Danube—the Raab. When the Hungarians first entered the lands of the Danube, in the reign of Arnulph the Child, the Ens was long the limit of their German kingdom. That a toll was long levied at Mauthausen, near the mouth of the Ens, as if entering a foreign country, was another result of the peculiar division of the land by the Ens. The same causes that rendered this place the centre of traffic, have also given rise to the many struggles and battles that have been fought for the possession of it. The mouth of the Ens has enough of such encounters to relate, from the uninterrupted hostilities of the Romans, to the last campaign in this place, where even Napoleon saw cause to shudder at the horrors of a battle-field.

The many fields and islands which the Danube forms here, present a countless succession of pictures in the Dutch style, producing most singular effects among the grand mountain-landscapes. A fisherman may be seen on the low shore, busied with the repair of a huge net, called in the language of the Danube a "*taubel*," an enormous drag-net, attached to the trunk of a tree sunk in the river. Here you behold a water-mill in the centre of a rapid stream, with a low island overgrown with willows and poplars close by, so little raised above the level of the water, that some of the bushes are washed by the rushing current. A miller is sitting on the end of a beam projecting over the water, busied in some repairs. There you see a little harbour for the shipment of wood. Now again, the broad stream is visible. Hard by is a store of wood, felled in the great watermeadows. Some people are engaged in loading a small vessel with this timber for Vienna. Around, nothing is to be seen but water and solitary wooded meadows.

And all these pictures have the advantage of being well preserved, the colours bright and fresh, the varnish incomparable. Even the beavers, which have their dwelling here, do them no injury, but, on the contrary, add to the effect. These wonderful animals are very numerous on the river between Linz and Vienna. It is singular enough that the progress of civilization should not have scared them away, and that they should be more numerous here than in parts so much wilder of the middle Danube; they are eagerly pursued, both for their skins and their testicles; and the worth of the whole beaver, when the latter are good, is estimated at from fifty to sixty, and even one hundred florins. The beavers build their dwellings mostly on the "breaking shores" before mentioned, and thence make excursions into the water meadows, where, like the wood-cutters, they fell the trees, especially the aspens and poplars, whose wood is not too hard, and of which the thick, fleshy, leathery rind constitutes their favourite food. These beaver-houses are difficult to find, as the animals place the entrance always under the water, and burrow upwards, and this upper part, which is properly their dwelling, is built with wood, and kept dry. Below, the door and fore-court of their house are covered with water, into which they plunge on any alarm. "One of the most interesting occupations to be met with on the Danube, is to watch these creatures at their work," said a gentleman to me, who, as a sportsman and lover of natural history, had paid great attention to them, and kept some beavers prisoners on his estate. "They are as comic in their gestures as monkeys, and as active and adroit at their work as persons who have not a minute to lose. With their really formidable teeth they hew down the trees like skilful wood-men, by a few well-directed strokes, and cut them into blocks. These blocks they carry like poodles to their dwellings, where they fix them with clay, which they lay on with their tails. They go splashing through the water pushing the blocks of wood, jostling and thrusting one another aside, as if they were working against one another for a wager. I have never seen them driving piles with their tails as some persons assert, nor do I think so soft an instrument adapted for such work. They are accustomed, however, to strike the surface of the water with their tails, sometimes apparently out of mere sport and wantonness, but sometimes, probably, when pursued by an enemy, it is done to cover their retreat under water by dashing the spray in the face of the pursuer. They are very difficult to catch. To dig them out like badgers is impossible, from the construction of their caves. To surprise them is no easy matter, on account of their quickness and foresight. They are generally caught in traps. As, unlike carnivorous animals, they find their food everywhere in nature, these traps cannot be constructed nor baited on the usual principle; the most delicate twig of poplar would be little attraction to them; it is therefore necessary to place a great number of traps in their way, and to be very cautious in so doing, as they scent iron very readily. I once laid fifteen traps in the neighbourhood of a beaver village, and was fortunate enough to catch a couple of thoughtless wanderers from the straight path. The next night I was unsuccessful, and so for ten successively. No doubt the mishap of their two comrades had become known throughout the colony, and all kept themselves within their houses. At last hunger or ennui drove them out once more, and on the eleventh night I caught another, evidently much reduced by fasting. But that was the last; the beavers took my intrusion so much amiss, that they abandoned the colony, nor could I learn where they had emigrated to;—in that neighbourhood no beaver has since been found."

The finest views on the Danube begin about six (German) miles below Linz, at Wallsee; and truly, I believe, the least enthusiastic person in the world must have felt himself enraptured at the sight of so magnificent a spectacle. Only in a series of dithyrambics, and to the accompaniment of the harp, are they worthily to be sung! I could have fancied myself sitting in some miraculous giant kaleidoscope; but ruins, castles, convents, palaces, smiling villages, snug towns, hermitages, distant mountains, towers, broad valleys, and deep ravines, steep precipices, fertile meadows, were the objects that produced these wonderful effects, instead of fragments of moss, beans, spangles, and bits of grass. Every stroke of the steam-engine wrought a new and yet more beautiful change, as if a magician had held the strings and pulled them always at the precise moment. Sometimes mountains hemmed us in on all sides, and we seemed carried over some mountain lake; another turn, and we shot as it were through a long chain of lakes. The steamer rushes on as if there were no such thing as a rock to be feared around. To a certainty we shall strike upon that at the corner!—no—a strong pressure from the hand of the experienced helmsman and we double the rock, a new opening is revealed, and new wonders displayed far and near. In such sudden turns of the vessel, often executed in a half circle of very short radius, we obtain through the sails and rigging and the twelve cabin windows, a *cascade* of views and images, if I may use the expression, in which all individuality is lost, and the effect of the whole upon the mind is perfectly intoxicating. A painter of any susceptibility must, I think, sometimes shut his eyes, that he may not lose all self-command, and leap over the side of the vessel.

The Volcanic powers, which, in the times of Olim, pierced and reformed the surface of our earth, shot across in the neighbourhood of Grein from the north, and threw up a dam from the Bohemian forest to the Alps, which formed a powerful obstacle to the waves flowing from the west. At this dam the waves long gnawed, till at last they made their way through. The lake, which had formed above the dam, flowed over, and the Danube burst through the narrow pass to a wider field beyond. Here and there, by the side of the cleft, fragments of rock had remained in and under the water, and so was formed the celebrated whirlpool called the "Strum of Grein."

Greinen in Austrian German means much the same as *weinen* (crying), and *Greinsburg* (or the castle of tears,) lies close by the entrance of the whirlpool, and bears this tragical name, in the midst of one of the loveliest prospects that crown the Danube. The river reflects the features of the fair castle and town in friendly greeting before it dashes its waters tinged with the melancholy hue of the pine forests, over the rock of the "Strum." This occurs at last by the little island Worth, lying like a fallen column of the old dam in the gate of the whirlpool. From this column low ranges of rock cross the river diagonally at both sides, and join the high angular rocks of the shore. Some are already so worn away that they are now under water, while others stand pointed and jagged above. The former are called "*Kugeln,*" the latter "*Kochelt,*" or "*Gehäckel.*" The mass of waters which passes to the south of the islet Worth, is called the entrance; that which passes to the north is divided by two lines of cliff into the "Wild cleft," the "Wild water," and the whirlpool properly so called, and through this the emperor Joseph, by the labour of thirteen years, succeeded in removing the most dangerous obstructions, and forming the main passage.

Firstly the Danube rushes foaming over the "*Kugeln*"—the heavy dash is heard from afar—then it plunges into the "*Gehäckel*," where it surges yet more impetuously, and shoots along with a rapidity befitting Neptune's team of sea-horses. Our engine was slackened; for my part, I would willingly have lain at anchor here a while to enjoy the magnificent spectacle.

The rock of the islet Worth is highly picturesque, it has several faces, and at the base, at the very extremity of the island, lies the old excrescence of a castle. On the summit of the rock, a huge cross rears itself, firm as faith in the midst of the storms of life, clinging fast to the rock. Several images of saints are niched about the rock, some adorned with the votive offerings of passing boatmen. Close to the entrance of the whirlpool, little boats row alongside the larger vessels, with pictures of saints, which they offer for sale as amulets. But our reprobate steamer shot past them with the speed of an arrow, and prevented the poor people from levying a small tribute upon the piety or fear of the passengers.

Opposite the rocks of Worth another mass shoots boldly into the water, bearing on its stern brow the ruins of the old castle of Werfenstein. Here it is said, Roman dust mingles with the German of the middle ages. The elsewhere broad Danube is here pressed within such narrow limits, that a bold Tell might almost hope by a daring leap to reach Worth.

The rocks of Werfenstein join the strong walls and abrupt precipices, of which they are only a small part, forming a dark pass of about half a mile. In the midst of this watery ravine, which must not be supposed to be *too* narrow, the stream dashes along with uncontrolled violence. Some of these rocks have particular names, as the "house stone," the "hare's ear," &c., and others are crowned with ruins, among others with those of the castles of Struden and Sarmingstein. Far above the cross of the rock of Worth, towers the church of St. Nicholas, the patron saint of the sailors. At the foot of this church, in the market town of the same name, is a hospital founded in the year 1144, for the relief of sufferers of whom the wild waters then furnished, probably a greater number than in these days.

The beautiful and romantic, the singular, the picturesque, and the incomparable in this part of the Danube, are so abundant, that it is almost as difficult to tear oneself from the description as from the contemplation, though we are apt to regret afterwards, the many words that have been spent in a vain endeavour to give an idea of the scene. A little below Werfenstein, the vessel struck against a rock; I know not whether from a change in the direction of the numerous currents in the "Strudel,"* or from pure awkwardness or carelessness of the steersman, or unmanageableness of the vessel; I thought at first, when I saw the bowsprit advancing nearer and nearer, that it was done in the most perfect security and boldness of design, and observed to an Englishman who was standing near me, "See how little danger the once so formidable Strudel has for our skilful and experienced navigators, and with what precision they steer in the very face of the rock." Scarcely were the words out of my mouth, when the vessel struck against that very rock, and a regular panic showed itself in the white faces and blue lips of the numerous passengers. The

---

* That such changes take place, is beyond a doubt; at every rising of the tide, the waters have a different motion on the surface.

bowsprit snapped short off, and hung on by the ropes, like a broken arm by the sinews. The ship being of course somewhat elevated in front, towards the rock, was proportionally depressed at the stern, so that the green waves of the Danube dashed in through the cabin windows. One large Englishman stood in the centre of the vessel, with his eyes riveted on the bowsprit and the rock, both hands in his pockets, and his legs apart, as if he hoped by this means to balance it. A young man curious to see what was going on, looked from the cabin window, and received the rough salute of the Danube over head and ears; and a lovely young married lady buried her face in her husband's bosom. Our vessel received a tremendous swing that brought the rudder round in front; the gilded bust of the Archduke Stephen at the prow, was also broken, and hung off to the side as if he declined having any thing more to do with us. "Stephen has got a good cuff," said a Linzer peasant, when the first fright was over. The whole was the work of a minute; like a waltzing couple, in the hurry of the dance, brought into sudden contact with the foremost pair, move crabwise for a few seconds, and then with renewed vigour, pursue their whirling course, we reeled awhile, staggered sideways and backwards through the vortex, then ploughing the waves with renewed vigour, brought the rudder once more to its place, and darted on in a straight line, as if nothing had happened. We passed Sarblingstein, built by the emperor Ferdinand, to fortify the Danube against the Turks; Freinstein, where Charlemagne overcame duke Tassito; and Persenberg, whose magnificent imperial castle of that name, is renowned in the olden time as the possession of the Margrave Engelschalk II., who, a thousand years ago, fell in love with, and carried off, the daughter of the emperor Arnulph. We could not, however, devote to these interesting objects all the attention they deserved, because we were still too much occupied with our vessel, and our terrified fellow-passengers.

Among the latter, in addition to the first intimate acquaintance, for whom I stood indebted to my collision with a travelling trunk, I had made several new friends. Nothing brings people so nearly together as a high degree of sympathy, either in joy or sorrow. The general lamentation over the rain with which the day began, had softened some hearts; the pleasure and excitement caused by the enchanting scenery, had assisted to thaw the icy incrustations wherewith fashion encases us; and after the accident in the "*Strudel,*" our souls all melted together into a sympathetic stream. How is it possible to resist when, on such occasions, a beautiful, timid woman, till then entirely a stranger to you, one with whom you have not before exchanged a word, and who has proudly and silently avoided every place where stood a stranger of the other sex, suddenly forgets all decorum, and seizing you by the arm, exclaims—"Ah, my dear good sir, *what is* the matter?" How can you do otherwise than immediately grasp at the proffered friendship. In one way or another, by the time we had passed the castles of Weins and Persenburg, we all felt to one another like friends of long standing. If it be hard to depict the beauties of nature, it is not less so to paint the joys of social intercourse, and I should esteem it one of the most difficult tasks I could impose on myself, if I were to attempt to give the reader a perfect picture of all the little occurrences and pleasures of our Danube journey. What the wise man says of the golden tree of life, and of the faint picture given of it in books, is true of the scenery of the Danube, and the sayings and doings of the company that filled the steamer. It follows, then, that it would be better to give up description of any kind, and leave off making books, and so it would, were it not that the reader has his own fancies, experiences, recollections, and wishes with which he supplies all omissions. If the author speaks of a castle crowning the brow of a rock, he is not satisfied, because he compares the meagerness of the expression with the image that memory brings before his eye; but the reader does not heed it; at these words he builds a castle for himself, and, perhaps, a much finer one than the reality. And it is the same thing with a picture of an agreeable circle or party, the reader feels all that the author says or does not say, and recollections or wishes supply the wants of the text.

We sat in the stern of our untiring steamer, and gaily passed the glass of social converse. London, Paris, and Vienna, had each its deputies in our circle; but Vienna, and I thanked heaven therefore, had the greatest number. The first deputy was a young actress, one of the most distinguished of the Burg theatre. She was returning from a professional tour, and related, with much talent and vivacity, some of her experience of life both before and behind the curtain. In her joy at finding herself once more in her fair Austria, she never failed to correct my false pronunciation (according to Austrian rules) of the names of the various places we passed. "Not Marbach, Moaba is the name of that pretty village we have just passed; you must not say Neustadt, but Neishtadel, and when you wish me joy on being at home again, you should not pronounce the word *heimath*, we call it *hoamat*." As the sun was then shining very brightly, I offered her my Austrian *lamprell*, or umbrella, and asked her if she could protect herself with that, using the Austrian word *protekiren*. This she found quite "*delizios*," and laughed excessively. "*Delizios*" is a very favourite word with the Austrians; and where we say I laughed (*da lachte ich*), they say *da bin ich lachend geworden*. This last expression pleases me extremely, and is, certainly, with many other Austrian phrases, a relic of the middle ages. I have no manner of doubt that Gotz Von Berlichingen and his comrades expressed themselves just so—"*Ich bin lachend geworden*."

Next to Miss Be——, I had almost betrayed her name—sat a fair native of Vienna, with her husband and a charming little daughter. She was returning from Italy, where her husband had filled some post in the Austrian service. We naturally spoke a great deal of the fair land "where the orange-trees bloom," and the young mother expressed herself on the subject with great animation. I found her, to my great astonishment, by no means inclined to do justice to the beautiful shores of the Danube. In the Linz theatre she had yawned over a farce portraying some of the local absurdities of Vienna, and which had made me laugh till I cried again. She thought it "all excessively trivial; such things, so full of equivoque, so offensive to all morality, would never have been permitted in Italy, where in this respect, as in many others, people were incomparably more delicate than in Germany." Her husband was more reserved in his praise and blame than his pretty wife. The little girl, a child about four years old, was a perfect Italian. She spoke not a word of German, but danced wildly about the deck, because she should soon be "*in casa nostra*." Her mother said that she understood German perfectly well, but would never speak, and had a decided aversion to it. I began hereupon in silence to ask myself, whether Austrians—even public officers who remained a long time in Italy—*all* returned such bad patriots? Did even this beautiful Austria look sad after Italy? Would the many and much vaunted enjoyments it offered, be looked on as trifling and insignificant? And is it peculiar to German nationality to exchange so lightly the mother-tongue for the more beautiful Italian; or do Italian children, brought up in Austria, imbibe a similar preference for German, and disinclination for Italian?

A tiresome Vienna dandy, who sat somewhat aside from us, mingled now and then in the conversation, but kept, for the most part, at some distance, and whispered to an elderly lady something mysterious about Countess Theresa, or the Princess Anna, or the Baroness Sophia, and made much mention of the Lichtenstein, the Starhemberg, the Fürstenfeld, and other such universally-known persons, who, according to the Vienna grammar, are to be named with the definite article. *C'était un commérage ennobli par les grands noms qu'on prononçait.*

Among the English there was a courier, who had come from England to Linz in six days. He kept looking at a book from which a friend was detailing the remarkable objects to be seen on the shores of the Danube; and they both read as diligently as if all these interesting places had been a hundred miles off, instead of lying right under their noses.

We had also on board a sister and a novice of the newly-established order of the "German Sisters." This order was once united with that of the "German Brothers" in the east, for the tending of sick knights, but did not long remain there. Lately, in our own time, when the Gothic style of architecture came into fashion again, these antiquities were also revived. They looked singular enough, in their twelfth century costume, among these Vienna and Parisian toilets. What I thought most disagreeable in the broad sunlight was, that their coarse white linen was not only badly washed, but horribly marked by the flies into the bargain. They told me that on the 16th of July in the present year, their first hospital in Bozen had been erected, after the pope's permission had been obtained in the preceding May. They were now on their way to establish another in Brunn, and to receive some new sisters, for which purpose they supplicated the assistance of St. Vincentius, the patron-saint of their order. The elder one told me she had removed to this order from that of the Grey Sisters, of whom more were to be admitted, that the new order might profit by their experience in the care of the sick.

In truth, no mammoth's tooth lies so deeply buried in the dust of ages, but our curious, prying age will ferret it out—no mummy lies hidden so closely in the depths of the pyramid, but our all-seeking curiosity will dig it into daylight—no nun is so snugly covered with the mantle of ancient and modern times, but she will be dragged from oblivion, have new life infused into her veins, and be sent forth a wanderer among the children of the present day. If it were possible to give life to the Egyptian mummies, we should see them among us again.

I was just about to leave the front deck, when, among the crowd, I observed two black figures, who suggested to me, for the moment, that my last notion respecting the mummies was already in the course of fulfilment. On inquiry, I learnt they were workmen from the celebrated plumbago mines near Marbach, a little picturesque village we had just left behind us. These mines have been worked from very ancient times; but of late they have acquired new importance. The English have found that this plumbago is well adapted to fill their lead-pencils, and they have, of late, imported it in tolerably large quantities. Last year two thousand hundred weight were sent to England. Since then the people of Vienna have bestowed a little more attention on the mines, and some new ones have been opened within the last two years. A company has been formed in Vienna for the exportation of this article, in which the Rothschilds had a share; and we had a young Saxon professor on board, who had visited the mines by the invitation of those gentlemen. It is remarkable that the Austrians do not rather make the pencils themselves; but the English understand these things better, and have better wood for the purpose. They get the material pulverized from Austria, carefully consolidate and enclose it in cedar-wood, and then supply all the artists in the world. Their own mines become daily poorer, while those of Austria increase, as the rich material, with which Nature has abundantly supplied them, becomes better known. Whilst the Saxon professor was obligingly explaining all this to us, the young German Italian took out her English blacklead-pencil and gave it me, that it might write its own history in my note-book.

The arrangements on board the Austrian steamers are apparently as good as those of the Rhine. To judge of the whole of a vessel, requires a long acquaintance, as it does to become well acquainted with a man; but the cabins, &c., left nothing to be desired. There were separate ones appropriated to the smokers, and abundant accommodation for the ladies. The business of the engineer, who had his own office, as the captain had, was promptly executed, and there was less trouble with respect to the baggage than in the Rhine steamers. Any one might take out, or put in, as it pleased him; a ticket being given, answering to that on the package. Neither was there any fault to be found with the fare. It is true, that our meals were so well seasoned by agreeable society, that some faults in the cookery might well have been forgiven.

The literature of the Danube may now compare itself with that of the Rhine. I do not mean in the larger scientific works, or those belonging to the *belles-lettres*, but the local information, which, at every place, in elegant little pamphlets, offers the necessary information to the traveller. The engravings and maps are not inferior to the letter-press. The whole course of the Danube is so fully and satisfactorily given, that it may have suggested to many the expediency of sparing themselves the cost of the actual journey altogether.

The sailors were Germans, Venetians, and Dalmatians. Many of the commanders of the Danube steamers are Italians. There is a great deal of courtesy shown by these vessels. When they meet, a salute is always fired, while the busy Rhine steamers pass each other without notice; indeed, there are so many of these, that there would be no end of the cannonading, if they observed the same practice. I noticed, also, that the ordinary boatmen always took off their hats to each other. The Danube millers alone, whose huge mills advance far into the stream, close to the channel, live on somewhat hostile terms with the watermen. The boatmen are angry that the mills sometimes narrow their channel, and the millers maintain that "God did not make the Danube for the boatmen alone," and assert that, in storms, their mills are often injured. Whenever we passed one of these mills, which the large waves we raised would set in motion, we were greeted with a jest or a grimace.

Of Great Pöchlarn I had only a passing glance through the cabin-window, as I rose to pour out a glass of wine for Mademoiselle B. Doubtless Bishop Baturich, of Ratisbon, examined it a little more attentively, when he received the place as a present from Louis the German, in the year 831. In spite of its high-sounding appellation, the place has only forty-five houses; nevertheless it calls itself a town, and so old a one, that it reckons almost as many centuries as it has dwellings. Under the name of Arelape, the place was known to the Romans, and in the Nibelungenlied it is called Bechelaren. These little paltry towns on the Danube play a more important part at the court of the River God, and vaunt of names more widely spread than the most important towns in Bohemia, which are like great spirits and men of mark lost in the provinces. Even the villages on the Danube consider themselves aristocratic, and in fact are so. Little Pöchlarn situated over against Great Pöchlarn, disputes with the latter its claim to the Roman name of Arelape, and to the epithet *praeclara* bestowed on one of them by the same people.

At every health we drank at our table d'hote we rushed by one or other of these old Danube castles; first, castle Weiteneck, then castle Lubereck, and at last some one cried out, "there is Molk, Molk, the finest abbey in all the holy Roman empire," and we all rushed up the cabin-stairs to look at it.

The beautiful abbey of Molk or rather to speak more correctly, the magnificent palace and cathedral of this stately old episcopal seat, sits proudly enthroned upon its granite foundation, the extreme promontory of an arm of the Alps, whose picturesque sides decline towards the Danube. On every side of the hill, a river pours its water into a mighty stream; on the one the Molk, on the other the Bilach, and their valleys lie in meadow and arable land at the foot of the lordly abbey. I did not see the interior. My intention was to have remained here one day, and to pursue my journey in the steamboat the day following. But when we have proposed to ourselves to see the whole, even so splendid an individual object as Molk vanishes like a point in the bewildering enjoyment. And then, honestly speaking, I felt unwilling to leave an agreeable circle in the steamer, which I might not have met with another day. In short, I allowed the abbey to pass by and remained with the gazing majority, instead of joining the minority, consisting of a Benedictine canon, and a young peasant, who got into a boat and left us here.

I thought at first to earn great praise from my fair travelling companions, when I told them that I had remained on board for the pleasure of their company. Quite the contrary. I heard nothing but reproaches. "There was a little laziness in the case," said they; "people like to sit still after dinner, and it is pleasanter to remain quietly here than to scramble up and down hills and steeps." I hid my embarrassment behind the friendly cloud of my cigar, but my reprover continued, "How, sir, you, an enthusiast for historical recollections, can pass the most remarkable point on the whole Danube with so much indifference, to drink coffee and smoke cigars! this famous Namare of the Romans, this mighty Mellicium, the chief seat of the powerful Hungarian prince Geisa, the original residence of the renowned Babenberg rulers, and where still the monuments of these illustrious lords are to be seen! the birthplace of Leopold, the patron saint of Austria?" "I esteem all these recollections, much," said I, "But

I can indulge them at least as agreeably in your society as in that of the reverend canon there; and after all, the living breathing world is beyond any other in my estimation."

"And what then is your mighty gain in this breathing world? A few silly, white-faced, gossiping women, that is all," said the Austrian. "And now listen to me, I will read to you from my Guide what you have lost. In the first place, a magnificent church treasure, with the costliest vestments, and a chalice made of gold found in the sands of the Danube."

"Ay, my dear madam, these splendours at least I cannot regret; I would much rather admire the ornaments you are now wearing on your neck and fingers, than all the jewels abbot ever wore, and this full glass is more to my taste than the empty chalice of Danube gold."

"Further; the pictures of all the Austrian rulers, painted by Grabner, and many excellent oil and fresco paintings by Scangoni, Lucas of Leyden, Schinnagel Querfurt, and a crowd of unknown masters, who, as everybody knows, have many more charms than the known ones."

"I have told you already this morning, that I have here a picture-gallery that interests me far more than all that Lucas of Leyden, or Schinnagel of Pöchlarn ever painted."

"Then the collections of coins, of natural history, the imperial chambers, and many other fine strangers' apartments, in one of which, no doubt, you might have lodged yourself. What do you say to that?"

"As for the chambers, I have only to say, that they are firmly attached to the rock. A stationary imperial chamber will not so easily allure me from a moving one."

"And last of all, listen now. A splendid library of twenty thousand volumes; and besides these, seventeen hundred rare manuscripts and incunabulæ. Now, sir, do not these twenty thousand volumes fall like twenty thousand ball cartridges, and these incunabulæ like so many bombs on your slumbering conscience?"

"A most energetic attack indeed! But, unfortunately, I must confess, I have wandered unmoved through libraries that could reckon hundreds of thousands. Give me but the short quintessence of all these books in your society, and I will leave the seventeen hundred incunabulæ of Molk without remorse, to slumber in their dusty cradles."

The reader will, at all events, have gathered from this conversation—and it was reported with that view—how well a visit to the Abbey of Molk would be rewarded, and he will the sooner make it himself, if he do not happen to come upon it as I did while on a rapid journey to Hungary.

Below Molk lie the ruins of Durrenstein, of all the castles of the Danube the most famed in song. Shortly before it reaches this point, the river makes a sudden bend, and a little further on, another, so that the castle presents itself suddenly throned on the frowning rock, and as it is closed in behind again by rugged mountain walls, it looks isolated in its rocky desert, although standing on the bank of the land-uniting stream. King Richard may have suffered all the more during his imprisonment here, for, if his apartment lay on the eastern side, although he might enjoy some distant view, it was a view into the heart of Austria, which he must have detested, whereas, on the side towards England, whither his longing wishes must have tended most, the prospect is most limited.

I should like to know more precisely what were the employments of the lion-hearted king in this stern rocky nest; how far he was at liberty to go, who spoke with him, and whether he learnt some words of Austrian German? Without historical record I can easily believe the noble warrior to have been kind and gracious to his attendants, the servants of Hadmar des Khuenringer, and that in the morning when they brought him—not his coffee—but his porridge, perhaps he would have answered their greeting with a " *Grüss di Gott Seppi.*"

It is a pity, however, that we cannot be sure of these things, and how thoughtless it was of Blondel not to keep a journal; no doubt his royal friend gave him an exact account of all that had happened when he was once more at liberty. What a precious, what an inestimable book would be " Blondel's Memoirs of the Fifteen Months' Imprisonment of King Richard Cœur de Lion." How seldom it has happened that such a royal prey, a lion, born for the most unbounded freedom, has fallen into such a trap. And how widely diffused is the story of this captivity, how for nearly seven hundred years it has been related and re-related by all European and American grandfathers to all European and American children! And yet, in how few words the whole tradition is contained! How much remains to be filled up by every narrator, according to his own fashion! Every one has his own image of Archduke Leopold, the cunning wolf, of the valiant, unsuspicious Richard, the suffering lion, and the gentle, tuneful Blondel, his faithful friend! The tradition, like every thing really beautiful, is so fine and touching in all its parts, that in defiance of the scanty data, it will remain as long as the rocks remain that echo it. As yet the story is in a measure new, and all the travellers thronged to the side of the steamboat to look at the ruins of castle Durrenstein, as if it related to some occurrence of recent date. The loophole, behind which the king was said to have sat, was sought for with glasses, and the broken column and wall of the knightly hall, where the hero walked with Khuenringer, and the fragments of painting in the ruined chapel, the cellars and the vaults. The castle will not last much longer; a couple of centuries at the most. Fragments of the wall will then be sought for on the mountain side, and the morsels will be enveloped in paper, on which may be inscribed, " a stone from the former castle of Durrenstein, where King Richard the Lion Heart was imprisoned," &c. And then the stone may vanish, and some thousands of years afterwards, perhaps, the vacant place may be pointed out, and strange tongues may speak of an unauthenticated story of some imprisoned king, in whom fewer and fewer persons are interested, until at last the lion-hearted king will be confounded with a real lion, and the story may run thus :—" In times of remote antiquity, when the people called Germans still inhabited this country, the last lion was caught in the wilderness, but afterwards escaped," &c. By the time Africa is cleared of its lions such a version of the story is by no means improbable.

As we passed Durrenstein, one of the Germans began to hum the air:

" O Richard, O mon roi,
L'univers t'abandonne."

I remarked that the words were strikingly correct, for the castle looks so solitary, that Richard must have really felt as if forsaken by all the world. " Yes," said the singer, " his spirit must have suffered the tortures of an impaled criminal, and that for fifteen months long! It is fearful, and almost moves me to tears." In fact the locality so seizes upon the imagination, that even I, though by no means sentimental, (the reader will permit this confession,) felt a certain creeping sensation coming over me. Strange! Had we not all heard this story a hundred times before, read of it, and related it again without any particular emotion; is not the whole an idea, an imagination! What was it then that so powerfully affected us in passing the place itself?

I used formerly when I heard the story of Richard's imprisonment, to feel mortified that it should be a German prince who played the ignoble part, and now it sounded strangely enough to hear a German singing in the French language the praises of an English king; but I might almost say, I was shocked to hear an Englishman, of whom I inquired the next verse of the song, answer drily, as he settled his cravat, "*Je n'ai pas l'intimité de toute cette chose.*"

Behind Durrenstein as we round the corner towards Mautern, is the last fine picture in this unequalled gallery, through which we had been running; a gallery so inexhaustible in beauties, that the hundred eyes of Argus would be wanted to discover them all. Mautern, and the opposite village of Stein, form a landscape in the style of Claude Lorraine, and seem placed here purposely to sooth the troubled spirit after the wild and savage Durrenstein. To the right and left lie the pretty little towns of Stein, Mautern, and Krems, all places sung in the Nibelungenlied, and here collected in the propylæum of the Danube temple. The river is crossed here by a bridge of boats, the first between this place and Linz; both the bridge and the town are interesting objects from their geographical position on the boundary, between the mountain territory of the Danube and its plains. In the foreground, from the window of a house advancing close upon the river, two monks were looking out on the unquiet steamboat; a terrace, belonging to the house projecting over the stream, was filled with flowers. In the background of the picture, on a rock seven hundred feet in height, rises a stately edifice, the Abbey of Gottweih, the third in rank of the ecclesiastical foundations on the Danube. It covers the whole tolerably broad back of the mountain, which stands in an extensive and beautiful plain. The hills rising at the sides of the little towns, are crowned with vineyards; and vessels are moving backwards and forwards on the winding river in front. What follows, is comparatively insignificant and uninteresting, partly from negligence, as I cannot but think, that with proper treatment and some pains, all these immeasurable water-meadows, morasses, and wastes, might be changed into pleasing pictures, were they only in the style of the rich marsh lands of Holland, dammed up by dykes, and spotted with a few comfortable houses, and some well fed cattle. But instead of that, these water-meadows lie bare and desolate among the many arms of the Danube, presenting a most unpleasing contrast to those before mentioned between the hills.

The beautiful Abbey of Gottweih, which drew many a sigh from the prisoners in the steamboat, alone remained long visible, a last consolation for all we had lost. Beyond the willow-grown meadows and islands of Hollenburg, we still caught sight of its distant buildings, till at last they vanished like a cloud in the grey horizon. Then, wearied out with the enjoyment of the day, we could recline on the elegant divans of the Archduke Stephen, and listen to him who related the pleasing story of the foundation of Gottweih. It is thus related by Bishop Altmann, of Passau, who lived in the eleventh century.

"In my youth, when I was still a travelling student, and when the deceased majesty the emperor Conrad ruled, I came into the most remote part of my new diocese, the country that we Germans took from the Huns and Avares, under our emperor Charlemagne, of blessed memory. I was in company with my dear brother and friend, Adalbert, bishop of Wurzburg, and Gebhardt, bishop of Saltzburg. They were then like myself, travelling scholars. We three passed many a cheerful and pious holiday together; but at times we shared nothing but labour, and want, and trouble; yet we went on our way diligently, prayed and sang, studied, and were followers of God's word. In that land, then, we came once on a high hill in the midst of fruitful plains, but one little laboured in, either in a spiritual or any other sense, on the banks of the broad Danube; and we poor scholars sat ourselves down and looked upon the country round about. As we three poor and insignificant people sat there on the summit of the hill, in the midst of free nature, there came upon us all three a vehement wish to be stronger and more profitable servants of God. We prayed to him that he would give us higher place in his service, and made a compact, each clasping the other's hand, that in all the roads and byways of life, that we trod in the name of God, we would faithfully stand by and help one another, and that we would neither halt nor rest, till each had the bishop's crozier in his hand, and a flock to pasture in the name of the Lord. Well! we have kept our bond truly, and our three bishoprics border on one another. And I, for mine own behoof, made a vow on that mountain, that if I became the bishop of Passau I would build a monastery on that same mountain, that the cultivation of the land and of the souls of the dwellers might be advanced thereby. I am now bishop of Passau, and the convent by the Danube has been long roofed in, and named by me, Gottweih, because I have dedicated it to the Lord and Creator of the world. And there my coffin is already nailed together, and my vault built, for I would fain be buried in the place of my fairest youthful recollections." Here may be added, that this wish also was fulfilled, and the traveller may yet stand and contemplate the grave of the poor scholar, Altmann.

The word meadow (Au) has in German a particularly friendly sound. The poet often makes use of it, and seldom without a loving predicate— the "charming," the "loved," or "lovely" meadows. But we have only to go from Stein to Vienna to be heartily sick of the name and the thing. I saw on this passage so many unlovely meadows, that I have the word regularly *en dépit*, and was not a little rejoiced when we came in sight of Leopold's mountain, and Kahlenberg, and when we passed Klosterneuberg, and heard at Nussdorf, "Halt—stop the machine." Nussdorf is the harbour of Vienna: it lies at the mouth of that arm of the Danube that branches off here, and flows through the imperial city. Here the greater number of the vessels navigating that river, land their passengers, and here, in consequence, is a never-ending turmoil and confusion of boats, men, and conveyances, to encounter which, one has to arm oneself beforehand with patience and watchfulness, in order not to be ingulfed in a vortex alike dangerous to purse, person, and baggage.

LOWER AUSTRIA.

VIENNA, OR BETSCH.

AND in this manner we reached the great city of Betsch, a name highly valued throughout the east, though wonderfully little known in Europe.

The city of Betsch has four hundred thousand inhabitants, and is the residence of a powerful Shah, who rules a land more extensive than Beloochistan and Affghanistan, called Nyemzestan. This land of Nyemzestan contains a number of kingdoms and principalities, over all of which the above-named Shah is master and lord. The greatest of these subordinate kingdoms is Trandebog, lying towards the north. Its inhabitants, the Trandebogians, amount, in number, to millions.

The language spoken in Betsch is a very singular mixture. It neither resembles the Turkish nor the Persian, but is said to have some affinity to German.

The Turks, the Hungarians, and all the nations beyond, far into Asia, call that Betsch which we christen Vienna, and signify by Nyemzestan, the whole of our German fatherland, of which they suppose his majesty of Austria to be sovereign lord. It is true, that the emperor Francis renounced this title, and the glory of the *German empire* has long since passed away; but it is long before the setting of a star is observed in distant regions, as its rays, once transmitted, still conjure up its image before us. Brandenburg is corrupted by the Turks into Trandebog. Betsch or Vienna is, to them, next to Trieste, the most distinguished place of traffic in Germany.

Two great water-roads connect Germany with the east: the Adriatic Sea and the Danube. At the head of the one lies Trieste, and of the other Vienna; and from these two places branches out the whole commerce of the east to the interior of Germany, as it develops itself from Constantinople to Trebisond and Smyrna. Vienna is the last westerly point before which a hostile Turkish army encamped, and the most western seat of an eastern commercial colony or factory.

The people who are the great agents of this commerce, through their own trade and their river navigation, are the Servians—the Rascians, as they are called in Vienna and Hungary. I could never discover, either from books or verbal inquiry, whence this appellation for the Servians was derived.* In Hungarian Latin, they are called Rasci, their country Rascia, and the King of Hungary is entitled "Rex Rasciæ."

The Rascians have their colonies in Pesth, Vienna, and other cities on the Danube, where they are mingled with the other inhabitants, as the Armenians, Bucharians, and Greeks, are in southern and western Russia, and as the Jews are in other countries; and are the principal masters of vessels on the middle and lower Danube. They are to be met with their wives in all the public places in Vienna, habited in a strange mixture of European and Oriental costume. After the Rascians, the Turco-Spanish Jews play the principal part in the commercial world of Vienna. This remarkable branch of a remarkable nation, was scattered over the whole Turkish empire after the most catholic kings of Spain had driven them from their dominions. They have commercial establishments in all the Turkish states of Africa and in Asia; and, as agents between the east and west, they have also fixed themselves at Vienna, where their houses are very considerable. Like the Servians, though in fewer numbers, they have extended their branches as far as Pesth, Semlin, Belgrade, and are more especially important in the relations of the Danube countries with Thessalonica.

These Spanish or Turkish Jews have adopted the eastern costume, probably because it was a *sine qua non* of their admission into the Turkish dominions, but they retain the Spanish language. They converse and correspond with each other from Belgrade to Salonica, and from Neusatz to Vienna in Spanish; probably it is found convenient here as a language very little known. They enjoy many privileges in Vienna, among others, that of being reckoned Turkish subjects, although established in Austria, and are consequently, under the protection of the Turkish ambassador, as independent of the native authorities as the Franks are under that of their consuls in the Turkish dominions.

Besides the above-named foreigners, there are many Greek and Armenian merchants settled in Vienna. The principal banker, Sina, is a Greek. Since the late improvements in the navigation of the Danube, which have made it possible to travel from Vienna to Trebisond within fourteen days, and to reach the interior of Persia in three weeks, traders from Asia Minor, and the Persian pointed caps, have made their appearance in the neighbourhood of St. Stephen's church, but they are only visiters in the city and not residents.

The whole number of Orientals in Vienna, is generally reckoned at about a thousand souls. In what degree their numbers have increased, with the still increasing intercourse with the east, I learnt in the office of the Vienna Foreign Police, where I had an opportunity of looking at the register of foreign residents. From 1822 to 1831 (in nine years), a large folio volume had been filled with the names and residences of Turkish subjects; from 1831 to 1836 (that is in five years), another as large, and in the following four years, a third was filled.

The register for the year 1840, gives the numbers of Turkish subjects trading *en gros*, whose firms are established in Vienna.

1st. Of the Greek religion (the fewest of these being of the Greek nation) fifty-two.

2dly. Israelite Turkish merchants (the greater number bearing Spanish

---

* There is a small river in Servia bearing a similar name, from which it may be derived.

family-names, as Somajo, Majo, Abeneri, Benturo, Major, Sabetay, &c.), forty-eight.

And 3dly. Armenian merchants, nine.

The greater part of these oriental inhabitants live in the neigbourhood of the old meat market. There they are to be met with, as grave as storks, slowly pacing through the bustle of a European street, or, reclining on the handsome red cushions with which the windows of a Vienna house are generally provided, they may be seen looking down upon the turmoil, and tranquilly smoking. Here also are the two coffee-houses most frequented by them, the "Grecian," and the "City of London." In the first, there is a constant influx and efflux of eastern merchants, mingled with Greeks, Jews, and Italians. The second, has been especially selected as the scene of their social amusements,—smoking and sitting still,—by the young Turkish students and the officers of the Porte, who of late have been accustomed to make the pilgrimage from the Bosphorus to the seat of art and enlightenment on the banks of the Danube. They learn German of course, and their pronunciation, seemed to me in general soft, harmonious, and agreeable. It sounded, however, comical enough to hear these foreigners take all imaginable pains to acquire the Austrian provincialisms, which they most conscientiously sought to imitate.

Surprise has been expressed (and with reason), that those of the Vienna coffee-house keepers who call their establishments oriental, take so little trouble to furnish them in the eastern taste. They have not so much as the broad divan always found in Turkish coffee-houses. Now, when we bethink ourselves, how much even we unquiet Franks value a comfortable seat, of which many of our proverbial expressions offer a proof, as "sitting in clover," "sitting upon thorns," &c. ; when we reflect that even with our inconvenient sitting machines, it is so easy to accustom oneself to one kind, that another becomes disagreeable, (I know a German lady, who told me, that being used to sitting on cane chairs, she could not endure cushioned ones, whereby I suppressed, just at the right time, a philosophical remark that came into my head, viz., that certain very distant parts of our physical organization must be capable of contracting habits, which, when opposed, excited disagreeable sensations,) when we consider these things, I say, we cannot feel otherwise than great compassion for the poor orientals in Vienna, mounted on our narrow, long-legged, unsteady, sitting accommodations, their hearts a prey to home-sickness, and their legs, the one tucked under them after the fashion of their fatherland, while its forsaken brother dangles solitary and stick-like in cold empty space!

VISIT TO ST. STEPHEN'S TOWER.

My best friend in Vienna was named Stephen, and when I heard he had become a widower lately, I went to pay him my visit of condolence. At first I did not very well understand the expression " become a widower," as, to the best of my knowledge, my friend Stephen, who was above four hundred feet high, and five hundred years old (being no other than the renowned steeple dedicated to the abovenamed saint) had never been married, although he had many brothers, as the double steeple in Rheims, the sister steeples in Munich, Lubeck, and other places. I asked, therefore, with some reason, "how he could have become a widower," and was answered

"Because it has pleased the fates, and the safety police to relieve him of his *cross*." So this was a piece of Vienna wit, which will not be taken amiss by any married lady in the world, I think, for the compliment implied is far greater than the discourtesy at first apparent. If it be maintained that every married man bears his wife enthroned in honour far above himself, as Stephen's Tower bore his cross, it must be admitted that the matrimonial burden cannot but be a light one to so great and portly a gentleman. This cross was also united with a double eagle, spreading its lordly pinions over the Tower, even as married ladies sometimes extend another pretty little instrument authoritatively over the heads of their wedded lords, or wedded servants as they should rather be called.

Stephen, as he is sometimes laconically styled in Vienna, is in general fanned by the pinions of more peaceful birds, or by the harmless, though, from its great height, sometimes outrageous god of wind; but nearly every hundred years this tower has had visiters of another description, lowering, black, hard-headed fellows, who cared little how they ruffled his carefully arranged toilet. Between the different bombardments, which Vienna and St. Stephen's Tower, in particular, have suffered from the Hungarians, Turks,—a second time from the Turks, and lastly from the French; exactly a hundred years have each time elapsed. Since the last shooting match, forty years have nearly flown away; from what direction the bombs of 1907 or 1909 are to whistle, it is not difficult to guess; for every traveller who visits Austria must ask himself why all the windows and loopholes, looking to the north-east, are not a little better fastened up. Perhaps Stephen may weather the bombardment of 1907, and, perhaps, a sixth or a seventh, but at last his courage may sink under these repeated attacks, till one day the old, crazy, useless Stephen, out of regard to the heads of the worthy citizens, will be ordered to be removed altogether. God be thanked, the hands by which, and the heads for whose sake this will have to be done, lie still in the darkness of the future. At present the good people of Vienna are busied in removing the old worn-out bones, and substituting new ones. I examined the work closely. The permission is obtained in the office of the church-master, where a printed passport for this little journey to the clouds is issued.

The church-master's office has its seat in the neighbourhood, and is in itself a little curiosity, for it is a question whether any other cathedral can boast so numerous a court. The venerable Stephen brings his middle age customs and usages into modern times, and has his own peculiar sources of revenue, which are as difficult to administer, as the Gothic caprices of building are to bring within architectural rules. The so-called giant door, one of its five entrances, abounding in all kinds of inexplicable decorations, is never opened on ordinary occasions, and seems to be quite rusty for want of use. It costs a considerable sum when, at the desire of some relative of an illustrious deceased, this door opens to admit the corse. The numerous death-bells have their different prices, and if it be desired that "Stephen" shall set his whole concert of bells in motion in honour of the departed, no inconsiderable capital must be expended. There are not less than twenty-one persons employed in the church-master's office; a church provost, a controller, four secretaries, a sexton, two upper vergers, two lower vergers, four assistant vergers, four guides, two reckoners. It must be observed that these form only one branch of the cathedral authorities, its police as it were. The cathedral dignitaries are many more, and then there are the female attendants or housemaids, to say nothing of the watchmen on the tower, &c.

Not far from the door, through which you ascend the tower, among the many monuments on the walls, there is one old stone with this inscription, "fortiter ac suaviter." I translated these words for the benefit of a pretty little Servian, who, with a train of brothers and kindred, was preparing to ascend along with me, and we took these words as a viaticum on our way. The young Oriental had the same detestable head-dress as the rest of her countrywomen in Vienna,—a cloth, bound flat and tightly round her head, with a bouquet of flaring flowers, like the feather in a soldier's shako. She was very pretty, however, in spite of her head-gear.

St. Stephen's Tower is inhabited from top to bottom by very different kinds of men and animals. At the bottom, strangers are under the guidance of two young ecclesiastics. Further up, as far as the roof, the church servants bear sway; we then enter the territory of the bell-ringers, and at the very top of the tower watchmen keep watch and ward. All, according to their own fashion, do the honours of the place, and levy a contribution on travellers. On all sides one is called upon to look and admire; here is the hole through which, some years ago, a man, weary of life, flung his hat down into the church, and then flung himself after it—there are the bells, cast by order of the emperor Joseph I., from the captured Turkish cannon—here is the great crescent, which the Vienna people fastened to their tower to induce the Turks to spare the splendid edifice—there are the twelve engines and thirty cisterns for the protection of the building against fire. In March they are filled with water strongly impregnated with salt, which is thus preserved throughout the summer. Admiration is also challenged for the great ugly double eagle lying with outspread pinions on the roof, probably the largest figure of a bird in the world. If it could rise into the air it might pass for the offspring of the far-famed roc; from the extremity of one wing to that of the other the measurement is one hundred and eighty feet. Each eye is formed of four gilded tiles, and each beak contains not less than thirty such scales.

People who are fond of taking exceptions against modern times, may find abundance of opportunity on the roof of this cathedral. In 1830 it was found necessary to repair a portion; the new tiles were shaped and coloured after the model of the old; but after the lapse of only ten years they are worn out. The glazing and colour is worn off the greater part, the white glaze turning quite red, and displaying the native hue of the clay, while the old tiles, the work of the middle ages, retain all their original tints and freshness. It is feared that the roof itself may suffer from the badness of the tiling, and a renewal of the work is already talked of.

No less than 700 steps must be mounted to reach the tower where the watchers have their dwelling and place of abode. The arrangements made for ascertaining the exact locality of a fire are very peculiar and interesting. On the parapets of the four windows, looking east, west, north, and south, are four telescopes. Each glass, or, as they call the whole apparatus here, every "toposkop" commands a fourth of the whole circular sea of houses, stretching on every side of the church. Each quadrant is divided by circles and radii into sections, and by the aid of the glass the section in which the burning house lies is easily ascertained. The individual house is discovered with the same ease. By every "toposkop" there lies a thick book

K

containing the names of all the house owners in each section; and thus the house can be not only ascertained, but named. When the name is found it is written on a slip of paper, which is enclosed in a brass ball. This ball is thrown down a pipe, and it passes rapidly, like a winged messenger of evil tidings, down to the dwelling of the sexton, where it is picked up by a watchman constantly in attendance there and carried to the city authorities. Here it is opened, and the name of the unfortunate house made known to those whom it may concern. In the description, this operation appears somewhat long, but it is performed with tolerable rapidity and certainty, and the " toposkop" can be used as well by night as by day. In the more remote parts of the suburb, the point is of course more difficult to ascertain, as the angles of vision and position become smaller in the " toposkop." Such an apparatus can only be used with advantage from towers as lofty as St. Stephen's.

The length of the piece latterly removed from the tower, from apprehension of insecurity, is about eleven fathoms; that is, as the whole tower contains about seventy-two fathoms, nearly a sixth of the whole. This piece had long swayed from the right line, in consequence of an earthquake, it was said, but at first with an inclination of only three feet from the highest point of the cross. At last, however, it was asserted that the highest point was a whole fathom out of the perpendicular. Many smaller parts had also been much injured, partly by time and natural causes, partly by the different bombardments. For example, the crowns of many little side towers had been split from top to bottom, and heavy fragments of stone hung threateningly over the abyss below swarming with life. The former repairs had been exceedingly defective; round many of these smaller towers only thick iron bands had been passed, which scarcely held the loose stones together. Others had merely iron staves and cramp irons to keep the runaway fragments in their places. In 1809, after the French bombardment, a great deal of money had been lavished on these cramps and holdfasts; but in 1838 the real repair now in progress was begun. From the main or round corridor, the tower is surrounded by eighteen galleries formed of strong beams connected by ladders, rising above each other to the top of the cross. The work was begun on the twenty-fourth of September, 1838; it was hoped that in three years it would have been finished, but it will certainly require three more to restore the noble building to its former magnificence and perfection. What a day of joy will that be for the people of Vienna!

The very solid manner in which the scaffoldings are erected, must have offered no small difficulty; from below, all this joinery cannot be looked at without a slight sensation of fear, lest some tremendous hurricane might in its sport scatter these beams like matches, and hurl them down upon the roofs and heads below. Whenever the wind is very high, the work must be discontinued, and the workmen retire. Hitherto all accidents have been avoided, but one of the men told me that the mischievous Æolus had once played him a trick, more dangerous than agreeable, in whirling him aloft and seating him astride upon a balustrade; fortunately, before the second gust came, he had clung fast to a beam, and, creeping down on the inner side, saved his life.

The difficulties experienced in the execution of the building may be estimated from this one circumstance, that half a day is required to raise the stones the same distance which the fire-announcing bullet traverses in a moment. The stones are all tolerably large, and eleven workmen are scarcely able to raise two in a day.

In order that the new stones used in the repairs may not be too conspicuous by the side of the old, they have invented a new colour, wherewith to stain them, but the right shade has not been caught, and the places repaired are easily recognizable from below. We pointed this out to the people about, but they assured us, that after many attempts no better colour could be found. It struck us at first as very extraordinary that it should be so very difficult to hit the colour of a mass of old gray stones, and began to examine them more minutely. We found such a variety of shades on every side and every stone, that it was clearly impossible that one and the same colour should suffice to blend old and new harmoniously together. The tints, moreover, depend partly on the vegetation, —the mosses which cover nearly the whole surface of the tower. In some places these mosses are withered and decayed; the stones are then covered with a dark gray coating that can be rubbed to dust between the fingers. Here and there occur patches of young moss, producing a grayish green tint; then come whitish grays, bluish and yellowish colourings. To give the right effect it would be necessary to lay on all these tints and blend them softly together; and even this would scarcely suffice, as the appearance of the whole changes with the weather. In rain and damp weather not only the bare stones change their colour, but also those covered with moss. The mosses attract the moisture, and many that look withered in dry weather seem to gain new life after rain. In a wet season the verdure of the tower on one side becomes extremely vivid, and it is impossible to follow all these changes with any artificial colour. It is a question whether it would not have been better to leave the new stones of their natural colour, trusting to time to assimilate them. Be this as it may, it is certain that the chosen colour is much too palpably blue, and ought to have been blended to a yellowish gray.

The flora of St. Stephen's tower is much more uniform than that of the cathedral of Cologne, where a hundred different plants grow in rich luxuriance. All the north side is covered with mosses. The south has little or no vegetation. The fauna of the cathedral is various enough. Of the human part we spoke before. The crows, jack-daws, hawks, &c., it has in common with all the church steeples in Germany; owls are very rare, the guardians of the place said there were none, which would be remarkable enough, but the bats are so numerous, that I was told on a late search for their hiding places not less than fifty had been discovered and killed, because the night patrols could no longer protect their lanterns or their faces from the assaults of these goblins. A worse plague than these are the *golse*, the little long-legged stinging insects of which all travellers and boatmen along the Danube complain so much. I should like to know what the swamp-bred animalculæ can think of seeking in these giant towers, where in summer time they swarm in such numbers that the people employed there are obliged to sleep with damp cloths upon their faces. Chamber flies are found also, but in no great numbers. Mice there are none. Spiders we found in prodigious numbers; they and the *golses* have been carrying on the war here these four hundred years, and doubtless much to interest the naturalist has occurred, meanwhile, in the world of spiders. In fact, a naturalist might take up his abode here for a time, with great advantage to science. Of the storms, the people say that nearly all come from the north. So soon as the weathercocks in summer turn suddenly to the south, a storm may be expected. One of the younger of the watchmen, who had been lately placed in this exalted position, told us, that the weather up here was sometimes awful. At his first watch the fearful band of wind instruments, whistling and howling in the numberless clefts, holes, and corners, the rocking and cracking of the tower pinnacles, the wildly driving ghost-like clouds, with the gleaming of the lightning, and the stunning kettle-drums of the thunder, filled him with such terror, that he thought he must have jumped out of the first convenient opening to the depths below. There must be here abundant field for observation on acoustics. In ascending, we remarked that the wind whistled through every opening in a different tone.

From the wooden galleries erected for the repairs, the panorama of the city of Vienna can now be enjoyed more conveniently than ever. I wished to look on this spectacle from the summit of one of the side towers. This summit is formed like the leaves of a rose flattened at the top and affording just space enough for two human feet. We ascended accordingly, and perched like squirrels on the topmost branch of a tree. The beautiful city of Vienna lay at our feet. It was a most beautiful, calm, clear day. We heard and saw all that was passing in the city; even the songs of the canary birds in the windows of some houses ascended to us, and we could see the butterflies fluttering over the house-tops in search of some green spot in this (for them) dreary waste. We could have told a gentleman we saw walking below, where the brother was of whom he was in search; for we saw him at the same time driving at his leisure on the glacis. This glacis, which surrounds the inmost core of the city, with its broad green ring, lends the panorama its principal ornament; it causes the whole picture to fall into picturesque parts, and permits the fine rows of houses in the suburbs to be seen to full advantage. They lie round the outer edge of the glacis like white flowers in a wreath of green leaves. The tower keeper named to us all the market-places, streets, houses, and palaces we saw beneath, showed us the Danube, the first range of the Carpathian mountains, the Styrian Alps, and the roads that led to Germany, Moravia, Bohemia, and Italy, and "that is," added he, "the high road to Hungary." Here was matter for a prophetic homily, but I did not preach it, for it would have been a voice calling in the desert. The little Servian desired to see the road to Hungary, which also led to her native land. I offered my hand, and she placed her little foot boldly on the edge of the stone flower-crown, and gazed on the fields of Hungary; and so we stood awhile, motionless, like two statues on a pedestal, neither felt in the least giddy, but I must not forget to say, that the place was firmly boarded up around us, so that the pleasure we enjoyed was unaccompanied by danger. When we, that is, my Servian and I, had satisfied ourselves with the spectacle, we turned with equal convenience to another, the manœuvres of the Austrian troops, which we contemplated quite at our ease from the altitude of the seven hundred steps above mentioned.

THE MENAGERIE AT SCHOENBRUNN.

That *man* should sometimes demean himself sensibly can be no especial wonder, since everybody knows that man is neither more nor less than a reasonable creature. But that the poor dim-visioned brute should do so, is a standing marvel and mystery of nature. Man has in his soul a clear light to lighten his path externally and internally; the Psyche of the brute is a small, feebly-glimmering lamp, shining dimly through manifold veils from a depth of darkness sending forth only occasional gleams. The Egyptians worshipped brutes as the marvels of nature; with us Europeans, they have fallen somewhat into contempt; yet amongst brutes and plants, which appear to owe so little to themselves, and to have received all directly from God, we seem often to be nearer to the divinity than amongst men.

For my own part, I can never look into the eyes of a sheep without feeling strange sensations in beholding this veiled mystery of the great soul of the universe. The reader will, therefore, not be surprised that I and my companion, Baron K——, in a short time after my arrival in Vienna, were to be found less frequently among the dandies, officers, ladies of fashion, market folks, fish-women, or by whatever other name the human chrysales may be called, than at Schönbrunn among the bears, apes, tigers, eagles, lions, and other disguises of the brute Psyche, having their abode in that garden.

We drove there one day in one of the many hundred public carriages, ready at all times of the day to go to all ends of the world with anybody and any baggage. One of our travelling companions was a smartly-dressed old citizen of Vienna, who, when he heard we were going to Schönbrunn, related to us *apropos*, that he had once refused a request of the emperor Napoleon when at the very summit of his power. He (the citizen) had a most incomparable horse, of Hungarian race, and Napoleon had seen it when the owner, as captain of the burgher guard, had defiled before him at the head of his company. The emperor had offered him 5000 florins for the animal on the spot, but neither the gold nor the entreaties of the lord of Europe could induce him to part with his admirable steed, and, as before said, he had refused his horse to this mighty potentate at a time when the Emperor of Austria had not dared to refuse the hand of his daughter.

The menagerie of Schönbrunn incloses a part of the imperial garden, near which there passes a miserable, scantily-filled ditch, that in summer smells abominably, and which it is amazing to me does not appear the frightful object it is, to the thousands of Vienna people who daily resort thither. The menagerie occupies a large circular piece of ground, in the centre of which, on a little elevation, stands a many-windowed summer-house, the abode of the gaily-plumaged parrot kind. If I were a courtier I should use all my influence to get these birds removed from so conspicuous a place, lest it should occur to some to draw odious comparisons between them and the court circle.

From this parrot centre the whole circle is cut by radii into numerous sections. All these sections are divided by walls and hedges, and broad walks. Each section contains the stalls, baths, ponds, pasturages, and pleasure-grounds of a particular species, and since the present emperor has filled up the places that had become vacant, there is a tolerable number of interesting furred and feathered creatures, to whom Asia, Africa, or America has furnished paws or claws, hoofs, horns or antlers, the appetite for bread or for blood.

The bears, tigers, and other carnivorous animals, are daily in view of the public; the prisons of the others must be especially opened to the curious. The brown bears sat, like poor beggars, in their dens, and received thankfully a morsel of bread. If it was thrown on the top, they climbed up the iron grating and thrust their paws through to reach it. One of them, when we took out some more bread, sat up on his hind quarters and moved his fore paws up and down like a petitioner till he got a piece. A tiger or a lion would never learn to do this. The nature of the bear seems to partake of the monkey as well as of the dog. The old bears in Schönbrunn are the grandchildren of bears likewise born in captivity, and have, in their turn, descendants, the fourth generation, therefore, of a tamed race. It would be interesting to learn, if in later generations the character of the animal will undergo any considerable alteration. But, unfortunately, the people here keep no exact account of their charges, which might be useful to the student of natural history.

It was a hot day, and the polar bears, the bloodthirsty animals, who wear on their body the colour of innocence, and cover their necks with the silver locks of venerable age, when all the while they have not an honest hair on the whole body, were splashing about in the water all the time we stayed. They are the only animals who do not require their dwelling to be warmed in the winter. Like their far more amiable brethren, the brown bears, they are fed only on bread and milk, which, it is said, enables them to bear their imprisonment better.

The beautiful royal tiger we found lying on one side with all his legs stretched out, but so that his hind legs rested between the two fore ones. The keeper said this was his ordinary position when at rest. We durst not disturb him, as he takes it very much amiss even if people only touch his den, growls fearfully, and is long before he can be appeased. His lady is of a much gentler character. The cages of the tiger, lions, and other wild cats, are divisible into two parts by means of sliding partitions, that the animals may be driven into one while the other is cleaned. A third division projects like a balcony, in which they can enjoy the sunshine and open air, and show themselves to the public. The bears have their baths in addition.

The story we heard in the next section concerning master Jack was distressing to a friend of humanity. Master Jack was an exceedingly well-disposed and well-bred youth, living quietly and respectably in his appointed dwelling. He was on the best footing with all his acquaintance, and particularly attached to his friend and servant, M. Henri, who had long been his companion and tutor in all the arts of life, wherein master Jack showed great address, succeeding in all he undertook. He could take the cork out of a rum-bottle without the aid of a corkscrew; beat a drum like the most experienced drummer, and blow a trumpet that, like the summons to the last judgment, pierced to the very marrow. If a lady visiting him let fall her glove or her handkerchief, master Jack dropped on one knee like a courteous knight, and presented it to her again. But who can enumerate all the virtues and accomplishments of this well-instructed young gentleman? It may be boldly asserted that master Jack was the first gentleman of the lion court of Schönbrunn, and surpassed even the politely soliciting bears in grace and dexterity.

An unexpected occurrence, or rather the consequences of a bad calculation, suddenly produced a melancholy change in the whole being of the gifted Jack. This occurrence was his acquaintance with miss Djeck, *vis-a-vis* to which viciously disposed lady, he had been unadvisedly quartered. Jack, who, receiving so many visits daily, might be said to live in the great world, had become acquainted with many a young lady without showing further civility than any cavalier might offer in pure courtesy to any lady. But this particular lady, who took up her abode in his very house as it were, produced a magical effect upon him. Her eyes, the ivory of her teeth, and the unspeakable charm of her gray cheek, excited in him the liveliest desire to call her his own. To the indescribable vexation of his tutor he forgot all his learning, all his accomplishments. His gentleness was changed to fury, his universal philanthropy to the most hostile feeling against all the world. In short, his mind which before resembled a well-cultivated field, now became like a garden laid waste. Ah, love, to what a condition didst thou not reduce this thy poor victim!

His faithful friend, M. Henri, dares no longer venture near him, for if he does, Jack immediately draws his sword, that is his club, which he whirls aloft in the air, threatening to crush to pieces all that approach him. I found M. Henri perfectly inconsolable. When I asked him why the female elephant had been placed so directly before her admirer's eyes, he burst out into invectives against certain persons, from which I gathered, that either there was no other place for the newly-purchased lady, or that they were in hopes of founding a race of Djecks and Jacks from a marriage between the pair. Packed up in his finger-thick hide, master Jack was moving his enormous mass of bone up and down the balcony of his house, throwing his weight now on the right, now on the left leg. Occasionally he tossed his trunk about as a man might bite his lips in suppressed anger. His little eyes looked quite calm, though his keeper assured us the creature was full of flame and fury. He seemed to take no notice of any thing, but that was, as we were assured, because, caged within his bars, he saw he could do no mischief. Any object, living or dead, that came within the reach of his trunk or his feet, would be dashed or trampled to pieces immediately. On the bread we threw to him, he never deigned to bestow the most superficial notice, while miss Djeck directly opened her soft fleshy mouth and snapped up every morsel of the roll.

At noon the lady was let out to take the air in the meadow. Behind the thick beams and trunks of trees forming the palisade we could watch her proceedings. She walked gravely down the path leading to the meadow, also strongly fenced, then turned to the left and stood awhile before the passage leading to Jack's apartment, as if to say, good morning, but as he did not appear, she went to take her promenade on the turf and finish her toilet, wherein she was assisted by a fresh breeze. It blew a thick cloud of dust and straws over her broad sides. Jack, we were told, they durst not let out if they would not expose both trees and walls to the greatest danger.

The larger species of animals have for the most part their separate sections of the garden, but of the feline races many specimens are lodged in one house. Among them is a lion, a born republican, for he is a native of Hamburg, not very imposing in size, but with a very fine expressive head.

There is certainly deeply rooted in the human soul a peculiar pleasure in the enjoyment of what is dangerous, and that with the timid as well as the courageous, with this difference, that the former love danger only when they are certain it will not affect them personally. Our companion in Schönbrunn who, if all signs deceived not, was an arrant poltroon, would persist, in spite of the intreaties and prohibitions of the keepers, in teasing the lions and tigers with his riding whip till they got up and showed their teeth. We on our side could not withstand the temptation of creeping into one of the cages to examine its internal arrangements. It was a leopard house; the walls were carefully plated with iron and painted light blue. The arrangements for carrying away all dirt, and the division into front and back dens, appeared to us to be very judicious. The leopards, it must be observed, for whom these apartments had been prepared, had not yet taken possession of them.

None of the animals assembled here have increased so much as the Brazilian hares. A few years ago, a single pair was brought here, and there are now thirty, and many have been given away. The wildest and most timid of all are the Sardinian moufflons. They keep at the farthest end of the ground allotted them; and we dared not invade it, as the keepers assured us, that on the approach of any person or thing strange to them, they would dash themselves in their blind terror against the trees and walls. Even their young display this extreme shyness the day after birth, and fly with such rapidity from all who approach, that it is impossible to catch them, while the young bears and lions will allow themselves to be taken in the arms like children.

Among the camels, who agree no better here than in Arabia, but live in a state of continual warfare, biting and striking each other with their forefeet, there was one so unbearably vicious that he was obliged to be kept chained in his stall. His bony figure, rugged and remarkably bare hide, faded yellowish gray colour, the flabby and diseased hump hanging down on one side of his back, his spiteful and venomous spitting and hissing when any thing human drew near him, and his self-contented ruminating when he was left alone, made him a most offensive image of the intensest egotism, all the more disgusting, that he was withal excessively dry and meager. But even the fat and well-fed of the camel kind look very little handsomer. The hair is seldom or never in good order, or sufficient to cover them entirely, so that the speckled parts of the body of a bluish colour show very disagreeably through the leathern skin. There was one such fat camel here, which had been brought from Egypt. Of all tamed animals the camel is perhaps the most malicious. The zebus,—tame, gentle cows, from the East Indies,—have a pond in common with the camels, which divides their territory as the Indian Ocean does the lands of their birth.

There are some remarkably beautiful zebras in Schönbrunn. One was with young. Another had already brought into the world a little one, that closely resembled its sire, a German ass. A few stripes on the legs only betrayed its maternal descent.

The birds are lodged and provided for in a similar way, and there is a fish-pond for the waterfowl. Carp are fattened for the spoon-billed geese, who will sometimes swallow a fish weighing three pounds, and measuring a foot in length, without betraying the least inconvenience. If the lion's capacity for swallowing were of the same relative size, he could dispose at once of a whole lamb. It must be an enchanting sight to see the ostrich run in his native deserts; for even the few light springs that he takes in his poor fields in London, Paris, or Schönbrunn, when the keepers allow him to escape from his narrow cage, afford a pleasing spectacle, in which the lightly fluttering plumage of his back plays a principal part. They have taken much pains at Schönbrunn to obtain young from the ostrich, but have as yet got nothing beyond the eggs. As the parents themselves do not understand hatching, and the German sun has not the life-giving power of the African, they put the eggs at first under a Turkey hen, who sat on them, but had not warmth enough to call forth such giant broods from the yolks. The heat of the oven was then tried, but with no better success. The parrots have laid eggs, but could never be induced to hatch them.

Of all the imprisoned animals none make so melancholy an impression as the eagles and vultures. These great, high-soaring, far-circling lords of the air, ought at least to have had their prison-house arranged in some measure according to their natural propensities. A wooden cage, with iron grating, is a fitter den for a lion or a tiger than for the rock-throned eagle's nest. In this narrow dungeon they cannot even stretch their pinions, and yet this motion is no doubt as much a necessity to them as it is to a man to stretch his arms and legs after long continuance in a sitting or lying posture : indeed it is evident, from the custom all imprisoned birds have of spreading their wings slowly and yawningly from time to time. The eagle and vulture sit upon their perches as motionless as if they were mere stones. One whom I was watching held his head on one side and his eyes immoveably fixed on the skies; another uttered a melancholy sound at intervals, and lifted his useless wing. Some of them are extremely old. I was told that one had been fifty years a prisoner. In fifty years, if we assume that one way or another an eagle can fly thirty miles a day, he might have traversed 500,000 miles; that is, he might have encompassed the earth a hundred times. Good God! what a fearful destiny to feel this power within, and be condemned for ever to one narrow dirty stinking hole! As the eagles are neither cheerful here, nor display their natural peculiarities in any way, they can yield neither pleasure to the lover of nature, nor profit to the inquirer into her mysteries; and people would do much better, I am almost inclined to think, to free them at once from the burden of life, and place them stuffed in a museum. A process to which the eagles, parrots, and some other birds are subject to in their confinement, is that of washing with an infusion of tobacco to free them from vermin. Their feathers are rubbed with it against the grain. They suffer more from vermin in captivity than in freedom, because they cannot guard themselves against them so actively.

The parrot-house, to which, as to a centre, all the sections tend, is adorned with the portraits of many animals. The birds themselves are as thick here as in some primeval forest of South America; they are two legged and feathered monkeys, for they are equally restless, teachable, imitative, and comic. To the stern motionless eagle they offer the strongest possible contrast, bearing captivity apparently with perfect contentment. They are in eternal motion, and seem to observe every thing with their ever-watchful eye, to meditate awhile upon it, and shriek and chatter without intermission. Sometimes the whole army of them would be suddenly as still as mice, and then break out all together into one fearful discord, as if they were put on a spit—an honour never yet accorded to their black tasteless flesh. The gardens of Schönbrunn are yet more distinguished for their plantations and their botanical collections than for the animals they contain. Not that the long avenues of beautiful, large, but most cruelly mutilated lime trees, are entitled to much admiration.

There is certainly a method of altering the natural growth and figure of trees to the advantage of garden decoration. Even the French style of gardening, as it is called, has its æsthetic and poetical side, for the trees, trained into pyramids, gates, arched passages, columns, and other architectural decorations, are made to produce some striking illusions, and as art has entirely changed the appearance of the trees, and left nothing natural about them, we forget the original form, and willingly give ourselves up to the sportive deception.

In Schönbrunn, however, by cutting one side of the trees and leaving the other in their natural irregularity, they have produced nothing but deformities, resembling high flat walls on one side, and wild forest denizens on the other. They are not even clipped of an equal height, but shoot up here more, there less, so that the image of the wall is not kept up, and nothing is to be seen but the mutilated tree. If any one should turn columns out of marble statues to form a portico with them, he would be cried out upon for his barbarism, but if he only half cut his statues, and then made them do service as walls, we should thank him still less for his pains. They take a great deal of trouble, however, to bring these trees into order, and have, among other machines, one fifty or sixty feet high, consisting of several stages, and rolled about on castors to enable the gardeners to reach the branches the better with their shears and axes.

But we ought not in gardens like those of Schönbrunn, where there is so much that is admirable, to waste much time in finding fault with these lime trees. We willingly abandoned ourselves to the guidance of the obliging attendants of the gardens, and followed them through their vegetable treasury, and if unable to give a satisfactory account of its wealth, we will at least attempt some description of the more distinguished objects.

There are many plants here, not in the greenhouses but in the open garden, which we should seek elsewhere in vain. One of the most splendid specimens is the *Sophora Japonica*, a large magnificent tree, with excessively fine feathery leaves. It stands on a beautiful lawn, and the windings of its boughs, and the whole figure of the tree, are so picturesque, that it has been repeatedly painted, and has its portrait in the emperor's collection of pictures of the plants and trees of Schönbrunn.

Artists are almost constantly employed in these gardens, in drawing either for the emperor, or with scientific objects in view. The green and hot-houses are all handsome and spacious, and a new temple of the Dryads in right imperial style is now in progress of erection. Whenever a branch is broken by the wind, the vegetable surgeon is directly at hand to assist with iron rings, ropes, and bandages. By the root of the orchidaceæ we saw a potatoe laid for those worms to creep into, which would otherwise attack the plant itself. For several trees standing in the open air, separate huts are erected in the winter, for example, the *Acaucaria excelsa*; and this must be elevated every year, as the tree grows rapidly. Every plant produces, or attracts, some particular species of insect, and every where we saw the most judicious arrangements for their destruction. From the Brazilian fan palm long threads depend, and every one of these threads is a panegyric on the vigilance of the Schönbrunn gardeners, for they are preserved in their entire length, neither torn nor in any way injured, as we so often find them in other green-houses. The palms in which this garden is richer than either the Jardin des Plantes at Paris, or Kew Gardens near London, have very long, very fragile roots, which require the greatest care in planting, and that that care is here bestowed the healthy slender growth of the palms bear witness. The *Stenia pallida* has a beautiful blossom, which has the appearance of being formed from yellow wax, and is very easily broken off. To avoid this, every blossom is provided with a prop composed of the slenderest splinters; many other plants had the like, with the addition, where the plant was very tender, of a little cushion of some soft material between the prop and the flower. I did not see a single neglected or sickly-looking plant.

Among the rarities shown are also some *Dendrobium Pierardi*, which require no soil for their growth, but are kept like birds in wire cages, and hung up at windows, where it is only necessary to sprinkle them at times with water; the climbing Vanilla grows also in the air, notwithstanding the thickness of its leaves, and may be suspended by threads in a room: Sagopalm, (*Cycas circinalis*,) whose yearly growth, even in a Schönbrunn forcing house, is six or seven ells; a rich collection of Ericas from the Cape; and, lastly, a *Cactus cerreus Peruvianus*, eighty years old, and which has therefore passed nearly a century of its bare, fruitless life, riveted like Prometheus to the desolate rock.

THE FRATSCHELWEIBER.—FISHMONGERS AND DEALERS IN GAME.

The most celebrated of all the women of Vienna is, beyond doubt, Maria Theresa, but the most noted are the so-called "Fratschelweiber." Like their sisters in the cabbage-market of Königsberg, and the Halles of Paris, they are distinguished for their eloquence, their presence of mind, and their inexhaustible wit. It is said that the emperor Joseph went once incognito among them, and purposely overturned a basket of eggs, in order to have a specimen of their oratorical powers. Their chief seat is in the "Hof," one of the largest squares of the city, where they deal in vegetables, fruit, cheese, and other articles of food.

What I saw and heard of these interesting persons gave me more amusement than I can hope to give the reader by a description, for when the naïve originality of the Vienna dialect comes into print,* it gives no more idea of it as spoken, than the printed notes do of the sound of a piece of music.

I must confess, that often when I returned from the "Fratschel" market I used to feel as if I had been in a mad-house, so incessant and clapper-like had been the chatter about everything in and about the world —about the "*Germnudeln*" which they were recommending to Herr von Nachtigall, an old hairdresser, whose poverty shone out from every side of his worn and rent nether garments, but on whom they bestowed the "*von*" nevertheless because he held a few kreuzers in hand; about the butcher, "the stingy hound, who had sold them such a miserable little bit of meat to-day." They spared neither the emperor, the pope, nor their ministers, and, least of all, the people of rank and fashion, whom they saw driving about. I was one day witness of the little ceremony used with the latter. At the corner of the "Hof," a careless coachman ran over a boy. In an instant a crowd of women and men were in full pursuit of the flying

---

* No attempt has been made to translate the Austrian provincial dialect, of which numerous specimens occur in this part of M. Kohl's work.—*Tr.*

vehicle, in which sat a lady and gentleman of the higher class. But the Fratschelweiber paid not the smallest heed to their high nobility. " Catch 'em there, bring 'em back, the quality candle-snuffers! bring 'em back! the scum of a dunghill! To run over the poor boy!" were the compliments that ran from mouth to mouth, as the mob ran bawling after the gentles, who would probably have fared ill enough, if they had fallen into the hands of the irritated rabble. This class of persons in Vienna are by no means the patient, respectful, timid herd to be met with in other capitals of monarchical states; for example, in St. Petersburg, Moscow, Prague, &c. The child, whose cause was so energetically adopted by the Fratschel women, was not even a countryman, but a little Croat, such as are met with in all parts of Vienna, selling radishes and onions. Beyond a bruise or two, he had sustained no injury; indeed, he had rather been knocked down than run over. The women put on his broad-brimmed Croatian hat again, wiped carefully his wide mantle of thick white wool, in which he looked like a diminutive Orlando in a giant's armour, and bought some of his radishes to console him. The child, who understood not a word of the Fratschel jargon, looked round him in a scared manner, and then resumed his monotonous cry, " *An guten ratti, ratti,*" (good radishes), the only German he knew. These Croats are very numerous in Vienna, and form no inconsiderable portion of the populace there. As they sell nothing but onions and radishes, the Fratschel ladies are persuaded that Croatia must be a poor country, and produce nothing else. In the suburbs, there are, in the public-houses of the lowest class, great dormitories for them which they call Croat quarters. There when the ravens return from the fields to Stephan's tower, the poor Croats huddle together after the fatigues of the day, and sleep in the same thick cloaks that have sheltered them from the heat during the day. " They live like so many cattle," said one of the Fratschel women to me, " they haven't even a bedstead, let alone a mattrass. They lie o' nights and holidays on their bellies, and are fit for nothing but to sell onions."

How long the peculiar habits and arrangements of a town will maintain themselves, and more frequently in small things than in great, is seen in the fish-stands of Vienna, which, in passing through Leopoldstadt, are discovered to the right of Ferdinand's-bridge. Although these stands are so easily moved, consisting merely of sheds upon floats, that look as if they were anchored by the river-side only for a time, yet they have made good their claim to the place for centuries, and as long as people have consumed fish in Vienna, so long has it been customary to offer it for sale at that part of the Danube-canal. The corporation of fishmongers belong, in many German cities built on rivers, to the oldest and most privileged bodies, from a very simple cause, namely, that they carry on a business which naturally was the first to arise in the immediate neighbourhood of a river, and one that often occasioned the foundation of a town there. In Vienna they enjoy great privileges, which have been ratified by all their emperors; yet, in modern times no trade, with the exception of that of wig-makers, has declined so much from its former splendour. The reformation, and the present more lax observance of the fasts, even in catholic countries, have greatly reduced the consumption of fish; and great are the complaints in this respect in Vienna.

" In former times," said an old dealer in fish to me, " there often came fifteen or sixteen waggons laden with fish to Vienna, and now they call out as if it were a wonder if only two or three come in one after the other. My late father, who lived in the good times, used to bring three or four hundred measures of sprats at once to market, and I, his son and successor, think myself extremely lucky if I can get rid of thirty, so much are the times changed. Formerly, I mean about forty or fifty years ago, people had some regard for religion and fast-days, and I know some great houses where on Fridays not as much meat was allowed as would go on the point of a knife. And then the convents in Vienna, what a consumption of fish was there! There were the Carmelites, the Augustines, the Minorites, the Barbarites, and all the rest of them! I recollect there was one convent where the monks used to fast the whole year through, and where we used to carry the most delicate kinds of fish by cart-loads. But that's all over now. The great people don't trouble themselves about fasting and eating fish, and even the monks are grown more impious. Nobody, now-a-days, knows what a fine fish is; my father used to tell me that in Maria Theresa's time as much as two and three hundred weight of *fokasch* would be sold at a time. Now when a great man buys a fokasch, it's easily carried home in a napkin, and they seem all to have made a vow to eat nothing but flesh.

"And then many changes in housekeeping have done a great deal of mischief to us fish-dealers. Formerly in most great houses the servants used to be fed by their masters, and then it was more with fish than with meat, which was dearer. Now the domestics have become more independent, they have more wages and feed themselves, and like better to eat flesh than fish. Formerly, a counsellor's lady would go herself to the market to buy fish; now she leaves a lthat to the cook, who is become a greater lady than the *court counselloress*, and people choose rather to buy from the game-market than from us. Then folks are all more disorderly and extravagant than they used to be. Once even poor folks would leave so much behind them that their children might at least have their dish of fish at the funeral—now they leave nothing but debts, with which the devil himself could buy no fish. In old times at every dinner some choice fish was always amongst the chief dishes—it is not so now. The Lichtenstein seldom gives a dinner, the Kollowrat only once a month. But such noblemen as old Zichy (God bless his memory), he used plenty of fish—liked it well, and knew when it was good—there are no such men now—at least not in Vienna, and it seems almost as if people thought God had put the fish in the water for nothing."

Up to the last point my worthy trader might be in the right, but there is after all, plenty of fish still eaten in Vienna, and even distant waters are laid under contribution. The Platten See in Hungary furnishes in great abundance the delicate fokasch.

In winter, oysters, lobsters and crabs are brought from the Adriatic, the former packed in ice, the latter in chests pierced with holes upon laurel leaves, on which they rest before they have reached them on the table of the gourmand. The ponds of Bohemia also yield a great quantity of fish, but the larger part of the consumption is supplied by that great arm of the Danube that passes through the city.

The fishermen, from whom there is as much to be learned now as at the time of the Christian era, gave me much interesting information concerning their trade. They told me that the sturgeons ascend to about sixteen miles from Vienna. Presburg is the highest point where they are caught;

the greater part come from Pesth. Four years ago they captured there a sturgeon of ten cwt., the largest that had been seen in Vienna for a long time. Up as far as Ulm, no eels* are found in the Danube or its tributaries. All the fish of this species, used in Vienna, come down from Bohemia. Neither is there any salmon in the Danube—it comes from the Elbe and the Rhine; salmon trout are caught in the lakes belonging to the estates of the Salt-chamber. *Kopen*, perhaps from *kopf* (head), are very small fish with very large heads. They are caught in the same waters as the trout, in the Traun and other mountain streams, and are animals of prey. When properly dressed it is a very well tasted fish, and is used sometimes as a garnish to dishes whereon larger fish are served. The finest fish in the Danube are the *schill* and *huchen*. The latter is like a trout in form, but weighs from fifty to sixty pounds. As the *kopen* are without bones, so the *huchen* have no scales, or scales so small as to be scarcely perceptible, for which reason they are the favourite fish of the Vienna Jews, who eat no fish with scales, and are, therefore, so in love with *huchen* that they will pay almost any price for it. The small sturgeon, often so strongly recommended by the hotel waiters to strangers in Vienna, come from the Hungarian Danube. They are easily entangled by the snout in a net, and caught many at a time. I was told some remarkable circumstances relative to the influence of the waters flowing through the city. The fish-dealers maintain that all water coming from the streets, canals, and sluices, is so poisonous, that it kills the fish in immense quantities. After a sudden violent shower in summer, when the whole town disgorges its filth, and the contents of all the drains stream at once into the Danube, many thousand cwt. (the fish-dealers weigh the creatures in thought, while they are still at large in their own element), are sure to lose their lives. In the summer of 1833, the Danube was extremely low; suddenly a violent storm of rain raised its waters nearly ten feet higher, and the stream from the city came out like ink. The fish, which are cleanly animals, rushed as if quite desperate to the surface, leapt high into the air, and fell in multitudes upon the banks of the river; a most stupid proceeding on their part, as by going up a little farther, they might have come to clear water.

The words that had escaped my friend the fishmonger respecting the great consumption of game, which it was evident had excited his envy not a little, induced me to think that I should find this branch of industry in a more flourishing condition than his own, and so in fact I did. When we consider the wealth of Bohemia in wild animals suited to the table—when we consider the numerous water-fowl that frequent the lakes of Hungary, the large scale on which the stag-hunts are carried on to the south of the Platten See, the chamois met with in great herds in the neighbouring Styria, and when we consider that Vienna lies exactly in the middle of these inexhaustible preserves, it may be readily believed that its markets are the best supplied with this species of *comestible* of any city in Europe. How great the quantity consumed was shown shortly before my arrival on the following occasion. The city authorities had subjected all game brought into Vienna to a tax of six kreuzers per head, and the impost

---

* There are no eels in the South Russian streams, nor in any of the rivers flowing into the Black Sea, till we arrive at a very considerable distance from the sea. So at least I was assured by a person well acquainted with them.

was levied even on every little wild duck and teal from the Danube levels. As these smaller articles could not bear so heavy a taxation, the trade in them ceased almost entirely. Hereupon the dealers found themselves obliged to represent to the authorities the greatness of the injury done them; that they had been accustomed to bring half a million yearly of these smaller birds to Vienna, which were now never brought at all; that numbers of persons who had gained a livelihood by catching teal and wild-duck, were now suddenly thrown out of employ, and that hence it would be necessary to impose the tax only on the larger kinds. The remonstrance was attended to, chiefly at the instance of one wealthy and influential tradesman, with whom I became acquainted, and I found much occasion to admire the vast nature of his dealings, and the extent and variety of his information. To buy a piece of game from the hunter, and give it to the cook to be dressed, seems so very simple an affair, that it is not easy at first to understand how it should give a man any position in the state. The links of our social transactions, however, are like those of the sciences, so intimately connected one with the other, that it is scarcely possible to carry on any one branch on a grand scale, without becoming in some measure familiar with others. It would be different if the stag had only flesh; he would then concern the cook only. But his antlers are wanted by the turner, his skin by the tanner. The feathers of the birds are of use in many trades; the naturalist is often indebted to the civility of the dealer in wild fowl. The grandees find it worth while to give him good words, to increase the profit of their hunting-grounds, or to secure the supply of their kitchens. His connexion extends even to the imperial court, for it is known that on extraordinary occasions, such as a visit from the heir to the Russian throne, he may be relied on for extraordinary supplies, such as a Polish elk, or a set of Russian heathcocks.

As I was already partially informed of these relations, I was not at all surprised to find my game merchant a clever, enlightened man, well acquainted with many branches of natural history, not ignorant of anatomy and geology, thoroughly informed of all that related to the chase, and the manner of life and habits of the animals; one who had studied the works of Cuvier and Buffon, and could severely criticize the exaggerations, flourishes, and extravagant assertions of the latter; who spoke of Count X., and Prince Y., as of persons with whom he was well acquainted, and related how the government had had it in contemplation to effect some change in the game *resources* as he called them, but had desisted on his representations. Nor did it afterwards excite my astonishment, when I found an artist employed among the antlers of various kinds, and among the plaster casts of different descriptions of animals. While I was with my merchant, there came a professor of natural history, and said to him, " I am come, my dear Mr. N. to *smell* about a little, and see if you have any thing new for me." And he was followed by a gentleman who also came to *smell* about, and invite Mr. N. to a hunting-party. These dealers in game are as fond of the peculiar odour of the wild creatures they deal in, as mariners are of their pitch and tar; and use the expression *smell* about as a technical term for a visit. I "*smelt*" often in at the house of Mr. N., and always found some interesting people there. Those who have much to do with nature are almost always interesting. One day I met there a Styrian chamois hunter, who related to me many interesting adventures he had met with in pursuit of those animals. Observing that I occasionally made a note of what I heard, he said, "Ah, write it all down, and I'll tell you something about the cunning of the chamois that no one has heard before." The previous year he had found a geis (female chamois) ready to bring forth. He had followed her for eight days to see where she would deposit her young. Sometimes he took off his shoes, and climbed on his bare feet like a cat; and once when he had to clamber up the steep face of a rock, he cut off all the buttons from his clothes that they might not make a "jingle." At last he discovered the two young ones in a niche at the top of a high rock, in a "*kästl*," as the hunters call it. The little ones were sporting around their mother, who glanced from time to time down into the valley to watch for any hostile approach. To avoid being seen, our hunter made a great circuit, and so reached a path that led to the "*kästl*." Exactly in front of the niche the rock descended perpendicularly to an immense depth. At the back was another steep descent. Some fragments of rock formed a kind of bridge between the larger masses, but these were placed too high to be accessible to the little ones, and could only be available for their mother. The hunter rejoiced as he contemplated this position, and pressed upon the animals, whose escape seemed impossible. When the old one caught sight of him, and measured with a glance the unfavourable disposition of the rocks, she sprung upon the hunter with the fury that maternal love will breathe into the most timid creatures. The danger of such attacks from the chamois is less from the thrust, which is not very violent, than from the endeavour of the animals to fix the points of their horns, which are bent like fish-hooks, somewhere in the legs of the hunter, and then press him backwards down the precipices. It happens sometimes that the chamois and hunter thus entangled roll into the abyss together. Our hunter was in no condition to fire at the advancing chamois, as he found both hands necessary to sustain himself on the narrow path; he therefore warded off the blows as well as he could with his feet, and kept still advancing. The anguish of the mother increased. She dashed back to her young, coursed round them with loud cries, as if to warn them of the danger, and then leaped upon the before-named fragments of rock, from which the second but more difficult egress from the grotto was to be won. She then leaped down again to her little ones, and seemed to encourage them to attempt the leap. In vain the little creatures sprang and wounded their foreheads against the rocks that were too high for them, and in vain the mother repeated again and again her firm and graceful leap to show them the way. All this was the work of a few minutes, whilst the hunter had again advanced some steps nearer. He was just preparing to make the last effort when the following picture, which was the particular circumstance he referred to in speaking of the chamois's cunning, met his astonished eyes. The old chamois, fixing her hind legs firmly on the rock behind, had stretched her body to its utmost length, and planted her fore feet on the rock above, thus forming a temporary bridge of her back. The little ones seemed in a minute to comprehend the design of their mother, sprang upon her like cats, and thus reached the point of safety. The picture only lasted long enough to enable their pursuer to make the last step. He sprang into the niche, thinking himself now sure of the young chamois, but all three were off with the speed of the wind, and a couple of shots that he sent after the fugitives, merely announced by their echo to the surrounding rocks, that he had missed his game.

The chamois are more numerous in the Tyrol than in Switzerland, and more numerous in the Styrian Alps than in the Tyrol. The wild goats come only as far as the opposite western end of the Alpine chain. They have been quite driven away from the eastern and middle portions, the highest and most inaccessible summits of the Savoyan Alps alone afford at present that degree of solitude and rocky wildness which is requisite for them. They are now protected in Savoy by a very severe law, which condemns to death any person who shall kill a wild-goat. Nevertheless, there are people who cannot withstand the temptation of aiming at these horned kings of the Graian and Julian Alps, and it is said there are at this moment in the prisons of Savoy several of these adventurous hunters, who have been condemned to death, and have had their sentence commuted into twenty years' imprisonment. Two years ago a couple of living animals of this species passed through Vienna on their way to Russia, a present from the ruler of Savoy to the emperor. I heard that some time ago a Vienna dealer had offered a large price for one, and that in consequence a Savoyard had shot an old one and delivered it in Vienna. The man was discovered and pursued by the royal huntsmen, but was lucky enough to escape by the glaciers into Switzerland, the paths being better known to him than to his pursuers.

My Vienna friend told me that by means of his acquaintance in Hungary and Bohemia, he often received rare animals, not directly connected with his business, and that scarcely an animal roamed the Austrian forests of which some specimen had not visited his shop. He took me afterwards into his ice-cellar, where I saw a great variety of creatures lying on the ice. He had had the cellar hung with Hungarian mats, and the ice was likewise covered with mats. He said that it was not sufficiently known to the owners of ice-cellars, that by means of these mats the ice could be much longer preserved than when it came into immediate contact with the air and the walls, and that a smaller quantity of it was therefore sufficient. Among his plaster casts of heads and antlers he had those of an enormous elk. He had given several copies of the latter to Austrian noblemen, who wished for them to decorate their castles, a fancy that never occurs to the gentlemen of Lithuania and Poland, the native country of these creatures. We may see by all this on how large a scale the game dealers of Vienna carry on their business, and how highly its resources are developed. It were to be wished that the learned and cultivated on their side would sometimes turn the knowledge and special details which such people have obtained from nature, a little more to account.

SUMMER-NIGHTS' DREAMS AND FLOWER FESTIVALS.

In the Sans-souci gardens at Mödling, there are nine tents of tastefully draped red and white cloths, pitched in a meadow, each of which is dedicated to one of the Muses, whose names, embroidered on flags, flutter over the tops: Calliope, Clio, Euterpe, and so on. In the centre stands a tenth, wherein a Vienna leader flourishes as Apollo, and regales the Muses with Strauss's waltzes. These muses are young maidens and old women, attended by cavaliers and children, who resort to those nomadic airy temples to drink coffee. Taking refreshments in this poetical style is quite in the taste of the Vienna people, whose oriental fancy delights in mingling the loftiest matters with those of every day life, and always selects the most high soaring inscriptions for the most trivial things.

The Vienna people are like great potentates, who will admit wisdom only disguised in the motley; but they have reflection enough to recognise the hand of destiny that mingles in the most insignificant occurrences of life. Therefore they will drink their coffee in the temple of the Muses, and swallow the bitter draught of truth sweetened with the sugarplum of cheerfulness. Hence the extraordinary dramatis personæ of Raimund's invention, the Sibyls as old maids, the Genii as bowling-green attendants, the conjurers and magicians from Warasdin and Donaueschingen, whopour forth unweariedly trifling jests and sportive wisdom in Swabian and Hungarian German. The titles of Raimund's pieces and their prevailing style are pretty well known amongst us, not so the style in which the proprietors of places of public resort invite the public to their enchanting popular festivals. I paid at first little attention to the announcements with which every corner of the streets was covered. But one evening late, *i. e.* at eleven o'clock, at which hour Vienna is as still as a mouse, I met a man laden with an enormous mass of printed paper, busied in pulling down the old bills and pasting up new. I asked him to let me look at some of them, and he threw down a whole bale before me. Herr Lanner announced a fête with new decorations and illuminations, under the name of " A Summer Night's Dream." Herr Strauss had found a yet more attractive title for another fête, which was to take place at Sperle. By the glimmering light of the lantern I read " Fancy and Harmony in the rose-tinted vestments of Joy, a rural flower festival and ball." On a third bill the " renowned Daum" promised a " Festive soirée and conversazione in his Elysium." Four characteristic bands were announced in the various localities, and further " the much admired original representations newly arranged for the present season," would take place as follows :

In Asia (one part of the gardens) would be displayed three saloons, brilliantly illuminated in the oriental taste, an avenue of palm trees as a promenade, adorned with the newly-invented transparent Iris garlands, and at the end the splendid principal view, giving an allegorical picture of Asia, beyond which the musicians would be heard but not seen.

In elegant Europe (another part of the gardens) a Roman triumphal arch would be changed in a moment to an amphitheatre, wherein the Olympic games were to be produced in appropriate costume.

In America (a lawn) would be performed the admired Railway passage to Australia, led by the gracefully adorned ladies and gentlemen, Apollo, Pluto, Diana, and Minerva.

In Africa (a fourth part of " Elysium"), beside many favourite performances, Herr Starsch, from Berlin, would have the honour of exhibiting many new feats of dexterity, and, in the splendidly decorated Harem, an African summer fête would be given.

As a souvenir of this conversazione, every lady would receive, " in a festive manner, two views of Elysium," with an explanation. For the greater gratification of the respected visiters, the atmospheric air would be impregnated with the newly-invented Schönbrunn flower perfume.

I believe that not in India itself could a fête for the multitude be announced in more pompous fashion. I noticed many others announced, as "Nights in Paradise," "The Dance of the Sylphs," &c. Each surpassed the other in high-flown fancies. The chief allurements to all these places are dancing and good music, and the proprietors endeavour on such occasions to procure some new compositions of the favourite composers, Lanner, Strauss, or Fahrbach, composed expressly for that evening. This music has generally some very striking title. A new waltz of Strauss's was called the "Electric Spark," another the "Evening Star," a third "Tears of Joy." Musical soirées and "Harmonious pictures" are almost always united with these fêtes, and how far the composers of Vienna go with their "harmony painting" may be seen from the following specification of such a "painting" produced when the archducal conqueror of Saïde was the hero of the day.

"Storming of Saïde (a new musical picture).
"First Part. Approach of the English Fleet.
"Second Part. Approach of the Austrian Fleet.
"Third Part. Characteristics of the Allies, and the Enemy.
"Fourth Part. Summons to surrender, refusal, disembarkation, attack, cannonading, bombardment, storming and conflagration.
"Fifth Part. Joyful demonstrations and thanksgivings of the Victors.
"Sixth Part. Celebration of Victory and triumphal march."

No parties in Vienna are so numerous as the musical ones, which have their ramifications from the highest society to the very lowest. Strauss, the most celebrated concert master, Lanner the most original, and Fahrbach, also well known to fame, are the leaders and demigods of these meetings, the tribunes of the people in Vienna. Like the Roman tribunes, they exert themselves to the utmost to enlarge and strengthen their party. When at Sperle, or in the public gardens, they flourish their bows in elegant little temples, amidst a grove of orange trees, rhododendrons, and other plants, and execute the newest and most effective compositions with their perfectly organised bands, (Strauss enrols none but Bohemians,) they seem in a measure the chiefs and leaders of the public. Before them stands a listening throng, with whom they are constantly coquetting, nodding to their friends in the midst of their work, and giving them a friendly smile as they execute some difficult passage. Every distinguished effort is rewarded by loud applause, and new or favourite pieces by a stormy "Da Capo." Even in the common dancing-rooms, the music is so little secondary, that the dance is often interrupted by a tumult of applause for the musicians and composers. Even at the fêtes of the Schwarzenbergs and Lichtensteins, a certain familiar understanding with the favourite musicians may be observed, which, among a people less enthusiastic in the matter of dance-music, would be thought out of place.

Strauss and his colleagues are always on the look out for new inventions in the field of music. In almost every season they produce some new clashing or clanging instrument, or some extraordinary manœuvre on an old one. Last summer, in a Pot Pourri, Strauss made all his violinists, violoncellists, and basses, lift up their voices and sing the Rhine song, "*Sie sollen ihn nicht haben*," which, with the basses especially, had a very comic effect. Lanner enticed the public by means of a young man, who sung a duet between a gentleman and a lady, in which the high and delicate tones of the woman were as accurately imitated as the depth and strength of the man's voice. No musical soirée ended without an imitation of the report of fireworks, wherein the rushing course of the rocket, and the sparkling hiss of the wheels, mingled in and died away with the musical tones. The next day then you are sure to read a long article in one of the journals beginning in this fashion: "Again has our justly esteemed, our inexhaustible Strauss (or Lanner or Fahrbach) astonished and enchanted us with a new effort of his admirable genius. All who had the good fortune to be among his audience," &c.

There is a printing-office in Vienna, the sole employment of which is the announcement of these fêtes, plays, and concerts, nothing else being printed there but placards. The proprietor of this establishment, Mr. Hirshfeld, has many people in his service, who thoroughly understand the most striking way of announcing such matters to the street public, by the judicious arrangement of the alluring words " Bal brillant," " Magic illumination," " Rose-tinted garments of pleasure," &c. I visited this printing office, where the readers were employed in correcting the style and orthography of waiters, &c., and preparing their eloquent productions for the press. The monster types are all of wood; the effect of the great black letters upon men's eyes and fancies is always speculated on, and the pictorial announcements of estates for sale by lottery, when all the letters are composed of pictures of castles and rural views, and where every million is represented entwined with the elegant flowery wreaths of hope, are really masterpieces in a psychological as in a xylographic point of view. The unusual words, or those that do not frequently occur, are composed, as occasion may require, from single letters, but the celebrated names, Strauss, Lanner, im Sperl,—Elysium, Prater,—Golden Pear, &c., are cut out of single blocks, and many duplicates are always kept ready for use at Hirshfeld's. It is the same with the standing phrases, such as " Splendid Illuminations," " Dancing Soirée," &c. Whoever has arrived at the honours of stereotype in Hirshfeld's printing-office, may deem himself a celebrated man within the walls of Vienna.

It is somewhat remarkable, although natural enough, that even these kind of announcements and posting-bills, on which the most innocent things in the world are made known to the public, are subject to the censorship, in fact to a double censorship; firstly, to the supreme censorial authorities who bestow the " Imprimatur," and secondly, to the subordinate police authorities who make any emendations held necessary according to circumstances and localities.

"They play them a trick for all that sometimes," said my bill-sticker, whom I encountered in the night as before mentioned. " Lately there was a ball at Sperl, where they danced till six o'clock in the morning, although they announced on their bill that it was to end after midnight; and when they were called to account by the police, they said that six o'clock in the morning was after midnight."

A Mr. von X. has farmed from the government, for the annual sum of five thousand florins, the exclusive privilege of posting bills about the town, and he has the right of suspending, on gates and public buildings, great wooden frames, on which bills are pasted. If he find, elsewhere, a suitable place for such things, the city authorities give him permission to make use of it. By Christmas presents to the upper servants, he also procures leave from the owners of houses to make use of their walls.

THE PROJECTED NEW QUARTER.

One of the most interesting things I saw in Vienna was the beautifully executed wooden model of the projected improvements and additions to the inner part of the city; five of the most considerable bankers in the city, Sina, Pouthon, Eskeles, Maier, and Corth, have united for the plan and execution. This plan is—in Europe at least—so unusual, on so grand a style, and so judicious, that one cannot but wish it success, and linger a little in the consideration of an undertaking, which has for its object so considerable an extension of the city.

Perhaps in no city of Germany does there exist so peculiar a relation between the city properly so called, and its suburbs, as in Vienna. Four-fifths of the population of Vienna live in the suburbs, &c. Prague, the city which offers the most direct contrast in this respect, is almost wholly city. The reason is that Vienna, notwithstanding its antiquity, attained at a later period the dignity of being a sovereign's residence than Prague. In the twelfth century Vienna occupied only the fifth part of the present site of the city, and only a fortieth of the whole space, including the suburbs; at that time Prague had nearly two-thirds of its present circumference. It is only within the last two hundred years, since the time of Rudolph the Second, whose general residence was Prague, that the Emperors have resided constantly in Vienna. From that period the extensive suburbs have grown around the heart of the capital, and hence the contrast between the commodiousness and regularity of plan in the former, and the extravagant maze of building within the walls of the city. The streets are narrow, the houses six, seven, and eight stories high, and buildings, whose grandeur demands a great public square for their display, are stuck into narrow alleys, and lost in a forest of houses. In many of the streets it has been impossible to make a trottoir half an ell in breadth, the carriages are often compelled to drive so sharply against the walls and windows of the houses, that it is an ordinary manœuvre of the pedestrians of Vienna, to save themselves from a crush by leaping on the steps of the vehicle. Carriages are sometimes to be seen with pedestrians clinging to it before and behind, and full often may they have occasion to thank heaven for having found a house-door open in time of need. The numerous thoroughfares, or *Durchhäuser*, through private houses and courtyards, to which the public has a conventional right of way, are of no small service to pedestrians. The whole city is pierced through and through with them, like an ant hill, and those who have the clue of this labyrinth, may run a considerable distance under shelter, and avoid the dangers of the carriages altogether. In no other city of Germany is there so great or so uninterrupted a stream of vehicles; the corner houses are, in consequence, particularly protected against this dangerous flood. All of them in the heart of the city have large stones placed slantingly, armed with an iron cap and rings, as thick as a man's finger, and the extreme smoothness which these coats of mail usually display, shows how often carriages must have ground against them. The unlucky pedestrian is provided with no such defence, and it may be a question whether more people have their limbs crushed by chariot wheels in Vienna or in Bengal.

All these evils have of late become more palpable with the growth of the suburbs, all of which naturally have their rendezvous in the centre of the city; not only have the people of rank who live in summer without the lines, their winter palaces within, but the merchants and manufacturers, although their dwelling-houses may be without in the suburbs, must have their shops, warehouses, and business localities in the city itself; and the majority of the inhabitants, for one reason or other, desire to possess a little *pied à terre* there. Shut up in its narrow middle-age armour of bastions, walls, and ditches, the city cannot extend itself as the suburbs have done, which have stretched further and further into the level country, and swallowed up village after village in an avalanche of houses. As in all other cities of Germany, the old wrynecked, crooked streets of Vienna have been patched and polished, the passage houses have been increased in number wherever it was possible; some buildings that were especially in the way have been bought at a high price and pulled down, all projections and excrescences have been pared away, and the pavement laid down is as good as can be wished. But in an old city like this, where the houses stand like rocks, and the streets run through them like gullies and mountain passes, improvement is no easy matter, and all efforts of the kind lag far behind the wants of the increasing population. The grand difficulty is the fortification of the inner city. This necessitates a breadth of space not less than from three to four hundred fathoms (the Glacis) between the wall and the suburbs. If the works could be done away with altogether, and the glacis built over, the city and the suburbs would form one handsome and commodious whole. The advantage would be immense for the inhabitants, for a very easy calculation will show, that the maintenance of the fortifications costs them millions yearly, directly and indirectly. Living would be incalculably cheaper, and great sums would be saved in conveyances and other matters therewith connected; they would live in handsomer houses, and traffic and population would increase from all these causes.

However, from political motives, the government cannot resolve upon giving up the fortifications, although we have abundance of unfortified capitals, and many are of opinion, that in case of a war, those of Vienna would be of little service. The part of the glacis between the Scotch gate and the Danube channel, is particularly broad, and on this circumstance the association of bankers have founded their grand plan for the extension of the inner city. They propose to destroy the old fortifications in this part, erect new ones beyond, and thus gain a free space for new buildings of not less than eighty thousand square fathoms. They have offered to effect the removal of the old fortifications at their own expense, and have had a plan drawn up by the architect Forster, according to which the new quarter of the city may be most commodiously united to the old ones. The public buildings, the churches, theatres, fountains, monuments, gates, &c., which the new quarter will require, these gentlemen will also erect at their own expense, and give compensation for the lost ground of the glacis, on condition that the sites for private houses shall be sold for their advantage. As before said, they have caused the plan, in all its details, to be executed in wood, and exhibited to the public. The old dark misshapen Vienna, in whose obscurities so many a fair pearl is lost, would thereby gain a bright regular magnificent appendix, whose equal might be sought in vain.

A large open place with monuments to the emperor Francis, and the first statesmen of his time, and a church in the Gothic style, is proposed as the centre of the new quarter. A splendid range of dwelling-houses, built in different styles, to avoid a disagreeable monotony, is to form a quay along the Danube, an ornament which at present is altogether wanting in Vienna; and those public buildings now in the worst condition, the Exchange, the Post-office, a theatre, with two supplementary buildings intended for institutions for the arts, and an extensive bazaar, are projected on a very grand scale. On the river they propose to form docks with large warehouses; and four new bridges, to correspond with streets already existing, are to unite the old city with the new. The projected new streets are to continue the old ones and yet maintain a symmetry with each other.

This model has been exhibited to the emperor and the archdukes, and admired by them, and therefore hopes are entertained that permission will be given to carry it into execution.

The chief subject of hesitation is again the fortifications; in removing a part, it is feared the whole may be endangered. Might not the invention of the archduke Maximilian, in the Towers of Linz, help them out of the difficulty. The whole city, suburbs included, might be girdled with them, and thus the whole brought within a circle of fortifications. With respect to the glacis itself, full of monotonous avenues of sickly trees, dusty spaces, and swampy ditches, there would be little loss. It is too large to be laid out as a garden, as has been done in some cities. But smaller and more modest spaces might be left free to be employed for this purpose.

THE QUARTER OF THE NOBILITY, AND THAT OF THE MANUFACTURERS.

The most animated parts of Vienna lie round Stephen's Place, the Graben, and the High Market; the quietest parts are the "Burg" from the Place of the Minorites, the Herrengasse, Teinfalt Street, the back and front Schenkengasse, &c. "Our great people live here," said a Vienna man to me, "and here it is still, still as a mouse." There is not a shop in the whole neighbourhood, no busy hum of traffic. It rains jolts and thrusts in the other streets, and one is put to it to keep from under the coach-wheels and horses' hoofs. It swarms there with Croats, Slavonians, Servians, Germans, and God knows what nation besides, while nothing is to be seen in the aristocratic quarter but silent palaces, before whose doors liveried laqueys are lounging as if they were masters not only of the houses but of the whole street. In this silent quarter—the Tein quarter—are the palaces of the Lichtensteins, Stahrembergs, Harrachs, Festetics, Colloredos, Esterhazys, Trautmansdorfs, and Schönborns. Antique escutcheons are displayed before the houses, dating from Rudolph of Hapsburg or Charlemagne, and the golden fleece gleams from the roofs. If the little sons of these grandees clamber over the roofs like the boys in other towns, they may gather all manner of aristocratic reminiscences among the chimney-pots. Here also stand the proud edifices of the Hungarian and Transylvanian Chanceries, the States House, the Court and State Chancery, the Bank, and several of the superior tribunals. The whole space occupied by buildings so important to the empire is not more than two hundred fathoms in length and breadth; there is more than one public square of that size in St. Petersburg, and it may be safely asserted that in no other European kingdom is the great nobility so narrowly lodged. There are, nevertheless, buildings here stately enough, if duly scattered, to adorn a whole capital. Not far from the Tein quarter, in the neighbourhood of the Jews' Place, is another where the manufacturers congregate. Instead of armorial bearings before the houses, we see the firms of cotton and silk manufacturers, warehouses for cloths, shawls, woollen fabrics, Fischamenter cotton yarn, white and coloured knitting-cotton, silks, stuffs, &c. These are only the warehouses from which goods are sold wholesale to the merchants; the retail dealers are to be found elsewhere, and the manufactories are in the suburbs. There, especially in the western part,—there are whole quarters of them, all of recent date. In times of yore Vienna was a Roman encampment, then the little capital of the Austrian dukes, among hundreds of others a German imperial city; and although as the imperial residence it became the centre of commerce for the empire, it is but very lately that it has been the chief seat of manufactories, whose articles of taste are scattered over all parts of the Austrian and a great part of the non-Austrian world.

Gumpendorf, Laimgrube, and Mariahilf, are the suburbs in which nearly the whole population is employed in manufactories. This is the case likewise in the villages of Funfhaus, Sechshaus, and others. Here the simple and uniform dwellings of the weavers and spinners are seen by hundreds, and on entering from the Tein quarter, we seem to be entering another world. The raw cotton comes here from two directions, from Egypt over Trieste, and from America and the West Indies over Hamburg. The yarn dealers, spinners, weavers, and printers, all live near each other, and the merchandise passes from neighbour to neighbour, or from quarter to quarter, till it reaches the hands of the merchants and consumers. Some of the manufacturers have also establishments in Bohemia, where wages are lower, and several have them on the Saxon frontier; but these are merely for show, little work being done there, though a great deal of English twist is smuggled over the frontier. The English can furnish yarn to the manufacturers of Vienna cheaper than these can buy it from their own spinners in the suburbs. The latter enjoy, therefore, a protection in a fifteen per cent. duty, which, however, is considerably reduced by smuggling. In consequence of this protection, which the weavers of Vienna do not desire, because, without it, they could purchase the English yarn more cheaply, they are constantly at feud with their neighbours the spinners. Both have their meetings and unions for the protection of their separate interests, and both seek to make good their cause with the authorities. The weavers have lately failed in their machinations against the protective duty; the spinners, nevertheless, entertain fears for its duration; without it, they would not be able to make head against the English. Be they as diligent as they will, and let their machines be ever so well constructed, the spinners of Manchester, at the fountain-head of the commerce of the world, would still possess advantages too great to be competed with by those of Vienna, though with the best will in the world. To mention one only: the Manchester spinners have a railroad to Liverpool, which enables them to purchase the cotton in smaller quantities, as they may want it. They may use it up to-day to the last thread, and send to-morrow to Liverpool for a new supply. It is, therefore, easy to follow every variation of price, buy small quantities when it is dear, and larger when it is cheap; whereas the spinners of Vienna, whether they will or not, must take large quantities at any price, lest their work should come altogether to a stand-still. The great speculators of England, also, have no existence in Vienna. These speculators make constant purchases of yarn, because the channels of the world are open to them, and they are, consequently, always sure of a market for their wares. In Vienna, they spin almost exclusively for the Austrian monarchy. There is no intermediate purchaser between the weaver and spinner, and the former will buy no more than he has an immediate occasion for.

The advantages which the English manufacturers have over those of Vienna, and indeed over those of the whole world, the manufacturers of Vienna have again over the other manufacturers of the Austrian monarchy. In Vienna, they have the best information of what is wanted by the Slavonians, Croats, Poles, Transylvanians, and from Vienna their wants and tastes are supplied. The old-fashioned gold stuffs used for the upper Austrian caps are manufactured in Vienna, so are the silver buttons in use throughout Hungary, and the black silk handkerchiefs, with red borders, which the Magyar shepherds twist round their throats. It is the same with hundreds of other articles. Being also the head-quarters of fashion, Vienna not only supplies these people with what they want, but with what they ought to want. Vienna fashions, and Vienna wares, exercise their influence not only along the whole course of the Danube to the Black Sea, but even in Poland and Russia, extending even in some instances into the Turkish territory.

Persons who understand these things do, indeed, assert that Vienna productions will not bear a very severe examination. " They are but trumpery fabrications," said a native, well acquainted with London and Paris. " Every thing here is, as it were, *blown* together. We of Vienna are frivolous and fickle, but our taste is good, and we look more to graceful forms than solid quality." Comparing them with what London and Paris can produce, this may be true ; but if a line were drawn from the Baltic to the Adriatic, no city would be found east of it which could compare with Vienna in the quality, taste, or low price of its manufactures. Their low price has often procured them a sale not only throughout Germany, but even in America. They make, for instance, ornamental clocks, of an elegance of which no drawing-room need be ashamed, for eight and nine florins each, and shawls for ten and twelve.

The shawl manufacture is one of the most considerable ; more so, indeed, than any other in middle or eastern Europe. The low price of the shawls has produced a great demand for them in Turkey. A shawl manufacturer, whose word I have no reason to mistrust, thought there could not be less than four thousand persons employed in Vienna on those articles ; and this fact is the more remarkable, as the rise of this branch of manufacture dates only from the year 1812.

THE SHOPS OF VIENNA.

It would not be possible to give a very detailed account of the shops of Vienna and all therewith connected ; but I must intreat the reader to accompany me into some, which afford abundant means for obtaining an acquaintance with Vienna life, and furnish better pictures of it than do the columns of the *Allgemeine Zeitung.* Of the shops for silks and fancy goods, none are at present in higher feather than the " Laurel Wreath," and it is worthy of a visit, were it only for the profusion of the stuffs of all kinds displayed there. Before the "Laurel Wreath" rose to fame, "L'Amour" was the repository honoured with the patronage of the fashionable world, for it must be observed that all the shops of Vienna have their signs, by which they are much better known than by the names of their proprietors. " L'Amour," however, has quitted the field, and retired to a fine garden and villa in the suburbs. In good time, the " Laurel Wreath" will likewise withdraw to repose upon its own glories; for in Vienna no one pursues this occupation long before he finds himself enabled to take his place among the " rentiers," and, in leisure and retirement, to exchange his shop for a palace.

Formerly, Augsburg was the German city most renowned for its silver chased work; now it is Vienna. The greatest establishment of the kind is that of Mayerhofer and Klinkosch, at the corner of the Kohl-market. Their manufactory is in the suburbs, and well deserves a particular description. The greater part of the plate, to be transmitted as heirlooms in the noble families of Austria, is made there; hence a long series of their coats of arms, which must be stamped on every separate piece, is preserved. A large service of plate for Mehemet Ali was lately bespoken at this house. The number of great families resident in Vienna renders it no matter of wonder that the number of engravers and medalists should be great likewise, or that the art of engraving and composing heraldic shields should be industriously pursued. "It is only at Vienna," said one of these artists to me, " that the real true spirit of heraldry is to be found. We do not even admit a coat pricked elsewhere to be correct." There is not only a constant manufacture of new coats of arms for the accommodation of those persons who are daily elevated from the public offices to be founders of noble families, but a never-ceasing demand for the reproduction of the old time-honoured shields in steel, gold, silver, and precious stones. On all sides we find hands, and sometimes fair ones, employed on these hieroglyphics of heraldry.

When we consider that the Dutch have carried on many a war about nothing but peppercorns, that the whole Anglo-Chinese quarrel turns on a few chests of opium, and that tallow, tar, and train oil, are not among the least of Russia's interests, and have often been objects of attention to emperors and their ministers, I shall not be reproached with an undue attention to trifles, if I enter a shop of more than ordinary elegance, for the sale of stearine candles, on the Kohl-market. Out of the white and delicate mass of stearine, they had formed a cavern full of stalactites, wherein was lodged a stearine ice bear. The candles were put up in trophies, like the weapons in an arsenal, and, here and there, piled into columns, whose capitals were crowned with flowerpots; indeed, the whole shop was adorned with flowers. By the invention of stearine, tallow may be said to have been ennobled, and thus rendered admissible to the most distinguished drawing-rooms. In Vienna, it has obtained admission at court; church tapers are also formed of it, although it is still a subject of discussion among the high church authorities, whether it be admissible, instead of wax, in places of worship. If I remember rightly, some of the bishops have prohibited it. In the Greek church it will certainly never find a place; there the ancient, noble labour of the bee will be always held in honour.

One of the later established shops of Vienna is the repository for bronze wares, kept by an Englishman of the name of Morton, of which there are now branch establishments in Milan, Prague, Pesth, and other capitals of the empire. The handsomest thing I saw there was a bronze aviary of slender gilded wires entwined with exquisitely wrought flowers in wreaths. The first cage of this kind was brought from Paris, for the empress mother; seventeen have been since made, ten of which were destined for Constantinople. As I left the bronze shop, I was witness of a little scene, alike honourable for the human and the feathered animals who figured in it. A couple of young sparrows, making their first essay in flying with their parents over the roofs of the capital, had fallen exhausted into the street, where they were picked up and carried off by a boy, in whose hand they fluttered and chirped most pitifully. The parent birds followed, uttering most sorrowful cries, fluttering against the walls, perching on signs of the shops, and venturing even into the turmoil of the street. I begged the lad to let the young ones go, and as the cries of the old birds had already excited his compassion, he did so, but the creatures flying awkwardly against the walls, fell a second time into the street, and were again picked up. " Give them to me, for my children, give them to me," cried some women; but the remonstrances of the feathered parents were so pitiful, that in the end the whole assembled crowd (all of the lowest class) raised a general shout of " No, no, let them go, give them their liberty." There were some Jews among the populace, who cried out louder than any. Several times the birds were flung up into the air, and as often fell down again, amid the general lamentation of all present. At last a ladder was procured, all lent a hand to raise it against a small house, and hold it fast while some one mounted it and placed the little animals in safety on the roof. The parents flew to them immediately, and the whole family took wing, amid the general acclamations of the multitude; even a couple of " Glacéfränzel" (*petits maitres*) stood still at a little distance, and eyed the scene smilingly through their glasses.

Among the articles made in large quantities in Vienna are theatrical decorations, wherewith it furnishes all the stationary and locomotive theatres of the Austrian empire. Many shops confine themselves to the sale of frippery of this kind, particularly diadems, and jewelled finery for the queens and princesses of the mimic scene. Great numbers of these diadems are made by the goldsmiths of Vienna. They make use of a peculiar composition of lead, tin, and bismuth, called " stage composition." It has so good an effect, that at a little distance the deception is complete. The small cut sides of the metal are not raised, but put together in a concave form; when the light plays on them, they have all the appearance of precious stones.

It is a remarkable fact that the people of Hamburg have learnt only within the last fifteen years how to bind a ledger. Before that time the great folios were generally sent for from England. The people of Vienna have not yet mastered this apparently simple art, for Girardet, the most considerable bookbinder in the city, who employs thirty-six journeymen, maintains among them three Englishmen for all the solid and difficult work, and nine Frenchmen for that requiring delicate handling and taste. These people understand their work thoroughly, and what they do is admirably well done. They work apart from the German workmen, in order to preserve the mystery of their craft. There are many kinds of leather used for this purpose, which are not to be had in Germany, so that the stuff as well as the tools and the workmen must be had from France and England. Nothing can exceed the beauty, elegance, and solidity of Girardet's bindings, and their variety is quite as admirable. Every two months there is a general clearance of old forms and patterns, to make way for new ones.

The last visit in my tour of shops was to one whose commodities were of a nature not usually made the subject of traffic in Vienna,—monkeys and parrots. The master of the shop told me that the bad weather of that year had been particularly injurious to them; he had lost monkeys to the value of one thousand seven hundred florins, all having caught severe coughs, of which they had died. One of the creatures was still coughing, and I was astonished at the similarity of the sound to a human cough. I saw here a number of close dark cages, which I understood to be the private studies of the parrots. In the evening their teachers shut them up in these prisons, and then give them their lesson. If the cages are not covered, their curiosity would make them busy themselves with other objects, and if they could see one another, they would converse in their wild American language. It is long before a parrot acquires a new form of speech. Some are sent to board and lodge with old women, of whom they learn the Vienna jargon. The majority had learned to scream out "Vivat Ferdinandus Primus."

RAILROADS.

It has often been matter of complaint, that the city of Vienna has not a more immediate connexion with the many rail and water roads radiating from it. The passengers by the steamboats complain when they find themselves compelled to leave their beds soon after midnight, if they wish to set off at five in the morning, and those by the railroads grumble equally at having to travel through the whole city, together with its suburbs and the villages beyond, before they can consign themselves to the energetic guidance of the locomotive. The various rail and steamboat stations lie two or three leagues apart, and some of them at that distance from the centre of the city. An incredible number of hackney carriages are constantly employed in transporting passengers to the several points. The magnificent terminus of the Vienna-Raab railroad lies at the extreme outer line of the city. The position is so lofty, that they might have continued the road to the very centre of the city without being in the way of the smoke of a single chimney. The terminus in that case would have reached about half way up to the summit of Stephen's Tower.

Before railroads were invented, many of the beautiful environs of Vienna were a forbidden Paradise to its citizens. Those who had no other means of conveyance at their command than what nature provided, never reached Baden, Stockerau, or any such distant point, from one year's end to another, or perhaps not in the course of their lives. Within the last few years the railroads have given them a key to these Elysiums, and at every opening of a new branch of road the newspapers of Vienna announce the fact in a style that might have suited some of Captain Cook's discoveries, new and most captivating descriptions of Stockerau, Briel, Helenenthal, &c., being put forth to entice people by thousands to the railroad.

The railroads have wrought a change in the whole environs of Vienna, and in the whole system of out-door pleasures. The Prater and the Augarten are lost, and comparatively empty now, when the seekers of pleasure can be carried away with so much ease to a distance of five or six (German) miles. The Prater had made the most extraordinary promises; it had announced a "Bacchus festival," to end with a faithful representation of the eruption of three volcanoes in Fernando Po. The three were to vie with each other in the splendour of their flames, and send forth smoke enough to darken the heavens. Preparations had also been made to blow up several masses of (pasteboard) rock. Nevertheless, the Prater was doomed to be deserted that evening, and the visiters were thronging to the railroads. On the other hand the invitations for more distant places of pleasurable resort were not less alluring. At Mödling, Strauss promised his newly-composed dances, "Country Delight," "Railroad Galopade," the "Naiads," &c.; and Lanner announced his musical conversazione, his "Eccentric," his "Reflex from the World of Harmony," to be given at Liesing. In Baden all sorts of "*Volksfeste*" were to take place. There was to be the "Dance for the Hat," a Milan dance, in which the ladies dance through a gate, and she whose transit falls in with a certain given signal obtains a hat by way of a prize. In the various "Arenas" (garden theatres), "The Bohemian Girls in Uniform," the "Elopement, from the Masked Ball," "The Maiden, from Fairy Land," and other attractive pieces, were advertised.

Around the last coach setting off for the Vienna-Raab railroad the people were thronging and steaming. "Pray, gentlemen, let the ladies go first," cried some voices in the crowd. "Yes, yes, the ladies first, the ladies first, they all say, and here am I shoved back again," cried a woman who had been pushed back from one of the carriages. She was launching in her despair into a high strain of eloquence when we invited her into our hackney-coach, and recognised in her, in spite of her shining kid-gloves, a Vienna cook. The cooks generally wear short sleeves, between which and their long gloves, a brown and scorched ring of an arm remains to reveal their calling.

The Vienna-Raab railway (now that its direction towards Hungary is given up, it will probably be called the Vienna-Trieste railway) is probably the most magnificent railway in existence. The terminus and intermediate stations are remarkable for their size and splendour. The waiting-rooms for the passengers of the first and second-classes are more like drawing-rooms than any thing else.

There are three classes of carriages; they are all extremely capacious, carrying not fewer than fifty-six persons. Besides these three classes, there are the, so called, "saloon carriages," furnished with looking-glasses, divans, tables, &c., and destined for persons of wealth and distinction. At present the lines of railroad are towards the resorts of pleasure, and have their names accordingly:—Mödling, Baden, Neustadt. The time will come when more important names will appear—the Adriatic, Venice, the East, the Levant, &c.

The banker Sina is at the head of the Vienna-Raab line, as Rothschild presides over the Vienna-Brunn line. At first the engineers were all Englishmen, but they have since been replaced by Germans. "The English have not the phlegm of the Germans," said a Vienna citizen to me, "they were rash, and careless, and many accidents were the consequence." The precautions observed on the Austrian railroads are so great as almost to counteract the main object of these roads—speed. Very slowly and very gradually the train is set in motion, countless are the whistles before it moves at all, and very moderate is the progress for some time. Long before they mean to stop, the speed is slackened, and astoundingly slow in its motion up to the terminus. It is true that if we could be assured that every new precautionary measure saved some lives, they could not be sufficiently commended, but the question will arise—do they really do so? It may so happen that the negligence of the lower functionaries increases in exact proportion with the extreme foresight of the higher. The surer the public is that precautions are taken by others, the less will they take care of themselves.

On the day I went on the Vienna-Raab railroad we had, in our train, fifteen carriages, full of people starting from Vienna in search of pleasure, consequently, seven hundred persons. We encountered similar trains several times, and, I believe, that the number of persons carried out that Sunday could not be less than twelve thousand. The direction of this railroad galopade was towards the plain at the end of the forest of Vienna. The hills are pierced by several valleys, beyond which lie the before-mentioned pretty villages of Liesing, Mödling, Baden, and others. Hundreds of men, women, and children, were disgorged by the train at the entrance of these valleys, and hundreds of fresh passengers packed in. Formerly a stranger required a week to visit all these vaunted places in their turn, now he can be whirled there, have a peep at them, and be back in a few hours.

We allowed ourselves to be complimented out of the carriage at Mödling, to enjoy the highly lauded views of " in der Briel." We found a dozen of asses ready saddled, standing at the station. One of the donkeys was named " Karl Wizing," another " Nanerl," and her gentle daughter " Sofi," so at least the juvenile drivers informed us. As we were just three in number, we chose these three animals, mounted them, and trotted away into the mountains. The father of the present Prince Lichtenstein first brought the neighbourhood of Briel into notice. He caused the naked declivities to be clothed with woods, paths to be cut, and the ground to be laid out with taste; adorned the summits with pavilions and summer-houses, built a magnificent seat in the neighbourhood, and abandoned the picturesque old ruins to the curiosity of the public. At this present time several yet wilder, woody and rocky valleys in the neighbourhood of Vienna are undergoing a similar transformation. Coffee-house civilization has put to flight the nymphs and dryads of the woods. The caves of the fauns have been fitted up for the sale of beer and wine, and where formerly a solitary lover of nature could scarcely force his way, the population of a whole quarter of the city are now gadding about in merry crowds.

The ruins of the old castle of Lichtenstein, to which Karl Wizing, Nanerl, and Sofi carried us, are *real* ruins, a fact worthy of remark, because the hills around are covered with a number of mimic ruins, placed there for decoration's sake. The old castle, one of the earliest possessions of the illustrious family whose name it bears, fell afterwards into other hands, and was subsequently re-purchased by the Lichtensteins, with the lands and vineyards belonging to it, for six hundred thousand florins. It is a regular, old, rock built, knightly nest. The dungeon lies right before the narrow entrance, and the first thing the stern old barons must have done on stepping over their threshold was to give a negative to the petitions for freedom which the captives sent up to them in groans from their prison below.

The hall wherein the ancestral pictures are suspended, has its walls partly cut out of the bare rock, and partly of freestone. The bare rock also forms the floor. The oldest portrait is that of John of Lichtenstein, who died in 1395, and the series is continued down to the grandfather of the present prince. The ladies hang in a neighbouring chamber, likewise carved out of the rock. It must be a real pleasure to be descended from this handsome, stout old race. They are all tall handsome figures, and the dainty ruffs, padded doublets, short hose, velvet caps, golden chains, and rich princely mantles of which they were never in want, sit on them in a most stately fashion. The handsomest among them is one " John Septimus von Lichtenstein, lord of Hanau and Ramsburg, son of Jörg Hartmann v. Lichtenstein of Felsburg, aged 35 years." One of them has a tiger which he is caressing by his side. Probably the present Lichtensteins would as soon adopt a tiger for a lap dog as resume this old rocky nest for a dwelling-place.

The archduke Charles is the owner of the lovely valley behind Baden. I never saw more courteous addresses to the public than those posted up in the grounds laid out by the archduke for the public. " The respected public are requested to make use of the paths laid down in these grounds, in order to spare the young wood." No doubt prohibitions of the kind would have a better effect, if such motives were always suggested.

The handsome castle, built by the archduke just at the entrance of the valley, is called Weilburg. Although we had the building constantly in sight, we were obliged to inquire the way to it twice, as we had got into some by-paths, and each time we received genuine Austrian answers. The first was, " I am not acquainted with this road ;" and the second, " This is the right road, the other is for *themselves*" (*i. e.* the owners). Schloss Weilburg is renowned for its collection of roses. The gardener told us there were not less than eight hundred species here, but in this bloomless season, they all looked as like each other as so many skeletons. To make us amends, we saw a plant but seldom met with in German greenhouses— the rose-coloured lily, with dark red spots (*lilium speciosum punctatum*). The site of the palace and garden is the most delightful that can be imagined. It lies on the borders of a hilly country, at the opening of a valley, in view of a richly-cultivated plain. On either side it is flanked by wooded heights, and behind is the narrow pass of the valley. Every thing required towards the formation of a fine landscape is here united: the elevating view over a distant land, rich in life and hope ; the warmly-tinted picture of the lovely valley close at hand, and the retreat into a friendly wooded solitude. The last was the particular object of my research, and I found at the end of the valley a beautiful meadow, in the midst of thickets, by the side of a river. This was called the house-meadow. Whilst Baden was swarming with people, but few found their way to this place. A little boy was exhibiting his skill on the violin, and received in reward of his masterly performance the large copper pieces of a few wandering Mecænas with the warmest gratitude.

On our return to Baden we refreshed ourselves with a cup of coffee and some excellent "*kipfeln*," which are better made here than in Vienna itself. They make them of all sizes, from half a kreuzer to five florins a piece. The more aristocratic among the bakers suspend a shield or crown of kipfel dough over their windows, in the manner of armorial bearings; the fresh baked are so much esteemed, that many bakers, not content with making them once a day, inscribe over their shops, "Here bread is baked three times a day." Baron Rothschild sent for a Baden baker to Paris, where his artistical performances were so much approved of, that he became a rich man in a short time.

Life in Baden has undergone a great change of late years. Formerly the emperor Francis lived here in the summer, and, like king Frederick William at Teplitz, assembled much of the great world around his person. Both places have lost by the death of those two sovereigns; nevertheless, now that the railroad brings, daily, thousands into the neighbourhood, and inundates it with smokers, drinkers, and cooks, the pleasures of the arenas have become of infinitely more consequence than those of the saloons. The baths will be great gainers. They are now within reach of many to whom they were before unattainable. Many invalids in public offices come with the first train, take a bath and return to the capital before their hours of business. Prince Puckler Muskau observes that, in Vienna, people talk about a "*lamprelle,*" or a "*parapluie,*" but know nothing about a *Regenschirm*. I also had opportunities enough of remarking the fondness of persons of the uneducated classes for sporting a few French phrases. While waiting with some hundreds of persons in the room appropriated to the second class, for the arrival of the train, I sat down near a very fat, very fine lady, who was parading her French to an acquaintance. "Comment vous portez vous?" said the lady. "Oh, ah, oui, bien," was the reply. "Prenez place ici, voulez vous?" "Non." "Pourquoi donc?" "Non! je, je,—Ah what shall I say, I don't know how to say it, but I'd rather stand," and hereupon he laughed out loud. "Il fait très chaud ici," persisted she. "Ay, you mean it is very hot, yes hot enough to stifle one." "Oui c'est trop," rejoined the fat dame, "it is *too* bad. If they would but collect the heat and put it into the engine they might save their firing."

The drive back, at eleven o'clock at night, was really brilliant, and the precautionary lighting of the road almost superfluous. The stations were illuminated with red and green lamps; the whole way along, lamps and torches were planted, and withal the moon shone resplendently in the heavens. Late as it was, we met several trains, and, without any exaggeration the engines were piping and whistling as numerously along the railroad as so many mice in a granary.

SUNDAY WALKS.

It was one Sunday afternoon that I walked into the streets to see what aspect the city bore at that time of the day. The workday and morning tumult had quite subsided, the constant "*Ho! ho!*" of the hackney carriages, and the "*Auf!*" of the car-drivers were silent, for 20,000 of the inhabitants of Vienna were rolling over the newly opened railway to the newly-discovered Paradise of Stockerau, and 20,000 were flying by the Raab road to Mödling, Baden, and the other valleys of the forest of Vienna; 50,000 more were gone into the country for the summer, and another 50,000 were gone after them for the day, to forget the troubles of the week in their society. Another not less respectable number of citizens and citizenesses were scattered over the gardens of the suburbs, the Prater, and the meadows, and thus I remained in possession of the inner city, with a remnant of lackeys, beggars, and sick; the Turks might have attacked and taken it at that moment with ease. The domestics were lounging before the doors and conversing with their opposite neighbours; the maids were chattering in the inner courts; the coffee-house of the "Orientals" was still full of company, for they were scarcely likely to approve of our way of keeping Sunday. In the cathedral of St. Stephen, a few old women were telling their rosaries, and screaming their devotions through the church; and one grating voice among them, louder than all the rest, repeated, at the end of each verse, "Holy, holy, holy!"

In the courtyard of one house into which I looked, I saw a little boy reading prayers aloud from a book. He told me that he was eight years old, and that he did this every Sunday. I took his book, and saw that he was reading the gospel of St. Luke, from the ninth to the fourteenth verse. He said it was the gospel for the day, and that many boys in a similar manner read the gospels on a Sunday before the houses of Vienna. When he had finished, there descended on him, from the upper stories, a grateful shower of kreuzers wrapped in paper.

In the usual tumult of the town, I had overlooked many smaller elements of the population, which I now discovered for the first time, as some inhabitants of the waters are perceived only when the tide has ebbed. I noticed for the first time the people who hawk Italian and Hungarian cheeses about the streets. They are chiefly from the neighbourhood of Udine, and also sell Italian macaroni. The greater number could speak as much German as they found necessary for their street traffic. There are in all not less than thirty thousand Italians in Vienna, and the passenger is not unfrequently accosted with, "*Poveretta! signor mio! la carita!*" Beggars should, out of policy, always speak a foreign language; it excites far more compassion than the language of the country.

Going farther, I found a man standing before a baker's shop, occupied in scolding a little maidservant. She was a Bohemian, he told me, and added, "That Bohemia must be a very poor country—every year there come thousands of them to Vienna—men and women, maids and boys. They learn as much German as they must, seek a service somewhere, are very moderate in their demands, will put up with a bed in the stable, or on the floor, and when they have earned a few florins, they go back to their own country." In fact, if we inquire of a hundred people we meet in Vienna what country they are from, the answer of twenty, on an average, will be "*Ich bin ein Behm*" (I am a Bohemian). The whole number of the Slavonians in Vienna is, it is said, about 60,000, and of other Non-Germans 100,000. In the highest circles as the lowest, the foreign element mingles everywhere. The number of Hungarians is reckoned at 15,000; but of these many are not genuine Magyars.

One could not in Vienna, at that time, speak three words to a man without coming to the name of Geymüller. My baker, whom I had requested to show me the way to the Glacis, told me, by the way, that it was the oldest banking-house, and had flourished for above sixty years. "The last Baron Geymuller, however," he said, "was no Geymüller at all, but an adopted son of his predecessor, and no baron properly, but they had made him one. He had squandered 150,000 florins yearly; many, both of the rich and poor, had been ruined through him; and now this mischief-maker had been politely shown the door; and allowed to go and live at Paris with his wife on the remains of his fortune, and they were not inconsiderable."

During this conversation we had reached the Saitzer Hof, where our roads separated.

At last I came to the end of the city, and went out upon the Glacis. Here seemed to be gathered together all whose legs were too short to gain the open country beyond the extensive suburbs of Vienna. It was the part called the Water Glacis, where there is some gay music every afternoon; numbers of little children with their nurses were lying and playing about the grass, and several schools under the guidance of their masters were doing the like. Some of them had pitched a tent in one of the meadows near which they were diverting themselves. There is no other city in Europe where the children have such a playground in the very heart of the town. The benches were bare of other visiters, with the exception of one solitary Turk seated among the children. He was taking his coffee, and dividing the "*kipfel*," that had been brought him with it, among the sparrows which are constantly flying in numbers round the Glacis. I sat down by him to share in both his amusements, and remarked a trick of the sparrows that I had never before noticed. Some of them were so greedy, that they kept fluttering in the air about us, and sometimes snatched a morsel of bread before it could even reach the ground, where the others were eagerly picking up the scattered fragments.

Like a polypus turned inside out, the inner life being displayed externally, the dead exterior skin turned within, even so is the life of Vienna reversed on a Sunday. The swarms that on other days are driving and bawling in the streets and public places of the city, are then singing, dancing, eating, drinking, and gossiping in the houses of public entertainment without. All this humming and drumming was so little in unison with my idea of a Sunday walk, that I was glad to take refuge from the noise in a place I was sure of having more to myself on a Sunday than any other day—the flower-gardens and churchyards.

Beethoven's monument stands in the Währinger cemetery. His simple family-name is inscribed in gold letters on the stone: but of late the growth of a bush planted near it has almost overshadowed the letters. I asked the sexton why he did not cut away the boughs that the name might be more plainly seen; he said the friends would not allow it to be done.

In every cemetery there is a certain form of inscription sure to be frequently met with. On half the gravestones in this place I read the word "Ever to be remembered!" (*unvergesslich*) which seems to me as unmeaning as it is short. On many of the graves lights were burning in small lanterns among the flowers. It is a custom in Vienna to light these on the anniversary of the death of the deceased. The Währinger cemetery is one of the most distinguished in Vienna; and many place on the graves of their departed friends flowers of a very costly kind, for the supply of which there is a greenhouse in the cemetery. At night two dogs are let loose to guard the property of the dead.

Nothing harmonizes better with a grave than flowers, and by way of a conclusion to my Sunday promenade, I went to look at the flower-gardens of Mr. N——, and Baron X——, and came at length to Rupert's nursery-garden, which for Hungary, and for all the other lands that receive the seeds of cultivation from Vienna, plays no insignificant part. It is said to contain not less than 2000 species of vine, and 400 of potatoes; the latter article must be particularly important for the before-mentioned countries, which are still very ill supplied with this vegetable. Rupert's garden is also celebrated for its dahlias, the flower now so passionately cultivated in all European gardens. The proprietor says that he has 900 varieties, with different names for each. As we find certain insects and butterflies hovering over certain flowers, so one is almost certain to meet in Rupert's garden some enamoured admirers of dahlias from different parts of the Austrian dominions on the hunt for some variety of [flower wherewith to complete their collections. Here, as in England, Hamburg, and Erfurt, they aim at the production of new kinds. The "Princess Kinsky" (white with lilac edges) is a creation of Vienna; "Baroness Herderfeld" (bright lilac with a dark violet coloured border), and "Count Fünfkirchen," are christened after Austrian nobles. The very newest productions of England and Germany find their way first to Rupert's garden. A "Charles XII.," a beautiful velvet violet, fading in the calyx to a tender lilac, and at the outer edge pure white, was now blooming for the first time in the Austrian territory. The last consignment had brought 84 new sorts, which were to come into bloom next year. It is worthy of note in how grand a style the English gardens carry on their trade with dahlia bulbs. To the name of the bulb, the name of the producers of its varieties is annexed, and usually a beautiful drawing added to show what the flower will be when in bloom.

Towards evening I returned by the Glacis, and there witnessed a scene I shall not easily forget. A sudden storm of thunder and lightning, that seemed to promise a second course of rain or hail, had scared all the juveniles encamped on the grass, and as I came up, all were in full flight over the narrow drawbridges and through the small gates. The nurses were towing along two, three, and four little creatures, and the schoolmasters driving their flocks before them. There was a thronging, bustling, and hurrying, as if the Turks had just entered the suburbs. "William, you stupid boy! what do you stand still to spell Franciscus Primus for?" (the name of that emperor is inscribed in golden letters over the gate,) "can't you spell enough at home? don't you hear the thunder?"—"Babette will you let go of that chain? this is not the time to count the links. See how you are keeping us."—"Good God! what's become of Seppi? He! child, run, run, the rain will spoil all your things." Thus screamed mothers and nurses, and all dragged on their small charges as if a second murder of the innocents was at hand. At the end of this century perhaps some grandsire of seventy will date his earliest childish recollections from this storm, and relate how in the long departed year of 1841 a storm drove him with others suddenly from the Glacis of Vienna, and his friend may likewise remember how he was there too, and how he got a box on the ear from his nurse for stopping to spell Franciscus Primus in the middle of the rain, and how a strange man dried his tears and led him by the hand after his attendant.

KLOSTERNEUBURG.

One day I went in a *stellwagen* that started from St. Stephen's place for the much talked of Klosterneuburg, in company with a pretty little girl and her mother, a pale young woman whom I took at first for a member of the corporation of semstresses, a little old mannikin, and some silent members on the back seats of whom no more need be said. The little girl had a basket with some linen on her lap which she held so negligently, that at the first jolt of the coach out it fell to the unspeakable terror of the mother, who announced the misfortune by a terrible shriek. The driver made a halt and I went in search of the basket, which luckily had fallen without tumbling out its delicate contents, and offered my services to hold it more securely for the future, through which small civility I won the hearts of my companions, and a conversation began that ceased not till we separated at Klosterneuburg. There was no want of subjects, for in a city like Vienna every night is sure to produce matter enough to employ, for the succeeding day, all the tongues that stand in need of exercise. We spoke firstly of Geymüller's bankruptcy, a subject which kept all the talkers in Vienna in full play for two months, and was introduced every morning as regularly as family prayers. It was maintained that it was the banker Sina, who had ruined Geymüller. The book-keeper of the latter had betrayed the embarrassments of his principal to Sina, who thereupon, to secure his own claims, had come forward, and anticipated the other creditors. The clerks of Geymüller had called the treacherous book-keeper to account for this, and even threatened his life. But Geymüller had said, "Let him live! for this man whom I have raised from nothing, and who has in return betrayed me, God will judge *him!*" Next, the last great fire was discussed, and some one related how the night before, a young man had been robbed and murdered in Leopolstadt.

"Ah, see there now! they are going on quite in the Galicia fashion in Vienna!" said the slim, pale, young woman whom I had taken for a modiste, but who afterwards gave us to understand she was the lady of a government tobacco agent. "Two fires in one week, a man murdered, Geymüller a bankrupt, it's regular Galicia fashion, upon my honour!"—"Were you ever in Galicia, if I may ask?" said I.—"Ah! yes, indeed, God help me, two whole years," was the answer, accompanied by a deep sigh.

Thereupon our conversation took another direction, for I too had been in Galicia,[*] and was interested for the country, and for the views others entertained respecting it. It may be easily imagined how longingly all eyes are directed from the provinces towards the warm high-beating heart of the Austrian monarchy; the far radiating centre of light, the seat of all that is noblest, fairest, and wisest, the imperial city of Vienna, and how its splendours and glories are magnified in the imaginations of those dwellers in the provinces, whose fortune it is never to see it face to face; and on the other hand, it is as easy to fancy how inconsolable must be the

---

[*] Mr. Kohl's tour in Galicia will form the close of the present volume, though in point of date it preceded his visit to Vienna.

man or woman destined to leave this temple of renown and source of all pleasure, for the comparatively joyless provinces. I never heard a Vienna lady more eloquent than when speaking of the Bohemians, Moravians, or even the Poles, Hungarians, Croats, and other remote people of the empire. As the wives of officers, military or civil, many a fair Austrian is fated to wander among these barbarians. Whoever has had occasion to listen to the complaints of those who have been stationed in Bukowina, Transylvania, or the military colonies, must confess that the *Jeremiade* of the Chinese princess married to a Mongolian prince, as delivered to us by Ruckert, in his Schi-king, was not more deeply felt nor more poetically expressed, nor is the joy of the princess when she returns to the capital of the Sun's brother, greater than the rapture of a fair native of Vienna, when she sees Stephen's tower again after a residence of some years in Hungary or Galicia. If any one be curious to know the kind of picture she would draw of the place she had left, let him listen to the account of the tobacconist's better-half, when the before-mentioned misfortunes and misdeeds awakened her recollections of Galicia.

"Yes, it is quite the Galicia mode, and we shall soon have in Vienna such spectacles as are to be seen in Lemberg every day. Whilst I was there, they hung nine men within six weeks. Once they hung up four on the same day. They were hung alternately, first a Christian and then a Jew, and then another Christian and then another Jew. Here, God be thanked, the punishment of death is pretty well laid aside, except among the military. But Galicia! Oh what a country! I had travelled before in Bohemia and Moravia; I thought the poverty and misery of the people was scandalous enough there, and far beyond what I had any idea of; but, Jesus Maria! I've learned more since; when I got to Galicia, I found what it was to be in a country so far behind in civilization! Such rogues and vagabonds as the people are there I never heard of! They plunder and pilfer, and commit all manner of excesses. At first we used to go by the diligence on the great high-roads, but afterwards we had a carriage to ourselves. *On* the high-roads you must have recourse to blows to get any thing, but *out* of them there is nothing to be had either for cudgelling or for money. One evening the Jew who was driving us, called out—' Look at the stars, do you see the stars? the sabbath is beginning!' and he actually wanted to take out his horses and compel us to pass the night in the open air! My uncle, who was travelling with me, gave him a beating and he drove a little farther; but my uncle was obliged to cudgel him six times before we got to our journey's end." Here I looked hard at the speaker, who had not asked me whether I had ever been in Lemberg, with a scrutinizing glance, but I saw that she was quite in earnest, meant *bonâ fide* what she said, and reckoned fully on our belief in her relation. "Lemberg," she continued, " they call their capital; but what a capital! Heaven help us! Here in Vienna if you have a florin in your hand you can do something with it, can have some diversion, can satisfy your hunger. But there, if you have two you can get nothing for them—nothing whatever; the coffee-houses are bad and filthy. A cup of coffee costs twenty-four kreuzers, and then it is good for nothing. A person in a public office, with a salary of 900 florins, cannot even say he has his own living out of it, not to speak of bread for his children. My uncle went from one coffee-house to another for two months together, when we were first there, before he could make up a rubber of whist."

Just then we reached Nussdorf, where a number of hackney-coaches were in waiting for the passengers by the Linz steamboats.

"There! In all Lemberg, a city with 80,000 inhabitants, if the people can be called inhabitants, there are not as many hackney-coaches as you see here in one place. I assure you there are not more than a dozen in the whole town. I lived with my uncle, and when the winter came we went to the assembly. My uncle had dressed himself of course, and so had I; I was quite bare, my neck I mean, and of course I had my hair properly dressed, as we should here in Vienna to go to an assembly. We drove there at half-past ten, that was soon enough, for who thinks of going to an assembly in Vienna before eleven o'clock? and all the company was assembled, and as long as I live I shall never forget it, all in their furs, some even in sheepskins, and boots and spurs, just as they go in the streets. As I and my uncle were taking our places, the people called to each other '*Schaut's die Schwab'n! Schaut's die Schwab'n!*' (Look at the Swabians!) My uncle, who understood Polish, translated to me all they said of us, the bandy-legged fellows! Jews and gipsies are there in abundance—gipsies (oh, it is scandalous) in whole gangs. They live in a state of misery that is not to be described, even when something is done to better their condition. But in that country each throws the blame upon the other. The nobleman says the peasant is lazy, and the peasant says the nobleman has nothing for him but a whip. And then sometimes the Jew's turn comes. The Jews, ah, I assure you this people—" Here the Austrian eloquence of our talkative companion whose innate antipathy to Hungarians and Galicians, excited by applause, ran on in a stream as fluent as molten wax, was interrupted by another description of oratory, that of the waiter of the Klosterneuburg inn, as he opened the door of the coach, and invited us to get out. We did so, and hastened to the convent.

The tradition respecting the foundation of this convent that it was endowed by Leopold the Holy, in commemoration of his having here found the lost veil of his consort the beautiful Margravine Agnes on an elder-bush, was repeated to us, as it is to all the thousands of travellers who yearly knock for admission at its gates. In the treasury of relics we were also shown a piece of the elder-bush, a rag of the veil, and a fragment of the skull, under whose protecting roof the thought of such a foundation was first hatched. The legends of the Catholic church are really sometimes inconceivably paltry. What a fuss they have made of that princely veil, whose loss was at once so very simple and so very insignificant? In a picture they have even represented a troop of baby angels busied in restoring the veil to the Margravine. And to found a convent on such an incident! The thing would be absurd, even if the veils of our Christian ladies had the mystic significance of the Mahometan veils, the loss of which might be supposed to include the loss of half their womanhood.

Put out of humour by these reflections in the relic-room, we requested to be shown the splendid library, that we might have something reasonable to look at; but the first book that fell into our hands was Chronica Austriæ by Johann Rasch, and the first remark that struck us on opening it was, that Noah must have been archduke of Austria, because when the waters of the deluge had subsided, and he as sole lord and ruler of the earth had taken possession, Austria must have been included. On a closer examination of this remarkable book, I found among other ante and post diluvian occurrences, not mentioned in any other history, a complete list of Austrian rulers in direct descent from Noah.

No less than forty princes (heathens) were enumerated, then several Jewish. Then the chronicler observes, "Heathen princes again ruled in Austria, and certainly not fewer than seven." To these succeeded the Christian rulers Rolantin, Raptan, Amanus, &c., a hundred princes in all, whom the crazy chronicler had invested with princely honours, down to the Babenbergers, eleven in number, and the Hapsburgers, fifteen.

The author of this book, a remarkable one in a psychological, if not in an historical point of view, was a teacher in the Scotch convent in Vienna, and the most curious part of the story is, that no joke is intended, but all is seriously meant. It is diligently compiled, and printed in the old, firm, careful, conscientious type of the last century. The exact date of every occurrence is carefully given: how long after the creation of the world, how long after the deluge, and how long before the birth of Christ. For example:

"In the year 1807, after the creation of the world in the 151st year after the deluge, and the 2156th before the birth of Christ, Tuisco brought a great people with him from Armenia, Germans and Wendes, among whom were twenty-five counts, and about thirty princes."

All the various readings of the princes' names, their sundry aliases, are also carefully noted. "In the year 2390, after the creation of the world, 734 after the deluge, lived the German Hercules, Hercules Alemannicus, also Hercule, Aergle, Argle, Excle or Arglon, the 'Hero with the fierce lion,' which he leads in a chain, and bears as a cognizance in his shield."

The whole is illustrated with pictures, and the coat of arms of every prince is given. Abraham's is a golden eagle in a black shield, placed obliquely.

Many historiographers have laboured for the glorification of the old house of Austria, but none have gone about their work in a way to be at all compared to Johann Rasch's. Can it be that in his time (he lived at the beginning of the 17th century) people were so far beclouded in the fogs of vanity and self-esteem, as to give currency to his book?

A further search in the magnificent rooms appropriated to the library of this convent showed that some really interesting books were to be found in it: Haufstangel's lithographs from the Dresden gallery, Salt's View of India, Denon's work on Egypt, and other splendid works of that description.

The Incunabulæ and manuscripts have all been lately bound in Russia leather, which is said to preserve them from the worms. There are some old missals and breviaries, and a costly edition of Pliny, on such indestructible paper, with so tasteful yet so clear a type, and with so solid a binding as in our times are no longer to be seen. The Incunabulæ must be very old, for the numbers of the paper, and the superscriptions are made with the pen. The old heathen sage Pliny was painted in gay colours in front of his work, with a glory like that of a saint round his head, writing his Evangelium, like St. John; proof enough how highly, even in the middle ages, the monks valued the classic works of the ancients.

There are also a great number of old German poems and legends. I took out one and found it gnawed by the mice. "Eh, eh," said the father, who was showing me round, " some wicked animal has been at our books again! It's very illegibly written. I can't read these old letters, and I don't care to read them, I like to read a plain good print!" Then stepping to the window, he hummed a melody which some organ-grinder was playing in the street below, and observed, " That is a pretty song. It is from the *Puritani.*" I rummaged further in the mouse magazine, and found another old dusty book. It was called, " On the German War of Hortleder," thus in Austria is entitled the war of Charles V. against the protestants. We may acquire a very sufficient notion of the contents of this book by only reading the title. It is alike characteristic of the manner of carrying on the war, as of the spirit of the times which dictated both the war and the book. It runs thus: "Of the German war of Hortleder, with the despatches, intelligence, instructions, complaints, supplications, written commands, summonses, counsels, deliberations, justifications, protestations, and recusations, replies, denials, details, alliances and counter alliances, orders and testimonials, letters of consent and dissent, challenges, admonitions, truces, battles, fights and skirmishes, with *one* word the causes of the German war." The mere reading of this title makes one feel quite Holy Roman and German *empire-ish.*

Klosterneuburg, as it now stands, is one of those stately giant erections, reared at the command of the greatest architect Austria ever saw on the throne—Charles VI. It is projected in the same grand style as all other architectural works of that monarch, and like many others also unfortunately (or fortunately?) not completed. Want of money, the sudden death of Charles, and the wars in the succeeding reign of Maria Theresa, prevented the completion, which was subsequently often attempted, but never achieved, as money no longer flowed so freely as under the administration of the former monarch. Much has been done, however, of late; the library is new, a magnificent staircase has been built at the cost of many thousand florins, the great marble hall is finished. The giant hall which has long remained as the workmen left it a hundred years ago, it is hoped, will be cleared as soon as the new church, which the convent is bound to erect in one of its parishes in the suburb of Hitzing, shall be completed. The cost has been estimated at 100,000 florins, but it will not be less than 150,000. The convent has the patronage of not less than twenty-five churches.

Klosterneuburg is particularly rich in vineyards, and their produce flows from the tuns of all the houses of public entertainment far and near. Hence it has acquired among the people the nickname of the "running tap" (*zum rinnenden zapfen*), just as Gottweih, on account of its abundance of ready money is called " the jingling penny" (*zum klingenden pfennig*); and even as the fathers of Molk are called the " lords of the jolly pecks" (*die Herren vom reissenden Metzen*), on account of the many fertile cornfields they possess.

The Emperor Charles VI. wished to make Klosterneuburg his usual summer residence, and built the convent for a château. Near the cells of the monks there is a range of magnificent apartments called the emperor's apartments, which are of no manner of use to them, but on the contrary, a great burden. The chief cupola of the building is surmounted with an imperial crown, and the lesser ones with the archducal hat. The imperial crown and the gigantic cushion on which it rests, is an exact copy in iron of the real crown at Vienna. Within, it is roomy enough to contain twenty men, and beams are stretched across to give it greater firmness. The precious stones are great bosses of iron-plate, painted blue and red, in which there are small windows or doors whence a wide prospect may be enjoyed.

The archducal hat on each of the other cupolas has here more significance than the crown, for Klosterneuburg is the principal convent of the archduchy, and is the guardian of the veritable hat itself, or rather, calls it its own. The monks maintain that the hat belongs, not to the imperial house, but to the convent, and when homage is to be rendered to the emperor as archduke, he must borrow the hat of them. The Archduke Maximilian dedicated this hat "*ex devotione*" to St. Leopold, the patron and immortal proprietor of the monastery. On the occasion of receiving homage, the loan of the hat to the new emperor, or archduke, is attended by a number of antique ceremonies.

Two imperial commissioners, generally noblemen of some old Austrian race, such as the Hardeggs, Schönborns, &c., come on the appointed day, escorted by a detachment of cavalry in a state equipage drawn by six horses, and are received before the gates of the convent by the whole chapter with the "reigning prelate" at their head. In the courts of the convent, the "*Bürgerschaft*" of the town of Klosterneuburg parade in uniform and armed. After a friendly welcome, the illustrious guests, attended by the whole company, go to St. Leopold's chapel, where they hear the service and sing a Te Deum, after which the "reigning bishop," in full pontificalibus and grasping the golden crosier adorned with precious stones, admired by travellers in the treasury of the convent, repairs to the throne-room where he gives audience to the imperial commissioners and demands their business. The commissioners in the old style make a speech to the "well beloved, pious and faithful," and declare therein that a new lord and ruler is minded to invest himself with the emblems and glories of majesty, wherefore he requests the convent will lend him the old hat. Then the bishop rises and gravely declares that he sees no reason to the contrary; whereupon the chapter willingly and submissively grant the request of the illustrious supplicant.

Here ends the first act of this important drama, and to gather strength and courage for the second, the party adjourn to the banquet-table, where the "Running Tap" shows itself no niggard, and many a glass is emptied to the prosperity of the old house of Austria.

After the banquet, the parties proceed to the delivery and reception of the hat; but in the first place, its genuineness and identity in every respect must be ascertained. The imperial commissioners draw out an old paper on which it is described in detail. The great blue sapphire on the top, in the centre the pearls, rubies, and emeralds, the sable tails, every thing is closely examined and certified, and then the hat is packed into its red leathern case, locked up, and carried down to the gate by the dean, assisted by two priests.

Here the case is delivered to the commissioners, who place it in a litter borne by two mules. The litter is followed by twelve of the Austrian "noble guard," all scions of ancient race; then come the commissioners in their carriage, then the empty carriage of the bishop, and behind it a part of his flock, the bürger guard of Klosterneuburg on horseback with their trumpets. The latter, and the empty carriage, only go as far as the Scottish gate of Vienna, where the national guard is stationed to relieve them and convey the hat to its destination. The return of the hat to the convent is conducted in similar style, but with somewhat less ceremony.

The archduke St. Leopold is the patron and protector of the Austrian archduchies, but Nepomucene and Florian are also supposed to watch over their safety. Leopold is buried here; the enamel-work on his monument is admired by all travellers, as in duty bound, although the place is so dark that scarcely any thing can be seen of it. But the beautiful stucco-work of the church really deserves the highest admiration, and I do not think that any thing so perfect is to be met with elsewhere in Germany. Such luxurious fulness of form, such correctness of drawing, such a solidity of workmanship, which, after the lapse of a hundred years, holds and looks as if it had been done yesterday, and such taste in the division and arrangement of the groups, make it really unique in its kind, and do the highest honour to the Augustine chapter of Klosterneuburg, if they had really a hand in the matter. I must confess that after I had seen all the splendours of this convent I felt as if I had enjoyed a banquet. Two gentlemen who were my fellow-passengers in the Stellwagen on my return, owned to similar feelings, only there was this difference between us, they had really dined. They had dined with the prelate and were full of his praises. On the way they pointed out to me a monument raised by a former prelate in commemoration of a great danger from which he had escaped. He was driving past the spot, when an explosion in a neighbouring Turkish redoubt, hurled some thousands of cannon-balls into the air. One of these balls passed obliquely through the roof of the bishop's carriage without doing him any personal injury, and, in memory of this preservation, he had had this ball riveted on the pointed summit of a column, with an inscription explaining the motive for the erection of so singular a monument, which seemed to me to announce more plainly than any thing else I had seen, the prodigious importance of a Klosterneuburg prelate.

HUNGARY.

OEDENBURG, ZINZENDORF, ESTERHAZY, AND THE NEUSIEDLER LAKE.

On leaving Vienna I took care not to leave behind the only Hungarian word I was master of,—namely, "*Yonapot*," signifying "good day;" for even a single word of the language of a country we are about to enter, is a precious little instrument for unlocking hearts, if one does but know how to use it. A hundred words and forms of speech form an inestimable treasure in such a case.

Immediately on passing the frontier, the village of Pötschking, where we stopped, presented an entirely different aspect from those on the Austrian side. The window-shutters of the houses were of iron, on account, I was told, of the frequent conflagrations; the stable-men wore the costume of butchers, and carried the implements of the trade, as they are required to exercise this twofold occupation, immense herds of cattle continually passing through the place. One of these men, whom I spoke with, proved to be an Austrian deserter, who had run away to evade the laws of recruitment; and when I asked him if he did not fear being discovered so close to Vienna, he answered, "Oh, they know very well where I am, but here in Hungary they can't lay hold of me. If they tried it, I could soon get together hundreds of the country fellows; there are plenty of us here without leave, but nobody says a word to us." Four German miles beyond Vienna, therefore, the Austrian police, and the social order dependant on it, loses its power. I met here many "*Zeiselwagen*," long carriages, in which the people sit back to back, crammed full of pilgrims for the shrine of Maria Zell in the mountains, and adorned with large nosegays. The driver sat in the front, driving with one hand, and holding in the other a prayer-book, from which he chanted aloud, what the pilgrims sung in chorus after him. Sometimes I met whole troops on foot, that entirely covered the road, broad as it was, men, women, and girls, mostly provided with great umbrellas to protect them from the sun, singing, and playing, led sometimes by a consecrated banner. They were principally Germans, as indeed are the greater part of the population for some miles beyond Oedenburg. The Magyars I was told did not join in these pilgrimages. The day (the 20th of August) was also, among these

Magyars, a great festival. It was St. Stephen's day, on which the hands, and I believe a part of the skull, of the saint are carried in procession through Ofen; and in all the villages we passed through, we found the people in Sunday clothes and making holiday.

At Drasburg, a village partly inhabited by Croats, we found some Croat girls assembled round a holy spring. Above it was an "Ecce homo" in stone, covered with dust and cobwebs, the water trickling out from under it. I asked one of them if the water was good. "To be sure it is," they answered, "doesn't it run off from God himself." As many as thirty or forty people were drawing or drinking the water, and one of the girls brought me her pitcher. To the great amusement of the bystanders, when I went to drink, I poured it all over me, not being yet aware that the Hungarian pitchers have a little treacherous hole near the handle, on which it is necessary to put one's finger, if one does not wish to enjoy the fluid inside and outside at the same moment.

Along the western side of the Neusiedler Lake, and the Styrian frontier as far as the Drave, the villages are inhabited by a mixed population of Germans and Croats. At that point begins the territory exclusively peopled by Croatians. In the Oedenburg Comitat, or county, there are 30 Croatian villages; in that of Wieselburg, 11; in Eisenburg 64; and in other counties not so many. Those on the Neusiedler Lake are called Water Croats. These Croats scattered among the Germans, are perhaps the fragments of the original population of the country; the dialect that they speak among themselves, is Croatian, but they almost all speak German, though not Hungarian. They serve as drivers and waggoners all over the country, but are said by the Germans to be too fond of their ease to devote themselves to agriculture.

The Croatian women wear very gay colours, the girls have bodices embroidered with gold, as stiff as coats of mail, and wear their hair in the fashion prevailing over the greater part of the world,—namely, hanging down behind in long plaits, and mingled with coloured ribbons. The women wear large hoods or coifs, from which depends a large piece of stuff decorated with rich embroidery and lace. They often come from the country with their gowns tucked up, and carrying their shoes and stockings in their hands, but sit down at a little distance from the church or village they are going to, make their toilets, and then march on in grand state. The Croatian men are attired in still more showy style than the women, with jackets and waistcoats covered with flowers and embroidery, and broad-brimmed hats with great bushes of flowers and feathers, in the number and beauty of which they take great pride.

They are very fond of warlike encounters among themselves, and those who feel especially that way disposed, stick in their hats a long glistening peacock's feather. These feathers are called "defiance feathers," and whoever mounts one of them must feel pretty sure of his own strength and skill, for he exposes himself by so doing to the remarks and attacks of all the rest. They often come to pitched battles on a very magnificent scale, and if they are interrupted by the police in towns, are sure to finish the engagement in the fields. The scenes which I myself witnessed in the Croatian villages were, however, of a very peaceful nature. In a lonely churchyard, in the vicinity of a solitary church, I found an old man lying prostrate in prayer upon a grave, on which stood a rough stone cross, with the inscription, "Here lies Agatschin Xaye: died 1839." The mourner informed us that this was his wife, who lay there with his two children, and that he was now left, as he repeated two or three times, "quite alone—quite alone." He showed us a cave in the churchyard entirely filled with human bones, said to have lain there from the time of the Turks. These bones were regularly built up into a wall, and some pious Croatian women had decorated the interstices with ribbons and flowers. To some of the skulls the hair was still hanging.

We met on our road to Oedenburg many waggons laden with rags, and my coachman informed me they were going to the Austrian manufactories; observing, "The Hungarians send us all their rags* and rubbish, that we may make something clever out of them," and it is characteristic of both nations, that a great deal of raw material is sent from Hungary to be worked up in Austria, whilst none ever travels in an opposite direction.

Oedenburg is the greatest cattle-market in Hungary, and most of the animals sold there pass on to Vienna by the road by which we had come. We frequently observed traces of their passage in little marshy spots, where the ground had been torn and routed up.

At length we discovered the town of Oedenburg lying in a plain, and surrounded far and wide with cabbage-fields. It is as old a town as Vienna, and dates from the Roman time, its present Hungarian name, Sapronia, being a corruption of its Latin one. The Germans have called it Oedenburg, or "desert city," on account of the desolate appearance of the country surrounding it. Coming from Austria, at all events, the name appears applicable enough, for there is more waste than cultivated land to be seen; but soon after passing the town, little vineyards begin to arise on the right and left. The most important lie in the direction of the Neusiedler Lake, where the air is milder than at Oedenburg itself, and where the inhabitants of the town have lands and vineyards producing the wines destined to slake the thirst of Moravia and Silesia.

Though the town of Oedenburg is principally inhabited by Germans, one meets everywhere with Hungarian appellations and inscriptions, especially at the inns. The one I entered was dedicated to the "Magyar Kiralyhoz," that is, to the "King of Hungary," and I drank my coffee in a "Kafehaz," on the sign of which a person in the national costume was depicted presenting ice and coffee. The company at table was various, consisting of some Polish cavalry-officers, who were marching through the town with their companies, a few Englishmen who were escorting twenty full-blood English horses to some Hungarian magnate, some nobles and citizens of Oedenburg, and lastly a Vienna merchant, a man of taste—at least he said so much about want of taste in others, that we naturally inferred that he regarded himself as in full possession of it.

Beyond Oedenburg we again passed through a Croatian village, where the church was full of pretty, clean, white-robed women and girls, praying to St. Stephen and the blessed Virgin. To this succeeded a German, and after that a mingled German and Croatian village, and at last we arrived at Zinzendorf, the first Magyar locality. This place belongs to the renowned Count S——, whose possessions extend along the southern shore of the lake, and join the Esterhazy estates. Near the town, in a handsome park, rich in fine old trees, lies the castle of this nobleman. It is of handsome

---

* The German word *lump* (rag) is also used to denote a scamp or vagabond.—*Tr.*

architecture, and fitted up in the interior in the English style with comfort and elegance.

The castle was occupied at the time of my arrival merely by servants and officers of the household, but the count who was in Vienna had had the kindness to give orders that my party, consisting of myself alone, should be invited to remain a day or two, and be treated as owner of the place. Some apartments on the lower story were opened for my accommodation. They lay among flower-beds in the middle of the garden. I found a sleeping-room with a bedstead of Italian proportions, a sofa of oriental luxury, and some lounging and rocking chairs, fit for the indulgence of a great grandfather. The dining and sitting rooms were of equally grand dimensions, all was in the most beautiful order, the furniture admirably kept, and even pipes stood ready filled, as if they had just expected such a guest as myself.

Several servants were always in attendance to fulfil all my wishes, and the cook begged to be informed what I would have prepared for supper, and what wine I was accustomed to drink. There are many people in the world who express a great deal of enthusiasm for solitude and a hermit life, and I believe such a hermitage as that in which I now found myself, would be exactly to the taste of such enthusiasts. The upper rooms, particularly, were arranged with a taste and elegance rarely seen out of London or Paris. The library had many magnificent copies of French and English books, besides an abundance of useful and interesting works on all subjects, from which, every morning and evening, I had some transported to my *cell*. One of the saloons had its walls adorned with portraits of the ancestors of the count's family; among others that of an archbishop of Gran, who had expended for the benefit of his fatherland, in bridges, fortifications, and other public works, no less a sum than "*vigesies et series centena triginta millia trecenti Floreni.*"

Hungary has at all periods boasted of disinterested patriots, who have laid these offerings on the altar of their country, and no family has produced more such men, than that under whose hospitable roof I now found myself. The present head of the family, as well as his father and grandfather, have all rendered their names illustrious by splendid liberalities of this kind, such as the foundation of the Hungarian Museum, of the Hungarian Literary Society, &c.

My abovementioned hermitage lay not far from the Neusiedler Lake, towards which led a long and beautiful avenue of linden-trees. I determined, therefore, to pay it a visit, and was attended thither by an English servant of the count's. Mr. John made me acquainted on the way with a countryman of his, employed to superintend the stud attached to my hermitage. It is a very common thing to find Englishmen in the service of the Hungarian nobles. Building bridges at Pesth, making roads over the difficult ground of the lower Danube, blasting rocks at the Iron Gates—everywhere one finds Englishmen, and everywhere is it all the better for the works that we do so find them.

As we rode along, Mr. John related to me his own history. He had formerly served in the English navy, and been in China and the East Indies, but had been afterwards wrecked in the North Sea. He had been hospitably treated by the Danes, who sent him back to London, where he was engaged as a working overseer of the Pesth bridge. There he met with a severe accident, and at length found his way to his present asylum, where he was occupied in constructing on the lake a little harbour for the yachts and boats which the count had had built on it.

The sides of the lake are at this part some hundred feet high, sloping, however, easily down to the low shore. The avenue I have spoken of leads to the summit of the bank, whence there is a fine view over the water. It terminates in a grove, where there is a little chapel, and a monument to a deceased count, who here met his death by a fall while hunting. We got some Hungarian boatmen, and rowed out a little way into the lake; the water was extremely smooth, but a mist lay on its surface, which was broken by no living thing but our frail canoe, and some flights of wild ducks. Mr. John informed me that they sometimes proceeded as far as the opposite extremity of the lake; and that a new yacht was soon to be launched, when a flag would be hoisted, the only one that had ever been unfurled on the lake. Mr. John was the admiral of the fleet of the "Ferto tava," (the Hungarian name of the lake,) and if, as a common sailor, he had formerly sailed over the great ocean, and round the wide world itself, he might now comfort himself like Cæsar with the reflection, that it was better to hold the first rank in a fleet of cockboats, than a secondary one in an English man-of-war.

The Neusiedler lake has the same colour as the Danube,—namely, a pale milky green. The sands of the river, also exactly resemble those of the shores of the lake, and it has been imagined that by means of the celebrated whirlpool, and a subterranean channel, there is a communication between them. This is very improbable, but there is another kind of subterranean connexion which is by no means so; namely, by the great marshes and the loose spungy soil, lying between the river and the lake. I observed that some piles, driven in for the intended harbour, had sunk considerably, a sure indication of the looseness of the soil.

Concerning the increase or decrease of the water of the lake there is a difference of opinion. The people on the lake assured me that, for several years there had been a regular decrease: in the deepest places it was not more than seven or eight feet, and in most not above five. Ten years ago it was at least seven or eight feet higher, and had a depth in some places of fifteen or sixteen feet. At that time it was constantly rising, and had covered a considerable number of acres with barren sand, so much so that several communes had determined to remove their villages higher up the bank, when, suddenly, in the year 1832, the water fell again; and since then, with the exception of an occasional rise, dependant on the season of the year, it has been regularly declining. It would be interesting to know if these risings and fallings occurred at regular determinate periods, but this I could not ascertain.

The Neusiedler lake in winter, is covered with ice as clear as glass; and, on account of its shallowness, it freezes in the mildest winter, and in summer is always lukewarm.

The only town on the lake is Rust, the smallest of all the Hungarian free towns, but the most celebrated for the excellence of its wines. We could distinguish, in the distance, its vineyards, where various kinds of fine grapes were growing. The lake should, in my opinion, rather be named after this town than Neusiedel, which is a little insignificant place, as, indeed, are most of the other villages and hamlets on the lake. These, although they are all inhabited by Germans, have all Hungarian names, and there are many little places inhabited by Hungarians which have German appellations; and, indeed, many Hungarian towns have not only a German and Hungarian, but also a Slavonian and a Latin name. On our ride back I found on the road a Magyar peasant-woman, reading aloud with great devotion, from a Hungarian prayer-book. She spoke no word of German, but I found means to converse with her, by means of my Englishman, who had learnt a little Hungarian. The different chapters of the book were inscribed—"The Liturgy," "Penitence," "The Holy Mass," &c. It was handsomely bound, and although the owner was very poor, it was very neatly kept.

I asked if it had been given to her; but she answered, no, she had bought it with three florins that she had saved up. At home she had another, called the Garden of Roses, which was still nicer and easier to pray out of. How gladly would I have given the good old soul, who seemed to hunger and thirst after righteousness, a better guide to the kingdom of Heaven than these books. Why was she not allowed the true spiritual nourishment of the gospel? She answered all our questions willingly, but was by no means inclined to gossip; indeed, garrulity is seldom the failing of a Hungarian; they are mostly characterized by a certain seriousness and dignity of manner, and their eloquence easily passes into pathos.

The costliness and splendour of the plate in which my evening meal was served up, dazzled my eyes. I felt somewhat like poor Hadji Baba, when they persuaded him he was a sultan. I was not much inclined to eat, but could not help enjoying the manner in which every thing was presented in my hermitage; indeed, I shall regard it as a point of more importance when I turn anchorite, to have my dishes presented in gold and silver, and richly-cut glass, than even to have them peculiarly dainty in themselves. Such things as golden pheasants, however, and pineapples, fruit, jellies, &c., might be required, on account of their beautiful appearance, as well as their perfume. On the following morning I paid a visit to the English horses under the guardianship of Mr. Robinson—or Robertson, and entered, for the first time, the houses of some Magyar peasants, in one of the neighbouring villages. They were all built alike, one story high, whitewashed, with the fronts not turned to the street, but to a little court. On the side next the street is a small window, and also a large thick beam running up through the wall, and supporting the roof. Below, this beam is let into a huge block, which serves at the same time as a house-bench. The interiors presented no appearance of extreme poverty, although it must be admitted that all Hungarian villages are not so well built as Zinzendorf. The peasantry of Hungary are, however, on the whole, better off than those of Esthland or Lithuania, though not so well, certainly, as those of Austria.

In the count's stables I saw none but fine English blood-horses, the most distinguished of which was "Christina," said to be the finest blood-horse in Hungary. Mr. Robinson showed me a printed genealogy of this celebrated lady, and I became very desirous to see her; but when I did, I must confess I felt, as I have done on being introduced to celebrated men, no little disappointment, for I could discover no trace of those admirable qualities for which she was famous,—nay, to own the truth, I thought her downright ugly.

"Oh! you must see her at work," said Mr. Robinson; "that's the way to judge." And even so is it with celebrated men. One must see them at work, for it is only then that one can recognise in them the genius or the hero of divine inspiration.

The English passion for horses and horse-races has been recently transplanted into Hungary, as well as some parts of Germany; but in the former country these things are carried on in grander style. In Zinkendorf alone, there were no less than two-and-twenty full-blood mares, each of which had her own stable, and her own groom. In currying them the fellows made a peculiar, inimitable kind of noise, to which they told me the English mares were so accustomed, that they would not stand still without it, so that the Hungarian grooms had been obliged to study to acquire the accomplishment.

Two German miles from Zinkendorf lies Esterhaz, formerly the principal seat of the princes Esterhazy, and as it would not lie in my road to Raab, I made an excursion thither. We met with a very friendly reception, and found some ladies from a neighbouring province, who had also come to see the castle. It is built in the Versailles style. During the last century enormous sums were expended upon it, by the princes of Esterhazy, in honour of the empress Maria Theresa, who frequently visited the place. A great saloon was built with this view, as well as a pleasure-palace in the park, in which *fêtes champêtres* were given. The saloon, however, was burnt down before the empress had seen it. The name bestowed on the pleasure-palace, it is said, was suggested by a casual question put by the empress, as to how much its erection had cost. The prince replied, " eighty thousand florins ;" and the sovereign observed, " Oh! for an Esterhazy, that is a mere bagatelle;" and on going out, she found " Bagatelle" inscribed in gold letters over the gate; since when it has gone by the name of " Castle Bagatelle."

In this palace is an apartment so constructed, that music played in the room beneath is heard as plainly as if played in the room itself. The effect may have been surprising, but I cannot help thinking, that the pleasure of music is increased by the sight of the instruments ; if not, we ought to sit in a concert-room with our backs to the orchestra. In the castle itself, although every thing has been of late much neglected, and many magnificent articles carried away to other seats, whose situations are preferable, there are still to be found many highly interesting works of art. It is impossible to enumerate them, for there are whole suites of rooms filled with them, and one cannot help wondering how they all found their way to such an out-of-the-way spot of earth, so little favoured by nature. In the vast tract of country possessed by the Esterhazys, there must have been many spots better adapted for the site of such a castle, than this sandy hill on the edge of a morass.

Among the curiosities exhibited, are two small figures of a man and a woman, of Italian workmanship, composed entirely of Venetian sea-shells. By an immense expenditure of labour, the lips, the cheeks, the eyes, the fingers, the dress, the boots, the buckles, have all been represented accurately by shells of different colours; even the hair of the head and beard, has been imitated. The figures are by no means beautiful, but they afford a striking proof of the variety and richness of the Venetian conchology. Twelve thousand florins were paid for them, but rather in compliment to a recommendatory letter from the empress, brought to Prince Esterhazy by the man who had them to sell, than from any desire he felt to become the possessor.

In Esterhaz also were many blood horses, and as usual, Englishmen in attendance upon them. I was told that the parents of these horses had sold for enormous prices in England, three and four thousand pounds sterling, whence I was led to infer the nobility of the children; I was nevertheless blind to their manifold perfections, and should have set more value on any good honest working horse. The great Esterhazy stud is kept in the Oseral district, to the south of the Platten Lake, and is said to consist of eight hundred high bred horses. Besides the stables, we visited the dog kennels, to which is attached a separate kitchen, a courtyard for exercise, and various accommodations for the different ages of the canine occupants. There were no less than ninety-two English dogs of fine figures, and with physiognomies expressive of their sporting capabilities, but I can feel no sympathy for these lordly hunting dogs kept in herds, and was not at all distressed, when the whipper-in cut in among them with a great whip to bring them into order, yet I should have grieved to see a blow aimed at a faithful house dog, or a shepherd's companion.

A manufactory of beet-root sugar has now been established four years in Esterhaz, and produces on an average every year, thirty tons of refined sugar. From a hundred weight of beet-root, from five to five and half pounds of sugar are made. This branch of industry is new in Hungary, having been first established there twelve years ago by the family of Odeschalchi, but there are now thirty-two establishments. The largest belongs to the Coburg Coharys, and there are some smaller than that at Esterhaz; but if we suppose that one with another, they make about the same quantity as is made there, we may calculate on a yearly production of a thousand tons of sugar. If we allow a pound of sugar per week to every sugar-eating individual, the wants of about forty thousand persons will be supplied, which is not an unimportant consideration. For every hundred thousand sugar-eaters, there are in Hungary, however, one thousand, who never taste such a luxury. At the end of the last century, there were only two sugar refineries in all Hungary, one in Oedenburg and one in Fiume.

It is not Esterhaz but the town of Eisenstadt, which is the chief seat of the Esterhazy *government*. At the latter town is the central-office of administration for all the vast estates, extending hence to the other side of the Platten Lake, as well as northward into the Slowack country. Each of the territories or lordships is administered by a president, residing in Eisenstadt, and four counsellors. The great mass of the estates is divided into five districts, to each of which a prefect is appointed and so extensive are these, that a prefect has often to travel two days to get from one end of his district to the other. Under the prefects again are the directors for each single estate, with their rentmasters, stewards, agents, &c. Some of the estates have from twenty to thirty villages and hamlets, and sometimes a town of larger size. On an average they contain about eight or ten.

The oldest castle of the Esterhazys—their hereditary castle of Galantha, lies in the Slowack country, but the greater number as well as the largest and newest are about the Nieusiedler Lake. The castle of Eisenstadt is celebrated for its park, and its numerous treasures of art. It is decorated on the outside with the busts of Attila and the leaders of the Magyars,— a sort of decoration not uncommon in the castles of Hungary. Among the various collections I was most interested by the great library of Church Music. There were two thousand compositions of various kinds,—Masses, Litanies, &c., besides two thousand oratorios, including several manuscripts of Haydn, written in a clear, delicate, elegant hand, very unlike the scrawl of Beethoven. At the time of the festivals given by the Esterhazys to the empress Maria Theresa, they had Haydn for a leader of their orchestra, and from 1806 to 1812, Hummel, to whom they are indebted for the rich and beautifully arranged collection of church music of which I have spoken. At this castle Haydn composed his celebrated " Nelson Mass," during a visit paid by the hero to Prince Nicholas. Another more recent English visiter, Lord Grey, procured for the composer a monument in the church of Eisenstadt, by enquiring after it before it existed. He was then told that such a monument had been long in contemplation, and it has subsequently been erected.

The castle and town of Eisenstadt, which I visited during my stay at Vienna, lie at the foot of the Leitha mountains, up the sides of which stretches the park, the largest and most beautiful in Hungary. It thus affords opportunities for the most exquisite groupings of trees and flowers, and its great extent may be imagined from a steam-engine having been put up for the purpose of conveying water to the flower-beds and greenhouses.

The walks leading up the mountains, the avenue of roses, the chestnut-avenues, &c., were, when I saw them, filled with promenaders, especially with pretty Jewesses. I was, however, less interested by the fair Israelites than by a Franciscan monk, Father Stanislaus Albach, of whose praises my companions were full. He had been a preacher in Pesth, and had there enchanted his hearers by his eloquence, but as his views had been thought too liberal, and he would not submit to retract any thing, he was, by order of his superior, banished from Pesth, and now lives in a very retired manner in Eisenstadt. He there occupies himself almost exclusively with plants, those harmless children of nature, the intercourse with which is best adapted to bring balm to a wounded spirit. He often wanders about botanizing for days together in the Leitha mountains, and among the marshy regions of the Nieusiedler Lake ; the rest of his time is employed in writing down his religious contemplations and prayers, of which he has already published a volume.

THE MORASS OF HANSAG AND THE GULYAS.

The Nieusiedler Lake is, as I have said, surrounded on the western side by the low vineyards of Rust. On this side, also, the water is deepest, as its basin slopes a little towards the mountains. On the east, it is shallower, and there occur sandbanks and islands of peat moss, which, at length, become united together, and a wide marshy district commences, which stretches as far as to the neighbourhood of the Danube, where the land rises higher, and assumes a firmer character. It is probable, indeed, that the river has formed for itself these high banks. The whole marshy tract lying between the Nieusiedler Lake and the arm of the Danube, which surrounds the island of Schutt, is called by the Hungarians *Hansag*, a name signifying morass, which has been retained in the Geographies as a proper name; but the Germans of the vicinity call it the " *Wasen*." The whole includes a surface of from eight to nine German square miles, and is, therefore, nearly as large as the Nieusiedler Lake itself, but affords only a scanty pasturage for cattle.

In some spots the soil of the Hansag is rather firmer, in others the water has collected in little lakes or ponds, the most remarkable of which is the one called the King's Lake. The greater part of the Hansag may be regarded as a floating bog; but, here and there, trees are growing, and nearly in the centre there is a wood of alders, which does not float. Over the whole surface of the morass lies a bed of moss, usually about six, but sometimes as much as from nine to twelve feet thick; and beneath this lies, almost everywhere, a stratum of bog earth, resting on a firm bed of clay, covered, like the bottom of the Nieusiedler Lake, with stones and gravel. In the spring, when the whole Hansag is overflowed, this moss covering (and sometimes also the stratum of turf) is loosened, and floats upon the surface of the water. If, in consequence, perhaps, of a favourable state of the atmosphere, the growth of the moss has been more than usually vigorous, it clings closely to the lower soil, and is overflowed; but it sometimes happens that large tracts are suddenly loosened, and what the day before was a sheet of water, becomes transformed apparently into dry land, in consequence of the moss bed having emerged during the night. If this account be correct, it is likely that the whole Hansag has been formerly a lake, and has been changed into its present condition by the growth of the moss. It may have formed, with the Nieusiedler, one great lake traversed by the Danube; and in the course of centuries, during which the river had formed for itself high banks, become reduced to its present size by the growth of the moss.

The accounts preserved in Oedenburg and Esterhaz, of villages swallowed up by the lake, and the very modern date ascribed to it, do not necessarily contradict this hypothesis; for this might have been occasioned by a sudden inundation, and the coarse sand of the Danube spread over the whole lower surface of the Hansag, is a surer record than these.

The greatest proprietors of the Hansag are the archduke Charles, of Altenburg, and prince Esterhazy; the latter alone claims three German square miles. The following table may serve to show the nature of the property:

Overgrown meadow and standing water	19,360 yoch.
Clear meadow land	11,700 ,,
Alder forest	8,190 ,,
Useful reedy tracts	5,700 ,,
Arable land	269 ,,

About three-fourths of the Hansag, therefore, including the reedy parts, are marshy, meadow ground; not quite one-fifth forest, and 1-160th arable land. This was the state of it fifteen years ago; but it is possible that it may, by this time, be somewhat improved, as the mere pasturing of cattle on it would do something, and the owners have been making some efforts to reclaim the wilderness; but there would probably be more progress made, if the land were divided among many small proprietors. Little or nothing, however, has been done by the government commission, established for the purpose, since the emperor Joseph's time. It has been supposed to be at work for fifty years, and it is impossible to find out what it has really done in all that time.

The greater part of what is obtained from the morass, is got out of it in the winter, and in very dry summers only is it possible to do any thing towards draining it by throwing up dikes or cutting canals. The princes Esterhazy have expended many thousand florins on these works, but they

THE MORASS OF HANSAG AND THE GULYAS.

might sink their whole revenues in such a swamp, without producing any great effect. One of their most expensive undertakings is a great dyke, which they have constructed as a means of communication between the north and south of the Hansag. This dyke has about twenty-three bridges, under which, in the spring, the water flows into the lake, *but it sometimes happens that the stream runs in a contrary direction.*

From the castle of Esterhaz the view ranges over a great part of this wilderness, where no trace of human habitation is discoverable. I was, however, as I have already said, desirous of taking a nearer view of the great marsh, and set out, therefore, for a drive along the dike, in the instructive company of one of the Esterhazy prefects, but was soon induced to leave the carriage, and proceed on foot over a path which heaved up and down beneath our feet. It is, nevertheless, possible to drive in a carriage to some of the hayfields and reed grounds, at least, with the light vehicles and skilful management of the Hungarian peasants. When we attempted it, however, one of our heavy horses fell through and remained sticking with all his four feet in the marsh as fast as if he had been nailed there. We left our coachman to pull him out, with the assistance of some herdsmen, and continued our way on foot. There was not the slightest danger, but it is a curious sensation to feel the ground everywhere shaking under one's feet, and to find it impossible to obtain a firm footing anywhere. We found workmen, reed-cutters, and mowers, provided with a contrivance of small boards fastened to their feet, to increase their security, while their heads and faces were covered with a kind of wig made of woven grass, to defend themselves against the bites of the small marsh gnats. They also stuff a quantity of grass into their hats to keep their heads cool during the heats of summer. The whole interior of the Hansag now lay stretched out before us, a boundless desert of reeds, interspersed with marshy meadows, and skirted on the distant horizon by the alder forest, which was just visible. The atmosphere was heavy and sultry, and countless myriads of gnats continued still more to darken the prospect. Besides these insects, there is another, called by the Germans *Minkerln,* which are a dreadful plague to both men and cattle, but which are occasionally very useful as leeches. My companion informed me, that the cattle here are liable to a peculiar malady, occasioned by the sudden change from the spare and scanty diet of the winter to the abundance of juicy herbs with which in the spring the marshes are covered, and many of them die suddenly in consequence. But after the month of June, when these insects make their appearance, the cattle are so plentifully bled, that the malady disappears, and the cases of sudden death occur no more. Large herds of what are called *wild* cattle live in the Hansag. They are called wild on account of their having never entered a stall. In winter the herdsmen drive them towards the borders of the marsh, into the neighbourhood of villages and forests, and place them in a roofless enclosure, where they remain till spring. The cows calve in February, and the young animals pass suddenly from the maternal warmth to the hardest frost, without suffering any harm. It is said, however, that only the cattle born in the Hansag can endure the hardship to which they are exposed there. Cattle that live thus always in the open air are called "Gulyas" by the Hungarians. For a tame herd they have another name. For the men who have the charge of oxen, sheep, horses, pigs, &c., they have entirely different words, and among all the south-eastern European nations, such as the Magyars, Tatars, and Wallachians, with the exception of the Slavonians, we find this rich pastoral vocabulary. This exception seems to me to afford a strong proof that the Slavonians were not so entirely a nomadic people as has been usually supposed. Whilst in Hungary, the words and phrases relating to agriculture are partly German, partly Slavonian, and partly Magyar, those concerning pastoral affairs are almost exclusively of Magyar origin. As we advanced further, we met a herd of four hundred young oxen and wild cows. As we approached, they started away and crowded timidly together, whilst some large white shaggy dogs of superior size came rushing towards us. We defended ourselves as well as we could, but the herdsmen had great difficulty in appeasing the terrors of their charge. The moment, however, they perceived their keepers advance to accost us, they became more tranquil, and as we continued to converse with the men, the cattle resumed their feeding, and evidently began to regard us as friends.

The herdsmen were two Magyars, in wide trowsers, short jackets, and broad-brimmed hats, with long black hair, sharply cut features, and sparkling eyes. Most of the German villages, on the Nieusiedler lake, employ these men as herdsmen. We accompanied some of them to their dwellings in the marsh. These were huts of a conical shape, built of reeds, with the floors also covered with reeds and straw. In the midst were some planks nailed together, and covered with hard beaten clay, which served for a hearth. Round this were laid straw beds, with pillows made of blocks of wood covered with sheep-skins. The inhabitants of these huts cannot even turn in their beds without feeling the ground shake under them, yet they occupy them all through the winter, and have a perfectly healthy appearance. Their principal nourishment consists of small pieces of beef, rubbed with onions and pepper and roasted; but the pepper—a Hungarian sort called "*Paprika*"—is used in enormous quantities. I swallowed a piece of the meat, and it felt as if I had eaten a burning coal. To this piquant dish they drink the muddy marsh water. When they wish to drink they lie down on their stomachs, and draw the water up by means of a reed. One of them showed me exactly how the operation was performed. He cut a reed, placed it upright, and then struck it about an ell down into the ground. He then sucked up the water and spit it out, as the first which came was thick, brown, and dirty. The more he sucked the clearer it became, till, at length, finding it drinkable, he drew out the reed, and wrapped a piece of rag round the lower end to serve as a filter. He then plunged it again into the hole and called on me to drink, saying it was delicious. I found one of these reeds sticking in the ground before every bed, and I was told that in the morning when they get up the first thing they do is to take a drink. On stooping to take a draught of this cool beverage I chanced to take hold rather carelessly of the reed, and they begged me to mind what I was about, as I might easily trouble the water beneath.

In the whole extent of the Hansag there are very few people who can read—read books I mean—but they can all read, with great readiness, in the physiognomies of their companions the oxen, and they can also read in the heavens the signs of the coming weather. It is not possible that the nomadic ancestors of these people, can have led a simpler and rougher life than their descendants do, and, perhaps, in all Europe one could hardly find within the same space a more striking contrast than that of these pastoral regions, and of the luxurious capital, which, with a railroad, might be reached in two hours.

Many a Vienna cavalier, however, comes to shoot in the Hansag, without taking any notice of it; and I am convinced that if a scene from the Hansag were cleverly represented at their theatre, the Vienna people would take it for a scene laid in some far distant country—perhaps in the jungles on the Delta of the Ganges.

How wild and barbarous this region is, appears sufficiently from the story of the celebrated wild boy found in the Hansag, and known throughout the country by the name of Han Istok (Marsh Stephen). According to the account given me, this boy was a perfectly brutalized creature, and was caught by some fishermen with a net, in the principal lake of the Hansag, in the year 1749. I saw his portrait in Castle Esterhaz, and to judge from the picture, he had a bald head, with a few hairs behind, broad features, resembling the lower animals, a thick under lip, large stomach, short legs, arms which he jerked about like a frog, and long fingers and teeth. In some particulars I felt inclined to distrust the accuracy of this portrait, his fingers and toes being represented as connected by a membrane like the web on the feet of waterfowl. His whole body was covered with a hard, scaly kind of skin, and when first taken, he would only eat grass, hay, frogs, and raw fish, from which he sucked the blood. After he had been kept for seven months in the castle, he left off sucking raw blood, and began to endure clothing; but they were obliged to keep him carefully from the water, as he made many attempts to escape by leaping into it. He remained fourteen months in the castle, and in the latter part of the time it was found possible to employ him in the kitchen, to turn a spit. They could not, however, succeed in teaching him to speak, and the only sound he uttered was a kind of hissing whistle. At the end of the time I have mentioned, he eluded the vigilance of his keepers, probably by springing into the castle-moat, and through that back into the wilderness of the morass. Prince Nicholas Esterhazy took much pains to recover him, and even had the moat and the neighbouring waters dragged, under the idea that he might have been drowned; but "Marsh Stephen" was seen no more. Three years afterwards, it is said, some one caught a glimpse of him in the Hansag, and as some old Frenchmen still doubt of the death of Napoleon, so many of the herdsmen believe that Marsh Stephen is still living among the waters. He has become, indeed, for the people of the neighbourhood a kind of mythic personage; at least I saw a poem in which he was spoken of as a kind of marsh king, who at times tormented the herdsmen and fishermen, and sometimes bestowed gifts upon them.

An official account of him has been drawn up in Vienna, which agrees perfectly with that which I have given. I find nothing incredible in the story, if we except the particular of his living *in* the lake; but as men have been known to live like squirrels on the boughs of trees, or like tigers and lions in dens, I consider it by no means impossible that a man might become accustomed to the mode of life of the beaver and sea-otter. Marsh Stephen, however, can only be considered to have carried the wild manners of the district a little farther than the rest of the inhabitants, of whose moral condition he was but an exaggerated specimen. Not only are the rational people here more uncultivated than any where else, but there are many who never attain to reason at all. In several of the villages round the marsh, there are numbers of Cretins; and I was informed by a lady, that in the island of Schutt, in the Danube, there were so many cripples, idiots, scrofulous patients, and Cretins, that it was quite disgusting to go there. She named to me also some races in the Hansag, with whom Cretinism was hereditary; and as far as I could judge during the short time I remained there, these Cretins have the same peculiarities as those of the Alps—idiotcy, large swollen heads, deficiency of speech, stupid insensibility, cunning, &c. It happens, also, sometimes here, as in the Alps, that the parents are perfectly healthy and rational, and all the children afflicted by Cretinism. This malady extends over the whole island of Schutt, and it may be doubted whether it have not some connexion with the water which they suck out of the marshy ground.

The sun had begun to sink, and, when we set out on our return home, innumerable flocks of birds were returning to their nests among the reeds from the distant cornfields on the firm land, where they had been feeding. We found with some difficulty the place where we had left our equipage. Several of the herdsmen hastened to our assistance, others had drawn our horse out of the mire, and pushed the carriage upon firmer ground. I could not help noticing as an indication of the abject slavery of the peasantry in Hungary, that one of the subordinate officials who accompanied us, as he was getting into the carriage, hit an old man a blow on his bald head with a thick reed, with which he was playing. I inquired what sort of man the peasant might be. " Oh, a capital fellow," was the answer, " one of our best herdsmen." " Why did you strike him then ?" " Oh, I don't know ! By way of taking leave." " Could not you have shaken hands with him ?" " Oh, no ! no ! not that either." This gratuitous insult to an obliging, bald-headed, old man, gave me as much pain as if I had seen a man receive the punishment of the knout.

One of the principal employments of the dwellers in and near the Hansag, and of the herdsmen, in their leisure hours, is drying the reeds and plaiting them into coarse mats, which are used in Vienna for packing and for other purposes. In the Venetian territory, the Black Forest and elsewhere, the shepherds make the finest and most beautiful straw mats, and if we compare them with those made in the Hansag, we shall have a fair standard for estimating the comparative skill of the different races.

On the eastern shores of the lake, in dry summers, soda issues from the ground, and the German inhabitants call this soda " *tsick*," in imitation of the Hungarian word *szek*, and call the places where it is found " *tsick earth*." The ground must have been tolerably dry, and its upper crust subsequently softened by light rains, before the soda can issue from it in abundance, and cover it for miles, making it look as if there had been snow. The people then collect it with brooms and boil it. The largest quantities are obtained between the Danube and the Theiss, but most of the little lakes in the Hansag yield soda when they dry up. In wet years it is found only on their margins. Since the year 1797 the Vienna soap-boilers have formed a company for the establishment of soda manufactories on the Nieusiedler Lake, and they understand getting the soda better than the prince's subjects. He would have been willing to farm out the production of the whole eastern shore, but could not come to terms with the Vienna company, which has now established itself near Nieusiedel, and must injure the prince's trade. Near the village Ilmick, on the lake, there is also found a fine crystal salt, which is partly sold and partly used for the cattle. On our return we brought the ladies of our party some forget-me-nots, plucked from the reed huts of the herdsmen in the marsh, where this tender flower blossoms in great abundance, and is eaten by the cattle. It was midnight when I mounted my horse to ride back to Zinkendorf, and as it was the night between Saturday and Sunday, we found, according to Magyar custom, all the villages full of life and movement, for on this night the young men pay visits at the windows of their respective damsels, and in many cottages lights were burning, and many happy pairs were standing in animated conversation before them.

At the castle of Zinkendorf all was dark and still. I had not been expected back that night, and every one was gone to bed. The doors and windows, however, were unfastened, and I found no difficulty in groping my way to my apartments. I was afterwards told that no one ever thought of locking up the castle, although it contained considerable sums of money. This is a fact which I found it hard to reconcile with what I had been told of the general state of insecurity in the country, and of the precautions it was necessary to take. It may be that criminals are too much dazzled by the halo of grandeur to venture to attack palaces.

On the following morning, while my carriage was getting ready, I visited the mulberry plantations of Count Szechenyi, a gentleman who has exercised a most beneficial influence on the cultivation and industry of his native country, by the benefit of his own example. In his nurseries near Zinkendorf he possesses two hundred thousand mulberry-trees, and he has planted out upwards of twenty thousand into the open field, which have now attained the age of from eight to twelve years. Should many of his countrymen follow his example, the growth of silk in Hungary may at no distant period become very considerable. There is scarcely any Hungarian town in which there are not Bohemians settled, and cultivating some branch of industry, and in Zinkendorf I found a Bohemian coachmaker, who informed me that he had already *launched* six hundred equipages. He also conducted me into the literary institution or reading-room of the place, for since the birth of Hungarian journalism, and the establishment of the Casino at Pesth, and the Hungarian Literary Society, these institutions have spread over Hungary with extraordinary rapidity, so that as I have said, even the little village of Zinkendorf can boast of one. I found there, the little Hungarian publications *Yelenkor, Villag, Hirnok,* &c., besides the *Allgemeine Zeitung,* and several other German papers. Like most similar institutions in this country, the reading-rooms had existed about three years.

THE RAABAU AND RAAB.

The whole country between Oedenburg and Raab is as flat as if it had been adjusted with a pair of scales. It forms a part of the western Hungarian plain, the lowest portion of which is the Hansag and the Nieusiedler Lake, and is bounded on the north-west by the Rosalia mountains, the Leitha mountains, and the Presburg branch of the Carpathians; on the north-east by the Neutra mountains and other spurs of the Carpathians; on the south-east by the Bacony forest, and on the south-west by spurs of the Styrian Alps. A figure whose boundary lines were drawn through the towns of Presburg, Pyrnau, Komorn, Raab, Körmönd, Güns, and Oedenburg, would inclose this plain comprehending a surface of about two hundred (German) square miles. With the exception of the Hansag this whole district is exceedingly fertile, and this fertility reaches its highest point in the island of Schütt. The Danube flows through the middle of this plain, dividing itself into several branches after passing Presburg, and uniting again at Komorn. This is generally called the Little Hungarian Plain in contradistinction to the great plain on the east, which might be called the plain of the Theiss, since that river flows through it from beginning to end. In the great plain the people are principally occupied with pasturage, but near Presburg agriculture is at least equally important. All the cattle and corn intended for exportation from Hungary is brought to the great staple places, Wieselburg and Oedenburg, and thence passed over the frontier.

The district between Wieselburg and Presburg, is called the "Haidboden," or Heath; that between the great and little Raab, the Raabau, and between the Heath and Raabau lies the Hansag.

It was on a tremendously hot day that I passed through the Raabau, which is like one large luxuriant meadow, mixed with cornfields. My coachman, a true Magyar, was tolerably well protected from the fierce arrows of Apollo by the immense brim of his hat, but I under the scanty shade of my travelling-cap, suffered much. Everywhere I noticed the adoption of defensive measures against the sun, and the other plague of these regions, the gnats. All the horses were armed with bushes of willow or other shrubs, and several shepherds with horses and sheep were often crowded together under the shade of a single tree, the horses being content if they could only thrust in their noses. Sometimes I noticed a still greater variety of animals, pigs, goats, geese, and oxen huddled together, and even from the middle of a hollow tree, popped out the head of a goat.

In all the doorways of the houses in this part of the country, wherever it is possible, curtains are used instead of doors, by which the double advantage is obtained of a greater circulation of air, and the exclusion of the gnats. Even in the castle of Zinkendorf, these door-draperies were employed. What are called fly-windows are also in use in all the cottages; and the master and mistress of the house often have the bed-matrimonial placed in the open air under the veranda of the roof, where they are shielded from the gnats, by a thick net hanging down, and enveloping them in its folds like Mars and Venus.

The most effectual method of defence against this plague of insects has been discovered by the buffaloes who wallow up to their necks in any dirty pool they can find. I got out of the carriage to take a nearer survey of these unclean animals, and perceived that though they were covered and dripping with mud, they were still chewing. From time to time they left off however, and putting down their heads into the puddle, took up a quantity of water, and threw it over the back of their necks, which stood above the water. Then they began to chew again, but repeated from time to time the same manœuvre, so as to keep themselves always wet. The sagacity of the ox does not appear to reach so far.

The more oppressive the heat, the more provoking became the false appearances of water which presented themselves to the eye on all sides, and there was a heaviness and gloom in the atmosphere although scarcely any clouds were perceptible. It was Sunday, and we met many smart-looking people; the broad hats of the Magyars, like those of the Croats near Oedenburg, were perfect beds of flowers, natural and artificial, intermixed with bunches of ostrich and peacocks' feathers. It appears that this custom has passed from the Croats to the Magyars, for I have elsewhere observed it among them. Some of them wore bushes of fine black ostrich plumes. Before the images of saints cut in stone, women were kneeling on the withered grass under the burning sun. They wore at the backs of their heads such a profusion of ribbons, bows, and lace, that if magnificence depended on the quantity of ornament, they were certainly magnificently dressed.

The shepherds whom I saw in the fields, resembled in dress and appearance the celebrated swine-herds of Bacony, and wore white mantles embroidered with red flowers, their hair plaited into two stiff tails that hung down over their ears. In some of the villages I noticed high thorn hedges, on the summits of which, great masses of thorns were piled up to keep out the wolves. These circumvallations of thorns are also in use in South Russia, and form the easiest and best defence against those animals.

In this district begins the cultivation of the fine Hungarian tobacco, the plantations of which my coachman pointed out to me. What surprised me was, to see potatoes growing among the tobacco, as well as among the maize, and indeed there appeared to be no ground devoted exclusively to their cultivation. Thirty years ago, potatoes were scarcely known in this part of Hungary, and the people are indebted to the Germans for the introduction of so useful a root. The Magyar peasants would at first have nothing to do with it, or at least only used it for their pigs, but they have changed their opinion since then.

Everywhere in passing though this plain, I could see on looking back, the distant snowy mountains of the Styrian frontier, commanding the country like a distant sovereign. I gradually lost sight of them, however, as well as of the prince Esterhazy, whose name is distinguished above all other names in this part of Hungary, as much as those snowy peaks above the Leitha and other mountains.

At Tshorna I took my dinner, and was exceedingly indignant at being asked by the monks, who I was and what I wanted, when I requested permission to see the library. If I had asked admission to a prince or a prelate, it might have been a different case, but the muses should require no such ceremonial introduction. I was even laughed at for wishing to see the archives, and told that the archives contained important state secrets, and that I could not see them without a written permission from the King of Hungary.

The church of the convent was filled with devout Magyars; the girls sitting in the front, the married women next, their heads covered with white handkerchiefs, and the men forming the outer circle, extending even into the cloistered walks, where they knelt in silent devotion.

Grapes are found in every village and hamlet, and if the traveller should complain with reason, that the soup is too watery, the meat too hard, and the cucumbers too sour, he has only to stock his carriage with Vienna rolls on setting out, and with these grapes he can indemnify himself for the bad cookery along the road.

I did not on the whole way to Raab, meet any carriages, or any people who appeared to belong to the higher orders, for the route which I followed, was a by-road leading through the interior of the country. We had continually to make our way through large herds of cattle, or flocks of geese, which are here larger than any where else, as it is the practice for the geese belonging to a whole village, to be confided to the care of one person. Sometimes we were stopped by a great drove of pigs coming from Turkey, whence they had been brought up the Danube in the steamboat to Raab, and were making their way to Oedenburg, one of the greatest pig-markets in the world. The plan generally adopted by the drivers, is for one man to go before shaking a bag of cucumbers, the odour of which is regarded by the pigs as especially enticing, while another of their guardians follows with a large whip, and thus between coaxing and threatening, the pigs advance on their way to the markets and the slaughtering-houses of Oedenburg.

Towards evening I saw the herds returning home to the villages; they consisted usually of two-thirds oxen and one-third buffaloes, and always appeared to observe a regular order of march.

The oxen came first in loose order, and the buffaloes, who never mingled with them, followed in close ranks behind. About half-way between Raab and Tshorna, we passed the large village of Enesh, whose inhabitants are exclusively Hungarian nobles; and whilst, at every other place, we had been civilly saluted, no one here took the slightest notice of us. It is said that, as they unite enormous privileges with enormous insolence and coarseness of manners, it is very necessary to be on one's guard in all intercourse with them. As we drove on, a young lady of high birth and ancient family was pointed out to me, engaged in cleaning out her father's stables; the Baron of K. passed us driving his team of oxen; and the Baroness Z. was sitting before her door, patching her husband's leather breeches. I drove respectfully and quietly by these personages, which it was so much the easier to do, as the road lay over a dunghill.

The sultry day brought forth, towards evening, a magnificent storm, and the incessant lightnings darted about like restless thoughts in the mind of man, lifting up various objects till, at length, the towers of Raab appeared in sight. As we approached Raab, the storm also came nearer; my Hungarian coachman urged his horses, according to custom, into a gallop, and we soon found ourselves in the middle of Raab, and in the midst, also, of wind, and rain, and thunder, and lightning, which made us all the better pleased to find shelter in the "Palatine" Inn.

Here, in the large hall, we found a grand dance going on, in which, after I had a little recovered from my fatigue, I heartily joined. The company, which was jumping about in such high glee, belonged mostly to the lower order of tradesmen and mechanics, ropemakers, grocers, butchers, &c., and Hungarian and German were spoken promiscuously. Most of them were dressed in the German fashion; but a considerable number were parading in the Hungarian national costume, which, for people in this situation of life, must be very expensive. It consists, in the first place, of very tight pantaloons down to the ankle, with short half-boots, and massive silver spurs. Over the waistcoat, hangs loosely on the shoulders a "*Dolman*" trimmed, as well as the waistcoat, with thick rows of massive silver buttons, and fastened by a silver chain that falls down over the breast. On the head is placed, rather on one side, a high Hungarian cap or *Kalpak*, and the hair hangs in small curls on the cheeks. They were mostly handsome young fellows who wore this showy dress, but not always native Hungarians, for it sometimes happens that German mechanics, on their travels, will take a fancy to display their persons to advantage in all the finery of Dolman and Kalpak, and silver spurs, although such a costume cannot cost less than 200 florins. The dances were often German, especially the waltz; but after each waltz there was a cry of "*Magyar! Magyar!*" as a signal that the Magyar dance was required. Sometimes they would not even wait for the German dance to be finished, but compelled the musicians to make a sudden change of tune by the vehement cry of "Magyar! Magyar!" (pronounced *Moyár*). The whole mass of the company then fell into pairs, the gentlemen placed themselves opposite each to a lady, whirled her round or danced round her, the eyes sparkled, the Dolmans flew about, and the chains and spurs clattered an accompaniment to the full but rather melancholy tones of the Hungarian music. The scene was not uninteresting, and I contemplated it a considerable time before I retired to my room, in the rather deceitful hope of a night's rest.

The city of Raab lies at the confluence of the river Raab and the Little Danube, and is of very remote antiquity; it is only in modern times, however, that it has acquired its present extent. In the year 1785, it had only 4,535 inhabitants, and at present it contains probably 20,000. There are in Hungary many instances of an equally rapid increase of population. The town is by no means poor in historical recollections, and indeed, after Pesth, is one of the most interesting I have seen in this country. During the wars between the Turks and Austrians, it was always regarded as one of the bulwarks of Christendom; but in the year 1595, it was taken by the Turks, and formed, for a short time, the extreme limit of their dominions on the Danube, being governed by a pasha. Since 1809, when the French were here, the fortifications have been for the most part destroyed. The French balls are still to be seen in the walls of the Evangelical Church and other buildings. There is also preserved in the Cathedral Church the iron gate and the petard with which it was blown in, when, in the year 1598, the Austrian generals Palffy and Schwarzenberg recovered the city from the Turks. The joy at this reconquest must have been very great, for to this day its anniversary is celebrated as the greatest festival of the year.

The Cathedral is said to have been the work of St. Stephen, and a large picture by an Austrian artist, represents him as presenting his son to the Almighty. The Turks filled the cathedral with earth, and made use of the high roof as a mound on which to place their cannon, so as to command the country for miles round. The story goes, that the Turkish general, Mehemed Bassa, one day said scornfully, that the Christians should have the town again whenever the iron cock on the top of the Carmelite convent should begin to crow; and that the day before the recovery of the town, the wind having suddenly changed, whirled the cock round, and made it utter a shrill sound, resembling a crow.

Among the things which struck me as remarkable in the town, were the *Curiae*, as they are called, of the nobility, that is, their town houses, which are privileged in the same manner as their estates in the country. According to the ancient laws of the place, a nobleman ought to be subject to the city police, and within the walls regarded as on an equality with every other citizen. Many nobles and magnates have managed to procure exceptions in their own favour, and have settled in the town, and bought land in it, without submitting to its regulations. "*Curia nobilaris*" is usually inscribed, or cut in stone over the entrance to these mansions, and within their precincts they enjoy, besides others, the enviable privileges of brewing beer, and distilling and selling brandy. They cannot be arrested by the city police, who dare not so much as enter these *Curiæ* which may thus afford shelter not only to their owners, but even to any criminals they may choose to harbour. The house of every clergyman, also, is, according to the expression here used, *Curia*.

Although Raab is by no means exclusively a Magyar town, being in a great measure inhabited by Germans, its citizens are renowned in Hungary for their patriotic zeal, which they are even said to carry to fanaticism. One circumstance, apparently trifling, may have contributed to this,—namely, that it possesses the best national musicians in Hungary. The gipsy bands of Raab are frequently invited to play in other places, and are always much admired.

If Raab were formerly considered as the last bulwark of Christendom, it may now be regarded as the ultimate refuge of Magyarism. It was the first town in which I was able to procure a complete collection of all the journals and periodicals published in the Hungarian language; and this I found in the Literary Institution, established on the model of the Casino of Pesth. The oldest Hungarian paper does not date back beyond ten years. Before that time, there were only a few, usually printed in Latin, which have since died away. The most distinguished of the journals at present in vogue, the name of which meets one at every turn, is the "*Pesti Hirlap*," or Pesth Journal, which has existed only a year and a half, but has already outstripped all its competitors. It keeps a vigilant watch over all faults and abuses of the government, and is the most liberal paper published in Hungary. Its editor, the darling of his countrymen, is the celebrated Hungarian noble, advocate, and deputy, "Koszuth." The other papers are, the *Hirnok* (the Messenger), the *Vilag* (the World), the *Erdelyi Hirado* (the Transylvanian Herald), the *Yelenkor* (the Present Time), the *Mult es Yelen* (Present and Past), the *Athenaeum*, the *Regelo* (the Romantic Tale-teller), the *Tudomanytar*, and some others. As I shall subsequently have occasion to refer to these, I must beg my readers, if possible, to keep in mind at all events, the names of the *Hirlap*, the *Yelenkor*, the *Hirnok*, and the *Vilag*.

The most magnificent residence in Raab is that of the catholic bishop, whose palace was purchased, by one of his predecessors, from the empress, Maria Theresa. The present bishop is said to be a very estimable and cultivated man. The Hungarian catholic clergy is almost the only one in Europe that still enjoys untouched and undiminished its former privileges and revenues, but a time is, probably, not far off when these golden days will be overcast, for there are evident symptoms of discontent at the little advantage to humanity or science derived from the large incomes enjoyed by so many very reverend but very useless gentlemen.

Far less of luxury and superfluity is to be seen in the abodes of the chief pastor of the evangelical or of the Lutheran congregation than in the splendid suite of dining-rooms, reception-rooms, libraries, and billiard-rooms shown to us at the palace of the bishop. So late as the reign of Maria Theresa, the Lutherans were forbidden the public exercise of their religion, and though Joseph's toleration edict removed this prohibition, they remained both poor and oppressed. The exact dimensions were prescribed to them for the church they were allowed to build, and it is, consequently, very small and low, and has neither bell nor steeple. These might now be added but that the means are wanting. The altar was placed immediately under the pulpit, and I was told that this was customary in all the Lutheran churches in Hungary.

Of the Lutheran school, as it was, unluckily, a holiday, I could not see much, but I saw here, for the first time, a complete and excellent map of the kingdom of Hungary, and there are now plenty of them to be had for all purposes. The most striking feature of a map of Hungary is the white space, destitute of names, that appears on the lower region of the Theiss and Danube. The Hungarians generally point to it themselves, and say—"Look! this white blank we owe to the Turks, who made a desert of these countries, and whose barbarism has retarded us for centuries on the path of civilization."

On one occasion there was shown to me the letter of a pasha from the time of the Turkish dominion in Raab, in which he addresses the citizens of a neighbouring town as "Hogs and Dogs," enquiring why they are so long in ransoming their girls whom he has taken in pledge, and threatening to take their heads off if they do not agree to his proposals. Similar records of the Turkish mode of government are found everywhere in Hungary in the archives of the cities, churches, and counties, and complaints are frequent of the outrages the country suffered from them. Almost every country in Europe has some foreign barbarian conqueror on whom it lays the blame of having retarded its progress. As the Turks in Hungary, so are the Mongols regarded in Russia, the Russians in Poland, the Austrians in Bohemia, the Germans in Italy, and the French in Germany.

At our dinner at the inn, an article from a Hungarian paper on the subject of mixed marriages was read and commented on, and then followed some recitations by two little girls of six and ten years old, of German poems, treating of the "consuming fire of love." I then ordered my calesch, and in the company of a courteous and learned Hungarian friend, drove to the abbey of Martinsberg, situated two German miles from Raab.

THE ABBEY OF MARTINSBERG.

This renowned Benedictine abbey lies on a spur of the Bacony forest, which stretches into the plain of Raab. Many a difference has been fought out on this plain, and neither Napoleon nor Charlemagne penetrated further into Hungary. After the battle in the plain the French were compelled to undertake a siege of the town and fortress, which lasted several days, during which they fired two thousand six hundred and sixty balls against the devoted city. After their conquest they blew up the fortifications, which have not been since restored. Their fragments and ruins lie around some three or four hundred houses which have sprung up on their site. Thus did the French render the same service to this as to so many German towns.

My esteemed companion was one of those Hungarian literati who prefer speaking Latin to any other language. He usually began by speaking German, but soon fell imperceptibly into Latin, finding it as he said so much more convenient and better adapted to conversation than any other tongue. He said that he knew many literary men to whom Latin was by far the most familiar, although on the whole it had fallen into disuse of late. He himself, as a Hungarian patriot, preferred as a matter of principle, the use of the native language, but when he wished to pour out his heart he could not help using Latin. Some, he said, carried their persecution of it to a pitch of fanaticism, "et illis nunc pudor est loqui Latine, et volunt ut canes nocturni vigilantes Hungariæ canant." With the human guardians of the night, in some Hungarian towns where they have been in the habit of crying the hour in German, this has really been required. I inquired whether, as I had heard, the Hungarian ladies spoke Latin, but he said he never met but one who was capable of doing so, and that was a lady from Presburg. The Hungarian magnates all speak it, but the Slovacks are considered better and more fluent Latinists than the Magyars.

As the abbey lies very high we soon came in sight of it, and I was really astonished at the size and beauty of this magnificent building.

"Non miroreris," began my friend. "You would not wonder at the splendour of the building, if you knew what revenues these gentlemen possess, and how they live. Their abbey is one of the richest in all Hungary, and the poorest of them drive out with four horses. Omnium rerum abundantiæ fruuntur, exempli gratia vini boni, equorum optimorum et totius vitæ apparatus ditissimi. The mountain on which the abbey stands, as you see, rises proudly from the plain, and has probably been since a very early period, dedicated to the service of religion. It was called by the Romans, and still retains the name of, the Sacer Mons Pannoniæ, and stands in the same relative position to Pannonia as Mount Athos did to Macedon. The first Christian king of Hungary, St. Stephen, and the first apostle of Christianity in our country, St. Anastatius, established here the first Christian church, and founded the abbey and the castle. Sanctus Anastatius primus fuit Abbas Sti. Martini, et mirum et inexplicabile est quantum nam in propagatione fidei orthodoxæ desudaverit." Stephen sent him as ambassador to Pope Sylvester II., who returned to him the crown and sceptre of the Hungarian kingdom, which the king had ordered to be laid at his holiness's feet. The pope afterwards raised the abbey to the dignity of a high or arch abbey, the only one of that rank in the Austrian empire. The abbot is "ex officio" a Magnate of Hungary, and he is chosen by the Benedictines from among themselves without the sanction or interference of pope or emperor. Joseph the Second indeed clipped the wings of these ecclesiastics a little, but Francis II. restored some of their lost feathers. Since his time they have begun to make great alterations and improvements in their convent, and although it is not yet more than half completed, this half has already a most magnificent effect. In the front of the building is a group of statues, among which those of Stephen and Francis, the founder and the restorer of the convent, are the most distinguished.

We left our carriage at the foot of St. Martin's mountain, and climbed up on foot. As we entered the courtyard, we were saluted by the busy hammering of half a dozen coopers, who were employed in fastening large oaken casks of most capacious dimensions, destined to be filled with the finest Hungarian wines. In the walls near the gate I remarked the loopholes, which in former days had been used by the abbots in defence of their abbey and their native country. The church of the abbey is adorned by the works of Maulbertsch. Many of the Austrian churches are full of the productions of his pencil; but the best are those in Papa, a town over which Prince Esterhazy exercises sovereign sway. It is said the prince was lately reproached by an Englishman in London, for not doing something for their preservation. In a chapel belonging to this church, a marble seat in a niche was shown to us, as that on which King Stephen was accustomed to sit, when he attended the service performed by St. Anastatius.

This marble niche and the seat are regarded by the Hungarians as their most interesting antiquities. "See!" said one of the monks, who accompanied us, "there our sainted king used to sit in person." The Hungarian peasants come in great numbers on the festival days, and beg for permission to sit awhile in king Stephen's chair, as they consider it very serviceable for many pains in the back. I took my seat there for a moment, but the very cold of the marble seemed to me more likely to give a pain in the back than to take one away. The chapel is built with six columns supporting the roof, which rests on them, and on twelve pointed arches springing out of them. The St. Martin's hill is connected with the mountain range, to which it belongs, by a long ridge, along which runs a footpath leading to the lonely little chapel of St. Emmerich, the son of King Stephen. This Emmerich was married, but during or immediately after the performance of the ceremony, made a vow of perpetual chastity. He was accustomed every evening to pass along this path to the chapel, in order to offer his prayers to the Blessed Virgin; and it happened that his wife soon began to harbour some suspicion concerning these nightly wanderings, and determined one evening to follow him and discover the cause. She did so, and peeped through the window of the chapel, and there she saw, by the light of the tapers on the altar, the handsome and devout Emmerich prostrate in prayer, with his head surrounded by a saintly glory. Struck by the sight, she also sank on her knees to pray at the door of the chapel, and embracing her husband as he came out, made a similar vow of perpetual chastity.

The library of this convent is as magnificent in its arrangements as those of the convents on the Danube, which I have before described. It is not possible to arrange books and manuscripts in finer or more picturesque order, and I did not venture to take one down for fear of disturbing the harmony of their position. In the great hall of the library were finely-executed statues of Stephen and Francis II. Joseph built his monument in the hearts of millions of his subjects, but if he had had a successor to have followed in his footsteps, his statue also, in bronze and marble, would everywhere meet our eyes. The collection of books amounts to eighty thousand, among which are undoubtedly many of great value.

In the museum which is connected with the library are preserved many Turkish and Roman antiquities found in the neighbourhood. In the Turkish time the convent had to pay tribute to the pasha of Stuhlweissenburg, and the correspondence between them was carried on in Latin.

The Turks had in Buda and Pesth also many German subjects who were made to serve as interpreters for them in their administration of these pashalics.

In the collection of coins there are some said to be of the time of Attila. They bear the portrait of a man whose features are those of a Faun, and the inscription "*Attila* 451." In other Hungarian towns I have seen more of these coins, but am by no means convinced of their authenticity. Some were inscribed "*Buda Dux Hunnorum.*" It is remarkable enough that the memory of Attila has been regarded with so much respect by the people of Hungary. There are here to be met with more representations of Attila, the "Scourge of God," than in Germany of *Karl den Grossen* or Arminius.

In the front of the convent is a high tower of considerable compass, from the top of which a truly splendid prospect may be enjoyed. The ascent is by a convenient gallery on the outside, and the eye can thence embrace the whole northern half of Pannonia, no fewer than fourteen of the fifty-two counties of Hungary being comprised within the view. Could we, as our eyes rested on this wide surface, have known all that was passing beneath them—could we have followed all the spiritual movements of the millions of beings whose dwellings lay in those gray, blue, green, and yellow patches, we should have seen cause enough for both joy and sorrow. How little can the individual embrace in his sympathies; scarcely his nearest friends; and what has he to do with the joys and sorrows of millions in a foreign land?

Some of the ecclesiastics soon joined me on the tower, and with them my friend from Raab, so that I had interpreters enough of the various objects that struck me. Many estates were pointed out to us as the hereditary seats of this or that family. Near the road leading from Raab to Buda, called here the Butchers' road, probably on account of the great herds of cattle driven along it to market, lie the ancient castle and convent of Dotis, in which Matthias Corvinus passed so much of his time. We could perceive also quite distinctly in the mountain perspective, the entrance to the celebrated grotto of Dotis, and we saw through the long vista of past years a horde of wild Turks, at the entrance of this grotto, driving in the inhabitants of seven Hungarian villages, and suffocating them there with fire and smoke. No less than twenty waggon loads of human bones were subsequently taken out of it. In the territories ruled by the Turks there are many such caves, filled with human bones by the tide of barbarism, as in various parts of the world other caves have been filled by natural floods with the remains of animals.

Not far off in the same range of mountains, we could with our glasses distinguish the stone quarries of Olmosch, whence the materials have been taken for the fortifications of Komorn. The environs of the towns of Papa, Güns, and Steinamanger, which we had before seen only marked with black strokes upon the map, lay now in vivid colours before us. To the south lay the neighbouring Bacony mountains, covered from their valleys to their summits with an uninterrupted forest of oak.

The convents of the Benedictine order are very numerous in Hungary, and like this Abbey of Willastins, usually built on the summit of a hill. They are, however, nowhere more powerful than here, where their possessions entered on one side into the Bacony as far as the Platten Lake, and on the other to the Danube and the Dotis mountains; three abbeys of inferior rank, also in this part of the country belong to them. On St. Martin's hill, there reside fifty-two of these reverend ecclesiastics, but in all there are one hundred and ninety-six monks who belong to the convent, which has the control of two academies, those of Presburg and Raab; eight Gymnasia, those of Raab, Komorn, Guns, Oedenburg, Papa, Gran, Presburg, and Pyrnau, and fifteen parishes, and the appointments of all the professors, teachers, and preachers, are made from among the inmates of the abbey. The arch abbot of St. Martin's, has accordingly charge of the spiritual, and in a great measure also of the temporal welfare of the inhabitants of two hundred German square miles; it is not surprising, therefore, if the election of a new abbot is matter of interest to the whole country round.

The afternoon had been wonderfully beautiful, and I could scarcely tear myself from the lovely spectacle presented from the top of the tower. The evening drew on, and we were still gossiping German, Hungarian, and Latin, all mixed together; as the Russians mix French and Russian, the people of Alsace French and German, so do the Hungarians in their conversation mingle together Hungarian and German, at least I should perhaps add, they do so in the presence of a German. An immense number of German words and phrases have at all events obtained currency, and although many zealous and persevering efforts have been made to hunt them out, they continue to maintain their ground.

The sun sank, and as I turned towards the Bacony forest it lay before me, an immense unbroken mass of gloom, not lightened to the mind's eye by its very equivocal reputation. My companions the monks, however, appeared to be acquainted with every "dingle and bushy dell of that wild wood," as one of the abbeys is situated on the opposite side by the Platten Lake, and another in the very centre of the forest. This is called "Bacony Bel," that is the entrails or kernel of the Bacony. The monks have therefore often occasion to cross the forest in every direction, and are intimate with all its wild population. These immense oak woods have been found very favourable to the rearing of hogs, and in this part of Hungary therefore, the swinish multitude takes precedence both of oxen and sheep. As children, the inhabitants of this forest learn neither reading nor writing, and very little religion, nothing but the management of pigs, upon whose existence indeed their own is based. They live in general, wholly on pork and bacon, seasoned so highly with the "Paprika," of which I have already spoken, that no one unaccustomed to these spicy morsels can venture to taste them. To this they drink the Hungarian wine in unlimited quantities, living, however, day and night in all weathers, entirely in the forest. They wear large thick white woollen mantles decorated with flowers and ornaments in red thread or fragments of red stuff. I mentioned to my companions a passage I recollected in Dion Cassius, in which he describes the Pannonians as wearing mantles of this kind. "It is very possible," he replied, "for these Kopenyegs, as they are called, with the large loose sleeves hanging down, are only worn in Pannonian Hungary, and are never seen in Dacia on the other side of the Danube. These mantles always appear to strike every stranger, and are therefore very likely to have been observed by Dion Cassius.

"It is often very difficult," continued my informant, " to say whether these Bacony foresters are swineherds or robbers. Their wandering and uncertain mode of life, and their superiority in strength to their more settled countrymen, are circumstances by no means favourable to their honesty. It is of them that the poet says:

"Fern von Liebe, Lust und Leben,
Weil' ich hier im düstern Wald,
Wo im Sturm die Eichen beben,
Und der Wölfe Heulen schallt.
Sonnenschein und Sturmeswüthen
Schwärzten Brust mir und Gesicht,
Und die borst'ge Heerde hüten
Im Gebüsch ist meine Pflicht.
Keine Menschenstimme dringet
Durch die Oede an mein Ohr,

Selbst das Vöglein flieht und singet
Lieber fern in Busch und Rohr.
Aus dem Thale nur zuweilen
Summt herauf der Glocke Klang, &c.*

"The bad character of these swineherds has given rise to a law in Hungary, that any one absent from his herd without permission, is regarded as a robber, and punished accordingly. These men, however, on the whole, are not so bad as might be supposed; they never harm the poor, and they pay proper respect to the clergy, confining their depredations to the rich nobility, for they are friends of liberty and equality. About two years ago they attacked a castle and plundered it of seventeen thousand florins; but within six months afterwards, I saw the sparrows build their nests in the skulls of those who had performed this exploit."

The principal weapon which the "*Gonasz*" (swineherd) carries, is a small, neatly made hatchet, fixed to a handle about three feet long, which serves as a walking stick, a pastoral crook, or to cut wood for fuel. When several of them meet in the forest, they often amuse themselves by throwing this weapon at a mark, and in this game they have attained an extraordinary degree of skill.

My companion went on to inform me he had once witnessed an instance of this in Pesth, whither two "*Gonaszi*" had driven a pair of buffaloes for sale. The animals had somehow become suddenly enraged, and had rushed down a hill and over the Danube bridge into the very centre of a crowded market-place. The one was soon taken, but the other continued overthrowing and treading down every thing in its way, and no way remained but try to hit him with the hatchet. This was accordingly done, and the weapon thrown so accurately, that the animal, though in the midst of a crowd, was struck exactly in the right place, and instantly fell to the ground. Their skill in the use of this weapon is, however, by no means always desirable, for they are often tempted to try it on men as well as on trees and buffaloes. In their quarrels among themselves, these hatchets often play as important a part as the daggers among the Spaniards. One may often observe them, when they are inclined to come to blows, suddenly turn round and wheel away to a considerable distance, in order to obtain the space necessary for throwing the hatchet, and if they have a mind to attack a stranger, they often throw a hatchet at him, as other banditti will fire a pistol.

It would be unjust to assert of the Bacony forest, that it is full of re-

---

* "Far from love and life and pleasure,
Through the forest's gloom I wend;
Listening to the wolves' wild measure,
Here my bristly herds I tend.
Storms and scorching suns have now
Swarthed my breast and burnt my brow;
Never human voice I hear,
Piercing through the gloom mine ear—
Never comes another sound,
Than the strong oaks breaking round.
Even the little birds will fly,
To sing where they can see the sky;
Only sometimes from the valley,
Comes the clanging of the bells," &c.

gular banditti, but it has always an abundant population of what may be regarded as dangerous characters. To those who are placed under their protection, however, or who visit them in their forest huts, or gossip with them over their forest fires, they are the most frank, honest, hospitable fellows in the world.

"I have often," proceeded my informant, "paid them visits and passed many interesting hours in their company. The last time was about two years ago, when the last of the great robber bands which had risen among them, under the guidance of the renowned chief, Sobri, had been taken and brought to the gallows. Sobri was a handsome young man of about twenty-two, who had, for three years, kept all the farms and castles round in terror, and a long time elapsed before he, and his most distinguished companions, could be arrested, for they were as cunning as they were bold, and the peasants, as is frequently the case, as well as the millers and landlords of the little inns, all round the country, were their friends. At length a considerable body of troops was brought against them, and after a sanguinary contest they were taken. There remained, indeed, to the last some doubt with respect to Sobri himself, as some asserted that he had escaped, with a large sum of money, and gone to America; but the probability is against this account, for a body was afterwards found of one of the robbers who had been shot, which Sobri's parents declared to be that of their son. Many of the band were killed, and others taken, but many quietly dispersed and took up again their occupation of herding swine.*

"It was a party of these whom I was induced by curiosity to visit, and I found them lying round their fire, not far from some huts built of straw and branches of trees. There were seven of them, and in answer to my salutation, they invited me to come nearer, but remained quietly by the fire, without disturbing themselves to do me honour. They were dark, wild, powerful looking men, wearing the national costume, with their coal black hair shining with hog's lard. I soon hit upon a plan of insinuating myself into their good graces. It happens that I am very strong in the arms, and seeing a very thick cudgel lying near them, such as they use against the wolves, I asked them whether they believed that I could break it into three or four pieces. They defied me to do it, and I broke it accordingly. As they are great admirers of bodily strength, they immediately stood up, made me welcome, and begged me to sit down with them. I replied I should first like to wrestle a little if they were so inclined, and did not take my place till I had thrown two, and been thrown by the third. We were now the best friends in the world, and I took my place among them. The fire was trimmed, and a large dry trunk of a tree was dragged forward and thrown on it, the small branches being broken off and serving to kindle the enormous stem.

"They now brought wine and "Paprika bacon," and as I began to speak of those of the band who had just been hung, they expressed great sympathy for them, and one of them said, clapping me familiarly on the back, 'Ah, sir, its always the choicest of the fruit that people hang up;' alluding to a custom of the country, during the vintage, of picking out the finest branches of grapes, and hanging them on a stick to be carried home to

---

* A paragraph went the round of the German press a few weeks ago, in which it was stated that the celebrated Hungarian bandit chief Schubri did really escape on the occasion here alluded to, and had, after a variety of adventures, settled as a druggist in Charleston.—*Tr.*

the sound of music. It was, therefore, with these choice grapes that my robber wished to compare his comrades.

"The pleasure which these people take in hearing and relating robber stories, and romantic legends of ruined castles, is a sufficient proof of their lively imagination, and there is no doubt that many a wild young fellow is inspired by them to deeds of similar daring. It really appears to be less either poverty or covetousness than love of action that makes robbers of them, in other circumstances it would as easily make them heroes.

THE DANUBE FROM RAAB TO PESTH.

In order to reach Pesth, I had the choice between the above-mentioned "Butchers' road," travelled by the herds of cattle, and the steamboat down the Danube. I was not long in deciding for the latter, although it was connected with some difficulties; for the steamboat cannot come up as high as Raab, but lies two German miles down the river, at a little place called Gönyö, which may be considered as a sort of suburb of Raab. For the sake of this two miles' journey, for which we had till two o'clock, we were obliged to get up at sunrise, and go on board a little yacht that was lying in the Raab arm of the Danube, called also the Little Danube. It was not till the yacht was crammed with boxes, and trunks, and portmanteaus and goods of various descriptions, and children, and fat women, and Hungarians, and Germans, till it seemed ready to sink, that our skipper gave the signal, and we were allowed to start. We passed out through what is called the "Water-Gate," through which the Turks effected an entrance when they took the town. There were many traces of balls on the stones by the gate, but I could not refrain from putting my hands on them, like an unbelieving Thomas, for a strange feeling of doubt sometimes comes over me concerning all the occurrences of past days.

From beneath this water-gate I obtained an interesting view, as well out of as into the town; for from this gate the market-women had ranged themselves on both sides, and formed a picture like the first scene in the second act of *Massaniello;* and they were offering delicious fruit at little more than the same imaginary price as that paid by the players: for instance, a penny for two large melons, or for seventy plums, or forty cucumbers. Two fine young fowls for less than sixpence. There seemed to me no longer any thing strange in the fact, that so many Hungarian kings had killed themselves by eating too much fruit. Matthias Corvinus fell sick and died after eating some fresh figs, and Albrecht after eating melons. On the other side of the water-gate lay the harbour, and all the far from inconsiderable bustle of the trade and commerce of Raab. The great tide of traffic does not, in this part of the Danube, pass up the principal stream, but into its smaller branches, for the real Danube between Raab and Presburg is full of islands, shoals, and sandbanks; and the vessels coming from the lower part of the river are willing to avoid the strong current of the main stream. The little Danube, although it has the disadvantage of innumerable windings, is deeper and more tranquil. Large vessels cannot, however, proceed farther up than Raab. Here they discharge their cargoes, and whatever is destined for Wieselburg, Presburg, or Vienna, is sent forward in smaller craft. The principal articles of commerce are corn and cattle, of which the former goes mostly to Wieselburg (on the Nieusiedler Lake), and the latter, as I have said, to Oedenburg, whence it is distributed over Austria. I could not very well make out why the corn did not travel the whole way to Presburg and Vienna by water, but I was informed that it was on account of most of the corn-mills lying scattered at very considerable distances round Vienna, almost as far as the Hungarian frontier; and that since land-carriage in Hungary is astonishingly cheap, the millers preferred fetching it from Wieselburg, to allowing it to go to Presburg or Vienna, where its price would be much enhanced. This can hardly be the only motive, nevertheless, it may be that beyond Wieselberg the navigation of the Little Danube becomes still more difficult.

As soon as the wished-for signal of our departure had been given, a little horse was attached to a long rope, and as he began to trot, we found ourselves moving very pleasantly down the narrow river, having on one side the highlands of the county of Raab, and on the other the " golden fruit garden" of the island of Schütt. Among those of the passengers who preferred the tarry deck to the confined air below, were tradesmen, servants, innkeepers, and clerks, Germans and Hungarians, all with mustachios, according to the custom of the country; merchants from Raab, a few patriots, an Austrian nobleman, and myself. We had scarcely opened our mouths before all the Hungarian topics of the day, the language, the constitution, the newspapers, literature, all came on the carpet, and occasioned that lively discussion which is sure to arise wherever two or three are gathered together in Hungary. The strife became particularly warm between the young nobleman and some of the Hungarians present, and I had several opportunities of displaying my impartiality, and playing the umpire. The Austrians are sure to see the shady side of every thing in Hungary, and the Hungarians find it very hard to approve of any thing Austrian, and as I was neither an Austrian nor a Hungarian, they found it convenient to appeal to me. The Hungarians believe that Austria exercises just as oppressive and restraining an influence on the western as on the eastern borders of her territories, and they are therefore disposed to a friendly sympathy with us Western Germans, whom they regard as hostile to Austria. The Austrian had begun the attack, on this occasion, by expressing great contempt for the state of Hungarian agriculture, which he had here for the first time become acquainted with, and by painting in harsh colours the state of slavery in which the country still remained, in spite of the favourable influence of the recent Diet. He then sketched the state of prosperity, order, and comfort of the Austrian peasant, compared with the backward and oppressed condition of the Hungarian, maintaining that in Austria the Emperor himself, even if he had right on his side, was not sure of being able to obtain justice against a peasant, whilst in Hungary the lowest noble could oppress his neighbours as much as he pleased. The Hungarians, he went on to say, were very ready to cry out " Liberty and Freedom," but it was really enjoyed by only the order of nobility, and these were often the cruelest tyrants to the oppressed millions. The Austrian peasant was made of better stuff than the Hungarian, for though he would not submit to tyranny, he was willingly subject to the law. If told such is the law, he was content, although even the law might be an unreasonable one; but of this voluntary submission no one in Hungary had any idea. Neither noble nor peasant would submit to any thing but force. He must indeed confess that in Austria there were many things that might be amended. It was not right that they (the nobles) should be free from military duty, nor that the peasants should bear alone the burden of many of the taxes; and all enlightened Austrians heartily wished for a representative constitution; but even with their arbitrary government, the people were infinitely better protected there than in Hungary.

The Hungarians defended themselves valiantly against these attacks, declaring that, although the lot of the peasantry had hitherto been bad enough, it had been entirely changed for the better by the acts of the last Diet, and that the fruits of this amelioration would soon appear. Very few of their nobles deserved to be called tyrants, and the conduct of many of them was really most paternal towards their peasants. Force must, indeed, they admitted, be sometimes employed, but the effects of the stick were not always prejudicial. That as to freedom, there could be no freedom where a despot was placed at the head of affairs; that the will of the emperor was omnipotent in Austria, but by no means so in Hungary. As soon as a man set foot in Austria he felt himself restrained by a thousand petty restrictions, but in Hungary he could breathe freely, and say and do what he would. Other ameliorations would follow. Much had been already done, and one of the first steps towards creating a national feeling, was the purification of the language, by ridding it of the German, Latin, and Slavonian words with which it had been contaminated.

Upon this hint the Austrian spoke again, and declared with rather a contemptuous smile, that if the Hungarians should be able to succeed in wrapping themselves up in their Asiatic idiom they would soon become complete Orientals, since it was only by means of the German and Latin languages that they had been able to maintain an intercourse with the entire system of European culture. Hereupon followed of course a very long and animated discussion, which lasted till we reached the point where the branch of the river we were on, entered the Great Danube, and where we were to exchange the little yacht for a vessel of sixty horse power. The sight of this majestic stream awoke in all a vivid sensation of pleasure.

On the one end of our little yacht were painted the Hungarian words, " *Isten velünk,*" that is " God is with us," and on the opposite end " *Senki elemink,*" (who then would be against us) and we certainly had some occasion for these excellent mementos, now that we found ourselves on this mighty stream, in a vessel that threatened to go to pieces with every stroke it received. It was well for us that God was with us, for we soon had to experience that we had, at all events, an enormous tow-rope against us. Just as we entered into the main Danube, and were driven not far from the shore, it happened that we met one of those large vessels from the lower part of the river called " *Hayos,*" drawn by fifty horses. The rope by which this great heavy three-masted craft was pulled along, was slackened, and the horses stopped at command, to allow us to pass across it as is usual in such cases, but I don't very well know how,—either because we were too slow, or the riders of the horses were too impatient, or too regardless of our safety,—but before we had crossed we heard again the wild cry, "He he! Ho ho!" with which these people urge forward their horses, and the immense rope was suddenly dragged up immediately before the prow of our vessel. Two inches further would have carried it under the keel, and our felucca with its whole contents would have taken a dip in the Danube. By great exertion we managed to stop just in time, but we were thrown against the other vessel, and its bowsprit entered our cabin, breaking down some stairs, perforating some boards and filling it with pale faces. I was told such accidents were not uncommon, as these enormously thick ropes drawn by fifty, sixty, or eighty horses, were able to lift a large vessel out of the water. The men engaged in towing on the Danube are a rough wild set of fellows, and are often enough in fault, especially when, as is frequently the case, they belong to the class of *nobles*.

We dined at Gönyö, and had two long tables quite full of persons who had come from Raab and the environs, in order to go by the steamer to Pesth, where a great fair was soon to be held. At our table a good deal of German was spoken, but at the other I heard only Magyar; and I noticed that, whenever my companions got merry, they slipped immediately into the mother tongue. I am sure I rose a hundred per cent. in the estimation of some of them, by a few words of thanks for a cigar, which I achieved in Hungarian.

"*En Magyar wagyok*" (I am a Magyar) is a phrase one often hears uttered with no small complacency, and "*a Schwoab*," ("the German there!") is equivalent to an expression of something like contempt. We never say in the same manner, "I am a German." I believe this is, in some measure, owing to a want of nationality, and also, in some measure, to what I must think our excessive modesty. We have certainly as much reason to be proud of our race as the Hungarians, and whenever it has happened to me, in a foreign country, to hear any one say, "*En Magyar wagyok*," or "I am a Pole," or "I am an Englishman," I have never failed to reply, "And I am a German;" and I think we should do well to accustom ourselves to do so.

After dinner, we went down to the river side to see a large steamer come in, which had brought no fewer than two thousand pigs from Turkey, distributed in three vessels which she had in tow. The boats built for this purpose are very conveniently arranged, and the pigs are undoubtedly far better accommodated than many of the poor negroes in the Spanish slave-ships. The pig-boats have two or three decks, one above another, covered with pigsties, divided by strong wooden palings, so that the fresh air can pass everywhere through, and spaces are left all round and among them, so that those who have charge of the animals may be able to get near and attend properly to them, not more than twelve or fifteen pigs being placed together. They are also well fed with Turkish wheat while on the journey.

All the countries on the Save, the Drave, and the lower Danube, Croatia, Slavonia, Bosnia, Servia, Wallachia, and Moldavia, possess immense riches in swine; and since in some of those provinces, and still more in others bordering on them to the south, there are numbers of persons who abhor this unclean animal, it follows that they are able to export vast numbers to their northern pork-loving neighbours.

I visited the vessels engaged in the conveyance of these interesting emigrants, in company with a young Servian, to whom the greater part of the two thousand were consigned. He was a handsome young man, wearing the Hungarian dress, speaking German, Servian, and other languages, and wearing a number of brilliant rings on his fingers. I drank a cup of coffee with him, and was thinking that, like Milosch, he might be destined to become a king of Servia; but his fate, poor fellow, was a different one, for a short time after he was murdered by a robber.

At length our steamboat came in from Vienna, and fetched us away from what we may call the golden strand of Gönyö; for here, as on the shores of the Theiss and other Hungarian rivers, gold is sometimes obtained from the river sand. This is an occupation exclusively of the gipsies, who deliver the gold to the government, as a sort of tribute, at very low prices. At Aranyos, near Komorn, we saw a number of them engaged in their interesting work. They place a board in a sloping position, on which there are several diagonal furrows or grooves; they then scratch up the sand of the river over the board, and pouring water over it, the gold dust, being heavier than the earthy particles, remains in the grooves. The gipsies then scratch out this sediment and mix it with quicksilver, which attracts to itself the particles of gold. These are collected and sold to the government officers in little balls of the weight of about three or four ducats. Goldsmiths and other traders are forbidden, under severe penalties, to purchase gold from the gipsies. The product of these operations is certainly very inconsiderable; but if we consider the proportion which these few shovelsfull of sand bear to the masses left lying in the bed of the river, we may reasonably conclude that immense treasures are still buried in the Danube. If the gipsies can get as much as the value of a ducat out of ten cubic feet of sand (which is less than they really do get), a piece of the Danube of a hundred German miles in length, and a thousand paces in breadth, taking the sand at five feet in depth, would give thirty thousand millions of cubic feet of sand, containing gold to the value of three thousand millions of ducats; and the actual depth of the sand is greater than five feet, and the extent of the goldbearing Danube is greater than I have assumed it to be. It is also to be recollected that the gipsies take the sand only from those parts of the river where they find it most convenient, as on sandbanks; and, gold being the heaviest material which the waters carry along, it is highly probable that the greater quantity lies in the middle of the river, and the comparatively lighter particles only are washed on the shore. I felt the "sacred thirst" awakening in me at the thought of the rich abundance of the precious metal—the three thousand millions of ducats that were lying below in the deep channel through which our steamer was cutting and foaming on its way. A single mile of this Danube sand might afford one gold enough for one's life, if one could but get it. How many individuals and nations, like the Danube, possess hidden treasures, of which only a paltry gipsy portion ever comes to light. Could they develope all the capabilities which God has bestowed on them, how boundless might become their physical and mental wealth!

We were received in grand style at Komorn by the whole of the military, in full uniform, with the bands of several regiments, coming to salute General Bagassi, whom we brought with us, and who had just been appointed commandant of Pesth, and the sound of the instruments carried me back in thought, to the days when the chiefs of the legions came down the Danube to inspect the numerous castles built by the Romans on its banks. The geographical position of Komorn is too important—it is too evidently pointed out by Nature for the settlement of man—not to have been occupied in the earliest periods of history.

The island of Schütt terminates at this point, and the arm of the Danube, which had separated from it at Presburg, as well as that called the Black Water, here unite again with the main stream, which also receives near this place the waters of the Neutra and the Waag.

From Komorn, therefore, there are navigable water-roads in many different directions; on the upper Danube to Raab, and on the lower Danube to Pesth and Buda, on the Waag and Neutra to the Carpathians in the north, and on the Black Water to the corn countries in the island or Schütt.

The Romans occupied this important position with their much-valued city of Brigantium or Bregetium, and it was garrisoned by the legio prima adjutrix. Roman fortifications were shown to me at Szony, opposite Komorn, and I had often occasion to notice here, as elsewhere along the Danube, the familiarity with matters connected with the Roman times displayed by people who did not pretend, as I did, to belong to the learned world, and yet often put my ignorance to shame. They talked of the quarters of the various legions, of the prima adjutrix, or of the legio decima in Vienna, of the legio secunda adjutrix in Buda, of the legio xiv. Gemina, near Presburg, as if they had heard it all from their grandfathers.

The town of Komorn, as might be imagined from its very advantageous position, has a considerable trade, and a population of twenty thousand inhabitants, without counting the military. Since the union of Hungary and Austria, the town has never been occupied by an enemy, not even by the Turks, who possessed all the country round. Had Komorn been lost, its fate would probably have been shared by all Hungary as far as the Carpathians.

On the strand were a great number of beggars, and amongst them a poor cripple on crutches, with two wooden legs. We threw him from the steamboat some copper money that we had collected, but unluckily could not reach quite far enough, for some of it fell into the edge of the water. The poor cripple was slowly stooping to pick it up, when a rascal with the full use of his legs and arms, pushed before him and snatched it away. The enjoyment of this, his ill-gotten gains, was, however, but momentary, for another lad, not a whit less needy-looking and tattered than either of the other two, darted forward, and bestowing some hearty cuffs upon the robber, forced the money from him, and gave it back to the poor cripple who could not help himself. Had Haroun al Raschid witnessed this action, he would certainly have made him Kadi of Komorn upon the spot. "Blessed are the just."

We had now again all the waters of the Danube united into one channel, to say nothing of the daily contribution of twenty millions of *Eimers* from the Waag and Neutra, and as we dashed along without any interruption, we soon lost sight of the great plain, through which we had been passing for several days past, and reached the mountains, through which the river finds or forces its way to Gran and Buda. In the whole of its course the Danube passes three of these mountain districts, alternating with the vast plains, through which it flows. First, below Ulm comes the plain of Bavaria, interrupted by some hills of little importance; then the beautiful range of mountains between Linz and Vienna; then the great Hungarian plain between Presburg and Komorn; then the mountainous region between Komorn and Pesth; again, plain as far as Belgrade; between Belgrade and Widdin again mountains; and, lastly, the great Wallachian and Bulgarian plain between Hungary and the Black Sea.

In some period, anterior to history, it is probable that the Danube formed three great inland seas, connected by cataracts and rivers, like the lakes Erie, Ontario, &c. Wallachia and part of Bulgaria belonged probably to the Black Sea. The part of the river lying between Passau and Vienna is the most beautiful as well as the most interesting in an historical point of view, but the narrow passes and cataracts between Belgrade and Widdin, far exceed any other in wild grandeur.

Immediately after passing Komorn, the right shore begins to rise, till at length, by Nessmeli, it swells into complete mountains. Near Gran the mountains begin to appear also on the left side, and they soon become so steep and rugged, and the river is pressed into such a narrow bed, that this may be regarded as the pass. These are the mountains which are called on the left side the Magusta, and on the right the Pilis range. The mountains near Nessmeli grow the wine the most widely diffused through the country, such as among French wines are the Graves or Medoc, or among those of Greece the Santorino. Throughout Hungary, Galicia, Silesia, and Moravia, if you ask in any inn for Hungarian wine, without specifying the sort, this, the Nessmühler, as it is called, is always brought. Near Nessmeli, stretching towards Dotis and Almasch, are also the celebrated stone quarries, which are of so much importance to the new buildings now in process in Pesth, and likewise to the fortifications of Komorn. There is found in them limestone, sandstone, and various kinds of marble, particularly a marble of a pinkish colour, which I noticed in Pesth, and which I shall have occasion again to refer to. A passenger in a steamboat, however, must pass over almost all that is interesting to the natural philosopher, the political economist, or the historian; his eye hurries from point to point, and he is borne in a few minutes past many a spot where Clio and her sisters would have lingered long.

The first sight of Gran is magnificent, and it is perhaps this fine position which has suggested to the Hungarian writers the notion that a town was established here a hundred and fifty five years after the deluge. In the first period of the Hungarian monarchy, Gran occupied the position, afterwards filled by Stuhlweissenburg and Ofen, and was the capital and seat of government of her kings. The sainted Stephen was born and crowned here, and up to the year 1241, when it was destroyed by the Tatars, Gran remained a rich and populous town, far exceeding in splendour all the other cities of Hungary. It was at the same time in possession of the most important trade of the country, and foreigners of several nations, French, Germans, and Italians, were numerous enough to have quarters or streets assigned to them; and on the high hill, where now stands the castle of the prince archbishop, the primate of Hungary, and a great cathedral, there stood even then a magnificent church in the old gothic style, with pillars of Indian marble. The place was in former times called, "par excellence," the Danube city, but its name has since been changed, not without reason, to that of the insignificant stream the Gran which here enters it. The population of Gran has been reduced to six thousand, and it bears few traces of its former greatness, except its fine situation, and the abovementioned castle and cathedral.

Soon after passing Gran the river begins to make its way with many turnings and windings through some difficult mountainous passes (like a wise man overcoming, by energy and perseverance, all obstacles to his progress), until it takes its great bend to the south. Whilst we were tacking this way and that, through this romantic mountain country, night came on, but the air was deliciously mild, and the promenade on the deck a real enjoyment. The stars glittered over our heads, and the moon poured her soft radiance over her heavenly flocks, and in various turns and corners of the mountains, lights twinkled from unknown villages and hamlets, that lay hidden in their clefts and hollows. We knew not even the names of these abodes, and to them our party of a hundred strangers, rushing hastily by, was, probably, of no more interest than a flock of wild geese passing over their heads.

At the narrowest part of the pass lie the ruins of the ancient castle of Wissehrad, which, as I have already mentioned, is a Hungarian word signifying "high castle." Many Hungarian kings have made it their residence, and it was the favourite seat of the celebrated and beloved Matthias Corvinus. It is said, by the people of the country, to have been so magnificent that a legate of the pope's, who visited it, called it a paradise, and the opinion of an Italian, in a matter of this kind, must be allowed to have some weight. Now, nothing remains of it but some scanty ruins, visible against the clear sky on the topmast peak of a lofty mountain, and Hungarian goatherds, clothed in skins, visit its grass-grown courts, in the place of princes and legates. Tradition also assigns to it, as an inhabitant, the unquiet spirit of a poor girl, who formerly dwelt on the other side of the Danube, and of whom King Matthias became enamoured, visiting her without disclosing his real rank. She regarded him as a simple huntsman, and hoped he would repay her tender confidence by one day leading her home as his wife.

It was, however, one day accidentally communicated to her that the lover, who rowed across the river to her at night, was no other than the crowned king of the country, and she was no less terrified than Psyche under similar circumstances. Like her also the maiden made a discovery fatal to her peace and her love. The impassable gulf that separated her from her royal lover, the impossibility of ever being truly his, preyed on her mind till she became insane, and threw herself into the river, across which he had so often hastened to her arms. Since then her restless spirit wanders for ever about the ruins of Wissehrad, mourning the loss of king Matthias and her unfortunate love. I must confess, however, I watched in vain for a glimpse of her white robes, as the desolate castle vanished behind us in the darkness. As we lost sight of it the moon went down, the whole scene assumed a drearier aspect, and I was glad to go down into the cabin, where, with lamps, and tea, and conversation, we might imitate the comfort of settled abodes, in the midst of the wild darkly dashing river. The company consisted mostly of Jews and Rascians, some of whom had paid their devotions pretty freely to the *Tschuttora*, but in one corner sat a boy and near him an old man, who spoke a dialect I had heard only once before, and who proved to be Swiss from the canton of the Grisons. The old man was a confectioner at Kaschau, and had been as far as Vienna to fetch his nephew, who was to be apprenticed to him. One might suppose from the numbers of natives of the Grisons whom one finds engaged in this trade all over Germany, Poland, Russia, and Hungary, that their native land overflowed, if not with milk and honey, with cakes and sweetmeats; but this branch of industry, to which they are so addicted abroad, does not, I believe, exist at all at home. The lads are, at first, employed in keeping cattle, and as they grow up, come out of the valleys of the Inn and the Rhine, and find their way to their uncles and cousins, already established in different parts of Europe, of whom they learn this, their favourite trade.

The old man, my fellow-passenger, seeming to think I must know as little of his country as the Danube sailors, informed me that it was a small but very ancient independent republic, which had formerly been allied to the great and powerful republic of Venice, and that they, the Alpine people, had furnished troops to the Venetians, and lent them valiant aid against the Hungarians and Turks, in return for which they had received the privilege of establishing themselves as confectioners, coffee-house keepers, and so forth, in the great city. In consequence, however, of some misunderstanding that had arisen between the republics, these privileges were not renewed after 1766, and a period was fixed within which they were to sell their goods and leave Venice, and thus it happened that they were scattered over Europe. I have vainly sought for a confirmation of this fact in the various historical works to which I have had access; but, to say truth, it is but seldom that historians condescend to bestow their attention on such little episodes of history as the dispersion of the sugar-bakers of the Grisons, and yet these little episodes are often replete with interest.

Of the town of Waizen our song is silent, for neither sun nor moon gave light, as we stopped at its harbour to put out some passengers; and the veil of night covered likewise the remainder of the Danube, as far as Pesth. Towards eleven at night we again saw lights; they increased, glittering before, behind, on every side, and over the hills and mountains down to the water's edge. They were from the towns of Pesth and Buda, amongst whose shipping we cast anchor, and soon after made our way to the hotel "The Queen of England," on the Danube Quay.

BUDA.—PESTH.

Buda (or Ofen) and Pesth are, in fact, but one town; one has arisen out of the other, the growth of one has been promoted by that of the other, and each is indebted for its greatness to its connexion with the other. They are united by a pontoon bridge over the Danube, and it is a pity that they have not been long since united under the same municipal government. Of such a union there is now great probability, and it is proposed to distinguish the one great city by the name of Buda-Pesth; and some Hungarian writers have even undertaken to prove that the twin cities were formerly one, known only by the name of Pesth, and that the other appellation was acquired from some German inhabitants of the right bank, who bestowed it on their quarter.

In old times, before the Turkish conquest, it is said to have had a period of splendour, like many other Hungarian towns; but the history of the present city can be dated only from the end of the Turkish dominion, for it passed from the hands of the Moslems into those of the Austrians as a mere heap of ruins. The city lay buried in filth and disorder, and the only buildings now standing which were then extant, are some low huts and stables. There were no suburbs, and the town did not extend beyond the narrow circle of its walls. Like Gran, Waizen, Belgrade, and other Hungarian towns, Pesth was, in the course of a century, bombarded, conquered, burnt, and re-conquered half a dozen times, and its aspect during that period probably resembled that of Belgrade and other cities of the Danube, on which the curse of Turkish dominion still rests. At the close of this period, as remarkable and sudden a rise took place in many of the towns of Hungary, as in those of Russia, after the destruction of the Tatar empire. So late as the commencement of the eighteenth century, Pesth could not be considered as freed from the barbarian yoke, for the Turks still continued to exercise a good deal of influence in Hungarian affairs. Down to that period, it remained one of the most wretched places in the empire; but in the course of the last hundred years it has become one of the stateliest of cities, not only of the kingdom of Hungary, for it will bear a comparison with some of the finest towns in the world.

We are accustomed to turn always to America for examples of the rapid growth and development of cities, but we have in Europe similar, and almost equally striking examples. In England there are many great towns which a hundred, or even fifty years ago, were exceedingly insignificant. In Germany, since the close of the last war, many towns have undergone remarkable improvements and extensions. In Russia, Odessa, St. Petersburg, Taganrog, and others, have been conjured into life; and in Hungary many have risen from dust and ruins to a considerable degree of prosperity.

The walls which encircled the old town of Pesth, do not now contain the seventh part of the surface covered by the modern city. It has four important and extensive suburbs, named after the four last Hungarian kings, and containing finer buildings than the city itself. Pesth is very regularly built upon a simple and intelligible plan, the old town forming a nucleus from which great broad streets radiate in every direction, and these are again united with each other, by concentric cross streets. In the Theresa suburb alone, this plan has not been regurlarly executed, and it is consequently out of harmony with the rest. As to Buda, it cannot be said to have any plan at all, for the unfavourable nature of the ground, and the obstacles to all regularity presented by the mountains, would scarcely have permitted the execution of such a design, had it been entertained. The whole situation and locality of Buda-Pesth, greatly resemble those of Prague, but in the former the new and elegant predominates, in the latter, the old and venerable; in their position relatively to the country surrounding them, there is also great similarity. The figure of Hungary, as of Bohemia, is compact, rounded, and almost encircled by chains of mountains, whilst both countries are cut nearly through the centre by the main river, —in Bohemia, the Moldau-Elbe, in Hungary, the Danube. The right angle formed by this river may be considered as the central and metropolitan district of Hungary. The Huns, Hungarians, and other conquering tribes coming over the Carpathians, made their first settlement on the banks of the Theiss, but Duke Geysa fixed the seat of his government at Gran, and it continued the permanent residence of King Stephen and his successors, till the attacks of the Tatars induced them to remove their court to Stuhlweissenburg, which, however, was merely a sort of Versailles, a place for ceremonies and coronations. Stuhlweissenburg was then to Buda-Pesth much what Presburg is now. The Diet, for instance, is held at the latter city on account of its convenient locality with respect to Vienna; nevertheless, Pesth, as the residence of the Palatine, of the Magnates, and of all the principal public officers, as the focus of national and scientific culture, as the seat of the universities and academies, the principal staple place of the foreign and inland trade of the country, and as decidedly the richest and most populous town, cannot fail to be considered the real capital of the country. The unexampled rapidity of its growth is a very accurate standard whereby to estimate the general development of Hungary, for the increase of population, of industry, and of general culture and activity throughout Hungary, must naturally manifest themselves most forcibly in the centre of their action, from which there is of course a re-action on the surrounding country.

Buda-Pesth has at present a hundred thousand inhabitants, whilst the number of hundreds it possessed a century ago is a matter of dispute. The Hungarians look with pride upon their capital, and dream that it may become once more the residence of kings; nay, they do not dream merely, but they say and maintain that it must be so. The town becomes every year more magnificent, more cultivated, more abounding in the means of enjoyment. Every year more and more of the Magnates come from Vienna to fix their residence here. " If our sovereign would but come and live among us," say the Hungarians, " we would build him such a palace as he does not possess in Vienna."

THE FAIR AT PESTH.

As geographical centre of the country, Pesth is also the centre of the Hungarian trade. It has four great markets or fairs, which, from their importance, might be called the royal fairs of Hungary. The most considerable is that beginning at the end of August, at which time all the channels of communication are in their best state, the Danube free, the roads dry, and at this time it is that the great purchases are made for the winter. As I fortunately arrived at this interesting moment I will endeavour to give some idea of the state of bustle and excitement that prevails during a scene which differs from any thing of the kind ever seen among us. The principal places occupied by the fair are—first, the Danube Quay, on which is erected a row of shops, and along which the vessels lie; secondly, the Jews' quarter, where every corner swarms with goods and buyers and sellers; thirdly, the market-places in the interior of the town, which are covered with booths; and fourthly, all the open spaces in the Joseph's suburb.

The Danube Quay is very broad and a German mile long, having on the side opposite the river a row of handsome houses, the ground floors of which only are used as shops. On the morning of the fair it was filled with thousands of busy traders, and the river was crowded with vessels of all kinds, including steamers. There were vessels from Austria, or the lower Danube, as far as Belgrade and Semlin, and from different parts of the Theiss. To the head of each vessel was fastened some article, such as a large pot, a wine bottle, a chair, a table, a broom, a wooden trough, a gigantic spoon, &c., which of course I took for a sample of the wares sold within, but which I found were intended to serve as signs or coats of arms, the only difference being, that instead of a sign-board merely painted by some rude dauber, the symbols of trade were represented thus bodily. The largest and most solid vessels seen in the middle Danube, the portion extending from Presburg to the cataracts below Semlin, are called " *Telyfohayos*," that is, complete or perfect ships. They carry from ten thousand to twelve thousand *Metzen** of wheat. They also go up the Theiss as far as Szegedin, where many of them are built. Others are built at Eszek on the Drave, where is to be had the fine hard oak, the material from the forests of Slavonia or Transylvania, chiefly used in their construction. They generally last, with repairs, as much as five-and-twenty or thirty years, and there is every year an evident improvement in their construction. Besides large vessels, there are others of a smaller size, broad and flat built, which carry furniture and manufactured goods to Turkey. Among the Germans living here I often noticed the terms "hard" and "soft" applied to various kinds of craft, and found that they were meant to distinguish the oak vessels from Szegedin and Eszek, from those made of deal which come from Bavaria and Austria, and especially a very slight kind of boat from Passau. These latter do not in general return up the Danube, but are sold as wood, or sometimes repaired again and sent to some place further down. I could not make out very accurately the relative proportions of land and water traffic at Pesth, but I believe, that of the two, the latter is at present increasing much more rapidly. The greater part of the navigation of the Danube, as I have already mentioned, is in the hands of the Rascians. Near the Quay was the pottery market, and never in my life did I see together so many pots and pans and clay vessels of every possible variety; a description of some of them may perhaps serve to illustrate some points of Hungarian manners and customs. First there were enormous piles of gigantic urn-shaped vessels, used for keeping the lard so much employed in housekeeping. Then there were earthen covered pans, for roasting or baking meat, and there were others called *Nudelseiger*, that were pierced through with many holes, for the water to run off from the Nudels or dumplings, which the peasants are wont to boil in them. Then there were mighty heaps of water-pitchers of a most peculiar shape, but one in general use here. These pitchers have a narrow neck, containing a sort of sieve to prevent impurities from passing into the vessel. The hole, out of which the people drink, is in the *handle*, which is hollow, and through this hollow tube the Hungarian sucks up the water, and praises the whole arrangement as calculated to keep his liquor cool and pure; but how such a pitcher is ever to be cleansed inside, is a mystery to me. There were also many thousands of a sort of bottle called *tshuttora*, in use every where in Hungary, among Magyars, Germans, Walachians, and Slavonians, to carry with them on a journey, or into the fields, when they are keeping their flocks and herds, or doing farming-work. The *tshuttora* is a round wooden vessel, of a corpulent shape, with a small narrow neck; it is generally turned out of one piece of wood, and has a hole at the top and another at the bottom, the latter closed with a spigot, and decorated with a rosette of coloured leather. It is also furnished with thongs, by which it can be hung round the neck, and has four little feet so ill proportioned to its portly dimensions that it hardly stands steadier on them, than its owner does on his legs when he has been too frequent in his applications to it. There is no Hungarian house that does not contain *tshuttoras* of all sizes, some of them as big as a small cask. The Hungarian magnates are equally enamoured of the tshuttora, and take them with them on journeys, or hunting-parties, and all similar occasions, and they are filled with every kind of liquid, from the wine of Tokay to the

---

* The Austrian *metz* is equal to 1¾ of a Winchester bushel.

dirty or brackish water of the marsh. In all songs in which the praises of the sparkling goblet, or the jovial bowl would be heard among us, those of the tshuttora resound in Hungary. These vessels were made in the earliest times exactly as they are now, and there is little doubt that the nomadic tribes who wandered first into Hungary came with the tshuttora round their necks.

Among the clay vessels was also one used for baking a sort of paste, the *tarhonya*, an indispensable article in the steppes of Hungary. It is composed of meal and sour milk, which is completely dried and baked over the fire, and then rubbed to powder. In this state it can be kept good a whole summer, nay, sometimes two or three years, and is a very useful article to shepherds, herdsmen, and others who lead a lonely life, especially as they are apt to live far too much on animal food and fat. A good handful of this farinaceous preparation, thrown over their dish of pork, tends, it is said, to preserve them from a disease very prevalent here, called "*tshomor*," and which is supposed to be occasioned by eating too much fleshmeat.

This malady is very generally diffused in Hungary. At the same time that I made acquaintance with the pottery I have described, I also saw the first instance of a man afflicted with *tshomor*. An old Hungarian was sitting not far off. He was yawning and stretching himself, and looked wretchedly ill. I asked him what was the matter, and he answered in a very melancholy tone, "*Ah Jesus Maria! megisömöröttem.*" (Ah Jesus Maria! I have caught a tshomor.) In its most common sense the word signifies disgust; but, as I say, it is also used to denote a peculiar malady, supposed to orignate in the consumption of too much animal food. The patient is often attacked by it very suddenly. He experiences a general sickness and feeling of disgust, loses his appetite, is constantly yawning, feels his limbs weak and his back stiff, and on his skin there appear a quantity of pimples or boils. The people will tell you that no physician and no medicine can afford relief, but that the malady must take its own course, which always lasts three days at least, and this time, during which they abstain as much as possible from food, is mostly spent in yawning. To rub the back and limbs is almost the only thing that affords relief. One peasant will even ask another to thump him and kick him in the side, or to pull his arms about violently, and from this ungentle exercise they profess to derive great solace. The German-Hungarians, I was told, were not subject to *tshomor*, but the petty country nobles, who generally feed high and lead a somewhat idle life, are subject to this visitation quite as much as the peasants. I was told of one of these little provincial aristocrats, who was very often afflicted with tshomor, and whose wife lived in constant dread of one of these attacks, as on all such occasions she had to make up her mind to three days of uninterrupted ill-humour; besides which, she was certain of having her whole time occupied, during those three days, in rubbing the back and kneeding the sides of a cross and grumbling husband.

The people who came with the goods I have mentioned for sale, were mostly Slavonians and Magyars; but there were also many Germans, colonists from the distant parts of Hungary. The weekly provision-market of Pesth is almost entirely supplied by Germans, as there are many German colonies in its immediate neighbourhood; and these men are so disguised in their Magyar costume—broad-brimmed hats, wide trousers, and mustaches—that one does not always recognise them. One of them, coming from the Bakony forest, whom I addressed, and who had brought various wooden wares, spoons, shovels, rakes, tubs, &c., confirmed to me the satisfactory information respecting the cultivation of potatoes, which I had collected on the Neusiedler Lake. The people are becoming everywhere reconciled to them, although here, as elsewhere, they were at first received with vehement dislike. He told me, as I had been told at the Neusiedler Lake, that thirty, nay, twenty years ago, the Hungarians attributed every imaginable mischief to potatoes, scarcely deeming them good enough even for pigs. At present, however, he added, they were raised everywhere in the Bakony country.

One of the most abundant articles in the market, and one of genuine Hungarian manufacture, was soap, of which the quantities were truly astonishing. This is all made on the Hungarian steppes, principally on the Theiss, and in Debretzin and Szegedin. The best has much the appearance of Limburg cheese, and comes from Debretzin, where there are no fewer than a hundred soap-boilers. There also are made the true Hungarian tobacco-pipes; and, according to recent statistical tables, eleven millions of them are manufactured every year, which would give one for every man, woman, and child in the kingdom. In general whatever is regarded as peculiarly Hungarian, is to be found about Debretzin—for instance, the finest and largest melons. The culture of this fruit, as well as the taste for it, however, has probably been brought from the countries about the Black and Caspian Seas, the native land of all cucurbitaceous plants. The usual plan of eating melons here, is to take one whole on one's plate, and scoop it out with a spoon, instead of cutting it in slices, and this although they are generally very large. A prize melon I saw exhibited by the Agricultural Society, weighed sixty pounds; and a Hungarian from Debretzin told me that in his country they sometimes reached the weight of one hundred pounds, and remained sweet, juicy, and finely-flavoured. The gourds, also, grow to an immense size, one of them often weighing as much as a hundredweight, and occasionally even twice as much. The common people eat them cut in slices, and roasted like chestnuts.

The fair at Pesth is not only important to the different parts of Hungary, as giving an opportunity for the interchange of commodities among themselves, but also to the neighbouring provinces of Turkey in the south, and of Germany and Poland on the north. Hungary is rich in the raw productions of nature, and the German provinces, as well as Austria, Moravia, Silesia, and the western part of Galicia, have surrounded this land of raw produce with a chain of industrial towns, busied in the manufacture of leather, wool, cotton, and silk. The principal articles which they come to look for at Pesth are wool, tobacco, cotton, skins, corn, wax, wine, and others of less importance. The persons principally engaged in Pesth, as agents from these provinces, are the Jews; and the greater part of the business is therefore carried on in the Jews' quarter, which is perhaps the busiest scene in the whole fair. The skins are brought thither in great waggons, drawn by four, six, or eight horses, near which several foals are often seen trotting; whilst behind comes a reserve team, either for relief or for occasional sale. In the inner courts of the houses, where the wares are unpacked, is a scene of litter and dirt, and uproar and confusion, that cannot be described, but which may be conceived, if we reflect, that among the chief articles bargained for are stinking hides and bed-feathers, and that the bargainers are Slavonians and Polish Jews.

On the first day of the fair, which was Sunday the 29th of August, I set out to see the fair in company with a Bohemian manufacturer, an excellent guide; for what the English are in Europe, that are the Bohemians in the Austrian dominions, the soul of every industrial enterprise, and the first to apply and bring into use all new inventions. He praised much, as we went along, the industry of his native country, and contrasted strongly the rough state of every thing we saw with what it would have been in Bohemia. In some parts of the city which we passed through, some houses that had been thrown down by the inundation, still lay in ruins, in others pretty little rows of new ones had been built in their places on high dikes. Crossing the feather-market, where feathers were flying about in all directions, and which was covered all over with huge featherbeds, we entered a street where the dust was thick enough to hide the afternoon sun. Abandoning ourselves unresistingly to the pressure of the masses, we were pushed in and pushed out exactly as we wished to be. The great stream of human animation was at this time flowing out of the town towards a large open space, covered with men and animals of all nations and races—not less, certainly, than thirty thousand persons being present. The ground was very uneven, and on one little hill, some hundred women had established a market for eggs and live fowls. Another hill was covered with droves of pigs; on the plain were vast troops of horses, and the valleys were covered with sheep. In some places were long rows of linen merchants from Slavonia, and on a grassy declivity, a showman had set up a flag and a barrel-organ, and was explaining in the Hungarian language, to the bystanders, four painted representations of the four last tragical periods of the life of the Emperor Napoleon. It is no trifling testimony to the greatness of this man, that at this distance of time and place, he should be thought the only one whose tragical moments were worthy of attention. At the entrance of the market was planted a cohort of dealers in Paprika, who had sacks full of this red pepper, so violently pungent, that a little on the point of a knife was enough, to our taste, to spoil a dish, but of which astonishing quantities are eaten by the natives. In the hotels, all sorts of Paprika dishes are brought—Paprika beef, Paprika bacon, Paprika fish, &c.;—but among the common people the Paprika is so universally understood, that it is seldom mentioned. One might think that every thing in Hungary grew seasoned with Paprika, bread being the only exception.

This plant is, I believe, the same as that called among us, Turkish or Indian pepper (*Capsicum annuum*); the kernel and the husk being ground up together for Paprika, both containing equally the fiery pungent quality.

The Slovaks are the principal dealers in linen, which they manufacture themselves in the north-western parts of Hungary, bordering on Silesia and Moravia, and this branch of industry has spread thence into other countries. As the Slovaks are the greatest manufacturers, the Hungarians are chiefly occupied in the breeding of cattle and horses; and in the energy with which they devote themselves to the latter, it would seem as if they had not quite forgotten the ancient mode of life of their forefathers on the Asiatic steppes.

I had opportunities enough to admire their horsemanship, in the feats exhibited by those who were showing off the capabilities of their several steeds, with a view to attract purchasers. One dealer, to whom it was objected that his horse was not quick enough in turning, made it rear on its hind legs, and pirouette three times running.

Some antiquarians have been of opinion that the present Hungarians and the ancient Parthians were the same people, and, in fact, the accounts given of the Parthians, by the Romans, will almost always apply to both. The Poles also, though of an entirely separate race, are in this respect strikingly similar to them, and Europe has received from these two nations two most important branches of her cavalry, the hussars and the lancers. It appears to me remarkable that the Tartars, Poles, and Hungarians, all such excellent horsemen, should so seldom have produced distinguished proficients in the art of horsemanship; but it would seem that the better a people in general ride, the fewer mere show riders are to be found among them. On the other hand, exactly those nations which make the worst horsemen produce the greatest number of these exhibitors, namely, the Belgians, the French, and the Italians. The Italians, indeed, who have given a name (Franconi) to the most renowned of the horsemanship race, are decidedly the worst horsemen in Europe. Thus it has been remarked that there are musical nations who have no composers, and poetical nations without writers, while those who have most of what is called "*bonhommie,*" have often the least of real and true virtue.

As we passed through the fair we remarked among the gipsies, by whom it was thronged, a pair coming towards us—a tall young man and a middle aged woman—both as black as Africa. The woman was lamenting and gesticulating violently. We accosted her to know what was the matter. She told us, immediately, that the object of her displeasure was her husband, a blockhead and a spendthrift, and a good-for-nothing fellow, and thereupon she began to cry most bitterly, adding, that he had gone, without her knowledge, and had bought himself a handkerchief, for which he had given twenty kreutzers. The handkerchief, moreover, was not even a good one; the colours were not fast; and so saying, she leaped upon his neck and snatched off the handkerchief, showing where his shirt was stained blue. The gipsy took all this very quietly, and laughed when she snatched away his handkerchief, and afterwards, without our asking for them, produced his papers, his passports, and so forth, which he kept carefully preserved in a bundle of rags. The possession of these certificates of legitimation often saves the gipsy from much petty tyranny, since, if he happen to be without them, every one is apt to think himself authorized to treat him in the most summary manner.

It was at this fair that I first heard the celebrated Hungarian gipsy music, in a large dancing-booth, where *déjeuners, diners,* and *thés dansants* were going on the whole day. The company was wholly composed of peasants; and the narrowness of the space in which they moved, was compensated amply by their zealous endeavours to make the most of it. They lifted up, swung round, let go, and caught up again, their fair ladies, in a most vigorous and praiseworthy style; and the noise of stamping equalled that of a hundred threshing-machines. The heat was overpowering, and the dust suffocating; for, besides what was raised by the toils of the dancers, clouds came in at the open doors and windows, from the fair outside, where herds of cattle were moving in all directions; and the sensations occasioned by heat and dust were not diminished by the clangour of the gipsy musicians, with their trumpets and cymbals.

Throughout Hungary the musicians are almost exclusively either Germans or gipsies; as the Hungarians themselves have in general little taste or talent for music. I do not mean that they are absolutely insensible to harmonious sounds, for what people ever was? but I speak only of the comparative susceptibility, and of their practical musical talents. The German musicians of Hungary hold, of course, the highest rank, and are met with in the principal theatres and churches, at the balls of the upper classes, and in the first-rate hotels; but the gipsies fill the lower appointments, such as those in the small theatres, and in the smaller towns they are the sole professors of the art. The Germans in general play none but German, French, or Italian music; but the gipsies the true national compositions of Hungary, which breathe a peculiar spirit, and are distinguished by certain original turns and phrases, which I never remember to have heard anywhere else. There is, however, a strong resemblance between all these Hungarian gipsy melodies, and it is easy for any one who has heard one of them, to recognise others. Among the Tatars, also, at least among those of the Crimea, the gipsies are the usual musicians; I had often heard them there, but could not recollect enough of their music to know whether it resembled what I heard in Hungary.

I could easily understand the partiality manifested by the people generally for this music, for there is something in its character so wild and impassioned—it has tones of such deep melancholy, such heart-piercing grief, and wild despair, that one is involuntarily carried away by it; and although, on the whole, the performance of the gipsies is rude and wild, many of them manifest so much of real musical inspiration, as may well make amends for their deficiencies in scientific culture. There are several gipsy bands which are celebrated throughout Hungary, and some of the patriotic journals even cite with rapture some performers of the last century. Anecdotes are also often seen in these papers tending to exalt these gipsy favourites above their more renowned brethren of the divine art. Thus, for instance, we are told of some pieces of Beethoven having been performed on a certain occasion, and received with immense applause, when some gipsy musicians entering, and playing some simple "Magyar Notas," the whole assembly was silent, and melted into tears. Even the German performers are sometimes compelled to learn some of these "Magyar Notas," with which they will often conclude, in order to leave a favourable impression on the minds of their audience, and "*Egy Magyar Nótát,*" (Now play us something Hungarian) is a common request at the close of more elaborate foreign compositions. There is, however, much monotony in this, as in all other national music, and the more cultivated even of native auditors are glad, after a while, to return to the greater variety and intellectual richness of our German compositions.

After I had refreshed myself by a bath and a supper at our hotel, the condescending "Queen of England," I set out again for a lonely walk along the Danube Quay, as well to enjoy the coolness of the clear moonlit river, as out of curiosity, to discover how some of the multitudes whom I had seen at the fair, were likely to be lodged. I found the whole strand covered with sleepers of all ages and both sexes, wrapped in blankets, mantles, or only in mats, stretched on the ground beside their wares. Most of them seemed to be enjoying a sound and refreshing sleep. Only a few of the more opulent or more effeminate, had let down a tent over their sleeping places, and lay with their goods under its protecting shelter. Those who had barges, or who could get a place in one, lay or sat sleeping about them, sometimes covering the whole vessel, where a fire was usually burning. I stepped in and out, wherever I liked, among the recumbent figures; now and then, one would raise his head, stare at me for a moment, and then let it fall again upon his sheepskin. Here and there were groups still awake, and occupied with conversation, singing, dancing, and play. In the vicinity of the new bridge was one party, more numerous and animated than the rest, whose character appeared a little equivocal. There were some merry noisy Magyar girls, performing a variety of gymnastic exercises and dances, not of the most decorous character, but undoubtedly national. Sometimes one of them would go and rouse a sleeping companion who was supposed to possess peculiar skill in a particular movement, and she would jump up quite willingly, rub her eyes, and begin to dance with the utmost goodhumour.

A long flight of steps leads down to the Danube from the quay, and even these were covered with people, Slovaks and Magyars, some sleeping, some waking. On the top of the steps stood one of the former imitating a bagpipe in a very comic manner with his mouth, and having some article of clothing tucked under his arm to represent the bag, blowing out his cheeks, and bringing out in a masterly manner, the nasal tones of his instrument. While he played his imaginary pipe, he also danced backwards and forwards on the little space allowed him, and his music served as accompaniment to certain " pas" executed by some women, who supported him occasionally with their voices. There could be no doubt of the country of these theatrical and comic bagpipe-players; for besides the difference of costume, and the circumstance of the bagpipe being a Slovak, and not a Magyar instrument, there is something too stiff and serious in the character of the Hungarians, for these lively exhibitions, but the Slovaks are in general a more gay, conversable people, more given to song and dance and poetry, than their ruder and more sombre Magyar neighbours. At the bottom of the steps on the sands, were assembled a group of Magyars, among whom an old man leaning on his staff, sent from beneath his broad-brimmed hat the melancholy sounds of a popular national melody, to which his audience were profoundly attentive, and when all other sounds had gradually died away, his low mournful tones alone broke the silence of the wide tranquil river, and the twin cities lay buried in sleep.

THE CONGREGATION OF NOBLES AT PESTH.

The provinces or circles into which, from the earliest times, Hungary has been divided, are called *Comitatus*, or counties, over each of which is placed, as chief officer, a Comes, or count, who is a Magnate of the empire and a person of great importance, notwithstanding the simplicity of his name; and who is assisted by two deputies, or *Vice Comes*, under whom again are placed many subordinate officers.

The whole division and organization of these counties resembles much that which was introduced by Charlemagne into Germany and France, and to understand more clearly those remote times, we need only study the existing state of things in Hungary. I believe that an exact comparison of what we have before our eyes in this country, with what we know of the Carlovingian institutions, would throw much light on both.

Like the counts of Charlemagne, the Hungarian *Comes* are appointed by the king for life. In Germany these countships soon became hereditary, and obtained princely and territorial power. In Hungary, however, up to the present time, only twelve out of fifty have become hereditary, and that not by gradual custom but by direct royal ordinance. All other officers from the Vice Comes downwards, are changed every three years, and new elections made by the nobility of the county. This three years' period of service, and the choice of new officers by the nobility, exists also in other countries organized on the basis of the feudal institutions.

The election takes place in an assembly of all the nobility of the province, at which every prelate, every magnate, every nobleman, and some few unnoticed and insignificant deputies of towns, are entitled to appear and vote. This assembly, which is called together for the choice of deputies for the diet, and also regularly four times a year for the regulation of matters of police and public economy, is called a congregation, though, as an Hungarian historical writer has observed, it might be named "*Status provinciæ*," since it stands in the same relation, and performs the same offices for the county that the "*Status regni*," or Diet, does for the whole kingdom.

The triennial elections for the various county offices, are called "Restorations," and one hears continually that, in this or that county, there is just now a "Restoration" going on. These Restorations, and the Congregations, for the choice of the deputies to the diet, are the most animated assemblies that Hungary has to show, and there take place those vivacious scenes, sometimes described in our newspapers, and which bear some resemblance to the English elections for members of parliament. At the regular assemblies of the principal nobles, recurring every three months, things are conducted in a more orderly manner, partly because private interests do not come so much into play, and partly because the uneducated class of peasant nobles do not attend them. At the elections these always take a prominent part, for though they really care little about them, they are pushed forward and made cat's-paws of by the great nobles. I have never witnessed one of the elections, but I have often observed the affable condescension of the high official personages, when one of these periods was approaching. With respect to dress, and deportment, property, education, and manner of life, these peasant nobles are not a hair's breadth above the common peasantry of Hungary, and their pride, presumption, rudeness, and incapability of improvement, place them far below that level; whilst, therefore, their privileges in the Congregations, place them on an equality with the prelates and magnates, and their yes or no has equal power, they are the most dangerous class of the community in Hungary, for they are privileged in their stupidity and ignorance,—an empty, presuming, puffed-up Ochlocracy.

The Hungarian patriots of the day, nevertheless, take a different view of this matter, and assert that exactly this class of peasant nobles, by their natural and healthy common sense, and their power of steady resistance, have often in moments of danger proved the main support of freedom and the constitution, and have hindered many abuses in cases where the royal prerogative has been stretched too far, and where the more powerful and better bred magnates have often been influenced or corrupted. If this be so, it is much to be regretted that the Hungarian constitution should rest on no better foundation than this ignorant peasant nobility. An enlightened middle class would form a basis equally firm, and one far more favourable to the mental and physical progress and development of the country.

Be this as it may, it is very curious to observe how the manners of the great nobility towards the little, become more and more amiable and gracious as the day of election approaches. They drive into their villages, visit their cousins and brothers, as they call them, on terms of the most friendly equality, solicit their " most sweet voices," and give no very delicate hints of the abundance of good things to be prepared for their banquets in the towns on the days of election. Carriages are sent to bring the voters, houses hired for their lodging and entertainment, and the day before the poll the candidates drive round to all the public houses to look up their constituents, and see if they are satisfied and in good humour.

The different parties are usually distinguished by wearing red, white, or blue feathers in their hats, and on the important day they vie with each other in early rising, for it is above all things of consequence to be the first to get possession of the county-house, where the election takes place. If they have not drunk too much over night, they often fill the hall as early as two o'clock in the morning, and though they cannot exclude their rivals, many of these halls are so small in proportion to the numbers of the nobility present, that a brisk, active party has often entirely filled it, and effectually prevented the friends of the rival candidate from getting near the polling place. Whoever is the most quick in his movements, splendid in his promises, and profuse in his expenditure, generally wins the day, so that the coveted posts are often dearly purchased. An election will cost as much as twenty thousand or thirty thousand florins and upwards, but the place of a Vice-Comes, by direct or indirect methods, is pretty sure to bring in again as much or more. The candidate is proposed by the " *Obergespann*" or Comes, and accepted or refused by acclamation, but should it not be easily determinable by this method, the votes are counted. On the announcement of the names each party seize their man, raise him on the shoulders of his friends, and exclaim " Vivat! Vivat! That's the right one—We'll have no other." The opposite party of course do its best to insult him, these insults are again resented, and such tumultuous scenes take place, that the prelates and orderly people in general are glad to make their escape. Even after his election, indeed, the " happy man" is by no means left to enjoy his success in quiet, for the congratulations and caresses of his adherents are often most inconveniently uproarious.

I attended many of the sittings of the Pesth congregation, and was present at their opening. In the antechamber of the principal hall several " *Haiducks*" were walking up and down. They were tall, distinguished-looking people, dressed in the handsome Hungarian costume, and fully armed. Several of them are always appointed to attend the Comitat, or county-house, and they are also placed at the head of the ordinary police of the county. They allowed not only every nobleman, but every decently dressed person to enter the hall, and even strangers were admitted to mingle freely with the speakers. There is indeed in every Comitat house a gallery for those who are not to take a part in the proceedings, but no one, with the exception of women, and those who are shabbily dressed, is obliged to confine himself to it.

The hall is fitted up in a manner which, though simple, is perfectly well adapted to the purposes it is intended for, and decorated with full-length pictures of the deceased palatines. There is also one representing the meeting of crowned heads at Paris in 1814, beneath which is an inscription that already seems to belong to by-gone times—" *Domita Gallorum ferocia usurpationibusque coercitis Vindices libertatis Europæ Felici fœdere juncti.*"

The hall soon became filled with nobles, young and old, officials and non-officials, many in simple surtouts, but most in the splendid national costume, and all of course armed. The conversation and movements of the assembly were perfectly quiet, and at length the president entered and the sitting was opened.

The President of the Congregation is the palatine of Hungary, who is also ex-officio, Obergespann of the Pesth Comitat. The archduke, however, has not attended the sittings for some time, but performs his duty by a deputy, or, as he is here called, "*Administrator.*" This administrator, a Magnate of Hungary, now entered, greeting the assembly with the ordinary Hungarian salutation, "*Alarzatos szolgaya,*" that is, "Your humble servant," of which one seldom hears much more than a hissing sound, and then took his place at the end of a table occupying the centre of the hall with the "*Vicegespann,*" secretaries, and other officers, on each side. The other nobles stood round or walked up and down the hall. There were indeed a few benches, but they were mostly used to stand on. Near the president lay a heap of papers, diplomas of nobility, protocols, and printed pamphlets, the latter on the subject of mixed marriages, concerning which a proposal was about to be made; and as the subject is just now exciting much attention in Hungary, all hands were immediately stretched out after them. The *Vicegespann* could not reach to give to every one, and when the pressure became too great, he seized a whole bundle of them, and threw them over the heads of the crowd into the middle of the hall, where they were laughingly caught by the bystanders.

As the discussions were carried on in Hungarian, I could not, unfortunately, understand them, but I was informed they related to some proposals that were to be made at the next diet, relative to a certain government officer, who had defrauded the treasury of fourteen thousand florins, and to the means of preventing such frauds in future, to the announcement of some patents of nobility granted by the king, and to the taxes on butcher's meat, which in Hungary are of as much consequence as the bread tax with us.

The diploma of nobility was written in Latin, and was of extraordinary length; containing all the long titles of the King of Hungary, and the Emperor of Austria, then the ordinary and extraordinary services rendered to the state by the individual to be ennobled, and then followed the names of the archbishops, bishops, prelates, *obergespann* ,and *vicegespann*, with all their titles, which are put in partly for the sake of ornament, and partly, as I was told, because these high and mighty personages are considered in some measure, to guarantee the validity of the patent.

Any person who wished to speak, called attention by exclaiming, "*kerem, kerem!*" that is, "I beg," and then approached the president's table, or sometimes spoke over the heads of those who were between. Almost all the speakers appeared to me to be characterized by a manly and dignified bearing; many spoke with great fluency, and some with what seemed like impassioned and fiery eloquence. Whenever any thing was said that seemed particularly to please, the gallery resounded with " *Elyen! Elyen!*" equivalent to our " Bravo !" or " Vivat !" Another word which I heard often repeated was " *Hayunk ! Hayunk!*" that is " Hear, hear !" but not used precisely in the sense in which it is employed in the English parliament, but rather in the sense of " Order! or Silence!" and these continual injunctions of " silence," did not a little to increase the noise always occasioned in an Hungarian assembly, by the moving about and clatter of sabres and spurs. It was sometimes impossible to hear the speaker for the vociferations of these lovers of order.

The best and most eloquent speaker among them was said to be the noble deputy, Kossut, who acquired so much fame at the last diet. He was, as must be known to a large portion of my readers, imprisoned for a considerable time, for having made public some discussions of the diet, is now editor of the most popular Hungarian journal, the "*Pesti Hirlap,*" which were forbidden to be printed, by distributing a considerable number of manuscript copies. He was subsequently liberated, and is now the most fearless and untiring advocate of all that tends to the amelioration and advancement of his country, the boldest and most unsparing denouncer of the errors and abuses in the constitution and government. He has made it his especial care to keep guard over what he considers the weak side of his countrymen—namely, the liability of the judges and other officers to corruption and irregular influences, and never fails to discover and expose offences of this description. Under these circumstances it cannot be but Mr. von Kossut, should have many enemies, but he counts a far greater number of friends, the whole public of Hungary being on his side, and he is the favourite and the political hero of the day. His Hirlap is the oracle on all occasions, and during my stay in Pesth, whenever any public matter was discussed I continually heard the eager inquiry :— " What does Kossut say of it ?"

I looked with much interest at this man, on whom the eyes of all Hungary may be said to be fixed. He is of middle size, and very agreeable exterior ; his features are regular and decidedly handsome, but strongly marked and manly. He is in the prime of life, with rather redundant hair and whiskers, but a mild and modest expression of countenance. He was rather pale when I saw him, and his features wore an air of earnestness, slightly tinged by melancholy, though lighted up by his fine flashing eyes. He spoke for full half an hour, without a moment's hesitation, and his mode of delivery appeared to me extremely agreeable. His voice is as fine as might be expected from so handsome a person, and the sounds of the Hungarian language, powerful and energetic, seemed, from his lips, I might almost say, warlike, although they come hard and harsh from the mouth of an uncultivated speaker. The "*Elyen! Elyen!*" frequently interrupted him, and the "*Hayunk!*" was scarcely heard once, for every one was attentive and silent of his own accord.

National pride, and the fiery zeal of patriotism in Hungary, tend much, I believe, to the improvement of oratory, and we Germans might take many a lesson in these things from our Magyar neighbours. I do not, however, mean to convey an impression that all the members of the Pesth congregation were orators ; many remained mute the whole time of the sitting, and others walked up and down, with their plumed Kalpoks in their hands, appearing chiefly intent on the display of their elegant costume. One did nothing but twirl about his rings, and another devoted himself to the unceasing brushing of his hat, and from many no sounds were heard but an occasional "*Elyen!*" or "*Hayunk!*"

The office of the vicegespann is something like that of speaker in the English parliament, as he calls to order those who require his interference, and, in case of contumacy, has the power to inflict pecuniary fines, or even to exclude the disorderly person from the hall. Among the anomalies which are everywhere discoverable in the Hungarian political edifice, is also this; that if the offender can make his escape from the hall before the vicegespann has had time to utter the words—" For this offence I sentence you to a fine of twenty-five florins," he escapes also the punishment. Should the Haiduck, however, at a sign from the Vicegespann, place himself before the door, the offender must remain and pay; and if he have not as much money, and that it is necessary to send an officer home with him, he must pay double.

I was told that one of the town deputies would very soon find himself subjected to this fine, if he presumed too far in his remarks on any privilege of the nobility, " for we deputies of cities," said one of them to me, " have a seat but no vote in these congregations." Upon this topic we were soon engaged in a warm discussion, in the course of which we found means to withdraw from the hall.

THE BRIDGE AT PESTH.

I know of no bridge concerning which so much has been in modern times said and written as the new one now building over the Danube between Pesth and Buda, and there are certainly few works of this kind whose execution has been opposed by so many obstacles political and physical. This truly gigantic work is deservedly regarded with pride by the Hungarians, and is, after the bridge of Trajan at Orsova, the only construction of the kind, the only permanent bridge, to which the middle and lower Danube have been subjected. With the exception of the Russian rivers, the Danube is one of the poorest rivers in this respect in all Europe, for whilst the little Thames counts almost fifty bridges, the mighty Danube from Ulm cannot number a dozen. The extraordinary breadth of the stream, the rapidity of its current, its irregular course, and the great inundations to which it is liable, have been the chief physical impediments to the erection of a permanent bridge, but something also must be attributed to the want of energy and activity in the people inhabiting its banks.

Between Pesth and Ofen (Buda) the Danube is about 1800 feet broad, and in early times when there was less intercourse between the two cities, the want of a bridge may have been less felt. Some barges tied together with ropes answered the purpose until seventy-five years ago, when about fifty pontoons were substituted, and these, diminished to forty-two, were moved to their present position by the Emperor Joseph. This contrivance, however, is very insufficient to the present wants of the inhabitants, and in winter is of no use at all. From December to March it is laid aside, and the communication between the towns wholly carried on by boats. This is occasionally by no means safe, and there occur days, from time to time, when the twin cities are wholly cut off from each other.

This bridge is besides much too narrow for the passage of great herds of cattle, large heavy waggons or bodies of troops, and on some of these occasions—the latter for instance—the bridge is for the time closed against other passengers. In summer when the water is very low, the bridge sinks so much in the middle, that horses are exposed to the labour of toiling up a wooden hill, and it has sometimes happened that waggons have broken through and fallen into the river.

These evils and inconveniences had often been made the subject of discussion, more especially about fourteen or fifteen years ago; innumerable articles had appeared in the newspapers, and debates had taken place in the diet; but the matter did not begin to wear a hopeful aspect till the zealous, patriotic, and influential Count Szechenyi placed himself at the head of the undertaking, and made a journey to England for the purpose of consulting the ablest architects. An official report was then published, and at length, after many and violent discussions in the diet, it was determined that the work should be begun.

It is hardly possible for us to imagine how the mere building of a single bridge between two towns, should be a matter of such violent interest to the whole kingdom, as to give rise to tediously protracted debates in the general diet, but this may be explained, partly by reference to the real importance of the undertaking for the whole country, and its great cost, and partly by certain existing political evils.

The importance of the undertaking is evident, not only for the two cities immediately concerned, but for all Hungary, since, for the extent of a hundred German miles (more than four hundred and fifty English) there is not a single standing bridge; those of Komorn and Peterwardein being bridges of boats, and those at Presburg and Gratz flying bridges; and at those periods when the Danube is full of ice, or the countries bordering on it inundated, so as to render the passage difficult or even impossible, the whole kingdom is rent into two parts, cut off from all intercourse with each other. The whole kingdom is, therefore, interested, that, somewhere or other, there should be a certainty of communication, and this is especially desirable in this heart of the country, this central artery through which pours the great tide of its commercial life.

The expense of the erection is undoubtedly a difficulty, for it is not easy to raise such a sum as £500,000 sterling, in a country which though rich in produce is so poor in money as Hungary. It has been accordingly found necessary to entrust the pecuniary part of the business to a Vienna capitalist, the wealthy banker Sina. Many over-zealous patriots have, indeed, uttered grievous outcries on this occasion. "Oh heavens, why did they not rather make a subscription through the whole country? The sum might have been easily raised, I myself would have gladly given a hundred florins, and I know many who would have given more, rather than have the whole country made tributary to a foreigner." It has been agreed, if Baron Sina advances the money for the bridge, he shall be allowed to erect on it a toll, for the space of eighty-five years.

It is possible that the patriotic plan might have succeeded, but whoever knows how little disposable capital there is in Hungary, and how very difficult these *easy* things are sometimes found to be when put to the test of experience, will not be disposed to regard with a jealous eye a plan by which so great a benefit has been secured to the country.

Another difficulty by which the subject of this bridge was brought before the diet, consisted in certain privileges of the nobility which it would be necessary for them to renounce. The whole body of Hungarian nobles, namely, have been hitherto entitled to pass either on foot or horseback over the Pontoon bridge, without paying the toll demanded of all unprivileged passengers. Baron Sina protested against any such exemptions in the case of the new bridge, and refused to advance the sum required, unless all persons whatever were subject to the toll. The said privilege, however, is so intimately connected with that of passing free over all roads, bridges, and highways of the kingdom, and finding, "I am a nobleman," accepted at all turnpikes instead of a certain amount of kreuzers, that the privileged orders dread of all things an attack upon this right (or wrong) as the first breach in their grand aristocratic circumvallation. Many of them, therefore, refused long and obstinately to make this concession; but their resistance was at last overpowered by the exertions of more liberal men, and the undertaking fairly commenced. The first shot has been fired, therefore, but it will be long yet before the breach is sufficiently widened. For my own part I own I could not witness without disgust the exercise of this petty but insolent privilege at the old Pontoon bridge. Let the reader imagine a row of mustached fellows, most of them (alas) speaking German, opening their barrier not only to every noble, but, according to a custom which has slipped in, to every well-dressed man, and seizing by the arm, and rudely demanding the toll of every poor working mechanic, every Jew or peasant boy that passed. These bridge-guards, by long practice of their trade, have acquired such a lynx-eyed dexterity, that even on Sundays and holidays, when the mechanic is often as elegantly dressed as the noble, they are never deceived. They know by sight almost all the inhabitants of Pesth and Buda, as well as their children and the inmates of their houses, and can tell in a moment who does, and who does not belong to the privileged orders. The rich Jews generally pay a certain sum yearly to avoid the annoyance of being stopped whenever they pass, and I have been informed, that, curiously enough, the gipsies enjoy the same exemption as the nobles. "*Les extrèmes se touchent*" or they are perhaps regarded as such complete nullities in society, that they are allowed like the free commoners of nature, the birds, to fly in and out as they please.

I cannot conceive how it happens that the upper classes cannot muster magnanimity enough to subject themselves voluntarily to this trivial tax, if it were only to avoid the disgrace of the thing; it is strange too to think, that any people should long submit to such a miserable species of oppression.

Many abuses are no doubt of more importance, but this is of so open and barefaced a character! The great man walks by unquestioned with his purse full of ducats, while the poor one, the very beggar, is forced to rummage among his rags perhaps for his last kreuzer. Blessed, therefore, be the new edifice which is to introduce a better system! Blessed be its foundation-stone, which is to be at the same time the foundation of Hungarian equality and true freedom!

I visited the works several times with a card of admission which I obtained at the "Bridge Office," for the correspondence, the management of the money, and other matters connected with the building, have occasioned so much business, that it has been found necessary to have an office, and a pretty numerous establishment of clerks and officers devoted to it. In order to support the weight of the bridge, which is to consist of a system of iron chains, four piers are necessary, two near the shore, and two in the middle of the stream. The four main chains which are to bear the greatest burden, are to weigh 24,000 cwt.; they have been made in England, as there do not exist in Hungary the machines requisite to try their strength, and subject every part to a rigid examination. This trial machinery is enormously expensive; but in England it is often wanted, whereas in Hungary it might never be wanted a second time.

The bridge was begun on the 1st. of May, 1840, and the part now erected, consists only of the coffer-dams, for two out of the four piers. The construction of these coffer-dams is in itself a gigantic work. They are temporary enclosures made in the river, by driving in a double wall of piles, pumping out the sand and water, and filling the empty space with water-tight clay. In order to give them the necessary strength to resist the pressure of the ice in the Danube, they are fortified by a system of cross beams in the interior. For the whole bridge, in the construction of these coffer-dams, no fewer than 7000 piles are required, each the trunk of a mighty pine-tree. Each of these piles is furnished with an iron point, weighing near a hundred weight, so that for these points only, 700,000 pounds of iron must be sunk in the bed of the river. Every pile has to be sunk eighteen feet deep into the bed of the river, and this is effected by the strokes of an enormous block of iron, every pile requiring about 400 strokes; yet all this toil is of course only to serve a temporary purpose, for as soon as the piers are completed, the piles are sawn away under the water, leaving only what is deep in the ground.

A steam-engine of twenty-four horse power has been erected to pump the sand and water out of the coffer-dams, and if the work proceed only at the same rate as hitherto, we may calculate that every summer one of these preparatory labours will be completed, and the people engaged on the works may feel tolerably satisfied, that for many years to come there is no fear of their wanting employment.

Some difficulties that existed, however, with respect to certain buildings belonging to the government, and which obstructed the works on the Buda side, have been arranged, and they will now proceed more rapidly.

I accompanied the principal architect to the place in the middle of the river, where they were preparing for the middle pier, and was much amused by the gabble of English, German, Italian, Magyar, and Slavonian workmen, swarming like ants over the scaffolding in the midst of the mighty stream. I counted above twenty machines at work, driving in piles at this one pier, and though it seems a simple thing enough to keep one's hands out of the way of a machine weighing ten hundredweight, and falling thirty feet, yet the people are so careless and thoughtless, that accidents are very frequent, and the loss of their hands and fingers is often the consequence.

The number of persons in the hospital of St. Rochus, who have been wounded and injured in this way, amounted to fifteen. At this rate we may calculate on seventy or eighty persons being more or less injured, before the bridge is completed.

The English workmen, whom the architect had brought with him, take precedence of the rest; next to them are the Italians from Trieste and

Venice, who have much experience in subaqueous building; and after these come the German, Hungarian, and Slavonian workmen. There was only one of the natives with whom the English architect professed himself satisfied, saying they were in general " stupid people," but of this one he said, " Yes, yes, he is something like an Englishman—there's some spirit about him."

I climbed upon the extreme point of a sort of bulwark erected to break the force of the ice, and enjoyed a magnificent panorama of the two extensive cities and the mountains around, from the middle of the majestic river; indeed I could not prevail on myself to leave the place till the evening bell sounded across the water.

Great anxiety prevailed in Pesth last winter, concerning this *ice breaker*, and it was thought it must be swept away, as well as the coffer-dam it was intended to protect. To the great triumph of the English, however, it remained uninjured.

As it was Saturday night I rowed ashore in the company of a crowd of the workmen who were going to get paid. Under a wooden shed, in the courtyard of the Bridge Office, where lay vast heaps of building materials, there stood a long wooden table, covered with heaps of money in various coins, of great and small value. " Precious burden!" thought, doubtless, the workmen, as they stood around contemplating it with eager glances. They were called up one after another to receive their week's wages from the hands of a smart cashier, who counted out the money with great rapidity, whilst a clerk sitting by entered it in a book. One might trace something of the character of each man in the manner in which he received his money. One would clutch it eagerly, as if afraid it might be taken from him again, another would come up with a saucy air, with his hat on one side, as much as to say, " Come! give me what belongs to me." A third, with a sullen and sinister look, would glance round at the cashier distributing all this money with so much indifference, as if he thought, "Ah! you rich rascals, you have money enough, but you give us poor fellows as little as you can—if I had but an opportunity!—"

I noticed that though they all took it without counting, probably out of respect, they stopped outside and counted it carefully two or three times over. Some would immediately begin to discharge little debts to their comrades, some would give it to their wives who were waiting outside, and others would go singing and shouting along, disputing as to which was the best public-house to spend the evening in.

THE RASCIAN TOWN.—TURKISH BATHS AND ORIENTAL PILGRIMS.

In the beautiful picture of Buda, on the opposite side of the river, presented from the windows of my hotel, I was particularly struck by a part of the town lying between the Observatory and the Castle Hill, covered with its churches and palaces. This was the district particularly inhabited by the *Rascians* or Servians, consisting of about a thousand small houses, occupying the side of a steep hill called the Blocksberg, with terraces rising one above the other. These horizontal streets, of which there are five or six, are connected by little steep lanes or flights of steps, and from the distance, the houses appear to have but one window each. The whole had very much the appearance of a great amphitheatre, in which the houses represented the boxes. I expressed to a Hungarian acquaintance my wish to take a nearer view of this curious quarter, and he answered according to the odd expression much in use here, " Well, dear *thing*, if you would like to go, go, but I shall not go with you, for I know there is nothing to be seen."

I may remark, *en passant*, that this word *thing* is used in a more extended sense, and made more universally serviceable, than, I believe, in any other country in the world. They not only use it as we do ourselves, to signify any inanimate object whatever, of which we cannot immediately recollect the name, but even extend it to persons and abstract qualities of the mind.

The Rascians have spread all over Hungary from Servia their native province, principally in the Banat, the Batschka and Syrmia, which we shall have occasion to speak of in the sequel; but in northern Hungary, the land of the Slovaks and Rasniaks, there are but few. They have established themselves as bargemen and traders on the Danube, and almost in every town on its banks a particular quarter is appropriated to them, as in many German towns to the Jews.

These people have been drawn into Austria by the spirit of trade, but also frequently driven into it by the oppressions suffered from the Turks in their own country. This migration of the Servians has been constantly taking place since the first appearance of the Turks in Europe—from the time when their first princes fled to Buda to seek the protection of the Hungarian king Sigismund, to the day when prince Milosch came to Vienna to solicit permission from the emperor to buy land in the Banat. Something similar has taken place with the Armenians, who also escaping from Mussulman tyranny, have spread over the southern provinces of Russia. They were Rascians and Germans, who, at the close of the seventeenth century, were taken as colonists to repeople Pesth, just snatched from the hands of the barbarous Turks. The Rascians chose the Blocksberg, the Germans fixed themselves on the Castle Hill, but these now so far exceed their fellow-townsmen in numbers, that the whole city may be considered a German one,—the Rascians themselves being half-transformed into Germans.

The quarter which they inhabit has no very attractive appearance, nor is the aspect of the houses much more inviting. On opening the door leading into a little courtyard of one of them, the first thing that met my eye was the pigsty, over which, as well as over a shed near it, a picture was nailed up, comfirming what I had heard of the fondness of these people for all kinds of pictorial representations.

The owner of the house, whose name was Bagdonovitsh, (literally translated,—the son of the one sent from God,) was not at home, being at work in the vineyard of a German neighbour. The rooms were very clean, and on one of the walls hung pictures of our Saviour and several saints, although the general character of the Rascians is by no means of a saintly order. The opinion entertained here of their cunning and roguery is pretty well expressed by the common saying, that it will take four Jews and five gipsies to make one Rascian. In this condemnation are included the modern Greeks and Macedonians; and there is probably some truth in the notion, for the very same opinion of them is entertained by the people in Odessa, and in other places where I have heard them spoken of: and it is pretty much in the same estimate that they were held formerly by the Venetians and Genoese, with whom they were engaged in mercantile relations; nay, even the Romans had the proverbial expression "*Græca fides nulla fides.*" One must not, however, suffer one's opinion to be influenced too much by sayings of this kind, for if we visit and observe these people in their homes, we find at least as much to excite interest and sympathy, as to awaken contempt or dislike.

The reputation of the Rascian town, in Buda, corresponds exactly with that of their countrymen throughout Hungary. If any inquiry is made concerning the conduct of its inhabitants, the usual reply is, "Well I haven't heard of any thing lately, but it's a bad place to go to at night; one's life's not safe there at night:" and my own experience did not tend certainly to contradict this unfavourable judgment.

It happened one evening that I was strolling rather late up the Blocksberg, on which, as I have already said, the observatory is situated, in order to pay a visit to an astronomer who had promised to show me something I wished to see on the disk of the moon, and as I climbed up the narrow crooked lanes and dirty paths which abound in it, I could not but call to mind some stories I had heard of its peculiar propensities. I came back quite safe and sound, but early the next morning, having occasion to retrace my steps, I saw the body of a murdered man lying exactly in the path I had traversed the night before. The police were occupied in conveying it into a house, and in answer to my inquiry I was told, "Yes, the Rascians killed a man last night! He was a dealer in wood, who used to bring Slavonian oak for the new bridge that's building. He had just been to get his money, and lay down in the moonshine to sleep. Silly enough, but they do it continually, to save the expense of an inn; the money's gone, and there's the man, and a pretty pickle he is in." "But, good God! how is it possible? here in the middle of the street, surrounded by houses!" "Oh, there are people here who never hear any thing, and there are plenty of bargemen or cattle-drivers that may have done it, and be far enough off by this time." I pitied the fate of the poor wood-dealer, and could not but feel that I had had an escape.

On one of my visits to the Rascian town, I entered a sort of eating-house, over which was inscribed, "This house is in the hands of God, and is kept by Maria Leitherin," and the Maria Leitherin was a German. The intimate association into which the Germans and Rascians are brought, has, however, by no means tended to abate the feeling of jealousy existing between them, and this jealousy is never more conspicuous than in the church, where the sermons are delivered alternately in German and Servian. In the pious processions this feeling of nationality often breaks out into indecorous squabbles; as each party desires to have the precedence, and both the spiritual and temporal authorities are sometimes obliged to interfere to settle the disturbance. A great number of the Servians of Buda do not belong to the Greek but to the Catholic church, having been converted by the Franciscan monks, but the Servians in general cling with great tenacity to their original faith. The Rascians or Servians (for these terms are in fact nearly synonymous) are said to be more devout than their German neighbours, and more rigid observers of fast-days, but at the same time far more addicted to brandy.

The Rascians have, like all orientals, a passion for warm baths, and it is not unlikely that they were induced to settle on the spot they now occupy by the temptation of the sulphur springs, since three out of the five which Ofen possesses, are to be found in the Rascian town, the King's Bath and the Emperor's Bath only, lying farther up the Danube.

These baths were known and used even in the Romans' time, and the Turks, as may be supposed, fairly revelled in them. To them, indeed (I mean the Turks), most of the improvements made in the baths are owing. They are frequented by all classes, and many visit them every day, sauntering away much of their time afterwards in the theatres and coffee-houses of the neighbourhood, or in loitering about in the sunshine.

A spacious building, enclosing several courts, has been erected over the springs, from which the water is carried in pipes into a great number of more or less elegant bathing-rooms, and finally into a great basin called the Common Bath, which is precisely in the state in which it was left by the Turks. Some of the baths cost as much as two florins the hour, but in the common bath one may sit the whole day for a penny. On visiting this we had to pass through several narrow passages before entering the chief apartment, where such a dim twilight prevailed, that for some time we could distinguish nothing, every object being veiled in a thick vapour. By degrees our eyes became accustomed to the light, or darkness, and we could perceive many naked figures, sitting or swimming about in the water, which flowed through the middle of a high-vaulted chamber supported on pillars. To the pillars were attached a few dim lamps, and two or three very small windows, deeply sunk into the very thick wall, admitted a scanty gleam of daylight. A broad stone pavement ran round the basin, and stone benches round the walls. Men, women, girls, and children, of all ages, were splashing in and out, and dressing and undressing themselves in various corners, and the boys were amusing themselves, by slipping about on the wet marble floor. My conductor informed me that he knew a painter who often came here to study the "human form divine," and it must be confessed there was plenty of opportunity. No one appeared disturbed by the presence of his neighbours, but packed up his or her clothes in a bundle, and placing them in a dry place on a bench, very quietly walked into the water, and after splashing about for a while, sat down under one of the pillars. I was particularly struck by a young and very pretty girl, who undressed herself in a distant and rather dark corner, and keeping on nothing more than a little short under petticoat (a remarkable instance of modesty by the by) very composedly jumped into the bath. No one of the men offered to approach her, every one keeping within the limits of his own domain. One only, it might have been her brother, or perhaps a bridegroom, did not seem to relish the curiosity with which we were regarding her, and came splashing up towards her. By the feeble light of the lamp we could see the girl looking anxiously and timidly in the direction in which we were standing, and the dark steaming face of her friend, whoever he might be, emerging from the flood, and placing himself between the girl and us inquisitive strangers. I cannot say, however, that I believe the girls who frequent these baths to be generally of immaculate character, but poverty and the passion for baths, does occasionally tempt even these to visit them.

The Imperial Baths, at the other end of the town, immediately on the Danube, resemble these in most respects, but are still more extensive. In the centre of this building is a kind of garden, where, when I visited it, numerous bathing guests—Servians, Germans, Hungarians, Jews, and even Turks, who often come to these baths from great distances, were promenading about, enlivened by the music of a gipsy band. The baths are as much frequented in winter as in summer, for many of the poor are glad of such an opportunity to get thoroughly warmed through, for three kreuzers, or rather more than a penny. I have been told that fish are sometimes found in the warm water of these baths, but I never saw any thing but some frogs, and that was in a particularly cool part of them.

The water flowing out of these baths serves to turn a mill, and a little further on, where it falls into the Danube, has still warmth enough left to induce the laundresses to take advantage of it to wash their linen. These springs never freeze in the coldest winters, and flow with equal abundance in the driest summers, for which reason the mill, an old Turkish fortress, with four towers, pays six thousand florins rent, and the miller is, consequently, to be considered as an opulent person, besides having a very agreeable though rather corpulent wife, and some very pretty daughters. I have, I must confess, an old prejudice in favour of the beauty of millers' daughters, and it was certainly strengthened by what I observed here. I made acquaintance with the family, and promised to pay them a visit in the evening after returning from a certain Mahometan house of prayer in the neighbourhood, respecting which many strange, but, I imagine, fabulous stories, had been told me.

The keys of this mosque are kept in Constantinople, and the pilgrims who visit the spot every two years, receive the keys on setting out upon their pilgrimage, for which they are equipped by some religious society in the Turkish capital. This mosque is, moreover, the most northerly point of Mahometan pilgrimages. We ascended the hill after passing the last straggling houses of Buda, and, leaving the broad road, entered a footpath, which led through the yard of a Buda vine-dresser, up a little flight of steps, and so close to a pigsty that when the Mussulmans pass by they must have some trouble to preserve their flowing garments from the contaminating touch of the unclean animal. The sacred building itself is a solid octagonal stone mausoleum, such as is often seen in Mahometan burying-grounds, and is the tomb of a distinguished pacha of Buda. The vine-dresser's wife, a worthy old German dame, who was in the habit of performing little services for the pilgrims, such as bringing them water to wash, informed me that there seldom came more than three or four in a year, but that this year, she knew not why, they amounted to fifteen.

Most of them appeared to be poor people, but some few brought servants with them. They all pulled off their shoes before entering the mausoleum, and those who had their servants with them, had their feet also fumigated with a costly incense which they brought with them. The pilgrims all appeared quite well acquainted with the locality, as if it had been previously described to them in Turkey.

When they enter the door, they place one foot closely before another, so as to count their steps, till they arrive at the spot where lies the head of the saint. They then fall prostrate on the ground and pray,—many with such devotion and exhausting fervour, that they are carried out fainting, when their companions or attendants rub them with a certain ointment which restores them to life. They come not only from Constantinople, but also from the distant parts of the Turkish empire, from Asia Minor, Syria, and even from the Persian frontier. Most, as I have said, are poor, and travel on foot from place to place, and are usually kindly and hospitably received by the catholic priests of the place, or by the convents, which liberally afford them shelter and support. The greater number of these pilgrims are modest and well-behaved people; but it occasionally happens that some are troublesome, and they are in such cases conveyed, at the expense of the city, back to the Turkish frontier.

We could not enter the mausoleum, as it is kept locked, but our conductor furnished us with a ladder, by help of which we looked in at some little grated apertures at the upper part, by which it was feebly lighted. The walls were whitewashed and hung with various articles,—a sword, a dagger, a banner, a rag of black cloth (probably from the renowned black mantle of Kaaba), and other things. I was told that there was also a stone suspended there, although from where we stood I could not see it; and that it was half-transparent and written over with sentences from the Koran.

It became quite dark and we were still lingering round the mausoleum, and among the boundless stretch of vineyards by which it is surrounded. Times were indeed changed since the Turks poured their conquering armies, with the sultan at their head, over these countries, where now comes only a solitary wandering pilgrim indebted for his bare existence to the descendants of those very Christians, whom his forefathers regarded as their slaves. Perhaps this lonely shrine hears many a fervent prayer, that Allah would be pleased to restore this land to the dominion of the faithful.

Our hostess of the mill informed me that a Turkish dervish was then living at the Imperial Bath, who after he had performed his prescribed devotional duties at the mausoleum, having had a desire to visit the far-famed city of Vienna, had set out to travel on foot in that direction; but, on account of some irregularity in his passport, the poor innocent dervish had been seized by the Austrian police as a suspicious person, and most unceremoniously marched back over the Hungarian frontier, as if he had been a person dangerous to the peace of the empire.

THE HOTELS AND THE CASINO AT PESTH.

I have often had occasion to be surprised at the immense number of hotels which have sprung up in Germany during these late "piping times of peace;" but I must confess, that what the last twenty years have done in this respect for Pesth, far exceeds any thing of the kind that we have to show. The grand style of these establishments, strikes us the more, when we consider what the town was even a few years ago; and it may serve also as a standard by which to estimate what it probably will be some years hence. Those of Buda, although twenty in number, cannot be compared with those of the sister-city in elegance. Those of the first class in Pesth are usually built round a quadrangle, with two great dining-halls, one below opening into a garden, furnished with an orchestra in the evening, and another on an upper floor, more private and more frequented by guests of distinction; the fittings up of both apartments being equal to any thing we should expect in Paris. There is always a coffee-room well supplied with newspapers, and (as far as I can decide the question) the *cuisine* is unexceptionable. The staircase is generally broad and handsome, being entirely of marble, decorated, wherever it is possible, with the Hungarian national colours—green, red, and white, the green being understood to designate the green hill on which the ancient kings of Hungary at their coronation were wont to brandish the sword ; white for the four principal rivers of the kingdom, the Danube, the Theiss, the Drave and the Save, and red probably to indicate the royal dignity. These colours meet one at every turn in Hungary ; the chairs and sofas are covered with red, green, and white stuff, and the rays of the sun enter through red, green, and white blinds ; the servants in all public institutions wear these colours in their livery,—and in the hotels and coffee-houses, where patriotism is "your only wear," they present themselves in every variety of form. I had some curiosity to discover the date of the commencement of this fervent nationality, and in the public shooting-gallery of Pesth, where the targets for a series of years are hanging up, I perceived that the appearance of the Hungarian colours began with the year 1829. On one of these, two angels were introduced, and they had had the complaisance to appear clothed in red, green, and white.

The new private houses in Pesth, belonging to the wealthiest citizens, are like the hotels, built in a very splendid style, and through the open house-door, the long vista of columns, and fountains, and beds of flowers, and magnificent staircases, formed out of blocks of red marble, is sometimes really surprising.

This peculiar marble, which is very abundant in Pesth, is brought down the Danube from the quarries near the villages of Neudorf, Kühgrand, and Domosloch ; it is used for every variety of purpose, from the palaces of the living, to the monuments for the dead. It is rather soft, and does not admit of a very brilliant polish, but it contains many shells and fossils, which often are made to produce a very beautiful effect. One piece, in particular, I recollect having seen preparing for the headstone of a grave. A stone-cutter was just then employed in carving the outline of a finely-drawn shell of three feet in circumference, and what was once the home of a snail, is now proudly enthroned over the remains of a human being. This marble appears to be very easily worked, for the letters "Louise Amalie Friedr" (I did not wait for the family name) were cut while I stood looking on.

Several architects in Pesth have already gained a considerable reputation ; some for the solidity, and some for the elegance of their structures ; and in general, it is to be observed, the city has been indebted for all its improvements and adornments, not so much to the magnates as to the commercial classes of her inhabitants. The finest house belonging to any of the latter, is that of the rich tobacco monopolist, U——n, and the most gorgeous of the palaces of the nobility is that of Count K——. The Hungarians just now think nothing good enough for their, capital, and a comparison of both public and private buildings of former times with those recently erected, will enable us to form a correct estimate of their progress in the arts during the last twenty years. The last tremendous inundation has, in its consequences, proved of no little service to the improvements, by sweeping away numbers of small old houses and hovels by which they were obstructed. Till then Pesth resembled a lady decorating her head with feathers and diamonds, while her feet were naked, and perhaps not over clean. The inundation has washed these feet, with a rough broom indeed, that in some places carried away the skin with it, but the wounds are now mostly healed, and in place of the miserable clay huts and wooden sheds that have been destroyed, there have sprung up rows of neat, pretty houses. It were to be desired that these dwellings might retain this characteristic of neatness; but if we call to mind the description given by Count Szechenyi of the manner in which a new and elegant steamboat was dirtied and destroyed by Hungarian travellers, we shall feel no confidence in the duration of the pleasing appearance, unless we suppose that the habits of the travelling Hungarian differ materially from those of his countrymen in their own homes. As this is not likely to be the case, it is probable that a new washing will be necessary before long, though hardly as rough a one as the town received on the last occasion from the Danube.

Notwithstanding all we have said of the beauty of the city there are portions of it which make a very unfavourable impression; which in summer are smothered with dust, and in winter half-buried in mud; and many parts, even including the palaces, have an uncomfortable air of newness, rawness, and want of finish. Another fault also, that should not be passed over while we are speaking of the new buildings, is their frequent want of solidity, and the haste visible in their construction; but it must be admitted that this is a failing exceedingly prevalent in our times. I have seen new houses here with cracks in their beams wide enough to put my hand into. The night before I left Prague, a large newly-erected mansion fell in; and there is at this moment an extensive building in Berlin with such a split in its walls, that it is a question whether it will be held up by the neighbouring houses or draw them with it into destruction. I pointed it out to a Frenchman, and he told me that these matters were not a whit better managed in France.

The new building in Pesth, the *Redoutenhaus*, devoted to balls and assemblies, contains two such magnificent rooms as are not often to be met with in our wealthiest and most luxurious capitals, and the dancing-room has a chandelier, requiring three thousand wax-lights. They are, however, never all lighted at once, as the heat they would occasion would be so great as infallibly to melt them.

The most important and interesting public building, however, is that of the Pesth Casino; which, as I have before observed, has given occasion to many similar institutions all over Hungary. This establishment—I mean the noble—or, as the people here say, the Magnate Casino—is devoted, in the first place, to social meetings, such as balls, concerts, and dinners; and secondly, to the purposes of a library and reading institution. It contains several comfortable and even elegant rooms, in which all Hungarian publications, without any exception, are taken in, as well as the best German, and several English, French, and even American papers. For the library all books published in the Hungarian language are procured as soon as they leave the press, and so are all those having any reference to Hungary that appear in foreign countries, besides many others of interest on general subjects. I must own that I consider myself as under particular obligations to this Casino, for I generally had the three pleasant and convenient apartments for my sole use and benefit. The thirty large handsome lamps shone for my accommodation, and the literary treasures of the bookcases and tables appeared to be laid out as tribute at my feet. Now and then a single reader besides myself would drop in, but he was sure before long to begin to yawn, and speedily disappeared. I cannot, however, affirm, that I should at all times have enjoyed equal opportunities for this luxurious retirement among books, so peculiarly to my taste, without being disturbed by the intrusion of any visiters; for I generally went there after the theatre was over in the evening, and it was the time of the year when many of the best families are out of town. In winter the institution is probably more frequented.

In one of the reading-rooms there stood always twenty pipes ready filled, and I enjoyed few more agreeable moments during my stay at Pesth, than when, kindling one of what I may call *my* twenty pipes at one of my thirty lamps, collecting a packet of interesting books and papers, and letting myself down into one of the luxuriously cushioned lounging-chairs, I proposed to dream over what was passing or had passed in the past or present world.

The great work of Count Marsigli, "*Danubius Pannonico Mysicus*," contains such exact and minute details of every thing connected with the rivers Theiss and Danube, that I was quite alarmed to find the field had been so laboriously tilled. Miss Pardoe's book on Hungary, like most English works on this country, is far too laudatory to be of much value ; and I do not think the lady can possibly be acquainted with the writings of Count Szechenyi, the deceased Count Desewfy, and other distinguished Hungarian patriots, or with the manner in which they have pointed out clearly and boldly all the evils and abuses of their native country, else she would scarcely have ventured on the exhibition of such an extremely flattering portrait. To show every thing in this deceitful "*couleur de rose*" style, is to do no true service either to the native or the foreigner.

The English sympathize readily with the Hungarians, not only from the commercial relations between the two countries, but far more on the higher ground of a similar enthusiastic love of political freedom. They are apt to overlook the vast differences between the Hungarian and English constitutions. While the power of the aristocracy in England is balanced by a nearly equal power in the third estate, that of the aristocracy of Hungary has no similar counterbalancing power at all. The nobility in Hungary $= 1,000$; the people $= 0$. In Hungary, indeed, there are counted four classes or estates, as constituting the diet,—namely, the prelates, the magnates, the knights, and lastly, the deputies of the towns ; but the three first have no interest in common with the latter, who may be considered to have a seat, but no voice, in the assembly. My favourite book, however, was the Collection of Acts of the Hungarian Diet, a handsome copy of which is always lying at the Casino, ready for reference, on a table appropriated to it. Whatever may be the defects of the constitution of Hungary, it must certainly be a great advantage for the people to be able thus to make out what is the exact state of the law on any subject. The title of this book is *Decreta, constitutiones et articuli serenissimorum et apostolicorum Regum ac inclytorum statuum et ordinum Regni Hungarici.* I seized on it eagerly, with a view to examine for myself, whether there really existed that remarkable hiatus I had heard of between the acts of the government of Maria Theresa and of Leopold II., and I found, indeed, blank leaves in place of the decrees of Joseph II., from the year 1791. It is well known that by a decree of the Diet, all the acts of this emperor were annulled, after his death, as illegal, on account of his not having been a crowned king of Hungary ; and this space in the book was, in consequence, left empty. Immediately after the decrees of Maria Theresa, followed those of Leopold II. Had the Hungarians merely objected to the form of these acts, which was certainly illegal, they might not have been to blame; but, especially after the advice given to them on this point by the dying Joseph himself, they should not have thrown away, along with the faulty vessel, so much that was excellent in the contents. Is it not to be regretted that there should remain in Hungary no trace of this excellent and admirable man; who, notwithstanding some occasional errors, was one of the most distinguished sovereigns that ever reigned over the country? Nowhere is his name breathed. It is as if he had never existed, or as if a curse lay on his memory. Will not posterity say that they have striven to annihilate the remembrance of the best and most enlightened ruler ever granted to them?

The extraordinary, the preposterous value set on the crown, is one of the most curious phenomena in Hungarian history and legislation. The "golden round" of the holy Stephen, studded as it is with pearls and diamonds, is after all nothing more than the outward symbol of that ideal crown which is the key and corner-stone of the whole edifice of the state. These types of sovereignty have a kind of sacredness even among other nations, but among the Hungarians this reverence for the tangible material crown is carried beyond all reasonable bounds. It is not only figuratively, but absolutely in itself sacred, and a consecrating power is supposed to go forth from it; it is called "*Sacra Regni Corona cum Clenodiis suis*," and according to the law of the kingdom, whoever has not literally and corporeally worn this metal ring on his head, is not the king. The principle that the king never dies is not recognised in Hungary; the king is allowed to die, but the crown which is spoken of by the Hungarians as a living, mysterious king, rules then alone till a new sovereign has united himself with it. He does not receive the title of "*Sacratissima Majestas*" till he has had the crown on his head; before that he is spoken of as "*Neo-coronata sacratissima Majestas.*"

The route which the Hungarian projects of law have to pass, through all the debates and stormy discussions which take place before they can reach the tranquil black and white of the paper code, is a very long and circuitous one. First comes the king with his postulates or "*Propositiones Regiæ*," and distributes them to the various estates or classes assembled round his throne, as the Hungarians say, "with becoming pomp."

These proposals are now taken into consideration by the two tables, that of the magnates and prelates, and that of the knights and town deputies, who discuss them among themselves, and consider the difficulties (*gravamina*) which they mean to oppose to the royal demands. The two tables then acquaint each other with their respective resolutions, and hold general sittings, (*sessiones mixtæ*, or *non mixtæ*,) until all, or at least a majority are agreed concerning the answer to be made. In all these discussions, however, the deputies of the towns are entirely innocent, let the issue be what it may. When the king and the states are not of the same mind, and at the beginning of the session, at all events, this is generally the case, there follow innumerable resolutions and representations, and negotiations interspersed with more debates and more *sessiones mixtæ* and *separatæ*, until at last they agree on some points, and agree to differ on others, which are then put off till the next diet.

At the end of the session, all that has been agreed upon is summed up in a paper entitled, "*Articuli dominorum prælatorum, baronum mag-*

natum et nobilium cæterorumque," this *et cætera* signifying the twelve millions of Hungarians who are not nobles.

These articles are then read to the king, and his assent required in a respectful manner, but this he does not grant till he has subjected the paper to another revision in his council. Should it be entirely approved of, he then has it put into the form of a decree, to which he gives his general and special sanction; declaring that he accepts, approves, and confirms what it contains, that he will observe the same himself, and will require it to be observed by others. To these decrees (*decreta serenissimorum apostolicorum &c.*) the royal seal is then affixed, and they are presented to the States with the same pomp with which these had received the royal proposals. These acts are then made public in all the comitats, and from that time they have the force of laws.

Among all the books, however, which occupied me at the Casino, there were none in which I was so much interested as in the writings of Count Szechenyi. This unwearied noble-minded friend of his country has been the author or promoter of almost every useful and valuable undertaking that it has witnessed for years past: steam-navigation, the making of roads as far as the Turkish frontier, the establishment of the Literary Society of Pesth, of the Casino, every desirable improvement brings the name of count Szechenyi prominently forward as a chief actor; he has found time, nevertheless, for a series of writings, all tending to the same noble end. The first, and most celebrated, is called "Credit," and under this title he treats of Hungarian affairs in general, of the sacredness of public duty, of agriculture, of the cultivation of the vine, of the wine trade, of trade in general, of road-making, of steam-navigation, and of all those things which would be likely to raise the character of Hungary in the eyes of the world in general.

The second work is called "Light," or information relative to the work called "Credit," and was called forth by an analysis or criticism upon it published by count Joseph Desewfy. These, I am sorry to say, are the only writings of Count Szechenyi which I have read; but I must own I felt some astonishment, that considering the home truths which he has spoken, and the free and uncompromising terms in which those truths are expressed, the countrymen of the count should not only listen to him with patience, but should even praise and exalt the author to the skies, should hang his portrait in their apartments, and "wear him in their heart's core" as the first of patriots. Had not the proof been before me I could not have thought that any one in Hungary would have ventured to denounce in such strong terms the national defects and errors. I could have fancied I was reading an oration of Demosthenes, or listening to a patriot of the Roman republic pouring out a torrent of indignant eloquence against the follies and vices of his countrymen. Nothing, certainly, could give a higher idea of the noble disposition, and great capability of improvement of the Hungarians, than the enthusiastic approbation with which they have received these writings, as well as those of Kossut and others, in which they are thus roundly taken to task.

These gentlemen, as I have before hinted, however they may agree in ardent zeal for the progress of their country, are by no means agreed on many other points. No two of them perhaps can be said to be precisely of the same opinion. The two counts Desewfy, are, however patriotic, decidedly aristocratic in their views, and, considering the Hungarian constitution as essentially such, desire to see it developed strictly in accordance with the intentions of their forefathers. Mr. von Kossut is a patriot of a different stamp, and of far more liberal principles. He agrees in the main with Count Szechenyi, and in his widely-spread journal, accessible to all, gives utterance to nearly the same views as those expressed in the more elaborate works of the count, addressed to a more select audience. There has been indeed some dispute between them concerning the mode in which von Kossut has deemed it fitting to utter his opinions; and this dispute, which may be considered either as a literary or a political controversy, formed, at the time I was in Pesth, a general subject of conversation. Two editions of Count Szechenyi's pamphlet had been sold off, immediately, and I remained long enough for the publication of von Kossut's answer. At all the corners of the streets I saw flaming on red and yellow paper, *Felelet, Grof Szechenyi Istvannak Kossut Layosto*" (Answer to Count Stephen Szechenyi, by Ludwig Kossut); and I heard continually the questions, "Have you seen Kossut's answer? What does Kossut say?"

We in Germany have no idea of the lively interest in all political questions that prevails at Pesth. It is only at Paris or Brussels that we ever see any thing like it. The public interested in these matters is also by no means as limited as might be supposed. The subscribers to the *Hirlap* alone amount to four thousand, and the editions of the abovementioned pamphlets, which were sold off almost as soon as published, consisted each of several thousand copies. Those who from their position in society can take no active part in political affairs, still look eagerly on as anxious and interested spectators, and read with avidity all that is written on the subject.

THE HUNGARIAN LITERARY SOCIETY AND THE HUNGARIAN LANGUAGE.

In the middle ages the city of Pesth was always designated as a " *Teutonica urbs,*" and even twenty years ago, it might still be considered as an entirely German town. In hotels and coffee-houses, at halls and public entertainments, or in private houses, nothing but German was spoken, and even those Magyars who had hardly any German to speak, were obliged to make the most of it. Not only many Hungarian Germans, but many even among the magnates knew nothing of their mother tongue. In the year 1825, a bookseller of Pesth published a Hungarian Lexicon, which had very little sale. All at once the tones of this language began to be heard, and since then the tide has risen higher and higher in its favour, until it threatens to overwhelm its Latin, German, and Slavonian competitors. The dictionary, of which, in three years, only a few copies had been sold, went off all at once, and another edition was called for, and disposed of in a very short time. Not much more than fifty years ago, there was not even a professor of the Hungarian language and literature at the Pesth University, and it was not till the diet of 1790, that a request was made to the king "*ut in Gymnasiis Academiis et Universitate Hungarica peculiaris Professor Linguæ et Stili Hungarici constituatur,*" and now it is required not only that every German, Slavonian, or other professor should give his lectures in the Magyar tongue, but that even the very peasant should take pains to acquire it. The demands of the Magyars, that the Germans and Slavonians should learn their language, may be regarded as an answer, though rather a late one, to the proposal of Joseph II., that the Magyars should learn German; the emperor was of opinion that not only the Magyar language, but the Magyar customs and privileges were altogether obsolete, and ought to be thrown aside, and dreamed not that beneath these ashes a spark still glimmered, that ere long would burst into a bright flame. Immediately after the death of Joseph, the Hungarian diet addressed his successor on the propriety of abolishing the use of foreign languages in public business, and imploring " *ut autem Nativa Lingua Hungarica magis propagetur et expolietur.*" It is from this proposal, doubtless, that may be dated the commencement of that enthusiasm for Magyarism, which would have reached its present height long before, if the French Revolution, at the period of Napoleon's power, had not been interposed. The impulse given by Joseph was, however, so much the more effectual, since the campaigns of Bonaparte had awakened a powerful emotion of nationality in almost every European state. There arose at the same time a similar feeling among the Germans, and even among the Slavonians.

The native language of the Hungarians had, in the mean time, been too little cultivated or developed to make it acceptable to other nations. No work of any importance had been written in it, and it could not, like the Bohemian and other languages of the Slavonian family, point to any past period in which it had been more flourishing. Nothing, therefore, it was thought, could better advance the proposed object, than the establishment of a Hungarian literary society, which, while it should take care to foster every remarkable manifestation of native talent, should encourage the publication of grammars and dictionaries, pursue various branches of grammatical and philological inquiry, should publish a literary periodical, and offer prizes for Hungarian works, and for essays on proposed questions relating to the native language and literature.

After the failure of many attempts, the society was at length established in 1825, Count Szechenyi contributing sixty thousand florins towards its funds, and inducing by this munificent example many others to offer similar sacrifices on the altar of their country. A president was appointed, and directing, corresponding, and honorary members were chosen. The society has now been fifteen years in activity, and possesses, besides a considerable library, a capital of four hundred thousand florins. Many philological, historical, and poetical works of considerable merit, have already been ushered into the world under its auspices, and their authors liberally remunerated, and the society is, therefore, with respect to Hungary, what the French academy is for France.

In the antechamber of the hall hangs the best portrait I have seen of Count Szechenyi, painted by Amerling, of Vienna, and I wish I could produce on my paper, as well as he has done on his canvass, the fine strongly-marked features, the eyes full of fire, and the whole manly, noble, energetic expression, which render it such an interesting specimen of Hungarian national physiognomy. May this portrait long remain in the antechamber—for it is a rule of the society that the picture of no living member shall be hung in the hall.

Much attention has been paid by this society to the dramatic branch of literature, and many translations from German and French, and some original pieces, have been produced, by the aid of which it has become possible to establish a national theatre at Pesth. Hitherto there existed none but German theatres throughout the country. A sum of four hundred thousand florins was granted by the diet for the erection of this theatre, but I cannot say it appears to me likely that these efforts will, for the present, at least, be crowned with much success. However great may be the enthusiasm for the cause, the obstacles, I fear, are still greater. There is an evident deficiency both of national dramas, and of actors and actresses, and the Magyars have certainly no peculiar talent for the art. I was told they succeed best in tragedy, which I can easily conceive; but I had the ill luck to see one of their comedies—a translation of Scribe's piece, "L'Art de Conspirer." It lasted, I do not know by what contrivance, from seven till eleven o'clock, though in Paris it never takes more than two hours and a half. Of the twenty-four boxes only eight were occupied, and the remainder entirely empty, but the pit and gallery were full. The more refined part of the public, it is said, frequent the German theatre by preference, but the young men, students, and others, prefer the Hungarian.

An Art Union has also been established in Pesth, upon the plan of ours in Germany, and I paid a visit to its exhibition. The pictures were mostly from Vienna; but partly from Munich and other German places. I found, I must confess, in the specimens I saw, neither excellence nor the promise of it, although I have met in foreign countries Hungarian painters of considerable merit; but they were of German and not of Magyar descent. A young German woman from Vienna, whose husband has an appointment here, informed me of an instance of a kind of national feeling against which, I trust, his countrymen in general will be on their guard. It was of a Hungarian from the interior, who had come to the exhibition expecting to find only genuine Magyar productions, and who was quite indignant at seeing so many pictures from Vienna. He objected, too, *in German,* to seeing the catalogue printed half in Hungarian and half in German, and began to tear out all the German leaves, without perceiving that in his rage he was destroying the alternate Hungarian pages also. The lady told me this in a whisper, and was evidently afraid of being overheard, as she said the Hungarians were exceedingly touchy on points of this kind.

Notwithstanding what I have said, I by no means wish to deny that Hungarians may attain to eminence in the pictorial arts, I would only suggest that they should not be too hasty to *tear the German leaves from their catalogue,* lest many a good Hungarian one should be lost in the process.

This remark may apply also to the great exertions now making to introduce the Hungarian language. The advantage of employing a language so far more cultivated than the Hungarian, as the German is, appears on many occasions so obviously, that the most determined patriots find it hard to avoid doing so, and to feel half-ashamed of their native tongue. They are often compelled to intersperse, in their conversation, German turns and expressions for ideas, which they cannot otherwise make intelligible. The town police of Pesth is in general compelled to speak German, as it cannot otherwise be sure of being understood by the great mass of the public; and this is also the case with another branch of the administration, that of the army, (that is the ordinary standing army, and not the militia or *insurrection,* as it is called,) in which German is so thoroughly established, that it cannot be displaced. I noticed also that of all fortresses, barracks, guard-houses, barriers, and gates, the Imperial Austrian colours, black and yellow, appeared in the place of the favourite red, green, and white, of Hungary. The banishment of what has hitherto been the political and diplomatic language of Hungary, the Latin namely, will be found an easier task; I say *will* be, for the whole matter is still to be spoken of as *in futurum*. The Magyar language has not, like the German, struck deep root into the hearts of the people, but rather resembles those plants which float loosely in the air. It has been by law excluded from the legislative assemblies, from diplomacy, and in a great measure from the sciences and from the schools. Even as late as the preceding summer, the university lectures continued to be given in Latin, but the beginning of this year was to be the final term at which the Latin language was to expire. It was thought that sufficient time would then have been given for the professors to make themselves acquainted with the Magyar tongue; but I fancy this will prove, in many cases, to have been a mistake.

The Austrian government has in general not opposed these attempts at national and provincial separation in the several states united under its dominion. It thinks perhaps, "*Divide et impera*," but in order to make sure of the *impera*, it is at least necessary to retain the use of its own language in the army. If every one of the nations composing an Austrian army were to be commanded each in its own language, the whole would become entirely unmanageable. The question of the employment of the Hungarian language, even in the army, is nevertheless to be discussed in the next diet, and the present difference of opinion on this subject with the government has occasioned the handsome building, erected for a military school in Pesth, to stand hitherto empty. The Hungarians have built it at their own expense, and will not consent to give it up, except on condition that the young officers shall be instructed in their native tongue; the government, however, insists upon German being *the* language, and between the two, the building remains totally useless. I shall be curious to see what will be the eventual fate of these now empty rooms.

OFEN, OR BUDA.

The passion for cold baths which prevails more, all over the Austrian monarchy, than anywhere else in the world, and to which Graeffenberg may perhaps have contributed, finds abundant opportunities of gratification in Pesth, and certainly if there ever existed a fashionable mania, which promised wholesome consequences, it is this warm attachment to cold water. Not only in the great cities, but even in many of the most insignificant towns of the empire, there are excellent establishments of this kind to be found. Not only are there baths on the Elbe, and the Danube, and the Moldau, but on the Save, the Drave, and the Theiss; on the Maros, and on the Koros, and on the Neusiedler Lake, so that the river-god may be said to pour his health-giving floods over the backs of the whole Austrian monarchy. In all public institutions, in schools, in hospitals, in madhouses, and more especially in the army, every measure is adopted to promote the abundant use of cold and swimming baths. In Vienna they are on the most magnificent scale, and the military man and the civilian, the rich and the poor, ladies and gentlemen, young and old, healthy and sick, find their way into the Danube. The river-baths of Pesth are of course on a smaller scale, and more unpretending in their style, but there is no deficiency of any real convenience. There are baths of all kinds and suitable to all classes, and as the entrances, on the rafts on which they float, are in general richly decorated with flowers, with a bright Hungarian flag waving from the top, they may be considered ornamental as well as useful.

The Vulcanic hot baths on the Ofen side, which I have already mentioned, are frequented by Walachians, Servians, and Turks, whilst the river-baths of Pesth represent the German or West European elements of the country. The former might be called the Vulcanians and the latter the Neptunists, among whom may generally be counted, besides the Germans, the higher classes of Hungarians. This difference in the two cities may be traced through many other particulars. The people of Ofen have built their city on Vulcanic ground, on chalk hills, and by the white dust on their clothes, they may generally be recognised; the inhabitants of Pesth have erected their dwellings on a sandy deposit from the river. The existence of the latter is based on commerce, for which they are indebted to the river; that of the former on their vineyards which cover their hills, and extend for leagues beyond the town.

The people of Pesth are in all things the great rivals and antagonists of the people of Ofen; and the people of Ofen, although they cannot get so much as a good pin or a ball of packthread without running over the bridge for it to their neighbours, and depend on those neighbours for the consumption of their wines, are never tired of disputing with and depreciating them. Ofen is built on the right bank of the river in Pannonia, which has always been the part of Hungary most influenced by Germany. Pesth lies on the left bank in the steppes of Dacia, and has thrown itself with far more ardour into the recent Magyar movement than its sister city; and has also, as the Americans say, "gone ahead" far more rapidly in trade, in the acquirement of wealth, and in general material development. Pesth has risen almost with the rapidity of an American city; whilst Ofen, occupied chiefly with the sacred arts of Triptolemus and Pomona, lies like a quiet country-town by the side of its bustling neighbour, and celebrates the mysteries of Ceres and Bacchus. As on most other subjects, a difference of opinion also exists between the two towns concerning their respective origin, each regarding herself as the original, and the mother of the other. As the early history of both is very obscure, it is not easy to decide the point with certainty, but the probability is certainly in favour of the fertile hills and sheltered valleys of Ofen, over the sands of Pesth, exposed to all the winds of the desert. The *Pesthians* are the stronger party, and now that they are advancing on their rivals over their new bridge, will probably swallow them up. The *Ofeners* are much opposed to the projected amalgamation of the two cities under the name of Buda-Pesth, as they consider that they would in that case become mere subjects of the Pesth burgomasters. I directed my steps one morning (after a preparatory dip in the Danube) through the silent, dusty, sunburnt streets of Ofen to that quarter of the town which may be considered as uniting the extreme ends of her history; abounding in Roman antiquities, Roman baths, Roman tombs, Roman fortifications, and having on the little island of Old-Buda which lies opposite to it in the river, the new dockyards, whence the new steamboats are launched into the Danube. These docks were built by a Pesth shipowner, and the whole island, which is overgrown with large trees, is occupied by them. There are not less than five hundred people constantly employed in them, from countries experienced in ship and boat building;

among them I found eight or nine Englishmen, fifty or sixty Italians, from the Italian ports of Austria, which furnish bridge and ship builders for the whole Danube, and some from the Rhine and from Switzerland, who have some experience in the steamboats used on inland lakes and rivers. There were also Dutchmen among them. Eleven steamboats have been launched from this dockyard, and there are not in the whole more than twenty on the Danube and its tributaries. It is a great disadvantage to these vessels, that if any repairs for the machinery are required they are obliged to be sent to Vienna. On the whole, according to what I heard from one of the Dutchmen engaged here, it appears that the engines are made too small, and the vessels are too heavily laden. No less than two million florins' worth of materials in iron, wood, ropes, chains, &c., have been collected on this island and these when made up into steamboats will, it may fairly be anticipated, yield to Hungary an ample interest for the capital invested.

Among the vessels still on the stocks, was one iron one, the thinness of which amazed us. Götz von Berlichingen, and Kunz von Kaufungen, wore thicker plates on their breasts. Some chains made in England, and others made here, were shown to us, and it was a difference like that of day and night. I trust I shall never have to lie at anchor with any but an English chain.

The Roman remains lie mostly sideways from Old Buda, and are said to be partly sunk in a marsh, but I did not reach them, having spent too much time in the Margaret's Island, searching for the remains of an ancient bath which are only visible when the water is low. As there is no reason, from the nature of the ground, to suppose it can have sunk, this might afford a standard by which to estimate how much the level of the Danube has been raised since the time of the Romans.

This Margaret's Island is about half a mile long, and very narrow; it belongs at present to the archduke Palatine, who has changed the whole surface of it into a beautiful garden, formerly open to the public at large, but now only to a few visiters, on account of some injury done to the plantations. A convent, a church, and some houses were erected here by the princess Margaret, daughter of king Bela IV., but these were afterwards laid in ashes by the Tatars.

Extending from the town along the whole shore of the Danube, lie vegetable gardens, producing principally cucumbers, melons, and immense quantities of *apples of paradise,* as they are called. They reminded me of the Bashtans, the Tatar vegetable gardens of South Russia. Every garden is provided with its own well, and at a certain time of the day hundreds of these wells are to be seen in full activity, as the soil is exceedingly dry. In the suburbs of Pesth are also many vegetable-gardens, but these are almost entirely occupied with cabbages, for which the people of Hungary have an extraordinary partiality. There are parts of the country where the peasants are in the habit of boiling a huge pot of it at the beginning of the week, and warming it up every day. They maintain, that the oftener it is warmed up, the better it is, consequently never so delicious as on the seventh day.

We passed to the Castle Hill through Neustift, and the Water Town; the two most villanous parts of the city, inhabited by a population made up of odds and ends, from all the nations of Europe, Italians, Germans, Spaniards, Portuguese, &c., fragments of the Austrian army which besieged Ofen under Charles of Lorraine, and recovered it from the Turks.

After the conquest of the place, they received grants of land and settled here, and have long since become so completely Germanized, that they can be distinguished by little else than their names.

These family names, and the names of the different hills, are nearly all that remain to speak of the days of deadly strife by which these fertile lands have been so often laid waste. The Swabian hill where the Germans were encamped; the Eagles' hill where the dead bodies of thousands of Turks were devoured by great flights of eagles; &c. Of all the buildings that covered the Castle hill—the castle of the Hungarian kings, the Christian churches, and the Mahomedan temples—scarcely one stone is left upon another. The terrible devastations to which Hungary has been exposed,—from the Tatars on the east, in the thirteenth century, from the Turks on the south in the sixteenth and seventeenth, and their fierce wars with the Germans and other European nations for its possession,—have swept away the traces of former greatness more completely than in any other capital of Europe. Moscow, Cracow, Warsaw, notwithstanding the terrible storms they have passed through, have still more antique remains to show than the principal cities of Hungary.

There is an armory on this Castle hill said to contain arms for eighty thousand men; and among the objects of interest preserved in it is some armour said to have been worn by Attila (probably not genuine, but interesting from the long-continued belief in its authenticity), and the armour of Ziska, the renowned Hussite hero, the iron of which is so thick that it seems scarcely possible that a human being could have worn it. Several of the pieces had to be screwed together on his body. There is also a relic of the French Revolution in the shape of a red cap of liberty mounted on a long pole, and a thick silk banner, once carried by the Austrian crusaders to Palestine—which, if it really made such a journey, is in surprisingly good preservation. There are besides, banners of the French Republic, of the Respublica Cisalpina, and of the Carbonari of Naples, the latter representing a cap of liberty between two daggers, with the words, "*Egualianze o morte! Subordinazione alle legge militari;*" a curious collection of trophies! but they may serve to point out the interest which Hungary has taken in these various occurrences.

There are in Ofen great magazines of saltpetre, an article produced in the steppes of Hungary in as great abundance, and of as good quality as in the saltpetre districts of India. The Hungarians, Slavonians, and Russians call this article *Salniter,* or in Magyar *Salétrom,* both which words are probably corruptions of the Latin words *sal nitrum*. But whence comes our word saltpetre? Does it, perhaps, originate in a confounding of the two words *nitrum* and *petrum*? The quantity of this article exported to Austria is usually estimated at ten thousand hundredweight, and smaller quantities are exported to Poland and other countries, the latter chiefly for the use of the druggists, but at Presburg a great part is made up into gunpowder.

The Castle of Ofen, the residence of the archduke Palatine, stands on the site of that of the ancient kings demolished during the Turkish time. It is a spacious and handsome building, and its position is commanding, but there is nothing very remarkable in the interior. The principal apartments are adorned with pictures, battle-pieces from the events of the thirty years' war, Maria Theresa in her coronation robes, &c. By a courtesy, which in Hungary is seldom denied to strangers, we easily obtained permission to visit the whole castle, including the apartments of the archduchess. On the table in her dressing-room, lay a portrait of Zinkendorf, a bible, and a petition to be presented to her on her return. In her usual sitting-room stood a spinning-wheel—and a little harlequin, and some playthings for her children were lying about. On the walls of this room hung the portraits of the archduke Stephen, and his twin-sister. He is an active, intelligent, amiable young man, and is a great favourite in Hungary, where he is regarded as the future palatine. Since the last inundation especially, in which he made great and benevolent exertions, he has been exceedingly popular, and his portraits have been much multiplied throughout the empire. The early death of the beautiful and amiable princess Helmine, his sister, has been a subject of general and sincere lamentation.

The prospect from the windows of the castle, the majestic breadth of the Danube—the magnificent quay running along the opposite shore—the city of Pesth with its far-stretching suburbs encircled by the distant forest, is truly magnificent.

In one wing of the castle resides no less a *personage* than the " *Corona cum Clenodiis suis.*" Whenever one hears a Hungarian speaking of this bauble, one can hardly help fancying it must be some beloved princess and her children. It has an apartment of its own which no one is allowed to enter, with an antechamber where two soldiers keep watch day and night. It has a guard of its own of sixty-four men, who have no other duty than the very entertaining one of relieving guard in this chamber. Their barrack or guard-house is situated opposite to that wing of the castle in which the crown *resides*. The windows of its room are walled up, leaving only two air-holes, and the door is of iron with three mighty locks, the keys of which are kept by three great officers of the empire. It lies in an iron chest with a costly lining, locked and sealed with the five seals of the king, the primate, the palatine, and the two other keepers of the crown.

At coronations it is taken out in the presence of all these officers, escorted by its own guard to Presburg, and received by the authorities at the boundary of each comitat. After the ceremony it is returned with the same pomp to the stately seclusion of its own apartment, before which two grenadiers again keep watch and ward.

In spite of all the care with which it is kept, there is, perhaps, no crown in Europe that has seen so many vicissitudes. It was once in pawn with the Emperor of Germany, once for a long time at the castle of a nobleman in Transylvania, once it fell into the hands of robbers, and Joseph II., to the great dissatisfaction of his Hungarian subjects, carried it to Vienna. Its return, under Leopold II., was like a triumphant procession. What appeared to me most curious about this crown was, that it comes half from the East—from Constantinople, and half from the West (the Germanic Roman empire), from Rome.

The golden ring or forehead band was presented to the Hungarian king Geysa in 1076, by the emperor Ducas; the two pieces arched over the top are fragments from the crown sent by pope Silvester, in the year 1000, to St. Stephen. Art and workmanship, language and characters, are also strikingly contrasted on the two sides, the one being Byzantine the other Roman, and thus the whole seems symbolically to represent no less the geographical position of Hungary between the east and the west, between the Italian and Greek peninsulas, than its religious and political relations connecting Byzantium and Rome.

PUBLIC COLLECTIONS.

The collections that have as yet been made at Pesth are not of much importance. This is owing partly to the Turkish spirit of destruction from the east, and the spirit of conservation of the Vienna people from the west. (It is strange that at every fresh topic that arises in Hungary, we can seldom shape our reflection properly, till we have cast one glance toward the rising, and another toward the setting sun.) The Turks have the destruction of innumerable convent libraries to answer for, as well as that of the celebrated library of Corvinus, which had been formed at Buda, and of which a part was burnt, and the remainder dispersed over all Europe. The zeal of the collectors of Vienna has, on the other hand, deprived Hungary of much of late years, for as soon as any thing interesting has been discovered anywhere in the country, Vienna has generally laid claim to it, better prices for things of real value being obtained there. Nevertheless, there is no lack at Pesth of curiosities of one sort or another that will well repay a stranger for the trouble he takes in visiting them.

My first visit of this kind was to the Hungarian National Museum, which was founded chiefly at the suggestion of Count Szechenyi, who advanced a considerable sum to start the undertaking. I was not able to see all the fine things preserved there, for in consequence of a new temple for the Muses being in the course of construction, the whole collection had been removed to another house, and many articles had been packed away. The collection, considered as a *national* museum, is still very incomplete, though it contains excellent specimens of the mineralogy of the kingdom.

Among the zoological specimens I saw the genuine Hungarian sheep, the race that the ancient Magyars brought with them over the Carpathians, and which is now becoming every day more scarce. It has large horns, more than two feet in length, standing wide apart. The people of the country know the animal under the name of the *Magyar koss*, or Magyar sheep.

All the Hungarian fishes of the Danube, the Theiss, and the Balaton, of which so many, well seasoned with *paprika*, had, at various times, figured before me on the table, were to be seen at this museum, either preserved in spirit, or carefully stuffed and nailed up against the wall.

The various descriptions of herons also were not wanting, the birds whose feathers are particularly sought for, as decorations for the *kalpaks* of the sons of the Hungarian magnates. The purple heron has only two or three black feathers on his head, and these, the most expensive of their kind, are destined only for the bonnets of the highest and most wealthy.

Among the specimens of the fine arts, I stopped to admire, with some interest, a piece of embroidery, representing the portrait of the King of Hungary. The artist, it seems, was possessed of a piece of white silk as a groundwork, but being too poor to purchase coloured silk, resolved to complete her work with her own auburn hair.

In one room there had been collected a multitude of things which could hardly fail to be of great historical value to the Hungarians; such as a silver shirt of mail that had once belonged to Stephen Bathory, and various other pieces of armour ennobled by those who in their respective days had worn them. Among the arms, the most remarkable are the sword, the bow, and the arrows of Attila, whom the Hungarians delight to designate as the Hungarian Napoleon. A banner is likewise shown of the celebrated insurgent Rakozy, with the motto, *Deus non derelinquet justam causam.*

In a few years, when the building I have spoken of is finished, this interesting collection will make a very different appearance from what it does now. It will, at the same time, be much enlarged; for several private collections have been purchased, with a view to their being added, and the Museum of Pesth will then be entitled to take a becoming place among the museums of Europe, and will present to the learned world many a treasure, the existence of which perhaps is at present scarcely known. The new building, which is rapidly advancing towards completion, will be a splendid pile of architecture, and no expense seems to be spared upon it. The only objection I have to it is, that it is placed too far away from the central part of the town, and in a quarter occupied chiefly by small and mean-looking houses. The presence of the museum, however, may have the effect of gradually improving the quarter.

The first hall, on entering, is to be a sort of Pantheon, in which the statues of Hungarian heroes and distinguished men are to be erected. Had the architect consulted me, an unprejudiced layman, respecting the proportions of this hall, I should have told him I considered it a great deal too lofty, in proportion to its length and breadth. The hall is only forty feet in diameter, and seemed to me to be ten or twelve fathoms high. It has, in consequence, the air of a tower rather than a hall, and two rows of long thin columns, one row over the other, have to support the whole. On leaving the Pantheon, you enter, right and left, upon long suites of rooms, running round a quadrangle; and as there are two floors, besides a basement story, there will be abundance of space to afford the Hungarians room, for many years to come, for the exercise of their antiquarian zeal.

Of the libraries of Pesth, that of the University is the most considerable. It contains 90,000 volumes, and, like most of the praiseworthy institutions of Austria, owes its existence to Joseph II. In the anteroom of the library is a relic of another great Hungarian collector of books, king Matthias Corvinus, namely his coat of arms, wrought in the red marble of Neszmely, which is still in such general use at Pesth for architectonic decorations. This coat of arms, I was told, was the only particle of the royal palace of Buda that was not destroyed during the period of the Turkish occupation. The crest of Corvinus was a raven with a ring in his beak. It seems that in his youth, a golden ring was stolen from him by a raven, which was said by his soothsayers to denote much and great good fortune. When, at a subsequent period, he had reason to believe the prophecy had been borne out, he took the raven and the ring under his especial patronage.

There was much analogy between the characters of Joseph and Matthias; and it might well reward the trouble, were some one to institute a comparison between them. Joseph, according to a well-known anecdote, once drew several furrows with a plough, in Moravia, that he might be able to judge from his own experience what the nature of the labour was. An anecdote of a similar character is told of Corvinus. When he was once holding his court in the Gömör comitat, he proposed, one day, after dinner, to his noble guests, to go and labour in a vineyard. The king himself, a vigorous and lively young man, went about his work with right good will; but his noble assistants were soon tired, and began to complain of the exertions required of them. Thereupon the king dismissed them, but urged them, at the same time, never to forget what labour it cost the peasant to produce what they often expended with so much levity. Joseph and Matthias both died in the prime of life, and the death of each was a signal for rejoicing to the prelates and the oligarchs; of sorrow and lamentation to the citizens and peasantry. At Joseph's death, the peasants cried out one and all, "we have lost a father;" and when Corvinus was taken from them, their saying was, "with him justice is now dead in Hungary."

In the large hall of the library, I found two old globes, executed at Venice at the time of the Doge Morosini, and two new ones of modern Hungarian manufacture. From these I was able to judge of the progress the Magyar language has made, the equator, the ecliptic, and most of the constellations having already received their several Hungarian appellations. Among the books I took up, was a speech by Count Bathyany, delivered on the inauguration of a monument of Joseph II. I expected to find an *éloge* of the deceased emperor, but found to my surprise one of the then living sovereign Francis.

With picture-galleries Pesth is very poorly supplied, those of the Hungarian magnates who interest themselves for the fine arts, having their collections generally at Vienna. The only fine pictures I saw at Pesth were those of a merchant, of the name of Isser, who is an enthusiast for the arts, and a member of no less than six foreign academies.

THE JEWS OF PESTH.

The whole kingdom of Hungary contained in the year

1785	75,000 Jews	} according to Schwartner.
1805	130,000 „	
1834	246,000 „	} „ Steller.
1837	254,000 „	

Accordingly in the year 1842, if we take an average annual increase of 3000 souls, their number must have reached 270,000. In fifty years, therefore, the Jews have more than trebled in Hungary, whilst the whole population of the country was in

1785	7,000,000
1839	11,973,000
1842	12,000,000

The whole population, therefore, has not nearly doubled, while the number of the Jews has trebled. This is a remarkable fact. Next to Galicia, Hungary is that part of the Austrian empire which contains the most Jews. Galicia indeed contains as many Jews as Hungary, while its entire population is only one-third as great.

Although there are parts of Hungary where they are by law forbidden to settle, such as Croatia, Slavonia, and the military frontier, yet the Jews have always played an important part in this country, and there were times when all the money and trade of the country was in their hands. In later times, Joseph II. in vain laboured for their social improvement, and the Diet is now occupied, in imitation of the other governments of Europe, in extending their rights, improving their character, and ameliorating their condition, by gradually blending them with the rest of the population.

Much is done by the Jews themselves towards the furtherance of this object, and the reform of the Jewish churches and schools at Berlin, Vienna, Prague, and other places, has given an impulse to similar reforms in Hungary. The Jewish congregation of Pesth, amounting at present to 1400 families, are following the example set them by that of Vienna. The Jews here are divided into two parties, like those at Prague and Vienna; those who support the new and those who support the old system of things. My learned Rabbinical friend, M. Schwab, plays the part of a mediator between the two parties, seeking to conciliate them by every means in his power.

The Jews here are similar to those of Bohemia and Poland, from which countries they have received the most frequent reinforcements. The Spanish and Oriental Jews, of whom there is a small colony both here and at Vienna, are said to be decreasing in numbers. These Spanish Jews came originally up the Danube from Constantinople. The immigration from an opposite direction, from Poland and Bohemia, continues even to the present day; and should the liberal intentions of the last diet, which would enable them even to possess landed property, be carried into effect, this immigration will continue to increase, and the Jews will keep flocking towards Hungary as towards another land of promise.

Four times every year a large number of Jews assemble in Pesth from Moravia, Silesia, Cracow, and Lemberg, many of whom form lasting connexions in this city, and remain here. The most industrious and enlightened are those who come from Moravia and Bohemia; indeed, the influence of Bohemia on Hungary is always beneficial and improving. I have spoken above of the influence of the Bohemian manufacturers who come to Hungary. Of the six teachers at the new Jewish school of Pesth, four are Bohemians, and only two Hungarians. The influx of well-informed and intelligent Bohemian Jews will probably be somewhat lessened by the circumstance, that for the future all teachers in these schools are to speak and teach the Hungarian language. The native Jews of Pesth have taken up the cause of Magyarism with great zeal, and there are many, among whom are several Jewish ladies, who speak nothing but Hungarian, take in only Hungarian journals, and affect to despise every thing German.

I visited the best Jewish boys'-school in Pesth during the writing, drawing, and history lessons. It contained three hundred scholars, among whom I saw little beggar-boys in ragged jackets, seated side by side with the children of the richest merchants in the city. The children who are taken in their eighth, ninth, and tenth years, speak only German, and seldom understand the Hungarian tongue; they learn it grammatically in the lower, and speak and write it in the upper classes. It is said to be very difficult to find competent teachers; for the Jews have never been accustomed to write the Hungarian language. The Jews of Hungary and Poland have a German and a Hebrew literature, but no other.

The method of teaching history used among the Jews of Pesth appeared to me very good. The teacher first dictated to the children a short skeleton of the subject in hand, containing the principal facts, with names and dates, which they wrote down and learnt by rote at home, after which he proceeded to relate the whole in detail. This is really the only proper method of teaching history in schools, and it is a great pity it is not more generally adopted.

I noticed that some of the scholars had written down a few Hungarian words on their slates. It contained a petition for some fellow pupil, but it was some time before the master could decipher and understand it.

The Rabbis of Pesth lead a very retired life, almost always at home, never going to any theatre, and very seldom to any other place of public amusement. My acquaintance, M. Schwab, told me that many learned Jewish books are now printed at Zolkier in Galicia; but the Talmud must always be printed either at Vienna or Prague. Sulzbach and Durrenfort are also places where many Jewish books were formerly published. The rule about the Talmud, probably owes its origin not to any distinct law, but to certain difficulties in the orthodox manner of printing it, which can only be overcome at the great printing establishments of Prague and Vienna. I saw, for instance, in my friend's library, a large Talmud in twelve volumes, printed at Vienna; it was a Babylonian Talmud, for that of Jerusalem is held in less esteem here, as throughout the Jewish world. The *Mishma* and *Gemara* were printed in large letters in the middle, and round it ran, in small letters, a broad border of notes, remarks, and explanations, by the celebrated French Rabbi Solomon Jarschi, whose opinions and observations are held in great veneration by his nation. Round this again, in still smaller letters, flows another border of learned annotations, by different other celebrated Rabbi's. Is not this symbolical in some measure of the whole Jewish system of religion—a little text of truth and wisdom lost amid a flood of learned wordy jargon?

THE HOSPITAL OF ST. ROCHE.

It is a somewhat melancholy fact, that the Hungarians, zealous as they are for the attainment and preservation of political freedom, have forgotten to take precautions for the bodily health and comfort of their poorer countrymen, and, whilst admiring the promptitude with which they furnished funds for the building of the national theatre, the Hungarian museum, and the magnificent bridge over the Danube at Pesth, we in vain inquire after the provision made for the comfort of their poor and their sick.

In all Hungary, there is not one hospital, poorhouse, almshouse, or lunatic asylum, supported or instituted by government. The care of the poor and the sick devolves entirely (with the exception of a few hospitals built by benevolent private individuals, or by the magistrates of towns) upon the monks and nuns; the state does nothing for them. This is not so much the fault of Austria, as of the Hungarian aristocracy. It is almost incredible, and yet it is a well-known fact, that in the year 1793, attention was first called to this state of things by Dr. Haffner, in a "proposal to the public of Pesth for the erection of an hospital." By the influence of this benevolent physician, the hospital of St. Roche was at last founded. It is now under the superintendence of the universally respected and esteemed Her von Windisch, the successor of Dr. Haffner. The present superintendent has very much enlarged the building. It is now capable of containing three hundred patients, and is the largest in Hungary. In

St. Petersburg, Vienna, and Paris, there are hospitals capable of containing as many thousands.

It is not my purpose here to give a full account of this hospital, which I am indeed not capable of doing, but merely to collect a few facts of general interest respecting it. It contains some rooms for lunatics, a very necessary provision, for in all Hungary there is no lunatic asylum, and lunatics are generally confined in the common criminal jails. This is intended perhaps to compensate for the practice pursued in Germany and some other countries, where criminals are often mercifully considered as insane, and sent to lunatic asylums. The Hungarians are said to be furious and mischievous when mad; a fact which their choleric and melancholy temperament renders very probable.

Sick criminals are also often sent to the hospital of St. Roche. This is not right, for all the common vulgar prejudices against hospitals are liable to be confirmed in the minds of the people, when they see them used, though only partially, as places of confinement for criminals. All prisons and houses of correction ought to have their own infirmaries. The present system is, besides, a great encroachment upon the benevolence of the founders and supporters of the institution, and a serious hardship to the excellent medical officers attached to it.

The *Hirlap*, a journal of which I have already several times made mention, records the astounding fact that no fewer than 250 corpses are annually found in the streets, of whom no one knows where they come from, or how they died! I was told at the hospital that this number was grossly exaggerated, and that an accurate computation would reduce the average number to little more than twenty-five. Even this number, however, appeared to me astonishingly large.

The country about the lower Danube, the Banat, the Batshka, &c., is known to be constantly liable to intermittent fevers. Temesvar is considered the centre of the fever district, but in proportion as we ascend the river we come to regions less and less subject to fever. The summer of 1841 had been one of the most healthy ever known at Pesth. The weather had been very hot, but free from any sudden variation. This must have been beneficial to general health, for the hospital throughout the summer contained less patients by one-third than the usual average. So small a number had never been known to be in the hospital since its foundation. On the 18th of July, the day on which I heard this, the thermometer stood at 42° of Reaumur in the shade.

During the terrible inundation of March, 1838, the Hospital of St. Roche, which was the largest and strongest building for some distance round, contained no fewer than 4000 inhabitants. All those who fled to the hospital as to an ark in the waters, were supported there for three days from the funds of the hospital. Their rations were dealt out to them in small and prudent portions, under the superintendence of an excellent, benevolent, and energetic lady, with whom I had the honour to become personally acquainted during my stay in Pesth. The flood rose rapidly, but the directors had had the timely caution to remove all the patients from the ground-floor. The situation of the hospital, with the mourning and despairing thousands of hungering, ailing, and dying human creatures whom it contained, must have been at the time indescribably dreadful. After the inundation was over, no less than 450 drowned bodies, mostly those of children, washed up by the waters of the river, or found in the streets, were laid out in the courtyard of this hospital alone, that they might be owned by their friends. I have often spoken with the inhabitants of Pesth of this calamity, and found they all remembered it only with shuddering and horror. They told me that no imagination could conjure up a picture at all equal to the terrible truth. I remember hearing an old apothecary of Buda exclaim, "No poet or novelist, or dramatist could possibly imagine or describe the actual horrors of that dreadful time. If a spectator had noted down the facts as they occurred, those who had not witnessed the inundation would never have believed him."

The water began to rise on the 12th of March, but it might have passed off as harmlessly as usual, had it not been that a little way below Pesth, the ice instead of melting began to accumulate, so as to check the progress of the rising water. The river now began to rise alarmingly, and the people prepared themselves for an inundation such as the city had often witnessed before, but they little thought they were about to witness one, such as Pesth is never supposed to have seen since it has been a city. A number of workmen were set to work to construct dams, just below the town, for, contrary to the course of nature, the water rose from below.

Thousands of citizens, urged partly by curiosity, and partly by anxiety, went out to see the building of the dams. It was a long earthen wall, to which numbers of workmen were busily adding, and against which the wild and rapidly rising waters beat incessantly. Already things began to look very alarming. The water rose and rose, the military were ordered out to assist in raising the dams. In vain! The angry flood despised the weak obstacles which human hands raised to oppose it. Whilst the workmen were busy piling up the dams, they suddenly remarked to their amazement and terror, that the Danube was already roaring behind them. The dams were undermined—they broke, and only a speedy retreat could save the terrified multitude. All fled to their houses, followed by the destroying waters, which rapidly gained upon them. The streets were completely emptied. The lower parts of the town were immediately taken possession of by the river. Every one began to fortify his own house, and to surround it with dams of earth, boards, and stones. The inhabitants of the Vaizner Strasse erected dams of particular strength. No inundation had ever been known to reach this street, and the inhabitants felt perfectly secure in this circumstance, and in the strength of their dams.

Their dams, it is true, held together and were not broken by the water; but as in great political convulsions, the stormy elements often scorn to attack the bulwark raised against them, when by passing round it they can accomplish their aim equally well, and baffle the shortsighted wisdom of politicians, so the Danube now began to show its strength, in a totally unexpected manner, namely within the houses themselves. All of a sudden the boards of the ground-floors began to shake, and little bubbles to appear all over them. A rushing, splashing sound was heard beneath, and all the little cracks and rat-holes became so many fountains of water. Very soon the Danube was dashing through all the beautiful shops, ground-floors, cellars, and warehouses, of the great Vaizner Strasse.

The inhabitants did not lose their presence of mind. They dashed into the water, and brought up their chief valuables into the upper stories. It was unheard of for the water to come so high; it could not possibly rise higher, and must soon sink. But the Danube now stood six feet high in the houses. To make assurance doubly sure, the inhabitants removed to their second floors; for the Danube had now risen ten feet within the houses. Many people had been standing up to their necks in water, in order to get at their deluged property; but the water was freezingly cold, like newly-melted ice, and they could bear it no longer. Poor and rich alike gave up the attempt to save their property, and thought only of life.

The ground upon which Pesth stands, is of soft alluvial formation, consisting only of mould and clay. The Danube was now only claiming its old rights; and it began to form subterranean aqueducts and canals. In one house which had deep foundations, the boards suddenly rose, and the flood threw up a large thick jar, the property of one of the neighbours. It had been torn along through one of the subterranean canals, and thus curiously restored to light. The apothecary of Buda told me, that, to his great surprise, a large piece of furniture, which had been left in the ground-floor when the inundation began, was afterwards found standing upright in his first floor, whither the torrent, dashing upwards, had carried it.

The thickness and solidity of the houses was no protection. Many of those most strongly built, were entirely broken up by the force of the river, and fell in. On the second day the flood was at its height. People began to doubt whether any of the houses would remain standing. The strongest buildings, such as the churches and hospitals, and the highest spots, such as the Neumarkt of Pesth, and the Schlossberg of Buda, were filled with fugitives. Great numbers of people put up tents in the Neumarkt, and fled there in spite of the intense cold of the weather; among these were many nobles and magnates. Whoever had not much to lose at Pesth, fled to Buda. The citizens of Buda sent over small boats, commanded by the Archduke Stephen, the Count Szechenyi, and other noblemen, who rowed about through the streets, and picked up every one, who was willing to leave his house.

The inundation had now lasted two days, and showed no signs of subsiding. Many began to imagine that the end of Pesth was come—that the Danube was forming itself a new bed, and intended to swallow up the city in its waves. It was generally believed that the whole surrounding district was changed into a great lake, which would never dry up again.

At length on the third day the waters began to retire. The icy barrier formed at the island of Czepel had probably melted, the river gradually flowed off in a southerly direction, and left Pesth to recover from its cold bath as best it might. Many streets were so choked with roofs, walls, rubbish, boards, and the bodies of men and animals, that it was not till after several days of hard work, that they were rendered passable. Nearly three thousand houses were destroyed; some had fallen in, and others had entirely melted away into the river. The silent gradual influence of water had in three days wrought more mischief than a hundred days of bombardment would have done. The appearance of the city after the inundation, was desolate, ruinous, and miserable in the extreme.

I do not know what appearance the other shops may have presented, but those of the booksellers, I was told, were filled with an extraordinary stock of *papier maché*, such as I never heard of before or since. Goethe,

Schiller, Shakspeare, Voltaire, Jean Paul,—French, English, German, and Hungarian books,—all were softened and melted together into one strange undistinguishable mass.

The cry for help of the poor ruined citizens of Pesth, resounded through all Germany, and generous assistance streamed in from every side. Half Europe assisted the rebuilding of Pesth, and though building materials were of course very dear, yet the city rose again from its ruins, its wounds gradually healed, and it became far more beautiful and extensive than before.

THE DANUBE IN THE CENTRAL PLAINS OF HUNGARY.

On the last day of August, we entered the steamboat which was to convey us down the Danube into Turkey, and the anchor was weighed at five o'clock the next morning. It was still night, and the moon seemed unwilling to yield dominion to the coming day. Seated upon a bench upon the deck, I viewed the river as it lay before me. The Danube is only 250 fathoms broad between Pesth and Ofen, but immediately below, it widens to three times that breadth, and enters the second Hungarian plain which stretches from the mountains of Central Hungary to those of Servia and and Slavonia. Between the Blocksberg of Buda and the hills behind Pesth, the two cities seem to lie within a huge gate, and the view is beautiful. The Schlossberg with its stately buildings is seen in the distance through this gate, and is the central point in the prospect. As the sun rose, every thing became more distinct, and at length it stood completely above the horizon, gilding the distant summits of the hills, and illuminating the whole landscape, as if to display it once more in all its beauty, to the gaze of the departing traveller.

These are the last hills seen, and we now entered the broad plains of the open country, and passed the large island of Czepel, with its fertile fields and meadows, interspersed with waving forests and smiling villages. Leaving this island behind us, we entered the most uninteresting district of all those watered by the Danube. No great towns enliven its banks—no picturesque hills or mountains vary its scenery; wide undiversified levels stretch away on every side, covered with marshy grass and shrubs, interrupted only here and there by barren deserts, with low monotonous banks. The right side of the river is higher than the left, and the villages which lie along the Danube, are all on the right side. The other side is almost entirely barren or marshy.

We did not, however, find our voyage at all tedious. We had more than 400 passengers on board, and such numbers of equipages and bales of goods, were piled up on deck, that we were rather crowded for room. Our fellow-passengers consisted chiefly of market people, merchants, tradesmen, Hungarian nobles, Servians, and Illyrians, who were returning home from the great fair of Pesth. We dropped them at different stations on the banks, from which they proceeded inland to their respective homes. Besides these, we had on board Walachian boyars, who were returning from a tour, Spanish Jews bound for Thessolonica, French and Germans bent upon seeking their fortunes in the provinces of Turkey, in a word, specimens of the population of most of the countries bordering on the Danube. In default of interest in the passing country, I turned my attention to the little community around me.

The quarterdeck on which we were seated, near the entrance of the first cabin, was the little capital, the court, and the citadel of our floating colony. Near us sat some Hungarian magnates, and among them the celebrated orator, B——, who so distinguished himself at the last [diet. He was a little man of a rather insignificant appearance. He spoke little, but was sometimes occupied in reading a newspaper and sometimes sunk in deep thought. He was very simply dressed and rather thin, and sat as little as he spoke. He was leaving Pesth to spend the summer in the enjoyment of rural tranquillity on his estates. "Have you seen B——? Do you know that B— is on board?" were questions continually put to me, which proved the popularity he enjoyed in Hungary.

The Walachian boyars, whose round faces and raven black hair showed them to be such, spoke only just German enough to get on with in an hotel or coffee-house, and by way of complement to these strangers a little circle was formed on the quarterdeck, in which French was spoken. To this circle a young Frenchman attached himself. He was travelling to Jassy for a Parisian house of business on whose account he was to form some commercial establishment in the Moldavian capital.

There were plenty of good citizens and citizenesses of Pesth, going to visit their friends and relations in the country. One group particularly attracted my attention, it was composed of a German lady of rank, with her charming children playing about her, and discovering every moment a thousand new sources of delight and amusement within the narrow limits of the quarterdeck.

The space between the quarterdeck and the chimney was crowded with wealthy merchants, Germans, Servians, and Turkish Jews. Among them was a pretty young Servian lady, who might have served a painter for a model of a Persian princess. She wore a Turkish *négligé;* her close silk underclothes, and upper pelisse edged with fur, became her extremely. Her black hair was laid round her head in two large plaits, like a turban, and was ornamented with gold coins fastened to large pins. She wore a red cap or *fez*, embroidered with gold, from which a bushy tassel of gold threads hung down upon her neck, around which she wore a long gold chain. A girdle embroidered with silver confined her slender waist,— so slender indeed, that I thought she could scarcely have more of a backbone than might have fallen to the share of a snake. I expressed some surprise at the splendour of her undress to a Servian gentleman standing near her. "Oh you should see her dressed for a gala, covered with gold and jewels!" replied he. "That would surprise you much more." She was past the bloom of youth for she was 22, and at that age Servian ladies are no longer young. She had, however, been married 14 years. "In Servia," continued my informant, "girls are often married while yet mere infants."

Among the passengers were also two Franciscan friars from Turkey, or rather from Bosnia. They wore broad-brimmed hats and mustaches, and spoke not a word of German, but were able to make themselves understood in Latin. They had finished their studies at Erlau in Hungary, and were returning thence to Czek in Bosnia. They told me that there were indeed schools in Bosnia, but that they could only learn there "*grammaticam, rhetoricem, poesiam; sed philosophiam et theologiam absolvere in nostris scholis impossibile est, et earum gratia in Hungariam venimus.*" I heard from these men that there are three convents of

Franciscan monks in Bosnia, and under them a little flock of about 1000 Catholics. In Turkish Croatia the number of Christians is said to be greater. The principal part of the population of Bosnia belonged formerly, and still belongs to the Greek church, but most of the higher classes are now Mahomedans. Bosnia was once a Hungarian dependency, the Hungarians are as eager to reclaim this old possession as the French are to be masters of the left bank of the Rhine. The Franciscans told me that their convents received an annual present of 300 thaleros from the Pope, and 400 thaleros "*a rege,*" that is from the Emperor of Austria, which presents went far to alleviate the extreme poverty in which they lived. It is singular that of all the numerous Catholic orders which formerly flourished in Bosnia, the poor, ignorant, and mendicant Franciscans have been the only monks who have kept their position, and been permitted by the Turks to remain. This is owing to the nature and character of the order; for its poverty did not excite the avarice of the Turks, as was the case with the many wealthier orders, and the striking resemblance of the Franciscan monks to the Mahomedan dervishes, may have contributed to give them a sort of sanctity in Turkish eyes. Be the reasons what they may, it is the Franciscan monks who alone nourish the feeble flame of Catholic Christianity throughout the Turkish provinces, and in Jerusalem the Franciscans are the only guardians of the Holy Sepulchre.

The Walachians were speaking French, the fair Servian and her coterie Servian, the oriental Jews Spanish, the Bosnian Franciscans Latin, the captain Italian, and different other passengers were conversing in the Greek, Hungarian, Walachian, and Illyrian tongues; but amidst this Babylonian confusion, German appeared to be the common neutral ground on which all met, and the tie which bound all together. German was spoken by ourselves, by the whole party on the quarterdeck, and by the crew itself. The Italian captain mixed up German naval terms continually with his Italian conversation; the Servians spoke very good German occasionally with other passengers; and even the Walachian boyars had a small smattering of the common language.

The steam navigation of the Danube has, I am aware, been looked upon with anxiety by the Germans, and with delight by Hungarian patriots, as likely to excite yet more the feelings of nationality and patriotism among the Magyars, but it appears to me far more likely to Germanize than to Magyarize the interior of Hungary. It will undoubtedly carry the seeds of commercial and literary enterprise into the remoter parts of the country, but it will likewise pour into Hungary a strong infusion of German manners and make the German language even more general than it is. The strongholds of Magyarism are in the barren plains and steppes of Central Hungary; and the more those plains and steppes are turned into fertile cornfields and pastures, and their straggling villages into prosperous towns,—the more the net of steamboats and railroads is spread over Hungary, the more it will assimilate with Germany, to which it owes these benefits.

Towards evening we landed at our fourth station at Baya, which lies on the left side of the river, at the distance of half a German mile from the marshes of the Danube. The buildings of the village peeped brightly through the bushes in their new white coverings; for Baya had the misfortune to be burnt down last year, and has been entirely rebuilt.

The destruction of Baya by fire, was contemporaneous with that of many other Hungarian towns. Indeed, at dry seasons of the year, a regular fire epidemic sometimes destroys half the towns in Hungary.

From Baya we proceeded to Mahacs (pronounced Mohatsh). The picture before our eyes remained always the same. Green plains with lime-trees and poplars to the left, high barren shores to the right, and before us the broad and beautiful Danube. As we sat upon the quarter-deck, an old soldier came limping on crutches towards us, and having made an appeal to our charity, he related the story of his misfortunes, which may serve as an illustration of the sufferings and dangers to which the soldiers who guard the military frontier are exposed. On the 31st of January, 1838, he had been sent to carry a message from one of the posts on this frontier to another. Night overtook him before his return, accompanied by a violent snow-storm. While he was struggling against the storm, he began to hear the howling of wolves around him. He at first went on as fast as he could without minding them, but they came nearer and nearer, and at last he was obliged to climb into a tree. He was indeed safe for the time, but he was a close prisoner, for the wild beasts came round the tree in great numbers. They kept walking round with wild and incessant howling, looking up at the tree, and sometimes crouching as if to make a spring upon him. He fired, but without effect. As he was afraid of their climbing up, he endeavoured to make a fire to frighten them away. He scraped together a few dry sticks and some moss upon the boughs, and with his flint and tinder he managed to kindle a small flame which warmed him a little; but the wild beasts did not leave him. The cold grew more and more intense, and he felt a numbness stealing over him. He therefore bound himself round the waist firmly to a strong branch, and clung round it with all his strength, in order not to fall into the jaws of the ferocious creatures. In this position he was found the next morning quite insensible, and to all appearance dead, by some comrades who came to look for him. He recovered, but remained a cripple for life, for both his legs were frozen and had to be amputated. He was now returning from Vienna, whither he had gone to petition the emperor for a small pittance which he had received. We collected for him a small pecuniary addition, and gave him two "pistoles" of "Turk's blood" to drink. It may be necessary, by way of explanation, to add, that in Hungary a small measure in common use is called a pistole, and a certain kind of red wine is designated by the tempting name of Turk's blood.

We had a painter on board who had often complained to me that he could find no picturesque subject for his canvass in any thing about the steamboat. I advised him to paint the soldier in the tree at the moment when he was cowering over his feeble little blaze, while through the darkness gleamed the fiery eyes of the hungry wolves, whose dark outlines as well as those of the forest trees covered with snow, would be partially seen by the light of the scanty fire. This appeared to me a very good subject for a night piece. He was, however, of opinion that a common story from an obscure and vulgar soldier could hardly be a fit subject for his pencil. I answered, that with such notions he would never become great; for the most beautiful subjects and situations were often associated with the most common events of life. Diamonds are not found ready cut and polished in the mines.

We reached Mohacs by nightfall. It was here that poor King Louis of

Hungary was betrayed by Zapolya, and defeated by the Turks, and died alone in a desolate marsh, to which he had fled for safety. The battle of Mohacs (which took place in the year 1526, on the 29th of August) decided the melancholy fate of Hungary, for its conquest by the Turks was the consequence of that battle. The young King Louis, after holding a diet whose sittings much resembled the uproarious merriment of a Bacchanalian festival, had marched at the head of 20,000 men against Sultan Soliman, whose army amounted to 200,000 soldiers. Louis's generals themselves saw the folly of their undertaking, and said in jest that whoever survived the battle should go to Rome and get all the rest canonized, for every one of them would certainly fall a martyr to the Christian religion. But, as if urged forward by an irresistible fate, they went cheerfully to meet their destruction; indeed, a Hungarian author exclaims, that surely no kingdom ever faced its downfall with such careless levity and merriment as Hungary. In this battle fell no less than six bishops and archbishops. It is a curious instance of retribution, that 200 years afterwards the Turks were defeated on this very field by the Prince of Savoy.

The former battle is celebrated here every 29th of August. The population of Mohacs and its neighbourhood assemble on the battle-field and make speeches in the Hungarian, Illyrian, and German languages to one another. Upon the spot where King Louis died, it is proposed to erect a small chapel. The palace of the Bishop of Mohacs contains many plans and pictures of the battle, and five cannons left behind by the Turks are preserved as relics in the town. As our steamboat stopped to take in coals at Mohacs, we had ample time to empty a glass of wine in honour of these interesting remnants of antiquity; yet of all moments the present is in fact the most interesting and romantic; for it is the flower and crown of all preceding moments, the youngest born of time, round whom is collected all the glory of the past, and before whom the future lies a dark unexplored abyss.

To the old Romans whose dull task it was to make a beginning to its history, how uninteresting must have appeared this Danube, which was to us invested with all the charms of a long eventful history! And how full of an interest surpassing all that we can now feel must that history be to a traveller 2000 years hence, to whom it comes laden with the rich fruits of the next twenty centuries! I always lament that I was born so early; of all things, I should like to have been born in the last age of the world, to have been the heir of all the ages in the foremost files of Time!

Towards midnight we proceeded on our way. The passengers began to retire to rest. The ladies' cabin and the state cabins were crammed full of ladies, and the deck was strewed with the peasants and others, who laid themselves down enveloped in their sheepskins. Some of the gentlemen lay down on the quarterdeck; others, among whom was I, preferred retiring to the gentlemen's cabin; but no sooner were all settled in their places, and silence began to prevail in the cabin, than certain mischievous and diminutive little beings began hopping about from one to another in a most tormenting manner. I could not conceive how the passengers could lie so still and even go to sleep while suffering from their attacks; for myself, I thought I should be eaten up alive if I remained much longer. I accordingly went on deck, preferring to spend the remainder of the night in walking to and fro, and contemplating now the dark river and shining stars, and now the various expressive countenances of the sleeping passengers. The human countenance is to me a source of endless interest and delight; and in the contemplation of the national and individual peculiarities of physiognomy around me, I found ample entertainment for the remainder of the night.

THE BATSHKA AND ITS GERMAN COLONISTS.

The morning soon dawned. It is always an interesting thought to me to remember, when the sun rises, that the day before me is the youngest day that has ever been. Yesterday (I speak of common yesterdays, undistinguished by any remarkable occurrence), yesterday is like an' extinguished light, an old newspaper, a piece of stale bread. It has been gathered away into the stores of the past, and we think of it no more. But the young day rises before us, fresh, beautiful, portentous. To-morrow is hidden in the dark womb of the future; the unborn child of Time; but to-day is ripe, ready, and near at hand. The warm rays of the sun shine over the broad Danube, and wake the sleepers with its kindly greeting, which announces the coming day; yet, near as it is, who knows what it may bring forth, what mighty events, what strange occurrences? How many future generations may labour to find out what this day was, and how it lived and died! how happy then ought we to deem ourselves, who are so soon to know its history!

Below Mohacs we entered a more interesting part of the Danube. It divided frequently into broad arms, which, after winding round large islands, again met and flowed together; so that we seemed to be passing through a gigantic park, with large rivers for little brooks, high grassy plains for smooth lawns, and vast forests for picturesque woods. At the union of the Drave with the Danube, however, this multiplicity of arms and islands entirely ceases. At this juncture an entirely new kind of country and population begins, both on the northern and southern sides of the river. On the northern side lies that interesting district called in geography books the Batsh comitat, but which the Hungarians never call by any other name than that of the Batshka, which name I shall here adopt. The situation of this country is as follows:

The parallelogram lying between the Danube and the Theiss, a desert level district frequented only by hunters and herds of horses, rises towards the south, into a low, barren plateau, which extends southward for some distance, of which a curve line drawn from Zombor to the mouth of the Theiss, would form the southern boundary. Between this and the Danube, lies a small alluvial plain, extremely fruitful, and watered by small rivers. This is the celebrated Batshka.

Most of the land in the Batshka is laid out in cornfields, and is in the possession of German colonists. Of its 120 little inhabited spots, only 29 are inhabited by Hungarians, and these places lie entirely in the northern and less fertile part. The Servians occupy 25 of its 120 divisions, and the Germans 41. An intelligent and amiable Hungarian nobleman, who lived in the Batshka, related to me many interesting particulars of the German colonists there. He said that the Germans often bought a piece of land for 100 florins, and by their good management and cultivation, were able to improve it so much, that after a time they could sell it again for several hundred florins. The German villages, he added, were all rich, not only in land, cattle, and stores of various kinds, but also in ready money. A German village in the Batshka was once condemned to a fine of 40,000 florins. Every one was curious to see what the peasants would do in this case; but the very day after they were apprized of it, the elders of the community came and laid the exact sum before the magistrate. On one occasion a nobleman of the Batshka laid a wager with another nobleman, who had doubted the vaunted wealth of the Batshka peasants, that at one day's warning he could obtain a loan of 100,000 florins from his German colonists. Before evening he had levied the required sum from five peasants alone. The next morning he told them of his wager, and would have returned the money, but they replied that they did not want it; they had bargained for the loan, and should insist on the execution of the contract.

Both the ancient Romans and the Hungarians, observing the singular fertility of the Batshka, cultivated and colonised it with great care. The Turks, whose devastating habits made no distinction between a fertile and a barren country, allowed this valuable and beautiful tract to run to waste and become a mere marsh. Under the hands of the German colonists however, it has reached more than its former state of cultivation and beauty.

SYRMIA AND PETERWARDEIN.

On the right side of the river, opposite to the Batshka, between the Danube and the Save, lies the land of Syrmia, a little paradise, about eighteen (German) miles long, and three or four broad. Through the middle of Syrmia runs a line of hills called the Frushka Gora, which are covered with picturesque forests, and beautiful vineyards. The grapes produced in these vineyards are much esteemed throughout Hungary. Another principal production of Syrmia are its hogs, from which are supplied all the principal hog-markets of Hungary. They are mostly of the Mongulitza race, short-legged, with woolly curly hair. They eat less, and can bear more fatigue than common pigs. No less than 70,000 of these interesting grunters are supposed to emigrate yearly from the land of Syrmia to the several markets of Hungary.

The first thing in Syrmia which we saw were the ruins of the Erdödy castle, belonging to a far-famed noble family of Hungary. It is almost the only Hungarian spot in Syrmia. We next came to Dallya. Here, as at all our landing-places in Syrmia, many Illyrian women had collected on the shore, to stare at us. It is now becoming more and more the custom, to call all the Slavonic nations of the Southern Danube, the Croatians, Slavonians, Servians, and Bulgarians, by the common name of Illyrians. This name pleases their national pride, for they believe, contrary to the opinion of the learned of other nations, that they are immediately descended from the old Illyrians mentioned by the Romans. The Illyrians of Croatia and Slavonia, are not without their provincial patriotism, and while they look down with contempt on the Magyar nationality of Hungary, they encourage an Illyrianism, to the full as hot in its patriotism as the former.

Beyond Dallya we came to Vukovar, or the town of the "Vuka," a small river rising in the Frushka Gora, and running into the Danube.

At Vukovar we took up two new passengers; two Syrmian ladies, young and pretty. Their costume, much resembling the riding-habits of German ladies, was of a light green colour, and set with rows of bright buttons. They said that this costume was very prevalent in Syrmia. They spoke good Austrian-German, and told us the language was generally spoken by all who belonged to the upper classes.

During the whole of the time that we continued to coast along the Syrmian district, I was surrounded by Servians, who were full of conversation about their native land. They were deeply versed in the ancient history of the country, and had an abundance of anecdotes to tell me about more modern occurrences. Of the new Servian hero Gregory Petrovitsh Tshornoi, they seemed to know quite as much as our own German newspapers. I asked them whether it was true that the Servians felt more sympathy for Russia than for Hungary. Their reply was, that the common people among them had a saying—" Never quarrel with him who drinks with thee out of the same cup at the Lord's Supper." We were engaged in such discourse as our vessel rushed past Opatovacz, past the ruins of Sharingrad castle, the Illock convent, and the castle and garden of Kameniz. Most of these castles and villages in Syrmia belong to the Duke of Odescalchi, Count Eltz, M. Yankovitch, and the Lords of Marzipani. The Odescalchis are not the only Italian family possessed of large estates in Hungary, but there are many of the great families, who, though their names have an Italian look, are of genuine Magyar descent. The Palfi and Sappari, for instance, are old and unquestionable Hungarian families, and the Marzipani, a family of which various branches exist in the country of the Slovaks, are genuine Slavonians.

The few great men I have named possess nearly the whole of Syrmia, except what belongs to the convents, and the peasants are all more or less serfs. This circumstance tends to deprive the people of all interest in my eyes. I can sympathize with the poorest labourer that maintains his wife and children with the work of his hands, but cannot help feeling something like contempt for the being who toils only for a master. The reflection has often occurred to me when I have seen German, Italian, and French peasants appearing as heroes on the stage; but as to the rural population of Eastern Europe, they are one and all unusable to the dramatist.

In the Slavonian provinces subject to Turkey, Bosnia, Servia, Bulgaria, &c., it is a remarkable fact that the principal nobility have all allowed themselves gradually to be converted to the Mahomedan religion. This will at least have one good consequence,—namely, that when these provinces are rescued from the Turkish domination, they will at the same time be freed from their nobles. Something of this kind seems already to be taking place in Servia.

It was some time before we reached Peterwardein, the most considerable town in Syrmia. Peterwardein and Neusatz are miniature counterparts to Pesth and Buda. Peterwardein, like Buda, lies round a fortress on the right side of the river; Neusatz, like Pesth, is a trading city situated in a plain on the left side. Again Peterwardein is as much older than Neusatz, as Buda surpasses Pesth in antiquity. Such pairs of cities are very common on the Danube; Belgrade and Semlin, Old and New Orsova, are other instances of the same kind. Of Neusatz we saw very little, for the ship lay so low, and the city so flat in its level plain, that the fronts of the nearest houses hid all beyond. Every river steamboat ought to have a convenient seat at the masthead, for the benefit of travellers who wish to see the country.

Peterwardein we saw pretty well, for the fortress rises from a hill of the Frushka Gora, round which the Danube makes a bend. A young German girl, who was on board the steamboat with her mother, shewed such enthusiastic delight at the sight of Peterwardein, her native city, that it lent to the place a peculiar interest in our eyes "Oh see, dear mother, there is our vineyard! And there is the summer-house round which I planted so many flowers last year! Ah, good Heavens! There is our dancing-master standing on the bridge. How he will wonder when he sees us back again! Come now, make haste, don't let us squeeze our bonnets in the crowd." They had bought two fashionable Vienna bonnets, as presents for the sisters at home. The traveller is often too much inclined to pass by with indifference the little home traits, which animate and fill with interest strange and foreign places. The idea of a dancing-master at Neusatz had never occurred to me, and Peterwardein gardens and summer-houses, tended with as fond a care as that felt at home, seemed something curious and unexpected to me.

Round Peterwardein grow the best wines of Southern Hungary. Passing Peterwardein we soon reached Karlovitz. These three cities are the three capitals of the Military Frontier; Neusatz is the trading, Peterwardein the military, and Karlovitz the religious capital, for it is the residence of the head of the Greek church in Austria. The Archbishop of Karlovitz, the Greek Synod, the Bishop of Montenegro, the Patriarch of Constantinople, and the Emperor of Russia, are the five independent heads of the Greek church in Europe.

A steamboat down the Danube tears along with such inexorable speed, that scarcely has an interesting object appeared above the horizon, when it already lies far behind, and scarcely any vigilance is sufficient to prevent the traveller from losing many objects of the highest interest. We were conversing with some entertaining young Austrians, who were describing to us the proceedings of a Hungarian Diet, at which they had been present, and while thus pleasantly occupied, the inexorable steamboat swiftly sped past the mouth of the Theiss, and when I turned to my map and to the river, I saw it lying far behind me, on the edge of the horizon. I had been particularly anxious to see this river, because I had hoped to discover the reason why the juncture of two such great rivers as the Danube and the Theiss, is not marked by any town or city. The confluence of the Danube with the Drave, and with the Theiss, are the only two exceptions I know of, in this part of the world, to the rule that all the mouths of great rivers are marked by considerable towns. These two mouths have not so much as a village or single house in their neighbourhood. The immense marshes which cover these two places may perhaps be the cause of this singular fact. The nature of the country made it, in consequence, impossible that large towns should arise exactly at the mouths of these two rivers. Nevertheless, their traffic required the existence of staple places, where the trade of the rivers might concentrate, and such places are Eszeck (the Mursia of the Romans) for the Drave, and Neusatz for the Theiss.

The corner of marshy land formed by the confluence of the Theiss with the Danube, is peopled by the Tshaikists, who form the crews of the Austrian gunboats on the Danube. Their territory belongs to the Military Frontier, and, like all the peasants of that portion of the empire, they are liable to military duties, with this difference, that it is not on land but on water that the Tshaikists are employed. Their capital is called Titel, and there is the chief station of their flotilla, of which, however, detachments are constantly to be found at Semlin, and at other points of the Danube.

The Tshaikists form a battalion of about 1000 men. They are bound to patrol about upon the Danube, and their services are sometimes taken into requisition for building bridges, passing troops across the river, and in case of inundation to keep up a communication between the different insulated points. The portion of the river on which the people are chiefly employed, is that which intervenes between Belgrade and Orsova.

THE MOUTH OF THE SAVE.

Passing between the marshy country of the Banat on the left hand, and the dry Syrmia on the right, we arrived at night at Semlin, at the mouth of the Save, opposite to which lies the far famed city of Belgrade. Semlin is the last town in Hungary, and Belgrade the first in Servia. At this point we passed through one of the principal openings into Hungary; one of those gates broken in its mountain wall, by the rivers that water its central plains. Hungary is a large and hollow basin of land, enclosed on the North and North-east by the Carpathians, on the South and Southeast by the Walachian and Illyrian mountains, and on the West by the Alps. The principal rivers which water it, are the Danube, the Theiss, the Drave, and the Save. The two former of these, which are by far the most considerable, have broken three gates or openings in the mountain wall which encloses the country. These three are,

1stly, that of Presburg, where the Danube enters Hungary, cutting through the northern extremity of the Alps, and the southern extremity of the Carpathians; 2dly, that of Belgrade, where the same river leaves Hungary, piercing the Servian mountains; and 3dly, that of the sources of the Theiss, where the valley of the Theiss winds through the mountain masses of Transylvania.

The first opening, that of Presburg, connects Hungary with the West of Europe. Through this passed the torrent of Huns, that, headed by Attila, poured forth to devastate Europe: through this pass swarmed the wild Magyars to torment Germany, and the fierce Turks to besiege Vienna. This was the gate by which the Germans entered Hungary to turn her wild nomadic robber hordes into peaceable and industrious citizens; through which the pious crusaders, the penitent princes of Germany, and the devout sovereigns of the West, journeyed towards Palestine; through which marched the Austrians to claim their hereditary rights, and finally the French under their great Emperor, to crush in Hungary the last remnant of Austrian independence.

Through the second great gate at Belgrade, passed the Roman emperors, and the generals of the Byzantine Empire, into the valley of the Morava. Through this opening the soldiers and janizaries of the Padishaw poured forth continually, to lay waste the Hungarian plains; here also the Hungarian and Austrian armies passed along to do battle against the Turks. It was through this opening, moreover, that the plague first entered Hungary from the East.

The third gate first admitted the Huns and Tartars, and afterwards the original Hungarian tribes themselves, into the valleys of the Theiss and the Danube; and through this gate it is the Hungarians already begin to dread that they will one day behold the armies of Russia enter the country.

The first of these openings leads into Germany, and may therefore be called the German gate. The second is flanked on either side by Servia, and may be called the Servian gate; and the third, where the Russians, or *Ruthenen*, may be said to hold guard, must be called the Russian gate.

Every thing now began to look very Oriental. Semlin resembles more a Turkish than an Hungarian town. The steamboat stopped here the whole evening, and we visited many shops, which were full of Turkish wares. Men in Turkish costumes sat cross-legged on the shore, smoking. The French consul of Belgrade came on board, and we learnt from him that many Germans emigrate to Servia from Semlin and Neusatz, as servants, innkeepers, and shopmen, and that they are much sought for, and well paid for their services. The Magyars, on the contrary, never cross the borders of their native land. A French courier also came on board here. He was a hard, cold, sharp, clever man, whose brown, spare, and weather-beaten countenance, bore marks of long exposure in travelling. He brought with him some excellent Turkish tobacco, of which he offered some to several among us. He had travelled in Africa, Europe, and Asia, namely in Algiers, France, and Asia Minor, and had journeyed eight times from Constantinople to Belgrade, and twice from Belgrade to Thessalonica. He told me that upon the Bulgarian roads, gipsies are the usual postilions, and that these, as well as the horses, are often beaten to death by travellers; in which case they lie by the roadside, and no one takes the least notice of the occurrence. He knew a Tartar who had in this way beaten to death three gipsies during his life. The whip, he said, and the Turkish costume, were indispensable appendages on that tour. Merchants, couriers, and now and then an Englishman, he added, were the only travellers along the road.

Early the next morning the tall white minarets of Belgrade lay far behind on the horizon. It vexed us that the wind, or the noise of the steamboat, hindered our hearing the cries of the Muezzins from the towers. This is the most northerly point, from which the Fateh of the Prophet is ever proclaimed, but it is surrounded by foes, and will probably not long remain a Turkish possession.

We now proceeded with the Turkish shores on one side, and the Austrian Military Frontier on the other. On the Austrian side all is level marsh; the hills of Servia give a far more agreeable appearance to the other side. Out of the Austrian marshes rise at regular intervals the solitary *Tshardaken*, or military posts, surrounded with bushes. They are all built of wood, and raised on piles, on account of the frequent inundations. The posts are placed near enough to one another for the soldiers to see from one to another in the daytime, and to hear each other at night. The situation of these posts during a general inundation, surrounded on all sides by water, must be tedious and monotonous enough. When smuggling or the plague demands it, the posts are thickened and the soldiers increased in number.

STEAMBOAT LIFE.

The Morava is the principal river in Servia, and winds through the whole of that province. At its mouth it divides into two arms, one of which is called the Yesoba. On this arm lies Semandria, a fortress of a very peculiar appearance and construction. Belgrade, Orsova, and other Turkish fortresses on the Danube, belonged formerly to Austria, and were altered and arranged according to the modern rules of fortification, and consequently do not differ much in appearance from those of Germany. Semandria, on the contrary, has remained unchanged and unmodified, from the times when cannons and gunpowder were unknown. The walls form a large triangle of great height, and are surmounted by rows of little turrets with loopholes. At the corners of the triangle are high sexagonal or octagonal towers, also surmounted with turrets, and between these at regular intervals along the wall, other smaller towers of a similar form. The walls and towers seemed to me to stand within one another in a double triangle. I counted twenty-five towers, but there appeared to be many more. The whole fortress was in good preservation, and was a beautiful object, with the morning sunrise shining full upon it.

The Austrian shores remained very military in appearance, and of stern, barren, warlike aspect. The Servian afforded more matter for description and for observation. There were cattle grazing in the meadows, and oxen drinking at the streams; there were villages, and women washing clothes in the river near them; there were Turkish and Servian boatmen, rowing boats, in which sailors in picturesque costume were stretched under the shade of bales of goods. All was peaceful, quiet, idyllic; and yet this harmless aspect concealed war, and pestilence, and tyranny, and social anarchy, while the rough bristling coast opposite, protected a land of peace, commerce, industry, and civilization.

At Drenkova, a new settlement recently formed by the steam navigation company, our number of passengers, originally 350, had dwindled away to thirty. The steamboat proceeds no further than Drenkova, where accordingly we were all turned out into a small convenient sailing vessel; but before quitting the agreeable and expeditious steamboat, the best vehicle certainly ever invented for river travelling, I cannot forbear recalling a few of its pleasant scenes and reminiscences.

The more the small community dwindled away, the more familiar and intimate with one another became those who remained. In the steamboats along the Rhine none of this amalgamation takes place, because at each station, the boat takes up as many new passengers as it deposits old ones. Not so on the Danube, where the intermediate stations are as yet of very little importance. As our journey was throughout accompanied by the most beautiful weather, we were almost always, day and night, upon deck. The German lady mentioned above always sat in her coach, which served her as an arbour, and protected her from the heat of the sun. The coach-doors were always left open, and her children were incessantly climbing and flying in and out, like pigeons in a dove cot. This little group formed the general centre of our conversation, and never failing topics arose from the countless objects of interest which we passed in our course. The watermills of the Danube, which occur in great numbers, afforded us frequent amusement. The millers appear to live in a perpetual state of hostility with the sailors. They watched us as we past their mills to make grimaces at us, and when they were sitting at dinner, they would hold out their plates and spoons at us with an air of grinning defiance, as much as to say, "Wouldn't you wish to have some? But you shan't!" Sometimes they would roar out as if in great terror, "the boat's lost!" "going down!" and when the passengers turned round with startled faces, the millers would laugh at them for their pains.

While passing the Batchka our discourse turned a good deal on the bad harvest of 1838, which was universally complained of. The summer had been so dry that all the corn had withered; and the Banat province, which usually sells 6,000,000 *metzen* of grain, had this year sold scarcely 1,000,000.

One day as we were sitting together engaged in cheerful conversation, the little painter of Pesth took out his apparatus and began to take our portraits. I told him that I would rather have seen him engaged on some of the more picturesque figures which abounded among the lower class of passengers. One day I led him aside and pointed out to him a poor sick Jew in Turkish costume, who was lying stretched on mats and sheepskins, but I could not prevail upon him to paint this man, and yet his appearance and ragged costume were in the highest degree picturesque and interesting. He wore a tattered turban and a faded old silk girdle, and his beard and hair were ragged and disordered. His countenance wore an expression of the deepest misery; his complexion was pale, corpselike, and white as marble; his eyes were dull and destitute of fire; the lines and features of his face were sharply cut but regular; his forehead and head were of a beautiful form, and the whole expression of his countenance was so noble that when young and in health he must have been remarkably handsome. I addressed the unfortunate whom, because he was covered with vermin, every one shunned, but I received no answer. I questioned some Jewish merchants about him, and was informed that he was a poor, sick, and distressed rabbi of Constantinople, who had been sent for to Vienna by some brother rabbis in the vain hope of his receiving relief from the skill of our German physicians.

THE CATARACTS OF THE DANUBE.

The Transylvanian and Walachian mountains, which branch off into Servia in a south-westerly direction, divide the great plains of Central Hungary from those of Walachia. These plains probably once formed great lakes, which gradually wore a pass through the mountains, and the pass so formed became the channel of the present Danube. This pass, through which the Danube winds in its serpentine course for eighteen (German) miles, is called the Clissura.

At Moldova the mountains on each side first begin to be of importance. They rise to a gigantic height, and if the river were narrow, these steep, bare, narrow mountain walls would be terrific in appearance, but the broad, calm stream which flows in tranquillity between them, softens their rugged grandeur. A little below Moldova, however, a very startling phenomenon makes its appearance, for to the height of twenty fathoms there arises from the very midst of the river a huge rock with frowning chasms, jagged edges, and pointed teeth. This rock is called by the inhabitants the Babagai, or "wicked woman." Immediately below it is the commencement of a series of perilous whirlpools and rapids.

I am unable to speak with any certainty of the height of the mountain walls at this place, but I was told by those whom I questioned, that their height could not be under 300 fathoms. Rocks and mountains then of the same height as these walls, similar in all respects, jagged and rough, and cut by deep ravines and valleys, are sown in the bed of the river itself, and tower out of the water on all sides. The highest of these is the *Tristovaczer Spitze*, below which the cataracts of the Danube begin. Scarcely had we passed this rock than we heard a dull hollow roaring in the water, and saw the dark heads of the dangerous reefs which here run right across the river. The rowers exerted all their strength and redoubled their exertions, for it is not enough that the excited waters drive on the boat till it flies before them with the rapidity of an arrow, the rowers must labour with all their might and main to increase this rapidity. If they were to proceed slowly and cautiously, by way of avoiding the rocks and reefs, they would inevitably be caught and swallowed up by one of the numerous whirlpools. The boat must cut them rapidly and decisively, like a knife, and the utmost precision, boldness, and local knowledge are required in the steersman. As in human life, wherever whirlpools and rapids lie in our course, the timid and fearful are sure to sink, while the courageous steersman, who redoubles his energy, and exerts all his experience and judgment, passes victoriously through every peril.

The transition from a quietly-flowing river to a wild eddying and whirling torrent, is, of course, gradual. At first the water only runs with greater rapidity. By degrees, small vortices and then greater ones begin to appear. As we advance, the pools increase in depth and circumference, and their edges lap over more and more upon one another till the whole becomes one vast, roaring, foaming, eddying, whirling vortex.

We all stood in the forepart of the boat, near where the rowers sat, many of us stretching our heads over the side, to witness the wild and awe-inspiring tumult of the elements. The children alone still continued to play with careless unconcern, regardless of the dangers around them. The steersman stood aft, gazing steadily upon the stream. Upon his energy and skill our safety depended. The measured, steady motion of the oars, as they cut the convex swelling bubbles in the whirlpool, formed a fine contrast to the wild, stormy confusion of the waters. I cannot say exactly how long the tumult lasted. It began three times anew, forming three separate whirlpools.

The breadth of the Danube, in the narrowest part of this pass, is only a hundred fathoms. Below Pesth it is 600 fathoms broad, and below Belgrade it is a perfect sea. This vast mass of waters, enriched by innumerable tributaries, is here forced through a channel so extremely narrow, and no vent is to be obtained either by inundation, or by any other means. It is this which gives the whirlpools, and the cataracts which follow them, such tremendous force and impetus. It is wonderful to see the whole united volume of water pouring itself down one steep and narrow defile with the rapidity of lightning, and more than the noise of thunder.

To estimate the exact quantity of water which is poured down the Clissura is impossible, for the depth of the river has never been ascertained with any degree of certainty; indeed it is so very various at different parts, that to find a just average is scarcely possible. At one place the boatmen said, "Here the river is forty fathoms deep;" and at another, "Here the rocks are only two feet below the bottom of the boat." Sometimes it happens that the boat, dancing wildly upon the waves, scrapes upon a rock, yet it is very seldom that an accident occurs. Out of 100 vessels,

99 got through the pass in safety. One may afford to risk life with such odds in one's favour.

Our *Tundér*, the name given to the description of large row-boat in which we were embarked, brought us safely through. We passed the *Islaz*, and the less formidable *Tachtalia* and *Yutz*,* successfully, and reached again a peaceful and quiet part of the river. At Svinitza, where stands a great rocky outlet called the Greben, the Danube flows quietly out into easy ground, and pursues a tranquil course. Svinitza is the southernmost point of the kingdom of Hungary. It was now evening between our rocky walls. The plains of central Hungary still basked in the rays of the setting sun, but gray twilight was spread over the gloomy mountain-pass. We had been told that we should reach Orsova that night, and were very much disappointed to see that the sun had set before we emerged from the Clissura.

It was a beautiful evening. The river was now three times as wide as before, and the mountains began again to be covered with green herbage. Here and there wild glens and defiles afforded a glimpse into the interior of the country. All was as silent as if we were travelling through the primeval forests, along some mighty American river. On the Austrian side the solitary fire of a military post lit up the heights here and there; and on the Servian side, the mountains were more frequently and brightly illuminated by fires kindled to frighten away the bears. We had all fasted the whole day, with the exception of our breakfast on board the steamboat, and all began to feel extremely well inclined for something to eat and drink. The children complained a little, though in a very modest manner, of being very hungry and thirsty, particularly as they were wrapped up in their cloaks, and forbidden to run about any more. One of our passengers, therefore, who had liberally provided for his own wants upon the journey, took pity upon us, and produced a little tea-service, with some sugar, biscuits, and glasses. One of the Jews on board struck a light, and lit a fire, another fetched water, and very soon a very comfortable kettle of hot water was boiling for tea, over a pleasant little fire.

The little ones were fed and satisfied: and we grown up children enjoyed our cups of warm tea that diffused more comfort, and good humour among us at that moment than the best champagne or tokay could have done under different circumstances. Here was again a picture I would fain have painted, but for want of a pencil, I contented myself with impressing the scene upon the canvass of my memory.

A NIGHT ON THE MILITARY FRONTIER.

As it grew darker, our boatmen took care to keep to the Austrian side. This was very necessary, for if we were not to keep within sight of the Austrian sentinels, we should be considered to have incurred infection, and should be subjected to quarantine on arriving at Orsova.

We could not get our boatmen to declare positively whether they thought we should reach Orsova that night or not. Our uncertainty was, however, soon terminated. " *Laij u krayi!*" shouted a sentinel from the Austrian side. I did not understand the cry, but the rowers did, and im-

---

* These are the Walachian names for the three principal whirlpools.

mediately rowed towards land. When we reached the post, we were at first forbidden to proceed, but on our using many persuasive remonstrances and arguments, the soldiers consulted together, and agreed that there was still light enough for us to reach the next sentry post, and that the sentinels there might decide upon our further proceedings. Accordingly they sent a soldier into our boat, by way of escort or spy, and we were allowed to go on. We proceeded with our tea-drinking in all possible good-humour, until the unwelcome sound, "*Laÿ u krayi,*" again resounded from the heights. Here we were compelled to disembark, and we did so in the confident hope of being allowed to proceed, under a guard of another soldier; but no—the corporal declared that it was too late, and we must spend the night where we were. In vain we pointed to the ladies and children, and remonstrated on the severity of compelling them to put up with the scanty accommodations of a military post. In vain we represented that they might send as many soldiers as they pleased with us, so as to hinder the slightest chance of any intercourse with Turkey. The sentinels were deaf to all arguments and appeals, replying that they could not take upon themselves the responsibility of allowing us to go on, and that we must stay where we were. We were therefore obliged to submit, and to surrender ourselves prisoners to the soldiers of the 13th military post of the Illyrico-Walachian frontier-regiment.

The post was called Plavishevitza, after a neighbouring Walachian village of that name, into which we now hastened, to endeavour to find some quarters more suitable to the sex and age of a part of our fellow-passengers, than the little sentry-house, filled with the rude soldiery of the frontier. We searched through the whole village, but found nothing except the most miserable huts, which were all obstinately closed against us.

At length we determined to look after the priest of the village. This seemed to us a capital idea. Where could we be more likely to meet with civility and hospitality, and where were we more likely to find fit lodgings for the ladies and children? We knocked. A gigantic man, with a gloomy countenance, and long ragged beard and hair, made his appearance, clothed in a coarse linen shirt and trousers of the same material, over which was thrown a loose caftan. We spoke to him in German, but the village priest, for such he was, appeared to know but two German words, which he repeated incessantly, shaking his head all the time: "*Nik's Wirthshaus! Nik's Wirthshaus!*" (No inn! No inn!) We began to speak in Russian, and entreated his hospitality, representing to him the helplessness of our situation. Our arguments, now perfectly understood, softened his heart, and he agreed for a reasonable remuneration to allow the ladies and children to occupy his two bedsteads, and the only room in his house, a miserable place enough; and moreover, he undertook to procure them a little milk and bread for supper.

The ladies who had remained on board the boat, were now fetched up, together with the children, of whom we each took one in our arms. The ladies and children took possession of the two beds; the priest with his wife and children stretched themselves in the ashes by the fire: our Ragusan lay down upon his cloak before the door, and I, my friend, and the Frenchman, returned to take up our quarters on the shore. Here we found two little carts, which the Walachian boyars had obtained, and in which they were determined to drive the remaining seven miles to Orsova. The Turkish

Jews and Servians were stretched on the sands by the river-side, wrapped in their furs, some smoking, some talking, and others sleeping. Some were lying on the benches and trunks in the boat.

The sentry-house or *Tshardak*, stood on the height immediately overlooking the sands. It had two divisions, one for the watchfire, and the other for the soldiers to sleep in. Before this little shed, under the projecting roof, the men had piled their arms. There were six or seven soldiers at the Tshardak, and their dress like their political constitution, was half military and half peasant-like. Over the usual peasant's frock they wore knapsacks, fastened to a leathern strap. Their legs were wrapped in linen or woollen cloths, and their feet covered with those sandals, fastened with red bindings, common to most Eastern Slavonian nations. They wore peasants' caps, and most of them had a knife sticking in the girdle. Those who were on watch, marched up and down before the Tshardak with a very unsoldierly gait, and with the long musket thrown clumsily over the shoulder. For the cordon service on which these men are employed they are admirably fitted; on parade they would certainly not show to advantage. They are truly a *rusticorum mascula militum prolas:*

All the soldiers of the frontier regiments are now taught the German language. Most of them forget it as fast as they learn it, except the few military phrases they are in the daily habit of using, but the non-commissioned officers generally speak German tolerably well.

We were very hungry and thirsty, and asked the soldiers whether we could have some bread (the Frenchman had actually the conscience to ask for white bread) or some dried fish, or a piece of bacon, or a glass of milk, or *Raki*, the common liquor of the country. They shrugged their shoulders, and said they had no such dainties, but they would get us plenty of water from the river, and would mix us some flour and water and boil it into a *mamaliga*. A fire was accordingly kindled, some flour and water put into a kettle, and a thick gruel soon prepared. One of the soldiers brought us a little salt in a wooden spoon, and another some powdered cheese. This supper was certainly no feast, but we were obliged to put up with it. As for the Frenchman, he protested that the first mouthful almost choked him.

As we were sitting round the fire, the cry of the sentinel, "Hold! Who goes?" was heard. It was a messenger with a letter. The corporal immediately despatched one of the soldiers with it to the next post. In a little while the sentinel hailed again. "A friend" was the reply. It was a patrol sent out by the chiefs of the Cordon, to see that all was right at the different posts. Sometimes these chiefs themselves make the circuit from post to post, without any previous warning.

Once more the unwearied sentinel repeated his challenge, and received a friendly answer. It was the new guard, come to relieve the others. No soldiers remain more than seven days together at a sentry post; they are then relieved by six or seven others, who likewise remain a week. Every soldier spends ninety days of the year on guard at these places. Each of the new comers had in his knapsack a bag, containing seven *Ocka* of flour, their sole provision for the seven days. Some of them had also a little powdered sheep's cheese, and some of them, though not many, were even without salt—at least so they assured us. Salt is very dear upon the Military Frontier, though extremely abundant on the Turkish side. The soldiers look with longing eyes upon the shiploads of fine green salt, which pass along the Turkish side of the river, and there is probably a little smuggling carried on in so tempting an article.

The soldiers had come very far that day, having set off early in the morning. They were very tired, and after throwing their thick brown cloaks over their weapons, they stretched themselves on the ground before the Tshardak, and immediately fell asleep. I never saw so little accommodation for a week's lodging. Their arms alone received any care or attention. We asked them why they did not sleep within the Tshardak, but they replied that it swarmed with mice and vermin, and that they always preferred sleeping in the open air.

The hardships and privations to which the daily life of these hardy and courageous men is exposed, even under the most favourable circumstances, is almost incredible. What must it be when bad weather renders the country entirely impassable, and shuts them up in the miserable Tshardak, and when the mere keeping of their weapons in good condition, requires incessant labour and care. But when the alarm-bell beats from the chief sentry-houses, when signal fires are lighted from the heights, when perhaps a robbery is proclaimed, and the soldiery have to roam the country for days together, in search of banditti, to recover perhaps some miserable cloaks and guns, then the frontier soldier is quite in his element! Then he sings the warlike songs of his country, and shouts the praises of the Austrian emperor, for privation and hardship are not felt by the hardy borderer, and war and tumult are his delight.

We seated ourselves on the edge of the height overhanging the sands, to enjoy our feast of *mamaliga* and water, and the corporal sat down beside us, with his knotted corporal's stick in his hand. The Corporal of the Military Frontier is a king whose sceptre is never out of his hand. There is no more certain way by which to win his royal favour, than to offer him a pipe of tobacco, as we now did. He immediately began to converse.

"We have had peace for some time with the Servians," said the corporal. "Under Prince Milosh they were kept in very good order, but since the new governor's accession we have been obliged to redouble our watchfulness, and we know not how it will be in future. The country is not as secure as ours just now, for even their officers of government must always go about armed."

Now and then from the Servian side we could hear the barking of dogs, the only sound which broke the silence around. We did not hear the howling of the wolves in the forests, although we listened for it attentively, for the barking of the dogs completely overpowered them. The fires in the Servian fields gleamed out here and there from among the dark trees. "There are plenty of wolves and bears over there," said the corporal. "We have some, also, but not so many. They have also more useful animals, such as stags and deer, than we have. Last winter they killed 300 stags and deer in the snow. Sometimes the bears swim over to our side, and the soldiers have to look after them pretty sharply."

It may be seen how various are the labours necessary to protect a civilized against a barbaric frontier. The usual number of soldiers kept constantly on watch along the banks of the Danube and Save is 6000, but when any peculiar danger demands increased vigilance the number is increased to 8000 and 12,000 men. The whole number of able-bodied frontier-soldiers is 60,000, and they keep watch in rotation as above described.

"As a German I feel proud of this institution of the Military Frontier," said I, turning to the Frenchman, "for it is one of the most remarkable projects which Germany has ever executed, for the defence of her own civilization and that of Europe."

"*Comment ça ? Vous étes fier ! je n'en comprends rien. Je ne sais ni comment ni pourquoi.*"

This phrase "*je ne sais ni comment ni pourquoi*," was continually on the lips of my Frenchman, who having lived all his life in Paris, was completely ignorant of every thing out of it. He turned round and went to sleep, while I continued to occupy myself with

THOUGHTS ON THE POLITICAL IMPORTANCE OF THE MILITARY FRONTIER,

which appears to me of the highest interest, as considered,

1stly. With reference to Germany as a German institution.
2dly. As a school of civilization for the neighbouring countries.
3dly. As a protection for the civilization of Europe against the barbarism of Turkey.

The foundation and development of this institution began with the fall of the Hungarian kingdom at the battle of Mohacs (1525), with the accession of the Austrian Emperor to the Hungarian crown, and with the beginning of the great war between the Turks and the Germans for the dominion over these Eastern countries, which lasted nearly two hundred years.

The Emperor Ferdinand, the brother of Charles V., first quartered German troops in those districts of Croatia bordering on Styria, in order to protect his new kingdom of Hungary against the incursions of the Turks. This garrison afterwards received numerous additions of Servian and Croatian fugitives from Turkey, who were endowed with lands, on condition of serving as military frontier guards against the Turks. In this manner was first organized the Military Frontier of Styria, which was afterwards formed into a distinct Margravate, under the name of "the one perpetual Generalty" of the Croatian Frontiers.

This Generalty is the basis and foundation of the whole subsequent structure. The more the conquests of Austria extended in Hungary, the more the frontier lines were lengthened. The more the Christian power became consolidated and strengthened, the greater was the number of Christian fugitives who took refuge on Austrian ground from the tyranny of the Mahomedan government. All these fugitives, Uskoks, Croatians, Albanians, Macedonians, Servians, and Walachians, were hospitably received by Austria, and settled as before on the waste lands of Slavonia and the Banat, for the defence of the frontier. As more and more provinces were added to the dominions of Austria, the frontier was finally extended to its eastern boundary round Transylvania, in the years 1765 and 1766.

It is probable that as civilization and culture spreads southward into the Turkish dominions, this living wall of protection against barbarism may gradually become unnecessary, but at present it is very far from being so. The internal disturbances and convulsions of Turkey, and the unsettled state of the Oriental question on the one hand, and the spirit of discontent, the passion for nationality now so dangerously prevalent in Hungary, on the other, render the preservation of the Military Frontier of the very highest consequence to Austria.

No one who has ever had an opportunity of comparing the state of civilization in the contiguous districts of Hungary and Turkey, can doubt what vast benefit this institution has conferred on the inhabitants of the countries immediately within its influence. In the first place the security of the inhabitants is placed upon a firmer footing than in the neighbouring districts of Hungary, to say nothing of Turkey. Within the Military Frontier very few robberies take place, and the traveller is as safe as in a German Province. To secure life and property ought to be the first consideration of rational civilization. The second is the security of judicial rights, and in this respect also the Military Frontier has an immense advantage over the neighbouring countries.

A great deal has also been effected for the morality and social order of the inhabitants. Their temperance, domestic peace, and the punctual fulfilment of their duties is subjected to a wholesome surveillance, but which must by no means be supposed to degenerate into a tyrannical and inquisitorial spirit of meddling. The highest as well as the lowest are restrained by military and moral regulations, of which they feel the salutary influence, and I myself, in the sequel, met with many Hungarian peasants who had taken refuge in the Military Frontier from the tyranny and severity of their masters, and who assured me that they were far better off in their new homes than they had ever been before. The frontier is, therefore, peopled from two sources, from Turkey and Hungary, by fugitives from oppression, who seek a refuge, in the order, security and peace established in the frontier districts.

Education has likewise been in many ways promoted here by the Austrian government, and if the schools of the Military Frontier do not yet quite answer their ends, owing chiefly to the want of qualified teachers, yet what I saw of these schools agreeably surprised me, and when we consider the state of education on the right side of the Danube, we cannot sufficiently rejoice at the mental illumination which has been shed on these dark regions by the Austrian government.

It is a no less agreeable surprise to the traveller coming from Hungary, or still more from Turkey, to observe the good state of the roads and bridges in the Military Frontier. The advantages which this institution has conferred upon the inhabitants, are the more striking, because the countries from which the different elements of the population are derived, lying so close to the frontier itself, invite comparison. Turkish Servia has founded a real New Servia in the Military Frontier, which might with more truth be called so than the Province of that name in Austria; Walachia, and Turkish Croatia, have also a little Walachia and a little Croatia, within the Military Frontier.

The work here accomplished by Austria, and indeed by all Germany—for it was only with the help of the money and troops supplied by the rest of Germany, that the Austrian government was enabled to found the Military Frontier—has been of the greatest service, not merely to Germany, but to all Europe; for it was this effective and energetic institution alone which formed a permanent rampart against the Turks, and preserved Europe from that dreadful disease to which it was so long subject, and which still rages throughout the East.

If, as is not improbable, the Frontier continues to advance in a rapidly progressive course of civilization and prosperity, it will perhaps gradually lose its military character, and blend with the rest of the peaceful and industrious Austrian community. It is remarkable to observe how the tables are now turned between Austria and Turkey. In ancient times, the lands of civilization and refinement lay on the right side of the Danube, and a frontier line, similar to the present Military Frontier, was drawn by the Byzantine emperors, to protect their dominions against the incursions of the Northern barbarians.

While I still sat on the shores of the Danube, making reflections upon the importance of the Military Frontier, the first gray light of morning began to dawn. The old corporal, giving up his post to his successor, took his departure with his soldiers. I observed that each soldier, as he went away, carefully took his cartridge from his gun-barrel, and put it into his cartridge-box. This is on account of the scanty supply of ammunition allowed to the frontier soldiers. On the Military Frontier, no unnecessary shot must ever be fired; the cartridges are sparingly dealt out, and must be used with equal parsimony. They are sometimes put three or four times into the gun, and then drawn out again, for the soldier must never go armed into the interior of the country. To any one not acquainted with these circumstances, the fuss made about a missing or spoilt cartridge, sometimes appears highly ridiculous.

We now set off for the village to look after our fellow travellers. When we arrived there, we found all still sunk in deep repose. The Ragusan lay sleeping before the door, and the window of the ladies was still covered with a little curtain. We went on into the village to try and obtain some warm milk for breakfast.

Here also all were asleep. No smoke yet rose from the chimneys of the little houses built of wood and clay, and in the narrow courts in front, surrounded with high basket-work, the little carts, ploughs, and agricultural instruments of the peasants, were still piled up together as if they too were fast asleep.

As the inhabitants, however, neither spoke nor understood a word of any language but Walachian, it was impossible to wake them in a polite and courteous manner. The only thing we could do was to break through a hole in the fence, and, putting our mouths to the door, to raise an inarticulate kind of cry. This we accompanied with a bombardment of kicks and knocks at the door, and after some time it was opened by a boy. The Frenchman began "*Eh bien! mon cher, faites vite! donnez nous un peu de lait! du lait—du lait!*" The Walachian lad was not much the wiser for this communication, and would doubtless have slammed the door in our faces, if I had not flown to Wallachian Latin as a last resource, exclaiming "*Lapte dulce! Lapte dulce!*" while the Frenchman held out some money.

The chink of money is the most intelligible of all languages, and it was not long before a slender Walachian girl appeared, leading some cows out into the courtyard.

We here saw for the first time the ordinary costume of a Walachian girl of these districts. Her head was bare, and her hair was laid round her head in thick plaits like a crown. These plaits are made so firmly, that the girls sleep in them. She wore a long, white loose chemise, decorated with pink threads, and over this, two long garments like aprons, one before and one behind. These aprons are the principal parts of the dress of a Walachian girl, who usually expends a great deal of care upon them. They are woven of bright coloured wool, and embroidered with patterns in yellow, blue, and white. They are called "*Pregacsen.*" The holiday Pregacsen are bordered with gold and silver thread. They are made quite alike, both being rather more than an ell long, and an ell wide. They are fringed at the bottom with an immense number of long tassels and ribbons, which hang nearly to the ground, and fly about at every movement. This is the part of their costume most striking to the stranger.

The cows, which the Walachian girl now began to milk, were miserably small, and she had to milk a whole herd to get a pailful. I remarked that these people, like those of South Russia, have never properly tamed their cows, or accustomed them to give their milk freely. They have first to put the calf to the udder, and then drive it away, while the milkmaid takes its place. The whole operation lasted an hour, at the expiration of which, we ran off with our milk, which we handed in at the little window of the priest's house, and which the ladies, being now awake, received with thankfulness.

THE LOWER CLISSURA.

At five o'clock we were again all seated in our *Tundér*, relating to one another the adventures of the preceding night. If our yesterday's voyage had been interesting, to-day's was no less so. Below Plavishevitza, the Danube is tolerably wide, but we soon saw before us a gate formed of two projecting rocks, beyond which the river ran through a very narrow channel. The place was beautifully picturesque. The broad Danube before and around us, the lovely verdure on the shore in the foreground, and in the background the gigantic gate, over which towered the highest peak in the whole range,—the Sterbezo al mare,—all this formed a beautiful landscape. Through the rocky gate we caught a glimpse of a further perspective, formed by projecting rocks towering over the troubled channel of the river, and terminated by light morning clouds and vapours.

We floated into the gate or *Kasan*, the water of which was ice-cold. In the middle of the stream rose a high rock, round which the angry surges foamed and dashed in wild fury. On each side of the shore lay gloomy caverns, and upon one of these rocks sat a majestic eagle, who did not deign to notice us as we passed. Crippled oaks and beeches nestled in ruts on the rocks. We glided quickly through, and though the river whirled and roared as before, this second pass, in which there are not so many little treacherous rocks, is not nearly so dangerous as that of the Islatz. We soon passed out again into the broad and quiet channel.

On the Hungarian side a new road is being constructed, which is to lead from Orsova to Uipalanka near Drenkova, along the Clissura. When it is finished the passengers and goods going to Orsova will proceed by this landway from the steamboat, instead of incurring the dangers of the Clissura pass. The work proceeds very slowly, because in many places the road has to be cut out of the solid rocks, and in others viaducts must be raised over clefts and chasms in the mountains.

On the Servian side may be seen the traces of an old Roman road, built by Trajan, and called by the Walachians the "*Trajan uht.*" I asked the Walachian boatman who Trajan was, and he answered, "*Imperator Rumanescu,*" which might mean either Roman or Walachian Emperor. It has been proved that the Walachians are far more directly descended from the Romans than the Italians. Their corruption of the Latin tongue bears a curious and striking resemblance to the Italian language.

"That road is Trajan's, the other is Szechenyi's," said one of my fellow-passengers. The road has been indeed built at the cost of the steam-boat company, but the noble Hungarian patriot, Count Szechenyi, is the life and soul of the undertaking, and the road is always called after him.

Again the Walachian boatman called out "*Ikonalui Trajan!*" (See the Tablet of Trajan.) This is the celebrated inscription cut in the rock by Trajan to commemorate the work of his legions. The point where it stands is extremely beautiful. Emerging from the narrow rocky pass, the wooded shore lay before us, and beyond, a little island, covered with shrubs, cornfields, and grassy meadows. The tablet was too high above the river for me to read, but the remains of the inscription, which are well known, will be found in almost every guidebook:

Imp. Cæsar. Divi. Nervae. F.
Nerva. Trajanus. Aug. Germ.
Pontif. Maximus. T. P.
Pater Patriae. Cos. P. P.
Monti D. . . . . . Bu.
S . . . . . . ati.

After passing the Tablet of Trajan we entered a broad and sunny valley, and in rather less than an hour we saw Orsova, the last town in the Military Frontier, lying before us on a bend of the river, at the entrance of a fertile valley.

VISIT TO A TURKISH PASHA AT NEW ÓRSOVA.

At Orsova we encountered our Walachian boyards again, but the most amiable part of our travelling society quitted us, to the regret, particularly, of the Frenchman and myself, who resolved to drive away our melancholy by some new expedition. We prepared accordingly for a visit to the neighbouring Turkish Pasha of New Orsova. A permission from the Austrian major commanding at Orsova was of course necessary (the superior magistrates of the military frontier are all military), and it was requisite we should have a double escort of health officers and custom-house officers, in order that we might not smuggle either the plague or a pocketful of salt into the country. The health office provided us likewise with a good boat and six oars, in which we embarked, well provisioned with grapes, cheese, butter, bread, meat, &c. We were soon again floating upon the centre stream of the Danube, whence the prospect is magnificent.

Austrian Orsova has the appearance of a flourishing place, stretching for some distance along the Danube, and to some extent into the country. Its trade is considerable, and was more so during the French continental system, when astonishing quantities of goods were sent up the Danube, and overland to Orsova, on account of the merchants of Trieste, who derived handsome profits from their speculations, though the merchandise was often doubled and trebled in price on account of the eccentric routes by which it had to be forwarded. This branch of commerce has now vanished, but the animation which it imparted to the trade of the Danube has not wholly disappeared.

Turkish Orsova lies on an island which divides the Danube into two arms of nearly equal breadth. The fortress was originally built, in a very solid manner, by the Austrians, when they were in possession of the island. It was then ceded to the Turks, but in the last war but one between the two countries was bombarded for several months, and was retaken by the Austrians after they had pretty nearly destroyed it. In this condition it was restored to the Turks at the peace.

On our landing, the health officers placed us between them, and marched us along to the pasha's house, which lay close to the water. We were shown up stairs, a health officer going before, sweeping and blowing the steps clean, and warning us, as we valued our liberty, not to touch any thing but what we received from their hands. We observed all possible caution, keeping our arms tightly pressed to our bodies, and the Frenchman, as he told me, was so careful of his extremities, that he did "his possible" to contract even his nose and ears to somewhat less than their customary dimensions.

A Turkish sentinel was walking up and down on the upper floor. In the background were some barefooted negroes and Arabs, staring at us with all their eyes. These were the household attendants of the pasha, their jackets and fezzes embroidered with gold, and their trousers of vast capaciousness. I was somewhat startled at seeing every thing so completely oriental. I hardly know what I had expected to see, but I had scarcely fancied I should so immediately find myself surrounded by African and Arabian elements.

It pained me to see the poor people shrinking timidly back, in their consciousness of our dread of coming into contact with them. Their notions about plague and quarantine are so different from ours, that I believe they think the Europeans hold them for unclean, and are too proud to touch them.

We entered the pasha's room, the doors and windows of which were standing open. It was a small apartment, and contained no furniture but a few chairs, and, in the corner opposite the door, a divan, on which sat the pasha and his interpreter. The pasha was a handsome man, about 45 years old, with a decided tendency towards corpulency. He had a red fez on his head, wore a blue frock coat with a standing collar, and from his neck hung a large crescent, radiant with jewels. This was a mark of honour bestowed on him, for his public services, by the late Sultan, for, it seems, we had now before us the architect of the fortress of Varna, a man distinguished for his military and mathematical acquirements, *enfin un homme de mérite pour la Turquie*, as some of my boyards afterwards expressed themselves.

In saluting him we took care not to strike out too far, either before or behind, lest we should fall into collision with some contagious object. The pasha returned our salute, and his servants placed chairs for us in the middle of the room, on which we were permitted to sit down, after they had been inspected by the health officers.

We expressed a wish to see the fortress, telling him we had come from Vienna for the purpose. He immediately said he would order one of his officers to show us over the works, but requested us, in the mean time, to remain with him a short while. There was nothing remarkable, he said, about his own house, but he had a better one in Constantinople, whither he was about to return, and where he prayed us to visit him. He said all this with the most obliging civility.

Pipes and coffee we were allowed to accept. The negroes handed them with outstretched arms to the health officers, and these presented them to us. The pipes were the costliest and most splendid articles of furniture in the house, and the coffee and tobacco were excellent of their kind.

The pasha told us he should very soon return to Constantinople, and had already packed up most of his things, or he would have shown us some fine mathematical instruments. He called our attention, however, to a fine Geneva watch, which he carried about with him, and also to a handsome telescope, through which we were all in turn requested to look. I, for my part, looked to the snug little houses on the Austrian side of the river, and felt as if from the very heart of Asia I was casting a glance into Europe. Nowhere, I believe, do the customs of the two continents meet so closely front to front, as in Turkish and Austrian Orsova.

After the pasha had made me give him the address of a good optician in Vienna, he offered us a second pipe and a second cup of coffee. My companion was for declining them, but I insisted on accepting the offered civility, as it might be some time before we should again have an opportunity of experiencing so courteous a reception from a Turkish pasha; the more so as in the interior of Turkey, travellers arriving from Germany were not likely to be so well received as on the Austrian frontier, where the pashas were often dependant on the Austrian officers for many little acts of kindness. My Frenchman grumbled, and was evidently out of all patience, but I was firm, and as he could not leave me, seeing he would then have been obliged to abandon the escort, he was forced to submit, though with a very bad grace.

I was particularly amused to see a copy of the Augsburg *Allgemeine Zeitung* in the room. The pasha told me he received it regularly, and that his interpreter had every day to read it to him in Turkish. It was his principal source of information, he said, with respect to what was going on at Constantinople. I told him he could not have chosen a better paper: that it was the one most generally read in Germany, and throughout the Austrian dominions, and even on the shores of the Black Sea, in all the best coffee-houses of Odessa. In Hungary I told him I had often seen, over the coffee-houses in small towns, a sign on which nothing was painted but a pipe, a cup of coffee, and a number of the *Allgemeine Zeitung*. I added that the paper was believed to have a circulation of ten thousand copies, and a public of at least a million of readers.

Thus conversing on various matters our second pipe came to an end, and the pasha, after thanking us for our visit, dismissed us most courteously. As we went out, I observed an enormous whip hanging against the wall: I was afraid to ask the use to which it might be applied.

A captain of a colossal size accompanied us as our cicerone. The town, we found, was thoroughly Turkish, the small houses lying concealed among bushes, trees, ruins, and heaps of rubbish. In the centre was a market with a number of stalls, and several streets, built with some regularity, ran off in various directions.

U

We were obliged to take especial care of the cats and dogs, and of the poultry, these animals being supposed to be particularly apt to carry the plague about in their furry and feathery habiliments. Our Turkish captain was kind enough to afford every assistance in these our labours, and was every moment taking up a stone to pelt some four-footed herald of the pestilence, that seemed disposed to intrude himself into our company. All strangers whom we met he beckoned with his sabre to keep out of our way.

In the market-place we found several merchants, who kindly invited us to sit down, and again presented us a pipe. I saw a public writer, in the old oriental costume, perched on a counter, and busily engaged with some manuscript that rested on his knee. We did not remain long here, as our conversation got on but lamely; we accordingly proceeded to the mosque, looking into a school on our way. The school was a low shed surrounded by trellis work. The little Turkish students were making a most heathenish noise, which contrasted amusingly with the quiet and sedate demeanour of their teacher who lay stretched upon a bench, where he smoked his pipe and said nothing.

The fortifications we found in a deplorable condition. The walls had not been repaired since the last cannonade, by which they had been all but demolished; or where a breach had been stopped up, it was only with a few wretched palisades, of which many were in a very dilapidated condition. Everywhere we had to climb over rubbish, dirt, and ruins; of cannons there was no lack, but there were few of which the carriages were not rotten, or that could have been made to bear on any object but the one immediately before them. Piles of cannon-balls of all sizes, covered with dirt and rust, lay about in all directions, and here and there we saw a sentinel, with his musket in one hand and his pipe in the other. They were mostly barefooted, and their clothes in rags. The force under the command of the Pasha of Orsova, to garrison the town and the two adjoining forts, consisted of two hundred men. Of guns, such as they were, there were upwards of eighty.

We made a present to the captain and to the interpreter, and embarked for Fort Elizabeth, or Shıstab, as the Turks call it. There we found about twenty-five soldiers smoking under a shed, and clad in uniforms, in the arrangement of which every man had been left to the free exercise of his own taste and ingenuity. Here also every hole and every heap of rubbish bristled with artillery, and on the ground lay a number of shells or hollow balls, which they assured us were filled with powder and other combustibles. Yet the soldiers smoked among them unconcernedly, and allowed us to do the same. Our Austrians assured us that we saw a fair specimen of all the Turkish fortresses along the Danube, and several travellers have assured us that we might see similar proofs of negligence and decay on every frontier of the Turkish empire. Exceptions, I suppose, there must be; it is scarcely possible that such places as Viddin, Varna, Silistria, and the Dardanelles, can be left in the same ruinous condition.

In the evening, when we had got back to Austrian Orsova, we found, with our Walachian friends, a gentleman from Constantinople, who told us that he had seen worse instances of carelessness in Asia Minor. He had there been one day in the tent of a pasha, where some wet powder was drying and being made into cartridges, and the men engaged in the work were smoking all the while. Our friend threatened to leave the tent if they would not lay their pipes aside, but they contended that as they were engaged in war they ought to accustom themselves to every kind of danger.

AUSTRIAN ORSOVA.

In Austrian Orsova, as in most of the towns belonging to the military frontier, many Turkish customs continue to prevail, particularly among the lower orders, although not the least trace remains of any Turkish, that is, of any Mahometan population. Even the Turkish weights and measures, the okkas, &c., have continued in use.

A proof of how the country must have improved of late years was afforded me by the complaint of a merchant. "Eighteen years ago," he said, "a man might go into the market-place and choose his workpeople; might say to one, 'You're strong, I'll give you eighteen *kreuzers*,' and to another, 'You're young, I'll give you only twelve.' Now, a mere child will ask you for twenty-four *kreuzers*, and a good labourer is not to be had for less than thirty-six. Land, too, is everywhere dearer than it was." Our Walachian boyards had several times made a similar report to us respecting their country.

In the market-place of Orsova may constantly be seen a number of Walachian women, selling grapes, peaches, and other fruit. It would be well if the dealers in the same line at Vienna would take example by the poor Walachians here at the extremity of the empire. Of the *Fratschelweiber* of the capital I have already spoken. Those of Orsova sit quietly by their baskets, quarrel neither with one another, nor with those who happen to pass by, but are almost always busy, either with their spindles, or embroidering their linen with red threads, which they work into an endless variety of neat patterns. Most of them, however, are engaged with their spindles, —the *furka*, of which I have spoken above, as being carved by the Austrian granitsharis, and from which the Walachian women seem incapable of separating themselves for a moment. The *furka* appears to be deemed an indispensable part of their costume. It is ever to be seen stuck in the girdle, and whether they be tending cattle, walking about, chatting with their neighbours, creeping behind the stove, or selling fruit in the market-place, the woollen thread never fails to dangle from the spindle. The Roman men were proud of saying that their swords lived in their hands as part of themselves. As far as the sword is concerned, the modern Walachians retain but little of the character of their Roman ancestors, but no Roman matron could have been more diligent with her spindle than are her Walachian descendants of the present day, and the idle quarrelsome *Fratschelweiber* of Vienna would find it for their own good, and for the good of all who come into contact with them, if they would take as diligently to the *furka* as do the poor market women of Orsova.

We made acquaintance also at Orsova with a teacher of the Greek language, who had arrived there from the islands about a year before. He had obtained an appointment to the city school, where I was told he received a salary of four hundred florins. In many of the Austrian cities along the Danube, Greek teachers are appointed in a similar manner. The want of them, it seems, had long been felt, but it is only within the last two years that regular appointments have been provided for them.

At present the Greek language is studied with great industry at many places all along the Danube, even as far as Vienna; and even at Neusatz I heard a mother complain grievously about the difficulty her son experienced in learning Greek, a language which it was so very necessary for him to know.

No where had I heard the subject of health so constantly discussed as at Orsova, and indeed throughout the Banat, whence I concluded that the country must be very insalubrious. It is so. Of the fevers in the districts, watered by the Theiss and Marosch, I shall have occasion to speak hereafter, but I was surprised to find that the marsh fever prevailed even among the mountains of the Banat. I was told, this might be owing to the want of cultivation in the valleys, where the waters accumulated in consequence, forming swamps, from which pernicious exhalations issued. Towards Mehadia the country becomes healthier, but on coming near Temesvar, we arrive again in a region in which fevers prevail to a serious extent.

On the following day, being market day, I had an opportunity of witnessing the singular manner of carrying on the traffic at the *Rastel* or *Skela*. The two words appeared to be used promiscuously. The *Skela* at Orsova is a large wooden shed, surrounded by a courtyard and an inclosure. The shed lies lengthways along the shore of the Danube, and is divided lengthways into three sections by two wooden railings. The Servians (or Turks, as they are here called) come to the railing nearest the river, after landing from their vessels, and the Austrian subjects come to the land railing. Both parties bring their merchandise with them, and show them to each other from their respective railings. The Austrians are at liberty to sell every thing to the Turks, but are allowed to purchase from the latter only such merchandise as are not deemed liable to infection, such as corn, fruit, meat, wood, and the like. As soon as they have agreed on the price, if it is the Turk who has to pay, he throws his money into a vessel filled with water, whence it is the Austrian's business to fish it up again. Austrian health officers and sentinels meanwhile are walking up and down in the intermediate inclosure, to see that the rules and regulations are strictly complied with. To me this was a highly interesting spectacle, and I thought the scene of the Rastel, if neatly produced on the stage, might be made highly effective as the opening of an act, provided the magnificent scenery of the Danube in the background was well represented, the Walachian, Servian, and Turkish costumes well preserved, the incessant border animosities between the Christian and Mahomedan population duly portrayed, and a little love story skilfully introduced, *he* being on the one side, *she* on the other, and the interest of the whole heightened by allusions to the dreadful pestilence, and the scarcely less dreaded severities of the quarantine laws. Indeed the whole military frontier is full of dramatic and poetical materials, and I believe a manager, a dramatic author, and a scene painter might find it well worth their while to journey hither together, and take a view of the whole country along the Danube, from Bosnia to Moldavia. It would be necessary, however, that they should travel on both sides of the river, for it is just the contrast between the Austrian and the Turkish sides, that might most effectually be turned to account.

THE HERCULES BATHS AT MEHADIA.

On the following day, I started in a carriage, to pursue the remarkable road along the Tsherna, with a view of visiting the celebrated baths of Mehadia. The Austrians have made an excellent road here. My Frenchman took leave of me with a promise to follow me to Mehadia, if his engagements allowed him to do so; but shortly after my arrival there, I received a friendly message from him, informing me that it would not be in his power to visit that interesting place. I am sorry to say I never saw him again.

Near Orsova, beyond the mouth of the Tsherna, is situated a small territory which is considered the common property of Turks and Austrians. It is a small uninhabited grassy marsh opposite the island fortress of Orsova. At ordinary times neither Austrians nor Turks must visit the place; but when the grass is ripe, the Turks come and mow it, and make it into hay. They then retire, and the Austrians proceed thither, divide the hay into two equal portions, take one of these away with them, and leave it to the Turks to come and fetch away the other.

Although the place lay a little away from our road, we visited the Austrian frontier post on the Tsherna, a post remarkable for being the place where all the Walachian cattle have to cross, that are constantly wandering into Hungary, to supply the deficiency caused by the demand of the Austrian market. The commandant of the post conducted us into his garden, in which there were excellent peach trees and Muscat grapes. The garden, and indeed the whole post, were situated on a small elevation, where there had probably been once a Roman fortress ; behind the garden we found some deep and solidly constructed vaults which the commandant made use of as a wine cellar. Beyond the Tsherna we saw immense droves of Walachian cattle. "They are still mixed," said the borderers, "but this afternoon they will be driven into the water, and after having been well washed, they will be considered to have been purified."

Mehadia is a large Walachian market-town in the valley of the Tsherna. In the time of the Romans the place was called *ad mediam*, which was corrupted, first into me-ad-diam, and in the course of time into *Mehadia*, by dropping the *m*, and introducing an *h*, to prevent the hiatus. The valley of the Tsherna to Mehadia is pleasing enough, but far less remarkable and interesting than the road farther up the valley from Mehadia to the Hercules baths. We remained, in the first instance, in the lower valley, whose several parts again have their different names, as the Shupanek valley, the Koramnik key, &c. In the Koramnik key, we descried, by the river side, a gipsy encampment, which we proceeded to inspect. There were about half a dozen families in as many tents. They were forging nails, and in doing so made use of a pair of bellows constructed of goat skins. Their domestic establishments were not a whit better than those of so many South American Indians, yet they cherish an extraordinary degree of pride, as I was assured by my companion, an inhabitant of the Banat. He told me, he had observed that the gipsies had even more national pride than the Jews, maintaining that they were the oldest nation in Europe. There are more gipsies in the Banat and in Transylvania than in any other part of Hungary. This is owing to the circumstance that the population is chiefly composed of Walachians, who more than any other people seem to harmonise with the gipsies. Schwartner, a trustworthy writer on Hungarian statistics, says—"The gipsy attaches himself more readily to the Hungarian than to the Slavonian, but of all nations he sympathises least with the German." Many Hungarians have made me a similar assurance, which, for my part, I am disposed to look on as a compliment, rather than otherwise, to us Germans. In the Banat, and, indeed, throughout all Dacia, the gipsies live under tents in summer, but in winter they have their particular places where they congregate, many hundred families living together in caverns and clay huts.

They all speak the Wallachian dialect, but among themselves they converse in their own gipsy jargon. The Walachians, who have most intercourse with them, have adopted a number of words by which to designate them and their doings. *Tshiganu* is the Walachian for a gipsy, but is meant as an opprobrious designation when applied to any one else. *Tshiganié* means gipsyism, or *ratio Zingarica*. *Tshiganosu* means importunate, or as importunate as a gipsy. *Tshiganescu* is used as a verb, to signify importunate solicitations (*petesco importune*), to beg as importunately as a gipsy. *Tshinganesce*, an adverb, means as much as gipsy-like or filthy.

If the gipsies are really of Indian origin, as there is every reason to suppose they are, and if they have left many kindred tribes in that part of the world whence their ancestors formerly came, the fact would say but little in favour of Indian susceptibility of improvement, seeing that the race has spent four centuries in the midst of European civilisation, without divesting itself of any part of its original barbarism. One thing, however, is certain. The gipsies are decidedly decreasing in numbers everywhere. At present, in Hungary, they confine themselves to the occupations of smiths and musicians, having lost the office of public executioner, which they formerly held. In the sixteenth and seventeenth centuries many Transylvanian grandees had their heads hacked off by the unskilful hands of gipsy hangmen, and it was by gipsy hands that the celebrated peasant king, Dosa, was placed on a red hot throne, and had his head encircled by a red hot crown.

We found it difficult to tear ourselves away from our gipsies; firstly, because I am never tired of contemplating this wild race, and, secondly, because they seemed in no hurry to allow us to depart. They had begun to beg, and as my travelling companion had shown himself tolerably liberal towards them, they redoubled their importunities, rushing out upon us *en masse* from all their tents. Their beggings and supplications increased in intensity till they had formed an impenetrable barrier around us, and, at last, they began even to lay hold of us by our clothes. We had the utmost difficulty in forcing our way through them, and our driver afterwards assured us, that if we had been stripped to the skin, we should not have been the first to whom such an incident had occurred.

Above the Koramnik key, supported by the steep wall of a rock, are the remains of a beautiful aqueduct. Eleven arches are still perfect, the others have been destroyed. Antiquaries are at variance as to the origin of this aqueduct. The magnificent style in which the work is constructed might lead us to attribute it to the Romans, still the details of the workmanship seem to argue against such a supposition. The arches are composed of large field stones and red bricks, a double stratum of bricks resting always on a fourfold stratum of large field stones.

Towards evening we diverged from the great military road which leads to the Terregova pass, and after passing several Walachian villages, and crossing the river twice by two elegant suspension bridges, the sulphurous smell by which we were assailed, announced to us that we had arrived at the main building of the great bathing establishment.

After having arranged matters a little in my room, I proceeded to read the laws and ordinances of the watering-place, a complete code having been suspended against the door. One of the first rules that caught my eye was the following: "Any guest wishing to a kill a lamb, a calf, or any other beast, is not allowed to do so anywhere except at the regular slaughtering-block fixed for that purpose." This article of legislation appeared to me to be characteristic of the kind of visiters in the habit of frequenting these celebrated waters. The Hungarian and Transylvanian aristocracy who come hither in search of health, are, of course, furnished with their meals by the restaurants of the place, in the same way as at our German watering-places; but, owing to the passion for sulphur baths, which prevails among all classes, there are constantly among the visiters many Hungarian and Walachian peasants, many townspeople of small means, and many of the petty boyards of Walachia and Servia, and these people, by way of economy, bring their own provisions and cooking apparatus with them, and to them it is that the ordinance I have just quoted is meant to apply.

This passion of the Walachians for sulphur baths occasions frequent disputes with the Austrians on the subject of the boundary. The Austrians have drawn their line on the top of a high ridge of mountains east of the river, while the Wallachians of the neighbourhood maintain that it should be formed by the river itself; but I confess I can just as little understand this claim as that of the French to the left bank of the Rhine, for the boundary as it exists was determined by the treaty of Belgrade, in the year 1739.

With the left bank of the Tsherna, however, the Walachians would gain some of those much coveted hot sulphurous baths, which they can now only enjoy after having performed quarantine, and the temptation has sometimes proved so irresistible that great bodies of peasants have gone out, armed with swords, pistols, cudgels, and pitchforks; have attacked, and sometimes driven back, the Austrian frontier posts, and have seized on the disputed territory. Only a few months ago, we were informed, the Austrian government had to send several companies of soldiers to drive them back. This little frontier war has been continually breaking out for more than a century.

Besides Mehadia, there are among the mountains of Transylvania many of these sulphur baths, which are much frequented every summer both by boyards and peasants, and as the Slavonian women of the military circles wash their infants with brandy to strengthen them, so the Walachians dip theirs in the sulphurous waters of these springs.

Even in the time of the ancient Dacians they were probably not entirely unknown, and the emperor Trajan discovered and took possession of them for the Romans, who erected here many buildings,—temples, bathing houses, and others, so that the whole valley is full of Roman antiquities.

An intelligent and well-informed Austrian colonel of the military circles assured me that he had never made an excavation in Mehadia, without some discoveries of coins, bronze statues or votive tablets. The present name of the Hercules bath has its origin in a temple of Hercules, that formerly stood here. The name is given particularly to the main spring, which is indeed a Hercules among all the sulphur springs in the world. It is larger even than the great spring at Ofen, and gives out no less than 5,045 cubic feet of water in one hour.

Many of the statues, inscriptions, &c., had been fastened into the rocks, and my Walachian guide spoke of some of them as familiarly as if he had been present at the time at which they dated. "Look there," he said, pointing to a half effaced *bas-relief* of two Roman women, "that's a lady and her daughter who came here to use our baths. The young lady had lost the use of her hands and feet, and before she went away she was able to dance." On one of the tablets a Governor of the Dacian provinces "*Præses Daciarum*" and on another a Prefect Mercurius and his family, returned thanks to Hercules and Venus, or to the Gods and Genii of the waters (*Diis et numinibus aquarum*) for restoration to health. Under Trajan, Hadrian, and the Antonines, up to the time of Decius, these baths continued to be used, but the great irruption of the Northern nations threw every thing into confusion, the place was forsaken, and for centuries a few huts or tents occasionally appearing among the Roman ruins, were the only signs of human occupancy which it presented. About a hundred years ago, it began to grow a little more animated, and at present the establishments are on so good a footing, and the reputation of the waters so widely extended, that it has become quite a fashion among the Hungarians of distinction to visit Mehadia.

Like every thing else in this frontier country, the whole bathing establishment is under military command. An Austrian captain resides here winter and summer, and is intrusted with the regulation of every thing. The two principal buildings, occupied by guests of the highest rank, are built in a long regular form, like barracks, on each side of a broad street, and their interior, it must be confessed, presents no more comfort and elegance than might be reasonably expected in a barrack. The attendants are mostly invalid soldiers. Further on are other buildings, inhabited by the gentlemen above mentioned, who are requested to slaughter their calves and lambs at no other than the appointed place. There are always a number of quite poor visiters, who come with their families and their whole stock of goods and chattels, and quarter themselves here for a considerable time; and there is a place appointed for the tents of the gipsies, who come in the bathing season to play music, tell fortunes, mend pots and pans, and beg. There are also shops and booths for the traders, who bring jewellery, manufactured goods, and various other articles, in the hope of disposing of them during the season.

We arrived at Mehadia at the end of the bathing season, when the little company that remained was expected to leave it the next morning. Among them was a Wallachian lady from one of the most distinguished Greek families formerly resident in Constantinople. She had been born and brought up to the age of thirteen in the Fanal, and had lived a most monotonous life, her only recreation being an occasional row on the Bosphorus. Since the revolution, however, all these families have emigrated to Russia, Wallachia or to Athens. The lady of whom I am speaking was herself married to a principal boyard of Bucharest.

I passed one very pleasant evening in this little circle, but the following morning came a row of carriages, each drawn by a team of horses, whose collective energies would probably be all found necessary to drag the vehicles through the almost bottomless roads of Wallachia and the Banat. I employed the rest of the day in rambling about the environs, and as far as the neighbouring frontier village Pechineska, which is reached by a pretty path along the banks of the Tsherna. We found this little place in a most extraordinary state of bustle and excitement, and all the inhabitants working away with a most tumultuous activity.

It appeared that an ordinance had been issued by the military authorities, directing the ruinous old hovels of the village to be pulled down, and new ones to be built in their stead. This was sadly in opposition to the favourite old Walachian saying, " So I have found things, and so I have left them," a saying that well expresses their partiality for the dirt and dilapidation inherited from their forefathers. In the neighbourhood of so frequented a watering-place as Mehadia, a different race of peasants would long since have bethought themselves of improving their houses, and rendering them attractive to visiters; but these people had to be driven by the hand of authority to care for their own convenience and their own advantage. A certain term had been fixed, within which they were required to complete their buildings, and they were therefore now toiling like so many ants, with beams and stones, and mortar. Even the women were helping, and some gipsies had been hired for a dram and a few *kreuzers*, to put a hand to the good work. "You are very busy here," said I. "Must be, sir—must be!" was the answer. Beyond the village, embosomed among the high hills that stretch towards Turkey, lay a lovely little valley, through which wound a silver streamlet that had just force enough to turn what is called a Walachian spoon-mill. The little wooden building, a sort of square box, stood click-clacking upon four tottering feet over the slender thread of water, and we ascended by a small ladder and through a low door into the upper part of the mill. Here we found a handsome young Walachian woman in full costume, with her beads, coins, long plaits of hair, her *Opinches* and *Opraches*, spinning away with her distaff, and at the same time looking after the grinding of her Kukurutz, or Indian corn. A mill of this kind usually belongs to a whole village, and every one, when he has occasion for flour, brings his sack of corn, and grinds for himself. The mill appeared to do its work very thoroughly, if we might judge from the slowness of its operations, for we could count each grain as it fell through, and it seemed to grind each separately.

As we left the mill, the Walachian woman began to relieve the tediousness of her employment by singing. Some goats, which she had brought with her, frisked about in the rich grass, and among the nut, plum, and wild cherry trees, that grew in abundance around; and the whole scene, enlivened by the click-clack of the mill, the murmur of the brook, and the warbled song, was really so pretty a picture of Walachian rural life, that I could hardly prevail on myself to return to the baths.

At every turn there, we were reminded of the Romans; the rocks are exactly in the same state as when the abovementioned prefect (*cum suis*) sought health among them. The people are dressed precisely as they are depicted on the Trajan's column at Rome, and much even of the language which the barbarians learnt from their conquerors still lingers in our ears. A letter which a *Dacian* messenger brought to a lady of our company began the address with "*Dominæ*," and when he had been waiting some time, he inquired if there were any "*Responsum*." He was answered in the negative, but money was given to him, which he was going to put up without counting. " Numera, numera!" exclaimed the Roman centur—I mean the Austrian lieutenant. It is to me inconceivable, considering the short time the Romans held Dacia, the torrents of different nations that have since streamed over it, and the storms of political anarchy, in which their empire has been wrecked, that so many traces of their existence here should still remain. Their language and character seem to have something of the tenacity of musk—where it has once been, its scent is left for ever, though all the winds of Heaven should blow over the place.

THE UPPER VALLEY OF THE TSHERNA AND THE LIFE OF THE BORDERERS.

On the following morning, which rose clear and bright after several rainy days, we prepared for an excursion into the upper, wild part of the Tsherna valley. Some of the mountain horses had been ordered by the officers who were to accompany us, and we found them at the appointed place, and at the time fixed on. These horses are as small as those of the Tatars of the Crimea, and distinguished by similar qualities, being surefooted, sagacious, and capable of enduring an immense deal of fatigue, but rather vicious in their dispositions, and ugly in appearance. They are native to the whole Alpine chain which separates Walachia from Transylvania, and are used by travellers and huntsmen on the military frontier, and for all kinds of transport;—for instance, for dragging timber out of the forests, which are inaccessible to carriages. They are called "*Morani*," that is, "inhabitants of the Alps." When we first set off, they kept continually kicking, and biting one another's tails, but as we began to climb the mountains they became quieter.

The groups of rocks which lie round Mehadia are piled up in enormous masses, above which some peaks rise still more conspicuously. The highest is the renowned Domoglett, from which it is said one can see into Roumelia. No geologist has ever yet described these rocks and mountains,—no botanist investigated their rich and interesting flora, no ethnographer explained the peculiar features of the life of man on these lofty regions. They offer a wide field for discovery in each of these branches of science, but the few observations I was able to make were directed only to the last-mentioned subject.

Along the topmost ridge of these mountains runs a chain of Austrian outposts, as far as Tsherna—the limit of her eastern frontier. From here the line runs along the western bank of the Tsherna, the upper part of which is on both sides Turkish! The lower declivities of the range present many abrupt precipices and rocky ravines, but the summits are finely rounded, and covered with beautiful meadows and pasture grounds. On these have been established little pastoral communities resembling those of the Swiss Alps; and the Germans of Transylvania never call these mountains by any other name than that of the Alps. These long grassy ridges usually belong in common to several neighbouring villages, and the manner in which the property is distributed is this:—In the spring of every year, a general assembly is held of the inhabitants of these villages, each bringing his flocks and herds with him to the place of meeting. These are counted, and, according to their numbers, a longer or a shorter period is assigned, during which the owner shall enjoy the whole produce and emoluments of the cattle belonging to the whole community; to one two days, to another three, to the richer a week. Each then proceeds in his turn with all the herds to the mountains, where he occupies a cottage, erected for the purpose, and makes into cheese and butter all the milk he can obtain from the cattle of the community, and then gives way to his successor. These general meetings (of which unluckily I have forgotten the name) are so important to the people that they serve them as epochs whence to reckon the different times of the year, as we do from Easter or Christmas. Their principal wealth consists in their flocks of sheep, as their horned cattle is of a small and poor breed. I was told they were in the habit of mixing the milk of sheep, and even of goats, with that of their cows. Here and there are herds of horses, of which the borderers have sometimes so many, that they scarcely know their number. According to Hietzinger, this military frontier, which has not more than one-fourth of the population of Bohemia, has 50,000 horses more than that kingdom.

The military frontier of Transylvania is not organised like that of Hungary. It forms no separate territory in which the whole population incurs the obligation of military service, but the troops, on whom this duty is laid, live scattered about in various parts of the country, and come at the appointed time from great distances to the "Cordon." The finest of these troops are the Szekler hussars, though the Szeklers have besides two infantry regiments. These Szeklers form one of the three nations inhabiting Transylvania (Saxons and Magyars are the other two), for the most numerous people, the Walachians, pass for no nation at all. The Szeklers boast of being the direct descendants of the men of Attila, although this can be just as little proved as that they are a Magyar people, as is asserted by the Hungarians. One thing, however, is certain, that the Szeklers speak the purest Hungarian, and have longest preserved the ancient customs of their supposed ancestors. Each of the houses on the frontier belonging to the Szekler regiment are obliged to furnish one hussar, and to equip him from head to foot. The officers equip themselves, and in consideration of this are released from all other public burdens.

The Szekler hussars have the best horses and the best uniform; and while the other eleven Hungarian regiments of hussars are said to excel all the other hussars in the world, these Szeklers again are considered to be the aristocracy of the hussars of Hungary. They are the lightest and most skilful cavalry in the world, and at the same time a bold, frank, and noble spirited set of men. Their high reputation, and their romantic life on these Turkish frontiers, has induced many English officers to join them. The whole regiment does not come together above once in every four years, but to those who take an interest in these things, to see the Szekler hussars go through their exercise, is counted one of the prettiest spectacles in Europe, and alone worth a considerable journey.

The whole valley of the Tsherna from the Hercules baths to the source of the river at Pietrilla Alba, a distance of eight German miles (nearly forty English), contains not a single village, nay, not a single house with the exception of the Austrian and Walachian guard-houses, and is a perfect wilderness bearing not a trace of human cultivation, but the paths trodden by the shepherds from the mountains to the river side, and the patrol-roads made in particular directions across all these desolate military frontiers.

The enormous rocky chasm which forms this valley, resembles in many particulars that of the Clissura through which the Danube flows. There are the same chalky cliffs, assuming the same forms, and about the same height, almost the only difference being that through the one rushes the mighty Danube, and through the other the little Tsherna. I should therefore think that, geologically considered, this valley must be a northerly continuation of the Clissura, and that both have had a common and simultaneous origin in consequence of some volcanic developments. In an historical point of view, this ravine is one of the most remarkable in Europe, and its appearance is the more striking, from the contrast of the dry and desolate character of its north-eastern parts to the well watered and cultivated country that lies on the west.

In proportion to the scantiness of the human population of this valley, —that being indeed no more than a few frontier guards, and wandering shepherds,—is the abundance of animal life, especially of the wilder sorts of each species: eagles, chamois, and bears. The eagles settle on the rocky peaks, and during our day's ride I saw several rise up rejoicing into those fields of light to which we can scarcely look up. The chamois, called by the Walachians "*capra de munte*," inhabits the whole range of Dacian Alps, and is found generally thoughout the Carpathians. With respect to the buffalo, it is singular that neither the natives of the country, nor those who have written about it, can agree whether the animal is really an inhabitant of these mountains or not. Bears are said to be very frequent, though I saw none; but there were many wild rocky caverns, which imagination might easily people with such tenants. The gates formed by these mighty masses of rock that lay across the valley, had seemed to close and open, and close and open again many times, showing at intervals long vistas of gigantic fragments and columns, at which the Cyclops might have toiled a long time, ere they had succeeded in piling them up. At length we reached the little frontier post which was to form the goal of our present journey. The sentinel who was pacing his lonely round, looking first into the Austrian, and then into the Walachian territory, informed us that the officer in command was unluckily, not at home, having gone out to inspect his cordon, but he might be back every moment. We entered his abode and found but little provision for the comfort of the lieutenant, beyond a wooden camp bedstead, and a small table on which lay some German books. The space allotted to him lay on one side of the door, and that to the common men on the other. The latter was almost taken up by a broad wooden bench without straw, for sleeping on, and on the wall hung a row of bags made of goat-skins, for holding flour, cheese, and even milk, which is always kept in skins.

The life of the officers of these frontier stations is extremely hard, and full of difficulties and privations of all kinds, and they doubtless often dream of the gay societies and balls of Karlsburg or Hermannstadt; but man accustoms himself to no kind of life more readily than to what is strange and peculiar, and there are many officers who have a passion for these frontiers, just as sailors have for the sea. If from their lonely posts they sometimes look with longing to the social joys of the town, it is no less sure that from the midst of these exciting pleasures, they often think with regret of the freedom of these romantic solitudes, and the unlimited power which they exercise over a great extent of wild country. Every officer is expected to keep a vigilant watch over the district intrusted to him, though the majors and generals do not, of course, visit the cordon so often as the subalterns. The most active and difficult service is at both extremities of the Military Frontier, namely, at the Bosnian and Dalmatian border, and at that of Transylvania. In the centre, on the Danube and the lower Save, it is easiest, partly because a water frontier is more easily guarded than a dry one, and partly because the people are more united and civilized. The dwellers on the western border are unruly and barbarous, and strongly inclined to a predatory mode of life: and as the Turkish government has not found itself strong enough to repress the excesses of the Bosnians, it has given the Austrians permission, once for all, to disregard the inviolability of its territory, and to pursue and take offenders on Turkish ground. Should the Bosnians, as it has sometimes happened, make an onslaught and burn an Austrian village, the Austrians are allowed, in their turn, the "gentlemanly satisfaction" of setting fire to a village in Bosnia, or driving off cattle, without incurring any danger of a war with Turkey. Such proceedings as these have been sometimes necessary among people who would be kept quiet by no other means. It is not long since two companies of the Austrian frontier guard crossed the border on an expedition of this nature, and, of course, on their return from Turkey, had to perform quarantine.

The Transylvanian cordon has also peculiar difficulties to contend with. In the first place the frontier is a dry one, and the line runs either through rocky ravines, or along the top of wild desolate and naked mountain ridges, where for leagues around no human creature is ever seen, but an occasional wandering Walachian shepherd. These mountains are said to be very insalubrious, and as liable to fever as the plains of the Banat. This information, at least, I had from an officer whom I met returning, sick and languid, from an excursion among those hills, where he had been inspecting his cordon. In the second place, the neighbours of the Transylvanians, the Turkish Walachians, are less peaceable and honest than the Servians. The Germans accuse them of being a mere nation of robbers, and certainly the stories of banditti, and of the famous band in particular which ravaged the country under the renowned chief "Harumbassa," to whom they had sworn obedience in life and death, are repeated till the traveller is weary of them. He must listen a thousand times to the narrative of all that took place, about two years ago, at Kimpolung— a sort of robber fortress on the borders of Bukovina, and how there was a certain chief at the pass of Boza, who made all the roads in the country unsafe for travellers.

"At Kimpolung," said an Austrian to me, "the robbers were whipt, broken on the wheel, hung, but it all did no good. About a year ago we had a great robber hunt. There was a numerous band which for months had scoured all the frontier countries. There was no finding out who they were, for they never allowed any of their companions to be taken prisoners, dragging them away when wounded, or if they could not do that, killing them and cutting off their heads, which they carried off, so that the bodies could not be recognised. At last when they had been driven into a corner, and much reduced in number, they mutinied against their captain, murdered him, and sent in his head, on which they imagined all their sins might be heaped. In time however they were all taken and hanged, for here on the frontier, every act of robbery is punished with hanging, even when unaccompanied by murder."

The Austrian posts are sometimes attacked by the Walachians, as I have already mentioned, without any view to plunder, but merely on the supposition that the boundary line has been unfairly drawn. One of the officers told me that only a short time ago, a mob of sixty Walachians had come to his post, and demanded that the Austrian eagle should be torn down, and the guard-house destroyed, since it stood on Walachian ground. Fortunately he had at the time twelve men with him, as the relief had come, and the old watch was not yet gone, so that he found himself able to resist force by force, and with his twelve men drove back the sixty, and pursued them far into the Turkish territory. He and his troop had then as a matter of course to march into quarantine. Along the whole Transylvanian frontier are little quarantine establishments for daily communication, such as the *Rastell* I have described at Orsova.

The Transylvanian Alps present many remarkable natural phenomena, such as the whirlwinds, which in hot summers are very frequent. An Austrian officer told us that he had been lately wakened in the night by a terrible noise, the cause of which he could not at the time conjecture, as the air and every thing around appeared perfectly still; but that on the following day he had discovered, not far from his post, a number of trees torn up by the roots, and lying in many places in a circle. Forest conflagrations also often take place in these woody regions in the month of August, and sometimes darken the sky with smoke, so that for weeks neither sun nor moon nor star is to be seen.

I was sitting with my companions the Szekler hussars, in a sort of little arbour, which the soldiers had built near the guard-house, when I heard the exclamation, " See there he is, and the Szeklers sprang up to meet their friend, a young Croat officer, who came well armed, and riding on a stout little mountain horse, over the high wooden bridge which crosses the rocky bed of the river Tsherna, meeting the patrol road on the other side. In his company came also two " *Serreshans*," mounted like himself, and completely armed. The Croat, who was the commandant, returning from a night patrol, bade us welcome to his hut in a most friendly manner. He appeared to be a well-informed, intelligent, and most amiable man, and spoke moreover very good German. I must remark, by the way, that though we were of various nations (Germans, Magyars, Slavonians and Walachians), yet our conversation was always carried on in German. We returned to the arbour, where after a time some wine, some good river water, and a sort of frontier national dish, made of lamb and bacon chopped up with onions and herbs, which must have been a most elaborate prepation, to judge from the time the soldiers were cooking it, was served up to us.

My attention was soon turned to the companions of our hospitable entertainer, the *Serreshans* of whom I have spoken, and with whom I had been much struck on account of the peculiar and very complete equipment by which they were distinguished from the rest of the troops on the frontier. Their uniform has been probably modelled on some national costume, which has now become extinct. It consists of a close doublet with four rows of glittering buttons, fitting like a coat of mail, and over this a wide cloak with a hood, which in rainy weather is drawn over the head. Their pantaloons were in the Hungarian fashion, very tight, of a sky blue colour, and gaily embroidered. Their thick stockings were also worked in coloured thread, and their hair, like that of the Hungarian shepherds, woven into thick plaits, and hanging down over their ears. Their features were the most regular and handsome that I had seen on the Walachian frontier. In their girdles they carried Turkish weapons, a yataghan and two very long pistols; a cartouche box hung down before, and a rifle, highly ornamented in the Turkish fashion, was thrown over the shoulder. Their whole dress and appearance was as picturesque and poetical, as that of an ordinary peasant soldier is prosaic.

These Serreshans form a separate corps in the service of the military frontier, and have had time out of mind their peculiar duties, and peculiar organisation. It may be that in them is to be sought the kernel of the old military inhabitants of the country, or they may be successors of the old frontier guard of Matthias Corvinus. They are in some measure the gendarmes of the frontier, and a small troop of them, a hundred or two hundred men, is attached to each frontier regiment. On the whole there are about a thousand of them, including a company on the Dalmatian coast. They are like bloodhounds in the pursuit of robbers and smugglers, and every officer takes some with him, on his visit of inspection to his cordon. They are as well acquainted with the ground and with the people on the Turkish as on the Austrian side; know all the affairs of all their neighbours; have immediate information of any design that is set on foot on either side, and are respected and feared by friend and foe; besides being the heroes of most of the daring feats that are performed in the frequent skirmishes with the Turks. Like all borderers the Serreshans serve without pay, service being, as the Austrians say, their "*robot*" or feudal service. Curiously enough, their officers are called by the Turkish name of "*Bassi.*" The colonel is called Haram Bassi or Upper Bassi, the subalterns Vice Bassi.

These Serreshans, the commandant of the Cordon, my Szekler friends and myself, the six soldiers who had returned from the patrol, and all our horses, made up a tolerably large party; filling not only the arbour, but also a little hut made of the bark of trees, such as the officers often put up near the guard-house, and where they like to pass the warm nights of summer. There we took our meals very pleasantly *al fresco*, and to me, the native of a Hanse town, it was a pleasurable circumstance that the watchword given for the night along the frontier happened to be. "The city of Hamburg." The *Hofkriegsrath*, or Imperial Council of War, in Vienna gives the word for every day in the year, and this passes not only along the frontier, but through the whole army. It is usually a proper name, of some individual or of a city, as for instance, "Aloysius," "Jerusalem," or, as to-day, "The city of Hamburg."

After the conclusion of our repast it was determined to pay a visit to the neighbouring Walachian frontier station, which lay opposite to the Austrian one of Tsherna where we were. We proceeded accordingly along the Austrian patrol road, and, crossing the Walachian boundary line, came to a high terraced land, covered with grass, behind which the rocks rose again to a giddy height. A more remarkable contrast, than that between the Austrian and Walachian station can hardly be imagined. The ancient Dacians cannot have existed in a more barbarous state than that in which we found the people on the Walachian frontier. We had scarcely entered the terrace or "*plateau,*" when three or four rough Walachian dogs, such as are always kept about their frontier stations, sprang at us. Our Serreshans kept them off with stones and cudgels, it being desirable, no less on account of the plague than out of regard for the safety of our legs, to keep them at a distance. A Walachian sentinel clad in sheep-skins, with a cap of the same material so covered with large woolly curls that it looked almost like a wig, was walking up and down before a hut made of boughs and moss; our call as well as the barking of the dogs summoned a few Dacians, also clad in sheep-skins, who came crawling out of the hut and approached us. We ordered them to stand still at a distance of twenty paces, which they immediately did, and called off their dogs. We entered into conversation with them and asked them how it happened that they, "*Romani*," that is, descendants of Romans, should not appear to be in a more prosperous condition. "Nay," they answered "*Domini! Imperatu nostru* is not so great and rich as your's. He takes our money from us, and never gives us any back." We asked whether their officers often visited them? "They had not been there for some weeks," was the answer; so that it appears that the Wallachians take their duties easily, whereas the Austrians patrol day and night on their border. "These Walachians, however," said one of the Austrian officers, "are good-tempered, obliging fellows, though somewhat given to thieving. They are often of great use when we want to have a bear or chamois hunt on their ground, for they trace the game with almost canine sagacity, and clamber up the steepest and most difficult paths to drive it down to us."

It is not surprising that a people so barbarous should be subject to the grossest superstitions. They believe, for instance, most firmly in the vampire, as it is called; that is, in a dead body which they suppose rises from the grave to suck their blood. Many who have believed themselves persecuted by such visitations, have even died from the effect of their excited imaginations. The idea that people can be rendered bullet proof is also common among them; and a frightful and disgusting notion prevails that this impenetrability can be obtained by eating the heart of a young child. This dreadful superstition is found also on the Austrian side of the border, especially among the *Serreshans*.

The Walachians brought from their hut a quantity of tobacco-pipe tubes, which they had cut from a very fine kind of shrub, called Weichsel, or Vistula reed, which grows all over these mountains. An extensive trade is carried on in this article to various parts of Europe, and visitors to the baths of Mehadia usually carry some of these tubes away as *souvenirs*. They are found also in the military circles, but the people are not allowed to gather them. They are of course much cheaper here than in Vienna and Leipsig, where an amateur would pay several florins for what here would cost only a few kreuzers; but like all that is rare in its kind, they are apt to withdraw from the common haunts of men, and are found best, and in greatest abundance, on the highest and most inaccessible rocks. We could not unfortunately make use of any of the pipes, but we presented our Walachians, on leaving them, with some tobacco, which they divided peaceably among them. On leaving them we passed up a little shepherd's path, through a wood, to another terrace similar to the first, and thence we had a most beautiful and romantic prospect of the wild valley beneath; the upper part of the Tsherna breaking through wild craggy rocks. At many apparently inaccessible points we noticed caverns, which, like those of some of our mountains at home, are full of bears' bones, with this difference, that our bears' bones lie buried in antediluvian clay, and those found in these Transylvanian caverns are covered with warm flesh and blood.

The bear of these regions is, according to the description of my companions, the Szekler officers, of a very large and strong race, but not the less on that account, like all his wild brethren, inclined to shun the face of man. Whenever he meets one he usually stands still, and, after reflecting for a moment, turns round and walks off. He eats almost every thing he finds; Indian corn, roots, fruits, goats, sheep, and even young wolves and foxes; but he is himself eaten by none in return, not even by man, for the people of the country have a superstitious dread of eating bear's flesh. He lives mostly in caves in the chalky cliffs; but in the valley of the Tsherna, there is some moist meadow land covered with fern of extraordinary size and thickness, among which, either to cool himself, or to watch some other animal, the bear is frequently found lying, and at certain times of the year he is never absent from it. He sometimes goes to the river to bathe, and sometimes to catch fish; and when the clumsy beast comes tumbling down over stock and block from his den among the high cliffs, there is a noise as if a fragment of rock were rolling down into the valley. The best fish in the Tsherna are the trout, and these are also the favourite morceaux of the bear, who sits watching his opportunity near the stones under which the trout lie, and from time to time hooks them out very cleverly, and tosses them on the bank. Sometimes he will strike on the stone where he suspects the trout are lying, in order to drive out the fish; and when he is pursued he will snatch up stones or logs of wood, to fling them at his assailants, not, however, until he is wounded, for till then he thinks only of making his escape. Many of the caverns in these mountains, from which bears or banditti have been driven, now serve as dwellings to the Alpine sheep or goatherds, and some of them even pass the winter in these holes, and keep their cattle the whole year out, feeding on whatever scanty herbage they can find. The goats are generally, in these cases, accommodated with the interior of the cave, whilst their herdsman lies by the fire near its mouth.

On one of the terraces above the Tsherna we found a little Walachian shepherd, who enjoyed the privilege of coming thus far, because he furnished the officers of the guard-house with goats' milk; in general the shepherds are obliged to keep at a respectful distance from the frontier posts, as it is feared the temptation to carry on a little smuggling trade with their Turkish neighbours would be too great for them to resist. A bag, or even a large lump of crystallized rock salt, that any of these poor fellows may be tempted to buy on Turkish ground, where they can get it so much cheaper, is sure to be spied out by the argus eyes of the Serreshans and frontier patrols. When they find themselves closely pursued on these occasions, they sometimes let it fall, taking care at the same time to leave some rags behind, or some piece of clothing, as these articles are supposed to carry contagion. A separate sentinel is then left to watch every scattered article, and the number of pursuers being thereby much diminished, the offender has a better chance of escape. Some very formal and elaborate proceedings are then commenced, to determine the proprietorship of the abovementioned rags, which, however, must only be contemplated from a certain distance, and after an immensity of writing, and long examinations and investigations, the question, who is the owner of the rags and the salt,

x

often remains undecided. The forest round has then to be scoured, to see if any more salt and rags can be discovered, and wherever they are found they must be left lying, and a guard stationed over them. A report must then be made to the nearest quarantine establishment, running nearly thus—" Yesterday evening certain Walachian smugglers attempted to carry salt across the frontier, but were detected and put to flight. They have, indeed, escaped, but they have left their salt behind them. One bag has been found under such a tree, a lump behind this or that rock—a cap or a waistcoat here or there. Proper persons have been stationed to watch these things, and it is now requested that some of the health officers may be sent to carry them away." After the lapse of a certain number of days the health officers arrive, and taking up the dangerous commodities with iron tongs, carry them to the place appointed for the purpose, where the rags are burnt, and water being dashed over the lumps of rock salt, it is regarded as purified by the baptism, and fitted for the service of western Europeans, who little think by what an expenditure of toil and trouble Austria defends them from the contagion of the plague.

Our friendly host the Croat commandant, with some of his soldiers and Serreshans, escorted us to the next post on our way back to Mehadia, but I was tempted to linger behind the party to explore one of the caverns of which I have spoken, formerly the abode of a renowned band of robbers. As it had by this time become late in the evening, my faithful guide, "*Juri*," (whom I had hired for the period of my stay at the Baths,) kindled a torch which he had brought with him for the purpose, and after tying our horses to a tree, we climbed a little way up the rock to the mouth of the cave. It is one of the largest in the whole Tsherna valley, being called, *par excellence*, the Robber's Cave, and must have been used as a sort of fortress or robber castle, as before the entrance in the rock are to be seen the remains of walls by which it was completely enclosed. In the interior it is divided into several compartments. We had to crawl on our hands and knees from one to another; but after passing through several, we arrived at a more lofty and spacious chamber, which may have been used by the robbers as a magazine, or a dormitory, or a banqueting-hall, or for all these purposes. The largest chamber is a hundred feet long, sixty feet high, and fifty broad, and the gentlemen of the road may have resided here with more comfort and convenience than their brethren, the robber-knights of Germany, within the narrow bounds of their castle-walls. In the background the cave narrowed to a mere cleft, which is said to continue quite through the mountain, and to communicate with other strongholds of the same description on the other side. My guide muttered to me, half in German and half in Walachian, something which I did not entirely understand, but as well as I could make out, he was informing me that in ancient times the famous *Robber Captain*, Hercules, lived in this cave.

As we rode on to follow our companions, I noticed a peculiarity in my little " Mokanu," (mountain horse,) that I had not observed before. While he was trotting along at a good pace, he held down his head as near as possible to the ground, and let me pull him up as often as I would, down went his nose again on the first opportunity. My guide told me the creature was tracking our party who had gone on before, as a dog would have tracked them, by the scent.

I could not hope to overtake my party after the time we had spent in the cavern, so I resolved to take this opportunity of visiting, before my departure, the cave of the Hercules spring. Through a narrow cleft in the chalk cliff, we penetrated to the spot where the clear hot water rushes impetuously out of a natural aperture, whence it is carried into the adjoining bathing-house, and distributed over various apartments, as well as into a large common bath. On the sides of the rock are inscriptions, as well ancient as modern, and near the common bath is a statue of him whom my guide, "Juri," persisted in calling the great *Captain* Hercules. Here was the greatest destroyer of robbers that ever existed, metamorphosed into a chief of banditti! The statue is always said to be of Hercules, but the lines and features are so much defaced as to be scarcely recognisable, for the Wallachians have a habit of scraping it, and drinking the dust mixed with the warm water of the spring, as a cure for some diseases.

The Romans, according to Mr. von Dorner, in his interesting work on Mehadia, as well as the moderns, esteemed this Hercules spring more than any of the other one-and-twenty. The cavern from which it proceeds, is said to perforate the mountain completely, and above is another opening from which sulphureous vapours ascend.

THE KEYS OF TEREGOVA AND SLATINA.

I had now reached the extreme limit of the Austrian monarchy on the south east, where it meets the Turkish territories, and I had to seek an interesting route for my return. I chose for that purpose the great diagonal running from this south-eastern corner of Hungary through the Banat by Temesvar and Szegedin, to the centre of the country, Pesth. It is both in an historical and a commercial point of view a most remarkable tract, being the way by which Trajan penetrated into Dacia, and that by which, in the last century, Joseph advanced against the Turks. The greatest part of the trade with Turkey also travels this road.

The equipage which I hired for this journey, was no other than a common peasant's cart, the boards of which, patched very neatly in various places, and covered with hay, formed a very comfortable seat. It was drawn by three stout little *Makanus*, harnessed together with ropes and thongs and strings of all kinds, whilst my own costume was not much more elegant; for, having found it rather too light for the cold of these mountain regions, I had supplied its deficiencies with various handkerchiefs and wrappers, and a large sheep-skin which the commandant of Mehadia had kindly bestowed upon me. It seemed to me as if I ought to be ashamed of such an equipage when I entered on the fine smooth road that might have befitted a very different kind of carriage. Since, however, no one here knew me, and no one could meet me the next day, and say, "My dear Mr. ———, what a pretty figure you cut yesterday," I managed to console myself, especially as the subaltern officers of the *Præfecti Daciarum* always travel in the same style; and I kept up my courage, even though I met several travellers differently equipped, who undoubtedly looked down upon me as a person of very little consequence. I met for instance the family of a great Walachian boyard, returning from where I know not, to their own country. They had several large Vienna travelling-carriages one behind another, each drawn by a dozen horses, and each crammed full of various members of the family, with their waiting-maids, valets, cooks, footmen,

&c. Behind came a waggon-load of hay, sacks of oats, kettles, pots, and pans, and all kinds of cooking utensils, on the top of which, other attendants were perched. This is the usual manner of travelling for the great in this country, and I can honestly say, I preferred my farmer's cart.

The valley of Bella Reka, although not to be compared with that of the Taherna, is pretty and variegated. The higher one rises, however, the more it assumes the character of a wild and monotonous highland. The hills are mostly steril with occasional intervals of wood, and some scattered patches of cultivated land, besides a few Wallachian hamlets, defended by high thorn hedges, against the wolves and bears, and the ill-attended cattle which are almost equally mischievous. On some of the hills we saw the remains of castles and fortresses formerly erected against the Turks. They were mostly of a quadrangular form, from ten to fifteen fathoms high, and divided into three compartments or stories, much like the towers now built as a defence against the Russians by the people of the Caucasus. These towers are met with as far as Karansebes, where the last bears the name of Ovid's tower, because it is said that Ovid passed here a part of the period of his renowned exile. From the Banat to Varna, and from Varna to the mouth of the Dniester (Ovidiopolis), every district seems to claim the honour of having inspired the *Tristia*, for there are no less than five different places where Ovid is said to have poured forth his melodious repinings over his misfortune of having seen at the court of Augustus more than he ought to have seen. It appears, however, tolerably certain, that the name of Karansebes, is not, as some learned patriots of the Banat will have it, derived from Ovid's *Cara mea sedes*, for he died seventeen years after the birth of Christ, and the Romans did not conquer Dacia till about a hundred years after our era.

The little thrashing-places of the Walachians in the open air, formed also a characteristic feature in the landscape, but on the whole we were less indebted to Triptolemus than to Pan for amusement on our road, that is supposing the latter divinity to take under his protection not only the Idyllic sheep and oxen of Arcadia, but also the great herds of Walachian cattle destined for the slaughterhouses of Vienna. In no country in Europe, perhaps, is so much butchers' meat eaten as in Austria, and, notwithstanding the quantity raised within her own territories, she requires a very considerable importation. It appears to me that as Hungary possesses about 5000 German square miles of pasture ground, it ought to be able to satisfy the appetite at least of the city of Vienna, but such is not the case, and the void created by the hungry tooth of man, in the great Hungarian herds, has to be filled up from foreign countries. The swine which come up the Danube we have already mentioned. The roads chiefly traversed by these great herds of foreign cattle, are two: the first from Moldavia, Bessarabia, and Southern Russia, through Galicia, Moravia, and over the Carpathians; and the second from Walachia by Orsova, on which we were now travelling. We passed continually great herds of beasts whose horns were all turned towards Pesth and Vienna. As we drove through them at a rapid pace there was usually a tremendous hallooing between the herdsmen and my driver, Martin, who I must confess was not over careful. The wild voices and gestures, and the barbarous exterior of these men, exceeded any thing of the kind I had ever seen, but their cattle were just as civilized in appearance as our own.

It is a well-known and indisputable fact, that all the herdsmen in the world are thieves; this phenomenon has never yet been sufficiently explained, but its truth is not to be controverted, and it may be inferred that a road, so much frequented by herdsmen, is not likely to be a very secure one. Fifteen or twenty years ago, I was told, even in broad daylight, it was dangerous to travel here without being well armed and accompanied. At present accidents of this kind only happen in the night; the police of the military circles is much improved, and the fine new road that has been made has contributed greatly to the security of travellers. As a proof of the necessity of vigilance, and, at the same time, as a guarantee that it is afforded, I noticed all along the road guard-houses erected, usually in the vicinity of the toll stations. Formerly the Serreshans patrolled here day and night, but this is now done at night only. What the Serreshans are in the military part of the Banat, the *Playashes* are in the interior of the province—namely, a police against banditti. The leaders or officers of these *Playashes*, I was told, had a Turkish appellation, and were called "Bulibashas," and throughout southern Hungary, almost every comitat has a different name for its gendarmerie. They are in some places called *Tshetniks*, from the Turkish word "*Tsheta*," meaning "the troop;" sometimes *Hadnagy*, *Haiducks* or *Persecutores*—words which have all the same signification.

We passed over a mountainous ridge, and arrived towards noon at *Teregova*, which lies near the source of the Temes, and at the entrance of the celebrated "Key," or narrow pass. The form of the country at this place is the following; the land is high, but still much lower than the mountain masses which lie on the east and west. The highest western point is the *Semenik*, and in the east the Sarko; from these two mountains, —the latter of which is seven thousand feet high, the former five thousand, —run three ranges of less elevation, which connect the two together. The first of these ranges—the one we had just passed over, has only a slight depressiom from which the waters on either side flow into the Danube and the Theiss; the second and the third range are broken through by rivers; from the Semenik flows the Temes, and from the Sarko the Hideg, which unite near Teregova, and force their way through the second and third ridges. The first of these is called the Teregova Key; the second, that of Slatina, and *key* appears to be the usual term for these narrow ravines, as "Irongate" is for the greater mountain passes.

At the desolate Teregova we found an inn kept by a handsome young German married couple, where we dined better than we had done in many a coffee-house at Vienna. They brought us, as a great rarity in these cold regions, some grapes, which had been sent to them from Orsova. A fellow guest, a huntsman, who was also going to Karansebes, determined to take a place by my side in the hay-cart, and only begged permission to take up with him a large sporting dog, alleging that the shepherds' dogs of Walachia were so vicious, that he could not venture to let him run behind, since a wolf could hardly defend himself against them, much less a sporting dog.

Our host informed us that if I had come a little earlier, I might have seen a waggon-load of leeches with which a Frenchman had passed by in the morning. He added, he had for many years furnished horses for these French leech dealers, and that these animals were obtained mostly from Walachia, Hungary being no longer able to supply the demand of Paris for leeches, any more than that of Vienna for beef. This leech trade is quite a separate trade, and the waggons pass from stage to stage through all Hungary, Austria, and Germany, direct to Paris. The French traders are supposed to belong all to one company, some members of which reside in Orsova, where they contrive to get the leeches smuggled in small parcels from Walachia, whence their exportation is prohibited. At Orsova they have a great pond in which they collect all they get, and from there they transport them to Paris, it is said, in fourteen days. The waggons are very carefully constructed for the purpose they are intended for, in the form of a huge chest pierced with holes, and divided inside by a kind of trellis work, into a great number of compartments, each capable of containing a bag weighing six Okkas, that is sixteen pounds and a half of leeches. This chest is very carefully placed on springs to avoid jolting. The leeches, when first taken from the ponds are put into the bags and hung up to dry in the air, for they must not be carried wet. They then roll themselves up like balls, and remain in a sort of torpid state during the journey. A hundredweight of leeches costs the French dealer in Orsova four or five hundred florins, and to the value of ten or fifteen thousand florins are often carried at one journey. The trade in leeches is one of the most delicate and critical that can be imagined. Should the weather be very sultry, the greater part of the cargo die on the road, and a frost suddenly coming on is equally fatal to them, moderately cool weather being the only weather that agrees with them. In order that there may be no delay on the journey, the traders agree with the peasants of the villages they pass, or with the landlords of inns, to have the required number of horses in readiness, and they send some one forward, or make some signal previously agreed on, such as cracking their whips in a particular manner as they approach, to announce their arrival. When this is heard, the people hurry out and have the horses ready on the road by the time the waggon comes up. In many places on the road by which the leeches come, as at Baya on the Danube, French traders are settled, who have ponds in which the leeches can be placed to be refreshed after the journey, and those who may have died on the road are carefully picked out. In this manner this description of merchandise is carried the whole way to Paris where the leeches are often sold at half a florin a piece.

In some places there are regular leech plantations in which the animals are bred; these are large ponds, the banks of which are covered with turf, and where the "Calamus Aromaticus," a plant considered to be peculiarly wholesome for them, is often planted. They sometimes, however, die by thousands, in spite of all the care taken of them, without its being possible to discover why. Much depends on the manner of catching them; the French often fish for them with Russia leather, probably smeared with something agreeable to the leeches, for they fall on it, and cling to it with the greatest eagerness. Others are caught with sieves, which some of the dealers regard as the best method. The growth of these creatures is astonishingly slow; in the space of five years, their increase of size is scarcely perceptible. In winter, it is necessary to take them from the ponds for fear of frost, and put them into vessels in underground cellars, with a layer of clay alternating with every layer of leeches.

There is a great trade in leeches from Wallachia and Poland, as well as from Hungary, where indeed the trade is falling off. Berlin, Bremen, Hamburg, and the whole North of Germany is furnished from Poland;

and many barrels of them go, viâ Hamburg to London, where they fetch a higher price than anywhere else—often five or six times as much as in Berlin.

Beyond Teregova we passed the first " Key," a deep narrow winding, woody ravine, about half a German mile long ; this led to a wide valley or basin, which again narrowed to the second " Key," or pass, that of Slatina. This place is called by the Walachians, " *Prolaz*," a word which like " Islaz," appears to signify merely a Pass or Passage. After passing Slatina, the valley of the Temes widens more and more, until it becomes a complete plain, on which is conspicuously placed the town of Temesvar.

As we descended into the valley, the mountains seemed to close behind us into a perfect wall stretching from summit to summit. Our eyes had so long rested on nothing but rocks, that they now wandered with delight over the beautiful surface. It was very warm—nay sultry, and Martin, my driver, stopped at a well to water his horses; our thirst also was no more to be extinguished than Greek fire, and most gladly would we have indulged ourselves with some of the fine blue plums with which the trees in every village were loaded. They were so covered, that the foliage could scarcely be seen for the fruit, yet we did not dare yield to the temptation, for the plum is said here to occasion fever. Our driver, who had but just recovered from this malady, made a wry face at the tempting fruit, and the delicious blooming plums proved but a deceitful Fata Morgana to our parched throats. Instead of refreshing the thirsty wanderer, the fruit serves only for the manufacture of a coarse spirit, the fatal and pernicious " *Raki;*" and for this purpose only, it seems, are the great plum orchards maintained, which soon began to weary me by their frequent repetition.

The last terrible Turkish deluge, that swept over this region, that laid its villages in dust and ashes, and destroyed or put to flight its whole population, took place in 1787, and many terrible scenes connected with it, are still fresh in the memory of some of its inhabitants. The landlord of an inn I stopped at, related to me that he and his parents had fled before the advancing Turks, and he remembered well, with what longing, they and countless other fugitives had daily watched for the coming of the Emperor Joseph, and with what fear and trembling on the other hand, for the approach of their barbarous enemies. On their return, after the Turks had been driven back, they had found their city razed to the ground, with the exception of the Franciscan convent, which was still standing. Before the altar of the church was found the body of the prior, in a state of decomposition.

The invasion of the Turks about fifty years before, in 1738, was so much the more terrible, that the plague broke into the country with them, and carried off six thousand persons in Pesth and Ofen.

At a village called Petroshnitza, Martin made another halt. He usually unharnessed the horses, and left us and the cart under a tree, while he took them to the water, and let them drink to their heart's content. The weather had become extremely hot, and my shawls and sheep-skins of the morning quite superfluous. The whole village seemed to be enjoying its afternoon's nap, for not a creature was to be seen; the cows dozed round the farms, and only the geese, the ever wakeful guardians of the capitol, screamed the announcement of our arrival. Two hogs, feeling, like the other inhabitants, an inclination to repose, lay down by the wheel of our cart. Like all their swinish brethren of this country, they had a long thick stick fastened in front of the breast by a string round the neck, to hinder them from breaking through the hedges into the gardens, which they are very fond of doing. At the window of a house a kitten was awake, apparently because she could not succeed to her mind in an attempt she had made to get a comfortable seat in the cap of an Austrian official personage, the said cap being too small and of too narrow a shape to answer her purpose. The bees, however, did not yield to the luxurious laziness of this "sleepy hollow," for they were humming away on the garden side of the houses as busily as ever.

"There will certainly be a storm," said the huntsman, my companion, as we drove away from this drowsy community. This was by no means agreeable intelligence, so I resolutely maintained there would be no storm.

The huntsman desired me to look back at "Muntje Sarko" and "Muntje Mik," how black the clouds were that hung over their summits, and besides, the lightning was already flashing among the mountains. Like certain statesmen, however, who, when they see threatening appearances in the political horizon, look the other way, and deny their existence, I kept my eyes resolutely fixed in the direction where the sun was still shining, and denied that matters looked so menacingly upon us. The dispute was over, however, by the time we arrived, wet to the skin, at Karansebes.

KARANSEBES.

The magnificent storm, which, however inconvenient in some respects, had certainly in others enhanced the pleasure of our journey, was so soon over, that I had time, on the evening of my arrival, to deliver a letter with which I was furnished to a worthy ecclesiastic of the place. In a country circumstanced like the Military Frontier, there can never be any want of subjects of conversation among those interested in literature and science. The materials are so abundant and so fresh, that two persons of any degree of cultivation meeting here soon become as of one heart and one soul, as I and my priest did when he invited me to spend the evening with him in his arbour. Our conversation naturally turned upon Trajan, for all who have been here since, have been, more or less, barbarians. The country belonged, it is well known, to the Roman province of Dacia Ripensis. It was conquered by Trajan at the battle of the Iron Gate, in which he totally defeated Decebalus, who, preferring death to slavery, put an end to his existence by poison. He and his predecessors,—Dorpora, Kotiso, &c., —must have been people of some character and energy, since they gave the best of the Roman emperors such hard work to subdue them, and it is but fair to conclude, that the people ruled by such sovereigns must have made some progress in civilisation. Yet of this people and of their civil polity no record has reached us, and of their history we know only the close! Here too Lysimachus waged war even before the appearance of the Romans. I know not whether our learned antiquarians have yet decided in what part of the country it was that he fought the disastrous battle which ended in his captivity; but it was probably in the neighbourhood of Karansebes, where some of the coins of Lysimachus continue to be found to the present day.

The whole country round Karansebes is so rich in coins of various kinds,—Thracian, Greek, Roman, and Byzantine,—that it does not redound much to the credit of our learned inquirers on these subjects, that the ground has been so much more diligently explored for purposes of pecuniary profit, as by mining operations of various kinds, than for those of science. To show how rich the field is for research, I may mention one fact, on the authority of my ecclesiastical friend. Four weeks before my arrival at Karansebes, it had been formally notified to the commanding officer that a quantity of silver coins had been found in a hole recently dug in a field in the neighbourhood. The coins were brought to him and recognised as Roman;— there were ninety-five of them of pure silver. A chest appeared at one time to have been placed in the hole, as the impression of its shape was still distinctly visible, and there were evident traces of its having been lifted out with a lever. The coins thus carelessly left by those who had taken it away, may give some idea of the number and value of the rest. From the apparent size of the chest it might have contained more than a hundred and fifty pounds weight of coins,—enough to make an antiquary's mouth water! But let him hear the end of this story, and the water will come into his eyes instead of his mouth.

Inquiries were set on foot to discover the thieves, and at length a woman, whose husband had absconded, confessed that he had been one of the treasure finders, and that he and some others had turned what they had found to their own use. They had intended to melt the coins, and sell the silver to a silversmith, and this had actually been the fate of a part of the treasure. They had melted *"about seventy* pounds." *Seventy pounds* of historical documents! Seventy pounds of finely-executed, speaking witnesses to a certain extent, of the state of things in that gray old time! Nor is this instance by any means a singular one.

Among the many remains of Roman enterprise and industry which this country presents, some of the most remarkable, perhaps, are the "hundred shafts" (*Centum putea*) sunk in the Banat mountains, which are cut, in a very laborious manner through the solid rock. As the Russians have their Siberia, so had the Romans their Dacia, and, with the one as with the other, to be condemned to work in the mines, "*ad metalla damnari*," was considered as a severe punishment. The wonderful works to which I have alluded, were executed entirely by poor "*ad metalla damnati*," under the guidance of Roman officers. I was unfortunately not able to visit either these, or the iron mines of Russberg lying to the right of Karansebes, and which have of late years again acquired celebrity.

These were formerly "*Ararisch*," that is they were worked for the benefit of the government. Such a mode of exploitation, however, is sure to be productive of little profit ; and, in this, as in many similar cases, the carelessness, indifference, or dishonesty of the persons employed, prevented any advantage from being derived from the mines. In the year 1826, they were, therefore, disposed of to private persons, and since then they have become, all at once, so productive, as to supply nearly all the most considerable iron-works in Hungary, and the iron mines of Russberg have, in consequence, assumed a very important position in the Austrian monarchy.

There are mines of all kinds in the Banat mountains, which are but a continuation of the Transylvanian chain, so abounding in metallic riches, a great part of them probably still undiscovered. Gold is generally obtained here, as in most other parts of Hungary, by the gipsies, from the sands of the rivers, no gipsy being suffered to continue in the military frontiers who cannot deliver at least three ducats weight of gold in the course of the year to the government at a very low price. Whatever they bring above this quantity is paid for *al pari*. The gold is usually procured from the sand in the manner I have already described, but they frequently dig for it in the mountains, where there are often found, very little below the surface, strata of earth containing the precious metal. In most cases the gipsies have much trouble to get together the required quantity of three ducats weight, but they sometimes make a lucky hit. Thus, for instance, a gipsy found, in the year preceding my visit to Karansebes, a piece of pure gold of the value of seventeen ducats.

On the following morning, by permission of the commanding officer, and in company with my new friend the priest, I visited the schools of the place. They consist, as in all the principal places on the frontier, of three classes, there being a girls' school, an upper or normal school, and several elementary, or, as they are here called, "*Trivial*" schools. There are also, for the whole Walachian-Illyrian military frontier, four division schools; and besides these there is, or *should* be, in every village, a national or commune school.

The normal and division schools are maintained by the government, and stand under the immediate superintendence of the War-office at Vienna. In these schools instruction is always conveyed through the medium of the German language. The "Trivial" schools are often private establishments. The commune schools, in the villages, though instituted by the government, are maintained at the expense of the parish, and instruction is given in the language of the place. Besides those I have mentioned, there are in almost every considerable town of the military frontier, German town schools. The same system prevails in the Transylvanian military frontier.

The school buildings which I visited at Karansebes, are not only good, but excellent. As it happened to be vacation time, I could not attend any of the lessons, but I saw some performances of the pupils, which were to be sent to the Hofkriegsrath in Vienna. They consisted mostly of specimens of calligraphy, exercises from dictation, themes, and mathematical and military drawings; and I must say that, had they not been provided with German teachers, I do not think Walachian, Slavonian, and Illyrian children could have produced such creditable evidence of their aptness to receive instruction. The object in view in their education seems to be, not only to educate them as men, but also, before all else, to make them good and well-taught frontier soldiers. For this purpose the subjects of the essays or themes, were very suitably chosen, such, for instance, as "Report to the captain concerning a case of smuggling," "Account of the damage done by a mountain torrent," &c. The maps and surveys taken, were also of the immediate environs, such as drawings of a neighbouring mountain, charts of the patrol roads of the frontier, and so forth. The mathematical pupils form a separate class of the upper school, from which the best scholars are taken for non-commissioned officers. From these posts it is possible for them to rise, even to the highest ranks, and there are many instances of Walachians of low birth who have done so. As there exists in the military frontier no class of privileged nobility, and as the noble officers of the Austrian army are not very fond of this frontier service, there prevails perhaps more freedom and equality of competition in this division of it, than in any other. In the mathematical class I have mentioned, there were in the year 1841, eighty-six scholars, and in the other three hundred. This number, I was told, was greater than it had been in preceding years. I was sorry to hear that a general aversion to these schools prevailed among the frontier population, and that it was generally found necessary to use some constraint to induce the parents to send their children. One branch of instruction appeared to me quite peculiar to these schools; that, namely, of "Instruction of the children in the duties of subjects," for which three hours in the week were set apart. This may perhaps be, among people whose notions of political institutions are so very confused and imperfect, and from whom, nevertheless, so exact and precise a fulfilment of duty is required, a very wholesome kind of instruction. It seems to me a very remarkable circumstance in the history of these frontier provinces, that the inhabitants have often appeared to prefer a military to a civil administration. On many occasions where parts of them have been placed under civil jurisdiction, the people have petitioned, of their own accord, against the change, and have received as a boon, a restoration of military rule.

LUGOS, TEMESVAR, AND THE BANAT FEVER.

After taking leave of my ecclesiastical friend, I ascended a vehicle belonging to my German landlord, who drove it himself. He had two fine horses that, to use an allowable hyperbole, carried us away with the rapidity of the wind, and for which he had paid only three hundred florins, Walachian money—that is, about fifteen Louis d'ors. On the right of the new Austrian road, after leaving Karansebes, are seen the remains of an old Roman road, partly covered with earth and grass, and in some parts completely obliterated by the plough of the husbandman. This country is the classic centre of ancient Dacia, and the spot towards which the wishes and dreams of Walachian patriots are oftenest turned, for we must not imagine the Walachian nation has entirely lost the remembrance of its former greatness. I have been informed on good authority that in Bucharest, the question of the revival of the kingdom of Decebalus has been seriously entertained. Its capital, destroyed by Trajan, was replaced by his flourishing colony of "*Ulpia Trajani Augusta, Colonia Metropolis;*" and a chain of Roman colonies ran thence through Transylvania, as far north as the sources of the Theiss, where the last was called "*Paralissum Colonia.*" The town of Hatzeg, in the Hatzeg valley, is supposed to occupy the precise spot on which stood formerly the capital of Decebalus.

As we were now crossing this chain of Roman colonies, the wars of Trajan naturally occurred to us, and certainly when we consider the enormous extent of the Roman empire of that day, it is difficult to conceive how so great a man could allow himself to be entangled in almost purposeless wars in this obscure corner. When we recollect the provinces of Spain, and Gaul, and Britain; of the Euphrates and the Tigris; of Egypt and Africa; and when we think of all that might be taking place over so vast an extent of the earth's surface, one would imagine the ruler of such an empire, to be desirous of occupying a central position, where he might receive information from all sides, and send forth his messengers to every quarter, instead of fighting among these obscure mountain passes, and exposed every moment to personal danger. My reverie was disturbed by an Austrian soldier demanding my passport, and reproving me sharply for not having had it visé at Karansebes. Through the whole Military Frontier, they are very strict on the subject of passports, and it is necessary to have them inspected at every turn, a thing by no means necessary in Hungary.

At this point the black and yellow flag of Austria appears for the last time, and is replaced by that of Hungary. The advantages of Austrian order and regularity are also exchanged for Hungarian freedom, which is sometimes very inconvenient in its peculiar mode of development. In the military frontiers, where the Emperor is the original proprietor of all land, which can only be held as a military fief; and where no officer can possess more than his fruit and vegetable garden, and is not allowed to hold other land even on lease, there is not a trace of a landed nobility. As soon as we cross the Hungarian border however, we hear on all sides of the great landlords and their estates. The principal nobility of the three comitats of the Banat, consists chiefly of new families, of Servian or Armenian origin. They are great cattle dealers, who, frequently amassing considerable wealth in this occupation, purchase estates in the Hungarian territories, where nobility is more easily obtained, and confers greater privileges than in any other country. These emigrations and settlements of Servian families in the Hungarian Banat, have been so numerous, that it has become quite a New Servia, the capital of which is Temesvar. Prince Milosch wished to purchase an estate in the Banat, but was not allowed to do so.

My coachman of this day had a very different opinion than he of yesterday, concerning the fine plums of which I have made mention. He said it was all nonsense and prejudice to suppose that the fever proceeded from the fruit, for that it was caused by the water of the Banat; and thereupon he plucked me a beautiful branch covered with plums as large as hens' eggs. He said so much, however, concerning the raki made from them, that I ceased to regard them with admiration. From the most beautiful and useful things, does man in all countries learn to procure this fiery poison; here from plums, in Russia from potatoes, in Sweden from corn, in France from grapes, in India from rice, and the Calmucks even from milk, apparently the most innocent substance in the world.

I heard a great deal of good of the Germans of the Banat, of their modes of agriculture, especially of their fields of tobacco, a plant which requires most careful cultivation; the Walachians think more of their fields of Kukurutz, or Indian corn. The warehouses for the preservation of this grain are peculiar to the country, and apparently well adapted to the purpose they are intended for. These buildings, which are seen by the side of every Walachian dwelling, and which, even on the estates of the great proprietors, occupy no small portion of the farm buildings, are called *Kukuruztkoras*, and are built in the following manner. A barn is constructed, exceedingly narrow,—about five or six feet in width, and from thirty to forty, or even as much sometimes as two hundred feet long, according to the wealth of the proprietor. This attenuated looking edifice is raised upon piles, to guard against damp, and is made of a kind of basket work, that the air and the sun may penetrate into it. The maize, which cannot, like other corn, be thrashed immediately after it is reaped, is packed closely in the *Kora*, and left there the whole winter to dry and ripen.

Walachian pigs, Walachian oxen, Walachian buffaloes, Walachian sheep, were our fellow-travellers the whole way to Lugos. In attendance on every herd, were commonly several Walachian drovers, wild ferocious looking half savages, though, perhaps, all the while, good honest fellows in their way; and some Servians on horseback, the owners of the cattle or their agents, armed with two or three pistols and a yataghan. Some of the animals had bells, which awakened pleasant thoughts of the Swiss Alps, till I came in sight of the bearer of the bell, when, instead of a comfortable-looking cow, adorned with garlands of flowers, I generally encountered a great ugly grunting sow.

One of these great herds, not long ago, actually broke down the iron bridge of Lugos, and it lay in lamentable fragments when we passed it, driving through the water to enter the town. It happened that just as a herd of buffaloes was crossing the bridge, they were met by some dogs who began barking at them. The front rank retreated, the whole was thrown into confusion, the noise of their trampling feet on the bridge rendered them still wilder, and at last they got wedged together in the centre of the bridge, where they stamped and raged, till down came buffaloes bridge and all, into the middle of the river. Many were killed, and others so badly hurt, that they had to be immediately slaughtered, and on many a table in Lugos, roast buffalo beef was had that day at a very low price. Some people maintained that the bridge had been badly constructed, others that the timbers furnished for the purpose had been bad and rotten, and the comitat which had furnished it must pay the damage; some laid the fault on the drivers, and some sought to find out the owners of the dogs, but on whom the responsibility was finally laid I know not. The case may serve to show that public works of this kind should be prepared for extraordinary, as well as for ordinary accidents.

At Lugos the mountains gradually sink into low hills, and thence, by imperceptible gradations, from hills to downs, from downs to mere slopes, until they gradually melt into a perfect plain.

At the inn at Lugos, not a creature came near us till we had stood a long time stamping, knocking, and vociferating, and this was the more inconvenient, as the rooms were all double locked. I recollect observing the same thing on my first entrance into Hungary at Eisenstadt, but no where throughout the whole military frontier. There we invariably met with good attendance, clean apartments, and excellent provisions. It would be strange if this were the result of mere accident.

Lugos is divided into German Lugos and Walachian Lugos, and this separation occurs in many of the towns of the Banat, nay, even villages are sometimes so arranged that the Germans live on one side of the street, and the Walachians or Servians on the other.

I was awakened on the morning after my arrival in this city, by a noise, which, however unpleasant, is by no means uncommon in the Hungarian comitats—the clank of fetters. Criminals are not only employed by the government, but are even allowed to go about to private houses to earn a few pence by their work, though never without their fetters; and, I have often met them clattering about the streets without any superintendence whatever. It was Sunday morning, and I visited the different churches of the place, both Greek and Roman Catholic. In the former, which is here called the Illyrian church. I found a few *Playashes*, in very showy uniforms, and many Wallachian men, but few women. In the Roman Catholic church, which I attended afterwards, the case was reversed. In the arrangements of the Illyrian church, the mode of crossing, the kissing of images, the manner of performing mass, and all but the melodies of the choirs, there seemed to me the most perfect conformity with what I had seen in the Russian and other Greek churches. The men all stood in front, and formed the main body of the assembly, while the women were scattered about behind. This circumstance also was precisely reversed in the Roman church. In the latter there are at least three times as many women professedly devoted to the service of religion as in the former. May not these differences be traced to the different spirit that prevails in the two religions? The Greek is by far the most prevalent form of worship throughout these eastern frontier provinces of Austria; in the "*Gespannschaft*," to which Lugos belongs, there are 156,000 Greeks, to 15,000 Catholics, and no more than eighty Protestants.

Among the few things worth mentioning, that my short stay at Lugos allowed me to see, I should not perhaps omit mentioning some pictures, by an Austrian artist named Prestel, not merely on account of their merit as works of art, which was considerable, but partly also on account of the local and characteristic nature of the subjects. The one represented a part of the Hungarian steppe, a wild boundless desert waste, over which hung the veil of evening twilight, rendered still more obscure by a low hanging cloudy sky, with only a faint streak of light on the distant horizon. In the foreground rides the principal figure, a Hungarian herdsman, on a wild, rough-looking animal, at full gallop. Before him, across his horse, lies a bleating calf, which he is carrying off like a wolf, having taken advantage of the twilight to steal it. The robber's hat is plucked down over his face, his spurs are plunged into his horse's side, and he is looking fearfully back to see whether he is pursued. The other picture also represents a part of the Hungarian steppe, on which a race of Walachian and Hungarian peasants is taking place; many of their waggons are seen in the distance, some drawn by as many as fifteen horses, three and four abreast, with troops of foals gambolling by the sides of their mothers. In the foreground is one, I believe a Hungarian waggon, drawn by only four horses, the long whip is flying about, the dust whirls up in clouds, the driver bends forward to animate his horses, who seem ready to spring out of the picture, for the painter has turned all their heads and breasts towards the spectator, and no foreground intervenes. The execution of both pictures is admirable.

I know not whether it was from the lively impression made by these pictures, or from any other cause, but I felt the greatest unwillingness to leave the hill country, and the greatest dread of the monotony of the desert steppe I was about to enter upon. It was a dismal rainy morning, and the little open waggon in which my goods and chattels were packed, looked uncomfortable enough. Remembering the manner in which the Hungarian peasants tear along the road, I was about to inquire of my landlord the Walachian word for "slowly." On glancing, however, at the little wretched-looking pair of horses that I had to draw me, I made up my mind that it would be more useful to have the command of some native word, or phrase, implying "get on."

On the road from Lugos to Temesvar, the greater part of the villages are inhabited by Walachians, but here and there already German colonies are met with. The Walachian villages are all, like the other villages of the Banat, built on a regular plan, and very few of them are older than the last century. Some are in the form of a square, or parallelogram, having a free space in the middle, for the church and government buildings, with immensely broad streets, regularly crossing at right angles, through their whole length and breadth. Some are built in a circle, with the church lying in the centre, and the streets radiating from it in all directions; and some form merely two parallel lines along the road; but since the ground of a great part of the Banat is as flat as a chess-board, any plan may be carried out without difficulty. I found the drive through these Walachian villages exceedingly amusing, and always rejoiced when I discovered a church steeple in the distance. The broad streets were usually covered with geese, turkies, pigs, and other animals, as far as one could see, and the women and girls diligently spinning their white wool, and twirling their spindles, moved about among them, gossiping with their neighbours, or carrying a meal into the fields for their husbands or sons. They all wore the hair in great broad plaits, and adorned with silver pins and buttons. The men I saw but seldom, partly because they were occupied with the vintage. It rained the whole day; but this to the Walachians was matter of rejoicing, for they say the skins of the grapes are softer, and that more wine is obtained, after a rainy vintage than when the fruit has been gathered in fine weather. The vineyards lay in the open field, and round them were drawn up numbers of small waggons, near which oxen were grazing. Upon these waggons were placed vessels for receiving the fruit of the grapes trodden out in the field, an operation usually performed with the feet, but for which there is also a wooden implement, divided at the bottom like the fingers of a hand. With this they crush the grapes, and then dip in a pot to take out the juice. This gives the best kind of wine; the grapes are afterwards pressed a second time, and from this second pressing an inferior sort of wine is made.

At one place I saw the vintage carried home. The master and owner of the vineyard walked in front of his waggon, drawn by four oxen, who followed, almost without any other guidance, precisely at the pace he adopted. On the top was seated a lad, his son, acting as driver; and the whole waggon-load consisted of three barrels of "*most*," or first juice of the grapes trodden out in the field, and these were covered with large branches of vines bearing the most magnificent bunches of grapes that could be found. These were intended to be carried home for a feast, and to make the vintage garlands, nevertheless, some of them were readily bestowed upon us wanderers. Behind the waggon came a row of gossiping spinning women, the wife, mother, and daughters, of the lord of the harvest, and near them the servants and assistants in the work.

The largest village between Lugos and Temesvar, is Rekas, an extensive colony, mostly inhabited by Germans, though partly also by another people called here "*Shokatzes.*" I inquired who these might be, whether they were perhaps Rascians or Servians? The answer was in the negative. One said they were Roman catholics from Illyria, another that they were baptized Turks; another and a better founded notion seemed to be that they were Dalmatians. I mention these various opinions merely to show the confusion of nations that has taken place in Hungary.

I stopped at Rekas to dinner, and found a very good inn, full of life and bustle. Here, as in most of the places I had lately passed through, I found a good German inn. The fever was said to have raged terribly at this place last summer, as well as over nearly the whole of the Banat. The Germans told me that every individual of their community, without a single exception had been attacked by it. Often not more than one third of the inhabitants of a village were capable of work at one time, and even at the period of my visit, not more than half of them were convalescent. Many had seriously injured their health by exerting themselves to work in the day, whilst they were suffering from fever every night. The peasant who gave me this information, said, that the fever had left him so weak, that he was hardly able to lift his whip to drive his horses. The hussars at the time in the Banat had also suffered severely, and the more so on account of the imperfect arrangements of their barracks. They had been incapable of performing their usual duties, and had been obliged to call in the assistance of a company of infantry to take care of their horses. This had not, however, been the sole misfortune to which the country had been exposed during the year, for the crops also had failed. The oat harvest had been the worst of all; and I saw on the road many of the peasants feeding their horses with gourds. The poor animals were very neatly gnawing off the rind from some halves thrown down before them on the grass. The Germans of the beautiful village of Rekas are "*Kammerbauern*," that is to say, they are obliged to pay an hereditary quit-rent to the treasury of the king of Hungary, and are subject immediately to his officers. Whether they are on the whole satisfied with their administration, I do not know, but as I stood before the door of the inn, some peasants who had been long looking at me, approached me in the most polite manner, cap in hand "They took the liberty—they begged I would excuse them, but they had heard—the report had been spread, that I was an imperial engineer, sent from Vienna to inquire into their condition. They begged that I would have the goodness to accompany them to their dwellings, and they would show me every thing, and explain to me all their grievances." I answered that as a simple traveller, desirous of all the information he could gain, I should be happy to accompany them. They accordingly told me many long stories of the injustice they had suffered, which I shall not repeat, as I had no opportunity of ascertaining how far their complaints were well founded. On my departure they stuffed my hands full of the finest walnuts I had ever seen, and would willingly have given me a sack full, possibly with some notion of winning me over to their side, for to the last they would not be persuaded that I was invested with no such dignity as they had attributed to me.

In no province of Hungary, perhaps in no province of the Emperor's states, does the treasury possess so many lands as in the Banat. These are called fiscal estates, and are distinguished from the Crown domains, which cannot be alienated, whereas the fiscal estates may be sold by the Emperor, or given away. From these estates, together with the produce of the Hungarian mines, the Emperor must derive a very important part of his revenue; the salt monopoly, however, is worth all the rest put together.

I have already had occasion to mention one instance of the fragile construction of some of the bridges in this country; and as I proceeded on my journey, I found that it was by no means a solitary instance. It was whispered that many official persons found their account in delaying the repairs of these broken bridges as long as possible, or leaving them to be done by their successors.

A bridge, in most countries, is considered to be a sign that in that place one may cross the river; but, here, it is on the contrary, rather regarded as a warning that one shall by no means attempt so rash an act. My Walachian and I always turned aside when we descried a bridge from afar, and sought for a place where we might drive through the water. It is only fair, however, to observe that I have occasionally met with very fine churches in this part of Hungary, and that all these things depend very much on the spirit which reigns in the comitat, and they vary exceedingly in the different comitats, which may be regarded as so many little independent republics.

Temesvar is the most important town in the whole Banat,—the principal place of residence of the Servian nobility of the province, and the head quarters of the Banat fever. All along the road I had been told, "When you come to Temesvar you will see what the fever is. The people there creep about with pale faces, and almost every one you meet is an invalid." This account I found literally true. At the very entrance of the town I met a waggonful of these poor fever-sick people, who, I was told were going outside the town to look for a certain herb, supposed to be more efficacious as a cure for the fever, than all the doctors' medicines.

After driving through a long suburb, and across a broad marshy glacis, I at length reached the inner kernel of the fortress, and stopped at a very excellent inn called "The Trumpeter," whence I went to pay a visit to an official personage, to whom I had a letter. His valet came to me with a slow heavy step and a dejected look, and begged I would be so good as to call the following day, as his master had the fever, and was just then in a paroxysm in bed. I asked what was the matter with himself that he seemed so cast down? "Ah, sir," he replied, "I've got the fever too." From this house I proceeded to another, where lived a lady, to whom I was charged, by some friends in Vienna, to pay my respects. "Oh, sir," said the waiting-maid, "my lady has had the fever these three years, and she is just now at her worst." Opinions are very various as to the cause of this distressing malady. By some it is ascribed to the fruit, especially to the water-melons; by others to the bad water, by others to the marshes, whence arise that other plague of the country, the gnats. The latter opinion seems the most probable, when the position of the town is considered. It lies, notwithstanding its name, not on the Temes, but on the Vega, in the midst of the many marshes which the latter stream forms. In summer the heat is suffocating, and for weeks together there is sometimes a perfect calm. An attempt has been made to remedy this evil, by means of a canal, twenty German miles long, which serves not only to drain the country, but from Temesvar downwards, is used for the purposes of navigation ; but one canal is quite inadequate to meet the extent of the evil. It must be intersected in every direction, like Holland or Egypt, before any good can be done. In this extremely hot summer, the fever had been dreadful. The inner fortress of the town felt like a baker's oven, and the air was so close and sultry, that a person coming in from the country could scarcely breathe in it. The great majority of the population had been attacked by the malady, and even those who were said to be free from it, felt more or less unwell. Of the two thousand soldiers of the garrison, nine hundred were in the hospital in one week, and there they had to lie or stand, and get through the fever as well as they could. The garrison became at last so enfeebled that it was found impossible to get through the

Y

ordinary duty. This Banat fever exhibits itself under forms as various as the gourds and melons that grow in the country. With some the attacks occur every day, with others every night. In some cases it appears as an intermittent fever, but the attacks return sometimes every second day, sometimes every third or fourth day, and these are said to be the severest cases. The symptoms also vary in almost every instance, some being attacked the very day they enter the city, others not till they have lived in it a considerable time. A journey to Pesth will often rid a man of his fever, but this rule is liable to exceptions, as there are instances of persons who have left the country, and yet retained their fevers for years. During the first days of my stay at Temesvar, I could absolutely find nobody who was free from fever, so I resolved to employ some time in rambles about the city and its environs. I was lucky enough to find a man in tolerable health, whom I engaged to act as *valet-de-place*, and fortunately he was able to walk pretty well, having now been free from fever for six days. He told me he was by birth a Croat, but could speak Hungarian, Walachian, Servian, and German, as well as his native tongue. Among us, a man who spoke five languages fluently might at least have had a decent coat on his back; but here almost every one can muster some half-dozen of these barbarous dialects, no one of which is of the least use to him when he comes to western Europe. German of course is an exception, being the language most cultivated in central Europe, and enabling one to enter into communication there with a greater number of people than any other language. With the knowledge of German one may travel with advantage in the following countries, in addition to all the German states: Holland, Denmark, Livonia, Esthonia, Finnland, Russian Poland; almost all the Slavonian countries as far as Servia; Hungary to the Black Sea; the Alps, Switzerland, and a part of France. Neither French, which is usually spoken only by the higher classes, nor English, which is confined to amateurs, nor Slavonian, which is not known out of the countries to which it belongs, can be made as extensively useful.

The town of Temesvar is one of the largest and best built in Hungary, and quite worthy to be placed in the same rank with Ofen, Pesth, Raab, and others, all of which have been built by Germans or under German administration. It has many fine streets and some really admirable buildings, especially the inner town or fortress. The inhabitants amount to nearly twenty thousand.

During the whole of my walk I had a perpetual vicissitude of sunshine and rain, and as during the rain I generally went in somewhere, and continued my tour of observation again when it left off, I might divide the result of my inquiries into chapters of fair weather and foul, somewhat in the following manner:

FIRST SHOWER.

I took refuge from this in the Comitat-house on the market-place. Here I found what in Hungary is common enough, a crowd of men and women heavily ironed going in and out, carrying water, dragging stones, &c. I inquired who they were, and was told they were people who had committed robbery and murder. "Such as hide in the forest and watch for a traveller, and when they see one, spring out and kill him. That's what they're put in chains for and obliged to work in the comitat's house, and every third year when it's congregation, they get whipped; thirty, forty, or fifty strokes, according to what they've done." It is an intolerable abuse that people thus circumstanced should be left to roam about the streets, instead of being confined in houses of correction. Their treatment too, as prisoners, is in many respects shameful. Here in Temesvar, where on account of the exhalations from the marshes, even the ground-floors of the houses are unwholesome; the cells of the prisoners are damp subterranean dungeons, a fit dwelling only for frogs and toads. From twenty to thirty criminals are sometimes crowded together into one of these dungeons; and in the preceding summer the typhus fever broke out in one of them, and threatened the whole city with infection. In order to bring a little fresher air into the prison, the holes in the wall were enlarged to something like windows; but no sooner was the fever over, than they were absolutely walled up again! Among the many improvements which the patriotic Hungarians are looking forward to introduce into their country, it is to be hoped they will not fail to devote some attention to the state of the comitat prisons and the sufferings of those confined in them.

FIRST INTERVAL OF SUNSHINE.

The rain ceased, and I continued my wanderings through the streets. Many, I might perhaps say most, houses in Temesvar are built upon piles, for the soil is generally marshy; turf and peat bog, or coal, which is certainly abundant throughout the Banat. A very considerable bed of it has lately been discovered in the neighbourhood of Lugos, near a spring, but it has not as yet been turned to any account, though it might be made most valuable for the steamboats on the Danube. Marshes were formerly to be found in the very centre of the town of Temesvar; and I was told that seventy years ago wild ducks might be shot within the limits of the fortress itself, on a spot now covered with good solid houses. The luxury of good water is not to be had in Temesvar, although many attempts have been made to sink artesian wells. In the suburbs only is there any water really drinkable to be had. At the best and most productive of these springs, the Empress Maria Theresa had iron pipes laid down to conduct the water into the town, but in summer it becomes half warm, and sometimes the pipes get stopped up, or there is something else out of order, so that no water, fit for drinking, is to be had; and the inhabitants are obliged to content themselves with what they can get from the canal. The unfortunate city, therefore, at such times, suffers simultaneously from too great a scarcity and from too great an abundance of water.

The fortifications are very extensive; so much so, indeed, as to make their defence no easy matter. I took a view of them from the low tower of a Roman Catholic church. Most of the churches, however, are Illyrian here, and one I noticed, which had just been freshly decorated, presented a most gorgeous appearance, glittering in pink, blue, white, and gold. The *Iconostas* was also adorned with freshly-painted saints, the work, I was told, of a young self-taught Walachian painter. I felt therefore the less inclined to blame some little faults of outline which I discovered, and admired the more the skill with which he had blended the bright and delicate colours.

y 2

SECOND SHOWER.

The sunshine had just lasted long enough to dry my umbrella, and to prepare it for the reception of a new shower, which did not keep me long waiting for its appearance, but soon came down so violently that I was glad to seek some better shelter. I found it in the house of a Servian merchant, with whom I entered into conversation on the subject of the commercial affairs of the Banat. Temesvar, lying nearly in the centre of the province, and enjoying besides the advantage of shipping goods on the Vega canal, is naturally the principal trading-place in the Banat. This canal traverses the whole province, and is the great medium of transport for all the commodities which the rich country yields. Through this canal, its corn and fruit can reach the Danube by a shorter road than through the Maros and the Theiss; and when once there, the corn vessels of the Banat proceed up as far as Raab, and thence to Wieselburg. Raab and Temesvar may be regarded as the two extremities of a line of navigation of which the one end, Raab, lies near a country (Vienna and its environs) where there is a great and constant demand for these blessed fruits of the earth; while the other end (Temesvar) lies in a country that produces them in abundance. Temesvar carries on a more active trade with the former city than with any other; and in both is established, in consequence, a considerable colony of Servian traders.

The second great commercial channel of communication from the Banat, although a less important one than the first, is up the Drave and Save, by the way of Semlin. By this road the corn of the Banat goes by the Kulpa, or the Upper and Lower Save, to Laybach, and thence to the ports of the Adriatic. The Vega canal has operated very beneficially on all this traffic; but, unfortunately, the canal shares the fate of the country through which it flows, and has sometimes too much, and sometimes too little water. The Vega is occasionally quite inadequate to feed it, and yet it sometimes overflows its banks and dikes; and it is less to be regarded as a canal regulated by locks, than as a river rendered navigable by artificial means.

SECOND SUNSHINE.

Like most things that are violent, the rain was of short duration, and I employed this new *intermezzo* in a walk on the glacis of Temesvar, which, like that of Vienna, is laid out as a garden. Some parts of it are very pretty, but the effect is injured by the myriads of frogs that hop about in all directions, as indeed they do through all the cellars and underground places in the city, as well as in the prisons. Along the glacis I made a short round, to the house of a lady to whom I had letters from Pesth, and through the kindness of one of her friends obtained permission to visit the arsenal. This interesting old building, which in many respects reminded me of the ancient castle of the kings of Poland, in Cracow, formerly belonged to Johannes Hunyades, the father of Matthias Corvinus, and was subsequently inhabited by the Turkish commandant of Temesvar. It now contains about thirty thousand stand of arms, and in one division, which particularly interested me, I found a mass of ancient lances, spears, and scythes, used for the Hungarian "landstorm" or militia, or for occasions when, as the sergeant who accompanied me said, "one wishes to arm the people." Even the old worn-out muskets of the soldiers are brought into the arsenal for this purpose. "They will serve," it is said, "for the peasants to shoot at the Turks." I do not know whether here, in the Banat, on the frontier of Turkey, the organization of the militia may not be different from that of the east of Hungary. There were many Turkish weapons also in the arsenal, which a hundred years hence perhaps, when the Turks shall have been expelled from Europe, may be looked at with great interest. On one yataghan was a pious inscription—" The Lord alone is my hope and my trust; may God bless the owner of this sword, Halil."

In Temesvar I also saw many beautiful specimens of the cannon of Charles VI., cast in Vienna, and remarkable for the beauty and elegance of their workmanship.

The sunshine lasted so long this time that I had still enough left to pay a visit to a highly estimable clergyman, in whose instructive society I passed a very agreeable hour. Knowledge and intellectual cultivation are always pleasant things to meet with, but never so welcome as in countries lying, like this, far out of the centre of European culture. This gentleman told me that a short time since he had had occasion to entertain one of those oriental pilgrims who often pass through Hungary to Ofen. He had been accidentally from home when this guest from a distant land arrived, and going to seek him in the garden where he was told he was waiting, he found him on his knees, on a mat, performing his evening devotions. The Catholic priest retired till the Moslem, having finished his evening prayers, arose and claimed his hospitality. On the following day the priest gave his guest a dinner, at which several other Catholic clergymen were present. He would not take any soup, but eat heartily of a sort of pudding presented to him; declined the fine Menescher wine, exclaiming, with an appearance of disgust, after having tasted it, "*Raki! Raki!*" —that is to say, "brandy," for which he probably took it, but he willingly drank champagne. He was asked whether he had money enough for his further journey; "No more," he answered, "than is necessary to enable me to reach the next town. Allah will provide for me then, as he has done to-day in bringing me beneath your hospitable roof. God is great, and nourishes all his creatures."

North of Temesvar, on the Maros, lies the convent of Radna, a celebrated place for pilgrimages. It is said to lie in a beautiful district, and is close to the Menescher mountains, where grow the delicious honey-sweet grapes, from which is extracted the wine that bears the same name. This range of mountains is one of the last spurs of the Transylvanian Alpine chain, as the Hegyallya is of the Carpathians; the latter produces the Tokay grape, and both border on the plain of the Theiss.

The convent of Radna, probably, owes some of its renown to the courageous and persevering conduct of its inmates during the time of the Turks. The monks, who belong to the order of St. Francis, found means to keep alive all that was left of catholicism in Hungary, under the Mahometan rule, and to defend it equally from the infidel and from the heresies of protestantism, which, partly perhaps out of opposition to Austria, had made great progress in the north of Hungary. Many attempts were made by protestants to spread their doctrines among the catholic subjects of the Turk, but the Franciscans, by some means or other, always managed to frustrate their designs. On one occasion in Szegedin, a protestant missionary presented himself to the pasha, begging permission to preach his new and excellent doctrine. The Franciscans begged the pasha would allow no such thing. The protestant said that if the pasha would allow a public discussion to take place between him and one of the monks, he would soon see who was in the right. The pasha agreed to the proposal, and listened to the dispute, which was carried on in the Hungarian language, usually understood by the Turkish officers, who, indeed, were often enough renegade Hungarians. The dispute was a very long one, and the pasha was not much wiser at the end than at the beginning: he therefore bethought himself of a clear and simple method of finding out who was in the right, and demanded of the protestant who were the greatest prophets the world had ever seen. The answer was, "Moses and Jesus Christ." "What?" screamed the Franciscan, "don't you reckon Mahomet?" This settled the business. The protestant was ordered forthwith to leave the town; the Franciscans rose high in Turkish favour, and the town of Szegedin gained the reputation which it has ever since retained, of being one of the most catholic cities of Hungary.

THIRD SHOWER.

Temesvar is, as I have before mentioned, the residence of most of the Servian nobility of the Banat, and it may be regarded as the capital of Austria, as Belgrade is of Turkish Servia. These are the two largest towns in which Servians play any important part. They are often very wealthy, dine off silver and gold, but have in general very little education or taste for inquiry. They are mostly of new families, and very devoted admirers of Russia. Their wealth is derived from the rich plains of the Banat, which for fertility can only be compared with Egypt. In the comitat of Torontal especially, which stretches to the mouths of the Theiss and the Maros, there are not less than sixteen or eighteen Servian families, each of which has a revenue of from a hundred to a hundred and fifty thousand florins; having, about a century ago, bought estates for a mere nothing, which now, by the colonization of the Banat, and the great increase of traffic, have risen six, eight, and ten fold in value. The repulsive force which appears to exist between the Servians and Hungarians (as between new and old nobility, new and old cultivation, the Greek and the Catholic churches) has hitherto prevented any of the ancient Magyar nobility from settling in this province, and as there are here many Germans, the language of the latter is more used, and the Hungarian less than in other parts of the country. This circumstance, is of course rather agreeable to a travelling German, and he is sure to meet in the Banat many well-educated countrymen. The phrase "countryman" is of course used in a rather more liberal acceptation than with Germans at home, who divide themselves into Prussians, Hanoverians, Saxons, Coburgers, &c., and find themselves separated by little national differences from each and all. When, however, the Saxon and the Prussian meet in Austria, they recognise each other as north Germans and brothers; and when the Prussian and the Austrian meet in Hungary, the distinction of north and south is forgotten in the common tie of Germanism. It is not indeed till a German has lived in foreign countries, that he becomes capable of a really patriotic feeling, and can embrace the whole German nation in the circle of his sympathies. If we go into still more remote lands, Germans begin to fraternize with Italians; and in Africa or distant Asia, the differences of Slavonian, Germanic, and Romanic nations are lost, and all may join hands as members of the great Caucasian family. Perhaps, should we journey among the strange and to us monstrous inhabitants of the moon, the differences and antipathies of European and Asiatic, African and Australian, North and South American, Christian and Mahomedan would be swallowed up in the kindness we should feel towards all terrestrial beings, and the heart of a Parisian dandy might overflow with brotherly love towards a Hottentot. Who can measure the powers and capacities of love and hate that fill the universe? Upon Sirius perhaps all who belonged to our Solar system would feel inclined to shake hands, and a native of Uranus be greeted as a dear countryman. Where is that centre of the universe where all these external differences sink into nothing; where the hostile separations of countries and systems are lost in all-embracing love and sympathy, where all these discords are resolved into universal harmony?

The last shower of rain I have recorded continued so long that night came on before it ceased, and I took refuge at length in the family circle of an amiable countryman, whose wife was busied as German housewives are wont to be, in domestic affairs. She was engaged, I was told, in the preparation of "Ribisel" and "Agresel," and as I had often heard these words without being able to make out what they signified, I begged to have them explained. I was accordingly introduced into the kitchen, and I there discovered that under these strange names were concealed dainties no less familiar than agreeable; that is to say, preserved currants and gooseberries. I here learned also some particulars concerning the preparation of the Hungarian wine, "*Ausbruch*," of which I had so often heard. It is only prepared from the finer kinds of wines, those of Tokay, Menescher, Rust, and Ofen, as the inferior sorts will not repay the trouble. It is made by first clearing the vines of all the poor and half-ripe grapes, and leaving all the fine rich and ripe ones hanging till they are almost as dry as raisins. They frequently hang till the month of November, but in wet and cold years, the "*Ausbruch*" cannot be made. When the grapes are considered sufficiently ripe and dry they are gathered, and good wine is poured upon them. They are then crushed and the wine drawn from them by the usual process. Wine is sometimes poured a second, and even a third time upon the dried grapes, but the first "*Ausbruch*" is of course the finest.

THE COLONIES AND LOWLANDS OF THE BANAT.

On the following morning I found that the showers which had been contending with the sunshine the day before, had now made common cause of it, and fairly beaten the sun; the blue patches of sky had all disappeared in one uniform gray, and the rain, which had been vainly invoked during the summer, poured down with a fury that seemed, now when it came *post festum*, to serve for nothing but to help to fill the wine-tubs of the Walachians, and to spoil the roads for us wayfarers. The rich, heavy soil of the Banat becomes in such weather as this almost impassable; the *made road*, as it is called, continues only a few miles beyond Temesvar, and thenceforward the traveller must struggle as he best can through the difficulties which nature has opposed to his progress. The diligence in which we were now to travel, was drawn by six stout horses, yet we looked forward to a very slow journey. My fellow-travellers were a poor sick young woman, going to Pesth to recover her health; a young German mechanic who had come to Temesvar four weeks ago, to look for work, but had found only the fever; a coachman who looked quite well every other day, but on the intermediate days complained grievously; an incredibly dirty Jew, also sick of the usual malady; and one passenger besides myself in health. With this cargo the six strong Hungarian horses plunged into the mire of the comitat of Temes. We soon discovered how fallacious had been our hopes of reaching Szegedin that day, and how fortunate we might esteem ourselves if we could even get as far as the intermediate station of St. Miclosch.

After passing Temesvar, the population of the Banat, always chequered enough, becomes still more diversified, and is nowhere more so than where the ground is most fertile, in the district of Torontal. This tract of country, lying between the Theiss and the Maros, is so extraordinarily rich, that it produces, year after year, the heaviest crops of wheat, without ever being manured, and is commonly called by Hungarian writers, the Egypt of Hungary, *ubertate locorum cœlique benignitate nulli terrarum secunda*. Thence to Pesth the fertility of the soil declines, until the comitat of Pesth itself presents nothing but a barren surface of sand. Under the Turkish rule, the rich plains were the least populous parts of the country, for the inhabitants naturally fled for protection to the mountains, and to the vicinity of the great towns. At a subsequent period an attempt was made to supply the difficiency thus created, by the establishment of colonies of Italians, Spaniards, Frenchmen, Germans, Servians, Dalmatians, Bosnians, and Bulgarians, and where, a hundred years ago, was to be found only a dirty shepherd's hut, an Armenian farmhouse, or a lonely well, are now to be seen villages of five thousand, six thousand, eight thousand, or even thirteen thousand inhabitants. Much, however, still remains to be done before the capabilities of the country can be developed to any thing like their full extent, and the comitats north of the Maros and Koros, where the influence of the Austrian government is not so powerful, are far behind those of the Banat. It is rather remarkable, that throughout the whole Banat, there is not a single Magyar village to be found, and the scattered families of that race, which may be met with, are so few as to be not worth taking into the account of the population. The Magyar population was entirely exterminated by the Turks, and the Magyars are now as firmly rooted to their native soil, as they were formerly restless and nomadic in their habits. The Banat may, nevertheless, be regarded as a part of the kingdom of Hungary; but I know of only three cases in which I have ever heard of Hungarian villages existing beyond the limits of Hungary proper: those I have already mentioned between the Drave and the Save, a few Magyar villages on the Dniester, and some in Walachia and Moldavia, which were originally colonies, forcibly planted there by the Turks. Very seldom, and with the greatest unwillingness, does a Magyar leave one comitat for another,—as if the restless, wandering spirit of the early Magyars, who changed their country at least ten times before they finally settled on the Danube, had rendered the whole nation so weary of change, that they never wished to move again.

The landed proprietors of the Banat, in founding new villages, (a work which is continually going on,) always seek for German peasants to inhabit them. One of these, a beautiful place called Shandorhatz, we passed about midway, between Temesvar and St. Miklos. It has a handsome spacious market-place, and a church with two towers, from which the streets diverge in a fanlike form, as in Karlsruhe. The houses are prettily painted in green and white, and the inhabitants are mostly young offshoots from the old German villages of the Banat. A particular term has been found here for the country-people, who come by agreement with the owner of the land to inhabit a spot of this kind: they are called "*Contractualists*," and they stand in various relations to the proprietor, according to the more or less advantageous bargain they have made.

On a "*Puste*" where we stopped, I met with a German schoolmaster, who, though he wore such a pair of mustaches, as many an hussar among us would envy, was nevertheless a very intelligent and well-informed man. He gave me a very good account of his school, which contained no less than six hundred children, divided into three classes. Of these, more than five hundred were from among the three thousand German inhabitants, and not above forty from the three thousand Walachians.

In the villages thus inhabited by a population half German, half Walachian, it is singular that they never mingle; they live on opposite sides of the street, and though handsome girls are to be found on both sides, Love has never been known to send an arrow across. Cupid is not so blind, it appears, as not to distinguish between Germans and Walachians, between Catholics and members of the Greek church. An inhabitant of the place assured me, that since its foundation no marriage had ever taken place between the opposite factions. "They do come together to fight sometimes," said my host, joining in the conversation, "but never to marry." In other villages we find similar relations subsisting between Germans and Servians, and Germans and Hungarians, but with the latter the distinctions are not so strongly marked. It is worthy of remark, that the Italians, Spaniards, and even Frenchmen, settled in the Banat, have all, more or less, merged their several nationalities in that of the Germans, which, considering that the Servians and Walachians, are in a decided majority, shows a far greater inclination of the Romanic people to the Germans than to the eastern nations.

The Italians were invited to the Banat, chiefly on account of the cultivation of rice and silk; but these branches of industry, like the cotton growing in the Banat, are as yet of very little importance. In the country itself, indeed, one scarcely hears any thing of them, and it gave me some trouble to make out where the plantations of rice and cotton and mulberries were really to be found. The Germans, it is said, are no friends to the rearing of silkworms, and often do no more than just plant the number of mulberry-trees agreed on with the owner of the land, and trouble themselves no more about them. Some are even so decidedly hostile to this branch of industry, as to root out the trees wherever they find them, and the country-people in general throughout the Banat, pay no sort of attention to it, so that it forms in fact little more than the employment of the leisure hours of a few widows, clergymen, and people who have places under government. Wheat and Indian corn, tobacco, wine, and potatoes, flourish abundantly under the hands of the Germans; the Magyars are almost exclusively occupied with the two last mentioned. The rearing of horses, is mostly in the hands of the Germans, that of horned cattle in those of the Rascians and Bulgarians. It is a remarkable proof of the great confidence entertained by the government in their German subjects, that these are allowed to carry a musket, while such an indulgence is positively prohibited to the Rascian and Walachian races.

It is said in the Banat that the Empress Maria Theresa, when distressed for money during some of her great wars, had offered to sell the entire province (or at least what she possessed in it, which was nearly the same thing) for three millions of florins, and that Prince Bathyany, had visited it in order to judge of the bargain, but returned, saying there was nothing to be seen but sky and boundless marsh, for which he could not agree to pay such a sum. The land was subsequently sold to Armenians from Transylvania, for incredibly low prices; the yoke of sixteen hundred square fathoms for two florins or even less. At present, by dint of draining the marshes and cultivating the land, the value has been so much raised, that a small estate possessed by Prince Bathyany in the north-west corner of the country, yields alone a revenue equal to half the interest of the above-named sum for which nearly the whole province might have been bought. Estates sometimes fetch even more than their real value, on account of the privileges of nobility which they confer, and the rich Servians often contend with each other in the purchase. There can be, however, no doubt that if these rich and fertile tracts were more favourably situated, in a country possessed of a better system of roads and canals, they would be worth four or five times as much as they are now. Nature appears to have been needlessly profuse in bestowing on the Banat a rich soil of four or five feet deep, so that six or eight oxen must be yoked to a plough, while some countries have scarcely as many inches. How many poor barren sandy regions might be clothed from what is here superfluity.

The description of the whole Banat given by Prince Bathyany, that it is nothing but sky and water, is in some measure confirmed by another saying, of I forget whom, concerning its roads, that they are strips of bog enclosed between two ditches. This definition I found perfectly correct, especially towards evening, when the last traces of the made road from Temesvar had long since disappeared. Notwithstanding the incessant cries of our lively charioteer, and despite the most heroic efforts on the part of our poor horses, our diligence *progressed* at about the rate at which an active snail might be expected to get on through a puddle of mud. In the mean time it grew completely dark, and the rain fell incessantly. All topics of conversation had been exhausted during the tedious day, and a moody silence settled gradually upon all my companions. They either slept, or abandoned themselves to their own thoughts. I was the sole occupant of the hindmost seat, whence I had a clear view of the whole contents of our vehicle, and I too gave myself up to my own reflections with tolerable resignation. They turned naturally towards the subjects that had occupied me during the day, namely the colonies of the various nations that had settled in the Banat. This led me to meditate on the entire system of colonization, and gradually my cogitations fashioned themselves into

THOUGHTS ON THE PEACEFUL MIGRATIONS OF EUROPEAN NATIONS, AND THEIR VARIOUS SETTLEMENTS IN OUR OWN QUARTER OF THE WORLD,

which, during my three hours of a nocturnal snail's gallop, moulded themselves into a kind of fragmentary essay, the defects of which my readers will perhaps overlook, partly in consideration of the circumstances under which it was composed, and partly, I hope, in consideration of the novelty of the subject.

There are in Europe several nations that form no establishments beyond their own borders, or at least none but insignificant ones. Let us commence with these non-migrating nations.

1. THE MAGYARS. They have founded camps, villages, and detached houses in the Slavonian and Dacian lands that they have conquered, and from these camps they have traversed half Europe,—Germany to the North Sea, Italy to the Adriatic and the Gulf of Genoa, and a large portion of France,—but without leaving behind them a single colony or settlement, or even a useful trace of their passage. They have at various periods borne sway in Bosnia, Bulgaria, and Servia, without forming a permanent settlement in any one of those provinces; even of those which they still reckon as a part of their own country, there are several where the main body of the population is entirely strange to them; as, for instance, in Syrmia, Slavonia, Croatia, the Banat, &c. Beyond the limits of Hungary there exists nowhere an important Magyar colony, except in Vienna, where about fifteen thousand Hungarians are said to reside; but even of these, probably, only a small proportion are of pure Magyar descent.

2. THE RUSSIANS. These also seldom leave their own country, and have nowhere beyond their own borders, formed any permanent settlement. The only exceptions I know of, are a few Russian merchants who reside at Berlin, and a small colony of Russian peasants near Potsdam. In Leipzig, to be sure, on account of the fair, several Russians establish a temporary residence, and the Russian aristocracy are incessantly travelling about in all parts of Europe. In Asia, and on the north-west coast of America, I am aware, there are Russian settlements, but these, as we are now confining our attention to Europe, form no part of our subject.

These few exceptions, however, are so trifling as scarcely to merit consideration; and taken on the whole, we must reckon the Russians among the nations that hold themselves aloof from the great European migrations. They keep themselves in general strictly within the borders of their "Holy Russia," and feel themselves nowhere at home where their czar and their church do not bear sway.

Within the range of their own empire, however, the Russians, in complete contrast to the Hungarians, manifest a perfect passion for migrating and colonising. They have covered the whole face of their vast territory with settlements of one kind or other, with colonies of hunters and of fishermen; with military and with agricultural colonies.

The Magyars are entirely wanting in industrial skill. They cannot, therefore, be useful to other nations; and this circumstance may contribute fully as much as their attachment to their native country, to keep them at home. The Russians are by no means without a taste for industrial occupations, but they can do nothing which is not done better by the inhabitants of other countries; and they are, besides, mostly *glebæ adscripti*, bound to the soil on which they are born. This is also true with respect to the nations subject to them, such as the Lettes and Lithuanians, who are devoted to agriculture, and are fettered to the estates of their masters by their political condition. The Tartars of the Crimea, and of the country watered by the Volga, are gradually disappearing. It is only in Russia itself, at Novogorod, Moscow, and other places, that little Tartar settlements are still to be found. They are thinly scattered all over the vast empire, as drivers, coachmen, and dealers in particular wares, such as shawls and dressing-gowns. Many Finnish races also appear to be dying away under the Russian sway.

3. THE POLES have certainly always taken more part in the movements of European colonization than the Russians, and all the countries of Europe contain, in the different branches of their commercial industry, a few widely-scattered Polish emigrants; but of voluntary Polish colonies, or of Polish settlements in foreign lands, we nowhere find a trace. The misfortunes and convulsions of their native country have been the sole impulses which have formed in modern times so many little communities of Polish exiles in Germany, France, England, and America, in the west, and in the desert plains of Siberia in the east.

4. THE SPANIARDS and PORTUGUESE, notwithstanding the grand scale upon which they colonised the new world, have taken but little part in the national intercourse of Europe. The Spaniards have founded no colonies in the other countries of Europe, with the exception of a few trading establishments in England and France, and a few military settlements in Austria, drawn together by the connexion of the royal houses of Spain and Austria. The whole energy of these peninsular nations was directed to the south and west, to Africa and America, where they founded large and powerful kingdoms, and empires peopled entirely by the Spanish race.

5. THE TURKS must occupy a part of our attention, in so far as they are now to some extent a European nation. In all the countries which have at different times been subject to them, they have founded only military settlements of governors, officers, and soldiers. They have very seldom been able to introduce their language, religion, and customs, into any of the classes of society subject to them, if we except the nobility of Bosnia and Albania, and whenever their yoke has been thrown off, as in Greece, Hungary, Servia, and Walachia, almost all traces of them have soon vanished, with the exception of a few military posts and fortresses. Those men, known among us as trading Turks, are mostly of other races subject to the Turkish government, such as Jews, Armenians, &c., and not genuine Osmanlis.

6. THE DACIANS, or WALACHIANS, are withheld by their political circumstances, and their want of culture, learning, and industrial skill, from often crossing the frontiers of their native countries; but they have founded a few agricultural colonies in Hungary, Transylvania, and the military frontier. The principal towns of these countries, particularly Vienna, Pesth, and Lemberg, also contain a few Walachian civil officers, and several Walachian noblemen have taken arms in the Russian service. These, however, are trifling exceptions.

The above-named nations, therefore, as well as a few others of less importance, may be distinguished as those who take little or no part in the national intercourse of Europe, and who, on account either of a natural distaste for emigration, or of a want of skill in the useful arts of life, or of the political circumstances which chain them to their native soil, seldom or never found colonies in the other parts of Europe; in short, as the non-colonising nations of Europe.

The following European races, then, remain to be considered:

1st. The Slavonians of Southern and Western Europe (Bohemians, Servians, &c.)
2d. The Greeks and Albanians.
3d. The Romanic races of France and Italy.
4th. The Germanic nations of England, the Netherlands, Denmark, Norway, Sweden, and Germany.
5th. The subordinate and dependant races; Jews, Armenians, Gipsies, &c.

THE SLAVONIANS.

Of the Slavonians, none are so much addicted to wandering habits, as the Bohemians and Servians.

The Moravians and Slovaks, who inhabit the north-western part of Hungary, are all minor branches of the great Bohemian race, which includes more than six millions of human beings, and plays no unimportant part in the national intercourse of other European countries.

At very various periods, from very various reasons, and for very various purposes, the Bohemian Slavonians have emigrated in large bodies to foreign countries. We find them settled in different parts of the Austrian Empire, as agricultural colonists; and in all countries of Europe, as religious fugitives; in some places as Catholics, seeking refuge from persecuting Hussites; and others as Hussites, seeking refuge from persecuting Catholics. Berlin and its vicinity still contain a little colony of Bohemian religious fugitives, and the most distant regions of the world, the far West of America, and the Hottentot lands of Southern Africa, are thinly sown with small communities of Moravian brethren.

The Bohemians are among the most industrious subjects of the Austrian government, and are settled in all the towns of the empire, as manufacturers and mechanics. The Bohemian colony at Vienna, is the most considerable of all, and they are there to be found in all classes of society, from the poorest day-labourers to the highest officers of state. Numbers of Bohemians emigrate annually to Vienna, stay there for some time, and return afterwards to their native country, with the fruits of their industry.

The valleys and mountains in Northern Hungary, inhabited by the Tshekhs, likewise send out numerous colonists southward. According to the account of a native Hungarian author, "of all the inhabitants of Hungary, they have the greatest industrial skill, the most energetic spirit of enterprise. Wherever they take root, they accordingly soon supplant and displace the original inhabitants, whether Germans or Magyars." There are, in fact, numerous examples of entire towns and villages, once solely inhabited by Germans and Magyars, but now entirely occupied by Bohemians.

The Tshekhs visit all parts of the Austrian Empire, and many parts of Poland, as retail dealers, with linens, stuffs, and other wares. As venders of medicine they are found even in the remotest parts of Siberia, and as mechanics and musicians all over the world. The Bohemian musicians traverse all parts of Europe and Asia, as veterinary surgeons; the Moravians are found in great numbers in Russia, and the Bohemian *Oleykari* (oil-merchants), *Safrannitschi* (saffron-brewers), *Platennici* (linen-dealers), glass-merchants, and wax-dealers, if they abound nowhere else, abound, at least, in all parts of Hungary and Galicia.

Next to the Tshekhs, the Servians are the most important of the colonising Slavonian races. They have, like the Bohemians, founded many agricultural colonies in the Military Frontier and the Banat. The persecutions of Turkish fanaticism have had the same expelling influence in Servia, which the Hussite tumults had in Bohemia. The Servians have fled into Austria in great numbers, at different times, and have settled there as agricultural soldiers.

The Servians have a great spirit of trade, and have founded many trading establishments in Hungary. Almost all the Hungarian towns have a Servian quarter, as well as a Jewish quarter. The Servians being a less cultivated nation, have less taste for the arts and manufactures than the Bohemians, and employ themselves almost exclusively as agriculturists, soldiers, and retail dealers.

Although the whole Austrian empire has been colonised in different parts by the Tshekhs, the Servian colonies are entirely confined to the kingdom of Hungary. Their most western settlement is at Vienna, beyond which no trace of the Rascians is to be found. In Russia and Turkey there are large Servian colonies.

The Croatians and Bulgarians are closely related to the Servians. The former people occupy several little villages in different parts of the empire, and the Bulgarians have formed agricultural settlements in Walachia, the Banat, and South Russia.

THE GREEKS.

The Greeks were formerly to southern Europe and western Asia, what the Germans afterwards were to eastern and northern Europe; namely, the founders of colonies, and the builders up of towns, in uninhabited or barbarous countries: but it is not here our purpose to speak, in detail, of the numerous, extensive, and important colonies founded by ancient Greece along the Mediterranean, and the Black Sea, and in the depths of Scythia. This colonising spirit, however, is far from extinct among the Greeks of the present day. Not only in all the towns of the Turkish peninsula, both in Greece itself, and in Macedonia and Thrace, but in the islands of the Egean Sea, the towns of Asia Minor, and the Russian cities on the Black Sea (Odessa, Taganrog, &c.), the Greeks still play an important part as merchants, bankers, and seamen. Even the great cities in the interior of Russia, as far as St. Petersburg itself, contain numerous large Greek trading establishments.

Another chain of Greek trading settlements intersects Walachia, Hungary, and the whole Austrian empire, as far as Vienna and Leipzig; but, with the exception of a few agricultural colonies in Russia, the Greeks are never the sole inhabitants of towns and villages. In Vienna, the greatest banker, next to Rothschild, is a Greek, named Sina, and Leipzig contains many Greek commercial houses of a high standing.

THE ITALIANS AND FRENCH.

The principal Italian colonies of the middle ages were trading colonies, and they mostly had their origin in the great commercial cities of Venice and Genoa. After the discovery of America, when their neighbours of the western peninsula turned their attention to grand schemes of colonization in the new world, the colonising Italians still concentrated all their energies in their trading settlements in Europe. Trieste, the Dalmatian harbours, Odessa, Taganrog, Smyrna, and Constantinople contain greater numbers of Italian merchants than any other foreign cities. All over Russia, Poland, Germany, and Hungary, certain branches of trade were, at one time, so exclusively in the hands of Italian emigrants, that the shops where the Italian and Levantine fruits and wines are sold, go still by the name of Italian shops, even when not kept by Italians.

In the fourteenth and fifteenth centuries, when it became customary to repair to Italy in search of kings and queens, many Italian priests emigrated to Hungary, where most of them were provided with lucrative benefices. Italian agriculturists have also settled in the Banat, to cultivate the rice-plant and the mulberry-tree. The inhabitants of Savoy and the Tyrol are plentifully dispersed all over Europe, as chimneysweepers, musicians, and dealers in images. The singers and musicians of Italy stand all over Europe at the head of their profession.

Widely and numerously diffused, however, as Italian emigrants are throughout the countries of Europe, they are always scattered singly. There are nowhere Italian quarters in the great towns of Europe like the German quarters in Russia, the Rascian quarters in Hungary, and the Jews' quarters in Germany; and they nowhere form large factories, like the English factory at St. Petersburg.

THE FRENCH.—It is a somewhat remarkable circumstance, that the French have upon the whole founded so few colonies, and that what they have done in this way can in no way be compared to what the Spaniards and Portuguese have effected in the new world, the Italians on the shores of the Mediterranean, and the Germanic nations in all parts of Europe. All the French colonies in other parts of the world appear very insignificant compared to those of the Spaniards, English, and Dutch.

Though a few colonies of French emigrants are to be found in London and the great cities of Germany, yet they mostly owe their origin to the religious and political disturbances of France, and not to a colonising spirit in the people. With these exceptions, the French residents in different parts of Europe, the French hairdressers, milliners, cooks, dancers, &c., who abound in the great capitals of Europe, are always scattered singly among the native population.

THE GERMANIC NATIONS.

We now come to the Germanic nations, of whom it is not too much to say that they now stand above all other nations, ruling and directing the great affairs of the world, and that no great event, no great movement of any kind, can take place in any part of the world which the Germanic nations, among whom we include the English,

Germans, Norwegians, Swedes, Danes, Dutch, and the Americans of the United States, do not directly or indirectly guide and control. The English, notwithstanding the immense extent and importance of their colonies in Asia, Africa, America, and Australia, have settled very little in the other countries of Europe.* There is no European continental district whatever, in which the English have established important agricultural or commercial colonies. Their whole love of conquest, their whole colonising energy, has turned to other parts of the world; and yet without possessing a single foot of land over the continent (with the exception of Gibraltar) they exercise an influence upon the rest of Europe equal to dominion over at least one-fourth of its soil.

Throughout Europe, English manufacturers, mechanics, and engineers, take a prominent part in all great public works and manufactories. They share in all our great companies for the construction of railroads, the starting of steamboats, and the lighting our towns with gas. Even in Russia they stand at the head of many public enterprises. The building of the great bridge at Pesth, and of a great Gothic palace in the Crimea, are conducted by Englishmen. There are also small bodies of resident English established in all the great cities of Europe, for pleasure or economy; but these classes of English residents in other countries are only passing visitors, and exercise no lasting influence on the places they inhabit. Far more important than these are the English commercial houses established on the continent, at Oporto, Lisbon, Cadiz, Gibraltar, Leghorn, Smyrna, the Ionian Isles, Constantinople, Riga, &c., and, above all, the great English factory at St. Petersburg. Many English missionaries also visit, and wander about, different parts of Europe, bent on the distribution of the Bible, the improvement of prisons, the conversion of the Jews, or some other work of piety or benevolence.

The Germans of Scandinavia are among the greatest of European colonisers. I shall not here go back to the old Northern colonists, after whom Normandy is still called, from whom the great English nobility derive their lineage, and the Neapolitan ducas and nobilis claim descent on account of their flaxen hair and light complexions; but, in more modern times, the colonies of the Scandinavians, in different parts of Europe, have been of great extent and importance. The Danes found a wide field for colonization in Iceland, and the Swedes in Finnland; which, although now a Russian province, is still Swedish in manners, customs, and language, and whose great towns are all of Swedish origin. They also established many colonies in Livonia and Esthonia, and exercised a considerable influence over those countries. The Scandinavians have, however, in later times, vanished more and more from the great European stage, and now play but a very inconsiderable part there.

The Germanic tribes of the Low Countries have always been much addicted to wandering habits. Not only have they peopled Java, the Cape countries, and other barbarous lands, but they have gone hand in hand with the Germans in European colonization. Frieslanders accompanied the Anglo-Saxons to England, and citizens, and peasants, from Flanders, settled in various parts of Germany during the middle ages.

---

* Yet there is scarcely a commercial city of importance, from Lisbon to St. Petersburg, in which an English colony may not be said to exist, to say nothing of the little communities of English residents scattered over France, Italy, and Switzerland.—*Tr.*

The German nation itself, situated in the heart of Europe, and thus connected by position with the French, English, Normans, Slavonians, Turks, and Italians, is calculated no less by its cosmopolitan character, than by its geographical position, to adapt itself readily to foreign lands, climates, and circumstances, and to amalgamate easily with other nations. The Germans are well acquainted with all the useful arts of life, and the variety of climate contained in their native country, renders them well acquainted with the cultivation of almost every European production, from the larch, the fir, and the pine, to the chestnut, the mulberry, and the vine.

The Germans are experienced and skilful in commercial enterprises, as the prosperity and reputation of the Hanseatic merchants sufficiently proves. They are vigilant and careful, equally willing to teach what they know, and to learn what they do not know, in their various avocations. Moreover, the saying concerning German faith and German truth, is no mere saying, but a real fact, soon understood, acknowledged, and valued by foreigners.

Although there is scarcely a country in Europe in which large numbers of Germans have not settled and prospered, yet their colonising powers have in modern times been chiefly turned to the north and east. They have settled in great numbers in Poland, Hungary, Turkey, Russia, the Baltic Provinces, and even in Tartary; and there is scarcely a branch of human industry which the German colonists in those countries do not carry on. They have established commercial seaport-towns all along the Baltic, and commercial houses in Novogorod and other Russian cities. They have introduced a better system of agriculture among the Russians, Poles, and Hungarians, and set them an example of industry, care, and honesty which they would do well to follow.

German miners have established themselves in Hungary and the Banat, as far as the Turkish frontiers, and in Russia and Tartary, as far as the Chinese boundary. The gardeners and vinedressers of Germany are to be met with all over Europe. German emigrants have established themselves in great numbers at Paris, as mechanics; at London, Bourdeaux, and Hull, as merchants; and in Northern Italy, as government functionaries. The broom-girls of Bavaria are scattered all over western Europe, and France contains great numbers of German cattle-drivers. The Tyrolese with their gloves and carpets, the Black Foresters with their watches, are often to be met with in France and Spain, and the German Military Colonists, the Swiss guards and others, have often played a conspicuous part in French history.

THE SUBORDINATE AND DEPENDANT RACES.

Besides the great nations of Europe, there are several subordinate races, who, although not originally belonging to this part of the world, have been long settled in great numbers in almost every country of Europe. The chief of these are the Jews, the Armenians, and the Gipsies.

There is no country in Europe in which the Jews have not established themselves, but it is in the Slavonian, Hungarian, and German lands, that they play the most conspicuous part. In Germany they are still mostly confined to certain branches of trade and commerce, but in the Slavonian countries they monopolize many other occupations, which nowhere else belong to them, such as those of the tailor and shoemaker. The Jews are always fonder of dealing with persons than with things. They never devote themselves to agriculture, or the herding of cattle, or the building of houses, or any kind of masonry or carpentering. In the Slavonian countries, they are still the only keepers of inns and alehouses, and formerly they monopolized in those parts of Europe the postage and tollkeeping departments. The transport of persons in those districts is still entirely in the hands of the Jews, but strange to say, they never meddle with the conveyance of goods.

There is a close connexion, and a continual intercourse, kept up between the Jewish colonies in different parts of Europe. Germany, as the mother-country of these various colonies, is continually sending out new reinforcements. The Spanish Jews, who established themselves in Africa and Turkey when expelled from Spain, and who have founded little colonies along the Danube cities to Vienna, where they form a separate congregation as subjects of the Turkish government, are a distinct and separate branch of the race; as are the Portuguese Jews, with their settlements in France and Holland; and the Caraïte Jews, who inhabit the towns of South Russia and the Crimea, and who possess small factories in Turkey.

The ARMENIANS are a far more modern appearance in Europe. They first entered it at the period of the conquest of Roumelia by the Turks; and when the Russians took possession of the Tartar kingdoms of Casan and Astrachan, and extended their dominions to the Caucasus, numbers of Armenians fled from the oppression of the Turks, and settled in Southern Russia. They afterwards spread into Poland, where they have a considerable colony at Lemberg; and in later times they have settled in various parts of Walachia, Transylvania, Hungary, and the Banat.

There are small commercial colonies of Armenians settled at St. Petersburg and Moscow, and even at Marseilles, Amsterdam, and London; but the countries of Europe most abundantly peopled by Armenians, are Turkey, South Russia, Walachia, Transylvania, Southern Galicia, and Eastern Hungary.

Throughout the east, the principal merchants are all Armenians; and in the Walachian countries, all the innkeepers who are not Jews are Armenians. In the steppes of Hungary and South Russia they are settled in great numbers as farmers and cattle-dealers, and the breeding and tending of bees is carried on by some of them on a very large scale. Wealthy Armenians have also often been admitted among the Polish, Walachian, and Russian nobility.

Of many other races, of whom small numbers have settled in different parts of Europe, such as the Persians at Moscow, Petersburg, and Astracan, the Bucharians who wander about Russia, and even sometimes come as far as Leipzig, the Parsees who have established a little settlement at Astracan, the negro communities to be found in so many great cities, the Arabs of Constantinople and Moscow, the Moors of France, the Malays of London and Amsterdam, we need not speak in detail.

The most extraordinary of all these subordinate races are certainly the Gipsies, who, living for centuries in the midst of civilized nations, have remained unchanged in their old barbarism and wildness, and have strenuously resisted all efforts for their improvement and civilization. There is no country in Europe which does not contain gipsies, but as Poland has become a second Palestine to the Jews, so the Walachian lands (Transylvania, Eastern Hungary, Moldavia, Walachia, and Bessarabia) have become a second native country to the gipsy race. Throughout Europe they only follow three regular occupations; those of the smith or tinker, of the horse-dealer, or of the musician. Otherwise they employ themselves in the more irregular professions of thief, soothsayer, and beggar.

I will conclude these observations by a statistical table, as accurate as I have the means of making it, of which the first column shall contain the names of the different races of whom I have spoken, the second the principal occupations which they follow in foreign countries, and the third the names of those foreign countries in which they have chiefly settled.

Magyars	Courtiers at Vienna or scattered in different villages.	Vienna. A few Turkish provinces.
Russians	Wealthy persons travelling for pleasure.	Germany. Italy.
Poles	1. Political exiles.	France. England.
	2. Emigrant nobility.	Lithuania. Podolia. Volhynia.
Spaniards	Political fugitives.	France. Italy. England.
Turks	Military colonists.	Along the Danube.
Dacians or Walachians	Civil and Military officers.	Austria. Russia. Turkey.
Tshekhs	1. Industrial colonies.	Austria.
	2. Musicians and retail dealers.	All Europe.
Servians	Fruit and cattle dealers.	Hungary.
Greeks	Brokers, bankers, and tradesmen.	Hungary. Turkey. Russia.
Italians	1. Commercial colonists.	The Levant.
	2. Chimney-sweepers, image dealers, musicians, dancers, &c.	All Europe.
French	Cooks, hairdressers, dancers, milliners, teachers, &c.	All Europe.
English	1. Sailors and merchants.	Portugal. Spain. Russia. Turkey.
	2. Manufacturers.	Germany.
Scandinavians	Agriculture and commerce.	Iceland. Finnland.
Netherlanders	Agriculture.	Germany.
Germans	Agriculture, mining, trade and manufactures.	Eastern Europe.
Jews	Money dealing and retail trading.	All Europe.
Armenians	Trade, agriculture, and cattle-dealing.	South-eastern Europe.
Gipsies	Music, horse-dealing, soothsaying, &c.	All Europe.

I amused myself with these reflections and calculations, on the long dirty road through the Banat, but could not thereby hasten the speed of our heavy coach through the wide waste of mud. We arrived at the village of St. Miklos time enough to witness the last scene of the *Gamin de Paris*, performed by a strolling company of players at the village inn. The part of the Gamin himself was represented by an old man nearly seven feet high, who moved about like a great awkward jointed wooden doll. The performance did not much entertain me, since I had seen the play both better and worse acted; but I was interested in the condition of the poor players. The sudden rise and spread of Magyarism, had done them much mischief, for the Magyar patriots although they have no native dramatic genius with which to supply their place, are very anxious to suppress the German actors in Hungary. At Pesth and other towns where there are many German inhabitants, the attempt has not succeeded, and the Banat, being the residence of many Germans, has also become a place of refuge for the poor German players, driven from other parts of the country. In one of the large towns of Hungary, a number of citizens lately agreed to subscribe a certain sum, in order to retain a regular German theatrical company in the town for the winter: but the patriots interfered; they also wished to have a theatrical company, but it must not be a German one. Being determined to have a Magyar company, the question arose how was this to be done. There are as yet so few Magyar actors in Hungary, that they rate their services very high; and in these egotistical days, expense is just the thing of all others, which the most rampant and noisy patriotism cannot stand. It was therefore decided to have an amateur company of patriotic Magyar ladies and gentlemen; the result of which, of course, is that the city must yawn all through the winter over stupid amateur performances, and that the poor German actors are turned out of employment.

The inn was full of Austrian officers, intelligent and agreeable men, with whom I passed a very pleasant evening. They related to me a curious circumstance which had lately occurred in a Hungarian village of nobles. These peasant nobles had for some time been in the habit of committing various offences with impunity. They had stolen cattle, insulted the commoners, and finally refused to furnish their quantum of recruits at the order of the last diet. The country administration, finding it impossible to bring them to order, summoned to their assistance the *Brachium*, or military force. These people, however, being nobles, and possessed of all the privileges of nobility, the commander of the military force was very cautious for fear of exceeding the limits of his authority. He received the written directions of the county magistrates, and then marched upon the rebellious village. He ordered his soldiers to load and present their muskets, and marched up the village street, where the belligerent nobles assembled, and began throwing stones at the soldiers, laughing at them, and defying them to fire, for their guns were sure to be only loaded with paper. The commanding officer, anxious to avoid bloodshed, gave a private sign to one of the soldiers to let fall his musket as if by accident. This was done, and it was eagerly seized by the rioters, who immediately examined it, and contrary to their expectations, found it laden with a solid leaden bullet. Their courage was wonderfully cooled by this discovery, and they quietly surrendered to the enemy. This *Brachium* is very often called to the assistance of the law in Hungary, but its operations do not always pass off so harmlessly, as on the occasion I have described, where the prudence and humanity *of the commander* prevented the bloodshed, which, under a less considerate officer, must have ensued.

THE BANAT.

The appearance of the Banat beyond St. Miklos, was very peculiar. The country is, as I have said, a perfect level. Many parts of Prussia and Holland are also quite flat and even, yet there is an immense difference between the flatness of those countries and that of the Banat.

The neighbourhood of Berlin, level as it appears, does yet contain small swellings of the ground, little insignificant hollows and rises, and here and there sandy hillocks six or seven feet high. If we view the country from a church tower, or any other elevated point, there are sure to be visible somewhere in the wide landscape hills thirty or forty feet high. Not so in the Banat, where every landscape is as perfectly level as if marked down with plummet and line. Here are no hills forty feet high; not even the smallest hillock or hollow is to be seen. All is smooth, unruffled, and flat, as the ocean during a dead calm.

The landscapes of the Banat might be compared to those of Holland, but there is one great difference between them. Holland is full of rivers, canals, ditches, and dikes; all the country is intersected by them, and the boundaries of the fields are everywhere marked out by water. This feature is entirely wanting in the Banat, which is a very dry country. From St. Miklos to Szegedin, nearly ten (German) miles, we saw, with the exception of a small arm of the Maros, on which Szegedin stands, but one trumpery little brook, which was running about, to what purpose I know not, and in all probability it would have been puzzled itself to assign a reason for its existence. No canals intersect the country; the fields are divided neither by hedges nor ditches; all is one monotonous, dry, unbroken level.

Holland is richly cultivated, and is thickly sown with populous towns and thriving villages. The whole Torontal province contains not a single town, and but one hundred and sixty villages and hamlets, making on an average about one inhabited spot in every square mile. These villages are very unequally arranged, lying sometimes close together, and sometimes three or four miles apart. Between them, all is one dreary and desolate plain, without bush or tree, without hillock or stone.

Among the excellent sketches of Hungary, lithographed by the Englishman Hering, which preserve the true character of the country with a remarkable accuracy and fidelity, unlike any other representations of Hungarian scenery, which I have ever seen, there is a view of one of the desolate plains of the Banat. The print although large, represents nothing whatever but one broad expanse of country, with a broad expanse of sky above; the only object of relief being a stork, who stands beside a well in the foreground. In spite of its monotony, the picture is striking, impressive, indeed I may say highly-picturesque and poetical, as every genuine representation of nature is sure to be. The sky is covered with light clouds, faintly tinted by the morning sun, which follow one another in long gradual perspective to the distant horizon. The plain lies quite desolate and level in the foreground, and further and further, the long even parallel lines repeat themselves again and again, fainter and fainter, into the boundless distance of the far-off horizon. As the eye follows these lines, it seems to descry continually a further boundless desert, beyond what at first seemed the horizon. The colours change on all sides in the same gradual manner, from the bright green of the foreground to a more bluish green, then to gray, and lastly to a pale distant blue. There is a strange dreary solemnity in the spectacle; not even one little bird is to be seen fluttering through the air. A slight line of shading on the horizon, alone indicates the possibility that some solitary herdsmen have kindled a fire at a distance. The lonely stork in the foreground stands motionless; the only living thing in the wilderness, save the frogs hopping about in the marshy ground around him. The pump at the well, is desolate and seldom visited, and the clanking of its handle as the wind moving over the plain raises and stirs it, accompanies the croaking of the busy frogs, and thus forms a dreary concert, which night and day is the only sound that disturbs the perfect silence.

This excellent picture of Hering, is a true representation of a great many scenes in Hungary. Let the reader imagine a great picture-gallery, containing 500 such pictures, each representing the same objects, sky, plain, pump, and stork, with only this variation, that in one picture the clouds shall be grouped differently from what they are in another; in one, the pump-handle is swinging to the right, in another to the left; in one the stork stands on his right leg, in another on his left; in one he is routing among his feathers with his beak, in another he has caught a frog. At every tenth picture, the prospect might be varied by the presence of a solitary herdsman with his herd, and at every twentieth by some distant village steeple on the horizon. The marsh in the foreground might here and there contain a few reeds and rushes, with which variation, however, the painter must by no means be too liberal; and finally, every hundredth picture might represent the interior of a village. Such a gallery would be a perfectly correct representation of the plains of Eastern Hungary.

It was the most beautiful weather possible, and the plain between St. Miklos and Szegedin therefore, appeared to the greatest advantage to us. The rain had softened the ground, and it was only at a very slow pace that we could crawl through the thick heavy mud. In Germany, when the roads are in this way almost impassable, there are many remedies. The traveller may, for instance, get out, and walk in some pleasant dry little footpath beside the carriage, or if none such is to be had, he can at least jump from stone to stone. In the Banat, where there are no footpaths through the fields, and no large stones in the roads, this is impossible. The grass by the roadside often invited us to try and walk there, but we found this to be quite out of the question. The earth everywhere was one thick pudding of mud, I even wondered how the blades of grass could stand erect in it. It is a most disagreeable situation to find oneself thus in the midst of a boundless expanse of mire, in which not one spot is to be found where a man can firmly plant his foot.

The warm sunshine only increased our difficulties, for the higher the sun rose the hotter it became, and the more the mass of mud thickened. The day before, the rain had kept it all fluid, and the mud was washed off our wheels as soon as it stuck there. To-day, on the contrary, the mud was thick, tough, heavy, and adhesive. As I had nothing else to do, I attentively watched the process of mud coating on the wheels. First, the iron wheelhoops were covered with slime, then the sides of the spokes: the coating became thicker and thicker, and heavy masses of mud clung to the axletree. From these small pieces continually fell, and clung round the spokes, enveloping the whole wheel with tough slime, and finally, all the spaces between the spokes filled up. The poor horses toiled and panted, the wheels grew heavier and heavier with their tough load, and at length they were no longer distinguishable as wheels, but appeared four, thick, solid, balls of heavy mud, in which, literally, no trace of a spoke was discoverable!

As in Russia people are sometimes frozen in, so in the Banat we were now *mudded-in*. It was quite impossible to get the carriage an inch further, and we had all to get down, and arming ourselves with hatchets and thick sticks, which had been taken with us in anticipation of such an emergency, we had to set to work at knocking and scraping off the mud from the wheels. This was to be done very quickly, for as the sun grew hotter and hotter, there was now some danger of our being *dried in*. The tough slime of a Banat plain very soon dries, and then becomes as hard as stone. We were in dread, every minute, of seeing ourselves locked in the stony earth, but we worked away on that very account, with the more activity, and in ten minutes the horses were able to proceed a little. Each of us taking a thick club in his hands, and walking beside the carriage, took one of the wheels under his protection, from which we were engaged incessantly in knocking off the adhering lumps. In spite of these precautions, however, we twice came to a dead lock, and had to stop and go through the old operation.

Such is travelling in the Banat, after rainy weather. Towards noon the fields by the roadside, to our great joy, became dry enough to walk in. We had been told that the by-roads were somewhat preferable, and had therefore abandoned the main road. Although we found ourselves miserably deceived in this respect, yet we were amply indemnified for our mistake, in my opinion at least, as it procured us the interesting spectacle of the great Bulgarian colony of "O Beshenyo," or "Old Beshenova." This place is inhabited by nearly ten thousand Bulgarians, although it is only called a village.

These Bulgarians emigrated to the Banat in the middle of the last century. Bishop Stanislavitsh, their countryman, who was living under Austrian protection, invited them over. They are said to have been tolerably wealthy when they came, but, having been endowed with large tracts of land, which they knew well how to turn to account, they have since then become much richer. Their principal colonies are at "O Beshenyo" and at Vinga. There are in all about twenty-five thousand Bulgarians in the Banat.

It was interesting to me to have an opportunity of comparing these Bulgarian settlements with those which I had formerly seen in South Russia. The manner in which the houses are built, their exterior appearance, and the reputation of the Bulgarians among their neighbours are the same in both places. In both the Bulgarians are considered frugal and penurious, but very industrious and prosperous in their dealings in corn and cattle. It happened that we arrived at the place on a market-day, and several thousand inhabitants, men, women, and children, were assembled in the open market-place. The appearance of the groups was pleasing. The women were all neatly and prettily attired in their national costume.

Little tents and booths were scattered over the market-place, and carpets and cloths were spread out on the dirty ground, upon which grapes, melons, fruits of all kinds, honey-cakes of all forms, pipes, pipeheads, sheepskins, and woollen garments, were laid out for sale.

A few venerable old beggars sauntered among the merry groups of chaffering bargainers and cheerful holiday-makers; and in several places sat a few blind singers and *gusle* players, sometimes on little grass hillocks, and sometimes on the muddy ground itself. I stood listening to one of these players, whose melancholy and monotonous voice was lost in the noise around, and attentively examined his instrument or *gusle*. It is a stringed instrument played with a bow, but instead of being held between the knees, or between the chin and shoulder, the player sits on the ground and lays the *gusle* on his knees. The case is shaped like a half drum, or something like a tortoise. This case is covered with skin, and over the sounding-board is drawn one long thick string, made of black twisted horsehair. It is struck with a strong bow, made of wood, bent into a crescent shape with light strings of horsehair covered with rosin. This bow is bound with iron, by way of greater security, and little iron rings are loosely hung along it, so that when the musician plays quickly, the song and the music is accompanied by a lively tinkling, like that of bells. The *gusle* is never played except as an accompaniment to the voice, and the slow, melancholy, but often pleasing melody of the voice, united to the monotonous tones of the *gusle*, and the quick tinkling of the iron rings, forms a musical ensemble, very peculiar, but by no means displeasing.

The poor blind singer whom I was observing, sat half-naked on the bare muddy ground. His bare feet and legs were covered up to the knees with the black thick slime of the marsh. His garment was all in holes and tatters, his long black hair flowed wildly over his naked shoulders, and his sightless eyeballs were raised to heaven, as if vainly seeking for light, while his voice gave forth in melancholy music, the words, " *O, velika Bogu slava! O, velika Christi ima!*" (Oh, the great name of Christ! Oh, the blessed name of the holy mother Mary!) These were the only words I understood of the song, and never had the praise of God's glory and the name of Christ sounded to me so touchingly as from the lips of this poor blind beggar, on whom the blessings of Providence seemed to have fallen so sparingly.

I asked one of the public officers of the village, who was pacing the market-place, whether they did nothing for these unfortunates. " Oh, yes, we do," said he, " but there are a great many destitute blind here." I remembered the numbers of blind beggars I had seen in South Russia, four or five wandering about together in a row, hand in hand, and I began to consider whether there could be any peculiarity in the climate of these Slavonian countries, or in the physiology of the race, to cause this frightful prevalence of blindness.

When we left O Beshenyo, and proceeded through the muddy plain beyond, I had occasion to notice the astonishing quantities of cattle owned by the Bulgarians. The wide grassy plain was covered, as far as the eye could reach, with herds of sheep, oxen, geese, pigs, and horses. I noticed that these herds were divided into innumerable small detachments, and was told that this was occasioned by the circumstance that a Bulgarian peasant when he dies always divides his land and live-stock into small portions, one of which he leaves to each child. The Germans of the Banat, on the contrary, always leave their property undivided to the eldest son, who pays to the other sons a certain compensation in money for their inheritance. I have seen three Bulgarians ploughing at the same time on a field which was scarcely a *yoke* in extent, but of which each possessed a separate corner.

After passing the last of these Bulgarian herds, we again entered the vast, monotonous, dreary marsh. One of my travelling companions related a curious anecdote of a wolf, which seems to prove the impossibility of ever thoroughly subduing the savage nature of these creatures. A herdsman had bought a young wolf with the intention of taming and bringing it up. The animal grew very docile, soon learning to come at his call, and to eat the bread, milk, vegetables, &c. which were offered it. As long as it remained young and small, the herdsman took it out with him on his rides through the steppes, putting the creature before him on horseback, where it clung fast to the saddle, and gave no trouble. As it grew up, he allowed the wolf to run beside him like a dog. When its master was absent for a few days, it gave every sign of sorrow and trouble; when he returned, it was beside itself for joy. The animal was now more than a year old, appeared totally to have forgotten the savage habits of its race, and was thought to have been thoroughly tamed and domesticated. All at once, and without any warning, it resumed its old nature. The herdsman came home one day from a long journey, and went as usual to caress his wolf, but the creature knew him no longer, it crept growling into a corner of the stable, and when its master approached, snapped fiercely at him. The herdsman adopted his former method of education; he gave his pupil a severe beating, left him to fast for three days, and then beat him again, and after this discipline, offered him food. The hungry wolf eagerly snapped up the food, but from that time forward became so fierce, untractable, and savage, that in the end his master was obliged to shoot him.

I soon after heard the melancholy story of the death of the young Servian above mentioned, with whom I made acquaintance at Raab. We were in the midst of a dreary waste or "*Puste*," as they are here called, when we reached one of those lonely pumps which I have mentioned in describing Hering's picture. To the right and left of these pumps are large troughs for cattle to drink at. Our horses were unharnessed and taken to one of these troughs: at the other sat some gossiping herdsmen beside their cattle. It was a tremendously hot day, and the bare unsheltered plain lay far on every side, scorched by the heat of the sun. I noticed at some distance a little hillock, upon which was raised a rude cross. I asked our coachman the meaning of it. He replied in broad Austrian, "'Tis the grave of a poor young Servian, who was murdered and buried here." "Did you know him?" "Ah, Jesu Maria! yes, very well. He was a good young man, and a great friend of mine. Four weeks ago he was in Raab, where he sold pigs, and got 17,000 florins ready money for 'em. He was going back to Servia with his partner, who was a rascal, and not contented with his own share of the profit, wanted to have his partner's 17,000 florins. He plotted with the coachman, and in yonder *tsharde* over there they settled all about it." As he spoke he pointed to a solitary tsharde, or wayside public-house at some distance, which was the only object that broke the dreary uniformity of the scene. He then proceeded to relate how the Servian wished to spend the night at this tsharde, but it was a fine night, and his treacherous companions persuaded him to proceed, as they had yet time to reach the next house. At this well the murderers fell upon and killed him. This, however, they did not succeed in doing at once, for the earth was found marked with footsteps, and traces of blood for some distance. He was a strong and brave young man, and probably defended himself gallantly for some time, so that the murderers, after stabbing him in several places had to despatch him with their pistols. They then threw his body into the well, and made off with his money. The next day some herdsmen coming to the well, found the water tinged with blood, and on examination discovered the body. "They pulled it out, threw earth over it, and stuck that cross upon the mound." "But the people at the tsharde must have heard the sound of the pistols?" "I don't know—they might." "Perhaps they were accomplices in the murder?" "I don't know—they might be." On inquiring the age, name, and date, of the event, I soon identified the unfortunate victim with my young acquaintance at Raab. I could not overcome for some time, the melancholy sensations excited by this story. The conversation having been led to this topic, my travelling companions continued all day long to relate various dismal stories of robberies and other atrocities committed in these lonely wastes. I shall not repeat them, partly because I am not sufficiently convinced of their truth, and partly because I take little pleasure in again occupying my mind with such revolting narratives. Certain it is, however, that these things are fearfully frequent in their occurrence in the Banat.

We had been told of a little sandy tract of country lying in the midst of the marsh, and in order to advance quicker on the sandy ground, we made a little round to pass over it. Such little sandy tracts are very scarce in the northern part of the Banat, though very common in the south.

At noon we reached a German village, where we dined. It was at this place that our coachman fell sick of a fever, and for the rest of the journey our Jew had to do his business. Here, as in South Russia, all the houses in the country, even those of the better sort, are made of earth. The manner of building them is as follows:—The extent and outline of the house to be built is marked out on the bare ground with a spade. Two planks are then stuck on edge, parallel to one another, leaving them as far distant as the wall is intended to be thick. Earth is next put in between those boards, and carefully stamped down. The same operation is continued with other boards, and more earth, till the wall is completed. The boards are fastened together with iron clasps. The earth very soon becomes extremely solid, and forms a good wall.

The further we proceeded towards the north-western extremity of the Banat, the more every thing began to wear a Magyar appearance. Even the German colonists became fewer and fewer, and the last few villages were almost exclusively inhabited by Hungarians.

We spent the night at one of the tshardes mentioned above. These tshardes all consist of two buildings, one for travellers, and the other for horses. Between these is a large courtyard, in the middle of which is a shed for carts and coaches. The whole is surrounded with a high wall, in which are two gates, one for ingress and the other for egress. These gates are regularly closed and barred every night, like the gates of a fortress; "Else," said our coachman, "no horse would be secure in his stable."

The courtyards of the houses in the Hungarian villages were all tapestried with quantities of tobacco-leaves strung together, beside which, busied in sorting and arranging them, sat the members of the household. In one of these villages I observed the manner in which sheep are milked in this district. The great, brown, cyclops-like shepherd, sat half-naked on a block of wood in the doorway of the courtyard, within which stood the sheep. A boy came behind and chased them out one by one. As each sheep came opposite to him, the shepherd seized its hind leg, forced down its head with his elbow, and squeezed the udders roughly in his other hand. This done, he let it go, and the boy drove out another, and so on, till all were milked. The operation was very rapidly performed.

We now passed the Bathyany estates, which I have already spoken of. The inhabitants of a lonely tsharde, near where our horses stopped to eat hay for the last time in the Banat, were ignorant whether there was any steward or administrator on the estate, or whether it was let on lease or not; they said they knew no one but the cashier, who came to them once a year, and who was the only person they had to do with. Near the borders of the Banat, we came to some bridges running over the now dry bed of an arm of the Maros, which I was told often rose high enough, in the spring, to overflow the surrounding country. The course of the Maros towards the Theiss is peculiarly calculated to promote inundations. Just before its confluence with the larger river the Maros makes a sudden bend, so the waters of the two meet each other, when they join. The consequence is, that when both the rivers swell, in the spring, the waters of the Maros have no chance of an escape, and are pretty sure to overflow the whole country. Dams and dikes, indeed, run along the banks of both these rivers, but they are very imperfect, and quite inadequate to the proposed end. A plan has long been on foot for conducting the waters of the Maros into those of the Theiss, in a more favourable direction, by means of a canal, but, practicable as the scheme appears, it has never been carried into effect.

SZEGEDIN, THE SODA MANUFACTORIES, AND THE ITALIAN PRISONERS.

Szegedin, the most important of the cities of the Theiss, is situated on the right bank of that river, at its juncture with the Maros, and contains nearly forty thousand inhabitants. We entered the town towards evening, accompanied by large herds of cattle, and by innumerable flights of starlings and other small birds, such as seldom fail to follow the course of great herds of cattle. In the suburbs we saw small parties of Servian cattle-dealers, all armed with abundance of daggers and pistols, riding out to meet their herds. In the suburbs of Szegedin, every thing we saw bore reference to cattle, cattle-dealers, and cattle-feeding. We observed large open spaces, in which several men were busied in sorting hay into small heaps for the cattle ; and in other places we saw the long grated barns, or *koras*, of which mention has already been made, and which were full of Indian corn gathered together for the consumption of man.

The suburbs of Szegedin, as well as the town itself, are very extensive; and the saying that Szegedin is as large as London, is no great exaggeration, though the population of the one town is nearly fifty times that of the other. This straggling manner of building is common to all genuine Hungarian towns, and such an one is Szegedin. Its insignificant little houses stretch along in broad, unvaried, unpaved streets, full of dust or mud. Not that these houses are in themselves ugly, for although they make no pretensions to solidity and architectural beauty, yet their coatings of green paint, and the trees which stand before many of them, give them a neat and cheerful appearance.

The principal streets are intersected by long wooden trottoirs or bridges, a very necessary precaution to keep the pedestrian from sinking into the heavy, tough slime of the unpaved mud. Upon these wooden bridges, the stranger may perambulate for hours through the wide, straggling, tiresome streets, till at last the city, without walls or gates, without prologue or epilogue, loses itself in the green plains around.

All genuine Hungarian towns are built in this manner, resembling, according to our ideas, not so much towns as immense villages, both in their appearance and population. Most of the citizens of these towns, the mechanics, tradesmen, and petty nobility, follow not merely a civic occupation, but also some agricultural pursuit, such as cattle-dealing, corn-growing, or vine-planting, which in other countries is exclusively in the hands of the country-people. Each of these towns has its so-called "*Határ*," or agricultural territory, or city environs, the lands of which are not occupied by agricultural villages, but are portioned out among the citizens and guilds of the town itself. The Határ of Szegedin contains more than twelve (German) square miles. Each citizen has here his little estate, with its lonely country-house, or *Szallash*, in the middle. Here the mechanics, tradespeople, &c., of the city, come out in the summer to live in their lonely *Szallashes*, and feed cattle, tend vines, plant tobacco, sow maize, &c.; and having thus provided themselves with a winter stock of health and eatables, they return in the autumn to their various civic avocations. Without the produce of these little estates, the business of the winter would scarcely suffice for the support of the town.

Passing over the long bridge of boats which crosses the Theiss at Szegedin, we entered an inn, whose spacious rooms, good beds, satisfactory cookery, and excellent company, left us nothing to desire. The next morning, I hastened as early as possible, to the fish-market to see the celebrated fish of the Theiss, which are to be had at Szegedin in the greatest perfection. The market was intersected by long rows of fishtubs and barrels, between which the buyers and sellers moved up and down, all noisy, busy, and animated, chaffering and bargaining, while fresh parties of fishermen were continually entering the market, lugging along heavy nets full of fresh, active, lively fish of all kinds. I was told that 100 large fat carp may be purchased here for a ducat! The prices of other fish are in proportion. Twenty-five fine crabs cost but one *Kreuzer Münze*. The fishermen told me that they often drew as many as 8000 crabs out of the water at once. A certain *embarras de richesse* arises in consequence; namely, the difficulty of getting consumers for this abundance of fish. The pigs are valuable assistants in this dilemma. All Szegedin smells of fish, and below the city the Theiss is continually casting up multitudes of the finny race to die and putrify along the banks. The consequence is, that at times the place stinks of fish beyond endurance, which is the more unpleasant, as the whole population is obliged to drink the water of the Theiss, the wells and springs of the vicinity being almost all bad or impregnated with saltpetre. Szegedin supplies all the Banat and a great part of Hungary and Turkey with fish. The Walachians dry fish in the open air, and eat them raw like bread. It is strange how much embarrassment and evil, her very wealth causes at present to Hungary: or rather, it is not strange; for Hungary, though rich in natural produ tions, is poor in human energy, power, and intelligence, in arts, industry, and cultivation; so that the teeming fertility of her soil, her rivers, and her mountains, is often worse than unavailing to her.

Having seen the fish-market, I proceeded to another of the important and interesting sights of Szegedin,—namely, the soda manufactories; with one of the inhabitants of the town, who was kind enough to give up his time to me, I drove out into the suburbs, where these manufactories are situated.

Not merely in the neighbourhood of Szegedin, in the great steppes between the Theiss and the Danube, but also in some part of the country on the other side of the Danube, as well as in all the flat country up the Theiss as far as Debretzin, the soil is more or less impregnated with alkaline particles. The earth, thus impregnated with mineral salts, is called by the Hungarians *Szek*, or *Szeg*, from which is derived the Hungarian name *Szeged*, afterwards lengthened into Szegedin. These alkaline particles are gradually conducted by a series of natural operations, to the surface of the earth. The frequent dews and rains are very useful in piercing and loosening the earth, in dissolving the salt crystals and drawing them to the surface; when these rains are followed by sunshine, the water evaporates, and leaves numberless little particles of alkaline salt on the ground, which cover whole tracts of country with a fine, white, crystalline powder.

Continuous rain and drought are alike unfavourable to the production of these crystals; but a gentle dew during the night, and fresh sunshine in the morning, ensure a plentiful supply. Early in the morning, the peasants sweep together the white powder, and take it into the city to sell it to the manufacturers. It is brought into the manufactories in a very impure state, of a gray colour, mixed in the proportion of one to three parts, with earth. The business of the soda boilers, is to separate the pure alkali from the impure alloy of earth. The *Szek* is often gathered from naturally damp places, marshes, morasses, bogs, &c., where the evaporation of the water effects the desired end without rain or dew. Nevertheless, a long drought is hurtful even here, because the salt particles cannot pierce the hard dry crust of earth. The Hungarians call these places " *Szekso-Stavaks*," which may be translated by " alkaline bogs." These alkaline bogs present numberless curious phenomena to the observing naturalist. Sometimes they become what is technically called " *blind*," that is, their alkaline stores having become, apparently, exhausted, they cease to be productive, though, generally, after some time, they begin to yield again. Sometimes soda appears in a place where it has never been found before. Most of these alkaline bogs appear to be inexhaustible.

The manufactories, in which the impregnated earth is purified and concentrated into good soda, are called in Hungarian, *Szekso-Gyars*. The soap manufactories of the city, of which I was told, though I somewhat doubt the fact, that there are no fewer than one hundred, prefer buying the impure Szek as it is brought to town by the peasants. This old custom is extremely injudicious, for a hundredweight of pure soda would go as far as three hundred weight of the impure Szek; besides, were it not for this habit, the process of boiling the soap would be considerably facilitated, and the soap itself would be better in quality; there would be less waste, and fewer pigs would be killed for soap. They, however, keep to their old practices with conservative tenacity; and the fine, pure, snow-white soda, produced in the manufactories, is sent to Vienna or Pesth.

The soda manufactories of Szegedin differ in nothing that I am aware of, from those of other places. The gray Szek is kept in great covered magazines, soaked in large wooden vats, and then boiled in great kettles; the dirty sediment is next melted in pans, and the earthy particles burnt or skinned off, so that the pure soda is at last collected, and poured into forms.

Driving back into town, we went to see the third of the Lions of Szegedin, namely the interior of its fortress, in which is situated the Italian Convict Institution. The fortress of Szegedin, once the residence of the Turkish Pasha and his janizaries, is a lofty building, with spacious inner courts, and two or three large gates. It lies on the banks of the Theiss, in the middle of the town, surrounded by the busiest part of the city. The fish, fruit, and vegetable markets stretch up to the fortress walls, and on the other side lies the public promenade of Szegedin, along which we now proceeded as best we might, by means of wooden boards and stepping-stones, through the mire and squash, into the fortress, with the purpose of visiting the Italian Convict Institution.

Szegedin is known to contain no less than 560 political Italian captives; a fact which occasioned a great deal of discussion in the last Hungarian diet, when the celebrated orator, Gabriel Klauzal, deputy for the Tshongrad comitat, in which Szegedin is situated, proposed a petition to government for their liberation. The motion was adopted unanimously by the Chamber of Representatives. Many dreadful stories are circulated in Hungary of the miserable situation, and of the ill-treatment which these prisoners have to endure. I shall here simply record the result of my own observations, which I think will suffice to prove the falsehood of some of these calumnious reports.

We passed through the old Turkish gate, and entered a courtyard full of Austrian soldiers, which was divided from an inner courtyard by a wooden grating. At this grating sat women with baskets of fruit, needles, cotton, and other trifles; the inner courtyard was filled with the Italian prisoners themselves. They looked neat and clean, and were dressed in strong gray linen, with caps of the same material on their heads. I had heard that their aspect would excite compassion and pity, on account of the harsh treatment it indicated. Compassion and pity their aspect certainly did excite, for these men were exiles from their country, and deprived of their liberty; but there was no sign whatever of their having suffered from close confinement, bad air, and scanty food. They all seemed in good health, and moved about in the large courtyard—I will not say with gaiety, for that would have been strange indeed,—but at least with animation and activity. They have plenty of time allotted them for exercise in this courtyard, during which time they can buy any trifles they want, of the women at the grating, and at the same time sell the products of their own labour. They manufacture many little articles of horn, wood, and paper, such as needlecases, saints' effigies, folding sticks, little baskets and boxes, little rings of plaited horsehair, &c. They were all standing about the grating, and as soon as ever any one appeared in the outer yard, they stretched their arms and hands out as far as possible, holding out their various merchandise, and screaming with much animation in a strange jumble of Italian, German, and Hungarian. "*Nobile! kaufend Nobile! gigi! gigi!* (*gigi* is an Italianized corruption of a Hungarian word for rings) or "*Nobile! kaufen! Napoleone, Napoleone!*" The countenance of the great Corsican is repeated upon almost all their little wares, and most of them had their hands full of Napoleons.

The fortress is commanded by an Italian general, who is the superintendent of the convict institution, which forms a regular little military community of prisoners, having its own priest, its own provision-masters, its own overseers, secretaries, physicians, &c. I presented myself to one of the authorities, and easily obtained permission to view the interior.

Round various inner courts were ranged the separate habitations of the prisoners, which were formerly the casemates of the soldiers. They were all above ground, very spacious and airy, and at regular distances from one another. The bedsteads were clean and good, and indeed I have seen many barracks in our best German cities, where the soldiers were not so well lodged as were these prisoners. Over each bedstead was inscribed the name and birthplace of the prisoner to whom it belonged: for instance, "Giovanni N. N. of Rodrigo;" "Martino N. N. of Verona;" "Ludovico N. N. of Venice," &c. "The national jealousies of these people are continued even here," said one of the Austrian officers to me. "The Milanese and Venetians here, for instance, are sworn foes to each other."

The casemates are lighted from the inner courts, but some of them have also strongly grated windows on the outer side. Many prisoners had hung up little stores of grapes on their window-bars, and others had little singing-birds in cages in their cells. I did not see their food, but their appearance proved that they did not suffer from hunger; and I have no reason to doubt the assurance of the Austrian officer, that they not only had abundance of meat and bread, but also a small portion of wine every day. They also procure themselves many little comforts, partly by the merchandise that they sell, and partly by the money sent them by their Italian friends and relatives. It is said that these 560 prisoners annually receive no less than 40,000 florins from Italy. If one could but learn the history of the various little savings which make up this important sum, what proofs of tender constancy, generous self-denial, and yearning affection, might they not disclose!

The workshops of the prisoners were separate from their sleeping-rooms. Their work is not voluntary but compulsory. Each is obliged to follow the profession or trade that he practised at home, or else to choose for himself another. This compulsion is truly a benevolent one; for nothing is more likely to render captivity endurable than regular occupation, particularly when, as is here the case, it is neither excessively laborious, nor continued for an undue length of time. Some work as carpenters, others as turners, and others, again, manufacture articles in papier maché, &c. They are divided into various workshops, according to their occupations, and over the door of each workshop the names of the trades carried on there are inscribed in Italian. In one of the turning-rooms I found a great many little busts of Napoleon in different stages of progression, in each of which the characteristic features, indelibly impressed on the retentive memories of the prisoners, were accurately repeated from recollection alone. "They often, sing, jest, and gossip, over their work," said the officer, "and sometimes they dance." Thank God, thought I, that their light volatile dispositions enable them so far to forget their unhappy fate and their dreary situation!

I had asked while yet in the Banat, of what crimes these people were guilty. "Oh, I don't know, I'm sure," replied every one; "probably they are gamblers, drunkards, and riotous persons, sent from Italy to Hungary to learn better manners. They are the refuse of their nation." I do not believe this, for the refined, intelligent, and cultivated countenances of many, proved to me that they were not of the lowest classes. They are accused of no crimes, at least of no legally punishable ones, and have never been regularly condemned. Many are only political enthusiasts and patriots, arrested in 1830 and 1831, and sent here for an indefinite time. This is the true misery of their situation, that for no definite offence whatever are they sent here, where none of them know how long they are to remain. They are tortured by continual suspense, doubt, and anxiety; by fear, lest perhaps they may never more behold their beautiful Italy, and by the hope that liberty perhaps may be each moment awaiting them. It seems to me that this agony of suspense must be a great deal worse than if they knew distinctly how long they were to be prisoners, were it even for 30 years; and it is dreadful to know that they are kept here by no law, but by the mere exercise of arbitrary power. It must be allowed, however, that these enthusiastic lovers of national independence, these haters of foreign domination, though we may regard them with pity, cannot be looked on otherwise than as necessary victims. It may fairly be argued that Austria, having once asserted her right to rule in Italy, she must vindicate her power there against that of France; that to support the existing order and peace, and for the sake of the Italians themselves, it is necessary to restrain restive patriotism; that consequently though the individuals may be pitied, the precautions of the government ought to be lauded. Still, allowing all this to be true, it remains certain, that in the absence of any regular trial, condemnation, or even accusation, many completely innocent persons, many, I mean, who are even innocent of the remotest approximation to rebellious or unruly patriotism, are probably suffering the pains of exile and captivity at Szegedin. It were more creditable, therefore, to the Austrian government, to institute a regular inquiry and examination, to find out whether it is really true, as is often stated, that many prisoners are at present confined here, who are as ignorant themselves as all the rest of the world is ignorant of any valid reason *why* they should not be at liberty.

When I picture to myself how many fond Italian hearts, now languishing in doubt and uncertainty, would have longed to accompany me in that day's walk through the chambers, courtyards, and workshops of the convict institution, to search out some dear familiar face, among those to me so unfamiliar and unknown,—when I reflect how dreary, how disconsolate, how utterly miserable and gloomy, is the life which those fond hearts imagine to be endured by their dear ones at Szegedin,—I feel no little pleasure in the hope that I am doing some good by recording in print what I saw and heard there (which I frankly confess was but little, and perhaps of no great value), in the hope that these pages may meet the eye of some who will derive consolation from the assurance that the necessary privations and sufferings of exile and captivity, are not, at Szegedin, yet further imbittered by unnecessary harshness, neglect, or cruelty.

I was informed that it was the intention of government very soon to send back to Italy eighty of the prisoners, who were considered as having sufficiently expiated their offences. May this prove no empty report, and may the rest of the captives soon follow them! I confess that I scarcely liked to meet the glances of those prisoners whom I saw, for I reflected how many of them, far less guilty than I was myself, might be spending their days in dreary captivity, while I, deserving it as much as they, enjoyed freedom to go wherever, and do whatever, I pleased.

"At Christmas we are very merry here," said the officer to me; "for then the prisoners have a little festival. The doors of the *Rastell* (so they call the wooden grating) are opened, and every one may pass in and out. Then the prisoners have a fair, and the townspeople come and buy of them, and talk to them. Both the townspeople and the Italians look forward to this festival with great pleasure! It may afford some little comfort to many a friend and relative in Italy, to hear of this Christmas festival.

The Hungarians, who are themselves such fiery patriots, such enthusiasts for political independence, are naturally very averse to having their country called the Siberia of Austria, and used as a place of banishment for the patriots of other countries. It was this feeling that occasioned the discussion in the last diet, and in the next the Hungarians will, no doubt, again exert all their influence in favour of the captives. The Hungarians themselves dread nothing so much as exile, and transportation would be the most terrible of punishments even to the vulgarest Hungarian criminal. It has long been the intention of government to constitute one of the desert islands on the Dalmatian coast, a place of banishment for Hungarian criminals. The bandits of the Bakonyer Forest, the cattle-stealers of the steppes, and the robbers and murderers of the *tshardes*, would certainly dread such transportation much more than the gallows.

The fortress, with its convict institution, lies in the middle of the town, surrounded by the *Palanka*, the original nucleus of Szegedin. This Palanka contains the principal buildings, the Town-house, the Gymnasium, the Guard-house, several good inns and hotels, plenty of private houses, and also the Military School, which was the next place I visited. Unfortunately, I could see but little of the school, a more important visiter than my humble self was there at the time. This was the commanding officer, who but seldom visits Szegedin, and in whose honour all the soldiers of the town, as well as the future soldiers of the Military School, wore on that day large oak boughs in their hats. This custom is observed on every festive occasion in the Austrian army. I do not know that any other army does the same, and yet no cheaper, handsomer, or, for German soldiers, more characteristic ornament could be devised. A branch of oak-leaves is a more really beautiful object than a plume of feathers, and great numbers of them together have a very gay and cheerful appearance. The oak is to the Germans what the laurel is to the Italians, and the olive to the Spaniard. Linden-leaves would be too large, birch-leaves too limp, and willow-leaves too fragile; but the graceful and elegant appearance, the durability, and erect stately position of the oak-leaves, no less than their symbolic attributes, make them a characteristic and suitable ornament for German soldiers.

At the military school all the scholars learn to fence, write, &c., with the left hand as well as with the right. This is certainly an excellent practice in a military school, whose pupils in after life may so often be exposed to lose their right arms. By this practice both arms are made equally useful.

After seeing the military school I went to that of the priests, who have a great Lyceum at Szegedin. Here I saw many interesting things; for instance, in their library, which consisted of six thousand volumes, was a coin of Rakostky, the celebrated Hungarian patriot, who at the beginning of the last century stood at the head of the Hungarian rebellion. This coin has the motto "*Pro Libertate.*" I was told the following anecdote of this coin:—The Emperor Leopold, during the insurrection of Rakotsky, took one of these coins in his hand, and turning to an Hungarian near him, asked the meaning of the words "*Pro Libertate.*" He was told that each of the letters stood for a separate word, and that the whole signified "*Princeps Rakotsky Ope Legionis Inclyti Bercaenii et Reliquorum Totam Austriam Trucidabit Ense*" (Prince Rakotsky, with the half of the legion of the illustrious Bertsheny and of his other companions, will destroy all Austria with the sword). The emperor laughed, and said that he had understood the letters to signify a different prophecy: "*Peribitis Rebellantes Omnes Laqueo, Igne, Bello, et Reliqui Toti Austriæ Tributarii Eritis*" (Ye shall perish, ye rebels all, by the rope, the fire, and the sword, and the rest will become tributary to Austria). Although Leopold, having been educated for the church, must have been a good Latin scholar, yet both the mental feebleness and the mild disposition of that emperor, render the truth of this story extremely questionable.

I dined with these ecclesiastical gentlemen, to whose learned provost I had been recommended. There was a numerous party assembled, and our conversation was animated and instructive. An old Swiss gentleman, the father of the provost, presided at table. The conversation turned on the great age which the Hungarians often attained; and a story was related of a woman who had died at Szegedin a fortnight before, at the age of one hundred and fourteen, and who was in good health to the end of her days. I was also told of another family now living, in which a brother and sister were eighty and ninety years old, yet their parents and grand parents were all living and in good health.

After dinner I viewed the town from the steeple of the parish church, and though the day was remarkably cloudless, to my astonishment I saw the whole of Szegedin enveloped in a thick, cloudy mist, precisely like that of Pesth. I know not what it is in these cities, whether perhaps it is a kind of dust from the steppes, or some other cause, that gives them this appearance.

Towards evening the sound of music attracted us to the Szegedin promenade. It is decorated with a few young linden and acacia trees, and though by no means an attractive promenade, it is a new and useful undertaking. The ladies of the upper classes at Szegedin do not as yet frequent its walks. The musicians were gipsies, of whose performances the Hungarians are passionately fond, but as they sat there in decent, regular, orderly clothing, playing the waltzes of Strauss and the airs of Auber and Bellini, they pleased me far less than when, clad in their own wild, picturesque attire, they poured forth the melancholy songs of their race. The musicians were close to the walls of the convict institution, and it is to be hoped that the sound of their cheerful melodies might reach the ears of the poor captives, and amuse their evening leisure; but the walls I fear were too thick and high.

It is strange that the province of Tshongrad should have been named after the insignificant town of Tshongrad, rather than after the far more populous and important Szegedin; and again, that the county assemblies should be held, not at Tshongrad or Szegedin, but at the village of Szegvar. This is the case in many other provinces; the reason being that the

Hungarian nobility, who conduct the county assemblies, are not fond of the cities, in which, like other citizens they are subject to the superintendence of the city magistrates and police. The magnates therefore prefer meeting in a village, where they are more free and uncontrolled.

Szegedin is one of the most patriotic cities of Hungary, far more so than Pesth. Indeed it often happens that provincial towns exceed the capital of the country in patriotism; besides, it has been often observed that the Slovaks and Servians converted to Magyarism, go further in their Magyarmania than the original Magyars themselves.

I spent the evening at the Szegedin club, in very entertaining mixed society. Throughout my journey in Hungary I always greatly enjoyed these clubs, which are now established in all the principal towns of Hungary, and I often anticipated during the whole day the pleasures of the evening's social meeting. Our conversation at these meetings turned usually on politics, and mostly on German politics. The Hungarians watch the proceedings of the Germans as we do those of the French and English. They take a lively interest in the proceedings of our constitutional states; receive with indignation the tidings of any unconstitutional or arbitrary movement on the part of a German government, and manifest the warmest admiration and sympathy when they perceive any evidence of high-spirited and independent patriotism in the people of a German state. I found all the Magyars full of admiration and delight at the noble bearing of the Hanoverians, and many a distinguished and warm-hearted Hungarian commissioned to carry back with me to Hanover the assurance of his hearty sympathy, and cordial admiration to Rumann and his noble associates. If Rumann were ever to come to Hungary he would be welcomed with the same universal respect and esteem which greeted Lafayette in America— but *certain other people who shall be nameless*, had better keep away from Hungary.

THE PUSTEN AND THEIR INHABITANTS.

"*Mektshemerek teck peck feck!*"

"Ah, my boy, what do you want? My clothes? There they are!"

"*Nintsh! Hayuk muk puk fuk tellemtalletell!*"

"What do you mean? Do you want my boots to black? There they stand."

"*Nintsh! Yöngörtöryöm függo mesh müggo!*"

"My good fellow, I don't understand a word of Hungarian."

Such was the conversation that I held at four o'clock the next morning (two weeks before sunrise, according to the Hungarian saying), with a little boy who approached my bed, and in vain endeavoured to express his meaning in this, to me, unintelligible gibberish. Seeing, however, that the little fellow was growing quite exasperated, and looked as if he was just going to cry, I sprang out of bed, and calling in the drowsy waiter, learned that I must make haste and dress, for the diligence would be there directly. My travelling companions were this day particularly agreeable; and, did not circumstances make it inexpedient, I could give the reader a very attractive description of them. As it is, however, I shall content myself with stating there were four of them, a lady, her little daughter, a clergyman, and myself.

The city of Szegedin soon lay far behind us, and we found ourselves in the midst of the Puste between the Theiss and Danube. The word *Puste*, is a Slavonian word, signifying desert, and has been adopted into the Hungarian language. They speak of the Sahara Puste, the Persian Pusten, &c.; but the word has also another signification. It stands for "empty," or "void," and is, therefore, used for a tract of country without towns and villages, in which sense it by no means necessarily implies a waste barren country. The Pusten of Hungary are often covered with luxuriant herbage, and inhabited by large herds of cattle; but they are always *voids*, containing neither town nor village, nor even a cluster of solitary farmhouses. The word is, in short, synonymous with the Russian *Steppe*. It has always struck me as somewhat singular, that while the words Steppe, Pampas, and Llanos have been regularly adopted among the terms of geography, that of *Puste* is nowhere used but in Hungary.

Immediately after crossing the Theiss, the traveller perceives that he has entered a new kind of country. At Szegedin, the first sand-plain begins, and the ground is no longer as perfectly flat as I have described it in the Banat. The plain is broken by little sand-hillocks; agriculture more and more gives way to grazing. The population consists either entirely of Magyars, or, at least, is thoroughly Magyarized. The sand of this district is very fine, and is mixed with fragments of shells. It extends so deep that nowhere have the inhabitants yet succeeded in boring through it, and reaching its clayey foundation. Large tracts are entirely desolate, without any trace of vegetation. In such places the sand is often raised by the wind into the air, as in the sand-storm of the Sahara. This sand-wind is much dreaded by the Hungarians, for in its course it often destroys the most fertile fields.

Among the remarkable attributes of these deserts, is the total absence of water. In the two hundred German square miles between Pesth and Szegedin, there is no trace of running water, no single brook, river, or stream, and not even a solitary well, with the exception of one little bubbling spring which rises in a marsh near Ketskemet. Another peculiarity of these deserts is the total absence of trees. Every thing is bare, desolate, and naked; nowhere rises a cooling grove, or even a solitary bush or tree.

Sand-plains with sand-wind, green patches with wild birds, marshes with cranes and storks, soda bogs covered with white powder, and occasionally meadows with fine cattle; such are the only varieties seen when travelling on a Puste. Occasionally a lonely Sallash or Tsharde, or a solitary herdsman's hut, gives token of human habitation; now and then a far-off pump, rears and sways its long arm before us, and sometimes, too, though more rarely, we behold the unfailing token of our approach to a town or village, namely a handsome, well kept, large, white—gallows!

The drivers of the diligences, unless they have very effeminate travellers, trouble themselves little about where they stop for the night. They do not look out for a tsharde, but when night comes on, they unharness their horses, and camp out on the plain. Some of them have their little holes or caves grubbed out in the sand, of which no one knows but themselves, and into these they creep for the night. A clergyman at Szegedin told me the following story of one of these campings out:

He was studying at Pesth, and wishing to make a short excursion into his native Banat, he engaged a driver and set off towards Szegedin. The driver was a dark, wild, fierce-looking fellow, and as night came on, seeing himself quite alone with him on the desolate Puste, far from any sight or sound of human habitation, and recollecting the bad reputation enjoyed by the Szegedin drivers, he began to feel very uneasy. He asked several times when they should come to an inn, without receiving any answer, and the driver at last explained that they were very far from any inn, and that as it was already night, they had better camp out on the Puste. He knew, he said, a place where this could be very conveniently done.

They went on for a little while, and at length stopped. "Here," said the driver, "is a hut where we can stop." The young ecclesiastic became more and more uneasy, for he saw no hut at all. He got out, however, and perceived, at a distance, a little straw-covered hole in the sand. He had, on the way, several times given the driver to understand that he was no rich merchant or nobleman, but only a poor ecclesiastical student, and he very emphatically repeated this assurance, as he saw the other disappear into his hole, and presently emerge with a hatchet, and a large knife. The driver replied, as he sharpened his knife, "that that was no matter, that if he had ever so little money, it should make no difference between them." The terrors of the poor ecclesiastic, now raised to the highest pitch, were, however, happily relieved, when he saw his suspected fellow-traveller again disappear in the sand, and fetch up the hind-quarter of a slaughtered calf, of which he cut off a large piece and reinterred the rest. He then made a fire, and roasted the meat on little sticks. The young priest produced a bottle of wine from the carriage, and his fears being allayed, they were very merry over their supper, which was eaten with a good relish, for the sand of the Puste cools and preserves meat extremely well. They then lay down peacefully together on the dry sand, and slept quietly till morning.

The driver's calf was doubtless not bought, but bestowed upon him by fate. He probably rode out one day merely to amuse himself, and it happened quite by chance, that a little calf met him on the way. He rode up to examine the animal, merely out of curiosity, and it chose to leap into his arms of its own accord. He took it into his hut and killed it, that he might examine it more closely.

The herdsman and drivers of the *Pusten* are all extremely hospitable in their way, and will rob their neighbours without hesitation to entertain a guest. An Hungarian gentleman told us, how, stopping once at a lonely Sallash in the Puste, he found there was nothing whatever to eat in the house. "That is no matter, I'll manage," said a little lad twelve years of age. The boy went out, and in a little while the traveller heard a sheep bleating, then a fire blazing, and finally a joint of meat crackling and hissing before the fire. This little urchin had stolen a sheep, killed it, lighted a fire, and roasted the mutton for the stranger's entertainment. The fact is, that sheep and oxen are looked on in this part of the world almost in the light of *feri naturæ*.

The herdsmen of the Puste are not only attentive observers of the course of the sun, but, by continual observation of the stars, they have become familiar with many of them, and can calculate to a great nicety the time of night by their position. They also practically carry out many scientific principles, which with us are never used in common life. For instance, when they wish to keep any thing cool, they do so by the aid of fire and in the following manner: They dig a hole in the ground, into which they put the milk or whatever else they wish to cool; they leave a long narrow opening at the top, over which they light a fire; this fire draws away all the heat from the hole beneath and leaves it quite cold. They then quickly cover up the hole, and in this manner preserve their food fresh and cool.

These people are very superstitious, and, probably, like all uncultivated races, they are firm believers in the power of the evil eye. They have many other ways of enchanting their enemies; for instance they write certain evil words on a little piece of paper, twist it up into a ball covered with cotton and throw it in their enemy's path; if he treads upon it, they confidently expect that the evil wish will be fulfilled. On this account, the Hungarians take great care to avoid treading upon any thing that lies in their path. Another favourite superstition of theirs, is a firm belief in the power of exciting love through the agency of sorcery. The process consists in boiling certain herbs by moonlight, at a certain hour, and immediately walling up the hot scum in the fire hearth. The name of the person whom it is wished to inspire with love must be solemnly pronounced over the operation, after which he or she so *ensorcelé* will be filled with an irresistible desire to share the said hearth with its possessor.

It is singular how many superstitions are common to all times and nations. Some incantations will be found in practice in the most distant parts of the earth, in precisely the same forms, often to the very same cabalistical words. This is often the case where it is as difficult to believe in a common psychological origin, as in an historical transmission from the one nation to the other.

The belief in witches has been prevalent even among the higher classes of Hungarians till very lately. There is an island on the Theiss, near Szegedin, upon which a lady of high rank, after a regular trial, was burnt as a witch, in 1746. This is, however, the less to be wondered at when we remember that in Holland, so late as the beginning of this century, a woman was drowned as a witch by some peasants. The general gathering place of Hungarian witches, bears the same name as that of Germany, It is the Blocksberg near Buda.

The weddings and funerals of Hungarian peasants, are conducted with the same stiffness, formality, and ceremonious etiquette, as those of a Spanish court. My ecclesiastical travelling-companion whiled away the tiresome journey over the dreary *Puste* for me, by relating the following particulars of an Hungarian peasant's wedding.

When a young peasant takes a fancy to a girl, either for her beauty, or her other good qualities, or perhaps from some prudential consideration, he imparts his wishes in the first place to some friends, whose duty it is to present themselves before the lady, and acquaint her with the amorous desires of their friend Andresh, Yanosh, or Petrushka. It is customary always to make this visit at twilight. The lady will, of course, not hear of it at first; she declares that she will never marry, and least of all this same unlucky Andresh, Yanosh, or Petrushka. This declaration is a matter of course and means nothing. The suitors must repeat their twilight visits, and use all their persuasive eloquence, to which the lady gradually yields, and at last declares that if they will have it so, the lover may present himself, and try his own powers of persuasion.

The lover's first visit is a very important step towards marriage, and is the stiffest and most embarrassing scene possible. The relations are all present, and present the young girl to him, who from this time forward calls him her *Volageny*, or bridegroom. It is etiquette for the bride to be extremely timid, shy, and bashful, during this visit. She has in the mean time embroidered a fine handkerchief, which she holds in her hand, till she can take courage to present it to him. This presentation of the handkerchief is the token of the bride's consent, and constitutes a regular engagement. The bridegroom places it in his bosom, but in such a way that a large portion of it may hang out ostentatiously, which it continues to do on every festive occasion in token of victory.

Many other visits follow, all of the same stiff and ceremonious nature, and all marked by various gifts, until the wedding-day. After the ceremony, the bride and bridegroom each return to their own houses to entertain separate parties of guests. After this has continued for some time, the bridegroom sends to the bride's house, inviting her and her guests to come and join him. She at first refuses to come. He sends a second time and she promises to come, but does not do so. It is not till the third invitation, that she leaves her paternal home, and enters that of her husband. Here a great feast is held, of wine, white bread, meat, fish, brawn, porridge, Belesh (a kind of cake made of twenty thin flakes of dough with slices of apple between), and other favourite Hungarian dishes. Etiquette, however, forbids the sad and timid bride to taste any of these dishes; if she were to do so, the whole Puste would be scandalized.

The wedding feast ended, one of the most important of the marriage ceremonies, the "binding of the head," follows. The bride's hair, which, until now, she has worn loose and hanging down, is gathered up into a very elaborate knot, and the plaits are smoothly laid round her head, after which the head-cloth, worn by matrons, is carefully folded upon it. This done, the friends of the bride go round, taking a washhand-basin, in which each washes his hands or affects to do so, and at the same time drops a small piece of money into the water. With this the day's ceremonies conclude. The next morning a grand breakfast concludes the whole wedding ceremonial.

It is customary at Hungarian funerals, for the sexton to make a long speech in the name of the deceased, taking leave of his relatives, and expressing all he might be supposed to feel on leaving them. This funeral oration the Hungarians call the *Butsusztato*, and they are very particular to have it of good quality, and well delivered.

For five or six miles, our way lay through the Hatar of Szegedin. All the land here belonged to the citizens, and many Sallashes were scattered around. These Sallashes sometimes contain nothing but a fire-hearth, and a single room, and perhaps a store-room at the side. Sometimes, however, they are convenient and handsome houses, with trees planted round, and a little garden.

At the end of the Hatar, stood a frontier hill, such as is used to mark all boundaries in Hungary. After passing this place, we entered the true Puste, inhabited only by solitary herdsmen. It became more and more dreary the further we advanced. Bare sandy plains, broken by little sand hillocks, stretched along on every side, and in many places the air was full of whirling clouds of sand. Here and there a little patch of bright verdure, generally situated in a hollow, where the moisture is better preserved than on the plain, gladdened our eyes and cheered the prospect. Towards noon the weather became extremely hot, and our horses had much ado to drag our coach through the sand. They did their best, however, as did likewise our lively coachman, Andresh, coaxing and driving them alternately. The Hungarian, like the Russian coachmen, have for their horses an infinite number of terms of endearment, with which they are at pains to enliven and cheer their cattle. The horses soon come to know their pet names, and certainly appear to redouble their exertions when addressed in these coaxing terms. Our five horses bore the following appellations. The first was called *Burkush*, that is, the Prussian, being a native of Prussia; the second *Keshey*, or the Piebald, on account of his colour; the third *Vidam*, the Cheerful, or the Merry, in compliment to his disposition; the fourth *Gyilkos* (pronounced Yilkosh), or the Murderer, because of the fierceness of his nature; and the fifth *Szikra*, or the Spark, in deference to his fiery courage and impetuosity.

At length our coachman, toiling with his weary horses through the hot sand, cried out with delight, "Ah! thank God, I see the gallows of Felegyhaz!" We knew that we were to dine at Felegyhaz, and stretching our necks out of the window, we saw the great white "hanging wood" of that city, rearing its stately head from a sandy hillock. It was a large, square, solid building. The lower part consisted of a square wall, in which there was a small door by way of entrance. At each of the four corners arose a stout pillar, and on the top of these pillars were laid crosswise the beams on which criminals are hung. It is extraordinary in what good condition these edifices are kept throughout Hungary.

We all heartily chimed in with the coachman, and cried, "Ah! thank God, there is the handsome white gallows of Felegyhaz!" as the low straggling capital of the *Kumanen*, began to emerge from the sandy plain.

THE KUMANEN, YAZYGEN, AND HAIDUCKEN.

Germans, in every grade of Magyarization, Magyars of all imaginable varieties, Russians, Slovaks, Servians, Walachians, Croatians, Slavonians, Dalmatians, Italians, Greeks, Armenians, Jews, Gipsies, Bulgarians, and Bosnians, such are the nations with whom we have as yet come in contact, during our course through Hungary. The Kumanen, Yazygen, and Haiducken, now demand our attention.

The territory of these two last-mentioned nations lies in the plain between the Danube and the Theiss, where the kings of Hungary at different times have assigned them considerable portions of land. The various districts inhabited by them may contain a superficial extent of about four hundred square miles, the population is reckoned at one hundred and sixty thousand souls.

The Slavonians maintain that the Yazygen, are the remnant of the old Slavonian nation, whom the Romans speak of, under the same name, as the aborigines of the country, and that they derive this name from the Slavonian word *Yasyk* (the tongue). The Hungarians, however, assert that the Yazygen are descended from a tribe of Kumanes, who, in the year 1125, made an incursion into Hungary under a leader named Tatar, and that they derive the name from an Hungarian word, signifying bow, their name signifying archers, or "shooters with the bow."

The Kumanes, a nation probably of Tatar origin, were formerly settled, like the Magyars, on the other side of the Carpathian mountains, in the southern steppes of Russia. Many of them, under seven leaders, whose names history has transmitted to us, passed with the Magyars into Pannonia, and Dacia, and became mingled with them like many other tribes. The greater part of the Kumanes remained behind on the other side of the Theiss. Individual tribes of them continued to make frequent incursions into Hungary; one for example, in the year 1074, under Oscu, another under the khan Tatar, in 1125. They were conquered or slain, or scattered as prisoners, and settlers, in different parts of the country. When the Mongolians broke in upon these eastern countries, other Kumanes flocked hither, as fugitives in search of protection, one great horde in 1227, another 40,000 strong, in 1239. The Hungarian kings received them willingly, because they found in them a support against their own discontented subjects, and also because they hoped to make a merit at the papal court, of their conversion to Christianity. One king of Hungary, Ladislaus, at the latter end of the thirteenth century, lived entirely among the Kumanes, let his beard grow as they did, and exchanged the close-fitting garments of the Hungarians for the wide oriental vesture of the Kumanes, wearing a pointed felt hat, and dwelling with them under tents of felt. They did the Hungarian monarchs good service as body-guards, but obliged them also, by their mutinous behaviour, to adopt severe measures, and even caused civil wars more than once. The extensive territory, and extraordinary privileges granted them in former times, are no longer enjoyed by them in the same degree; they are now, for example, compelled to pay a tax to the king from which they were formerly exempt.

Their peculiar rights and immunities confirmed to them by Maria Theresa are principally as follow:—Firstly—as free men they are subject to no lord of the soil, have their own tribunals, and even exercise the *jus gladii*, having a chief or captain named by the Palatine, and choosing their own subordinate officers.

Secondly. Their territories, Great Kumania, Lesser Kumania, and Yazygia, are represented by two deputies in the Hungarian diet.

Thirdly. Like the Hungarian nobles they are exempt from all land or water tolls, from episcopal tithes, and exercise various regalities in their own land.

The Haiducks have a different origin from the Kumanes and Yazyges. They are called in the Hungarian language "*hajdu*," and in the Hungarian Latin *haidonici*. The name comes probably from the Hungarian word *hajadon* (an unmarried man), and the *haidonici* were probably young bachelors who took service with various leaders, or condottieri, in Hungary. They were also a kind of "*landsknechts*," like the* Cossacks, in South Russia. The word *kosak* has much the same meaning as *haiduck*; that is, free, unmarried man. The kings whom they served in war bestowed lands on them. The people now known under this name inhabiting an extensive swampy district to the north of Debrez,—the six Haiduck towns (*oppida haidonicalia*), as they are called,—are descended from a free corps of foot-soldiers, formed in the beginning of the seventeenth century by a prince of Transylvania, Stephen Botshkai, of Servians, Walachians, and Hungarians, whom, when the wars were ended, he rewarded by grants of land, particular pri-

---

* Many kinds of troops have been formed in Hungary, several of which have become renowned in Europe as the Haiducks, Hussars, Redcloaks, Browncloaks, Serreschans, &c. The Haiducks of Botshkai were good foot-soldiers, and, perhaps, were originally employed in Hungary as messengers for the tribunals. A messenger of a court of law is still called in Hungarian a Haiduck; the majority of them, however, are now mounted.

vileges, and the right of choosing their own chief. These privileges were subsequently confirmed by the Hungarian kings, and these Haiduck's also send two deputies to the diet of Hungary.

The Haiducks who, as before said, are of Magyar origin, and the Kumanes, probably a kindred race, are now in speech, costume, and manners, completely *Magyarized*. This is the case, also, with reference to their religion; and although they remained heathens longer than any other part of the population, they, as well as the Hungarians, took a zealous part at the time of the reformation. The Haiducks and the people of Great Kumania, are nearly all protestants; the Yazyges, nearly all catholics; the inhabitants of Lesser Kumania are divided pretty equally between the two religions.

Nevertheless, pure Magyars, as they are all esteemed, there exist, I think, many differences, though they are little heeded. That their free constitution, and the warlike spirit yet alive among them, must call forth such differences, may be *à priori* understood. That they have had this effect was made evident at the time of the last recruitment in the year 1840. In other parts of Hungary the recruits, although chosen by lot, were occasionally brought to their colours by force. The Kumanes (those of Lesser Kumania at least) took up the matter in a more soldierlike spirit. All the male population, capable of bearing arms, were called together, and assembled with drums and military music, on the market-place of Felegyhaz. Here a table was placed, at which their captains, with their secretaries, presided. Near at hand uniforms, with shakos and arms, were displayed; all who felt a desire for martial glory came forward of their own accord, and had their names inscribed. A uniform was then fitted on, and the new candidate for military honours marched off, fully equipped. In this manner their whole contingent was furnished.

While we were at table, at Felegyhaz, an article in a Transylvanian journal, similar to one I had heard of at Szegedin, was spoken of. "Ay, the Transylvanians have whistled our Hungarians handsomely off their mountains once more," observed one of the guests. I noted this characteristic expression, but could not obtain a sight of the article; the paper that contained it was not forthcoming.

It is delightful to find in these Hungarian wastes, even on the heaths of Ketskemeter, such fine grapes and cherries. In this they enjoy a great advantage over the heaths of Lüneburg, and the sandy plains of Brandenburg. The finest, freshest grapes were offered for sale on all sides. The *pujhas* (turkeys) likewise deserve honourable mention for flavour, although not to be met with in such numbers as in the Banat, and in other places inhabited by Walachians, who have taken these feathered productions of India, as well as its corn, under their particular protection. In their villages large flocks of these fowls are to be met with. These "*pujhas*" are called "*pockerl*" by the Hungarian Germans, and this makes the seventh or eighth German name for one and the same domestic fowl, which seems to have propagated itself with tolerable rapidity over all Europe. What, in Hungary, is called a *pockerl*, is a *puter* in Berlin, a *kalkuhn* in Courland and Livonia, an *Indian* in Austria, in other parts of Germany, a *truthahn*, a *welschhahn*, a *kabkuter*, and a *consistorial bird;* while the goose, the duck, the stork, the swallow, and other domestic birds, have the same name everywhere. How happens it that this bird rejoices in such an abundance of appellations? It is more unaccountable with a tame animal than with one in a wild state. The latter comes from various lands unannounced, but the turkey, owing its increase to the fostering care of man, might, one would think, bring its name with it, to pass from seller to buyer. It is certainly a bird that seems entitled to some distinguishing appellation.

It is not long that Felegyhaz, Szegedin, and the majority of the genuine Hungarian towns, have had any other chimneys than wooden ones. At present they are for the most part constructed of stone. However, the beneficial metamorphosis of wooden cities into cities of stone, which progresses so rapidly in Russia, makes a slower advance in Hungary, where commands are neither so roundly given nor so promptly executed. The greater part of the houses are roofed with shingles; very few have attained the dignity of tiles.

THE HEATHS OF KETSKEMET.

After dinner we advanced farther into the deserts with our "sparks," "murderers," and "Prussians." One of the most remarkable features of these wastes is, the non-occurrence of scattered fragments of rock; and it is often as interesting for science to know what a neighbourhood does *not* as what it *does* contain, but the former point is more apt to be overlooked by travellers than the latter. The Hungarian plain between the Danube and Theiss is, after the North German or Baltic plains, and those north of the Black Sea, the largest in Europe. It has a superficial extent of more than a thousand (German) square miles. There is nothing similar to be met with in England, Spain, France, Italy, Turkey, or Southern Germany. It is surrounded by high mountains, the Alps, the Carpathian, and their several spurs; but none of these mountains have scattered their fragments over the plains, and if the presence of these rocky masses in North Germany, Switzerland, and other countries is enigmatical, and has given rise to a variety of theories to account for it, we ought to be equally curious to know whether the newest of these, the ice theory, can explain the *non-appearance* of such masses here, or whether this circumstance be a new enigma and stumbling-block in the path of inquiry. That the Carpathian mountains have never scattered their fragments around them I would certainly not venture to maintain, and of course such fragments, forced down by torrents, are to be found in the valleys; but so much is certain, that in my travels through Bessarabia, Galicia, and round the Carpathians, I have never seen such masses of rock in the fields, nor have I ever found any person in the larger or smaller plains of Hungary who could show me any, after all my inquiries. The plain of the Banat, although it lies close to the mountains, has not, I believe, anywhere a cubic inch of rock lying on its surface. The same may be asserted of the plains of Southern Russia.

Our next station was Ketskemet, the largest and most noted market-town of Hungary. *Ketske* signifies the goat, in the Hungarian language,—is there a connexion perhaps between the name of the town and that of the animal? This town has above 30,000 inhabitants, for the most part employed in the breeding of cattle. The fields are the pasture-grounds of countless herds of noble oxen, spirited Hungarian horses, and long-horned sheep. The whole surrounding country is called the Ketskemeter moors, and includes, under this name, a considerable portion of the plain between the Danube and Theiss. It is difficult to comprehend how so many human beings have congregated, in a neighbourhood, where there is neither a river to afford facilities for commerce, mountain or rock whereon to erect a fortress, or any other relation subsisting that could tend particularly to the promotion of social communion. The existence of 32,000 townspeople in this place is a riddle hard to be explained by a geographer.

The inhabitants are nearly all genuine Hungarians, noblemen, artisans, and peasants. The nobles have established a Casino. The most striking thing about the peasants—the same dark-skinned, dark-haired race we had seen in Pesth, but more properly belonging to these plains—was the short shirt. It does not reach so far as the middle of the back,—sometimes the whole garment is nothing more than a narrow middle piece, connecting the sleeves. As in this fashion a broad strip of flesh between shirt and trousers remains undefended; the sun burns it into a dark-brown indelible girdle, by which the Hungarian peasant will, in the Elysian fields, be distinguishable from all other peasants of the world. The Hungarian shirt, indeed, deserves particular mention, as it is certainly the most peculiar of its kind to be met with in Europe. Another odd fashion of these peasants is that they stick their short pipes not in front as other people do, but behind. The waistband of their trousers, in the middle of the back, is the chosen resting-place for the familiar fumigating tube. Some, however, prefer the brims of their hats.

At Ketskemet we were present at a review of Italian cavalry quartered there. These people, who, it is well known, are very bad horsemen, no doubt afford abundant diversion to the Hungarians, who are the best in the world; and the Italians on their side may revenge themselves by a comparison of these Ketakemeter moors with their lovely fatherland. To us Germans, Ketskemet is an ungenial spot; with us there would be more joyousness in a town containing 30,000 human beings. Nevertheless, the place is not to be despised. If it be measured not by a foreign but an Hungarian standard, its handsome town-house, reformed and catholic gymnasium, and many gaily-painted houses, possess a claim to admiration, as well as the richly-filled gardens without the gates. The fruit we tasted there was excellent, and the wheaten bread of the town is celebrated throughout Hungary. The Hungarians are great consumers of white bread like the French; even the humblest enjoy daily their white bread in considerable quantities. Perhaps this is the cause of their indifference to the potatoe. It has been said that the potato rarely finds a ready admittance into a wheat country.

Between Ketskemet and Pesth, a distance of eleven (German) miles, there are only three villages, Orkeny, Ocsa, and Soroksar. We passed the night in a solitary inn, named Fuldeak (Student's Ear), an extensive building enclosed by walls like a fortress. The host and waiters were Germans. The establishment, on the whole, was a very tolerable one, and the guests numerous: the supper might even be called good, and the conversation was agreeable. Many things, highly characteristic of the country, were mentioned in the course of it. But this a traveller seldom finds wanting, for every thing he sees and hears is more or less characteristic; the difficulty is properly to retain and arrange the materials that present themselves constantly in the greatest profusion.

Only one anecdote related that evening has retained a place in my memory. It is of an Hungarian scholar, who found means to administer a lesson to an Hungarian nobleman. The latter had built a magnificent house, and misused his poor peasants most cruelly while erecting it. When the house was finished, he desired to have a Latin inscription for it, for which he applied to our scholar, who happened to be known to him as the author of some happy Latin verses. The inscription was promised for the following morning. But in the morning the scholar had vanished, and over the door of the house, written with a coal, were found these lines:

> Congeries lapidum, multis congesta rapinis,
> Corruet et raptas alter habebit opes.*

The anathema, I was told, pronounced in the middle of the last century, has already been fulfilled. The nobleman is dead, his race extinct, and his estates have reverted to the crown.

The mounted patrol who guard the moors from Sallash to Sallash, had done their duty, and we found, on the following morning, that we had been neither robbed nor murdered during the night, but were all alive and merry. A thick fog that hung over the fields soon cleared away and gave us very fine weather, which our driver assured us would continue. We should have a beautiful autumn, he added, because the "*pipatsch*" (red field poppy, *Papaver Rhoeas*), remained so long in bloom; which was looked on in Hungary as an unfailing sign.

We saw on the way a pond of a milky whiteness, coloured by a chalky earth which abounds in the country. This earth is dug from the Pusten, and is used to whitewash the houses that have, in consequence, the same freshness of appearance which I had before noted in Southern Russia. There are many points of resemblance in the nature of the soil, and the customs of the people, between the Hungarians and the natives of Southern Russia.

The water of the steppes impregnated with salt, is sometimes made use of by the people for household purposes. Salt is dear in this country, as it is a royal monopoly, and the people of the steppes have often recourse to the expedient of digging for salt springs, in order to boil their food in the waters. This practice is said to be injurious to the health, and has, therefore, been prohibited.

In Ketskemet, and other places in its neighbourhood, there are numerous establishments for soap-boiling. The soap is made mostly of hogs' lard, and candles are generally composed of goats' tallow, either obtained from their own animals, or, what is more frequently the case, from the goats of the mountains of Servia and Transylvania, of which I had seen numbers at Orsova. Pomatum for the hair is also made of hogs' lard, which is held to be very wholesome, both for the hair and the head, and is, therefore, sometimes used in such quantities that the locks fairly "drop fatness" in very warm weather. With us, pomatum is more used by women than by men; here, on the contrary, it is the men who anoint themselves rather than the "ingrins," as the women of Magyar race are termed throughout Hungary, where they generally envelop their heads in a quantity of handkerchiefs.

At one station, where we stopped to breakfast, we saw a couple of Hungarian shepherd-dogs. These animals, who, when they are left alone to guard the flocks, show no mercy to either wolf or stranger, are called in

---

* This pile of stones, heap'd up by many a wrong,
  Shall pass away to stranger hands ere long.

Hungarian, *Szelindek*. They have long hair of different colours, white, gray, and brown, and look very like wolves themselves. The same likeness may be traced in the large dogs which the *Tshabanas* of Southern Russia lead in chains when they pass inhabited places. I was told that an Hungarian once travelled into Italy with four of these dogs, and exhibited them as wolves. The shepherds make use of these Szelindeks only as a guard against the wolves; for the purpose of keeping their flocks together, and directing the sheep, they have generally a common kind of small dog called a "*kuty.*"

In the steppes where so many genuine Magyar physiognomies are to be met with, I found a further confirmation of an opinion I have before expressed,—namely, that the Hungarian physiognomy in its principal features, is a very handsome one, and has no trace whatever of the Mongolian, as some have asserted.

As the gibbet is to be seen at every Hungarian town, so the ugly form of the stocks or the block of punishment (*strafblock*, or *schandklotz*) presents itself in every Hungarian village. The Hungarians call this instrument "*Kaloda*," a Slavonian word in use among the Russians, Moravians, Illyrians, and Croats. It differs in form from similar instruments of chastisement among us, consisting of two thick planks fastened together like the two halves of a pair of scissors. In the lower plank are two semicircular holes, through which the feet and legs of the delinquent are passed; similar holes, corresponding to those in the lower, are cut in the upper plank; the two are secured at the ends, and the poor captive, with his limbs thus confined, lies for twelve and twenty-four hours together, stretched on the ground, exposed to all the inclemency of the weather and the gaze of the passers-by. Such a "*schandklotz*" figures before the courthouse of every village. However, I must admit I never saw the apparatus decorated with a prisoner.

Stealing of cattle is as common an offence in these steppes as stealing wood is in many parts of Germany. Robbery of the person is far less frequent here than in the Banat among the Walachians, and therefore the comitats, through which we were now driving, are not under martial law, while the Torantal comitat in the Banat has not been free from it for years. When a number of robberies take place in a comitat, and the neighbourhood is unsafe in consequence, such a comitat can, on application to the king, have martial law proclaimed. Immediately very summary proceedings are adopted; criminals caught *in flagranti delicto*, are not even brought under a roof; the legal authorities repair to the spot, and when sentence is passed the unhappy sinner has only three hours to live: whereas, when this law is not in operation, he has three days granted him. The clergy (and the nobles?) are exempt from martial law. This law is never granted to a comitat for longer than three years; application must then be made for a renewal of the favour. When I was in Hungary, I heard of three comitats in which martial law had been proclaimed. Notice of it was sent to all houses of public entertainment.

On our road we came upon the settlements of a gipsy colony. There were a considerable number of *putri* and *gunyho* (clay and reed huts), and in one I found, to my great astonishment, a German woman, who assured me that she liked the gipsy life and would not quit it. I should have liked to have had a longer conversation with her, for, in the course of her constant rambling with the gipsies, she had acquired a considerable knowledge of the country. She said that the worst and most vindictive people in Hungary were the Zinzari. Their first word when affronted was "*otyespantiti*" (you shall remember it), and they mostly kept their word by setting the house of the offending person on fire, or doing him some other injury. She also mentioned some peculiar customs of the Servians. They have regular lamentations for the dead, and at funerals serve up a particular dish, composed of wheaten flour, mixed with raisins. (The Russians do the same.) The seventh, fourteenth, and the anniversary of the funeral are days kept sacred, but this only among the wealthier classes. Among their many church festivals, they have the "Blessing of the Fields." On this occasion, persons place themselves in the churchyard to scatter wheat in the path of the procession as it passes round the church.

It can scarcely be imagined with what joy a German greets a German village, after seeing, for some time, nothing but gipsies, Sallashes, and Pusten. Ocsa, a place, according to all accounts, highly interesting for more reasons than one, we saw only in the distance, because, as I have before said, we drove, according to the good pleasure of the Szegedin driver, through all manner of by-ways. The first German town we reached was the market-town of Soroksar on the Danube, the population of which is German. It was Sunday, and the German maidens were coming out of church, all clean and neat, and clothed in their native costume. The men had adopted the Hungarian *bunda* (fur garment). It is singular enough that in Hungary and Southern Russia they should never lay aside the sheepskin even in summer.

God bless the German nation and all that belongs to it, thought I in my heart, and added, aloud, "*Vivat Soroksar.*" "Not so loud, don't say that so loudly," said one of my travelling companions, "some of these worthy people may take it amiss; in Pesth they make use of that expression, Vivat Soroksar, to tease the natives." The phrase, at full length, runs "Vivat Soroksar, Maria Theresa is a market-town;" and it refers to the time of that empress, when this place from a village was raised to the dignity of a town. When this grace was made known officially, the honest folks of Soroksar meant to cry "Vivat Maria Theresa, Soroksar is a market-town!" but, unluckily, in their joy, they made a slip of the tongue, and shouted unanimously, "Vivat Soroksar, Maria Theresa is a market-town." They were so laughed at in consequence that the words "Vivat Soroksar," are, at any time, enough to throw a native of the place into a rage.

The road from Soroksar to Pesth is paved, and on this *chaussée*, which runs along the Danube, there is an active and constant traffic. We were driving in company with a number of coaches, with five and six horses, and some waggons, and the nearer we approached the capital the harder they drove. At last, as it generally happens with Hungarian drivers, and their fiery steeds, our course became a regular race. The Hungarian drivers carry enormously long whips, as they seldom drive less than six, and sometimes more horses from the box. The whip is flourished continually over their heads, the driver playing constantly with the immeasurable lash, which waves at one moment freely through the air, and then, by a dexterous movement, is as suddenly twined round the handle of the whip. We represented at last a *tableau vivant*, almost a copy of the painting we had seen in the Banat. Our coachman, having once made a silent wager with another coach-and-six, was no longer to be restrained; nor were his horses, although, after their toilsome journey, we had supposed them to be quite exhausted, and thus *ventre à terre*, and veiled in a cloud of dust, our great clumsy vehicle lumbered into Pesth, we insides panting for breath and shaken to a jelly.

STUHLWEISSENBURG.— VESPRIM.

The forest of Bakony stretches in its chief direction from the south-west to the north-east across the Buda mountains to Buda and Pesth. On the north lies the great artery of the Danube with the towns of Raab, Gran, and Waizen; to the south the long Platten see lies parallel to the Forest, which in its length skirts the southern plains at the foot of the mountains as far as Buda. In the same direction runs another of the most considerable Hungarian roads, leading over Stuhlweissenburg, Vesprim, Schumegh, and Kormond to the Styrian Alps; and for the sake of those noble objects, I chose this road to return to my dear German fatherland.

There is no regular communication between the places lying in this direction and the capital, but carriages may be hired at a tolerably reasonable rate, expressly for the journey. On the morning of the 26th of September, I began my journey in one of these. So thick a fog from the Danube veiled the cities of Buda and Pesth, that after we had driven a few yards from the gates they were no longer to be seen. The pain of parting was thereby greatly shortened and we soon found ourselves in a new country. There are many villages peopled by Germans on this side of the Danube as well as on the Pesth side. We passed among others Hanselbeck, a German village with a Turkish name. Like St. Petersburg and Odessa, Tiflis and many other cities of the East, the Magyar capitals have planted German colonies in their neighbourhood, in order to provide themselves with milk, butter, and other dairy and garden produce. In St. Petersburg and Odessa pleasure-parties are made to the German villages of Pawlowski and Lustdorf, and the same thing is done at Pesth and Buda to the German colonies. Our horses took fright at a variety of objects on the road, among others at a comitat Haiduck, who passed us at full gallop. These people patrol the country day and night, to the no small hazard of their lives: many are "*blown* away by the robbers," we were informed. The second alarm of our steeds was a drunken mail-driver, who had let the reins of his solitary steed fall, and drove up against us. In endeavouring to catch at the reins he tumbled from his seat, and he might have lain a long time on the ground if our people had not been good-natured enough to pick him up, replant him in his place, and put the reins once more in his hands. I understood, from this incident, how the correspondence of Hungary might easily be somewhat tedious. In the mean time the passengers in our carriage were frightening each other with their horrible stories of robbery and murder. These passengers were an Austrian, highly disdainful of every thing Hungarian, the ancient chamberlain of an "*Excellenz Graf,*" (a count who has any office constituting him "*Excellenz*" is always thus spoken of in Hungary and Austria,) and an Hungarian excise-officer. They told of a *tsharde* that had been completely plundered, although there were fourteen persons in the house at the time; of a lad of eighteen who had murdered his master's whole family; of a man who had killed his own brother because the latter had formerly committed a murder, the remembrance of which tormented the other and demanded vengeance; of a family in which murder was hereditary. The details of these horrors, although some were extremely curious and interesting, I purposely omit, as they were not, to speak it mildly, exceedingly edifying.

I really felt uncomfortably for the poor exciseman, obliged to listen to us Germans enlarging on themes so little to the credit of his country and his class. I tried several times to turn the conversation to other subjects, but the speakers always returned to the same "raw-head and bloody-bones" stories in which they seemed inexhaustible. I learnt here the various appellations for the different species of rogues, and was glad to inquire about them, hoping by this means to lead the conversation by degrees to the subject of language. The terminology runs thus: *Tolvai* is simply a thief; *Rablo* is a general term for robber; *Haramia* is a highwayman or a marauder, who conceals himself in a forest; *Gyilkos* (pronounced Yilkosh) is a thief and murderer by profession.

Towards evening we came in sight of the city of Stuhlweissenburg, in Hungarian Fejervar, in Slavonian Belgrade, and in Latin Alba regia, all of which signify nearly the same thing. There is something very peculiar in the aspect of this city. It lies in the midst of a swampy plain, with its vineyards, or rather vine-hills at some distance from the gates. On these vine-hills, each citizen has his little possession, and each contains a house. These vineyard-houses are so numerous, and some of them so large, that they form a town in themselves, so that the vineyard town and the town Stuhlweissenburg properly so called, which are divided also by a portion wholly uncultivated, of the swampy plain, are completely distinct from each other.

We drove first into the vineyard-town. Right and left lay the vineyard or press-houses as the Hungarians call them. The vineyard-town is surrounded by them as the cattle-breeding shepherd towns of the *Pusten* are with the *Sallashes*. The arrangement of these houses is also similar to that of the *Sallashes*, insomuch as they contain a hearth and a dwelling, and that the whole population of vinedressers take possession with bag and baggage in the season of the vintage, and there abide till it is over, as is done by the cattle-owners in the *sallashes* at one time of the year. They have generally but one or two windows, one large room with a press, and a large door leading into a cellar, and are one story high, but in the larger possessions of the wealthy owners there are some houses of considerable size and elegance, as the bishop's for example, which may almost be termed a palace. Around the bishop's press-house are those of several nobles; then come the houses belonging to the trading part of the community, and to the left of the road the Rascians of Stuhlweissenburg have theirs. The vineyard-town is a faithful reflection of Stuhlweissenburg itself.

The fortnight or three weeks spent among the vineyards in the vintage time is a season of great gaiety and enjoyment. The labours over which Bacchus presides are in themselves more of a festival than a toil. Every leisure hour is devoted to merriment, especially when the vintage is as abundant as it was this year. Gipsy musicians were roving about from house to house, the vinedressers danced in the open air, and in the midst of the treillage of vines a temporary saloon for the same purpose was erected for the more aristocratic part of the assembly. The bishop has built a chapel among the vines in which service is performed on Sundays. At the commencement of the season, when the "vintage is opened," numbers perform a pilgrimage to this chapel when there is service.

We came unfortunately too late to witness these joyous labours; the vintage had taken place in this hot year two or three weeks earlier than usual, and was just over when we arrived. The press-houses were all locked and barred, and stood among the despoiled vine-branches, like bodies whence the spirit has departed. Only here and there the door of some lingerer remained open, and a few poor girls were diligently employed in seeking the remaining grapes among the waste leaves. Some of the wealthy owners permit these gleanings.

The vintage of Buda was formerly one of the most celebrated, and the gayest in Hungary. No vinedresser formerly omitted to twine his vine-wreath from the finest branch of the vine, and bring it home in triumph with song and dance. This custom has now fallen more or less into disuse; the vineyards of Buda have increased enormously in extent, wines are cheaper, times worse, and the vinedressers no longer so gay and frolicsome as they were.

In Hungary they do not in general allow the plant to shoot up to any great height, but cut off the shoots of the year close to the ground as is done in Provence. In consequence, the stem swells to a thick knotty growth from which in spring new shoots burst forth. These knotty stems naturally assume various and sometimes very extraordinary forms. These too figure sometimes among the emblems of the vintage feast. Pieces of these strangely distorted stems are often carried home with the vine-wreath and preserved as memorials, like the antlers of the stag in our hunting-seats. Some of the pieces are occasionally fashioned into drinking-cups.

The wine of Stuhlweissenburg is not one of the most distinguished kinds in Hungary. It is said the cellars are not well constructed for its preservation. The quantity, however, is considerable, and a large portion is consumed in Stuhlweissenburg itself in *Johannissegen* and *Stehwein*. This *steh* (standing) wine is what a person takes at a friend's house without sitting down; and there are people, it is asserted, who often swallow so many drops of "standing wine," that they lose the power of standing altogether. The *Johannissegen* is another "drop" offered at parting. "Well, you must drink the St. John's blessing with me," says a man to his friend, when he sees him preparing to depart. "The origin of the expression," said a Stuhlweissenburger to me, "is derived from a custom which prevails of taking some bottles to a priest (on St. John's day?) to be blessed, a portion is then poured into the various casks, and from these the *segen*, or blessing, is offered to the guests."

As before mentioned, a wide, uncultivated plain lies between the vine-hills and the city. A few hundred paces from the gates, we came upon the ruins of a church, and were told that the city had formerly extended thus far. The great morass of Stuhlweissenburg is called the Sarret Marsh. The larger portion, three German square miles in extent, lies to the west of the city, and another, of considerable extent, stretches to the east. The city, between the two, stands on perfectly dry ground; formerly it stood on islands in the morass, on which account its different divisions were called *Szigeth* (islands), in the old chronicles. One great suburb, (the Buda suburb) was a short time ago all swamp. By means of a great canal, the Sarvitz canal, which crosses the swamp in several directions, and descending the Sarvitz valley carries off the waters to the Danube, a considerable portion has been drained, and a quantity of arable and garden ground reclaimed. This draining might be carried much further; "but," said a Stuhlweissenburger to me, "we have so many lovers of the chase, and there is such excellent wildfowl shooting in these swamps, that many people dislike the drainage. There are here multitudes of black and white billed bittern, geese, swans, and ducks of all kinds; even stags and wild boars are very plentiful. Part of the swamp preserve belongs to the town, and part to the nobles; and some of the citizens are as passionate lovers of the chase as the noblemen. Our city-hunting parties in the swamp of Sarret are often as gay as our vintage; we have built a saloon for dancing there; and on grand occasions we take the ladies and the gipsy musicians out there. Besides this, many small houses have been erected in the swamp, in which to pass the night occasionally, and for snaring birds, &c. People who have laid out money on these things, and take pleasure in them, of course are not very fond of the draining: and then, we have vine and arable land enough without it."

West of the Danube, and north and south of the Platten Lake, lie the most productive hunting-grounds in all Hungary; and there, on the lands of Esterhazy, in the Oseral district, are held those grand hunting-parties of which so many incredible stories are related.

Stuhlweissenburg was formerly the coronation and burying place of the Hungarian kings, and, for a short period, their residence also. For five hundred years it was for Hungary what Cracow was for Poland, Upsala for Sweden, and Rheims and St. Denis together for France. It is singular enough that the burial-places, residences, and coronation towns of kings, should be so often separate from each other. The first king buried in Stuhlweissenburg was Stephen the Holy; the last, John Zapoyla. The last king crowned there was Ferdinand, brother of Charles the Fifth. The same ceremonial was observed then as is now observed at Presburg. The new king ascended the "coronation hill," and waved his sword towards all four points of the heavens; the oath was taken upon a lofty scaffold before all the people, the red velvet carpet, over which the king rode to church, was abandoned to the populace, &c. Of all these details scarcely a trace is now remaining. I asked in vain for the "coronation hill." The noble old cathedral in which the monarchs were crowned, and which contained their mausoleums, was entirely destroyed. Where it once stood even is now a disputed point. A priest told me that the Turks, not content with levelling it with the ground, had filled the vaults with powder, and blown them into the air. In the course of five hundred years, a long series of kings had not only bestowed so many bright ducats on their coronation day, but had adorned the cathedral with so many royal gifts, as to render it one of the richest in Europe. On a pallium of Stephen's, now in Vienna, it is said, a picture of the cathedral, as it then stood, was embroidered by the royal hand of his consort, Gisela. It is known that the first queen of Hungary embroidered the mantle now worn by the kings of Hungary at their coronation—is this the pallium meant, perhaps?

Lately, on boring for an artesian well, the skeleton of a headless corse was discovered; and, close to it, several golden buttons and fringes, and on its finger a gold ring. A red stone containing a drop of some fluid matter, in a little cavity, was set in the ring. From the ring it was concluded that the body was that of King Charles Robert, of the Neapolitan house of Anjou, who died of hunger and poison in the castle of Vissegrad, and who, dying under the ban of the church, was left there to decay unburied, till the remains were subsequently removed to Stuhlweissenburg, and placed in the royal mausoleum. This skeleton, and a piece of the skull of King Stephen, brought with his hand from Ragusa to Hungary, are the only relics of the royal race who moved and had their being here for so many centuries. The brethren of the Hungarians, the Poles, have more carefully preserved historical monuments so dear to them; the walls and statues of their royal mausoleums are yet standing. The Hungarians, on the other hand, have preserved in a most admirable and remarkable manner the venerable edifice of their ancient constitution; while that of Poland lies in the dust, the Hungarian remains nearly unimpaired.

The present city of Stuhlweissenburg is quite modern; nothing antique is to be discovered in its architecture. It is built like all the new Hungarian cities, but has a far more stately appearance than Szegedin, or the other Pusten cities. The population is half Hungarian, half German, and has a Rascian suburb. In one of the gates some Roman stones with inscriptions are inserted, perhaps remains of the ancient Floriana, which formerly stood here. The invention, or rather the generally extended practice of boring for artesian wells has been of immense benefit to this city; formerly it contained but one well that afforded really good water for drinking, now there are ten. In boring for one of them, the labourers pierced through the ruins of some building a fathom and a half below the surface.

In Stuhlweissenburg, I learnt one Hungarian phrase by heart which displeased me excessively—"*Nintsch haz,*" (not at home). These fatal words wounded my ears the first time from the lips of Frau von N.'s servant. I had a letter of recommendation to her, but she, with her whole charming family, were gone on a visit; I heard them next from the maidservant of a French gentleman whose leech-pond I wished to see, but he too was absent on business; and lastly from the haiduck of Herr von C. to whom I brought a greeting and an introduction from a friend in Pesth. I felt myself the more forlorn and abandoned, as I had reckoned upon enjoying a pleasant and social evening with one or other of these good people. The city of Stuhlweissenburg contains twenty-three thousand souls, and yet I could not get at one! I felt the despair of one pining for water in sight of a stream he cannot reach, and prayed fervently to Heaven to warm some heart in my favour. It occurred to me, that the same laws are not valid for the hungry as for the full, and hearing that there was a Cistercian convent in the place, I knocked at its gate without further ceremony, begged the superior for the charity of a little society and conversation, and was bade kindly welcome.

The Hungarian clergy are very hospitable, and like all their countrymen have something frank and cordial about them. The shadow side of their life has been often enough brought forward and insisted on; but with all the shades, which are undeniable, I have always found so much light, that, for my own part, I am right well pleased with them. There is a great difference between the catholic and the reformed clergy in Hungary: the former are immcomparably more learned and more imbued with the west European civilization than the latter; a circumstance which arises probably from the fact, that while the latter have almost confined themselves to the study of their own language and literature, the catholics, in the study of Latin, have prepared a soil more favourable to further cultivation. There is also more knowledge of Germany and German literature among the catholics, owing to their connexion with the Austrian clergy; while the reformed ministers rather keep aloof from them, and call their own doctrine in opposition to that of the German reformers "*Magyar hit,*" or the Magyar faith.

The noble and learned Hungarian priests look down somewhat scornfully upon the simplicity of their reformed brethren. It is somewhat different with the Lutherans in the Slovak country. These live in another and very dissimilar spiritual element. I was assured by many enlightened catholics, that taken on the whole, the protestants in Hungary were far more intolerant than the catholics. " It never occurs to a catholic," said they, "to inquire after a stranger's religious belief, which a protestant would do immediately; the protestants keep much together, and are far more exclusive than the catholics." A lady assured me that although she had been brought up in a convent, she had never till her eighteenth year known any difference between protestants and catholics: the former bandy the reproach of heresy amongst each other far more than the catholics do towards them. I give these remarks as they were made to me, having had no experience on the subject myself; so much, however, I must say, that no question respecting my religious faith was ever put to me, go where I would.

When I told the Cistercian that I was a native of Bremen, he began to question me about the schism among the clergy there, and I found to my surprise that he was far better informed on the subject than I was. They also made some inquiries respecting the lead and wine cellars of my native city. I told them that I was astonished things so insignificant in themselves should have obtained so wide a celebrity, and spoke of some other peculiarities of the place which seemed to me far more deserving of notice.

In this convent I read for the first time the celebrated ninth article in the first part of the Hungarian code of laws, containing the four fundamental rights ("*libertates fundamentales*") of the Hungarian nobles. They are as follow:

1. That every nobleman has a voice in the enactment of the statutes of his comitat;

2. That before conviction of a crime, and before a legal sentence has been pronounced, a nobleman cannot be arrested;

3. That a nobleman alone can possess a landed estate; and

4. That none but the king is above him.

"The sum of which is," said the priest, " that with us a nobleman *by law,* may do every thing that pleases him." These famous articles are familiarly known throughout Hungary by the name of "*Primæ Nonus,*" by which every one understands "*Primæ Partis Codicis Articulus Nonus.*"

Formerly a clause was inserted in the fourth privilege, that the noble might oppose lawfully the reigning unconsecrated king. This clause was struck out of the statute-book by the emperor Leopold, since it not only made the nobleman the judge of the king's actions, but tended to the destruction of the state altogether; but as it still remains in the *Tripartitum* of Werhotzy, a law-book written by the celebrated prothonotary and palatine Werhotzy, which is so esteemed in Hungary, that its dicta have almost the power of law, many of the Hungarian nobles bear it well in mind, and will still appeal to it.

I found a copy of the *Allgemeine Zeitung* in this convent. My spiritual friend thought that about twelve copies were brought regularly to the city. It may be a question whether in Northern Germany more than one city of 20,000 inhabitants may not be found, where a smaller number of this journal would be sufficient to supply the demand.

The next morning I drove with a pair of fleet horses (easily obtained here) to Vesprim. To the right I saw the Verteach mountains, in which there is a very remarkable break at this part. It cuts through the mountain back of an extensive valley, leaving the hill standing at a considerable distance on either side, like a vast portal. Through this gate runs the highroad to Raab. Much merchandise from Pesth takes this circuitous route over Stuhlweissenburg to Raab and Vienna, because the roads are better than those leading more directly through the Buda mountains. Leaving the mountain gate, and the city of Stuhlweissenburg behind, the road passed along the skirts of a branch of the Bakony forest. The hills were for the most part planted with vines. Our horses took objections to a dead dog and a dead horse, both of which lay across their path, and then to a gipsy-cart drawn by an ass. The cart was two-wheeled, and about large enough to accommodate a couple of flour-sacks, but three gipsy-women with their children, had contrived to pack themselves in it, a young lad sat on the animal's back, and an old gipsy squatted behind it on the pole; the boy held the reins, and the old fellow retained the executive power in the shape of a knotted stick. They were all as black as if newly imported from Africa.

In Polota, a town subject to the Zichy family, I saw a synagogue with a modern inscription, in the Magyar language, a sign of great patriotism among the Jews of the place. I doubt whether we could find in Germany one synagogue with a German inscription; the churches of four other religious sects were all dwelling in peace with one another. The situation of the town at the foot of the mountain was not bad, and beetling over the habitations of men, enthroned on a lofty rock, two castles of the counts of Zichy, an old and a new one, reared their stately heads. From this place, castles and the ruins of castles met us at every step, by the side of the forest.

One of the curiosities of Polota, is a lawsuit which was commenced in the year 1727. The exposition and settlement of various pleas and counter-pleas occupied a hundred and eleven years down to 1838. It is said that it will come to an end at last; the litigants, made wiser by more than a century's experience, have resolved to come to an accommodation. This is not the only "monster" lawsuit that exists in Hungary.

There are more pictures by Rosa di Tivoli in Hungary than in all the German picture-galleries, plentiful as the sheep, oxen, and herdsmen of this industrious artist are there. On every side we saw also the finest groups of cattle and figures. Wrapped in their sheepskins, the Gulyasses were either cooking their noonday meal by a fire kindled in the open air, or stretched under the shade of a tree, enjoying an enviable state of do-nothingness, while their herds grazed around. Almost all the oxen were handsome, indeed to be handsome is the ordinary condition of the inferior animals; man alone enjoys the privilege of being occasionally ugly. However, I saw one exception to this rule, in a most hideously ugly ox. His mouth was widely distorted from the regular line usual in the physiognomy of his race; his teeth were awry and ill formed, and his horns, which have generally so stately an appearance, especially with the cattle of Hungary, were frightfully twisted, and his eyes had a most repulsive expression. His skin was very ugly, and his head, white on the other oxen, was covered with a nasty-looking dark-brown mole. The ugliness of the brute was so striking, that it was impossible to overlook it. Perhaps there may be apparent to the cows' eyes many shades of beauty and degrees of ugliness that are overlooked by ours.

Below Polota we passed a very singular-looking wall. It was low, several hundred feet long, built of fine freestone, from three to four ells wide, and screened a quantity of marsh-water, that issued from the mountain. The people here attribute the building of this wall to the Turks, and say it was a bath; but it requires little consideration to induce one to reject this supposition as extremely improbable. The wall seems built for eternity, and was, I doubt not, a Roman work. It strongly resembles those reservoirs built by the Roman emperors on the declivities of the hills of Constantinople, which were called "ὑδράλια," and are in existence to this day. Unfortunately there was no inscription, but it is known that in this part of Pannonia coins of the emperors down to Constantine have been found. The fine upper stones of the wall were partly loosened, and some lay on the ground. I was told that the whole had been sold to the Jews, who meant to make use of the stones. They have a handsome piece of work before them in the destruction of this Roman work, which at all events they will not effect without some trouble.

The nearer we approached Vesprim, the faster our driver urged his horses. At last he began a race with another carriage like our own, with two horses. "I know him," said our man, "I will *sekiren* him a bit." "And what is *sekiren?*" I asked our Hungarianized German driver. "*Sekiren* means to get the laugh against any one; when it is done only with words they say *sticheliren.*" After a time he turned again to me. "What do you think, shall we overtake him? I think we are gaining on him." And in fact we had the pleasure of seeing the *gallows of Vesprim* before him; there were two of these pleasing objects, one of stone and the other of wood, on a hill near the city. When I inquired about them in Vesprim, I was told that one was the town, and the other the bishop's gallows, both bishop and town exercising the *Jus studii.* Another account was, that two years ago so many criminals were executed that the one stone gibbets had been found insufficient, and therefore a supplementary one of wood had been erected. I know not which of the two accounts was the correct one, both parties seemed equally likely to be well informed.

I had an introduction to the Piarists who have a large college and seminary in Vesprim. One of the subordinate officers received me, and, as the rector could not immediately be spoken with, remained with me in the anteroom. My companion entertained me in Latin, affording me another opportunity of studying the very peculiar Latin spoken here, which is a literal translation of Hungarian or Austrian German. The first question of my man was, "*Cum qua occasione advenit?*" It must be borne in mind that in Hungarian Latin, the third person singular is used in addressing any one, the words *Dominatio vestra* (your lordship) being understood. The Austrian word *Gelegenheit* (opportunity) was understood here to signify what kind of vehicle, and was literally translated by *occasione*. "*Num propriam occasionem accepit?*" continued my Latinist, and I replied, "*Ita propriam occasionem accepi.*" We understood each other capitally, but no European scholar of the west would have dreamed what he meant by his question, or I by my answer. He intended to ask whether

I had hired a carriage for myself, my reply was intended to be an affirmative.

"*Num dignabitur ecclesiam nostram inspicere?*"* quoth he again, and sometimes a sentence was patched with a pure Hungarian word, for countless are the Latinized Hungarian expressions in use amongst them; but, perhaps our middle age Latin was not much better. The Latinized names of the Hungarian dignitaries are quite unintelligible, to those unacquainted with the Hungarian language: for example, "*Agosonum Regalium Magister*" (Archchamberlain), "*Pincernarum Regalium Magister*" (Archcupbearer), "*Banus Croatiæ*" (The Ban of Croatia), &c. It is well known, however, that the educated clergy speak very good Latin, and the educated among the laity, speak it very fluently at least.

At last the reverend gentlemen to whom I was recommended made their appearance, and had the goodness to escort me about their town. Vesprim has the most peculiar site of any Hungarian town I ever saw. It is said to resemble that of the mountain city of Schemnitz. It lies in the upper valley of the Sed, near the sources of that river. The high land has several very deep indentations, owing either to the river or to some volcanic convulsion, and the serpentine lines of these indentations meet at the end of the valley. In consequence a number of tongues of land or promontories are formed, and perched on these promontories, and buried in the depths of that valley lies Vesprim. In the centre, on the long promontory of a steep chalk hill rise the bishop's palace, the seminary, the gymnasium, the comitat-house, and all the principal buildings of the city. The cliff ends with a long, high, narrow edge of rock projecting far into the river. From this point is obtained the best view of the city. On this elevated ridge many ruins are to be seen, memorials of Turkish ravages. Here too, the Turks put many of the chapter to death.

The bishopric of Vesprim is one of the richest in Hungary, and the bishop is so much of a great man here, that almost every thing that is good in the city is ascribed to him. The bishops of Vesprim belong to the most ancient and most distinguished dignitaries of the kingdom. As early as the thirteenth century, a high school, the oldest in Hungary, formed on the model of the University of Paris, flourished here under their protecting care. At that time the city contained twenty parish churches: but the splendours of Vesprim, like all other splendours of Hungary, set when the Turkish half moon rose above the horizon; all that is now to be seen is the work of the last century.

The bishop's palace contains many beautiful works of art. There are some excellent pictures by French artists of the time of Louis XV. In the chapel we saw and greatly admired a Christ crowned with thorns, said to be Titian's, and the admirable execution and exquisite expression of suffering in the face of the Saviour were certainly not calculated to throw a doubt on the conjecture.

Among the portraits of the bishops who have held this see, may be seen those of members of the most distinguished families in Hungary, the Esterhazys, Szchenyis, &c. The present bishop is also primate of the kingdom. The revenue of the bishopric is said to exceed 300,000 florins— a magnificent *vinea Domini!* In France the revenue of an archbishop is

---

* Will your lordship condescend to look at our church?

fixed at about 25,000 francs, that of a bishop at 15,000. In Hungary there are many chapters, the income of whose individual members exceeds that sum. The chapter of Vesprim is one of the richest.

One of these dignitaries of Vesprim, founded in the year 1811 an educational institution of a peculiar kind. It admits now but the children of mixed marriages "because," as my priest observed, "the education of such children is naturally much neglected," and brings them up in the Catholic faith of course. The founder gave a sum of 300,000 florins for this purpose; but the "Patent" edict having sunk the value of these 300,000 to 60,000, the plan could not be brought into operation till another wealthy dignitary of the church came to the assistance of the pious undertaking in 1827. Twenty girls, and as many boys are educated here. If the girls marry, they have 100 florins given them as a dowery. The director seemed to be a learned and well-informed man. It is said that the institution is indebted to him for many services which are little known, and for which he receives but little acknowledgment.

Christianity was brought to Hungary, as to Bohemia and Moravia, from Greece. Several Hungarian chiefs and dukes were baptized at Constantinople. In the time of Sarolta, the mother of king Stephen the Holy, there were yet several Greek convents in Hungary. The ruins of one are still to be seen in a narrow valley near Vesprim. Happily for Hungary, she allowed herself to be won over to the Latin church by Italy and Germany. This it was that decided that Hungary should belong to Western Europe; and this also affords us the best security, that through all the changes of destiny she will hold with us against the East.

It was already twilight when I set out to pursue my journey towards the Platten Lake, and it soon became pitch dark. The only objects I could recognise in the obscurity were a waggon drawn by four fine oxen, and laden with corn, flour, and hay, for the use of the bishop, and some carts, each drawn by four horses, and packed full of fowls, also for the bishop, and going to Vesprim.

Late in the evening we reached the famous bathing-place of Fured, and long and loud we had to knock and call at gate, wall, and window, before we could get admittance. We began to think the inhabitants had all given up the ghost, when a man made his appearance with a light, and having satisfied himself that we looked like harmless people, opened the doors. We asked the people of the house if they had not heard our noise before.

"Oh yes," was the answer; "but you must not take it amiss. By night all cats are gray, and it is impossible to know directly whom one has at the door. So late in the year no guests to the baths were to be expected, and the Bakony forest, *antiqua silva, stabula alta ferarum*, was near." Therefore it was they had hidden their lights; for sometimes foolish, drunken people would come and make an uproar, and quarrel, and the like, so he hoped we would not take it amiss.

I tranquillized the worthy people thoroughly, and assured them they had done my valour too much honour in taking me for a bold captain of banditti; that I was by nature of a most peaceable disposition, and rejoiced from the bottom of my heart when others let me alone, instead of nourishing evil thoughts of attacking them. I was very glad to find myself among them, and begged them by all means to bar the door carefully again.

My hosts called me on all sides "gracious lord" (*Gnädiger Herr*) wherein I begged once more to correct them, as it would puzzle me to say of what I was lord, and I was conscious of as little grace as might be. Hereupon the two pretty daughters of the house tuned up their guitars, and while I regaled myself with the culinary works of art set forth by their worthy old aunt of seventy-six, and with a glass of excellent Hungarian wine, they sang me an Hungarian song entitled "The Balaton," that is to say, the Platten Lake.

Unfortunately I did not perfectly understand this song, as it was sung in the Hungarian language; but its words were something to this effect: "God once sent two angels down upon the earth to see if his name was held everywhere in honour. The angels found it held in high honour among the burgers and peasants; everywhere as the messengers of God they were received with joy and veneration. At last they came to the palace of a great lord, and a wealthy lady. Here the servants drove them away, and would not hear of them or their sender. The lord and the lady refused the strangers an alms, although they were wearied by their journey. A poor shepherd, whom they met in the fields, gave them of his bread and his drink, so that they were refreshed and could fly back to Heaven. They related what they had found below, and complained of the hard-hearted lord of the castle. Then was God wroth, and again sent down messengers, who utterly destroyed the castle, and, that the place where his name was held in honour might vanish from the face of the earth, he caused waters to flow over that land, and thus was formed the Balaton or Platten Lake. Since that time, where once a lordly castle stood, is now the habitation of mute fish; but round about the Balaton, God-fearing men have increased and multiplied."

I requested my obliging young hostesses to sing me another song, which they immediately did. As I am not able to render this in a good metrical form, I translate it literally. The title is

MENET A KEDVESCHER.
(The Ride to the Beloved One by the Platten Lake.)

1. On the dry earth falls the hoar frost. Eat not, dear horse, it might give pain. Dearest, I will buy thee a silken bridle and a velvet saddle, so thou be to my delight.
2. Hard roll the clods under thy feet. Dear horse, heed well thy feet; fly me to my heart's dear Rose, for away from her my soul pines in deep sorrow.
3. See the moon begins to shine brightly; so pure it never before appeared, shed thy beams on me, that I may not lose myself in the darkness.
4. See the Balaton glances brightly before us. Thou sparkling lake, thou wilt not pour thy waters over the land, and bar my path. O beautiful Balaton, shed not thy waters o'er my path. See, I should bring my poor horse in danger.
5. Hold my good steed, we are at our goal. Look there, a light glimmers feebly through her window. See, there sits a young brown maiden slumbering. What ho! my sweet girl, slumber not, thy lover waits without.

"You must know," said my kind and song-loving *Ingrin*, "that the Platten See, in some places really overflows its banks, and makes the road often impassable; and moreover our Hungarian youths have the custom of modestly visiting their mistresses at their windows, and there conversing with them."

I told them that Shakspeare had chosen the same situation for his two lovers in "Romeo and Juliet." In the fourth verse, I added, there was a particular delicacy in the rider's petitioning the lake, not for himself, but for his horse; and I was pleased with the fancy of trying to make the animal believe grazing would be hurtful to him, and with the flattering promise of a velvet saddle and silken bridle.

"Note also the dark maiden," said the singer, "the Hungarians love nothing but brown or black hair. Fair girls do not please, and the poor, pale, light hair seems downright ugly to them. You will never hear the charms of a blonde extolled in an Hungarian, as you do in so many a German song." "And still more in an Italian one," said I. "The modern as well as the ancient Italians hold light hair, and especially the golden locks, to be the most beautiful. The Roman ladies wore false locks of the favourite colour, and the painters of Italy, who have represented their ideal of beauty with fair hair are numberless. The portraits of Petrarca's charming Laura, one in particular in the Berlin gallery, have light, indeed almost white hair."

"Nay! that is too shocking!" said my horrified *Ingrins*. I tried to explain the matter, and represented to them that fair hair resembled silk; that the play of colour in this tender material was generally softer and finer than in dark hair, and might, therefore, be more attractive to a painter; lastly that the soft and gentle tints of blond tresses had more analogy with the character of women than the abrupt contrasts of the dark hair which seemed more suitable to the man. Perhaps the Hungarians dislike the light colour because it approaches the gray of age; while the full raven black hair suggests the idea of youthful prime and freshness. The dislike of the Hungarians to the Germans will not explain their dislike of blond beauty, for the Italians admire it, though they have looked on the Germans time out of mind with hostile feelings.

My harangue was too long for the damsels; they tuned their guitars again to a song of mourning and lamentation, composed by Count Wesseleny in his captivity, no part of which, unhappily, I retain, and concluded with the song of an hussar, who is setting out for the wars, and entreats his mistress for a flower and a parting kiss. She answers she has no time now; she must give the flowers to her mother, but when he comes back from the wars she will give him both. The hussar answers that perhaps he never will come back, perhaps he shall be left dead upon the battle-field. "Then will I plant the flower upon thy grave, and bestow a kiss upon thy cross," she answered, and melting into tears, permits him to take as many kisses as he likes.

THE CONVENT OF TIHANY, AND THE PLATTEN LAKE.

The next day, in company with some public officers, and the obliging father of my pretty vocalists, I visited the bathing establishments of Füred. They belong to different persons who possess land in the neighbourhood, and who have a claim upon the springs and their produce. One bathing-house was erected by the Benedictine monks of the neighbouring abbey, another by the Esterhazy family, and a third belongs to forty of the peasant-nobles in common. All these buildings, some of which are very large, together with some places of amusement, a theatre, public gardens, avenues of trees, &c., form a very pretty settlement close to the shores of the Platten See. In the background there is a beautiful oak-wood, and in front the expanse of the magnificent lake which forms a small bay in this part, with the peninsula of Tihany sweeping round.

As Trentschin in north western, and Mehadia in eastern, so Fured is now the most noted and best frequented bathing-place in South Western Hungary. Its "*Säuerling*"* is excellent, and it is strange that its merits should have been acknowledged only so very lately. The Hungarian travellers of the seventeenth century have spoken of these springs, and lamented that none but the neighbouring shepherds should come to enjoy their delicious waters. It is only since the time of the emperor Joseph II., that any thing of consequence has been done for the convenience of guests, of whom the yearly number now exceeds a thousand.† The wholesome taste for cold bathing has also taken root, and besides the arrangements for the drinkers of the *Säuerling*, there are baths on the Platten See, and they are to be greatly extended this year.

The little theatre is exclusively devoted to representations in the Hungarian language; the inscription in front is likewise in Hungarian. It is said to be very bombastic, and a gentleman who was about to translate it to me, declared that it was impossible to render it in German. The shorter sense of it was, "the fatherland to its sons." I should rather have supposed "the sons to the fatherland," but as the theatre is really a poor insignificant affair, either would be absurdly pompous and swelling. Every thing about Fured, however, is excessively patriotic. All the fences round court and garden are painted of the national colours, red, white, and green; the little garden bridges, and the pavilion over the springs, are emblazoned in the same hues. The previous year a company of Tyrolese who had descended from their Alps to Fured were not even allowed to sing there, out of pure patriotism. No one will think of blaming the Hungarians for loving their native land; but in the midst of our wonder, we can scarcely admire a zeal for nationality carried so far as to prohibit the innocent pleasure of listening to a few Tyrolese singers, because they happen to be foreigners. We Germans love our country too, but we can enjoy an Hungarian song for all that. Even as a matter of policy the Hungarians should not carry their patriotic feeling to too lofty a height, for a building raised to an unreasonable elevation is apt to topple over, and is, at all events, sure to impair its own durability.

I set out early after dinner that I might reach the famous abbey of Tihany in time, and deliver my credentials from a friend in Pesth to the abbot. The figure of the Platten Lake is a long parallelogram, and the shore is a tolerably straight line the whole way; the only exception occurs about the middle, where a considerable peninsula runs so far into the lake that between its point and the southern shore opposite there remains only a narrow channel, thereby dividing the lake into two, the eastern and western lakes. This remarkable peninsula is evidently of volcanic origin; it consists plainly of two deep basins, probably extinct craters, with a steep descent towards the water. In the bottom of one of these hollows lies a small lake, the other is moist meadow-land. These two basins are connected with the shore by a swampy level, which probably lay altogether under water when the lake was higher, and completely insulated the pe-

---

* Those mineral waters are called in German *Säuerlinge*, which contain carbonic acid gas, or fixed air, as one of their chief component parts, throwing up bubbles when poured out, and mantling like Champagne when mixed with sugar and wine. Among the best known German mineral waters of this kind are those of Selters, Eger, and Salzbrunn.—*Tr.*

† In 1840, there were above 1800.

ninsula. On the steep declivity of the second basin stands the mistress of the peninsula, and, indeed, of half the country round, the abbey of Tihany.

I drove there in a little Hungarian carriage that made a music on the uneven road like the jingling of the brass-laden harness of our German drivers. What we hang about the horses, the Hungarians of the Platten See hang to the carriage itself. A number of small iron-plates, strung on an iron rod, fastened obliquely from the pole to the fore wheel, clattered and jingled backwards and forewards with every motion of the vehicle, as if it could not make noise enough by itself. Cheered by this agreeable harmony, we reached the isthmus that joins Tihany to the mainland, and there sunk deep into the mire; for, as before said, the ground is swampy, and as level as a table. The ascent begins as soon as the peninsula is reached, and here are to be found the remains of the defences ascribed to the Romans. It is certain that the Romans made use of this peninsula as a military post, although there may be no foundation for the tradition that the empress Valeria, the consort of Galerius, in whose honour this part of Pannonia was called the Valerian province, retired hither, with her mother, Prisca, after the death of her lord, to lead a life of seclusion. The peninsula itself has rather a desolate appearance. The two volcanic basins are nothing but bare pasture-lands with a small portion of arable. The basaltic elevations on the southern and western sides are wooded; those to the east are bare. We drove through the first hollow, then ascended, and entered the second. Here the abbey comes in sight, situated on an elevation, at the foot of which, on the sides of the basin down to the small inner lake, lies an Hungarian village. The Benedictines have a pleasant lodging ready for guests who have any kind of recommendation to them, and here I passed a few very agreeable days.

The abbot who was busy when I arrived, made me over to a subordinate officer who was to show me the curiosities of the place, and whose talkative humour and very original German, amused me exceedingly. "How I envy you to be able to travel so much!" said he, as we set off to explore the peninsula. "How much experience and knowingness one must gather in travelling! It is true that it can only benefit clever people; ignorant people may travel as much as they will, they are none the better for it. As we say in Hungary, 'Send an ass to Vienna, and you will not make a horse of him;' and many stop at home and become wise people notwithstanding. There is our great poet, Kisfalndy, for example, who lives at Schumegh, not far from here. He is our Hungarian Orpheus, and something more perhaps, and he has never been out of Hungary. Do you know his writings? What noble thoughts! His last publication, and the best of all, was a collection of songs about the environs of the Balaton. Well, if I were to go on my travels I should know when to stop, for I was well instructed in religion by my father, and that's the principal thing. My father made all his children very religious; we were all obliged to learn by heart every point of Christ's genealogy, and of God's providence: and when one knows all that, and can keep it fast, one can go through life safely enough."

"And where were you brought up?" I asked.

"In Debrezin, where they do not speak much German. I learnt it here. The Hungarian language also is differently spoken in Debrezin, coarsely and not at all flowingly; here they speak finer and more *affectedly*: and where do you come from?"

"*Bremiabo!* from Bremen," was my answer, "*Nemet szabad varos,*" (that is, a free German city).

"Where is Bremen, right or left below Trieste?"

"Neither, but at the back of it, if you will consider Trieste as standing with its face to the sea. Bremen lies high up in the north of Germany."

I have often noticed that the uneducated Hungarians make use of very extraordinary expressions in German; if they have not the right word they take another, or coin one for the occasion; they are probably led to this by the facility they enjoy of making new words in their own language.

The curiosities of Tihany peninsula consist, firstly, of an echo, which, under certain favourable conditions of the atmosphere, will repeat a whole distich. My companion amused himself by repeating at least ten times, the Hungarian style and title of my native city, "*Bremia Nemet kiralny szabad varos!*" (Bremen the German royal free city!) secondly, of some caves in which the monks are said to have hidden when the Turks held the country round; and lastly, in some singular petrifactions called the "goats' nails," from the striking resemblance they bear to a goat's feet; they are probably petrified shells. The people take them for the feet of real goats belonging to the primitive inhabitants.

As we returned home my companion gave me some information about the Hungarian cookery, in which he seemed quite at home.

The chief dish of all Hungarians, at least in this part of the country, he said, was dumplings with curdled milk. This dish made its appearance every day at every man's table, even on the nobleman's, and if not served up at dinner, it never failed to figure at supper. Roast or boiled meat, roasted horseflesh, pork, or bacon, almost every one eat every day, even the poor had their bacon and white bread. The vegetable part of the meal varied every day according to old established custom. On Sundays, generally sour kraut (*Toltett kaposzta*); Mondays, sweet cabbage (*Olasz kaposzta*); Tuesdays, another kind of sour kraut called *Savangu kaposzta*; Wednesdays, yellow turnips, cabbage, or lentils; Thursdays, *Savangu repa*, or white turnips preserved in vinegar; Fridays, yellow turnips, and Saturdays, spinach, and so on. The first part of the week may therefore be looked upon as sacred to cabbage of different kinds, and the latter, till *Szombat*, (even the Hungarians have adopted the Hebrew word, Sabbath, for Saturday, like almost all the eastern Europeans,) is devoted to turnips.

While pursuing these valuable inquiries, we came back to the abbey, where in the evening I made the acquaintance of some of these dishes, while enjoying conversation a little more instructive.

It was a beautiful evening, and I had a good opportunity of enjoying it, when I retired to my cell, a large, Gothic, vaulted room, commanding a view of the lake, wherein the moon's sickle was reflected in a thousand dancing, sparkling waves. On one side lay the deep shadow of the Bakony forest, on the other the bright mirror of the lake was gradually lost in the distance, and a vague, uncertain line only marked the place where the Romans had attempted to unite the lake with the Danube by means of a canal. No sound broke the silence, save the murmuring of the waters; not a voice, not an oar. The convent was intensely still, I felt alone with the genii of the lake.

In many respects the Balaton or Platten Lake is the counterpart of the lake of Geneva. They lie at the two extremities of the Alpine chain, and between them a chain of lakes winds along the northern and another along the southern line of these mighty hills; on the one side the lake of Constance, the Swiss lakes, those of Bavaria, and the Neusiedler lake; on the other the Italian and some small Illyrian lakes. I should like to know whether there exists any geognostic connexion between these lakes and the chains of lakes near them; I mean whether they have any common reference to the elevation of the lofty Alpine range between them. I do not remember that this point has ever been cleared up, or has even induced an inquiry.

Many peculiarities, as my readers are no doubt aware, have been ascribed to the Platten See. It has been described as constantly agitated even in the calmest weather, as foaming and fretting, and dashing its waves incessantly against the shore; the ebb and flood as being very trifling, but its waters as rising or sinking according to the changes of the moon, at particular hours. The evaporation of the surface, we have been told, is replaced by subaqueous springs, which have their sources in the neighbouring limestone mountains, and bring with them a quantity of carbonic acid which is disengaged in the lake, and thereby occasions the effervescing of its waters. The colour of the water is said to be generally a clear white, but when storms are approaching, even when no clouds have yet appeared in the heavens, it assumes a dark hue, and forms thus a convenient weather-gauge.

The whole nature of the Platten See has never been properly examined, and therefore I believe that the few facts related to me on the spot may offer something of novelty. The evening I speak of, when I looked upon its waters, waves were constantly beating against the shore, although the atmosphere was perfectly still. The following morning I went down to the ferry at the extremity of the peninsula. This ferry unites the comitat of Salader, at the north of the lake, to that of Schomoty, at the south. A road leads through the peninsula, over which the people who wish to go "*in's Schomoty,*" pass as over a bridge. On the Schomoty side there is an Hungarian, on the Tihany, a German ferryman. The walk from the convent to the ferryman's cottage is nearly a mile. His name is Dicker, and he has held the ferry over this lake for nearly eighteen years. He assured me that the water was never still, not even when there had been a calm for fourteen days. He also confirmed what had been told me respecting the changes in the weather to be foretold by the appearance of the water. "Even when the storm is in Germany," said he, "the lake has got it in its stomach, and foams and grumbles beforehand." In the little strait at the extremity of the peninsula, where the lake is only two hundred fathoms wide, the motion is the strongest; and in addition to the agitation of the waves on the surface, there is a strong current, strongest in the middle of the strait, where the water is not more than seven fathoms deep at the utmost. The current flows sometimes from west to east, and sometimes in a contrary direction; the people could not say whether there was a double current as in other straits. The monks thought this current was caused by the superfluous waters of either part of the lake, and that if the wind blew long from the east the water was driven into the western part, and *vice versâ*; but the boatman was of opinion that the stream was continual, even when there had long been no wind to impel the waters to one part or the other. After a long continuance of wind the water became troubled, but in general, even among the reeds, it was as clear "as aqua fortis."

The people employ a curious terminology for the different winds. The north wind, which blows from the Bakony forest, is the *upper* wind; the south, from the Schomotyer plains, the *under* wind; the west wind is the *Saler*, because it blows from the Salader comitat; and the east wind the Calvin wind, probably because it comes over the Hungarian steppes, where there are more Calvinists than in any other part of Hungary. The " Saler wind," from the Alps, sweeping along the whole length of the lake, is the most violent; it raises the waves mountain high, and brings with it the greatest number of storms. As to the story of the rise and fall of the waters with the moon's changes, no one knew any thing about it.

The foaming of the water may arise from the quantity of carbonic acid gas carried into it by the springs. The Platten See is so strongly impregnated with this gas, that Professor Schuster thinks the whole lake may be looked upon as one great receptacle of a much diluted acid. Yellow paper becomes pretty quickly of a brown red tint in its waters, and red is changed to blue. The taste is strongly astringent, and the skin, after washing in it, becomes rough and breaks. The eyes, after bathing in the lake, become sensible of great irritation, which sometimes even amounts to inflammation. Horses driven to swim in the lake would lose their hoofs if fat were not rubbed into them. The water may be preserved for a long time without becoming putrid, and it will even preserve meat and other substances completely fresh for several days. The fish found in this lake are said to differ greatly from those of the same species in other waters. The flesh is finer, firmer, and better flavoured.

The Romans dug a canal from the eastern corner of the lake where the little river Sio runs out of it, and afterwards, uniting with the Sarwitz, flows into the Danube. The Sio, I was told, is an intermitting river; it does not always flow, but forms at times only a lengthened swamp. The Romans are said to have gained much ground on the shores of the lake, by means of the Sio canal, which was subsequently inundated in consequence of the canal becoming choked up. As no navigation would be ruined by the draining of the Platten See, and nothing worse would ensue than the non-appearance of the delicate *fogasch* on the tables of Pesth and Vienna, the whole lake would be no great loss, and the Hungarians could not do better than tread in the footsteps of the Romans, and clear out the canal once more.

The boatmen at the Tihany ferry assured me as a positive fact, that since 1834 the lake had sunk five feet. During three months of the present summer, which has been a very dry one, it has lost five inches more. I asked them how they knew that, and they showed me a scale which they had made on the beams sunk here, to form a sort of quay for the ferry-boats.

I could learn nothing certain respecting the height of the water before the year 1834, and the question remains, whether the lake be really diminishing, or whether, as the people here seem inclined to think, a periodical increase and decrease takes place. It was remarkable that what I was told of the decrease of the Platten See, and also the epoch of its commencement exactly tallied with what I had previously heard of the Neusiedler lake. In winter the lake rises from six to twelve inches, and reaches its highest point in March.

The south-western end of the Platten See loses itself in swamps, through which several small rivers find their way to the lake. In later times many attempts have been made to drain these swamps. Has the quantity of water in the lake perhaps been affected by these? It is very possible if we assume that a part of the lake water remains in these swamps; but the contrary may be the case, there may have been an increase of the quantity when we reflect that the whole waters of those small rivers now flow into the lake, part of which formerly the swamps must have absorbed.

There are a far greater number of species of fish in this lake than in the Neusiedler. Two of them are of importance; one because it is so highly valued by the epicure in fish, the other because it is caught in such vast quantities. The former is the renowned *fogasch*, the latter the *garda*. The fogasch, a kind of sand eel (*Perca lucioperca*) is only found in this lake. It is from seven to ten, and 15 lbs. weight, and is most frequently caught in the western part, chiefly near the market-town of Kesthely, a possession of Count Festetiz. It usually keeps in the deepest part of the water, and is consequently very susceptible to the hostile element of fish, the air. As soon as it is taken out of the water it dies. Clear water and a sandy bottom are its delight; in reeds and swamps it is never to be found. The flesh is very white and firm, and much more "corny" than that of other fish, as my ferryman of the lake expressed it.

The *garda* has a most fraternal resemblance to the herring, but is somewhat smaller. The Germans in the neighbourhood generally call it a herring. It is very delicate, but is little else than bones. Whilst the fishermen esteem themselves fortunate if they catch a couple of fogasch at once, and very seldom indeed capture as many as five or ten in their nets, the garda is to be had by fifties and sometimes even by hundreds of cwts. Small as this water kingdom of theirs is, these lake herrings, like their brethren in the ocean, appear to have a taste for wandering, and move about incessantly in their basin. By what passion they may be urged I know not, but they are not unfrequently to be seen in shoals on the surface of the water flying from the eastern to the western side and back again. The state of the weather may perhaps have a great effect on them.

The gardas are caught most frequently during winter, and in the following manner: A number of small holes are made in a circular figure on the ice, and pretty close together. Opposite to each other, in the circle, two of the holes are made much larger than the others; through one the net is lowered, through the other it is drawn up. The draught is sometimes so abundant that the net cannot be drawn up, and the fish must be taken out singly.

As it is easier to describe the labour than to execute it, and the circle and the net are very large, a great number of persons are required for this kind of fishing. The best time for it is in the beginning of the winter, before the ice becomes too thick, and many accidents, sometimes fatal ones, take place in consequence. I was told that on one occasion, nearly fifty persons lost their lives. The fishermen are generally native Hungarians. Indeed the towns and villages round the Platten See are all Magyar, in which point this lake differs materially from its brother the Neusiedler See, which is surrounded by German towns, and at the utmost can be considered as Hungarian only at its south-eastern coast. The Neusiedler, however, can bear no comparison in interest with the Platten lake, partly from this very cause. The natural-historical, the picturesque, and the historical associations are all in favour of the latter; hence it is far more renowned in Hungary, and more glorified in the national poetry. Among the Romans also, the Balaton was the more noted; it is not certain what name they bestowed on the Neusiedler, and some even assert that it is not certain that it existed at that time. The Romans called the Platten See *Pelso*, probably a corruption of the ancient Slavonian word *Boloton*, which has much the same signification as the Latin *Palus*, and like this, is no doubt a verbal root. The *t* in *Boloton* might be easily changed into an *s*. The Romans called it also *Volocea*, which may be only another corruption of *Boloton*. The Germans make *Blatten*, or *Plattensee* out of the same word; the same old Slavonian word seems a foundation of all. The Hungarians have also another name for it; they call the lake *feyer tenger* (the white sea).

I returned from my visit to the Tihany strait, in time to play a game at billiards with some of the monks. They called the game "*Ludus tudicularis;*" I asked for an explanation of a name so new to me. "*Quia tunditur*," was the answer. Out of politeness they persisted in styling me "*doctissime*, or *clarissime*," although I assured them that I was far from deserving the distinction, as in the first place I was every day discovering monstrous gaps in my learning, and in the second, no university had ever conferred that dignity upon me.

The game of billiards is known all over Europe, and the Russians have carried it far into Asia; its terms are familiar to every man and nearly to every lady, but few, I believe, are acquainted with the Latin expressions invented by the Hungarians, and I therefore subjoin those I learnt on this occasion as curiosities.

The balls are called *globi*, and, according to their colour, *cæruleus*, *ruber*, and *flavus*.

"*Ubi globus Dominationis?*" (Where is your ball?)

"*Ibi! incipiamus*" (Here! let us begin).

"*Dignetur præcedere?*" (Will it please you to go on?)

"*Dolendum est! Si cæruleus huc veni sset*" (What a pity! If the blue had but come this way).

I made a miss. "*Fallit! fallit!*" was the exclamation that followed.

"*Nunc flavus recte ad manum mihi est*" (Now the Caroline lies right to my hand).

I made a good stroke. "*Bene, bene! Nunc Hannibal ad portam.*" (Very good! There will be the devil to pay now.)

"*Dignetur Dublé?*" (Will you please to double?)

"*Fallit!*" (A miss!) "*O si homo nunquam falleretur, esset invincibilis!*" "*Reverende Pater! Nunc tota positio difficilis est.*" "*Nil video! nisi cæruleum et rubrum percutere velles*" (I see nothing particular except a cannon on the red and blue).

"*Ah, ah! subtiliter volui et nil habeo!* (Alas! I wanted to do something very clever, and I have done nothing!)

"*Bene, bene! Nunc si adhuc illum faceris. Fecesti! Finis ludi!*"

We were called to dinner. The party was pretty numerous. There were other guests besides myself; a priest of the neighbourhood, and some students who often met at the tables of the abbots in Hungary, as friends or relations of some of the community. The conversation was extremely lively, and to me, highly instructive; and seemed the more interesting when I thought of the peculiar position of our dining-room, on the summit of a mountain, with on the one side the broad still prolific lake, on the other an immense forest filled with herdsmen and their grunting charges. An animated and highly cultivated circle has under such circumstances far more charm and worth than it would have in the centre of a large capital.

The abbot and the prior were, among the inmates of the convent, those who pleased me most. The latter had been formerly Professor of Poetry and Rhetoric at a gymnasium in Raab; he was a man rich in knowledge, of a fine taste, and apparently of an ardent and energetic character. His conversation was so agreeable to me, that after dinner I followed him to his cell, or rather his very pretty chamber. If conversation were not so capricious and intangible a thing, I should attempt to give the reader some idea of mine with this learned monk, from which might be gained much new information respecting Hungary; but conversation, animating, kindling as it is when we take an active part in it, is ordinarily but a lifeless wooden thing upon paper, because it is nearly as difficult to follow its many and often graceful turns, as to describe the evolutions of a dance. We spoke of the old times of Hungary in the days of the *Augsburgi Uthözet* (the battle of Augsburg); of the proceedings of the last diet; of Kisfaludy's artless but inspired verses, which ring in one's ears and bewitch one like gipsy music, and particularly of his principal production, "Himfy's Love;" of the young poet Zuzor's lyric and erotic songs, some of which, however, as the production of an ecclesiastic, have been exposed to severe reprehension; among his best are "The Sleeping Beauty," "The Little Window," "No Subterfuge." From this native poetry we came to that translated from the German, including nearly all the poems of Schiller, but scarcely any thing of Göthe; and passed from Hungarian literature to Hungarian ethnography, to national economy, the condition of the schools, the manufacture of wine, and the natural history of the country in all its various relations, a width of range that may appear marvellous and unlikely enough to the reader, but in which the subjects followed each other naturally and unconstrainedly through all the mazes and regular confusion of an unfettered conversation.

BAKONY FOREST, ITS POETS, CASTLES, AND ROBBERS.

It was no easy task for me to tear myself from Tihany, where I would willingly have lingered a little longer; but as my friends in the convent told me that if I wished to reach Schumegh in the afternoon I had no time to lose, I left them the day after that of which I have just spoken, descended the steril mountain of Tihany, and leaving Fured to the right, pursued my way through the two volcanic hollows, over the swampy isthmus, and proceeded along the road by the lake, whose whole western division now lay stretched before me, glittering in a splendid sunshine.

The Platten See, like the lakes of Constance and Geneva, and, indeed, like the majority of large lakes, has one high mountainous and one level shore. Its mountain side, like the Neusiedler lake, boasts an admirable vine culture, while the low and swampy coasts are brought under the plough, and used for pasturing cattle. Between the vine hills of the two lakes there is this difference, that those of the Platten See stretch from east to west, consequently face the south, while those of the Neusiedler extend north and south, and are, therefore, not so well protected. Hence, it might be concluded that the produce of the Balaton vine must be superior to that of Neusiedler, but this is not by any means the case. The wines of Ruster and Oedenburg have a far higher reputation than those of the Plattensee; to the former, the Hungarians themselves assign the second rank after Tokay, whereas the Platten lake has only one kind that can bear any comparison with those of its rival. Are the German cultivators on the northern lake, perhaps, better skilled than their Hungarian brethren? The best wine of the Platten See is the produce of Badatschon, a high mountain on the northern coast, of which we frequently caught sight as we drove along. Like most of the mountains north of the Platten See, Badatschon is round, high, and pointed. The vine clusters round it nearly to the summit. The grapes improve as they ascend to the middle, where they attain their perfection. Near the summit they ripen too much it is said, and in consequence impart a certain bitterness of flavour to the wine. On Badatschon, in addition to wine, a kind of wine decoction is made, known under the name of Badatschon wormwood, and as renowned in Hungary as the Menescher, or Tokay essence. To make it the juice is boiled with certain herbs. The same thing is done with the best of the Schomlau grapes, to produce the Schomlau wormwood. Schomlau lies not far from the Badatschon. This wormwood is not made in any other wine district of Hungary.

The vintage of Badatschon is one of the most celebrated throughout Hungary, and may be almost considered as a national festival. Friends and acquaintance are invited far and near. Portions of the Badatschon vineyards are held by proprietors resident at a great distance; the abbots of the surrounding convents, and the nobles from afar flock to the mountain in the season, and for a fortnight together it is nothing but grape-gathering, music, dancing, and feasting. The goodness of the wine, the beauty of the surrounding scenery, and even the form of the volcanic mountain, which brings all the vineyards to a common centre, and thereby favours social intercourse, have no doubt given Badatschon its merited reputation.

My equipage was one of the same ring-furnished, rattling, peasant carriages, I have before described; my driver was a genuine Hungarian, who understood not a syllable of German, and was, moreover, a peasant-noble of a village near Tihany. I had taken up a countryman of my own, who wanted to go to Kesthely, and requested a seat on the straw by me. He was from Zips, as they call the land inhabited by Germans at the southern base of the Carpathians, where he had been long settled. These Zips Germans, although originally from different parts of their common country, have contracted in their new one a certain peculiarity shared by them all. They are in every way unlike the Saxons of Transylvania; even their dialect differs. My companion could not pronounce an r. I took this at first as a personal peculiarity, but I was afterwards told it was common to all the Zips Germans, and that in fact they used no such letter in their language. This strange habit rendered many of his words quite unintelligible to me at first.

The village where we breakfasted lay somewhat away from the lake, in the middle of a broad valley of the Bakony forest. The inhabitants were partly Catholics and partly of the reformed church, and their places of worship stand close together. I went to look at the reformed church; it was very simple, and had an air of antiquity about it. The seats for the women and girls were below, and near them were those for the married men. The unmarried men and the children sat in a wide gallery over the heads of the others. The font was a tin vessel carefully wrapped in a rather ragged black cloth. The pulpit was likewise hung with black. The sacred books had all been printed in Debrezin.

The sexton told me that Catholics and Protestants lived on very good terms with each other ; but that in the neighbouring village dwelt the Lutherans, with whom neither Catholics nor the other Protestants could agree. Nothing was known here of the disputes relative to mixed marriages. It was an old established custom that of the children of such marriages, the boys should be brought up in the faith of the father, and the girls in that of the mother. I asked him whether Catholics were not sometimes converted to the reformed faith. " No, never," was the answer, " but the contrary sometimes happens; a ' reformed' nobleman (the peasant-nobles are nearly all of the reformed faith) when he is on his deathbed will sometimes send of a sudden for a Catholic priest, but it never occurs to a Catholic that a Protestant minister can be of any service to him."

At this place I parted from my German companion, who was going over the mountains to Kesthely. At parting I begged him to teach me a few Hungarian words, that I might at least say what was absolutely necessary to my driver, and the result of my studies was *frischen* (drive quickly); *laschan* (slow); *meggai* (halt); *mi osz?* (what village is that ?) Sometimes I was told I must scold and call names for a variety, but I might do that in German, with a tolerable certainty of being understood. "But as a nobleman would not he take that amiss ?" I asked. " Oh no," was the answer, " that will not be taken amiss, but you must not say " hell ;" that would be sure to give mortal offence ; that is a word he will not be likely to put up with. There is another word which equally enrages their wives ;" and this word my informant also favoured me with, but I am not inclined just now to be equally communicative.

Furnished with these valuable instructions, I drove on, although I did not feel altogether comfortable in having for my only companion in the Bakony forest so privileged a person that he could not be hanged like other people for any crime he might commit, for it was his privilege as a noble to be beheaded, and to have his hands tied before instead of behind his back. I could not hope for the consolation of getting him arrested, however unjustly he might act towards me, for he might have protested against any constraint by his " *En nemes ember*" (I am a nobleman) which is as much as to say, " I am a being of another species from you." I must, however, confess that I had no cause of complaint against my noble driver. Our whole conversation was "*meggai*," "*laschan*," "*frischen*," and these magic words, to my great surprise, were always followed by a prompt obedience.

The country, as far as the town of Tapolza and its immediate neighbourhood, is highly interesting. The ground is on the whole flat, but many singularly formed isolated hills rise on its level. Some are pointed like a sugarloaf, others have rounded summits; some are long and four-cornered, like giant graves. Many have extensive ruins on their summits, formerly the residences of old Hungarian families, who once led their own retainers to the field, but are now nearly extinct.

Behind the town of Tapolza, the Bakony forest, properly so called, begins; that is the chief ridge of this mountain range, which is almost every where covered with oak. In Tapolza the German landlord told me that the banditti, of whom nothing had been heard for some time before, had lately completely pillaged the old pastor of a neighbouring village, an old man of seventy. On the following Sunday he was to have celebrated the jubilee of his fifty years' service. The robbers probably conjectured that he must have saved something in the course of that time. Ten men, armed with blunderbusses, pistols, clubs, knives, and hooks, had broken in upon him, not in the night, but at ten o'clock in the morning; had bound all the family, and so ill used the poor old man to make him discover where his valuables were hidden, that he was not expected to live, and had already had the sacraments administered to him. They had robbed him of 1800 florins and all his plate. Martial law had been proclaimed, and every person convicted of stealing above the value of five florins would now be hanged within twenty-four hours. "This," added my informant, "is the boldest exploit they have performed this year, but they will go on with it now they've begun."

The drive through the forest lasts about three hours. In the forest itself the elevations are slight. The higher mountains lie further to the east. For these three hours nothing is to be seen beyond the thick oak forest, and this would be enchanting but for the thought of the banditti that haunt it. On the other side of Bakony, another isolated mountain, its summit crowned with ruins, shows itself while the traveller is still in the centre of the forest; when it is passed the vineyards begin to appear, and hidden within them lie the little press houses of Schumegh.

The sun was already setting when I drove out of the forest and came in sight of "*Schumegi var*" (the town of Schumegh), with long ranges of vine hills to the right; and on the left, in the distance, the Castle of Patika and its ball-shaped mountain, which, by a wonderful effect of the light, looked of a perfect indigo blue. Beyond lay an extensive plain.

In Schumegh I went to pay my respects to the old poet, Kisfaludy, who resides there. Hungary has two poets of the name: Kisfaludy Carl, and Kisfaludy Schandor (Alexander). The latter is the most esteemed, and him I went to salute at his seat in Schumegh. His family belongs to the oldest in Hungary, and is descended from one of the seven dukes who came into Hungary with Arpad the Magyar. *Kis* signifies "little," *falu* "village," and *y* "of." In German the name would be "von Kleindorf" (of Little Village). It is difficult to trace a Hungarian family, because, to mention one cause among many, the younger sons at a former period often took different names from the villages the family possessed, and still, when an individual is ennobled, he always assumes an additional name from some such possession. Kisfaludy Schandor is, however, far more distinguished by the nobility of his poetry than by that of his birth.

When I entered his house a maidservant gave me the unwelcome intelligence that her master was at his vineyard. I would not be put off, and requested that a servant might accompany me thither. The maid did not understand a word of German, and I had to make myself understood through an interpreter. To my great surprise, however, I heard her speak to the house-dog in German. The animal wanted to go with us to the vineyard, and jumped upon her; she drove him back with the same expressions a German would have used. This was a new discovery. German, I found, was used here in speaking to dogs, just as we make use of French for the same purpose. How comes it that languages, generally considered so refined, should on the other hand be used so ignobly? Did the Romans speak Greek to their dogs and horses?

I found the old man among his vines; he received me kindly, as I came in the name of the muses, to whom he had devoted himself. He said visits of this kind were rare things in this remote corner of the world. Three years before, an Englishman had called upon him, since which time I was the only visiter of the sort he had seen.

The sun still afforded light enough to make the tour of the beautiful vine-clad hill, where he showed me his little Tusculum, a press-house surrounded by a wooden balcony, hidden among the vines. In this charming solitude Kisfaludy wrote most of the beautiful lyrics which enchant his countrymen. He spoke much of his youth to me. In the year 1809, in the last insurrection of the Hungarian nobles, his comitat chose him for their major, and the palatine made him his aide-de-camp. He and the palatine had surveyed the Bakony forest, and ascended the highest mountain, the Somhegye. It had then some magnificent oaks growing on it. The palatine caused them to be measured, and found that some of them had attained the height of twenty fathoms. No pines were found throughout the whole extent of Bakony, except a few here and there which had been planted.

Kisfaludy took me afterwards to his house, where, unhappily, the hand of the directing housewife, who had preceded her husband to the long repose, was wanting. He intended next morning to set off for the beautiful vine-clad hills of Schomlau, between which place and Schumegh there is almost an uninterrupted succession of hanging vineyards; and his sister in the mean time was to have the charge of his house. As I saw the preparations were not all completed, I took leave and returned to my inn, where the disagreeable task awaited me of choosing a driver for the next day. One, out of several who presented themselves, was warmly recommended by a gentleman who had supped with me, and whose eloquence owed something to the Badatschon, or Schomlau, unlocker of hearts. "Take this man," said he, "he is a German, and you can trust him; he will not give signals to the robbers, and afterwards help them to murder travellers. I've often been driven by him, and nothing ever happened amiss."

As this extraordinary recommendation really deserved attention, inasmuch as it put me on my guard as to the kind of people I was likely to meet with here, and as Joseph's face pleased me, I made a bargain with him. He demanded twelve florins a day; I offered him six; he abated his demand by two, and I advanced one, and thus our agreement was concluded. I gave him a shake of the hand, and he gave me two florins by way of *earnest*, which is here paid by the driver instead of the driven, and promised to be punctual the next morning.

I asked the nobleman with whom I had supped, whether it was really such unsafe travelling here? "Oh, it is always better to be on one's guard," was the answer. "Our peasants are becoming bolder since our diet has thought fit to limit the application of corporal punishment."

"Is not the stick soon to be laid aside altogether?" I asked.

"Heaven forbid! my child," said my companion, "that will never do. Our Hungarians are much too fiery, much too sanguine in temperament; they are not so easy to rule as your phlegmatic Germans. They are more like the French and Italians, with whom they are always ready to fraternize when they meet. No, no, without the stick there is no getting on with them; they would all cut each other's throats, if they were not ruled with a tight rein."

I retired soon afterwards to my sleeping-apartment, the way to which led through a yard filled with horses, cows, sheep, swine, dogs, and other animals, and then up a ladder into a gallery piled up with maize straw to the height of four feet. Before I could reach my chamber-door, I was obliged to disturb a number of the quadrupeds, goats as it appeared, who had taken up their quarters comfortably in the straw. Just as I had made myself room to enter, my attendant let the light fall among the straw; it caught fire directly, but we were fortunately able to extinguish it, before much mischief ensued. I went to bed, but the goats did not, and their ceaseless trampling in the wooden corridor, and the rustling of straw, made an unbearable disturbance in the stillness of the night. Now and then a difference of opinion seemed to arise among them, and in the scuffle they came thump against my door. I got up to drive the brutes to the other end of the corridor, and the noise we made together set the dogs in the yard barking, which was quickly responded to by all the dogs in the neighbourhood; what was worse, I did not succeed in driving away the goats, for as often as I drove them off, back they came again. Heartily tired was I of the night's amusement, and right glad when the morning broke. I dressed myself in haste, and went to inspect the ruins I had observed on the mountain of Schumegh as I issued from the Bakony forest. This mountain is a solitary rock, steep on all sides, and rising abruptly from the plain, with a flattened cupola-like summit. There is no other hill near it. The powerful bishops of Vesprim had formerly a castle and fortress here, and maintained a garrison of two to three hundred men. The fortress is in ruins; not so the wealth and consideration of its spiritual lords, as the beautiful chateau they have since erected at the base of the mountain shows. A wide archway and broad road lead to the summit of the hill, whence there is a beautiful view over the fields, with the Platten See to the south, and to the east the vineyard hills of the poet of Schumegh.

My new driver, Joseph, was a goodhumoured brisk lad, of six-and-twenty. As a boy he had come with his father from Styria to Hungary, had served as waiter at an inn, and had now set up as driver on his own account. He owned a pair of Transylvanian horses, with which we drove from Schumegh to Grätz, twenty-four German (about one hundred and eight English) miles, in two days, without much distressing the cattle or fatiguing ourselves. I believe he might easily, in the north of Germany, have obtained one hundred dollars for each of his steeds; in his own country Joseph said he was ready to part with horses, harness, and carriage for one hundred and twenty florins if he could get them. Joseph was now clad in the German fashion, but at home he wore the Hungarian costume, and had two "dolmans" of the finest cloth at fifteen florins an ell, one trimmed with black lace, the other with silver. They were also decorated with silver buttons, amounting to nineteen ounces weight, at six florins an ounce. He had moreover silver spurs worth thirty-two florins, and his whole costume, when he was equipped in full Hungarian trim, was worth 300 florins, and was worn only on holidays at the public dancing-houses. Joseph was a *Nyalka legeny* (a smart handsome fellow), a description of persons who, like the *majos* of Spain, play the principal parts at the places of public amusement in the little provincial towns, and display a finery and pride of which we have elsewhere no idea. Such a *Nyalka legeny* was the celebrated Capitan Pacha Piale, the son of a shoemaker of the town of Tolna on the Danube, the conqueror of Chios, to whom Suleiman intrusted the storming of the arsenal of Constantinople, and who has perpetuated his name by building one of the finest mosques in that city. Joseph had a good deal of the assumption of these gentry about him, as I remarked particularly in Styria, where he found a great deal to reprove. In Styria I should perhaps not have been long without quarrelling with him occasionally, but in Hungary he was German enough to sympathize with, and we got on well enough together.

There is a constant influx of people into Hungary from Styria, as we had occasion to note as we proceeded. We met numbers of persons coming from Germany with wine-casks; these were the "*Weinschwärzers*," who buy the fine Hungarian wine at the place of its production for four or five florins the eimer, and then smuggle it over the frontier into Styria, where the law subjects it to a duty of two florins and thirty kreuzers, or about one-half of its value. It was the vintage season and we met whole trains of these Styrian wine-smugglers, mounted on carts laden with large empty casks. In Hungary of course no one would inform against them, and they proceeded openly in great caravans. How they manage on the Austrian frontier is more than I can tell.

We also met considerable bodies of thrashers from Styria, who leave their steril mountains to find employment in the thinly-peopled Pusten of Hungary. They go to the neighbourhood of the Platten See, and then farther down the Danube. On the other side of the Danube, in the Hungarian steppes, they are not to be met with, because there the primitive Asiatic mode of husbandry prevails, and the corn is trodden out by horses. From nearly all Alpine countries such periodical wanderings to the surrounding fertile plains take place.

It is true that the majority of these people return with their earnings to their native country, but many of them remain; whereas there is no business or employment that tempts the Hungarians to move westward. "Nothing comes from the east but the wolves in winter," observed Joseph; "in summer they hide themselves in the Bakony forest, but in winter they find their way even into Styria."

By noon we were in Pasvar, but found no great reason to rejoice at our speed, for the inn was detestable. The only thing of interest I found was a portrait of Attila! I do not in the least exaggerate when I say that in the Hungarian towns I heard and saw far more of this ancient conqueror than of Napoleon. The Hungarians reckon him and his Huns among their nationalities, and are even, I think, somewhat proud of the exploits of the "Scourge of God." I do not speak of what the learned say on the subject, but the common Hungarian's constant boast is, "We Magyars came twice to Europe, and have twice conquered Hungary; once under Attila, and once under Arpad."

Our admirable painter, Kaulbach, in his celebrated picture of Attila, has represented him treading on a shield, and wielding his many-thonged scourge. In the picture at the inn, the hero was on horseback, tossing victoriously a banner aloft in the air and about to cross a river, just where its waters are pouring down in a mighty cataract. I have met with similar portraits of Attila in Hungary much oftener than I have with those of Arminius or Charlemagne.

A dirty tablecloth, watery soup, hard tough meat, raw potatoes, sour wine, dirty butter and half-baked bread, fairly entitled an unfortunate traveller to say as I did, without tasting a morsel, "I have done, waiter, take it all away."

While Joseph was feeding the horses I paid a visit to a neighbouring Franciscan convent. There I found much more to remind me of St. Francis than of Christ. A St. Veronica was holding the handkerchief in her hand, on which was impressed, not the face of our Saviour, but the head of a Franciscan. In another picture, a Franciscan was raising the dead; in a third, another Franciscan, instead of an angel, was represented bearing a lily, as a heavenly messenger of peace, and many other objects in the same taste. In every religious order it seems the fashion to glorify those miracles alone which were wrought by one of their own order, but I had never found anywhere such flagrant self-idolatry as among these Franciscans. I saw in this convent a book I never met with before, a so-called "*Modus dicendi missam.*" In this book was minutely described, not only what the priest was to say, but how he was to hold himself, how to lay hold of the bread, how it was to be given, how the fingers were to be held in bestowing the blessing, &c.; and to aid the description, pictures of priests in a hundred different attitudes were given. The different parts of the hands, fingers, &c., were numbered with reference to the text. It struck me, that even supposing it were necessary to enter so much into the details of these mysteries, it would, at all events, be better not to print them.

As I was not fortunate enough to find a reasonable being either in the convent or the inn, I retreated to my carriage, which stood in one of the huge sheds to be seen in every Hungarian-inn yard. Here I found company enough. Many travellers in Hungary when they find the inn bad, dine and take their afternoon's nap in their carriages. To the right of mine, a German peasant family had just finished their potato dinner; in one to the left, the party, consisting of an old father, a young woman and her husband, were comfortably asleep. Before me stood an elegant equipage, in which sat a lady with her interesting little daughter, who was amusing herself by jumping in and out. She held a small earthen cup in her hand, which she exhibited to me, calling out "*Pohar, pohar*" (drinking cup) and then hid herself in her mother's lap. "My little girl cannot comprehend how her Hungarian jargon should not be intelligible to you," said her mother; "she has not yet learned that there is any other language than her own." The pretty little *Ingrin* seemed to be quizzing me, and I felt exceedingly stupid in my inability to make any return to all her quips and cranks.

The poles of all these carriages lay quietly in the dust, and our horses were calmly disposing of their oats and hay in the stables beside us. There was something droll in the appearance of so many peopled vehicles remaining so motionless in their places, all changed for the time into sofas and divans, things not to be found in the miserable *tsharde*. Some oxen occasionally thrust in their muzzles among the carriages to enjoy the shade, and near them against a pillar lay three Slovacks sleeping on some straw and their travelling-sacks. If they had not been so shaggy, so oily, and so very tarry in their appearance, I must have admitted them to be remarkably handsome fellows. The Slovacks generally are handsome; I have never seen a finer regiment than the Slovack infantry regiment, with respect to carriage, form, and martial expression of countenance.

Such a picture as I have just described is constantly to be seen in the yards of all Hungarian "tshardes." I should add that our host stood in a corner, skinning a newly-slaughtered sheep, and that such bloody spectacles are also common to the place; there seems no end of the sanguinary work.

My Joseph was the first driver ready, but I was almost sorry that we had all to go different ways, and did not set off in company. He chose to drive me the back way out of Hungary, through a variety of fields and forest paths.

The forests were nearly all of oak, under whose shade great herds of swine, oxen, and buffaloes were feeding. In this neighbourhood, the valley of the upper Raab, I saw the largest herds of the last-named animal that are to be found in Hungary; in middle Hungary there are none. Joseph told me that the herds were sometimes as savage as their keepers, particularly the swine and the buffaloes. The herdsmen know how to set their cattle at both man and beast, and make use of them for their own defence. They teach the swine by first throwing young dogs among them, which they eat up, and then older dogs are sacrificed, but these are often first cruelly mutilated by the herdsmen. By these means the swine soon lose their fear of dogs, and learn to eat up young and old; and a swineherd is almost as thankful for the gift of a dog, as of a piece of money. The object of this training is to teach the swine to defend themselves against the wolves and sheep-dogs. The wolves soon become aware of the danger that threatens them from the swine, and only attack them under peculiar circumstances. Upon occasion the herds make use of their unclean charges as a protection against men; they have certain calls, to which the animals answer, and if they are not exactly set upon men, the smell of a stranger allures them: they like flesh, and will readily attack, if they are not prevented. It is the same with the buffaloes. They collect readily at the herdsman's call, and fly at a stranger, if not held in check. Push with their horns they cannot, but they will trample dog, wolf, or man, or to death with the fore feet. "A friend of mine and myself," said Joseph, "once laid a wager with a buffalo herdsman, that we would venture armed with good clubs among the herd, even if they were set upon us. The wager was a barrel of wine. We took our clubs, and the herdsman raised the cry, 'Ischtennem, ischtennem,' which is their call for help when attacked. The brutes advanced slowly, after their fashion; we advanced to meet them before they had drawn their circle too close; some of them came closer to smell us. 'Ischtennem, ischtennem,' cried the herdsman again, and the buffaloes prepared to attack us: we stood with our backs to a tree. About two hundred paces farther there was another tree, and at a like distance a third. If we fought our way to the third tree, we were to have won our wager. I had thought to cripple the brutes by aiming at their legs with our clubs; but our blows had no more effect than if they had been bestowed upon so many iron posts; so we threw them away, and trusted to our address and fleetness. I must own our courage sank rather sooner than we had expected. The snorting brutes pursued us so sharply, that I began to think of reaching the second tree, and climbing up to save myself. I saw my friend already running for it, closely pursued by the buffaloes. 'Will you ask for quarter,' called out the herdsman; I said 'yes' to save my friend, and he shouted '*Hei, jae, jae!*' threw himself among the herd, and drove them off my friend, who was already down! Our wager was lost, and I have hated the sight of buffaloes ever since. They are detestable brutes. They have never been able to teach so much vice to oxen and horses."

I told him that he had run a very foolish risk, and that, for my own part, I would much rather have been torn by a lion, than be trampled to death by buffaloes, or eaten by swine. All the buffaloes we saw were extremely fat. "These brutes," said Joseph, "get fatter upon straw than oxen upon clover."

Travelling along byways, as I have described, we had the better opportunity of seeing those scenes of national life which a traveller most delights in. We surprised the herdsmen by their fires, the women and young girls at their domestic occupations, the children romping under the chestnut-trees, and the old people chatting at their house-doors. The landscape became more and more pleasing as we advanced; the country more animated and populous. A little way before arriving at Körmönd, we saw a wisp of straw dangling from a tree, to mark the border of the Eisenburg Comitat, the last through which we had yet to pass. It is one of the most populous in all Hungary; and indeed it may be taken as a rule, that the comitats bordering on Germany are always more thickly peopled than those of the interior. Joseph complained of the increasing prices of corn and hay for his horses; but this to me was only one of many gratifying signs that we were approaching a more prosperous country. Handsome chestnut-trees became more common by the sides of the houses, the waste pieces of ground less frequent, and smaller in extent. In short, in proportion as we ascended towards the German hills, I felt that the country was also advancing in an amending scale of cultivation.

We reached Körmönd shortly before sunset. This town; perhaps the Curta of the Romans, lies in the valley of the Raab, with the Styrian Alps in the background, the last spur of which loses itself in the valley. The towns of Guns, Steinamanger, Oedenburg, and Eisenstadt, have the same mountainous background in the west, and the same level foreground in the east, and form the first chain of western towns in Hungary. They occupy the ground where the mountain disappears and the level land begins.

It was Sunday evening, and all the people seemed to be employed in roasting and eating chestnuts. In this part of the country there are whole forests of chestnut-trees, planted, as some Hungarian authors assert, by the Romans, who, it is well known, had some fine colonies here: Sabaria, Scarabantia, and others, the same chain of towns whose Hungarian names I have given above; but as to the chestnut-trees, seeing they extend through the whole Alpine range, their appearance here is better explained by the geology than the history of the country.

In Körmönd I saw again a park and garden. They belong, with a castle in the neighbourhood, to the wealthy family of Bathyany, and join those of the Esterhazys, of which I spoke in Eisenstadt. In this part of the country is to be found all that Hungary has most distinguished in the way of gardens. The cultivation of gardens and trees is much attended to here; in the central parts of the Magyar land there is scarcely a trace of a garden. The fruit of this district, and there is an astonishing abundance of it, is generally brought into the market in a dried state, and is known by the name of Oedenburger fruit. Vienna is principally supplied with the article from this part of Hungary. In the Bathyany garden I saw the most magnificent wall of *Hedera quinquefolia* I had ever beheld. The gardens were full of promenaders from the town.

As our horses were fresh again after sunset, Joseph proposed to drive farther. It was already twilight, and I hinted at the chance of robbers. "All that's nothing," said he, coolly, "and, besides, I have got my *hackerl* with me," drawing out from under the straw a handsome sharp axe with a very long and slender handle, which he had never before shown me. "I always keep this by me in the straw when I drive," added he, "I like it better than two pistols; if any attack is made upon me in the carriage, I give them a taste of that, and whip on the horses to a gallop. I can hit better with that than with a pistol, and, then, it makes no noise."

On the road he related a number of exploits of bandit heroism of Sobri (pronounced Shobri) and his comrades, and of a certain Laketos Istvan. The latter hero and two of his companions defended themselves once against fifty peasants, who had given them chase, and drove back the whole party to their village. At last soldiers were sent out against him, when Laketos Istvan, seeing escape impossible, shot himself through the head before them. It is said that Hungarian robbers have often preferred a voluntary death to an ignominious imprisonment. How much the people of this country assist in keeping up this kind of heroism among the robbers, we had an opportunity of seeing in the inn at St. Mihaly's, where we stopped for the night. On the walls of the principal room there were various fresco paintings; on one side the portrait of a former king of Hungary, and on the other that of the robber chief Sobri, not any way in connexion with the gallows, but armed, and in full costume. The painter had, to the best of his ability, which was not much, given him a very handsome face, besides a pair of prodigious spurs, a tight-fitting jacket, and a cap set jantily on one side, and embroidered with red flowers and fancy patterns. In his girdle were stuck a pair of pistols, and he was leaning on his *hackerl*, similar in form to that of my friend Joseph.

"Was he really as good-looking as he is there painted?" I asked the cook.

"Yes, he was then a handsome fellow of about two-and-twenty," she answered. "He may be six-and-twenty now."

"Now? I thought he had been long dead?"

"Eh, my conscience, no! He is alive still, and is gone to America. He was a shepherd's son, and born in the Comitat of Tolna. Many a priest and nobleman has he robbed, but he never touched the poor; nor ever killed any one himself—he let his people do that—unless he were attacked, and then of course! Twice he got away from the people that had caught him. Once they thought to have him in a village, but he flung off his cap, disguised himself and got clear off, and when they came to the house where they thought he was, and asked, 'Well, where is Sobri?' he answered by firing off his pistols at the edge of the forest, and was off in a twinkling! Another time they really had him fast, but the wife of the Burggraf (governor of the gaol) who had him in charge fell in love with him, and let him escape. At last they got a whole pack of haiducks, peasants, and soldiers, and had a regular battle. Some say he was killed then, and that his old father and mother were brought to recognise the body of their son. But *I* don't believe it. He would not let himself be caught so! I think he is only keeping quiet because he sees there's nothing to be done."

"Here," thought I, "it is easy to perceive the train of argument by which an honest man allows himself to be transformed into a robber chief."

While the cook was telling me this story, she was engaged in preparing for me a "*bocken händel,*" ground some Transylvanian rock-salt in one of the small salt-mills to be seen in every Hungarian kitchen, placed a little bread-mountain, such as is usually baked in every Hungarian household, on the table, and invited me to do justice to these viands, a request I was not slow in complying with.

The next morning Joseph and his brisk Transylvanians were early ready to set off, and I did not keep them waiting. We continued to ascend the Raab valley, and the scenery was beautiful. At Körmönd the white Hungarian oxen had disappeared, and their place was supplied by the Styrian and German teams. The Hungarian ox is a handsome animal, but the Styrian has more expression in his physiognomy, and more strength in his bones. He is a far better worker than the Hungarian, who is accustomed to be yoked with five and even seven of his brethren, while the Styrian has frequently to work alone.

At length we reached the parts inhabited by Germans alone, the land of the Hienzes, or Hänzes, as they are called. Here, in the time of the Roman domination, began another province, Upper Pannonia. The *Hienzes* or *Hänzes* (I could never learn which was the right word) are a very peculiar race of Germans, and their reputation does not stand high, either for mother-wit, or acquired knowledge; when a *Hienze* is spoken of, the hearers involuntarily smile. I once heard a citizen of Guns disputing with one of Steinamanger, whether Guns or Steinamanger, were properly the capital of the Hienzes, and neither seemed desirous of appropriating the honour to his own town. I asked the landlord of a large inn, where we breakfasted the next morning, why the people were called *Hienzes.* "Why," replied he, "because they speak so *hienzish.* They live here on the frontier, and are neither Germans nor Hungarians, but all *hienzish.*"

I believe great injustice is done the *Hienzes.* As far as I could judge, they have as much understanding as their neighbours. How far they are really a mongrel race, must remain a subject of future inquiry. To me they seemed perfect Germans, a good and vigorous stock, and true brothers of the Austrians and Styrians. I found every thing about them—their architecture, their husbandry, style of dress, &c.—so perfectly German, that Hungary was just as completely out of my head as if I had not been in the country.

There are some Croats mingled among the *Hienzes*, "Water Croats," as they are called, as there are among the Germans of Eisenstadt and Oedenburg. The Hienzes are now expected to learn the Magyar language. "Nobody understands it here," say they, "but the schoolmaster is to teach our children. Unluckily he does not know a word of it himself."

I went into one of the houses of the village where I found a woman reading a religious book. I opened it at the article "Purgatory." Under this head there were was a most grisly and awful picture of hell, founded on the relation of a priest, who had undergone three days' punishment, and then returned to earth, and on that of a soldier who had passed two days and two hours in purgatory. Every thing said to have been witnessed there was most minutely described, and in a style perfectly adapted to the " million." The soldier and the priest vied with each other in the little details of their descriptions of the torments to which the souls were subjected by the devil. It is impossible for me to transcribe the exact words in which all this was given in the book, meant for, and, in style, suited to the multitude. A thousand times in one day a soul was said to be eaten by some indescribable monster, and again vomited forth, rent in pieces, gnawed, burnt, crushed to atoms, and again renewed, again to undergo these tortures. The soldier saw a fearful dragon, in whose entrails other monsters generated and devoured a second time the souls he swallowed, and which were again served up as a third course to a third brood of intestine worms and griffins. The sufferers, moreover, according to these veracious and trustworthy reporters, were a thousand times more susceptible to the tortures they endured than we on earth could at all conceive. One single moment of the pains of hell exceeded in intensity a thousand years of earthly pain. This pleasant description closed with a supplication from the poor tortured spirits, that the pious would, by prayers and gifts to the church, labour for their deliverance. This precious book was by no means an old one, and a woman was actually reading it.

I was really shocked, and could not help asking the woman whether she believed that the "good God" permitted such horrors to exist? "Ah, no sir, I don't believe it," said she; "but you know, sir, if people that make books told nothing but the truth, nobody would buy their wares."

It is consoling to think that hard as the authors of such books labour to insult God's goodness and mercy, the sounder sense of the people in some measure defeats their aim, and that the results are by no means what they desire, perhaps for the very reason that they have spiced the dish too highly. Strange indeed is the difference between the grim atrocities invented by these book-makers in Christian Europe, and the simple chastisement imagined by the old Greeks in their Tartarus. Let us think only of the vessel of the Danaïdes, the stone of Sisyphus, the fruit trees and fugitive waters of Tantalus. To me these punishments appear not only less incredible, but far more impressive, then this everlasting burning, crushing, and swallowing. As these punishments, moreover, were more mental than physical, they display a more elevated spirit in those who invented them. There are at present a number of persons engaged in the distribution of the Bible and other useful books. It would be worth their while to visit this part of the world, in order to wrest such detestable absurdities as these from the hands of the people. They might silently buy them up wherever they found them, and destroy them even if circumstances did not permit the replacing them with other and better books.

The country of the *Hienzes* is about twenty or twenty-four miles in width. Our little Transylvanians were fleet, and it was not long before I perceived a little bridge, whereon stood the Austrian custom-house officers. I was prepared for a long and tedious search after sundry excisable articles, and made Joseph a sign to halt, when the officers at once stood aside, and pronounced the welcome words, "You may go on." Not a hair belonging to us was ruffled. Our carriage rolled over the bridge; I breathed more freely, for, Heaven be praised! I was in Germany again.

STYRIA.

FURSTENFELD TO GRATZ.

Arriving from the frontiers of Turkey, and after having traversed Hungary, I re-entered the Central Empire, a title to which our Germany may certainly lay a fairer claim than China. Oh, if it had but had a face, I could have kissed the dear, snug, comfortable-looking little frontier town of Fürstenfeld, perched upon its hill, with its houses and its streets, and the people that moved about in them, together with the cheerful and inviting hostelry at which we put up. I seemed to have got among friends and old acquaintances again, and I almost wondered, when I told the people I had just returned from Hungary, that they did not seize me by the hand and wish me joy. Even the Austrian wine, which I had always thought before was more acid than agreeable, rather pleased me now. Its golden colour looked to advantage with the rays of a German sun playing through it, and I arrived with little trouble at a conviction that Austrian wine, mixed with water, was an excellent beverage, and decidedly more salubrious and better calculated to quench the thirst than the more fiery wines of Hungary.

My inn was almost a nunnery, being presided over by a widow, under whom all the offices of the household appeared to be discharged by a numerous array of daughters and assistant damsels. I dined in company with some Austrian officers, who commanded the frontier post, appointed for the protection of the Imperial Tobacco Manufactory, at which no less than 45,000 cigars are daily made, chiefly for the accommodation of Trieste and the southern provinces of Austria. To Trieste alone, I was assured, more than 600,000 imperial cigars were sent every month from Fürstenfeld. In the whole year, at this rate, making a trifling deduction for holidays, fifteen millions of cigars are manufactured at this place. Now these are all of a villanous quality, such as few will be able to smoke without making wry mouths; the Austrian government, moreover, to protect this manufacturing monopoly, has to maintain a little army of clerks, and other public servants, besides a military detachment for the protection of each separate establishment; and if the monopoly were done away with, a countless host of custom-house officers and excisemen would become superfluous, endless temptations to fraud would cease, and in the place of a few wretched retailers of tobacco, a prosperous class of dealers and importers would immediately arise, men that would not only sell better cigars and tobacco for less money, but would extend and animate the general trade of the country with foreign nations. Under these circumstances, it is really difficult to understand the motives that can induce the Austrian government to cling to a monopoly, the revenue of which would be amply replaced by a more regular tax, levied upon the lovers of the weed, in the shape of an import duty.

In passing from Hungary into Styria, a number of little contrasts immediately strike the traveller. The Hungarians appear to have rooted out all their pine forests. At Fürstenfeld these present themselves again in all their majesty, and continue to characterize the landscape, all the way to the borders of Bavaria. Such a thing as an umbrella is seldom to be seen in Hungary; in Styria, on the contrary, people are seldom seen without them, and this is the case in most of the Alpine countries. Buckwheat is found growing in every valley of the Alps, but it is never to be seen in the wheat-growing plains of Hungary.

The road to Grätz runs for several leagues over a flat but elevated ridge, with few indentations, like a huge dam constructed by the hand of Nature. To the left and right, the eye ranges over smiling valleys and startling abysses, and beyond these arise more lofty hills to enclose the picture. Our two black Transylvanians did their best to carry us over these mountain roads, but it was after midnight before we reached a gate, which opened to afford us a passage, when we were kindly informed that we had now arrived at the city of Grätz. After a little while we stopped again, and were told that we had come to the *Jacominiplatz*, the handsomest square in the city, and that from the said *platz* there issued the *Herrengasse*, the handsomest street in the city, and that in the said platz there stood the *Stadt Triest*, and that the said *Stadt Triest* was a very excellent inn. We immediately resolved to subject the last piece of information to the test of a more close inquiry, but to take the remaining assurances on trust at least till the return of daylight.

GRATZ.

Of all the Alpine cities between France and Hungary, none is so populous as Grätz. It contains 48,000 inhabitants, and may therefore be looked on, in some measure, as the capital of the Alps. Situated halfway between Vienna and Trieste, the town serves as the centre of the inland trade between Germany and Italy, and being a cheap and agreeable place to live in, many families, both from Trieste and from Vienna, are induced by considerations of economy to fix their residence at Grätz. Many civil and military officers, who have retired on pensions, reside here; many Italians come here to study German, and many are glad, during the heats of summer, to quit the sunny plains of Lombardy, and seek refreshment in an Alpine atmosphere. There are several other cities among the Alps that serve as places of transition between Germany and Italy. One of these is Bozen, between Inspruck and Verona; I found one family from Dalmatia at Grätz, and another that had come all the way from the Ionian Islands. Formerly, a great number of young Italians studied at the University of Grätz. This continued till 1831, in which year, out of the thousand students then frequenting the university, no less than 200 were Italians; agreeable, well-bred young men, and sufficiently well provided, in a pecuniary point of view, with the means of making themselves agreeable to the townspeople. The cholera frightened them all away at once, and they have never returned in equal numbers. At the period of my visit, there were only twelve Italian students there. Inspruck also had formerly a little colony of Italian students; but, at present, it appears that the young men who come from the south in search of German erudition, give the preference to Vienna.

Grätz is a large handsome city, and offers all the conveniences of one, without either the drawback of a court, or the noise and bustle of a large commercial community. It is a favourite residence, not only for retired officers, but for those also who have retired from yet higher stations, for those who have stood near to thrones, and would fain forget the height from which they have fallen. I allude here particularly to the Duchess of Berry. The Archduke John also, who loves the atmosphere of the Alps better than the atmosphere of a court, spends his winters here, and his example is imitated by many nobles of congenial tastes. A few English and French families are also found to mingle with the other elements that constitute the society of Grätz. The place is a kind of harbour of refuge for numberless old vessels that have been damaged among the hurricanes and whirlpools of the world. I found, for instance, many noble and forgotten wrecks cast ashore here by the Polish storms. Among others, the fiery, old, grayheaded Ostrovsky may daily be seen at the theatre, in the second stall to the right of the stage. There was a time when upon the theatre of the world many an anxious eye was turned upward towards him; now, the strutters on the stage look heedlessly over him away, and only here and there are a few to be found who still remember what the sorrows were that bleached those noble locks.*

---

* Count Anthony Ostrovsky was born at Warsaw in 1782, and was distinguished throughout the greater part of his life by his ardent and disinterested patriotism. He studied at the University of Leipzig; and when the French army entered Warsaw in 1806, he was one of the first to inscribe his name among those who composed the guard of honour. When Napoleon retreated from Moscow, Ostrovsky attached himself to the French army, and very narrowly escaped with his life at the battle of Leipzig. He returned to Poland at the peace, and was elected a Senator Castellan in 1817, in which dignity, notwithstanding the personal animosity of the Grand Duke Constantine, he was confirmed by the Emperor Alexander. Ostrovsky now became a leading member of the Polish opposition, and drew upon himself more and more the hatred of Constantine. Ostrovsky was at Leipzig, on his return from a tour through England, France, and Switzerland, when he heard of the insurrection at Warsaw. He was detained for some time by the Prussian authorities, but succeeded in reaching his native city towards the close of December, where he was immediately appointed commander-in-chief of the National Guard. From this time forward he continued to play a prominent part in the two campaigns that terminated so disastrously for his country. When Kruckoviecki was invested with almost dictatorial powers, Ostrovsky withdrew from the diet. On the 6th and 7th of September, he fought upon the ramparts of Warsaw as a private soldier, and quitted his post only for the purpose of voting in the diet to defend the city to the last extremity. It was too late, however, Kruckoviecki having already issued orders to withdraw the troops. Ostrovsky continued nevertheless, to exert himself to the last to support the hopes of his countrymen, and was one of the last among the leading men of the revolution to quit the country. At the head-quarters of Swiedzibno, on the 4th of October, 1831, he drew up the last official document of the Polish nation—namely, the celebrated Manifesto to the Kings and Nations of Europe. He was accompanied into exile by a wife and ten children.—*Tr.*

Of the exiles, none attracts more attention than the Duchess of Berry. I asked where she lived. " In the *Sack*," was the answer. Strange mutability of fortune, thought I, to quit the stately Tuileries of Paris, and take shelter in a sack at Grätz! The sack, however, in which the princess lives is rather a roomy one. It is a street of imposing breadth at one end, but extremely narrow at the other, where it is compressed between the river Mur and the rocks on which the castle stands. The Duchess lives at the broad end, in the house of the ancient Counts of Herbertstein. The mansion is of great antiquity; but old-fashioned though it be, it has been filled by so many objects of interest, that the collection is one it will not be easy to find equalled elsewhere eastward of the Rhine. The Duchess's private property in France was not confiscated when she herself was banished, and the objects that served for the decoration of more than one palace in France, have now been concentrated within the venerable halls of her present dwelling " in the Sack."

Her pictures, mostly by the best modern French painters, as well as a multitude of things to which historical associations alone impart a value, are arranged with a degree of taste, the like of which we should vainly look for at Vienna. Among the family relics are shown—a sword of Francis I., a shoe of Henri IV., a pair of golden stirrups of Louis XIV, &c.

It must not be supposed that in their banishment the Bourbons have abandoned the hope of a second restoration. On the cushion of a sofa I saw a beautiful piece of embroidery. It consisted of the words " *Ils reverdiront,*" encircled by a wreath of white lilies. On another cushion I saw, in letters of gold, " *Vaincre ou mourir pour Henri.*" A picture of a Chouan kneeling before an image of the Virgin, hung close by the sofa, with the words " *Marie, bénis nos armes !*"

Among the paintings are several which, through the medium of lithography, have become familiar to every part of Europe, such as Vernet's " *Chien du régiment,*" " The Trumpeter and his Horse," and " The Mendicant Musicians of Benneford."

I was so much delighted with the taste displayed by the Duchess of Berry in the arrangement of her own magnificent collection of pictures, that I chose her for my guide when I visited the picture-gallery of the States of Grätz; that is to say, I directed my attention to those pictures of which the Duchess had chosen to have copies painted for her own palace. They were four in number. The names of the masters I have forgotten, but the pictures themselves are indelibly fixed upon my mind.

There are other collections in Grätz, but I visited none of them, with the exception of that of the old castle of Eggenberg, now the property of the family of the Herbertstein's, who, with the Trautmannsdorfs and the Dietrichsteins, may be considered the most ancient and most eminent races of Styria. In Russia the name of Herbertstein is even better known than in Germany, for a count of that name having been sent on an embassy to Russia, about 200 years ago, wrote a book, which still passes for the best account of the ancient condition of that country; so much so, that a Russian antiquarian, when he wishes to decide any point respecting a question of bygone times, generally refers to his Herbertstein, as the most convenient and most authentic guide.

The castle of Eggenberg lies at about a league from Grätz, on the edge of the plain, and at the foot of the vine-covered hills that bound it. A stately avenue leads up to the castle, a large square building, with four principal wings, and a park surrounds the whole. What gave the place a peculiar interest in my eyes, was that it stood there, not the result, like so many modern palaces, of one man's fancy or caprice, but a genuine piece of hereditary architecture, handed down to us by the protecting legislation of successive centuries. From the chairs and bedsteads in the rooms to the trees and bushes in the garden, every thing stands under the guardianship of the law, and may not be altered according to the whim of the temporary possessor. A hundred years ago, the entailed property passed to the Herbertsteins from the Eggenbergs, and the old bed in which these slept is still carefully preserved with its canopy and hangings, nor will the terms of the entailment allow a fraction of it to be removed. The present possessors seem to have thought that bedsteads of a more modern make might be more convenient to sleep in, and have accordingly caused new state-rooms to be fitted up for their accommodation; but they have not dared to alter the arrangement of the old state-chamber.

The catalogue of all the objects of art and *virtu* in this interesting old mansion, fills a large folio volume. I would gladly have turned over this catalogue a little before I proceeded to inspect the collection itself, but finding that at the third page of the introduction I had only got to Cadmus Milesius, and at the twelfth no farther than Macrobius, I began to think I should scarcely have time to read on till I got to the artistical heirlooms themselves, and so determined to proceed to their examination without waiting any longer for the directions of so ponderous a guide.

The ceilings of the rooms are ornamented with designs in stucco, among which various paintings are introduced. The stucc-owork is different in each room. Here the pattern represents broken crowns, and hearts wound round with thorns; there hands grasped in each other, or globes with serpents twining about them. Everywhere may be seen an abundance of moral sentences, such as—" No heart is free from sorrow ;"—" Fortune awakens envy;"—" Crowns also are perishable." I have seen few castles decorated in so significant a manner, and if the children who grow up among these heirloom moralities—for the owner of the castle for the time being, cannot legally alter one of these mottoes—do not become wiser and more right-minded than other men's children, it can hardly be said that the blame lies with their ancestors, who have provided for their daily study such an abundance of excellent precepts.

The names of the rooms are as genuine German as the fine old oaken furniture, which is, moreover, elegant and solid in its way. The antique chairs are as perpendicular in the back, as were the stiff old nobles for whose accommodation they were manufactured, and the rooms are *Sitzzimmer*, *Arbeitszimmer*, and *Betzimmer*, and not *salons de conversation*, cabinets, or chapels. In the chapel are some beautiful pictures of Guido's.

Grätz boasts of a *casino*, to which neither beauty, talent, good fame, nor any of the qualities most valued in other parts of the world, can obtain admission for their owner, but for entering which the one great qualification required is noble birth. Only twenty-four families of the place are considered of spotless nobility, and so strict are the laws of the casino, that the loftiest patrician who allies himself with a family of inferior rank cannot introduce his wife there. In the north we talk of the urbanity of the Austrian nobles, and of the unreserved manner in which they mingle with the other classes of society, and if the remark is intended to apply to coffee-houses, and places of public resort, there may be some truth in it;

but there is no country in which the private circles of the nobility are of so exclusive a character. Regulations so strict, or rather so ridiculous, as those enforced at the casino of Grätz, are not known at the casino of the Magnates at Pesth, nor at the casinoes of the nobles at Dresden and Berlin, nor at those of Livonia and Courland. It is strange that any thing so absurd should still maintain its ground, but the fault lies with the families of plebeian rank, who seem to be destitute of every feeling of self-reliance, and disgrace themselves by their habitual veneration for rank, and the surprising value which they attach to an admission to a patrician circle. What they ought to do, is to found a casino of their own, and make it their first law, that no one shall be admissible who cannot show that he is not of noble descent.

Every traveller who has visited Styria, is loud in his praises of the Archduke John. It was impossible for me to visit all the schools, museums, and other public institutions, directly or indirectly called into life by this high-minded prince, but I endeavoured at least to see the most important ones, and the first to which my attention was directed was the JOHANNEUM, the national museum of Styria, containing various distinguished collections of natural history and the fine arts, together with a library, a reading society, and a technical school. The collection of Styrian mineralogy is a remarkably fine one, and in the arrangement of the specimens their geographical position has been kept in view as well as their systematic grouping. In the botanical department, the fungi and other plants which do not admit of being dried, have been beautifully modelled in wax by Stoll, of Schönbrunn, an artist of high eminence in that line. In the zoological collection, the mixture of foreign animals with those of Styria is decidedly a fault, but in other respects nothing can be better than the system of arrangement. Thus by the side of every stuffed bird or serpent, may be seen its skeleton, and by the side of each butterfly, its eggs, caterpillar, and chrysalis.

The technical school of the Johanneum is considered one of the three best in Austria; the other two are those of Vienna and Prague. In the lecture-room I saw drawings of all imaginable agricultural implements; and specimens of every species of grain grown in Europe, were carefully arranged in flowerpots.

The reading society of the Johanneum has been the result of circumstances rather than design. A few scientific and technological periodicals had been subscribed for, and placed in a separate room for the accommodation of the teachers, and of such private persons as took an interest in the subject. There was a constant wish to increase the number of periodicals, and at last the Archduke John placed himself at the head of the society, and obtained from the government permission for the importation of a number of English, French, and German works. This permission has been more and more enlarged, till at last the reading society of Grätz has become, by far, the most important of the whole Austrian empire, no less than 170 periodicals, in German, Hungarian, English, French, Croatian, and in various other languages, being provided for the instruction and entertainment of the subscribers, who are by no means idle in availing themselves of the opportunities thus provided for them. The regulations by which the society is governed, were drawn up by the archduke's own hand, and are considered so judicious and practical, that many German cities have applied for copies, with a view to the establishment of similar institutions.

Societies of this kind are always able to procure many books that, in circulating libraries, would not be tolerated by the Austrian police. Throughout Austria, indeed, circulating libraries are in a very depressed condition. In Grätz, a place of nearly 50,000 inhabitants, there is but one, with about 3000 volumes, and those wretchedly arranged. A poor widow carries on the hazardous concern of lending out books. I asked her for something good and new to read, before going to bed, and she handed me some of Clauren's novels! I asked her for something of Victor Hugo's, but his works were prohibited; of James's, but he also was prohibited; of Bulwer's, but he was only partially tolerated. There was no lack of indecent books, but those I did not want. "For morals," said the old lady, "they care less than for opinions." These libraries, however, rarely fail to have a private corner, in which the forbidden fruit is kept for the enjoyment of those in whose discretion confidence may be placed.

In all Vienna, there are but two circulating libraries of any respectability, and four minor establishments, something like that of Grätz. In Ollmütz, in Moravia, there is one of the latter class. In Insprück, the capital of the Tyrol, there was one a few years ago, but there is none now, the man who kept it having given it up, and no new one having been established, owing, I was told, to the opposition of the Jesuits. In Munich there are no less than six excellent establishments of the kind, besides several smaller ones, and for the 80,000 inhabitants of Dresden, there are no less than twenty, large and small included.

To some extent the want of circulating libraries in Austria is supplied by the liberality of the owners of private collections. I was told of gentlemen in Grätz, whose books circulated as freely as though they each gained a livelihood by lending them.

Among the public libraries of Grätz, that of the university is the most important. It contains about 40,000 volumes, and had in the preceding year (1840) been visited by 8000 readers; that is to say, one book or other had been asked for 8000 times. At this rate there must have been a daily average of twenty-five to thirty readers. This is little enough, considering that the students are not allowed to carry any books home with them. Nevertheless, it was a considerable increase on the preceding year, when the readers had amounted only to 7000. The library contains many very curious things, but at all these provincial libraries in Austria they are very cautious of showing their principal treasures, lest these should be demanded by the leviathans of the capital. Several of the catalogues of provincial libraries begin with a lamentation over their lost riches, remorselessly snatched from them to enrich the libraries of Vienna.

A second great public institution, established by the Archduke John, is the *Inner Oesterreichische Gewerbe und Industrie-Verein*, a kind of polytechnic association. It is intended to assist and encourage artists and mechanics, by means of exhibitions, prizes, collections of models, &c., and is one of the largest associations in the Austrian empire, comprising already 1218 members, though only established since 1841. The collection of models and specimens interested me greatly. Among other matters, it contained samples of all the different kinds of scythes used or manufactured in Styria, Carinthia, and Carniola. This is an article with which Styria supplies all its neighbours, and many distant nations. I saw here Hungarian, Russian, and Polish scythes; marsh scythes for northern Italy, and articles of a different construction to suit the real or imagined convenience of the mowers of Bosnia and Bulgaria. Most of these forms are of great antiquity, having been carefully handed down from one generation to another; but new inventions are sought after with the same zeal.

If there is an article of spotless fame in the commercial world, it is the steel of Styria, for inquire about it where you will, and you will hear it spoken of with commendation. Its fame extends much farther than the manufacturers themselves are, probably, aware of, for they send their merchandise only to Trieste, and have very little notion of what hands it passes into, out of those of their Triestine consignees, by whom it is sent to Egypt, Turkey, America, and indeed to all quarters of the globe. The people in those remote regions, who buy the steel of Styria, know often as little whence it comes, as those who manufactured it know whither it goes. In Mexico, Cuba, Venezuela, and most parts of Spanish America, the article passes by the name of *Acero de Milano*, or Milan steel, the only material of which the Mexican miners like to have their *barras mineras* made, large crowbars, for breaking the ore after it has been softened by fire.

One of the oldest of the archduke's institutions is the Agricultural Model Farm, with a central school for agriculture, a building for the annual meetings of the agriculturists of Styria, and a few fields for practical experiments. The archduke has prevailed on the Styrian states to support the institution by a public grant for the support of ten poor students, with the view to their being educated as good practical farmers. This institution has already led to the establishment of twenty-six branch establishments in different parts of Styria and Tyrol.

At the period of my visit to Grätz, the annual fruit and flower-show of this institution was just open, and a very brilliant show it was. I saw there eighty-three different descriptions of apples and pears, one hundred varieties of grapes, and no less than ninety kinds of potatoes. Of the last-named fruit there were Brazilian, Scotch, Polish, Crimean, and even Algerine species, but to my astonishment not a single *German* potato had been sent for exhibition. *En revanche*, there was a magnificent specimen of a pear, to which the grower had given the name of the *German National Pear*.

The art of rearing fruit has been wonderfully improved in Styria during the last thirty years, though it has not yet been carried so far as in the archduchy. The Etsch valley, and particularly in the neighbourhood of Meran, is celebrated for its fruit, which is carried for sale to Vienna and Munich in great quantities; some people assured me, it was taken even as far as to Odessa. The grapes and apples, carefully packed at Meran, are carried over the mountains on men's backs to the Inn, where they are shipped, and forwarded by water.

The fruit and flower show had been arranged in the *Rittersaal* of the provincial House of Assembly for Styria. In this building the states of Styria hold their meetings, which exercise but little influence over the weal and woe of the province. In ancient times these states were a much more important and powerful body, and like the Cortes of Barcelona, allowed no prince to enter on the exercise of power till he had taken the prescribed oath, and made certain concessions to the people. Much as the princes of the House of Habsburg boast of the love and loyalty of their faithful Styrians, the history of Styria is by no means wanting in instances of firm resistance to arbitrary power, and it is only by the suppression of insurrections that the country has been reduced to its present political insignificance. The history of Styria would be well worth writing, and there are men enough in the country very well able to write it, but they know they would not be allowed to write it in the only manner consistent with truth, with the dignity of letters, and with the honour and interest of the province. The last time that the Styrian states did homage to their prince according to the old prescribed form, was in 1728, when Charles VI. received their loyal assurances at Grätz. With Maria Theresa, what had already become little more than a ceremony, ceased altogether, and Styria lost her last security against arbitrary power; the aspirations after a better order of things, I was assured, were not few and far between; time alone can show what fruit these aspirations will one day bear.

FROM GRATZ TO LEOBEN.

Early in the morning of the 11th of October I pursued my journey, which, as a matter of course, carried me up the valley of the Mur, for from Grätz, encompassed as it is by mountains, there is no road into the more level part of Germany, except that which has been constructed by the waters of the Mur. Indeed of such importance is the river to the country, that Styria might with great propriety be called Murland; and in the same way Carinthia might be named anew the Land of the Drave, and Carniola the Land of the Save. The Mur rolls rapidly down from its native mountains, and our little carriage rolled rapidly up to meet it.

The Schöckel mountain is a kind of barometer for the good people of Grätz. My driver, Frances, shook his head as he looked at this barometer, telling me the mists were rising up its sides, and would come down again about noon in the shape of rain. The Schöckel was not the only mountain enveloped in mist; to me they all appeared to be tapestried with the same kind of decoration; and a heavy mass of clouds hung threatening over the plain of Grätz. It required no great wisdom as to the ways of the weather to prophesy the approach of rain, and as the clouds are at all times fond of opening their hearts over the said plain, I bade Francis enliven his team a bit, in the hope that our prospects might improve in proportion as we came upon higher ground.

Immediately on leaving Grätz, the plain (*das Grätzer Feld*), in which this beautiful little city has located itself, is closed in, and the traveller enters through a mountain-pass into a narrow valley, that stretches away, about six (German) miles to Bruck, widening here and there into a kind of amphitheatrical basin, in which a little market-town rarely fails to have taken up its station. These little enlargements of the valley, miniature repetitions of the *Grätzer Feld*, have each a separate name. One is called *Auf dem Tratten*, another the *Zeckenfeld*, &c. This compression of the valley of the Mur, between Grätz and Bruck, is, no doubt, the origin of the geographical division of the country into Upper and

Lower Styria. Not that the people themselves have drawn any definite line of division, for wherever you happen to be along the Mur, all the country above that point is called Upper, and all below it Lower Styria.

Several little market-towns lie along this valley, as Gradwein, Peggau, and Fronleiten. The last of these, where we dined, is beautifully situated, like all the little towns in these lovely Alpine regions, and the mind would gladly abandon itself here to the enjoyments which the magnificence of Nature provides with so much prodigality, were it not that the awful mental degradation in which so many human creatures exist there, tends very much to imbitter the pleasure. On leaving Grätz, we enter the country of the *Cretins*, which are here called *Troddeln*, or *Trotteln*, and in Carinthia, *Kocker*. In Lower Styria, a land of vineyards, and hills of moderate elevation, and where the life of man is one of less labour and endurance, *Cretins* are seen but rarely, and where the Mur enters Croatia, they cease altogether; but in the higher regions, where subsistence is more difficult and the customary food less nutritive, there is scarcely a village in which these frightful objects do not present themselves, with abashed looks, staring eyes, crooked legs, and often as many as three or four huge wens to their necks. It is the most appalling shape in which human deformity ever presents itself, for mind and body seem to be crippled alike. Generally speaking, the Cretins are cruel, malicious, and revengeful. They devour every kind of food with a sort of animal voracity, and their every impulse, or natural desire, manifests itself in the most revolting manner. Their scent is usually very quick, as with animals, but they are generally more or less deaf. Their growth is slow, and they seldom attain an average height, which is fortunate, for the sight of a full grown *Cretin* would be altogether unendurable. On the other hand, they frequently live to a considerable age, many of them dragging their miserable existence about with them for seventy years, and more.

Upper Styria is the chief seat of *Cretinism*, which diminishes as you approach Lower Styria on one side, and Bavaria on the other. In and about Salzburg a few Cretins may still be met with; in Linz and in Bavaria there are none.

It is a singular fact that some villages and valleys appear to be quite free from the affliction, while in others again it prevails like an epidemic. Not far from Fronleiten, for instance, there is a small district, called *In der Gams*, where there is scarcely a house without two or three *Troddeln* in it. Many attribute this to the influence of the soil. Here, as elsewhere, people imagine they have observed that near mountains of clay-slate, the population has always a decided tendency to *Cretinism*, and that in the vicinity of limestone-rocks very few cases of it occur.

Popular belief, however, assigns a multitude of causes to the malady, and the poor water is made to bear most of the blame. Some springs are regularly shunned, as living streams of wens, imbecility, and Cretinism. About three leagues from Fronleiten there is one of these springs; its water is transparent as crystal, and delicious to drink, but is held in horror, nevertheless, far and wide, under the name of Wen-spring, or Kropf-quelle. The cattle drink the water without any evil consequences resulting to them. Other springs are pointed out, with equal confidence, as yielding a water certain to act as a preservative against the malady.

Beyond Fronleiten the valley becomes more narrow again, and the Röthelstein, and some of the other mountains, lean over as if they were just on the point of rubbing their foreheads against each other. The Röthelstein owes its name to the deep red hue of its rocky summit. Caverns abound in all directions. Some have been described so often as to fatigue with the repetition, but the greater part have never been explored by science. Many are filled with ice in winter, and harbour little lakes in summer, and the warmer the summer the greater will be the masses of ice in winter.

Among these wild Titanian scenes, the peaceful works of man acquire a double interest. The houses and the narrow strips of pasture-ground seem perched upon the rocks, or losing themselves among the chasms, and the mind naturally ponders over the daring of those who selected spots so difficult of access, for their dwelling-places, and settled fearlessly among hosts of surrounding giants. Rafts of wood are moving rapidly but skilfully down the Mur. The river is little indeed to look upon, but it has its perils, and requires an expert steersman quite as much as the Danube.

A few leagues beyond the Röthelstein the narrow character of the Mur valley changes, and at Bruck we enter the Upper Valley. Bruck and Leoben lie at no great distance from each other. At these two cities, the roads meet from Vienna, Linz, and Salzburg, and continue then in an united line towards the south. The road from Vienna through the Mur valley to Grätz, and thence on to Trieste may be compared to that from Munich, over Inspruck to Verona. Between these two great roads that intersect the Alps from north to south, there is no third that comes at all near them in importance.

We drove on to Leoben through the dusk of the evening. We were lighted on our way by a multitude of little lights. First we had the stars twinkling in a bright sky, next we had countless numbers of lights shining out upon us from the dwellings of man as we passed them, then we had glow-worms in the grass, and lastly the pipes of Francis and myself. Various as were in themselves these light-giving objects, they produced all, strange to say, much the same effect, when seen through the darkness of night. They seemed all to be only so many illuminated *points*.

In Leoben I supped with some officers and a surgeon, on a numerous array of savoury Austrian dishes that are nameless out of the country, and would not be recognised beyond the emperor's dominions by the names under which they pass current with his subjects. The officers complained sadly of the physical defects that prevailed among the population. At the last recruitment, they told me, among sixty recruits they had been obliged to refuse twenty-five, on account of ruptures, distorted joints, wens, Cretinism, or other bodily defects, and often the proportion of the rejected was still greater. The strongest and finest men of the neighbourhood, they said, were the woodcutters, and those who floated the rafts down the river; the least healthy were the charcoal-burners and miners, among whom Cretinism was particularly prevalent. The evil, they added, was less than it had been. Formerly a few Cretins constituted a regular appendage to every inn or tavern, where they were kept as servants of small cost, and to serve for the amusement of the guests! Nor are they by any means useless as servants, for in spite of their apparent imbecility, when once they have learned any particular kind of work, they will often perform it with greater regularity, than servants who have the use of all their senses.

Throughout my whole journey, from Grätz to the Bavarian frontier, everywhere I heard the people joyfully declare that Cretinism was on the decline. If so the evil cannot be an unconquerable one, nor can it depend on the unalterable influence of the soil. It may like most of the ills that owe their being to human barbarism yield to the intelligence of a more enlightened age, to the gradual influence of education, and the improved condition of the humbler classes. How must it not incite governments, as well as private individuals, to increased exertions, when they see that the little that has already been done has not been done in vain!

EISENARZT AND THE EISENBERG.

The road which leads to Salzburg and the Salt districts, is called by the people of the country the Salt Road. We quitted it on the following morning to visit the celebrated mines of Eisenarzt and Vordernberg, which lie away to the side among the hills, and, after having satisfied our curiosity there, it was our intention to return to the Salt Road by the way of the Admont convent.

The upper valley of the Mur and the upper valley of the Ens run parallel with each other, from west to east, and are formed by three parallel ridges of the Alps. The Mur, turning to the south near Bruck, forces its way through the southern ridge; and the Ens, in the same way turning towards the north, breaks through the northern barrier, and rolls on to join the Danube. The central ridge, which divides the two rivers from each other, remains unbroken, but has several passes, one of which occurs between Vordernberg and Eisenärzt, and to this pass on the following morning we directed our course.

All the mountains seemed to have grown into the firmament, for the latter was hanging down over them, wrapped in a close veil of mist, and where, here and there, one of the tall gentlemen allowed us to get a peep at his head, we saw it had been lightly powdered with snow during the night. To the eagles, and chamois, the sun was probably visible, but he appeared to trouble himself very little about us humble wayfarers in the mist-hidden valleys below. The valley, or ravine, up which we travelled, was very narrow, with a small stream, the Berger Bach, running down it, and huge masses of rock scattered on either side. The place was full of ironworks, which continued all the way to Vordernberg, where there were no less than fourteen furnaces, from which upwards of 300,000 cwt. of pure iron, I was told, were annually obtained.

I went over a few of these furnaces, and also over a new mining school, established through the exertions of the Archduke John. Here I found the most complete collection of iron ores that I had ever seen. They were doubly arranged ; first, geographically, according to the places whence they came, and secondly, according to a geological system. The school receives its pupils from the polytechnic institutions of Vienna, Prague, and Grätz, where they have generally been well prepared to perfect themselves in the science of mining by practical studies on the spot.

From Vordernberg our road ran farther and farther up into the region of pines. The higher we came the clearer grew the weather, and by the time we had reached the mountain pass—the Prehbühel—we had as beautiful a day as we could wish for. A few *Sennhütten** here called *Schwaigen*, abandoned already by their fair occupants, were scattered about the

---

* *Sennhütte* is the German name for the summer cottage among the Alps, erected as a shelter for the herdsman who drives his cattle to the mountain pasturage. In French Switzerland the word for one of these huts is *chalet*. The French word is

edges of the mountains. The *Sennerinnen*, in some places also called *Schwoagerinnen* and *Brentlerinnen*, had left their summer abodes to take up their quarters for the winter in the valleys.

At the loftiest point of the pass are large magazines of ore; for within this pass are the celebrated works whence an ore so rich is obtained, as to be unmatched by any other mine on the European continent, with the exception of those in the Ural mountains. The metallic mass seems to have laid itself like a thick mantle over the northern declivity of the pass, and to rise, moreover, like a vast cupola within the pass itself. On the summit of this cupola, a large iron cross has been erected, and thence the Eisenberg (or Iron Mountain) descends with tolerable regularity into the Münchthal to Eisenärzt.

The summit and the upper half of the mountain belongs to the Vordernbergers, the lower half of the mantle of iron belongs to the Eisenärzters; the former are a company of private speculators, the latter the officers of the government. From the summit of the pass, a railroad runs into the mountain, and by this railroad the ore is brought to the magazines of which I have spoken, and is thence conveyed, in common carts, to the furnaces. After leaving Leoben, it appeared as if there would never be an end to the carts laden with ore. This road, therefore, is very appropriately named the Iron road, in the same way as the road to Salzburg is called the Salt road.

I sent my charioteer, Francis, on to Eisenärzt by himself, and committed myself to the railroad which was to carry me quickly into the bowels of the mountain, and thence out into the open air again on the northern side. I went with a train of returning ore-carts, of which there were nine or ten, and these were drawn with great facility by a single horse. On the last of the carts sat one of the superintendents, a few workmen, and myself.

Cold it was in this elevated position, but the view was magnificent. The *Hohe Schwab* (the Tall Suabian) rose with all his pinnacles and promontories, and formed a truly wonderful panorama of rocky elevations and fearful abysses. The Erzberg himself is about 3000 feet high, but the masses round about rise to an elevation of more than 7000 feet. Having arrived on the Vordernuberger side of the mountain, I commenced my inspection of the remarkable works which have now been in full activity for so many centuries, tearing the dull ore from the entrails of the mountain.

There is reason to believe that the nature of the Eisenberg was known to the Romans, though it is asserted that no mine was worked there before the year 712. The mass of iron accumulated here by the hand of nature, is truly astonishing, and the ore is obtained with little trouble, compared with other mines, on account of the trifling depth to which the miner has here to descend. The circumference of the hill is 6000 fathoms, its height 3000 feet; and the whole summit of the mountain, and the covering of one side of it, form one mass of iron ore, and that of so rich a quality, that two hundredweight of ore yield one hundredweight of clean iron. If we suppose the stratum of ore to be everywhere 200 feet in thickness, it will follow that we have here a stock of millions upon millions of tons of iron;

---

probably better known to the majority of English readers; nevertheless, in the present translation, the German word has been preferred. In Styria, it would appear, the cattle, during summer, are confided to the care, not of men, but of women. These women are called *Sennerinnen* (in the singular, *Sennerinn*), and the herd of which they have charge, the *Senne.—Tr.*

quite enough, at all events, to provide the world with needles, ploughshares, and swords, for a tolerably long time to come.

I have spoken of a mantle of iron as covering one side of the mountain. This expression must not be taken so literally as to suppose that the ore lies on the side of the mountain in one stratum of a uniform thickness, like a cloak on the back of a fine gentleman. Here and there this covering of iron disappears altogether, and in other places it sinks to a great depth into the interior of the mountain, or runs through it in the shape of veins of greater or less size. Moreover, when I say the ore lies on the surface, that too must not be taken literally, for the mountain is everywhere nearly encrusted with a covering of vegetable mould, sufficient to afford sustenance to a number of pines and other trees. The way in which the work has usually been carried on, has been to clear away the mould, and then to pick out the ore. This system has led, in the course of centuries, to the formation of a multitude of spacious caverns and grottoes, similar to those we see in stone quarries. Of these grottoes there are at least fifty in different parts of the mountain. Where the ore runs into the heart of the mountain, the miners have sometimes followed its course, and long subterranean passages have been formed in consequence.

Some of the caverns (*Tagbauen*) of which I have just spoken, have been worked for more than a thousand years, and present a most interesting appearance. They are large irregular halls, or rotundas, with floors and walls that make not the least pretension to smoothness. Blocks of ore, of various sizes, lie scattered about, some because they have not been thought rich enough to be worth carrying away, others because no convenient opportunity has yet presented itself. Columns and arches of ironstone are seen on every side, and clinging to the walls the busy miners are working away with their hammers.

Paths lead from one work to another, and here and there lie the little huts in which the miners pass the night, ten or twenty together, as long as their working week lasts, for the dwellings for their families are mostly below in the valleys. A few of the superintendents, however, have their houses up on the mountain itself.

Travelling from cavern to cavern, I arrived at a projecting ledge of rock, whence the view down to Eisenärzt and the Münch valley was more magnificent than I could have imagined. Round about rose the steep sides and the huge stony masses of the Pfaffenberg, the Seemauer, and the Reichenstein, of which the last named is by far the highest. Among these mighty works of nature,—and the same, to some extent, may be said of the colossal piles reared by human hands,—one is apt very much to under-estimate distance and size. The walls of the mountains around me seemed quite even and uniform, yet my companions assured me, there were ledges, and promontories, and abysses, to look upon which would make my hair stand on end. They talked much about the chamois that frequented those rocks, so I asked them whether they, with their practised eyes, could detect any of the creatures. At this they all laughed, and said, if, on the mountains I was looking at, there were hundreds of chamois I should not be able to see one, even though provided with a good telescope. To me the mountains appeared so close, that I should have expected to see the nightingales fluttering about the bushes, if there had been any. How paltry the pyramids of Egypt would look if placed among these hills!

The mountains had all wrapped their summits in veils of snow. Deep down below, with the huge giants crowding around, lay the little cheerful, cultivated valley of Münch, with the smoke curling up from the houses of Eisenärzt. As we proceeded, the same view presented itself with endless variations at each new projection, and with every step we approached nearer to the peaceful valley, and seemed to be receding more and more from the frowning mountains around us.

On my arrival at Eisenärzt, the director of the ironworks, to whose polite attentions I was soon to be indebted, was still occupied in his office, so I took a walk, to while away the interval, with Völkel, a chamois hunter of great renown in this part of the world, from whose conversation I derived much entertainment. The chamois is a creature so light, graceful, and sagacious, and the places it frequents offer such an endless variety of situations, and such frequent motives for exultation in success, that the chamois hunter never fails to be passionately fond of his occupation. If the chamois lived in the plains, this would not be the case. The whole of the Noric Alps to Maria Zell and the Schneeberg, are full of chamois, "but round about Eisenärzt," said Völkel, "they have become scarcer, for the Archduke John has his Brandhof at the foot of the High Alps, where he coaxes them over to his own side."

The Brandhof is an estate which the archduke has bought and fitted up as an Alpine cottage, and there he has occasionally chamois hunts on as large a scale as the king of Bavaria, near Berchtesgaden, where more than a hundred of these beautiful creatures have sometimes been killed in the course of one hunting expedition. The Archduke John has become a thorough Styrian. At the popular festivals which he gives at his Brandhof he dances with the hunters and their damsels, wears the Styrian costume, and the people, when they speak of him, generally drop his title, and call him plain "John." "Ah!" said my companion, "that John's a man, and there would be as much of the man left if you could strip him of all that birth and fortune gave him."

I have always found the civil servants of the Austrian government extremely obliging, and much more unreserved in their communications than I could have anticipated. My director was no exception from the general rule, but, on the contrary, gave me so much information about the works placed under his superintendence, that if I could have retained half of what he told me, I should have been in a condition to write a very instructive book on the subject. It was already evening, so we proceeded with lighted lanterns to pay a visit to the furnaces.

Each of the three furnaces of Eisenärzt produces yearly from 60,000 to 64,000 cwt. of iron. The thirteen furnaces of Vordernberg produce each 20,000 to 30,000 cwt. The poorest ore yields forty per cent. of metal. Poorer ore is found, but is not considered worth melting. The richest ore yields seventy per cent., but the average is from fifty to sixty per cent. In England there are single furnaces that do as much work as all those of Eisenärzt put together.

We supped at the inn, where our conversation turned upon the customary Styrian topics: iron, chamois, and Cretins. I mentioned what the officer had said at Bruck, and asked whether his account was likely to be correct. My present companions thought he must have spoken within the mark; about Eisenärzt, they were sure, it would be a wonder if, out of sixty recruits, twenty were found fit for service. Wens, ruptures, and an enlargement of the veins of the legs, were the rule, and the absence of those deformities the exception. Wens, moreover, appeared to be ordered in various classes, according to their size, and a woman with a "quite clean neck," I was assured, was almost a rarity in that part of the country. Not far from Eisenärzt, it seems, there lies, at a considerable elevation, a valley called the Radmer, where there are more Cretins than in any other place of equal extent. I was told of a young man who lived there, and who had been a fine intelligent boy till his eighth year. He was making admirable progress in his education, when suddenly his eyes began to lose their lustre and to assume that ominous dulness of expression, which to the practised glance announces the approach of mental darkness. As the fire of intelligence became gradually extinguished in the boy's eye, his features assumed a staring, stupid expression, his knees bent inward, his walk became slow, his memory and all desire for information left him, and his poor parents saw their child sink irrecoverably into the night of Cretinism, into a creature destitute of thought or feeling, though continuing to drag a worthless life about with him.

In Styria, as in Switzerland, the Cretin is invested with a kind of sanctity, and an insult to the poor "*Troddel*" is sure to be followed by the resentment of all his relatives. This is partly owing to a belief that the poor benighted being is paying the penalty of the sins of his family. The worst of it is, that marriages between Cretins cannot always be prevented. I was told of two farms, for which no purchaser could be found, because it had been observed that every family that had occupied them, had sunk into irrecoverable Cretinism. It may be some compensation for this grievous affliction, that Upper Styria is quite free from the fevers which prevail to so great an extent in Hungary, and from which even Lower Styria is not exempt. The people of Lower Styria often travel into the upper part of the country to escape the pestilence of these fevers, or to recover from their effects.

THE STYRIAN ROCKS.

Francis and I resumed our journey the next morning, with a parting blessing on all the iron, still slumbering under the Prehbühl. Heaven bless the work of all those numberless busy needles that are still sticking in the mountain, but which one day, centuries hence, perhaps, will be taken out and delivered over to the diligent fingers of our German housewives and maidens! May the scythes and the ploughshares, that yet lie dormant in the Eisenberg, know none but a peaceful duty when called into activity, and may it never be their fate to be bent into more warlike instruments! or should such be their destiny, may they, at least, never be raised in strife, unless for the defence of our common German fatherland!

The air was tolerably cool in these valleys, a thing not very surprising in the month of October, seeing there is always more cold than heat there, though the thermometer rarely falls so low as in the valley of the Danube. The temperature in winter seldom falls below $-4°$ of Réaumur. The preceding winter had been one of unusual severity, and one morning the thermometer had been down to $-11°$, which was something quite extraordinary. In Vienna, during the same winter, the thermometer had been down to $-15°$ and $-16°$ for several days together. Yet Eisenärtz lies at a much greater elevation, and is quite open to the north.

Our road led through the loftiest and wildest rocks. Beautiful and of endless variety as they were, presenting themselves at every step in a different grouping, still their wildness and magnificence had an overpowering effect. There seemed to be something intolerably insolent in the human pigmy that presumed to wander amid piles, fit only for the housing of giants. In some of the villages I saw sundials, on which the hours had been marked only from seven in the morning till four in the afternoon; because before and after those hours, no ray of sunshine ever found its way into the valley.

I passed a group of rocks to the left with a narrow pass leading to the Radmer valley. This pass was called "Between the Walls" (*zwischen den Mäuern*), and another, a little farther on, was called "In Time of Need" (*In der Noth*), two denominations highly characteristic of the country, for the people seem to me to be always living between walls, and every day with them is more or less a time of need. A man does not require to have himself experienced all the hardships of such a life, to enable him to judge of the delights of a seven months' winter, of a modicum of oatmeal as the recompence of a hard day's toil; of ploughing through a thin covering of mould, over a stony bottom, at the edge of a precipice, with the prospect that the harvest will fail six years out of ten, and seldom yield more than two bushels of corn for one of seed; of the wintry labour of climbing up the hills, amid hurricanes of snow, to cut wood, and thus amid toil and danger seeking to obtain the subsistence which the land has refused to yield. No, it does not require to have undergone all this to understand the mountaineer's notion of a fine land, one in which the life of man and the course of the rivers roll along over more easy and less precipitous paths. My charioteer, Francis, though a native Styrian, seemed to be as much overpowered by the wildness of the rocky labyrinth as myself. "Nay, I would not live here," he cried, "this is an appalling country!"

So thoroughly was I satiated with rocks that when I arrived at Hiflau, on the Enns, and was told there were two roads to the monastery of Admont,—a short one through a rocky ravine, and one, three miles longer, over a beautiful plain,—I hesitated not to choose the longer way. I found out afterwards I had done wrong. What I ought to have done, was to go through the ravine on foot, which would have led me through scenery more awfully magnificent than is to be seen in any other part of Styria.

We continued for some time, after leaving Hiflau, to pass one colossus after another, but we reached at last the plain of which so inviting a picture had been given us. We broke forth into a cry of exultation on beholding it, and, after passing our ocean of rocks, we exclaimed "Land, land!" with something of the feeling of delight with which Columbus may be supposed to have hailed the first sight of a new world, after traversing his ocean of water. The mountaineers, when, in autumn, they have brought their cattle in safety down from the Alps, or when, after a wolf or chamois hunt, they spring from the last rocky ledge down upon the plain; or when, in winter, returning from a woodcutting excursion, they come rattling down the snowy path in their little wooden sledges, and arrive at last without mischance upon horizontal ground again, no doubt raise their eyes to Heaven in gratitude, and exclaim, "Land, land!" Hence perhaps this little oasis of a plain has so appropriately been called, *'s Landl*. The Styrian poets call it the Noric Tempe, which is a *leetle* bit of an exaggeration, for in Tempe there were cities, whereas *in's Landl* there are only two very pretty little villages, one of which is called Landl, and the other Reifling. The latter lies at the entrance of the Salza valley, up which passes the path to the celebrated place of pilgrimage, Maria Zell. I will not attempt to estimate the extent of the plain, for the rocky masses, and the mountains towering into the clouds, may easily have deceived my unpractised eye, but it seemed to me to be a pretty little inviting miniature dukedom; and our eyes, imprisoned as they had been for several days among cyclopian walls, revelled with delight over the green meadows, like little birds just escaped from captivity.

We remained, however, but a short time in the valley of the Enns, but proceeded onward to St. Gallen, where we already found ourselves within the influence of the widespreading lordship of the monastery of Admont, which in the surrounding country owns a very pretty little portion of iron-works, castles, and tributary villages, to say nothing of the patronage of sundry excellent ecclesiastical livings. St. Gallen was founded by the abbots of Admont, and the castle of Gallenstein was built near it, as a residence for their officers, stewards, &c. These gentlemen have since found it more convenient to take up their abode in the town itself, and the old castle stood for some time abandoned to the ghosts and goblins who have, time out of mind, been the legitimate occupiers of all forsaken mansions. Of late the castle had been honoured with the visits of a very active fraternity of moneydiggers; and to prevent these busy speculators from bringing an old house about their ears, the abbot adopted the prudent course of selling the ruinous old concern to a smith, on condition of his removing the materials. When I passed the place, he had been already two years at work, breaking up the old walls, but seemed to have made little progress for the time.

After passing St. Gallen the road became steep, and I walked on, leaving my driver to follow. It was a beautiful evening, and a range of lofty mountains towered up on one side of me. Seen from below all mountains appear of immense height, as to the clown all those above him are great men: it is only when we rise ourselves, and have an opportunity to make our observations from an elevated point, that we come to distinguish the mighty among the mighty.

The play of colours and the effects of light on these mountains were wonderful and of endless variety. One colossus I watched particularly as the sun was departing from the horizon. The foot of the mountain was plunged in the sombre hue of a black pine-forest. Higher up were light bushes, and the upper part was covered with white snow. On the summit the snow seemed to be tinged with yellow, and a glowing red cloud hovered over it. The cloud became redder and redder, till at last the yellow summit became likewise red, and the rest of the snowy covering assumed a deep orange tint. This went on for a while longer, till at last the whole mountain seemed to be burning with a deep, fiery, purple red, as if a divine spark had suddenly kindled a glowing flame within the colossus. The magnificent spectacle was just at its height as I reached the summit of the Buchau pass, and the beautiful upper valley of the Enns presented itself before me. The river here traverses a vast basin, formerly, no doubt, a lake, but now a smiling valley, with the wealthy abbey of Admont in its centre, and mighty mountains and picturesque ranges of rocks rising like an amphitheatre around. At the top of the pass I found my charioteer awaiting me. I mounted my equipage accordingly, and over a convenient road I rolled past the rich fields of the monastic lords, through the little market-town that depends on the abbey, and up into the magnificent courtyard of the convent palace.

THE ABBEY OF ADMONT.

Admont is by far the most important and the most celebrated religious community in this part of the Alps. Its wealth is great, and the abbots, who played a prominent part throughout the history of Inner Austria, have still a seat and vote in the States of Styria, and at one time bore the style and designation "by the Grace of God:" as—"*Adalbertus Dei Gratia Abbas Admontensis.*" No less than thirty-six churches receive their spiritual directors from this monastery, and two gymnasia and several schools are supplied from it with teachers. The design of the monastery itself is on the same vast and magnificent scale which I have already described when speaking of the convents along the Danube. Like them it began to be built in the middle of the last century, and like them it has never been finished. Wars under Maria Theresa, reforms under Joseph, and revolutions under Leopold and Francis, left neither money nor leisure to proceed with the pious work. Incomplete, however, as it is, the convent is still a splendid building, and of the abundance of spare room within it I had soon an opportunity of judging, when I was conducted to the spacious apartment designed for my accommodation, and in which I was left to await the return of the prelate, who had driven out a few days before to a chamois hunt, but was hourly expected back.

I could walk twenty steps in my room in any direction I chose to take, and I did so some dozens of times while examining the arrangement of the place. It was an antique and venerable apartment, such as we rarely see nowadays, except in Austria or on the stage. The thick oaken door was adorned with carvings of angels' heads; the huge stove of Dutch tiles was surrounded with arabesques in iron, that made it look like a harnessed knight with a stiff-starched standing collar. On the lofty walls hung nothing but a small Venetian mirror in a massive metal frame, before which stood a crucifix, and a little desk for prayer. The windows were large enough for a church, but the glass was in most diminutive panes, that rattled in their leaden casements when shaken by the night wind. A large balcony without commanded, no doubt, by day, a splendid prospect, but the October wind and the darkness of the night were not just then calculated to induce me to satisfy myself on this point; I found it more agreeable to court the vicinity of my irongirt stove, who soon began to glow for me with a friendly and inviting ardour, and I was just beginning to abandon myself to the train of pleasing thoughts which the genial warmth of my companion was awakening within me, when I heard the coach-and-four of the prelate, and the hunting equipages of his suite, rolling into the courtyard.

My presentation followed almost immediately. I found in the prelate a venerable man of about seventy, but full of health and activity. He ushered me, without delay, to the supper-table, where I found several monks assembled, whose conversation was full of the events of the chase whence they had just returned. Some of the finest chamois mountains belong to the abbey, and the learned monks of Admont have in consequence been, at all times, great chamois hunters; a circumstance that may have had its share in giving them that air of vigour and sturdy health of which it was impossible not to take notice, and may also have contributed to maintain in them that taste for study and learning which has always characterized them quite as much as their love of sport.

Among the inmates of the convent I found twelve Cretins. It seems that some centuries ago one of these poor creatures was able to render an important service to an abbot of Admont, by apprizing him of a design of some enemies to surprise and pillage the place. Out of gratitude for so well-timed a communication, the monks have ever since entertained a dozen of these benighted beings, and whenever one of them dies, a number of candidates are always sure to apply for the vacant place. A number of poor Cretins are also supported by the monks without the convent walls.

After supper, when the prelate had dismissed me for the night, the Father Steward accompanied me to my roomy cell, and kindly bestowed an hour of his time in conversing with me about all the distinguished and excellent men, who had at various times adorned the community, or still continued to adorn it. Of these, there was none whom I valued more than the deservedly respected historian of Styria, Albert von Muchar, whose acquaintance I had had the good fortune to make at Grätz, and to whose kindness I now stood indebted for my introduction to the convent. I make it an all but inviolable rule not to mention by name any of the persons with whom I become acquainted on my travels; for even my warmest and best deserved praise might sometimes be any thing but welcome; but this excellent man I hope will excuse the exception I have here made. There are men for whom one feels an impulse of friendship at the first glance, and the impression made upon me, during our brief acquaintance, by that pious, learned, and benevolent Benedictine monk, is one that no time will ever be able to efface. I regretted missing his company here in his own splendid convent, but he is at least as usefully employed in his vocation at Grätz, where he has for many years graced the chair of Professor of History. Nor was I allowed to experience any inconvenience in consequence of his absence. Every possible attention was shown to his friend. On the following morning, I was invited to inspect the collections of the house, and afterwards to make a little excursion through the romantic environs.

The library of Admont is said to contain 100,000 volumes, many of very ancient date, for while the convents of Hungary and Lower Styria, have frequently been plundered and destroyed by the inroads of a barbarous foe, Admont, in its mountain-circled valley, has always escaped unscathed, nor has its peace been broken by any of the great European wars that have shaken the nerves of all the rest of the world. Twelve times the Turks made inroads into Styria, but they never came so far as Admont. The French were there indeed in 1806, but only in peaceful quarters.

Many buried treasures might be found in this library. Sir Humphry Davy spent several weeks in examining it. The other collections of the convent are but of trifling value, and I bestowed, therefore, but little time upon them, for the sun was rising gloriously above the mountains, and making his toilet for a real holiday.

The convent garden was beautiful enough in its way, but I was anxious to contemplate the more magnificent garden laid out by the hand of Nature. My Benedictine friends, accordingly, conducted me to a little *château de plaisance*, the property of the monastery, and fitted up at times for the reception of illustrious and distinguished guests. From this château, where I was entertained with an excellent glass of wine, we had a view of all the surrounding mountains, with the names of which I was duly made acquainted by my reverend hosts.

A stranger must not suppose that he has made himself master of the nomenclature of a range of mountains, when he has graven on his memory the names of the principal masses that present themselves to his view. A mountain has a number of peaks, ravines, abysses, and other component parts, and each of these has its distinct appellation. In short, a mountain has generally as long a list of names about it, as a ship with all its masts, spars, and ropes. Every point, every wall, every path, every patch of pasture-ground has its separate name, and its distinct character. Not that these names are always known to all the country round. The hunters have explored and christened spots which the husbandmen have never seen, and in the same way the *Sennerins* are familiar with places known only to themselves.

On our return, we looked in at some houses situated on the side of a mountain. These Alpine habitations in Styria rarely contribute much to the picturesque effect of the landscape. They are generally covered with rough pine-boards, which, as they are never painted, soon from the exudation of resinous matter, acquire a sombre brown hue on the sunny side, and a yet more gloomy gray on the shaded side. The architecture is much the same as that which prevails in Switzerland; a large projecting roof, and a balcony running round the whole house. We drank some milk with the worthy inmates, who kissed our hands and arms on taking leave, and before re-entering the monastry we went to see a manufactory of scythes, an article, in the construction of which neither the English nor the Swedes can excel the Styrians.

The scythe smiths, in Upper Styria, are mostly wealthy people. I was told of one who gave away yearly one thousand florins to the poor. "There were millionaires among them formerly," said one of the monks to me, "and there may be still, but luxury and extravagance are beginning to creep in among them. Some must have their equipages forsooth, and their daughters must dress like princesses, and then, you know, the hoard is apt to melt away."

The truly infernal din of hammers and grinding-stones, in one of these scythe manufactories it is impossible to describe, and those constantly subjected to it, I found, were all, more or less, deaf. The master of the establishment at Admont told me that the greatest demand for Styrian scythes was from Brody in Galicia, whence they were exported to Russia, to arm the mowers of the steppes. To Turkey a great many used to be sent, but he supposed that the trade had fallen into the hands of the merchants of Pesth, for a great many scythes went to Pesth now, and very few to Turkey. What seemed most to puzzle the worthy smith was the complete cessation of the Frankfort trade, which was formerly of greater value to him than any other. He seemed to imagine that the scythes had been generally shipped from Frankfort for America, and that that market had, perhaps been occupied by the English. It amused me to hear the good people speculating here, in their mountain fastnesses, on the political and commercial revolutions of the world, but I was unable to solve their doubts.

I was heartily tired of the noise of the scythe smiths, and felt most agreeably relieved when my friends ventured to hint that it was near dinner-time, and that we ought to return to the monastery, that we might not keep the prelate and the other gentlemen waiting. There was no lack at table of a spirited and instructive conversation, and after dinner I took leave of my reverend hosts, to whom I had much pleasure in giving the assurance, for which they so eagerly pressed me, that, if circumstances ever brought me into Styria again, I would not fail to repeat my visit to their beautiful convent.

THE UPPER VALLEY OF THE ENNS.

A beautiful road leads from Admont, along the upper valley of the Enns, to the Dachstein glacier, the mighty mark set up to show the border between Austria, Styria, and Salzburg. This is the most delightful of all the Alpine valleys. It is large and broad enough to afford a convenient field for the cultivation of man, and yet it has an abundance of picturesque beauties, the mountains, variously grouped, rising on each side to the height of 7000 and 9000 feet. A traveller among the Alps, however, where nature herself speaks in so sublime a language, must keep a tight rein upon his words, or he will always be feeling, thinking, and talking *superlativo* and *superlativissimo*. We northern Germans, when we leave our heaths and sandy plains, are apt to launch forth into esthetic raptures at the sight of the Elbe hills near Meissen, and if we go on heightening our expressions of delight as we get farther south, we are sure to be out of breath by the time we reach Styria. I must therefore content myself with saying that the upper valley of the Enns is full of interesting and beautiful objects, is about half a league broad, and being tolerably straight, enables the traveller to command an extensive view. The soil must be extremely moist, since all the ground is laid out for pasturage, and not a single human dwelling stands by the side of the river. The villages are all built a little way up the hills.

I was so pleased with my drive up this valley that I was by no means sorry when Francis told me we must spend the night in the little hamlet of Lietzen, a necessity to which I submitted all the more willingly, as I heard the sounds of music and dancing issuing from the little inn at which we stopped. I had had an opportunity at Grätz of spelling out the rudiments of a Styrian dance, and was well pleased to avail myself of so fair a chance to con over my lessons once more. I have seen many national dances that have pleased me; as, the Hussar dance of the Hungarians, the vigorous Mazurka of the Poles, the poetical Kosakka of the Russians, and the original Dioko of the Walachians. I have also seen the voluptuous Fandango of the Spaniards, the stormy Gallopades of the French, and the say-nothing Waltzes of Germany; but I must say that, for grace, decorum and good-humour, nothing can exceed the national dance of Styria. It is a near relation to the Tyrolese dance, or to the Austrian *Ländler*, but more graceful than the former, and more significant and varied than the latter. The movements are sufficiently slow to allow of their being beautiful, and the figures and positions are full of delicate allusions to the soft sensations of love; the whole dance, at the same time, breathes such graceful gaiety, that at the first glance you see it is more to the Styrian than a mere measured movement of the feet.

Other national dances, I admit, are beautiful in their way, when they are beautifully danced; but the fandango easily becomes *too* voluptuous, the Hungarian dance clatters too much with the spurs, the Polish is apt to become *too* wild, and the Russian is deformed by gestures and distortions of the limbs, grotesque rather than graceful. Now the Styrian dance, as far as I have seen of it, is free from all these excesses, and I am pleased to think that it is a German race that has invented so beautiful a dance, at the same time that I am at a loss to understand how it is that it should not have become more general in Germany. The music that accompanies it, is as graceful and characteristic as the dance itself, and in proportion as the dancers become excited, they set their voices as well as their feet into motion. I was so well pleased with the scene, that I had the greatest difficulty in tearing myself away from it. The ball, however, bade fair to stretch tolerably far into the night, so, giving the merry party a farewell blessing, I retired to bed to arm myself with a few hours' repose, against the next day's journey. May Heaven long preserve the worthy Styrians in the enjoyment of such graceful expressions of unsophisticated pleasure, and keep afar from them the levelling flattening influences of our age! To be sure the Alps are a tolerable bulwark against the levellers, and will take them some time to flatten down.

THE SALT DISTRICT OF STYRIA.

At Mitterndorf I stopped to look at a nail manufactory, a branch of industry, which, next to the making of scythes, is perhaps the most important in the country; but after leaving Mitterndorf, we quit the regions of iron, to enter upon those of salt. Arriving from the east, Aussee is the first place where this wide-spread fabrication is carried on. Western Styria, eastern Tyrol, south-eastern Bavaria, and what is called the Austrian Salt District, (*das oesterreichische Salzkammergut*,) are all parts of one vast country of salt, in the centre of which stands Salzburg, a town that probably owes its name to the staple commodity of the surrounding regions.

Here I determined to send Francis with our equipage on before me to Gossern, on the other side of the mountains, and to follow on foot, making one or two rounds; partly to have an opportunity of enjoying the view of the delightful valley of Aussee from an elevation, partly to pay a visit to a Styrian *Sennhütte* or *Chalet*. I found some kind friends at Aussee, to whom I had letters from Grätz, and who recommended me to a hunter of the Alps, who in his turn undertook to introduce me to a fair *Sennerin* of his acquaintance.

The young lady for whom our visit was intended, resided on a mountain called the Pflindsberg Alp, and the name by which she was known, was the "Külml Miedl of the Grundl Lake." Külml, it seems, was the name of her father's farm, which was situated close to the Grundl Lake; and Miedl is a kind of abbreviation for Maria. Some of these Sennerins, I was told, had titles quite as long as some of our German counts.

Külml Miedl has her *Sennhütte* on the side of a mountain, particularly well situated for affording a view of the Aussee panorama. The consequence is, that she frequently receives visitors, and for their accommodation a few boards have been nailed together into the shape of tables and benches, in front of her hut, so that she is always prepared to see company, and being a goodhumoured, merry girl, and famed far and wide for the beauty of her voice, she is seldom long without seeing strange faces in front of her elevated habitation. She is already beyond her "first youth," being about thirty years old, an age at which the female voice is best suited for the Alpine melodies, for the voice of a very young girl is seldom powerful enough for them. Strong lungs and long practice are absolutely necessary for the proper management of the voice among these hills.

They have three different sorts of song: the *Jodeln*, the *Johezen*, and the *Jauchzen*. The *Jodeln* is tolerably well known all over Europe, being the kind of song we have most of us heard from the itinerant Alpine singers who are constantly on their travels. The other two, however, can be heard only in the mountains.

The *Johezen* is a sort of melodious recitative, in which they contrive to make themselves heard from mountain to mountain; the *Jauchzen* is a call, challenging or inviting one on another mountain to enter upon a conversation, or, rather, a duet. A native writer expresses himself thus on the subject:—" A *Jauchzen* is an invitation which the *Sennerin* gives to her distant friend to enter on a dialogue in song. Hereupon follows, in sharp, lengthened tones of harmony, and distinctly articulated words, a recitative expressive of salutation, reproach, or intended to convey an invitation or a narrative. As soon as the first singer pauses, the other takes up the strain, and this interchange of song will sometimes be carried on for hours, and at astonishing distances, if there happens to be no wind, and the atmosphere is tolerably clear."

Having spent several months among the Alps at one time of my life, I am able to speak of these musical dialogues from experience. Sometimes a *Jauchzer* is raised merely to exchange a good morning, at other times by way of a warning that some cattle are going astray on an opposite hill. This song can be distinguished at a much greater distance than any mere scream or call, and when the *Sennerin* therefore gives her orders to her *Haltern*, (the lads stationed on the mountain as her assistants,) she does so mostly in song.

The Küml Miedl, I was told, was confessedly the best Alpine singer, or *Jauchzerin*, in all Styria, and I was anxious to hear the nightingale warble among her own bushes. We had been told she was still up on her mountain, but was expected to come down for the season that day or the next. I hurried my hunter, therefore, in the hope of reaching her hut before her departure. We started accordingly upon our mountain expedition, but had scarcely got halfway up when we met the Küml Miedl on her way down. Her cows were driven on before her. A horse, with her luggage packed upon it, was led by one of her lads, her sister carried a few bundles, and the fair *Sennerin* herself closed the procession. My hope of spending an idyllic evening with the Alpine shepherdesses on their mountain was frustrated, and so vexed was I at missing the anticipated enjoyment, that I felt half-inclined to give the girls a good round scolding for not having waited one day longer. Indeed, I did not altogether forbear from reproving them for their haste. I produced, however, some fine imperial pears, which I had brought with me from Aussee, for the express purpose of entertaining the *Sennerin* on her chamois meadows. The fruit was thankfully accepted, but I could not prevail upon my new acquaintance to favour me with a song, and as I did not expect much pleasure from an Alpine melody, if accompanied by any thing like constraint, I did not long continue to press the lady, but, wishing her a good day, pursued my walk towards her cottage, which was already in sight, and at no great distance.

We had not, however, proceeded far when we heard suddenly two voices raised in song. I looked back, and saw the Miedl and her sister on a projecting point of the mountain engaged in a regular Alpine duet. They had probably seen by my looks that I was in earnest in my wish to hear them, and they were perhaps not altogether insensible to my present of pears, which had proved an agreeable refreshment on their journey. We sat down and listened. The girls, pleased in their turn to have attentive and admiring listeners, went through their song, each singing alternate verses, and closing with a vigorous *Jauchzer* that rang through the mountains, awakening echoes far and near. I would have gone down to thank them, but they ran off to follow their cows that had meanwhile been driven on before them.

I was delighted to know that I had now heard a song from her who was confessedly the best singer of the Noric Alps, nor did I allow my pleasure to be disturbed by the remark of my hunting companion, that the song must be heard on the top of the mountain if I would judge it properly. To me it seemed a farewell greeting to the departing year, and some such feeling may have mingled in the song of the two fair mountaineers, who really sang with exquisite pathos. The *Sennerin*, though exposed to many hardships during her summer residence on the mountain, is almost always passionately fond of the unconstrained life which she leads there, and while her songs in spring are full of joy and exultation, they seldom fail to assume a serious and melancholy tone as autumn advances, and warns her down into the plain. As she drives her herd down into the valley, she decorates the horns of her cows with garlands, and her friends come forward to greet her with music and song; her return has the air of a holiday or a bridal, but she herself is often, all the time, sad and dejected as the bride about to exchange the poetry and freedom of maidenhood, for the cares of a household, and the embraces of one entitled to exact obedience.

The descent of the Sennerins from the mountain is always made as festive as possible, and for this purpose they generally contrive it so that a number of them, eight or ten perhaps, shall bring their herds down on the same day, when perhaps two or three hundred cows are driven into the valley at the same time. The cattle have garlands of flowers wound about their horns, the oldest cow and the oldest bull—the patriarchs of the herd—being always decorated with the utmost profusion. These garlands are of such splendour that the decoration of a cow, on her way down, will often be worth ten or twelve florins, that is to say it will often sell for that price, on account of the quantity of Alpine herbs which are collected on the mountains, and for which the apothecaries are always ready to pay liberally.

The young men, with bands of music, usually meet the descending procession at the foot of the mountain, and each Sennerin is conducted to her own house in a kind of triumphal procession. A horse, also adorned with garlands of flowers, is brought for her to ride home on, and her kettle and milkpails, are hung round its sides as the insignia of her triumph.

On every farm the Sennerin is always the most important and most highly considered member of the establishment; for it is she who has the most important part of the farm property under her care, and moreover a great deal of courage, prudence, and intelligence, are indispensable to a proper discharge of her duties. Many a fine Alpine meadow lies in a situation in which the utmost vigilance is required to prevent the cattle from falling down a precipice. A meadow of this kind may sometimes be made safe by means of a good strong hedge or other enclosure, in which case the Sennerin is bound to see that the hedge is at all times in good condition. Some meadows cannot be secured in this way, and then a constant eye must be kept on the cattle to prevent their straying into dangerous places. Other meadows may be safe enough in fine weather, but extremely dangerous if the ground has been made slippery by rain, or when the precipices are concealed by a mist. All these things the Sennerin must constantly bear in mind. Then again the patches of meadow ground lie scattered in small bits about the mountain, and some judgment is required in determining in what succession each shall be depastured or left to be mown for hay. Nor is it only the cattle that is exposed to danger; the Sennerin herself has often to venture upon ground, where for one false step she may have to pay the penalty of her life.

For any accident to her cattle, the Sennerin is held responsible, and if as much as a calf has been suffered to fall down a precipice, she to whom such an accident has happened, is not allowed to return home in triumph in autumn. She must wear no garland herself, and instead of flowers, she may only bind a rope from the stable round the horns of her cows. A good name also is requisite to entitle a Sennerin to be received with music and rejoicing at the foot of her mountain, and she who has the reputation of neglecting her work, or of *too often* encouraging her sweetheart to go up the mountain to her, must not hope for such a compliment from her fellow-villagers, but must go stealthily home, like her unwary sister, and when she and her cows have reached the farm, she must *open the stable-door with her own hand.*

We had a splendid view of the Aussee valley from the top of the Pflindsberg Alp. This valley, with its lovely little lake, combines almost every ingredient that goes to the composition of a beautiful landscape, and its inhabitants are equally distinguished for their fine forms and their industrious habits. Their houses are handsomely built, well kept, and every spot of ground is maintained in the highest possible cultivation, circumstances which, no doubt, contribute materially to the decoration of the landscape. Some of the mountains round about are nearly 10,000 feet high, but only one, the *Thorsteiner,* is of a construction to allow of the formation of glaciers. This mountain is of so difficult ascent, that it is only at long intervals, that individuals are found hardy and expert enough to reach the summit.

After enjoying for a long time the splendid panorama formed by this and several other valleys of which we were able to obtain a glimpse, we went to pay a visit to the *Sennhütte* of the Külm-Miedl. It was really a handsome little house, two stories high, every thing, apparently, in the best condition, but doors and windows were all made as fast as locks and bars could make them. The only *living* thing near the now deserted dwelling, was a spring of water, that splashed into a little natural reservoir, and will probably long continue to yield its quickening waters, when the present owner of that house, and many many successors, will long have closed their busy careers, and long have slumbered under the turf of the valley.

It was getting dark before we set out on our return, but as the path down was easy and safe, my hunter and I lighted our pipes, and pursued our conversation without interruption. When we had done talking of the Sennerins, I encouraged him to tell me of the manners and habits of the chamois. The story that a herd of chamois will post sentinels to give warning of approaching danger, he treated as a fable; but " the mothers while they have little ones," he said, " are always more vigilant than the others. The notion, I believe, has arisen from the practice of the old bucks to graze apart from the herd, particularly after they have once been beaten by younger or stronger bucks, when they often become *misanthropical*, and wander about alone till they die or get shot. The strongest buck, for the time, is always king of the herd."

" Have you ever watched such a solitary buck ?"

" Jesus Maria! to be sure I have! Once I observed an old buck yonder on the Trisselwand. It was a huge creature with a voice like a bear. He soon saw us down below, and began to walk up and down watching us, for they never run away when they see danger coming, till they have stopped some time to consider which way it is best to run. But man is cleverer than they. I had two lads with me, and told them to stop where they were, and keep the buck in their eye. I, meanwhile, crept up, by paths known to myself, till I got above the creature that had continued to watch my lads, and, as soon as I got a good aim at him, I shot him right through the heart. To be sure, I had the wind in my favour. Had the buck been to leeward of me, my cunning would have been of little use to me. Oh, the wind is of great importance to the chamois hunter; and he must not wear showy clothes or bright buttons. That is one reason why we old ones mostly shoot more game than the smart young hunters, with their fine jackets and their new hats."

" You say the old bucks keep themselves away from the herd; do the old does never do so ?"

" Oh, the old does, you see, are always the most important people of the herd. Every herd has an old doe, who marches on before, and whom all the rest follow. We call her the *Vorgeis*,* and her we take care never to shoot, for then the herd choose a new *Vorgeis*, who leads them by new ways, which we are then obliged to study afresh. Kill the *Vorgeis* of the herd, and it's a long while before you know the rights of your hunting-ground again. Sometimes the herd breaks up altogether, or splits into two or three, and it's a long time before you know what's become of them."

A herd of chamois, he afterwards told me, is seldom more than fifteen or twenty strong. Not but that eighty or a hundred may sometimes be seen together, but then it may be taken for certain that several herds have met, and will soon part company again. Each herd has its " home" in the most inaccessible parts of the mountain, whither it retreats on the approach of danger, and when a herd has once accustomed itself to its home, it seldom leaves it for a long time together. " It's not easy to get at a chamois in its own home," continued my companion, " for that's sure to be a dangerous place. Some of our young men, however, follow the creatures even there, and many a hunter pays for it by taking his

---

* Literally, the "leading doe or mother."

last tumble. Ay, and it has happened more than once that a hunter has climbed to places whence neither he nor his friends could get him down again, and there they must either starve or get some one to shoot them."

" And who shoots a man in such a case?"

" His friend if he has one. To be sure, such a thing doesn't happen often, but it does sometimes. People in the valley, sir, have little notion of what goes on in the mountains. It's none but a true friend, none but a sworn brother will do a man a service like that. Another turns away, and says he won't charge his conscience, but the true friend will not leave his brother to linger in torments."

Amid conversations such as these, passing through little woods and along meadow-paths, of which, owing to the darkness of the night, I could see but little, I arrived with my companion at the height of Petschen, which, with the exception of the Sömmering, is esteemed the most elevated mountain-pass in Styria. Hence a paved road leads into Upper Austria. The Styrian side of the pass is covered with a pine wood, where the glow-worm's was the only particle of light I was able to see, but from the summit of the pass, whence we looked down into Austria, lights enough were visible from the windows of the several villages of St. Agatha, Obernsee, Reitern, and Goisern. Here I took leave at once of my Styrian hunter of the Alps, and of his native land that in so short a time had become so dear to me. We stepped into an inn by the roadside, to take a parting glass of Italian wine, he to strengthen himself for his nocturnal walk homeward, and I for mine into

THE AUSTRIAN SALT DISTRICT.

On issuing from the darkness of a pine-forest, the piece of Austria into which I looked down from my mountain-pass, seemed as if it had been lighted up for an illumination. And an illuminated land it was in more senses than one. Not merely on account of the gay lights twinkling from the windows, and reflected in the smooth mirror of the Hallstadt lake, but on account of the comparative enlightenment and intelligence of the people. With all their many good qualities, the Styrians, it must be owned, are a marvellously simple race, and even the Upper Austrians appear knowing and acute in comparison. The Styrians appear to be perfectly aware of this. Nothing is more common than to hear one of them say, "Ay, the Austrians are more clever than we ;" and this they say without a particle of illnatured feeling. There was another circumstance that made me look upon the banks of the Hallstadt lake as an illuminated spot: the majority of the inhabitants are Protestants.

In the sixteenth century, Protestantism had spread far and wide in Austria and even in Styria. Nearly the whole nobility of the country had embraced the reformed faith, and Maximilian II. was a while undecided whether he would not receive the communion under both forms. Even in the seventeenth century, the Austrian nobles had Protestant chaplains at their castles; at first openly, and afterwards secretly. What a glorious event would it not have been for Germany, if Maximilian had yielded to his better impulse, and joined the Protestant cause! Germany, from one end to the other, would have been a Protestant land, a united land, and the wars of the seventeenth century, against the lights of Luther, would never have desolated our fatherland! Those wars made the Austrian nobility Catholic again, and brought the population back to the church of Rome ; but remnants of Protestantism have remained, chiefly among the mountains, and along the borders of some of the secluded lakes, particularly those of Aussee and Hallstadt. A Protestant clergyman told me, and he had the best means of being correctly informed, that in Upper and Lower Austria the Protestants number 17,000, in Styria upwards of 5000, and in Carinthia and Carniola about 18,000. In Vienna alone there are 12,000. Joseph II.'s Edict of Toleration, in 1781, made many Protestants throw off the mask of Catholicism, so much so that one Catholic priest near the Hallstadt lake, found a very numerous congregation reduced to two or three families.

It was late in the evening before I reached Goisern, where I found Francis waiting for me. I lay down in the hope of enjoying on the following morning the scenery of the lake, but a soaking rainy day dispelled all these dreams and drove me on to Ischl and thence to St. Gilgen. Here the rain ceased; so, selecting a guide, and sending Francis on to the Fuschel lake, I resolved to make up in some measure for my disappointment by ascending the Griesberg, a mountain of moderate height, but whence a fine view is to be obtained of all the lakes of the Salt District.

We were met, quite unexpectedly, on our way up the mountain, by a little herd of about twenty cows, all gaily garlanded. Here, as in Styria, the *Sennerin*, or the *Alpendirne*, as I found she was here called, must hang no garlands round her cows if she has had " a misfortune " during the season. "The young men mock her then, I suppose, and tease her when she comes down?" "God forbid, sir!" answered my guide ; "is it not bad enough for the poor girl that she may wear no flowers as she comes home? No, sir, no one would have the heart to mock her ; no one says a word to her."

From the summit of the Griesberg the view of all the surrounding lakes is ravishingly beautiful. There is something at once beautiful and interesting in a lake. It affords to the eye something of the same delight as an island does at sea, and is in fact itself an island of water surrounded by land. The lakes of the Salt District are just of the right size to harmonize with the surrounding scenery; a river flows from lake to lake uniting them, and by the side of each watery mirror stands a cheerful little town to complete the picture, to which the surrounding mountains furnish a magnificent frame. The Thorsteiner, with his glaciers and perpetual snow, forms of course, a prominent feature of the panorama.

All the *Sennhütten* of the mountain were already locked up and bolted, in the same way as I had seen the house of the Külml Miedl near Aussee. All at once my companion, an Alpine hunter like him of the preceding day, started and cried out, "The Alp is peopled still! if there's no *Sennerin* here, there are poachers here!" He had observed a little wooden vessel by the side of a spring, and this was enough to assure him we were not the only people on the mountain. My hunter looked so gloomy and serious at his discovery, that he was evidently prepared to encounter poachers rather than pretty girls. The poachers, it seems, often take shelter in the huts of the Sennerins, and these, in their womanish kindness, are but too apt to harbour those whom the law declares war against.

Like a lion ready to pounce on his prey, my hunter glided stealthily but rapidly towards the cottage which lay a little concealed. On arriving at the door we knocked, but received no answer for some time. At last, however, we heard some one stirring within, and a young girl of about nineteen admitted us, reproving us mildly for our impatience, and for the noise we had made. My hunter's brow was smoothed in a moment, and he explained his conduct by stating the suspicions he had entertained.

"I peeped through the window a bit," she replied, "before I opened the door; but I see you are honest people, so come in." She had kept her cattle in doors on account of the stormy weather of the morning, and had just been milking them. There was one Sennerin on the mountain beside herself, she told us; all the others had already gone down. Her meadows, it seems, were of a nature to afford good grazing for her cows for a little longer. To our habits there seems to be something strange in the fact of two young girls remaining alone upon a mountain, with not even a dog by way of protection, and we are surprised when we are told that such a custom has been preserved unchanged from one generation to another for centuries. To my mind the fact speaks volumes for the uncorrupted manners and kindly disposition of the people.

The Sennerin lighted a fire, produced milk, bread and cheese, and seasoned our repast by her unreserved gaiety, and by singing us several pretty songs that, to me at least, had the additional charm of novelty. In the mean time, night crept on, and she made no hesitation in allowing us to take up our quarters in her cottage till morning.

We arranged ourselves for the night on the floor, as well as we could. Our hostess retired into a back room. Early in the morning we were awakened by her song, and found her engaged in milking her cows. We breakfasted on some new milk, and on the crusts that remained from our last night's supper, and then parted with a mutual exchange of good wishes. We climbed over many an enclosure, wandered along many a path that the cows had been kind enough to mark out for our convenience, and at about nine o'clock, by various byways and crossways, and roundabout ways, we reached the Fuschel lake, where my hunter delivered me over safe and sound to the care of Francis, whose joy at seeing me again, indemnified me in some measure for the pain I felt in parting with my acquaintance of a day. He was a strong, active, handsome young fellow, and I had been delighted with his intelligence and his readiness to oblige. His name is Joseph Bader the Obenauer, but "the Obenauer" is the name by which he is best known in the country.

Francis told me the people at the house where we had stopped, had celebrated the *Almentanz* the night before, and the place had been full of *Diandl'n* and *Bub'n* (lads and lasses) dancing and making merry. I have witnessed an *Almentanz* more than once. It is a festival given to celebrate the return of the Sennerins. It is at these dances, generally, that marriages are made up, and wedding-days fixed; quarrels of long standing too are sometimes brought to a crisis at an *Almentanz*, and settled by a fight.

THE GAISBERG.

Before reaching Salzburg we came to the Gaisberg, which rises at only a little distance from the city. Uninteresting as is this hill to look upon, the panorama from the summit is not the less magnificent; so I again sent Francis on by himself, and having obtained an experienced guide, started on my upward journey.

My guide on this occasion was what is called "of a certain age." He had seen much of the world in his various capacities of herdsman, hunter, and cicerone of the mountains: besides having, as I suspect, made acquaintance with many parts of the Alps in the less legitimate character of poacher. Such a man is often invaluable to a stranger desirous of information; a veteran of this sort will often possess far more knowledge of the country, its people, and its productions, than can be collected from any book; and for my part I valued my introduction to him more, than I would have valued one to the Prince of Salzburg himself.

The view from the Gaisberg is known to half Europe, or at least to all Germany; for I doubt whether there is any well-educated German who has not either seen it himself, or heard it described by a friend. The first object on which the eye rests is naturally the city of Salzburg, lying in the plain, apparently close to the foot of the mountain. You seem to hover over the place, and to look down perpendicularly into its streets.

Salzburg has a situation peculiar to itself. It lies in a broad, convenient, level valley; but out of this valley, and close by the river side, there rises a little range of hills, that forms a semicircular dam, within which the city is enclosed as in an amphitheatre. These hills form a kind of natural rampart to the city, and the passes through this natural rampart supply the place of city gates, through which the citizens may pass by convenient roads into the plain. That part of the city which lies on the other side of the river, is compressed between the Salza and the Mountain of the Capucins. The plain without the city is highly cultivated, and dotted with villas, castles, and pretty villages.

The panorama from the Gaisberg has a twofold horizon. That to the north-west embraces the city and the plain, that to the south-east comprises the mountainous country whence I had just come; and this combination of mountains and level land it is that constitutes the great beauty of the view. You overlook the Salza, in its countless windings, for many miles, till at last you lose it in the remote mist, and for one arriving from Styria, where his eyes have been somewhat satiated with mountains and wild scenery, the highly cultivated plains of Bavaria, with their teeming fields, their handsome villages, and their little patches of woodland, have a double charm.

Towards the north-east, the view into the Salt District bears considerable resemblance to that from the Griesberg, and comprises a large part of the same country. I had no objection, however, to a repetition. While my look was fixed upon the Mond See (Moon lake) my ancient companion told me of a mermaid, who had been haunting its waters several times within the last two months. Many of the hunters, he said, had seen her, but had been afraid to shoot at her. Marvellous tales of this kind are frequent among the lakes and mountains. When we see these beautiful and majestic objects lying before us on a fine sunshiny day, we wonder how these superstitious notions can become connected with them; but the people of the country, it must be remembered, see them under very different aspects, and under very different circumstances, from the sightseeing traveller, who chooses fine weather and the best season for his visits. On a stormy wintry night, and seen from rocky heights, or through the gloomy opening of a pine-forest, the lakes now so placid may put on a very different look, and may be well calculated to conjure up all kinds of fantastic visions, to a mind predisposed to the impressions of superstition.

Among the popular superstitions of Styria is that respecting a four-footed dragon, called the *Bergstutzen*, supposed to lie in wait among the mountains, where he bites people, who are certain to die when bitten by him. The Archduke John, by way of discouraging the belief, has offered a reward of thirty ducats to whoever will shoot the monster, and produce his body. He has also offered a high reward to any one who will kill a monstrous snake, said to harbour in one of the mountain lakes. These rewards, however, are not, I fear, calculated to produce the intended effect. If the monsters are not caught, that will be no reason for the multitude to disbelieve in their existence, and the very circumstance of a reward having been offered, will be looked on by the people as a sanction of their superstition.

While reviewing the surrounding mountains with my telescope, the conversation with my guide turned naturally on the chamois.

" In those mountains yonder, there are more chamois now than in any other hereabout. You may now and then see some snow-white ones up there, but that's seldom. In winter, when the *Sennhütten* have been abandoned for the season, the chamois come lower down, and graze on the meadows where the cows have been."

" But what can the chamois feed on in the depth of winter ?"

" Oh, there's always a little green on the edge of the snow; and then the deeper the winter, the farther do the chamois come down. There are warm springs, too, in different parts, where there's green all the year round. Nature is never quite dead among the mountains. Where the snow lies thin there's always moss below it, and when they are hard pushed, the creatures eat the young boughs of the dwarf fir."

" You have hunted the chamois yourself, sometimes, I suppose?"

" Oh, Jesus Maria! how often! Many's the creature of them I have shot by the start."

" What do you mean by the start ?"

" Oh, you see, when the chamois takes fright, she darts away over stock and stone like the wind; yet every now and then she stands still for a second or two to look round. That's what we call the start. The hunter must seize that moment, or he has very little chance. Oh, the dear time! Many's the creature I've shot yonder among the rocks of the Stony Sea !"

" And do you ever venture into those parts now ?"

" No, not now; my head won't hold on any longer."

This is an expression very common among the hunters to express a liability to giddiness, to which old men are more subject than young ones, and which completely disqualifies a man for chamois hunting. Their limbs are often powerful enough still, when they are obliged to renounce the favourite pursuit on account of the giddiness which seizes them, and which to mountaineers is the most serious infirmity that can overtake them. Among the mountains, to be free from giddiness is looked on as the same thing as personal courage, and is held to be of more importance than experience and a sure foot. Some of the mountain-paths, indeed, are enough to make the stoutest man reel. A path that affords breadth enough for the entire sole of the foot is considered amply large;

in general, the thorough bred mountaineer considers a path perfectly practicable, on which there is everywhere room for half his sole to rest upon.

The Gaisberg, on which I was now standing, is 4000 feet high, but, seen from Salzburg, has an insignificant look on account of the much greater elevation of many of the surrounding masses. On some of those mountains, rich Alpine meadows, fit for the grazing of cattle, are found at the height of 6000 feet. Some of these meadows are famed throughout the country. Thus the Kor Alp, on the borders of Carinthia, is celebrated for the beautiful herbage of its pastures, its magnificent situation, and the merry life which the Sennerins and the cows lead there. Notwithstanding its great elevation it has the advantage of being sheltered against the north winds by still higher mountains. There are many other mountains of which the pastures are highly prized; and in general it is found that the higher the meadow lies, the finer is its herbage, and the more strong and thriving is the herd that feeds upon it. The best herbage of all is said to fall to the share of the goats, who can climb where the cows cannot venture to follow, though Alpine cattle are tolerably skilful too in clambering where no cattle born and bred on level ground would have the least notion of venturing. Sometimes the Sennerin will climb herself where she would not venture to drive her cows. This is done to cut some favourite grass to throw before the creatures while she milks them, and many a poor girl has paid with her own life for her desire to minister to the gourmandise of her milk-yielding charges.

The nature of most animals appears to be modified after a long residence among the mountains. A dog, for instance, accustomed to live in the valley, is of no use among the rocks, where his tender feet begin to bleed almost as soon as he gets there. The oxen and cows, accustomed to a mountain life, will sometimes go with perfect security along paths where none but a practised mountaineer can follow them. Yet the people will tell you that a cow, though less liable to giddiness than a man, is not quite free from it, and will sometimes tremble all over, at particularly dangerous places. Sheep are the most helpless creatures of all, and are therefore seldom driven up to very high ground. It is even said that when a flock has been driven along a dangerous road, if the leading ram has fallen down a precipice, the sheep have all followed out of mere stupidity.

One thing that always struck me about the cattle of the Alps, was their remarkable gentleness and goodnature. An Alpine cow appears to have no notion of shyness, and though, of course, there are exceptions, yet, generally speaking, you may go up to any of the cattle among the mountains, and stroke and caress them without the least apprehension. I have often done so myself, and the creatures have generally left off grazing, and looked round at me with a most winning look of gentleness and satisfaction. Professor Schotkey, who knows the Alps well, goes still farther. " When the stranger," he says, " comes to a pasturage that is but rarely visited, the goodhumoured cattle will come up to him and caress him with such evident expressions of welcome and kindness, that one is tempted to fancy the pretty cow is some enchanted princess."

The character of animals is, in my opinion, always influenced and modified by the character of those under whose care they are placed. The fondness of the Sennerin for singing is not without its due impression on her cows, who learn to listen with pleasure to her song; the proof of this is, that many cows cannot be brought to stand still when milked, unless their mistress will sing to them.

In spring, when the time for going out to the mountains approaches, the cows manifest the utmost impatience to get out of their stables, and this increases when they hear the Sennerin preparing her implements, and trying the little bells which she contemplates hanging round their necks.

My guide led me down by a shorter though less convenient path than that by which we had ascended. At the foot of the mountain we parted ; he to return to his mountains, I to betake myself to the ancient city of Salzburg : and, as I had so long consorted with, and grown so fond of, my lowing friends among the Alps, I chose for my temporary residence in the old episcopal capital, a mansion which displayed, as its ensign, the image of a " golden ox."

SALZBURG.

I believe there is scarcely any part of Germany, that, during the first fifteen years of the present century, was as often taken to pieces and put together again, or passed through the hands of so many different masters, as the territory of Salzburg. Till 1802, it still belonged to an independent spiritual prince of the empire, who in that year resigned, and the country was given to the Archduke Ferdinand, as a compensation for his dukedom of Tuscany. The archduke reigned there till 1805, when Salzburg became a part of Austria, and continued so till 1809. Then a provisional French government was established there. In 1810 the country was incorporated with Bavaria, and in 1815 it was restored to Austria. The more we contemplate the fair, though uniform, days of these piping times of peace, the more strange does that rough period seem to us, when countries and nations were so unceremoniously shuffled up together, and dealt out first to one partner, and then to another.

The golden time of Salzburg, the time to which its aged inhabitants still look back with regret, was the time of its spiritual princes. The city prospered under the crozier, and the archbishops ruled their subjects with great mildness, all but the Protestants, who were driven out of the country. From 798 till 1802 did the archbishops bear sway in Salzburg, and during those thousand years, sixty-four princes occupied the spiritual throne. Among them we find the names of most of the princely houses of Germany.

The Archbishop of Salzburg is still one of the first ecclesiastics of the Austrian empire. I say " one of the first," because the Primate of Hungary, and the Archbishop of Ollmütz, are considered of equal rank. He is called Primate of Germany, (I wonder how many Germans there are who could name the Primate of Germany, if called on to do so,) and he is, moreover, *legatus natus* of the Apostolic See at Rome, and the spiritual head of all the mountains and valleys of the Eastern Alps. His suffragan bishops are those of Trient, Brixen, Gurk, Seckau, Leoben, and Levant.

If those, however, were golden days for the good people of Salzburg, I must say that I saw no symptom of their passing at present through the ordeal of an iron age. It may be inconvenient to them to have ceased to form a centre of government, and to be obliged to refer so many of their concerns to the superior authorities at Linz, but this is a misfortune that they share with many German cities that were formerly the capitals of principalities, and the residences of courts. For the sake of German unity, it were perhaps to be wished that similar complaints were more frequently heard in Germany than they are. With this exception, however, and always bearing in mind the constraint under which all those live in Austria, who occupy themselves with speculative researches, the Salzburgers appear to me to be a very happy little people. The constraint I have just alluded to is, indeed, said to be felt very sensibly here on the Bavarian frontier, where the censorship is much more severe than at Linz, while at Linz again it is far less indulgent than at Vienna. Many a play may be performed at Vienna, too, that would not for a moment be tolerated by the authorities of a remote provincial city. When I was at Salzburg fourteen years ago, the people still looked back with regret to the period when they had been under the Bavarian rule. Of this I discovered now no trace, and I rejoiced at the change. The Bavarian may have been an excellent government, but it is a bygone government for the Salzburgers, and the best thing that can happen to these is to find cause to love the government under which they are to live. God preserve the *status quo*, and teach princes and nations to become more and more reconciled to it!

It was at Salzburg, as most of my readers are probably aware, that Mozart was born. The house is still in existence where Mozart's parents occupied rooms on the third floor. The spot where his mother brought him into the world, and the place where his piano stood, are shown to the curious. The walls are said to have been covered at one time with his compositions, but of this there is now no trace, all the rooms having been freshly papered. I could not visit these rooms without a feeling of reverence. Hence it was that this brilliant genius departed at five years of age to astonish and delight the world, and to acquire a claim to the monument which, after an interval of nearly one hundred years, his native city is about to erect to his memory.

I went to see the place. The preparatory excavations have led to the discovery of some interesting Roman mosaics. No less than five of them had been completely cleared when I saw them, and two of these, by far the largest and the most beautiful, had been found lying one over the other. Between the two there had lain about a foot of earth, and as the lower pavement was found in excellent preservation, and of very beautiful design, it is difficult to imagine what could have induced the Roman architect to cover his floor with rubbish, and have a new one laid over it. The stones, used to form the design, are small pieces of marble of various colours. The principal figures are two combatants in three different positions. In the one compartment, they are just about to attack each other; in the centre, they are in the heat of battle; and in the third, one of them has just succumbed.

I watched with much interest the manner in which these fragile monuments of ancient art were displaced. The small pieces of marble had simply been pressed into a layer of clay, which lay immediately upon the ground. To displace this layer, the whole mosaic was divided into partitions, mostly of a square form, and generally about an ell in length and breadth. Those stones which fell immediately on the frontier lines, were carefully picked out and numbered, so that their proper places might easily be found again when the whole came to be readjusted. As soon as a square piece had by this means been isolated, a flat wooden frame was placed over it, and over the whole a quantity of plaster was poured, which soon hardened into a mass with the mosaic below. The square piece thus prepared was then detached from the ground with flat iron instruments, and, having been carefully turned over, received a coating of plaster below, corresponding with that which it had received above. The whole compact mass was then packed in a box, and put by, to remain till a suitable spot had been fixed on where the whole mosaic pavement might be put together again. I believe the process is the same as that used in Italy for the displacement and removal of large mosaics.

The fragments of marble of these Roman pavements, and many other pieces of marble large and small, that the Romans worked up in Juvavia, came from the celebrated quarries of Untersberg, which still contribute to the architectural decorations not only of Salzburg, but even of more distant cities, the Untersberg marbles being sometimes sent even to Hungary. The marble is generally of a light flesh colour, but some completely white is occasionally obtained. The Untersberg stands upon the border between Austria and Bavaria, the frontier line passing over the summit. The larger portion of the mountain stands in Bavaria, nevertheless several of the quarries on the Austrian side of the line are the private property of the king of Bavaria, who uses up a good deal of marble in the decoration of his capital. When I visited the hill, a block of marble had just been detached, six fathoms long, six broad, and three deep. The weight of this enormous mass was estimated at 22,000 cwt. The people fully expected to get this huge piece down without any accident, and when down in the plain they intended to saw it up into pieces of 300 to 400 cwt. Many pieces of this size were lying about at the entrance to the quarry, and were mostly destined for Munich. At the foot of the quarry I found a sawmill, where such pieces as were too large to remove, were reduced to a more convenient size.

What contrasts we often find side by side! After having admired the colossal mass of marble that had just been detached from the mountain in one quarry, my attention was called in another to a man who was collecting small fragments for the construction of a toy, the use of which is very generally diffused throughout the juvenile world—I mean those little marble balls, with which there are few boys in Germany who have not frequently amused their leisure.

This little article is apparently of trifling import, but it is destined for a very extensive public. Here in Salzburg these little balls are called *Schusser*. They are chiefly made at Salzburg, and at some of the quarries of Saxony, and find their way into all parts of the world, being sometimes even carried to India by way of ballast. The machinery by which the requisite rotundity is given to these popular little spheres is moved by a watermill. The owner of the mill collects the broken fragments of marble, which none but himself thinks worth carrying away. These are broken, as nearly as possible, into square cubes, that are then thrown into the mill, where, between cylinders of stone and wood, they are soon rubbed into a round form. The article is cheap enough here in Salzburg, where you may have thirty *Schussers* for one kreuzer, or less than an English halfpenny.

I had every reason to be satisfied with the choice I had made of the "Golden Ox" for my head-quarters at Salzburg, for I found there assembled every evening, a very agreeable circle, composed of amateurs of mountain excursions; men who seemed to be upon intimate terms with all parts of the Alps.

In every country, a traveller who wishes to learn any thing about the region he travels in, must cultivate native society, for there only can he ever hope to obtain information about the details of the country. There are some countries, of which the physiognomy is flat and uniform, and easily learned by heart. Not so with the Alps. There, every hill, every valley, every spot of ground has a character of its own, often a distinct climate, and a peculiar population. In one place we find the men chiefly occupied in tending the vine; elsewhere they are hunters, farmers, or manufacturers. The most striking contrasts are everywhere found side by side, and each valley, each hill, has so many details to be studied, that a stranger will never know half of them, without a frequent intercourse with the people.

The most north-easterly mountain of the Alps, towards Vienna, is called the Schneeberg (snow mountain); and a man who knew this mountain well, told me, he could point out twenty different paths up to the summit, of which each should present a distinct esthetic and scientific interest. Yet these, he added, were only the principal paths of the mountain, and a man who knew these must not suppose that he had made himself acquainted with the hill in detail. Now the Schneeberg is only one of many hundreds of summits that go to form the Alps, and, at this rate, it would take a man the life of a Methusalem, to make only the principal tours over each mountain. This may suffice to show the importance, in such a country, of cultivating the acquaintance of the natives.

A man well acquainted with the surrounding mountains may generally be found in every village. The mountains lie so close to them, that the men who live among them, whatever their occupation may be, cannot help acquiring an intimate knowledge of them. The herdsmen, hunters, woodcutters, and charcoal burners are continually up the mountains, and exploring their inmost recesses; but even the farmer who cultivates his fields in the plain has frequent occasion to go into the mountains, where he probably has his cattle out for the summer, or where he must provide a stock of wood for his winter wants.

The information which these people acquire about the mountains is often of the highest interest, but at the same time very difficult to get out of them. They have grown up amid these stupendous works of nature, and often what the stranger sees with awe and admiration, is to them so familiar, so hackneyed, that they feel almost ashamed of talking about it. They have never dreamed of instituting comparisons, or of forming any thing like comprehensive views; and therefore, though they may be consulted with perfect reliance respecting the objects immediately within their reach, the traveller must not content himself with their instructions if he would obtain a general knowledge of the country. This must be obtained from the more cultivated inhabitants; from men who have studied the Alps, and whom education had qualified for the study. Such men are to be met with everywhere among the Alps, if the traveller will take the trouble to find them out. I do not merely speak of such men as Saussure, who devoted his life to Mont Blanc; or as Agassiz and Hugi, who have sacrificed nearly all their time to an investigation of the glaciers; but in every little town there are men who take a delight in climbing up the hills, as botanists, zoologists, or geologists, in search of rare plants, curious insects, and new specimens of rock. Then there are philanthropists who come into the mountains to study the condition of the Cretins; and there are ethnologists who ramble about to discover in some sequestered nook, a remnant of one or other of the various races that have overrun Europe in turn, and have most of them left little specimens of themselves among the Alps. In one valley may thus be discovered a population evidently of Slavonian descent, with coal black hair, and in the adjoining valley a blue-eyed and light-haired race, the descendants probably of some Saxon or Celtic tribe. Lastly come a very numerous class, who love to climb the mountains for the mere pleasure of overcoming difficulties; men whose great pleasure it is to discover new places, and to reach summits never before trodden by mortal foot. Such virgin mountains are still numerous among the Alps. The Hohe Venediger, in the Pinzgau, a mountain 9000 feet high, was ascended for the first time a few years ago. The summit tapers to so fine a point, that there is said to be scarcely room at the top for more than three people to stand upon it. The first man that succeeded in getting to the top was seized with such giddiness that he did not remain there more than two minutes, and was obliged to creep down upon his belly.

Another class that must not be forgotten here, is composed of the landscape painters of Munich, who seldom fail to spend a part of the summer among the Bavarian highlands, or among the Alps of the Tyrol and Styria, and return with sketch-books full of cattle-groups, chalets, glaciers, waterfalls, and forest scenes, to be worked up or filled out during the autumn and winter. These artists the stranger should visit in their painting-rooms, or listen to them at their evening meetings, talking of their adventures among the hunters, poachers, and sennerins. A man may obtain many an useful hint from such conversations.

These mountain-exploring painters, these impassioned climbers of the Alps, are a race of modern growth, for there was a time when we knew more in Europe of the Andes than we did of the Alps. The Romans never appear to have had any taste for such investigations, and the gloomy forest-covered mountains of those times were less inviting than the pastoral scenes which we now find there, than the smiling cultivation which now greets us in every valley. When Saussure, Bourit, and Bonstetten travelled into the Alps, they may be said to have gone upon voyages of discovery.

It is now no longer so. Valuable observations have been collected. The periodicals of Austria, Styria, and Carinthia, have accumulated an immense mass of varied details respecting their several mountains. The military maps executed for the Austrian and Bavarian governments are masterpieces in their kind, and will certainly not soon be excelled. The writings of Leopold von Buch, von Schultes, Haquet, Kochsternfeld, Hormayr, and of various others, have thrown light upon many points that were formerly obscure. Our German painters have furnished an abundance of excellent pictures, and some of our writers of fiction, as Zschokke and Schotky, have painted pictures quite as attractive, in their pretty tales illustrative of Alpine life. Still, all that *has* been done, is little compared to what *remains* to be done. No one yet has done justice to the Alps, and colossal though the labour would be, I cannot help wondering that no one has yet undertaken a comprehensive work on the subject. The man even who added no fresh materials to the stock of information already collected, but simply brought that information into a comprehensive and convenient form, would deserve the thanks of his fellow-men, if he performed the task successfully.

FAREWELL TO AUSTRIA.

The month of October still continued to vouchsafe us bright and cheerful days, so I determined to proceed leisurely on towards Munich, and to linger among the mountains on my way. A man seldom flirts or coquets with the Alps without falling in love with them, and after that he finds it no easy thing to tear himself away from them. I found a gentleman at Salzburg of congenial taste, who, like myself, wished once more to have a nearer look at the Bavarian highlands than could be obtained from the Gaisberg, even with the assistance of the best telescope; so, one fine October morning we packed our little travelling encumbrances into the carriage of a Salzburg driver, who maintained that he was familiar with every road and byway in the mountains, and thus prepared we rattled gaily along the valley of the Achen towards the Austrian frontier, which we were able to reach in two short hours.

We crossed the border without any difficulty. Our horses thrust their ears into the atmosphere of Bavaria; their legs trotted after, as if of their own accord; our coachman enthroned upon his box, was not long in following; and in due course, we two, seated as we were in the after part of the carriage, rolled majestically into another kingdom, and found ourselves safely landed within the territory of the German Zollverein.

BUKOVINA.*

THIS pretty and pleasant little district, which is twenty-four (German) miles in its greatest length, fifteen in its greatest breadth, and which contains about one hundred and eighty (German) square miles, lies at the Northern extremity of that great tract of country inhabited by the Walachians, which stretches itself southward one hundred and fifty miles, crossing the Danube, and terminating in the Greek peninsula. Like all frontier countries, it has often changed its masters during the political storms and convulsions which have agitated these now peaceful regions, and has been frequently conquered by the Poles, and reconquered by the Moldavians. Bukovina, however, belonged mostly to the latter, for not only is the principal population Moldavian, which it has probably been from the remotest ages, the names of all the mountains and rivers in the country, being, with few exceptions, Moldavian, but both the physical circumstances and social condition of the country, are the same as in the rest of Moldavia. In Bukovina as in Moldavia, the peasant labours for his lord twelve days out of the year, according to the laws laid down in the *Ghika Chryson;* here as there, an autumn day's work is decreed for the threshing of sixty *Mandeln* of corn, each *Mandel* containing fifteen sheaves, and each sheaf so thick that a man can scarcely span it; and here as there the spring and summer day's work is fixed in a similar manner. Here as there, the lords are always trying to enlarge the number of serving days, and to increase the thickness of the sheaves of corn.

The family names of the noblemen of Bukovina, are the same as in Moldavia and Walachia: they are pure old Walachian names of the most ancient origin, or else Greek names dating from the days of the Byzantine emperors. These families have been Hellenized for many generations, and the nobles generally converse with each other in the Greek

---

* The concluding part of the present work, comprising a tour through Bukovina, Galicia, and Moravia, formed originally a portion, not of Mr. Kohl's work on Austria, but of his "Travels through the Interior of Russia." In collecting and condensing that gentleman's volumes on Russia, that portion which referred to Galicia and Moravia was naturally omitted, not on account of any deficiency of interest in the subject, but because it was thought that a description of Austrian provinces would have been out of its place in a work professing to treat only of Russia. We have much satisfaction in availing ourselves of the present opportunity to atone for our former omission.

language. The influence of Vienna has at last begun to Germanize the[m] a little; they learn French and German, call themselves *Baron* and *Gr[af]* and dress in the German fashion. Many of these noble families, t[he] *Mikultshas* for example, have estates in Moldavia, in Bessarabia, and Bukovina, at the same time, and are thus subject to three emperors [at] once.

It is characteristic of the geographical position of this country, that [its] present name, Bukovina, which signifies Beech-forest, arose out of [the] battles between the Poles and the Moldavians. "Towards the end of [the] fifteenth century, in the days of the Polish king Albrecht," says K[an]temir, the well known historian of Moldavia, "there was here [a] great open plain lying along the Pruth. When the Poles pitched th[eir] tents here with a great army, Stephen the Great, prince of Molda[via] attacked and beat them, took their camp, put the Poles to flight, kil[led] the greater part of them, and took twenty thousand prisoners, who we[re] principally nobles. When the king of Poland afterwards offered a lar[ge] sum for their ransom, Stephen refused to take it, being anxious to er[ect] such a monument of his triumph as would commemorate it in futu[re] centuries. He therefore harnessed the whole of the twenty thousa[nd] nobles and serfs alike to ploughs, and made them plough the wh[ole] field of battle, and sow it with the seeds of the beech-tree. These seed[s] grew up in time to a beautiful and extensive forest, which the Poles hav[e] named Bukovina, and of which they never speak but with tears." This battle-field, and the *Dumbrevile roshe* or Bloody Beech-forest (as the Moldavians named it) which has risen upon it, lies on the strip of land between the Pruth and the Dniester, near Chotim and Tshernovitze; and the remains of numerous ditches, trenches and fortifications still bear witness to the many battles between the Turks, Poles, Hungarians, Moldavians, Russians, and Tartars, of which these beautiful frontier plains have been the scene.

A part of Bukovina on the northern side of the Pruth, has become Russian, but the rest has been Austrian ever since 1775. That upon the whole, the country has improved under a German government, cannot be doubted, when we contemplate among other signs of prosperity, the extraordinary increase of its population. According to a census taken not long after the country became subject to Austria, namely in the year 1788, the inhabitants were only one hundred and twenty thousand, whereas in 1838 the number amounted to two hundred and eighty thousand. During a space of fifty years, therefore, the population has nearly trebled, a circumstance which could not be paralleled either in Russian or Turkish Moldavia. This extraordinary increase in the population may be partly owing to the influx of German emigrants, who have settled in the cities as merchants and mechanics, and of the Rusniaks, who are preferred to the native Moldayians as labourers; but certainly it is more to be attributed to the better political order which the Austrian government has introduced into all classes of society, and particularly to the improvement in the condition of the lower classes, whose cause the imperial government has energetically taken up, and who have increased and flourished under the shadow of Austrian justice. The loss of several of the nobility, who, displeased with the new order of things, have preferred quitting Bukovina for Turkish Moldavia, where their noble relatives still rule with undiminished splendour, has not been felt to be any very serious calamity.

The inhabitants of Bukovina are, as has been said, principally Moldavians and Dako-Romans,* and foreign elements are mingled as in the rest of Moldavia. The Armenians form about a hundredth part of the inhabitants of the cities, and are merchants, innkeepers, &c.; the Jews, about a tenth part of the town population, are brokers, mechanics, &c. Among the other elements of population in Bukovina, are the Germans, who are settled in the towns as mechanics and officers (Tshernovitze indeed, the capital, is almost entirely German), a few Magyar settlements on the Transylvanian frontiers, some Russian colonies founded on the Pruth by emigrants exiled on account of religious opinions, and finally a Slavonian race of mountaineers called "*Huzzulen*," settled among those mountains whose highest points belong not to Bukovina but to Transylvania, and who are different in all respects from the Walachian population. The name "*Huzzulen*" is probably only used in Bukovina and Moldavia. It is derived from the old Dacian word "*Huzz*," which signifies robber, and may therefore originally, like many other names of nations, have rather been used as a *Nomen Appellativum* than as a *Nomen proprium*. The *Huzzulen* inhabit the southern part of the Carpathian mountains. They live principally by rearing cattle. They burn charcoal, fell wood, and make all kinds of wooden wares, which they convey on one side down the Dniester, Pruth, Sereth, and Moldava, into the plains of Moldavia and Bessarabia, on the other side down the Theiss, Samos, and Bistriza, into Hungary and Transylvania. These mountaineers are easily to be recognised throughout Bukovina by their more ample clothing, their firm gait, and the formidable hatchets always slung to their girdles, which they could as little dispense with as their right arms.

The fertility of Bukovina is famed throughout all the neighbouring countries. The Galicians always speak of it as a Land of Promise, and the Austrians regard the turkeys and capons of Bukovina, which are fattened on Turkish maize, as the greatest delicacies of the kind known throughout the Austrian empire. The soil yields twelvefold for all that is sown, the pastures in the valleys are extremely rich and fine, nay, the very clouds of heaven rain *honey* and *butter* in this land of abundance, at least so say the Prince Kantemir and the historian Sulzer. Sulzer says—" Often in summer time, clear honey rains down from heaven, which the inhabitants erroneously call manna." Prince Kantemir remarks of the butter rain, which he naturally terms "an extraordinary spectacle," "Before sunrise there falls a dew upon the leaves and flowers in the mountains of Bukovina, which the inhabitants collect in vessels; after a time they find floating at the top of the water the most beautiful butter, which differs from common butter neither in taste, smell, nor colour. This butter contains so much nourishment, that if the sheep were driven to the pastures at the time of this butter dew, they would in a few days become so fat that they would die of suffocation; so that the shepherds keep their sheep at the foot of the mountains during the months in which it is most abundant." Even fables generally contain some shadow of truth, as the most tasteless fruit contains a kernel, and so we may take the Prince Kantemir's account as testifying to the nourishing qualities of the Bukovinian pastures; that in the wilder parts of Bukovina buffaloes are still sometimes found, is probably a fable. Bears, however, are plentiful in the moun-

---

* They call themselves Rumanyos (Romans), and the Italians call them Romani.

tains, while wolves seem to be more abundant in the plains. It cannot be of much use for the Austrian government to set prices on the heads of these animals, as long as it takes no measures against the continual inroads of wild beasts from Poland, Russia, and Turkey. The *Huzzulen* are said to be very bold bear hunters; they generally attack these creatures armed only with their hatchets, and sometimes, it is said, they will even rush at a bear with their arms merely wrapped up in cloths, which they thrust down the animal's throat, and so choke him. The *Huzzulen*, like the Walachians, are skilful bear tamers (*ursaren* in their own language, from the Latin *ursus*); the credible Sulzer gives an account of a festival which a Walachian prince once gave in honour of his sister-in-law, at which forty bears danced a ballet, accompanied by the tambourines, drums, and songs of their teachers.

Of the tame animals of the country, the pigs are numerous and excellent. Every house in Bukovina is surrounded with these dirty but delicate grunters, and every village swarms with them. They are indeed plentiful enough in all the neighbouring countries, particularly in Russia; but they prosper and fatten so amongst the oaks and beeches of Bukovina, that they are numberless as the sands of the sea, and are continually on the increase. Turkeys are also extremely numerous and excellent throughout Bukovina, Moldavia, and Bessarabia, almost every peasant possessing herds of them. They are to be seen also in Bessarabia, but in Russia and Poland it is only the nobles who possess them. They are common domestic animals throughout all the countries subject to the Turkish sceptre.

Bukovina has, properly speaking, only three towns: Tshernovitze, Sereth, and Sutshava; therefore only one town to sixty square miles, all the rest being mere villages. These villages have undergone little change, and both the peasants and their dwellings resemble exactly those of other Moldavian villages, but it is otherwise with the solitary country-houses of the nobles, and with the larger towns. The latter have been quite Germanized, both in outward appearance, and in internal organization, under the Austrian rule, so as to bear some resemblance to the smaller towns of Germany, while those Moldavian towns, which have remained in the Russian territory, still preserve their Turko-Moldavian character, and have lost none of their Oriental features. Of the three towns of Bukovina, Tshernovitze, Sereth, and Sutshava, one lies in each of the principal divisions of the country; Tshernovitze on the Pruth, Sereth on the Sereth, and Sutshava on the Sutshava.

According to Prince Kantemir, the old capital Sutshava once contained not less than 16,000 houses. At present it is an unimportant place. Tschernovitze, now the capital, is the largest and most populous town in Bukovina, containing about 15,000 inhabitants. It has attained this importance entirely under the Austrian rule, for Sulzer mentions nothing remarkable about the place, except that it contained two very beautiful Jewesses. Tshernovitze is its Slavonian name, but the Moldavians call it "*Tshernauz.*" The town lies on the right bank of the Pruth, and is built in the style of the old German cities, with long narrow streets, high pointed houses, and still higher churches and steeples; and seen at a distance from the plains of the Pruth, it has a stately and imposing appearance. The Moldavian huts and cabins have disappeared from around it, and the whole is built of stone. Good roads and avenues of poplars and linden trees lead to the pretty and cheerful houses which form the suburbs.

Coming from the valleys of Bessarabia, and the shapeless, disorderly towns of Podolia, the sight of this handsome and pleasant town seemed to us a glimpse into another world, and so it certainly was. The crossing of the frontier line between the Russian and Austrian territories, seemed at once to have brought us sóme hundreds of versts nearer to Germany, Vienna, Berlin, nay, even to Paris, Spain, and Italy. At the sight of Tshernovitze, the whole west of Europe seemed before our eyes, and we fancied ourselves close to Vienna, the Alps, and Italy; for large as the Austrian dominions appear compared to the other German states, they seem small enough to one coming from the immense Russian empire, which appears to stretch out boundlessly around the traveller, on every side. After being accustomed to reckon by thousands of versts, a hundred miles seems nothing.

But we had to struggle through many difficulties on the Austrian frontier, before we could freely give ourselves up to these agreeable ideas. Austria is very suspicious and inhospitable to all travellers entering Bukovina from the Russian side. Her ambassadors and consuls are very sparing of their visas to Austria, and give them only to those particularly recommended to them. The recommendation of the Russian authorities alone is not sufficient, and if the traveller has not the visa of the consul-general, his passport is sent to Lemberg or Vienna, and he must wait a week or two, imprisoned within the Russian frontier line, before the gates of the Austrian Paradise are opened to him. The boundaries of Bukovina are surrounded with a threefold Cordon, and we were obliged to pass through so many offices, custom-houses, and inspection-houses, that I could not number all the stamps, seals, marks, and signatures which were put on our luggage. But the worst of all was, that all our books and papers were sent to the *Hofrath* at Tshernovitze, who, instead of returning them, sent them to the authorities at Lemberg, who, serving us in the same way, sent them finally to the higher authorities at Vienna.

On these frontiers we were incessantly obliged to ransom ourselves from further importunity, with *Zwanzigern*. " Sir, you have still two cigars and a half there." " Hold your tongue, and here's a Zwanziger for you!" —" What papers are those? They must go with the rest." " Never mind, here are a couple of Zwanziger."—" And these boxes, have they been searched?" " Yes, take these three Zwanziger." What can the Russians think of the good old German honesty and truth, of which they are so fond of talking, when they contemplate these frontiers? Yet all the officers at the boundary line are Germans.

Every thing, however, has its end, and so had the search on the Austrian frontier. We rolled quickly and joyfully over the stone bridge of the Pruth, which is kept in order alternately by the Emperors of Russia and Austria, into the luxuriant meadows and forests of Bukovina, and into the city of Tshernovitze, the residence of the redoubtable *Hofrath*. The *Hofrath* is here, in fact, the governor of the province. In Russia a Hofrath would hardly be allowed the care of a village; but here no one named the Hofrath but with the greatest respect. The Hofrath had done this—the Hofrath had ordered that—were sounds that met us on every side. The nobles have generally many matters to settle with the Hofrath, for the Austrian government wisely sides with the unprivileged classes against the nobles.

We found the town busy, cheerful, and lively. Little as the rest of Europe knows of Tshernovitze, yet the little place enjoys a great reputation, far and wide around, for excellent wares, good cakes, and merry festivals, and whenever the Russian public officers of Chotim, Kamenyez, and other neighbouring villages, wish to enjoy themselves for a little while, they get leave of absence, and come to Tshernovitze for a few days, to drink the good wines of Hungary, and buy pretty trinkets for their wives. Nowhere are Russian and German life brought into such close neighbourhood, and such striking contrast with one another, as here. The town seemed to us like a suburb of Vienna, though one hundred and fifty miles from that city. All the shops were filled with Vienna wares, and large gaudy inscriptions on the houses invited the passer-by to enter and purchase the wines, the trinkets, the cakes, and other goods within. Though it was not market-day, the streets were full of *Huzzulen*, who had descended from the mountains to make their purchases, and sell their wares.

The inns were full of life and bustle. There was a long table d'hôtel, at which Germans, Hungarians, Poles, Armenians, Jews, and Walachians, mingled together ; there were billiard-tables, musicians, and waiters with white aprons—nay, even two pretty Vienna chambermaids—things to which we had long been strangers. As we entered our hotel, the smell of roast-meat met us from the kitchen, and made us sensible that we had again entered the land "where it is always Sunday, and the roasting-jack twirls for ever." It is astonishing how the festive character and light-hearted gaiety of the Vienna people are diffused throughout the countries o'ershadowed by the Austrian eagle—every province partakes of them.

"*Bassa manelka ! Teremtata !*" and other unintelligible maledictions from an Hungarian nobleman, saluted us as we seated ourselves at the table to despatch one of those excellent capons, whose delicacy and fine flavour are so peculiar to Austria, and which are nowhere else to be tasted in full perfection. " Gentlemen, I am the noble von Hagymas Pentek !" cried our Hungarian, who was already several degrees removed from sobriety ; and who then went on, in tolerably good German, with his opinions upon roasted capons, religious differences, and the blacksmiths of Tshernovitze, who were accustomed to shoe his horses, when he made his annual journey from Transylvania, over " those horrid mountains." Hungarian wine and smuggled Hungarian tobacco, are the principal articles of trade between Bukovina and Hungary ; but many others are brought over the Carpathian mountains. Galician plums and Hungarian leather, Galician tallow and Hungarian hemp, Galician honey and Hungarian hops, Galician salt and Hungarian gold and silver, are all so many links which bind together the two countries. Still they are more united by the tie of a common population. Not only do the Bukovinian Walachians, and Galician Rusnaks, extend far into Transylvania and Hungary, but the Hungarian Slovaks stretch on their side into Galicia, and many Magyar colonies are established in Bukovina. In this manner the interests of the two countries are bound together in many ways, and there is a strong sympathy between them.

Our evening companions interested us far more than our dinner society. They were two well-educated young Moldavians in the Austrian service, and were enthusiastic patriots. They told us many stories and legends of the golden age of their country, of the Moldavian, or as they said " Dako Roman" mythology, and of Stephen the Great, and other heroes of Moldavia. We had never before seen Moldavian patriots ; and like many other ignorant people, we did not even know there was such an article as Moldavian patriotism. To our surprise we now encountered it everywhere, and met many people even in Lemberg, glowing with tender enthusiasm for the great days of the Dacian Empire, under Decebalus the Great. Dacia is now surrounded with mighty and powerful neighbours, which do not permit its nationality to obtain a free voice. The country has been torn up and partitioned quite as much as Poland, but it obtains less general sympathy, because its situation is not generally known, and yet the Moldavians, Walachians, Bessarabians, and Bukovinians are men—nay more, they are countrymen, fellow-citizens, and patriots.

To read or import into Austria, the journals published in Moldavia and Walachia, is strictly prohibited by law.

GALICIA.

FROM TSHERNOVITZE TO LEMBERG.

DURING the sixty years they have ruled over Galicia, the Austrians have supplied it with many excellent roads; and this is not the least important of the benefits which the Poles have received from the Germans. The course of these roads is directed by the course of the Carpathian mountains. Galicia is an oval, or rather a crescent-shaped country, with its straight side resting on its firm mountain-wall. The rude character of these mountains, makes this side less passable and habitable, and the population increases in density, the further we recede from the Carpathians. The mountains themselves contain only solitary huts and a few small hamlets. Where the valleys widen, small towns and villages make their appearance, and at the foot of the mountains, lies a line of larger towns, connected by the great road parallel to the Carpathians. This great artery of Galician life and commerce begins at Sutshava, the furthest town of Bukovina, where the wild untraversed Moldavia touches on Austria, follows the Carpathians northward to Tshernovitze, passes through Kalomea in the valley of the Pruth, and then through Stanislavov, in the valley of the Dniester, crosses Lemberg, the central point of Galicia, and then bends round like the Carpathians, and passes through Cracow towards Moravia and Vienna. On this road lie the principal market-towns of the country, and not only the goods which the nineteen circles of Galicia exchange with each other, but also those which Moldavia sends to Austria, the cattle which the inhabitants of the steppes send to the markets of Brunn and Olmütz, the carts of fancy wares which Vienna manufactures for Russia, the furs and the tea which the inhabitants of Kiev send to the west, the Moravian-Silesian manufactures which the Jews of Brody smuggle into the Russian empire, —all these are conveyed to and fro on this road, which is of the greatest importance to the commerce between the two mighty empires, and particularly to the intercourse between the cities of Vienna, Odessa, Lemberg, Prague, Cracow, Kiev, and Moscow. It is the more frequented because it is the only great road within a considerable distance. It is one hundred and thirty (German) miles long. Smaller roads run from place to place, parallel with it, but none of these are of any considerable length.

There are besides, three principal roads which intersect the country in a transversal direction, cutting through the Carpathians; one at the eastern end running from Bukovina to Transylvania, one at the western end from Cracow to Hungary, and one in the middle from Lemberg to Hungary. The Carpathian mountains offer one great facility for road making, by their quantity of mountain streams, which are so useful for conveying the materials required into the plains. In Northern Poland, the sea has assisted the work, by scattering over the plains fragments of rock and masses of stone, but the eastern part of Russian Poland is without any such advantage.

As the bad roads of Russia had damaged our *kalesch* so much that a fundamental repair was necessary, we were obliged to part with it in Bukovina, that it might be sent back to its native country. We had now the choice between the Lemberg diligence, which goes only once a week, and had set off the day before, the Galician extra-post which is but a very inconvenient and disagreeable vehicle, and a Jewish hackney-coachman, whom we eventually decided upon choosing. His coach was covered, had three horses, was so large that we might have lived in it with all our families, and was driven by a Rusniak enveloped from head to foot in black sheep-skin. These people always drive quicker than German coachmen, though not quite *à la Russe*, and with our Rusniak *matvei*, we daily travelled from twelve to thirteen (German) miles. This kind of conveyance is certainly not very elegant, but it is large and convenient. The vehicles are called in German "*brodyer bauten*," and in Rusniak "*budas.*"

As we had plenty of room inside, we took up tired pedestrians, for a lift, every now and then, and thus had the advantage of learning much of the condition of the country, from the lips of the people themselves.

Our travelling companions of the first day were three Walachian noblemen, from Bukovina, stout gentlemen, with long thick beards, who sat, wrapt in thick furs, in an uncovered droshky, and were driving to Vienna to make complaints against the *Hofrath* of Bukovina, in the name of some nobles who had been offended by him. They spoke tolerably good Vienna German, and were obliging and friendly towards us.

The kingdom of Galicia with its dependencies, Lodomiria and Bukovina, may be divided into four principal parts, through each of which flows a large river. These four rivers are the Pruth, the Dniester, the Bug, and the Vistula. The district of the Pruth contains about two hundred square (German) miles, with 300,000 inhabitants; the district of the Dniester, six hundred and ten square miles, and 1,800,000 inhabitants; that of the Bug one hundred and ninety square miles, and about 450,000 inhabitants; and that of the Vistula, six hundred and sixty square miles, and 1,900,000 inhabitants. The population of the country groups itself in masses round the rivers, as is generally the case.

The district of the Pruth is all but entirely occupied by the Moldavians or Walachians; the Rusniaks have taken possession of the Dniester, and all its tributary rivers; and the lands of the Bug and Vistula are occupied by the Poles. The proportions of the different elements of the population in Galicia, are about as follows:

Walachians or Moldavians	300,000
Rusniaks or *Ruthenen*	1,800,000
Poles or *Masuren*	2,300,000
Total .	4,400,000

It is among the heights of the Carpathians, that these races offer the most striking contrasts to one another; for those who are settled among the solitary mountains differ strikingly from the inhabitants of the valleys and plains. The Huzzulen of the Black Mountains differ greatly from the Walachians, the Goralen of the central Carpathians from the Rusniaks, and the Slovaks of the Western Mountains from the Poles. The Rusniaks inhabit that part of Galicia which gave the whole country its name, the old Russian Grand Duchy of Halitsh, which was, for some time, united with the Grand Duchy of Kiev, afterwards flourished as an independent kingdom, and was then conquered by the Poles in the fourteenth century. These Rusniaks are a small Russian race, related to the Cossacks and Malorossians, as the Bavarians are to the Saxons. Though they call themselves Rusniaks, I was told, by an intelligent and well-educated man among them, that it was considered more accurate and refined to call them *Ruthenen* or *Russinen*. The Hungarians call them "*Orashoks*," as they do all the Russians. Their total number in Galicia is nearly two millions. A smaller mass of 400,000 Rusniaks has spread into Hungary across the Carpathians.

Their language differs much from that of Great Russia, and yet with our Moscovite Russian we could make ourselves understood. The inhabitants of Little Russia are perfectly understood by the Galician Rusniaks, yet many things about them, their costume for instance, prove there is a great difference between the two races.

The Rusniaks, like other Malorossian races, are wanting in that agreeable and obliging manner towards strangers, which distinguishes the Great Russians. They appear unfriendly, cold, and reserved towards those whom they see for the first time. It may be that the long pressure of the Polish yoke has operated disadvantageously on the development of their character. In the mountains, they are said to have preserved their ancient manners in greater purity. Robbery and murder are very rare among them, and the statistics of the Austrian criminal courts prove that crimes are as uncommon among the Rusniaks of the east, as they are plentiful at the opposite end of the empire, among the Italians of the west.

Some races among the mountains are said still to preserve a purely patriarchal state of society, a family remaining as long as possible under one roof—sons, daughters, nieces, nephews, grandchildren, and great grandchildren, all living together under the dominion of the patriarch head of the family.

Like the inhabitants of Little Russia, the Rusniaks live better and are more cleanly than the Poles. Their tables also are more abundantly supplied; in this particular, the lower classes of Galicia retrograde as we go from east to west. The inhabitants of Bukovina live best, the *Masuren* worst, and the Rusniaks are between the two. Here bread, soup, meat, fish, and cakes, are all Russian, both in taste, appearance, and mixture. Brandy is as much in request as among the Russians, and drunkenness very common, as is always the case in those regions of ice and snow, where the poor frozen serf flies eagerly for refuge from the cold, to the deleterious "*fire-water*."

The Rusniak peasant, like those of Little Russia, makes all his furniture and household utensils himself: he is his own architect, carpenter, coachmaker, and shoemaker. He is generally very frugal and careful (except where brandy is in question), and in every Rusniak household will be found a little box, to which the master of the house alone has a key, where he deposits his savings, often a considerable sum, with whose amount, however, not even his wife or children are acquainted.

Formerly all the inhabitants of this country,—nobles, priests, princes, and peasants,—were all Rusniaks. Many noble families even now claim descent from the princes of Halitsh, as Galicia was formerly called. The Poles have Polonized the country during their four hundred years of dominion over it; but it is only with the nobles that they have completely succeeded. The old Galician families of Potocki, Jablonowski, Dieduskicki, Skarbeck, &c., were originally Russian; but by intermarriage with Polish families, by continual intercourse with Polish grandees, and by sharing their privileges, rights, and constitution, they have become so assimilated to the Polish nobility, in language, manners, and customs, and finally by their adoption of the Catholic religion, that they are no longer to be distinguished as belonging to a separate race. The great Rusniak nobility, therefore, has lost all its Russian character, and become completely Polish. It is different with the petty nobles, the *Schlachtitzen*, who stand nearer to the people, and with the people themselves, that is the peasantry. The Poles who did not, like the Germans, encourage the education and civilization of the people, had not means enough to assimilate the lower classes of Galicia to their own. The Rusniak peasant clings with warm attachment to his old habits, and unlike the Poles, Magyars, Slovaks, and other neighbouring nations, seldom intermarries with foreigners; above all things he avoids connexion with the Poles, whom he hates and despises as much as the Russians do. The peasants, the *Schlachtitzen*, and the clergy, have remained completely Rusniak here, in dress, language, and habits. The Rusniaks, immediately after the introduction of Christianity among them, adopted the Greek religion, in common with all the Russian nations, under Wladimir the Great. Under the Polish dominion, they clung constantly to this their chosen religion. The utmost which the endeavours of the Poles could accomplish (even in the last days of the republic, when they were most energetic and successful) with the assistance of the jesuits, was a union of the Catholic church with the Greek-Rusniak church; *i. e.* an acknowledgment of the supremacy of the pope, all the practices and privileges of the old Greek-Rusniak church being preserved unaltered. This union took place about one hundred and forty years ago, with the consent of the reigning Metropolitan: "a traitor, a bad man, the betrayer of his church he was," said a Rusniak priest, with whom I once conversed on the subject.

The work of union proceeded, although very slowly, on account of the aversion of the people to Polish Catholicism. The uniting Metropolitan was succeeded by others who refused to unite, and the people repeatedly protested against it. The present Metropolitan is only the fifth who has consented to the union. In this way the work of union proceeded but slowly, though its progress continued under the Austrian sceptre. Many congregations, in particular that of a very wealthy church in Lemberg, founded by some Walachian nobles, resisted for a very long time, and have only very lately united themselves with the Catholic church. Some have not yet yielded. Catholicism is at the same time advancing and retrograding among the Russo-Slavonic races; for whilst Austria is uniting churches with Rome in the south, Russia is attacking her in the north. While Catholicism advances from the west towards the east, the Greek church proceeds from the east towards the west. The two millions of

Rusniaks subject to Austria, have long kept their eyes fixed on the occurrences of the east. They feel an unconquerable hatred to their beardless priests of the union, and will stretch a friendly hand to the Russian Greeks, when they advance towards them, were it only that the venerable old beard might again grow on the chins of their priests. It was a great mistake in Austria to seize the sovereignty over so many Rusniak Poles. The sympathy towards Russia is as deep-rooted as the antipathy felt towards that country by the Poles. The clergy of the united Greek church in Galicia, is entirely Rusniak; the Polish tendencies of the nobility have had no influence upon them. As is universally the case in the Greek church and throughout Russia, the Rusniak nobles have never sought admission into the church; on the contrary, the priests have invariably risen from among the people. In the Polish Catholic church, the heads of the clergy are all the scions of noble families; whereas the supreme head of the Rusniak Greek church, the Metropolitan himself, is generally the son of a peasant. In the same manner and in the same degree as the Poles succeeded in Polonizing Galicia, they assimilated to themselves various other parts of that vast tract of country lying between the Baltic and the Pontus, which had fallen to their share in the prosperous days of the republic. Everywhere they made the Lithuanian and Russian nobility completely Polish, by placing them on an equal footing with their own, and giving them a share in all the rights and privileges of native Polish noblemen; but everywhere, beneath this Polish surface, the people, with whom the Poles used no such assimilating means, remained untouched and unchanged in manners, customs, language, and ideas. Polonization, however, succeeded best with the Lithuanians, the race least related to the Poles, for the Lithuanian clergy became Roman Catholic; it succeeded least with the Russians and Rusniaks, whose Greek clergy offered a permanent and effectual opposition.

Still less did the Cossacks become Polonized, who were never thoroughly subjected to the Poles; and the influence of the latter upon the German provinces of the Baltic, Prussia, Courland, and Livonia, was very slight. In those countries, Lutheranism and German nationality were preserved in all their purity. It is interesting to observe how, during the events of later years, the sympathy for the misfortunes and degradations of Poland has been awakened in these different countries, in precise proportion to the Polonization of each. In the last insurrection of Poland against Russia, for instance, Lithuania immediately rose with her; the half Polish Podolia and Kiev murmured, and conspired, and designed, but never came to open rebellion. Polish-Rusniak Galicia sighed and applauded, and lent the assistance of pecuniary contribution, and silent prayers. The Baltic provinces were indifferent and inactive; though Courland contained more friends to the Poles than Livonia, where the traces of their old dominion were quite effaced. The Cossacks willingly aided the Russians with their pikes, in the subjection of the Poles, to whom they had often lent a forced and unwilling help.

SNIATYN AND STANISLAVOV.

We arrived late in the evening at Sniatyn, the first town in the land of the Rusniaks, where we drove up to a Jewish hotel. We found a beetroot-sugar manufactory at this place, and learnt that these manufactories are numerous in the district and pay well. We here drank a "*Seidel*" of Hungarian wine, and as we found it very refreshing, we took a "*Pfiff*" in addition. *Seidel* is the Austrian word for measure, and *Pfiff* for glass. Hungary supplies her neighbours so well with all kinds of good and bad wine, that we appeared to be in a land of grapes and sunshine, instead of ice and snow. In Southern Galicia, however, we had, sometimes, to drink sour Moldavian wines.

Upon the table in the inn lay a piece of paper, on which some fair Polish hand appeared to have been trying her pen. Such pieces of paper have often a value and interest in the eyes of a traveller, as unconstrained manifestations of the national mind. There was the name of the writer, written two or three times over—Elizbieta Visnievska. Then came *Yasnie* (Most Illustrious) twice over, and finally the connected words "*Povinszovanie dla Yasnie Velmoznei Pani naszei Matki—*" (Humblest representation to our illustrious and powerful lord Matki—) the name was unfinished. The fragment, however, was sufficient to open to us a long perspective into the feelings and ideas of the people, whose fears, hopes, and cares centre so exclusively in their illustrious and powerful lords, that even in trying their pens, their lord's name is the one which occurs to them. Coming from the south, Sniatyn is the first town which, soul and body, from the houses and steeples down to the dogs and cats, is the property of one nobleman.

In the evening we had badly baked *Kulatshi* with our tea, an odd kind of cake, common throughout Rusniak Galicia. The soft dough is first drawn out to a long pliable string, and then twisted into the shape of a crown of thorns, and so put into the oven. The inhabitants of Little Russia make a similar cake, which they call *Kulitschi*, but the *Kalatchi* of the Great Russians is differently shaped. This night in bed we recognized an old northern acquaintance, in the *Tarakanen*, a disgusting, great, long-legged insect, common among the Lettes, Esthonians, Great Russians, and Poles, but never seen among the Little Russians. They are here called *Tshipalki*, and in Poland *Prussaki*.

The way to Stanislavov led us the next day along the Pruth, through Kolomea, the last town on the Pruth, and over an elevated road dividing the valleys of the Pruth and the Dniester. In the valley of the Pruth the high summits of the Tshorna-Gora towered at our side, but in the valley of the Dniester the Carpathians were quite hidden from our sight. This is the case the whole way from the Pruth to Stanislavov and Stry, where the highest points of the mountains are never more than seven or eight miles from the traveller, and yet are never visible to him. No mountains were to be seen; we appeared to be travelling continually in a plain, and not even on the horizon could we discover any traces of mountains. This is the case throughout Galicia, till we come to Cracow. It may be partly because the Carpathians rise highest at their two extremities, in Bukovina and Moravia, and have in the middle no towering pinnacles rising above the rest; and partly because the whole of Galicia is a high country, gently rising from the Polish plains to the mountains. On the Hungarian side the Carpathians rise much more abruptly from the plains stretching away at their feet, and in that country the horizon is everywhere bounded by hills.

In the Pruth valley we noticed the peculiar race of fat-tailed sheep, common in Walachia; they are plentiful here, as throughout Moldavia and Walachia, and from these districts they have spread through South Russia, where they are known as Walachian sheep. In the interior of Galicia they are unknown, and only the common Polish sheep is there to be seen. Towards the west the Carpathians have checked their spread; for the *Huzzulen* and *Goralen* have not the fat-tailed, but the common sheep. The cattle here is not so fine as in the Russian and Moldavian plains. The large silver-gray oxen of the steppes are still to be seen, but they are mixed with the small black cattle of the Carpathians. The still larger Hungarian race is never seen on this side of the mountains.

Many a *seidel* and *pfiff* were emptied by our Walachian fellow-travellers, before we stopped for the night; particularly at the Armenian publichouses by the wayside. These Armenian publichouses alternate in Galicia with the German and Jewish inns, but are in smaller numbers than the last named. The Armenian hosts are generally mere wine dealers, and do not let lodgings and beds to travellers. Many of them have become very rich in this country, and a few have even been raised to the rank of nobles. There are several powerful Armenian noblemen in Poland. In the same way the Poles have sometimes raised Jews to the rank of nobles, and allowed them to share all the privileges of the aristocracy.

The Jewish inns are the oldest in the country; the towns are full of them. Their accommodations are such, that they can provide the traveller with nothing but a roof; provisions and beds he must bring with him or seek elsewhere. The houses are large, the courtyards and stables spacious and convenient, the rooms small, but better furnished than would be expected. Bedsteads there are, but no beds, because their usual customers either require none—the Polish servants, coachmen, and peasants, usually sleep in their clothes and furs—or if any are required, the traveller brings his own with him. As we were in neither of these positions, many expedients were proposed. Some proposed to buy beds for us, some to borrow them of their neighbours, others to vacate their own to us; we however generally preferred a clean sheet spread over some hay and straw. Regular inns, with beds, we did not find till we came to Lemberg.

Provisions were as scanty as beds; when we asked for them we were referred to the neighbouring *tracteur* (traiteur), who would provide us with what we wanted. The man who mediates between the traveller and the host in Galicia, who acquaints the traveller with the advantages and capabilities of the inn, and sees to the fulfilment of his wishes, is called the *factor*, and is always a Jew. The word factor is no doubt an abbreviation of *factotum;* for as the inn itself has nothing, and does nothing, it is the factor who procures and arranges every thing for the traveller.

In the Galician towns, particularly in the more western ones, German inns, ("Catholic inns," the people call them), are fast rising to rival these Jewish hostelries. When we came to a town, we were always asked whether we would drive to the Catholic or the Jewish inn. We always decided for the Catholic, but our Rusniak servant was a Jew, and always arranged matters so that we were obliged to put up with his Israelite brother.

A few miles before Stanislavov, we came to a pine forest, the first we had seen in coming from the Black Sea. In Bessarabia and Bukovina there are no pine forests, and the sight of these beautiful, dark, leafy masses, supported on tall, smooth, stately columns, was an agreeable surprise to us.

From the upper valley of the Dniester the pine forests stretch, one after the other, in close succession to the land of the Esthonians and Finns, where they border on the northern birch-forests.

The town of Stanislavov, has now no fewer than 15,000 inhabitants, and is the second town of Galicia. It lies between two small rivers, both called Bistriza, in the valley of the Dniester, and is, without doubt, the most respectable of all the Dniester towns, from Sambor and Stry, to Chotini, Bender, and Ackermann. It formerly belonged to a Count Potocki, whose family is widely spread, wealthy, and powerful, in all the countries from Bohemia to the Pontus. The people of Stanislavov still speak of a Countess Potocka, who, after the custom of Polish nobles, kept up a little standing army in the town, and the ruins of a fortress, which she erected for her own ends and those of the republic, are still shown to strangers. Stanislavov is now a free imperial city. It carries on an important trade with Galicia and Podolia, has a good gymnasium, is the capital of a large circle, and is the residence of many far-famed noble families, among which those of the Counts Idushicki and Yablonovski may be named as the principal. The town is, on the whole, well built, and rich in elegant buildings, palaces, churches, &c. The fancy shops, plentifully fitted out with the pretty toys of Vienna, astonished us not a little. The apothecaries' shops were orderly and good, and the coffee-houses splendid, and I think a traveller, coming from the west, would be just as much astonished to find so elegant and refined a little city on the borders of civilized Europe, as I was to find western elegance and luxury meeting me so soon after my leaving the dreary steppes. Walking through the streets in the evening, we found every place well lighted, and met German watchmen continually; and late at night felt quite at home, on hearing a horn blown from the towers. In one of the public-houses, late guests were still carousing together. We entered, and found the place full of Jews, in long black silk talars, with long, flowing, black beards. They were half tipsy, and were singing loose drinking-songs, to the same peculiar tunes to which, in this country, they chant the psalms of David in the synagogues.

The next morning public worship was performed in the churches; but it was also market-day, and business proceeded as usual in the "*ring*," as the market-place is called in all Galician towns. The word is no doubt a Germanization of the Polish word for market, "*Rynek;*" but the people of the country believe it to be a genuine German word, and the expression may have arisen from the *rings* of booths and shops, which surround the market-places. On the corner houses of the market-places in Galicia, is always inscribed the Polish word Rynek, and under it the German "*der Ring*." The streets, like the market-places, have always both German and Polish names inscribed at their corners, and are paved with flint from the bed of the Dniester. The market-places and streets swarmed with a gay and busy crowd of Armenians, Jews, Poles, Germans, Rusniaks, *Goralen*, and Hungarian soldiers. From the market the flood of life poured on to the churches and to the public houses. We entered the principal church of the town, a Catholic one. Its size and architecture merited the name of a cathedral, and we were pleased no less by the beautiful organ and other decorations, than by the noble style of building and its vast extent. The chancel, choir, organ, and altar, were adorned with various valuable and excellent carvings in wood, and the church was as full of statues in stone and wood as of men and women. A curious fancy of the priest's was displayed upon the altar. It was decorated with large glass bulbs, containing blue, red, and yellow fluids, behind each of which stood a lamp, whose rays streamed through the church with all the colours of the rainbow. In Russia apothecaries have similar glass bulbs before their windows.

In the market-place, rock salt from Rossulna and other places at the foot of the Carpathians, was one of the most abundant articles for sale. It is the custom here to cut this salt into all kinds of elegant shapes, like cream cheese with us. We saw these little snow-white forms arranged on all the tables of the Jewish merchants. They have fine saws, with which they cut the large pieces into smaller ones.

At Stanislavov we enjoyed again the satisfaction of feeling ourselves in a town, which sensation one quite loses in the great, dreary, desert Russian cities. The houses were here close to each other, and stood in crowded groups; high roofs rising above lower ones, and churches and steeples towering over all. The streets ran all manner of crooked ways, and even the avenues of the town (the Russian towns have none), the long poplar avenues, and the dusty roads, spreading out in every direction, appeared to us both cheerful and stately, as did the view of the whole from the western heights, over which our *Broder Baude* rolled away, the next morning at eight o'clock.

Upon these hills the road divides itself. The principal road goes on towards Stry by a circuitous route. A bad by-road leads to the town of *Halitsh*, which although much famed in the Russian annals, is now no more than a small place inhabited only by Polish Jews, and bears no traces of its former greatness. This is the case with all Russian towns of bygone prosperity, which, not being built of solid stone like our old cities, do not bequeath to posterity any tokens of their ancient splendour. We had hired our coach and its driver for the longer road, and had paid him extra money on purpose; but the shorter suited him better—he had laid a plot with a brother driver who was going the same way, and when we came to the cross road, both turned off towards Halitsh. We screamed out of the carriage windows—so did the passengers in the other coach, but as persuasion and threats were in vain, our only way was to get out, and seizing the horse's reins, to turn them back again by main force, which done, the ill-humoured Jewish drivers, after much noisy altercation, submitted, and quietly drove down the prescribed road.

FROM STANISLAVOV TO STRY.

Behind Stanislavov, we saw the first manured field. In the valley of the Pruth and throughout Bukovina, no manure is ever used, because the soil is so rich and productive that it needs none, as is also the case all over Moldavia and Southern Russia. This kind of soil ceases in the valley of the Dniester, and, as we proceed north-west, every thing grows more and more barren and scanty, till we reach the sandy plains of Poland, which partake of the desert nature of those of Brandenburg and Prussia. In Bukovina six or eight oxen are always harnessed to the plough, after the custom of South Russia and Moldavia. Here the plough is driven with only a pair of oxen or horses, and sometimes only with one. The whole state of agriculture and housekeeping is different here from what it is in

Bukovina. Grain is no longer threshed by horses in the open air, but with flails in large barns; hay or corn are no longer kept in great heaps in the open air, but in sheds and barns; nature appears more niggardly and less liberal, man more careful and painstaking. The furrows are drawn in the peculiar manner common throughout Poland; six small furrows lie close together, and then comes a great, broad, deep one. This gives the fields a curious but not unpleasing appearance.

Maize is no longer cultivated here, and consequently we no longer meet with any of the national dishes prepared from it by the Moldavians. The potato, on the contrary, becomes more and more plentiful; in no part of Poland, Posen excepted, is this root so much eaten as in Galicia. The Germans, as everywhere, are zealous partisans of this vegetable. "The people here," said a Galician to us one day, "eat very little bread on weekdays, though plenty on Sundays; and they only eat meat on high festival days, at weddings, christenings, and so forth, while the Moldavians and South Russians, eat meat every day."

The slavery of the peasants here is still very abject, as it is all over Poland. Monsieur Dupin has drawn a map of civilization in France, on which he has shaded the wild and uncultivated regions quite dark, the more cultivated, lighter, and so on to the white regions of perfect refinement and civilization. If a similar map to indicate the extent of slavery in Poland were to be drawn, the whole country ought to be painted black as ink, without a single white spot; no doubt, however, there would be gradations in blackness. The blackest hue of all would be found in Lithuania, where the slavery of the peasants is of the most oppressive character, and where the timid yielding pliable nature of the people offers no resistance to oppression. In Galicia—particularly in Rusniak Galicia, a few faint streaks of a lighter shade might be admitted. Slavery is older in Poland than in Russia; the Poles first introduced it among the Malorossian races, and history shows how much trouble it cost them to do so. The Russians have always kept within bounds in the infliction of their fetters upon subject nations. The effect of this is manifest among the Rusniaks of Galicia, in a certain independent and lofty bearing, whilst the Lithuanian serfs, prostrate before their masters, seem to have lost all dignity and self-respect.

In northern Poland, two thirds of the time and strength of the peasant is at the disposal of his lord, whilst in Galicia he has only to work for his master from sixty to one hundred days. They call this task work "*Robbot.*" Only fifteen or twenty days in the year are exacted as Robbot from the crown peasants. Besides the Robbot, there are many irregular tasks and services of different kinds, and tributary offerings of butter, eggs, fruit, money, &c., which are not regulated by law, but by a vague rule of custom, liable to be interpreted according to the will of a tyrannical and oppressive master. The Austrian government is unceasing in its endeavours to change these undefined duties, but much remains to be cleared away in this Augean stable of Polish slavery, and in most instances, the Galician, like the Lithuanian master, can do pretty much what he pleases with his serfs.

An important innovation in Galicia is the general prevalence of German agricultural colonies. They have entered the country partly at the invitation of private noblemen, and partly at that of the government. North of the Carpathians, among the Poles and Russians as far as the Caucasus and the sea of Asoph, these German colonists are always called *Suabians*, whilst south of the Carpathians, in Hungary and Transylvania, they are everywhere known by the name of *Saxons*, whether they come from the Elbe, the Rhine, or the Danube. The study of the German colonists in these countries, of the old customs which they have retained, and the new ones which have crept in among them, the different influences of the different races among whom they have settled, upon their costume, language, and manners, would be one full of interest. Whoever imagines Galicia to be an uninteresting country is very much mistaken. The mere contemplation of the influence of the different elements of the population upon each other, cannot fail to be deeply interesting to every thoughtful mind.

The road from Stanislavov to Stry passes through Kalush and Boletrov, and through the valleys of the rivers Lomiga and Striza. In the first valley we dined, in the second we passed the night. All these Carpathian mountain-streams are pretty much alike. They are each ten or twelve miles long, and flow very rapidly in a north-eastern direction into the Dniester. Each consists of two streams which unite together about two miles above the spot where they flow into the Dniester. Each has a town at its mouth, and another further up the valley.

The *Mogilos*, or grave hillocks of the Mongolian races, are very abundant in Bukovina and round Stanislavov, but here they appear to cease altogether. Southern Galicia is almost as thickly sown with these *Mogilos* as the steppes of Southern Russia.

In every village and town we found, in the middle of the market-place, a large stone effigy of some holy martyr, or canonized hermit, or a Madonna, clad in nun's attire, bearing the infant Christ, or a priest, bearing the consecrated Host; all so many monuments of the supremacy of Catholicism over the Greek religion, for the latter, not approving of sculpture in the service of religion, has banished all such images from the churches, streets, and market-places. Throughout all the countries subject to the Greek church, such monuments are never found in the towns and villages, and an oil painting here and there in some chapel, a fresco painting on the wall of some church or cloister, or, oftener, a simple cross, made of two pieces of wood, rudely nailed together, are the only visible symbols made use of. The catholics taught the Rusniaks to erect effigies of this kind, such as are to be seen in Bohemia and Bavaria; but they do not appear to be much reverenced by the people, for I never saw a Rusniak cross himself before any of these images, although he does so in every church, and before every old Greek picture, as piously as any Russian.

At Kalush we dined at a Jewish *tracteur's*, named Schnitzle. A few Austrian soldiers were playing at billiards with some civilians, and a Jewish marker was calling out the numbers in Polish. The Austrian soldiers and officers in Galicia always appeared to me merry and cheerful; Poland appears to agree with them very well. They are always making a noise, and are to be met with at every billiard, card, or dinner table. There is something complacent and self-satisfied about them. This cheerfulness and merriment of the Austrians in Galicia must be a thorn in the side of the Poles. The German traveller, on the other hand, might rejoice at seeing his countrymen living here as rulers and conquerors, did not many a disagreeable conviction disturb this feeling; among others, the knowledge that the Austrian has no feeling of national patriotism about him, and if commanded, would just as readily direct his musket at a Saxon or Prussian, as at a Russian or Pole.

This place had been half burnt down a week before. The wooden walls and roofs of the houses had been entirely destroyed, and only a row of tall chimneys, with the ovens and hearths to which they belonged, still towered like pillars from the dust and ashes beneath. In Northern Poland I had often seen villages destroyed by fire, which always presented the same appearance.

It was Sunday, and in the market-place of the little town I appeared to be in the middle of Germany; for German peasants were standing everywhere around, dressed in blue cloth, the young in jackets with silver buttons, the old in long coats. Some were standing in groups, others leaning against the wooden railings in long rows, and all enjoying the Sunday *dolce far niente*. They told us that they got on very well, and that by feeding and selling cattle, they earned a good deal of money. "The Germans are the only people in Poland who eat meat every day," said a Jew to us once. It must be confessed, that upon the whole, it is very pleasant to be a German, for a German patriot has a very extensive fatherland, and everywhere finds his countrymen prosperous and respected.

We drank tea at *Dalina*, a little town lying between two hills of the Carpathians. Though it was Sunday, we found the market-place of Dalina full of life, bustle, and traffic. The law forbids the holding of a market on a Sunday, yet, all through Galicia, the principal business of the week is carried on on Sundays, probably according to the old Malorossian custom, for we remarked the same thing throughout Southern Russia, Odessa not excepted.

It is much to be wondered at that more ethnographers and travellers do not visit these countries, to give us some account of the life led in these cities of the Carpathians, and to perpetuate a few of the interesting pictures which daily present themselves. In fact, while sitting on the wooden bench at the door of the little inn, we could in a few moments, with a little portable camera-obscura, have collected several pictures, wanting neither in general nor in picturesque interest. We were particularly struck by the universal cheerfulness which appeared to animate all; not only the leisurely buyers and promenaders, but the merchants and men of business, seemed full of Sunday gaiety. The round satisfied countenance, merry eye, and white uniform, of the Austrian soldier, contrasted agreeably with groups of dark-furred Rusniaks. The young Rusniak girls, arm in arm, promenaded in long rows up and down before the gay booths, richly stocked with fancy wares. Their peculiar head-dress, a long white handkerchief, fastened together at the forehead, and waving behind and by the side like a long banner, became them remarkably well. The *Goralen*, a poetical and musical race, of great physical strength, and much given to tobacco smuggling, had descended in great numbers from the mountains, to trade in cattle; and both men and women were easily known by the two thick plaits in which they arrange their black hair, and which they wind round the head from the forehead to the ears. Here and there a tall Magyar, of slow gait and dignified manners, wandered through the crowd, and here and there was a barefooted monk in his great brown cowl. The long black talar of the small, meager, Polish Jew, an indispensable agent in Polish commerce, was seen on every side. The Jew arranges and consolidates every thing, forms and witnesses agreements, and holds together the whole fabric of society; every thing moves and lives here in a Jewish element. The Jew is either himself the merchant, or the broker who mediates between him and his customers; the Jew guides and settles all business, the Jew pours out the brandy which gives the purchaser fresh courage for bargaining, and it was a Jew who brought us the coffee which sweetened our contemplation of these interesting groups.

Near Dalina we crossed the Sviza, one of those little rivers of the Carpathians spoken of above, but which was now a lifeless insignificant piece of water. In spring, however, when the melting of the mountain snow swells its current, it is, like all these rivers, very useful to the *Huzzulen* and *Goralen*. The Huzzulen float the wood of the Carpathians down to the Dniester, where they dispose of it to the inhabitants of Halitsh, who convey it to its further destination. Great orchards of plums are to be seen in all the villages here; this fruit thrives amazingly in Galicia, where it yields the far-famed *Zvetschenmuss*, which the Galicians call *Povill*, and which forms no inconsiderable article of commerce with Hungary, Northern Poland, and the Ukraine. This Galician *Povill* is everywhere welcome as an agreeable and nourishing kind of food, and Lemberg contains large warehouses full of tubs of Povill. While travelling in Galicia great plum orchards were often shown us, which brought in annually many thousands of florins. This cultivation of plums decreased as we proceeded northward.

In the evening we drank tea at *Balekhov*, for we had not yet learnt to dispense with this agreeable Russian custom. The Polish word for tea, "*Herbata*," signifies more properly *herb*, and in fact there is little more of the genuine Chinese beverage in the article itself than in its name; so that we often thought with longing of the delightful Russian "*Tshai*," genuine in word and fact.

The harmonious but monotonous and melancholy tones of an Harmonica attracted us from our tea-table to the lawn before the house, where we saw two or three German carriers lying on the ground. They were Silesians from *Teschen*, handsome, powerful men, in short blue jackets and trousers, all richly set with large silver buttons, and with gay woollen caps on their heads. They were conveying cloth from the farfamed manufacturing town of Biala to Tshernovitze, in Bukovina, whence it is sent to Russia, Walachia, and Turkey. Both the Silesian and Moravian carriers travel through the whole Austrian empire, from the confines of Russia to the Adriatic Sea. They use the same great waggons covered with white linen cloths which are common in Germany. With these heavy vehicles they can only travel on regular roads, and though with their powerful horses and great strong waggons, they can transport heavy and bulky goods with greater ease and security than the native carriers, yet in districts unprovided with roads, they are obliged to yield to the latter. The Rusniaks and Slovaks are the only native Galicians who carry on this business on a large scale. Where there are good roads the German waggoners are preferred, but everywhere else the Rusniaks. The Russians everywhere seem to have a particular tendency to this wandering way of life, for as in Galicia, the Moldavians, Poles, and *Masuren*, always stay at home, while the Rusniaks are found wandering about everywhere; so in Lithuania, Livonia, and Esthonia, the carriers and drivers are all Russians. The restless, busy, nomadic life of a waggoner or driver suits the Russian character. Breslau, Posen, Warsaw, Kiev, Bukovina, Ofen, and Pesth, may be named as the boundary points in the great circle which the Rusniaks frequent as carriers. Laden with wine, salt, honey, corn, and *Povill,* they intersect the Carpathians, where their light little carts, built in the Russian fashion, are better than the heavy, solid waggons of the Germans. The making of roads, however, is narrowing their territory more and more, and enlarging that of the Germans. It may be imagined, therefore, with what unfavourable eyes the Rusniak regard the fine new " Imperial road," as it is commonly called, which intersects the whole of Galicia.

The different branches of transport in Galicia, are divided among the different elements of the population, in about the following manner. The Germans convey the produce of Austria and Silesia along the high-roads to Turkey and Russia. The Rusniaks travel about in the interior with home produce, along the natural paths of the country. The Jews never convey goods, but only travellers. The *Huzulen* and *Garolen* are in possession of the rivers and streams, and occupy themselves with water carriage.

STRY.

We set off from Balekhov at three o'clock, the next morning. Every thing still slumbered under the black veil of night; the Carpathians seemed to have unquiet dreams, for a storm was raging among them. Every thing was dark and silent in the Rusniak villages, and only here and there the forge of some industrious smith gleamed through the night. We shuddered with cold and drowsiness, and were very glad when we arrived to breakfast at " the Imperial free city of Stry."

Before the gates of the city we saw a board stuck up, on which was written in large letters *" Hier ist Viehseuche."** A great herd of Podolian oxen stood lowing before the gate, and an Austrian soldier was translating the melancholy inscription for the Malorossian cattle-dealers, who then sorrowfully turned away with their beasts to avoid the town by a circuit. At the inn of Stry, a Polish lady of rank, with her attendants, was just entering a huge old-fashioned coach, such as we had not seen for a long time. Five horses were harnessed to it; three before the other two. The host was putting some packets of "Stry sausages" into the lady's carriage, assuring us at the same time that we must take some with us, as no travellers ever left Stry without some specimens of this esteemed and farfamed delicacy.

Stry is a Polish city, but a good deal *Germanized,* that is to say cleared of all its Polish dirt and rubbish, furnished with proper gates and walls, and with a few good buildings, and well paved throughout. The old Polish dustholes, once so common in Galicia, have all been swept away by the Austrian government. To see them in their old unchanged, unsophisticated condition, the traveller must go to Russian Poland, particularly to Lithuania. Stry is, as has been said, a free city, " *Volnoi Gorod.*" This name must not call up in the reader's mind the image of one of our German free cities. The expression has in Hungary and Galicia nothing to do with political freedom and independence, but merely denotes that no private nobleman is master of the place. The Imperial free cities are

---

* Here a contagious epidemic is raging among the cattle.

called so as opposed to the *Dominikalni Gorodi*, or cities belonging to private persons. Next to these private cities, where the one nobleman possesses all the land and houses, where all the citizens pay their rent to him, where he names the magistrates and Burgermeisters of his own authority, and where criminals are tried in his name ; next to these come the *Cameral Städte*, (*Kameralni Gorodi*), where the emperor is the same to the towns, as the private nobleman is to the *Dominial Stadt*.

As the morning dawned, the market-place of Stry became more and more filled with Jewish brandy dealers, and bread-selling Germans. As the sun rose, the Jews began to pray, and while pouring out brandy for the peasants, popping their money in their pockets, and going up and down into their cellars to fetch fresh bottles, they continued gabbling over their prayers, uninterrupted by their various avocations.

FROM STRY TO LEMBERG.

From Stry our road lay through the valley of the Dniester. It is here a fine broad river, bordered by beautiful meadows, which are flooded every spring. On the other side of the Dniester arises that narrow range of hills intersected by many small streams, which spreads out from the Carpathians, dividing the Dniester from the Vistula, and proceeding further in a south-easterly direction towards Podolia, separates the valley of the Dniester from that of Bug. The Dniester is here, as everywhere on its course towards the Pontus, very deep and rapid. I now crossed this river, over which I had passed so often, probably for the last time in my life, at the little fishing village of Rosvadov. Even here, scarcely ten miles from its source, the river already contains a great quantity of fish.

The Jews of the Dniester pay four thousand florins rent for the bridge and road tolls of this district, and they make scarcely as much profit as is necessary to enable them to live a miserable life of dirty squalor, with their wives and children. Throughout Galicia the Jews generally rent all the tolls of the roads and bridges.

At Nikolayev, or Mikolayev, as the Poles say, who always turn the Russian *ns* into *ms*, we saw a very old Greek Rusniak church. This little building rests, like most Rusniak churches, under the shade of a grove of venerable oaks, whose lofty tops far overshadow the old towers. The church is entirely built of wood, the walls of great trunks of beeches laid crossways on one another; the three towers which rise into the air, like old decayed branches, are built of pinewood and covered with wooden shingles. The roof of the church was so low, that my head reached up to it, and when at last the priest drew back the curious old bolts, and the thick oaken door grated like that of a prison as it opened, we felt as if entering the interior of a hollow tree. The church was filled with a dim twilight; for the only apertures for light were the little windows in the towers, and the waving shade of the dark oak-trees playing round the place, weakened the effect of the few rays of sunshine which shone down through these apertures, upon the glittering pictures of saints on the walls. Before the door was inscribed upon the walls, in old Slavonic numbers, rough as if hewn with an axe, the date 1633. The church was dedicated to the famous Russian saint, Nicholas, who stands in high veneration with the Rusniaks. His picture hung in the centre of the Iconostase, and had just the same physiognomy and the same decorations as in Russia. Iconostase, altar, and holy vessels, were just as we see them in all old Russian Greek churches, and scarcely any traces of the modifying influence of Catholicism were to be discovered; a little sculpture had, however, crept in here and there. The image of Christ upon the crucifix, carried by the priest, was not merely traced as the Russians, in fulfilment of the commandment against graven images, are accustomed to have it, but stood out in relief from the cross. I pointed this out to the priest. He said, certainly this was wrong, but it could not always be helped, for those crosses were often presents from Catholics. I also noticed two or three insignificant modifications in the service; for example, the altar remains visible to the congregation during the whole service, whilst in Russia it is hidden from them at certain times by the drawing of curtains, and the closing of the doors of the Iconostase. In the middle of the church was a great stone, about a foot and half high; this was the pulpit. The priest told me that every Sunday he stood upon this stone, and preached some moral discourse to the congregation in the Rusniak language, although he could speak Polish, and his congregation could understand it. Behind the altar was a collection of old Slavonic church books browned and blackened by time, which were all printed in Lemberg or Kiev, and the older ones in the far-famed Russian monastery of *Potshayu*. The whole Iconostase stood awry, and the pictures hung awry on the walls, which, like the whole church, looked as if about to fall in. The patron and owner of the church was one of the wealthiest nobles in Galicia, Count R——. For thirty years the congregation had in vain been endeavouring to get their master to rebuild the church. "That man is a freemason and jacobin," said the priest. "He has built mills, manufactories, breweries, and a great theatre at Lemberg, but not one church. Six of his churches are already in this deplorable state; yet he prefers paying the fine imposed by the Metropolitan every year, to laying out any thing upon rebuilding them." I could find it in my heart to wish that the count may not alter his mind; for if a new church were to be built, what would be the consequence? It would be made larger than the present one, and then the old overshadowing oaks with their venerable thousand years would fall, the old stone would be replaced by a mahogany pulpit, the old well thumbed Slavonic books would give way to new ones in elegant bindings, and the interior of the church would bear witness only to the skill of the Lemberg masons, and not to the thousand heartwrung sighs and fervent prayers, which have ascended to Heaven from beneath the lowly roof of that little old, time-worn Rusniak temple. I could not help wishing therefore that the church might long preserve its uneven walls and old oaks, and I told the priest he would do wisely not to mourn over the backwardness of his patron, but rather to do all he could to preserve the old church in its present state. It is always easy to build a new church, but very difficult to build one two hundred years old.

In this church we copied the title of the Metropolitan of the United Greek church, which is interesting on account of the present position of that church. It runs thus:—"*Michael Lewicki z Bozega Milosierdzia i zu wladza S. Stolicu, Apostolskiei Metropolita Halicki, Arzubickup Lwowski, Biskup Kamenicki.*" (Michael Lewicki, by the Grace of God and under the sanction of the Holy Apostolic Chair, Metropolitan of Halitsh, Archbishop of Lemberg, and Bishop of Kameniez.) In his official German title, the following words are always added to the foregoing:—" Excellency, Privy Councillor, and Doctor of Theology." Although he now resides in Lemberg, he is always styled Metropolitan of Halitsh, the old capital. His old Bishopric of Kameniez, has long ago fallen to Russia; still he does not regard it as " in partibus infidelium," but as " in partibus fidelium," and would much like to join it. The united Greeks are far from bearing the Union with patience ; on the contrary they bear it only as an unavoidable necessity. In the publications of the Metropolitan, the Pope is always called " *Nashu Pasterz Grzegorz XVI.*" (our Pastor Gregory XVI.) The Priests are not called *Popes*, but pastors (*Pasterz*), or clergymen (*Kyonzui*.) The word " *Pope*" is here used only as a contemptuous appellation. " A man is fined a ducat here, if he call a Priest *Pope*," said the Priest, " but if any one just fresh from Hungary or Russia calls me so, I do not complain." This feeling has probably arisen from the influence of Catholicism ; and may not be shared by the people, who are very much attached to their old Popes. To our surprise, we found the common Russian superstition, that the chance meeting with a *Pope* is an evil omen, prevailing here also. If a Rusniak meets a Pope in going out, he spits to avert the threatened evil. There is another superstition current here, which I never met with in Russia, namely, that to meet a Jew forebodes good fortune and prosperity. This reminded me of many similar strange prejudices in Germany, such as that to dream of a fire signifies money, and that it is unlucky to wish a hunter success when he sets out.

That remarkable tract of country which separates North from South Galicia, the land of the Poles from that of the Rusniaks, commences behind and Nikolayev, is about 700 or 800 feet above the level of the sea, and 400 or 500 feet above the valley of the Dniester. It is very bare and quite flat, and consists of masses of chalk, full of petrifactions, as in Podolia. The little rivers which rush down from it into the Dniester, flow through deep sharply cut channels. We saw no trees but birch trees. Towards Lemberg the road became a little less even, and we drove over the wave-like undulations, now up and now down. The roads were here paved with the soft chalk of the *Plateau*, and were therefore very bad. On this table land the races began to mix. We entered a village which was peopled half by Poles and half by Rusniaks. Upon the whole, however, the Rusniaks form still the majority. We now, for the first time, met with the small Polish horses, and in the inns and public-houses Polish landlords became more frequent.

Here also, for the first time, we again enjoyed the long unseen spectacle of a smooth mirror-like lake. Throughout Moldavia, Walachia, and South Russia, there are no good sized inland lakes. It is a remarkable fact, and not a little characteristic of the structure of the ground, that throughout the whole extent of the Carpathian mountains, a district more than 100 (German) miles long, and fifteen or twenty wide, there is not one considerable basin of water, while the Alps are full of them. Not one of the numerous streams, which flow down from the Carpathians into the Dniester, forms a lake.

In our *Broder Baude*, we had taken up, from time to time, specimens of all the different classes of Galician population ; giving a lift now to a Rusniak, now to an Armenian, now to a Jew, now to a priest, and now to a German mechanic. We found the more opportunity for this, as the land of pedestrians begins at Bukovina. Throughout Russia, where there are scarcely any footpaths, no one goes on foot ; neither tradesman nor peasant, neither monk nor pedlar, except perhaps the poor hardworn soldier. A few miles from Lemberg, we gave a lift to an Austrian soldier. He was a Pole, but spoke German; he had served for ten years, and was to serve four more. He looked very well off. He told us that he rubbed his white clothes over every week with chalk. The coat given him by the Emperor was to last him two years, the cloak three years; he received three shirts for two years, two pair of trousers for each year, and one pair of boots every nine months. There is no doubt, that the Polish soldiers in the Austrian service are three times as well fed and clothed as the Russian soldiers.

Here we again saw the genuine old Polish bow, which we had never seen since leaving Poland. The Polish peasant never bends forwards when saluting another, as we do, but sideways, in the most extraordinary manner. When they do the thing quickly, it is only a jirk of the left shoulder. Generally, however, the Poles bow so low that they almost lose their balance, bending over sideways, and kissing the hem of the garment of the saluted person, sideways. Even the very dogs do not approach their masters strait forwards, but creep sideways towards them. The usual Polish salutation which accompanies the bow, is "*Padam da nog*," (I throw myself at your feet,) or else still more strongly, "*Padam pod noshig*," (I throw myself under your feet). These phrases are continually used in common conversation; for servility is as inherent a part of the Polish, as obedience of the German character. Even the young Polish *élégants* at the balls of Warsaw, Lemberg, and Wilna, talk of throwing themselves "at the feet" and "under the feet" of their partners. The Polish beggars also sometimes place their caps on the ground, and bow down low over them, in saluting a superior.

At Brodki, a village near Lemberg, a young Jewish barmaid, who wore a hood decorated with pearls, worth a hundred ducats, told us that the Jewesses of Lemberg often wear jewels to the value of from one thousand to two thousand ducats, about the head. She also made us acquainted with a Polish beverage called *Malina*, made of the whitest and sweetest honey, and the best raspberries. This beverage is as common here as mead is in the north.

Late in the evening the bustle and crowd on the road, and the noise and tumult of the public-houses, showed us that we were approaching the capital of the country, the far-famed and much praised city of Lemberg or "*Lvov.*"

LEMBERG.

Lemberg lies in a small, deep, round valley, surrounded by hills, which just enclose the town sufficiently to allow it the necessary room for spreading. Its suburbs stretch up the sides of the hills, so that the whole valley is filled with buildings, streets, courtyards, and gardens.

We entered the city at nine o'clock in the evening. Every thing was illuminated in the most splendid manner, the lofty houses were lighted from top to bottom, far and near the streets glittered with long rows of brilliant lamps, and even the hills around sparkled in every direction, and yet all this was but the illumination of every day. On high occasions of rejoicing, when the city is festively lighted up, the spectacle from the hills around must be really magnificent. It was long since we had seen any thing so beautiful, and our hearts leaped with joy as we rolled in through the gates of the city.

A few *Zwanziger* warded off the threatened search of our effects. The Austrian soldiers quietly let us pass, and our *Baude* soon stopped before the door of the handsome *Hôtel de Russie*, where we found a fine house, an excellent *table d'hôte*, attentive servants, and in short, all the accommodations of the best Austrian inns, at very moderate prices. Here we spent the five days of our intended stay at Lemberg very comfortably, and when we bade our friendly host farewell, we promised to chant his praises for the benefit of all future travellers. In the luxurious beds of the hotel (I speak here with the feeling of one just come from the steppes), I dreamed very agreeably of the *Goralen* and *Huzulen*, of conquered difficulties and expected enjoyments, till late in the morning the sun of Lemberg awaked me to fresh activity.

It was the 20th of October which, contrary to expectation, rose with the mildest and pleasantest air, and the brightest sunshine. We wandered through the long streets of the town, towards that old kernel of the city, round which has grown up this mighty crystallization, of not less than six thousand houses, and eighty thousand inhabitants; I mean to the ruins of the old *Löwenburg*, which is built on the tops of the high hills, overlooking the valley in which Lemberg is situated. On a steep sandhill from five hundred to six hundred feet above this valley, stand the ruins of a castle, built about five hundred years ago, by a prince of Halitsh named Leo or Lvov. The town, which soon grew up under the protection of this castle, received thus the name of Lvov, or, in German, Löwenburg, shortened into Lemberg. The ruins are not very important. Only a few walls of the old castle remain upright, but fragments of other walls are scattered all over the mountain. There are various little houses on the hills, in which the Austrian soldiers keep their powder. From these ruins an excellent view is obtained of the whole city and its suburbs.

The amphitheatre of hills, by which Lemberg is surrounded, is one of the most regular I have ever beheld. It forms a perfect circle of about a German mile in diameter. The wall of hills around is from 300 to 400 feet above the city, which in its turn, is 102 fathoms above the level of the sea. Lemberg looks as though it lay as snug as an egg in its nest, in this basin of hills. Parts of the suburbs spread up these hills, and the highest summits are adorned with churchyards, convents, and ruins. Over these hills spread out the four great roads, which connect Lemberg with the rest of the world; the one towards Cracow, the second towards Warsaw, the third towards Russia, and the fourth towards Hungary. The road towards Warsaw has become the least frequented of late, and that towards Hungary is not of much importance; the principal one is that leading to Cracow and Vienna. The road towards Brody and Russia has also become more important of late years.

The sides of the hills are covered with beautiful gardens and promenades. On the other side of the Löwenburg, I looked down into a wide open plain, through which winds the road towards Warsaw, and the little river Poltev. It is easy to see that this plain lies much lower than the valley of Lemberg. Probably the latter once formed a little lake, which has gradually flowed away on one side. In one corner of the basin rises one of the sources of the Vistula, called the Poltev, which flows into the Bug, one of the tributaries of the Vistula.

The whole spectacle from these ruins is magnificent. The situation of Prague resembles that of Lemberg, except as regards the river of the former city; but the situation of Cracow exceeds that of both in beauty. At Lemberg the view is everywhere wanting in extent. Of the architecture of Lemberg, it is not sufficient to say that it is infinitely better than any thing we Germans ever imagine the Poles to be capable of; for not relatively merely, but positively the appearance of the place is far more elegant and pleasing than that of many great cities in Germany. The open squares are large, the public walks, boulevards, and gardens numerous and extensive. The houses and churches, the manner in which the buildings are arranged, the development of the complicated web of streets, all this in the great Polish cities, such as Wilna, Cracow, Posen, Gnesen, Stanislavov, Lemberg, &c., remind us far more of the old German cities of the middle ages, than of the Russian cities. There are parts of Lemberg, where the traveller might fancy himself in Magdeburg, Nuremberg, or Frankfort on the Maine. This is probably owing to the close connexion which has so long subsisted between Poland and Western Germany.

Lemberg, which became important in proportion as Halitsh declined, contains many old buildings. Round the market-place stand many antique palaces of the Polish nobles, among which is the large black house of Stephen Bathory, built in the noblest old Gothic style. The ruins of John Sobieski's house were pulled down a short time ago. In the old Polish times Lemberg contained from 15,000 to 20,000 inhabitants. Under the Austrian dominion, its population rose rapidly to 30,000, 40,000, 50,000, and now numbers nearly 80,000. No other Polish city approaches Lemberg in this rapid increase. Cracow, Gnesen, and Wilna, have sunk more and more from their former greatness, during the last hundred years. Warsaw, as the central point of the whole, has also lost a great deal. Posen has risen, though not at the same rate as Lemberg, which—with the single exception of Warsaw—is now the greatest and most important city of Poland.

Nothing surprised us more in Lemberg, than the number and richness of the old churches. The Catholic cathedral is the largest of these, and is filled with monuments of Polish nobles, marshals, generals, and ministers. The church is dedicated to the Virgin Mary, whose miraculous picture hangs above the altar. The walls of the choir are all covered with little paintings representing the various miracles wrought by the picture of the Holy Virgin, to whom the church is dedicated, on beggars, counts, field-marshals, and nobles, under each of which is a Latin inscription. Near the altar is a fresco painting of a gigantic angel, turned towards the Virgin, with the following words proceeding from his mouth— the letters painted in the freshest and brightest gold: "*Regina regni Poloniæ, ora pro nobis.*" It is strange that the Austrians have not long ago erased this inscription, as of seditious tendency. Perhaps the Polish priests protect it. What can the prayer of the queen of the kingdoms of Poland be, except that it "may please God to have compassion on the oppressed and divided nation, to restore its independence, and chase from the fair land its triumphant foes, the Russians and Germans?" The cathedral, like all the churches of Lemberg, is adorned as gaily as any Italian church, with pictures, statues, monuments, artificial flowers, splendidly dressed wax dolls, and coloured and illuminated glass.

The church of the Jesuits is built in a very simple and beautiful manner. The great Jesuits' college, has been turned into a *Gubernium*, that is, a residence of the principal civic functionaries. Most of the sculptures we saw in the churches showed a greater state of advancement in the fine arts than we had imagined to exist in Poland.

Near the cathedral stands a little Gothic chapel, both the internal and external sculpture of which is very good. There are paintings of the founder of this chapel and his wife on the outer wall, with the inscription " *Georgius Brimow consul Leopoliensis, fundator istius capellæ* 1617." It is surprising that the Poles could build so well in the Gothic style, at so late an era. The Lady *Burgermeisterinn* of the seventeenth century is represented as wearing the dark short gown, and the white handkerchiefs round her head, formerly worn by all Polish ladies, and even now by the peasant-women round Lemberg.

The kings of Poland used to bear the title of " the orthodox," and with justice, for they were, as the Poles still are to the present day, zealous adherents to every Ultramontane article of faith. They were accustomed, when elected, to submit the decision of the elective council to the pope for approval, and all spiritual dignities in Poland were conferred by the pope alone. The papal nuncio at Warsaw was all powerful in spiritual affairs, and the order of Jesuits succeeded so well in Poland, that in a short time after their first introduction, they had accumulated property nearly to the amount of 40,000,000 florins. The fasts are nowhere kept more strictly than in Poland; for during the great fasts, the Poles deny themselves even butter, milk, and eggs. During one half of the year, the only kind of grease that either the Poles or Russians indulge in, is hemp or linseed-oil, which they eat quite rancid, and which tastes abominably. They might have escaped the necessity of using this detestable condiment, if Count Ossilinski, who was sent to Rome in the middle of the last century, to implore the pope for an alleviation of the severe fasts in favour of the Poles, had understood Latin a little better. The pope, who was a very bad geographer, but who considered that in countries not blessed with the olive-tree, the fasts must be very difficult to carry out, asked the Count, " *Num habetis olivam?*" (Have you the olive-tree?) which the latter understanding to mean "Have you oil?" replied " *Habemus*," without adding, as he should have done, " but only rancid and filthy linseed and hemp oil." The pope replied " *Ergo potestis jejunium quadragesimale observare*," and he adhered to this decision.

Shortly before our arrival in Lemberg, a new Catholic archbishop had been appointed, namely, M. Pistek Franz de Paula, Bishop of Tarnov. In one of the churches, we saw a calculation of the sum which his promotion had cost this bishop, and it amounted to no less than 16,702 florins and 59 kreuzers. This cannot, however, be a very important sum to the prelate, for the yearly income of his see amounts to 28,912 florins and 30 kreuzers. The pope is said to have formely received upwards of a million of florins a year from Poland.

Next to the Catholic archbishop, the most important spiritual dignitary in Galicia is the Greek Metropolitan, also Archbishop of Lemberg. The convent in which he resides, according to the custom of the grandees of the Greek church, (the Metropolitan of Petersburg resides in the Nevski convent, and the Metropolitan of Kiev in the Höhlen convent,) offers little worthy of notice.

The richest and most interesting among the Greek churches of Lemberg is the Vlokhsky Zerkva. It was founded by two Walachian princes, who escaped from Turkey with their treasures to Lemberg, and it was so richly endowed by them, that it still possesses the principal part of the quarter of the town in which it lies. Of its moveable treasures it has, however, lost a great deal. This is the church which was the last to yield to the pope, and it did not do so without stipulating for certain privileges. For instance, it was to be subjected only to the papal chair of Rome, and not to any other bishop or archbishop. The Metropolitan is very jealous of the independence of this old Walachian church, and looking upon it as a rebellious sheep in his flock, exerts himself much to bring it under subjection to his pastoral staff, which he will probably in time accomplish, for the pope himself would perfer such an arrangement.

Lemberg has no fewer than three archbishops. Two of them we have already spoken of. The third is the Armenian archbishop, Cajetan Vartarasivitsh, who presides over all the Armenian congregations of Galicia. Galicia and Eastern Hungary are the most western countries inhabited by this remarkable race, which bears so great a resemblance to the Jews, both in its attachment to commerce, and its wide diffusion throughout foreign lands. The Armenians, like the Jews, have very seldom enjoyed political independence; Persians, Turks, and Caucasians, have successively forced them into exile. This is the reason that the Armenians are found scattered through all the towns of the east, throughout Persia, Syria and Asia Minor, and also through the greater part of European Turkey and Southern Russia. Some towns in the latter are wholly occupied by Armenians, as for instance Natshitshevan, a town containing 12,000 inhabitants. The Armenians enter Galicia on two sides, from Turkey and from South Russia. They have been settled in Lemberg since the seventeenth century. They possess many churches there, in which the service is performed both in the Armenian and Polish languages. All of these churches are small. These Armenians do not wear their national costume, but they are easily recognised by their physiognomies. The Armenian language is still used among them. In the little churchyard surrounding their church I saw tombstones as old as 1630 and 1648.

Lemberg has plenty of convents—Greek, Armenian, and Catholic. We went to see some Catholic convents, as far as a convent can be seen by profane eyes. Among others we saw the Convent of the Holy Sacrament, in which we were told the richest and most distinguished nuns took the veil. We heard a very melancholy story connected with this convent. A beautiful Jewess, only fourteen years old, the only daughter of one of the richest jewellers and bankers of Lemberg, had made acquaintance with a young German officer, and the two young people fell in love with each other. The parents, zealous adherents to the Mosaic law, forbade their daughter all communication with the young German, as soon as they discovered their mutual attachment. The beautiful Jewess, however, whose passion was only the more excited by this opposition, and who now valued the solicitations of her Christian lover above the law of Moses and the prophets, with his assistance fled from her father's house, and took refuge in the Convent of the Holy Sacrament, declaring her intention to become a Christian. In vain the despairing parents demanded the restitution of their child; the laws declared that no Jew or heretic taking refuge in a Christian convent, with the declared intention of becoming a Christian, could again be given up. The aged mother, however, implored an interview with the fugitive, and the request was granted. She packed up in a casket all her pearls and jewels, 30,000 ducats in value, and appeared with them before her daughter, who had in the mean time been instructed in the Christian religion by the priests. The mother heaped caresses and entreaties upon the young girl, reminding her of those holy laws and doctrines which her father and mother, her grandfather and grandmother, had faithfully followed, and which had been carefully transmitted to their child. She spread out before her the snowy pearls, the sparkling diamonds, and glowing rubies; she decked her out with them, and promised her that they should all be her own, as well as every thing else that her aged parents possessed; she should be the one beloved daughter, the treasure and darling of their hearts; she should be petted, caressed, and humoured in every thing, if she would only forget the young Christian, and return to the faith of her fathers. She implored her not to load her family with shame and grief—not to draw down upon herself the curse of her father and mother—not to bring down her old parents in sorrow to the grave. Bribes, threats, and entreaties, however, were alike lost upon the obdurate child. "Mother, I belong to a Christian, and know you no more," was her cold and hardhearted reply to all. The father threw himself at the feet of the archduke governor of Galicia, and prayed for help to regain his lost daughter—his only child. He implored the assistance of temporal authority in aid of his paternal rights, and that the priests should be forced to yield up his daughter, whom they had no right to keep; but the archduke, although well inclined to favour him, dared not violate the privileges of the clergy, and decided that if the girl did not wish it, she could not be given up to her parents. Thus far had this affair, which engaged the attention of all Lemberg, proceeded on our arrival. The instruction of the convert was proceeding, and the day of her baptism and confirmation had already been fixed. The parents and the whole Jewish population were in despair. Of the bridegroom nothing certain was known. Perhaps he hoped for a compromise with the parents. What afterwards became of the pair, I never learned. Perhaps the parents renounced all intercourse with their disobedient child; the love of the young Austrian for the rich Jewess may have cooled towards the poor Christian; the unfortunate proselyte may have lived in remorse and died in despair. At all events, the unsolved enigma admitted of many a melancholy solution.

Of the buildings in progress during our stay in Lemberg, the most remarkable was the great theatre built by the Count *Skarbek*. This is a remarkable undertaking for the richest of all the Galician noblemen. He bought a large piece of ground, on which formerly stood a royal Polish castle. It had been built by Sobieski, who was born at Zolkiev (an estate belonging to him near Lemberg), and who often, when king, visited Lemberg and Zolkiev. Next to the ruins of the Löwenburg, this is the most classical spot in Lemberg, and on this spot stands the nearly completed Skarbek theatre, which is destined to enrich the Galician capital with a temple worthy of the drama. The theatre is to have many dependent buildings. One is to contain a spacious hotel, and another an elegant coffee-house. Baths, confectionary shops, and wine cellars are included in the ground-floor, and furnished lodgings are to occupy the upper rooms. Vacant spaces will be let by the count to watchmakers, jewellers, and dealers in fancy wares, so that the great institution will contain every thing to be desired by a stranger. The count has obtained various government privileges for his several speculations, on condition that after fifty years the whole building shall become government property.

The present theatre of Lemberg is insignificant enough, compared with that of which we have been speaking. The performances are generally in German, and only twice a week in Polish. The middle classes, the German civil and military officers, the merchants and mechanics of the city, form the theatrical public here, as at Warsaw, Petersburg, &c. The magic circle of blooming Polish beauties, surrounded by romantic young patriots, which Schulze tells us he saw at Warsaw in the last century, would now be sought there in vain. These, like so many other garlands, have since then been torn and trampled down in Poland.

On the curtain of the Lemberg theatre is a painting of Apollo descending in his chariot. The celestial horses of the sun have been endowed with very earthly desires by the painter, for while one is drinking at a stream of water flowing by, another is grazing on the fresh and verdant grass. Here we witnessed the performance of the "Maid of Orleans," which, of all Schiller's pieces, is the greatest favourite with the Austrians, as being the most loyal. The heroine was performed by a Demoiselle Roland, whose figure was very well suited to the part, for she was very handsome, and the shining armour became her extremely well. The Israelites are great patrons of the drama here, and the pit was as full of the black talars of the Jews, as the boxes of the glittering jewels of the Jewesses.

The town-houses of the great Polish cities generally stand detached in the middle of the *Ring*, or market-place; this is the case at Warsaw, Cracow, Wilna, and Lemberg. The *Rathhaus* of Lemberg is a more stately and handsome building than most of our German civic dignitaries can boast of. Its four long and lofty wings enclose a large square quadrangle. Round this building runs the ring, generally full of life and bustle, and bordered by the best houses and shops of the city. The four sides of the Rathhaus have each a large gate opening into the quadrangle, which is a busy thoroughfare, always full of passengers. At the four corners of the building are four large stone basins of water, with colossal statues of Neptune and the Naiads in the middle; the pedestals consist of gigantic lions and sea-monsters, who spout forth water into the pitchers of the Lemberg water-carriers. The market-places of Leipzig and Dresden have been described repeatedly, but I do not remember to have seen a description of the Lemberg market-place, and yet it is far more interesting than either of the other two.

In the courtyard of the *Rathhaus* we saw many colossal stone figures of lions, eagles, and the city arms. These had served as decorations to a former building, but had found no place about the more modern one. Among them was a large statue of the Goddess of Justice, but without hands or feet, and with a broken sword. The Austrians did well to remove this melancholy caricature. They have supplied its place by something better; for if there is any thing for which the Galicians ought to be grateful to Austria, it is for the improvements that have been made in the administration of the law.

Not even the smallest Polish town is without plenty of confectioners' shops, public-houses, billiard-rooms, coffee-houses, &c.; for a Polish town is never wanting in loungers, revellers, and idle people. It was certainly a mistake to make Bacchus a Grecian divinity, or to suppose the celebrated "*dolce far niente*," to be a saying of Italian origin. Lemberg has better and more elegant coffee-houses than Dresden, and other towns of equal size. The best is that of Wolf in the market-place. It contains a fine suite of rooms, which are always found filled with Poles and Austrians, at all times of the day, as if there had been a perpetual holiday at Lemberg. In the middle of one of the rooms was enthroned the coffee hostess, surrounded by cups, glasses, sugar-basins, teapots, coffee-pots, and milk-pots. Three sorts of coffee are known here, "white," "brown," and "black;" according to the quantity of milk added, Chess, draughts, billiards, and smoking, are the usual pastimes. In some private rooms, however, gambling is carried on; of which the Poles are still so fond, that now, as formerly, many poor people are to be seen who have lost all at play, and many wealthy men who owe their palaces and estates to their success at the gaming-table. I have often seen beggars in the streets, by turns throwing dice, and begging alms of the passer by.

French and German costumes are worn here as throughout Poland. We saw the beautiful old Polish costume nowhere, except in two pictures of a young Pole and a Polish lady, which hung before a coffeehouse in Lemberg. The paintings were deservedly admired, and the nationality of the costume probably gained the landlord many a patriotic customer. The young Pole was represented sitting negligently on a sofa, with a cup of coffee in his hand, and chatting with a Turk who stood behind him. His four-cornered Polish cap, edged with fine fur, was adorned with a waving heron's plume, fastened to the front of the cap with a golden agraffe. The long silk "*Contusche*," with slashed sleeves, fell in waving folds around the well formed limbs, which were here and there displayed, and which were covered with tight white silk hose. A large jewel confined the shirt upon the breast, the short boots were decorated with gold lace, and all the borders and edges with the finest embroidery. It is a great pity that so splendid a costume should have given place to the detestable French swallow tail. The Poles, however, retained their national costume longer than any other civilized nation of Europe; longer even than the Spaniards, Swedes, or Russians. The *Contusche*, the "*Kurtka*," the diamonds, and the plumed cap, vanished only with the independence of Poland. Even at the last diets of Grodnov and Warsaw, the rich old costume was worn. Even at the last partition of Poland many old nobles sought and obtained the privilege of appearing at the assemblies of the nobility, in the national dress. I never passed the picture of that handsome young Pole, without thinking of the former splendour of the country, the wealth and luxury of her aristocracy, and the mad follies of her young nobility.

Everywhere in Lemberg the Polish and German nationalities manifest themselves side by side. All inscriptions on the streets and marketplaces, and over shop-doors, are written both in German and Polish. The book-shops contain as many German as Polish books, and in the streets I heard the two languages continually mixed up together, so that every thing wore a double aspect—half Polish and half German.

The German of Lemberg is an offshoot from the Austrian stem, and contains, besides many words and phrases peculiar to the Austrian dialect, many others which are not found in the Austrian or in any other German dialect.

It is well known how fond the Austrians are of unwieldy and ridiculous titles. In the churchyard of Lemberg we found "resting in the peace of God," a *Tabacks-blätter-Einlösungs-Magazin-Verwalter*," who was lying close beside the " *Herr Gubernial-Bittschriften-Einreichungs-Protocoll-Director R——*" ! * The churchyard of Lemberg, however, deserves respect; for, firstly, it has a very pretty situation, rising gently up the hill side, with a fine view from the top; and secondly, it encloses the bones of many estimable men. Among these is the Baron von Hauer, the last Governor of Galicia, but one who has left an excellent name behind him. Every one speaks with respect and veneration of this excellent Austrian statesman, who died in the prime of life, who was the shield of the oppressed, and defended the humbler classes, as if their cause had been his own.

Lemberg is the third city for Poland in a literary point of view. Most of the productions of Polish genius are published at Warsaw, next comes Vilna, then Lemberg, then Cracow, then Breslau, and last Leipzig. We admired the excellent printing and getting up of the most recent Polish publications, which adorned the booksellers' windows of Lemberg. That energy which cannot manifest itself in action, finds a vent in books, and thus gives some token of remaining vitality. The booksellers of Lemberg, however, are far better provided with German than with Polish books.

The streets of Lemberg, as of all other Polish towns, are very busy and noisy. Schulze long ago remarked that the Polish nation was a very noisy one, and that in no royal antechamber did he hear so much gossip, quarrelling, and noise, as in that of the Polish king. The Poles talk very fast and loud; particularly the common people, who do not *speak* but *scream*. The Poles also drive and ride a great deal; the ladies drive with four horses, and the gentlemen ride with two mounted servants behind them. Even the peasants take many things to market in carts, which German peasants would carry on their backs. In Poland, as in Russia, a dozen hands are put in motion, where *one* would elsewhere be thought enough. Above all, however, it is the Jews who make the Polish streets noisy and busy; for they are always out of doors, running about, asking questions, and imparting news.

Among the most interesting sights of Lemberg, are the reviews and parades of the Hungarian soldiery quartered there. Austria treats the recruits from the different parts of the empire, whom she incorporates into her army, very differently from Russia; partly because the laws and privileges of the different countries subject to her sway, force her to do so. She keeps the different races divided as much as possible, into separate regiments. Every nation has its peculiar military characteristics, which can only develop themselves among compatriots; and Austria considers that she can effectually prevent the political sympathies of her soldiers from becoming dangerous, by sending the Austrian and Bohemian soldiers into Hungary, the Hungarian and Italian troops into Poland, and the Polish regiments into Italy. This is the reason why there are far more Hungarian and Italian, than Polish troops, in Galicia.

After being accustomed to the brilliant appearance of the Russian officers, their military carriage, and stately and regular movements, the

---

* These titles are somewhat untranslatable. The first signifies, literally, a "director of a magazine for the clearance of tobacco-leaves;" and the second, the "director of an office for the reception of petitions to the government.'—*Tr*.

first impression of the Austrian officers is not pleasing. There is something stiff and awkward about them. With the common soldiers the contrary is the case. In long defiles and lines, the Russian soldiers may be superior, but taken separately, every German soldier is worth ten Russian ones, both in appearance and action. The Hungarian soldiers, however, in all situations, in the line, on parade, or taken singly, always enchant the spectator. The Hungarian soldiers are not large, but of good proportion, handsome appearance, and elegant carriage. The features of those we saw at Lemberg were pleasing; they had all dark eyes, finely shaped noses, black hair, and handsome beards, so that we never saw them pass without looking at them with admiration. Their uniform becomes them, and their march is proud and stately, as that of the victorious young French guard used to be. They look particularly well on horseback. They are in fact a nation of equestrians, taking great pains to get into the cavalry regiments, and doing all they can to escape the infantry.

Hungary and Poland are the two European countries in which Latin continued longest to be used as an official, diplomatic, and even conversational language. The nobility of Galicia generally speak Latin well. In Hungary even the ladies very often converse in Latin, and at Lemberg we met with an Hungarian peasant who understood Latin. In the Galician courts of justice, Latin is always used, and all decrees and proclamations are issued in this language. All the judges and courts of justice have Latin titles by which they are commonly known. For example, the Upper Adels Gericht of Galicia is called, "*Cæs. reg. in regni Galiciæ et Lodomiriæ judicium provinciale nobilium.*" From different reports of this court stuck upon the gates of the Judgment Hall, we saw some strange specimens, however, of Polish Latin. We learnt for instance, that "*Metrica*" signifies *archive*, and that "*Tenutæ*" comes from "*tenere.*"

THE POLISH JEWS.

If any thing is calculated to make a residence in Lemberg, or indeed, in any part of Poland, disagreeable, it is the Jews, those torments of peasants and travellers. During our stay we were generally surrounded by them, even before breakfast. While we were yet in bed, slumbering drowsily on our pillows, they were generally round us screaming their various offers into our ears. Three factors, each of whom at the same time announced himself as the one real factor of our hotel; ten drivers who offered to convey us safely and comfortably to any part of the world at a moment's notice; and whom we in vain assured that we had as yet no intention of proceeding further; a dozen brokers, who offered to transact business for us anywhere, of any kind, and innumerable venders of old and new wares, who importuned us to purchase goods we did not want—these officious tormentors often plagued us so, that we sought refuge in the street, in sheer despair. There, however, we were no better off. The stranger has no chance of escaping the eyes of these pitiless vultures, who follow and fasten upon him like a swarm of bees. Nothing can exceed the officious and tormenting importunity of the Polish Jews; no assurances, no declarations suffice; one may wish them all at the devil a thousand times a day, without getting rid of one of them.

The increase of the Jewish race in Poland is one of the most remarkable phenomena in the history of nations. Although in modern times, their increase has been somewhat checked by the measures of different governments, yet from the Black Sea to the Baltic, from Odessa to Riga, Königsberg and Dantzig, the Jews possess an influence and importance which they possess nowhere else, and form a larger proportion of the population than in any other country. In all the towns of these districts, the Jews are the only agents and brokers, and all the mechanical trades, except those of the smith and the carpenter, are in their hands. No business, important or unimportant, is transacted without the mediation of a Jew. The nobleman sells his corn to the merchant through the mediation of a Jew, and it is a Jew who procures for the householder his servants, his housekeepers, his cooks, nay even the tutors and governesses of his children. Estates are sold, money borrowed, provisions bought,—in short people eat, drink, ride, lodge, and clothe themselves through the agency of the Jew. Formerly the Jews were the only tollkeepers and renters of the salt mines in Poland ; but the Austrian government has altered this in Galicia. It has not, however, totally changed this state of things, and it is still principally the Jews who rent the tolls on roads and bridges, and the government distilleries. Every Polish nobleman retains a Jewish broker on his establishment, and in the towns which he is accustomed to visit, who follows his master's footsteps incessantly, and without whom the nobleman can do nothing. The Jews have so completely monopolized this kind of occupation, that no purchaser can find a seller, nor any seller a buyer, without the help of a Jew. Although at Lemberg we had engaged a German driver for our journey onward, yet we could not manage to deal directly with him, and all our intercourse with him was carried on through a Jewish broker. We afterwards asked why, as he knew where we lived, he did not come to us himself to arrange his terms. He replied, that the Jews being once in possession of this brokerage business, if he were to refuse them the accustomed per centage, they would refuse to assist him the next time he came to Lemberg, and he dared not offend them, as they were always the best informed respecting strangers and their plans.

The extraordinary increase and spread of the Jewish nation in these countries, and their remarkable position in the kingdom of Poland, is an interesting enigma in the history of Europe, the best solution of which will be found in the peculiar character of the Polish nation. The boundless ambition, the wild passion, and love of lawless power on the one side, and on the other (for extremes create their opposites, and as the wealth and luxury of the few is always allied to the want and misery of the many, so the slavery of the many is a necessary condition of the excessive privileges of the few), the low servile spirit, and the want of independent feeling, which are fundamental elements of the Polish character, have influenced their political organization and divided the nation into two extreme classes : an arbitrary and oppressive nobility, and a tame, spiritless, and enslaved peasantry. Between these two there remained an immense chasm, making it difficult for any middle class to arise, on account of the violence of the Polish character, which will be either master or slave, and cannot endure the moderation and independence of an intermediate station. The nobles were determined to keep all others beneath them, the peasants were accustomed to see all others far above them. As long as the old barbaric Sarmatian kingdom existed, as long as the wants of the nation were simple, and its intercourse with foreign countries slight, the chasm remained unfilled, without causing much inconvenience; but when in the middle ages, Poland grew stronger and more important, and entered regularly into the list of European nations, when she made conquests and carried on commerce, when a taste for luxury and a consequent demand for greater perfection in the useful and ornamental arts arose within her; when, in one word, the want of a middle class began to be felt, for which Poland herself possessed none of the elements, the Jews presented themselves as wonderfully well adapted to supply the want. Driven from their native land, despised and oppressed by all other nations, the Jews had learnt in the hard school of adversity, that patience, fortitude, pliability, and servility, which the Polish nobleman expects from all beneath him. The state of affairs too at the time naturally led them towards Poland; and scarcely had they touched Polish ground, when they spread with astonishing rapidity, over all the countries subject to the Polish sceptre.*

An examination into the Polish and Jewish national characters, will show how well calculated they are to get on together. The Jew is dirty, so is the Pole, and therefore neither is disgusted with the other. The Pole is furious and passionate, the Jew mild and patient. The Pole is extravagant and generous, none knows better than the Jew how to take advantage of these qualities. The Pole is careless and ignorant in arithmetic, the Jew skilful and exact. The Pole lives in the present, and never thinks of how he will get out of a scrape; the Jew is slow, cautious, and full of resources. The Pole is proud and impetuous, the Jew humble and obedient. The Pole is idle and lazy, the Jew industrious and toilsome. It would have been impossible for the stiff Polish pine to grow up beside a noble oak, but it was easy for a flexible and clinging parasite to entwine itself amongst the branches of the stately tree.

A detailed history of the Jews in Poland, by the hand of any one who knew and understood them, would abound in extraordinary and interesting events and anecdotes, and a description of their present condition would combine pictures of the most squalid misery and of the greatest luxury. The extraordinary privileges which the Polish nobles have sometimes granted them, and the degrading treatment with which they have at other times loaded them, have given rise to the greatest extremes in their condition. Sometimes the Jews, who had their own deputies at Warsaw, and their own marshal over them, appeared to form a state within the state, preparing to face the Poles as nation to nation; sometimes, on the contrary, they were made the slaves of slaves.

The affairs of the court at Warsaw have often been guided by some fair Jewish Esther. Conspiracies and insurrections of the Jews have often taken place, and in the wars of the Poles for independence, the Jews, who mourn with them for the downfal of the old republic, have taken an active part. Casimir the Great, upon whom a Jewish mistress exercised great influence, enacted many laws highly advantageous to them. He gave them a privileged court of justice, for settling their disputes with Gentiles, and other courts of their own for settling their disputes among themselves; he freed them from all state burdens, and endeavoured to relieve them from the tyranny and oppression of their masters. This

---

* No further, however, for on the Russian frontiers their territory entirely ceases. The Russian character, similar in many respects to their own, did not offer them similar advantages.

tyranny and oppression has, however, continued ever since to be exercised upon them, and the nobleman has always done whatever he pleased with the Jews upon his estate. He fixes and increases at pleasure the taxes which they pay him, and the fear of driving away these useful slaves by overweening tyranny, is the only restraint upon his despotic caprice. The law forbids the nobleman to flog his Jews, but the Jew—dependant upon his master's humour in so many respects, dares not claim the protection of the law, and in reward for his endurance, he is allowed to tyrannize over the peasant, as the noble tyrannizes over him.

It was formerly a common custom for the Polish nobles to keep Jews at their castles as fools. Even now these Jewish jesters are often met with in great families; they bear every kind of insult and ill-treatment with patience and servility. They are treated just like house-dogs, eat and sleep in their master's rooms, but are the butts and scapegoats of the whole family, on whom each throws his own sins, and vents his own ill-humour. In a certain Polish household there lived lately a *house Jew* of this kind. He had received the brilliant name of Prince Friedrich, and was never called by any other. He was as elegantly dressed as the master of the house, and was fed by every one like a pet parrot. Each member of the family was continually popping things into his mouth, which he was compelled to swallow; if he was in favour, it was a lump of sugar, if they wished to tease him, rhubarb and magnesia, and sometimes a rap of the knuckles at the same time. He was obliged to be alternately rocking-horse, dancing bear, draught-ox and jackass, for the children, as they and their play required. On Sundays they dressed him up and masked him, now as a negro, now as a Brahmin, now as a he-goat, and now as Jupiter, or Pluto. The master himself often played tricks upon his fool, even more *piquant* than those of his children, for they did not always pass off without bloodshed. One day the Jew met him in the castle-court, just as he returned from the chase in a great ill-humour, having shot nothing. "I hope the *gnädige Herr* has had a good day's sport," said the fool, bowing low. "The devil! Jew! I haven't so much as shot one chattering magpie. My gun is still loaded. But stay—I think I can bring down a magpie yet! Up into the tree, sirrah! Up! no flinching! Higher, higher, or I'll give you the ball in your head! Up into that branch—now sit still, magpie!" So saying, he discharged the contents of his gun into the leg of the screaming Jew, who fell down from the tree into the courtyard, and the nobleman rode past him laughing heartily, and fully content with his day's sport. The Jew was taken up, cured, fed with honey and bonbons, and remained in the house as before.*

At Lemberg we were told of two young noblemen who had, a short time previously, played the following trick, by no means the worst of which I was told at the time. They had been riding along a very dirty road, and came to a Jewish village, where some Jewish families, men, women, and children, all attired in their Sabbath splendour, were walking along the clean pathway, while the young noblemen were splashed with mud from top to toe. "Look at the Jews how fine they are, with their white stockings and bright black shoes. They go in finer clothes than the nobility of the country." "Let us make them dance in the mud a bit,"

---

* This anecdote was related to me at Lemberg, of a nobleman residing there. I afterwards learnt that the same story has been told by Solomon Maimon of a Prince —i—.

proposed one. The proposal met with the greatest approbation. "Down Jews, down from the footpath. You shall have a fine Sunday's sport. Come, dance a Mazurka here in the mud. We will provide music." The Jews prayed the "good gentlemen" to have mercy, and not to turn the merry jest into mournful earnest, but the latter ordered their servants to blow a Mazurka on their hunting-horns, and driving the Jews into the mud with their horsewhips, forced them to dance in pairs, to the united music of the hunting-horns and the horsewhips, until they were covered with mud, when the young nobles rode on, delighted with their practical joke. To the honour of the Austrian government, however, it must be added, that such things very seldom happen in Galicia.

The language of the Jews is a corrupt German. In the Baltic provinces it resembles that of Prussia, in Galicia that of Austria; and these circumstances seem to indicate the German origin of the Polish Jews, while their costume, on the contrary, would appear to confirm the conjecture that they came originally from Greece. Perhaps they entered Poland, at about the same time, from both countries. The dress of the Polish Jews is purely oriental. It is totally different from that of their German brethren, and bears no resemblance to that of the Poles. But throughout Poland, from the Pontus to the Baltic, it never varies; an uniformity the more remarkable in a nation which has no political unity.

All the Polish Jews have tall meager figures, that is to say the men, for the women, probably on account of their inactive way of life, are often stout. The men are wrapt in a long caftan, generally of silk, and always black, which is confined round the waist by a silken girdle. Their complexion is always pale, and this does not appear to be occasioned by personal cares and troubles, but to be the common colour of the race. Their complexion, however, is at the same time delicate, so that their faces often look as if they had been carved of alabaster. Their hands are, in general, remarkably soft and delicate, and I have seen such brilliant eyes, such bright dark hair, such beautiful forms, such noble countenances, among the Polish Jews, that I have often wondered how such beings could grow up in such deep social degradation and abasement. There are parts of Luthuania where every Jew is a handsome man. Under the most miserable rags they often display the noblest forms. They generally wear their black hair short behind, but in front they allow a few ringlets (*Priessaken* they call them) to overshadow the ears. How the Italian painters created so many beautiful Jewish heads, as patriarchs, apostles, or as Christ himself, without ever having been among the Polish Jews, I am at a loss to understand. A painter wishing to produce countenances of the same exquisite beauty, need only come here, and faithfully copy the physiognomical treasures presented to him. The contrast between these noble figures and the occupations in which they are found, is a matter of incessant astonishment to the traveller. It is as if one saw King Solomon or David selling old clothes, or the patriarchs and apostles higgling with peasants about the price of beer.

The head-dress of the Polish Jews is a high fur cap elegantly shaped. The Jewesses wear flowing dresses, and brightly coloured turbans; those of the wealthier among them are richly adorned with pearls and diamonds. The whole costume is so oriental, that one might fancy them just arrived from Syria. Both men and women wear shoes or slippers; I never saw a Polish Jew in boots. Even the beggar finds means to decorate his person a little; but no one can imagine, who has not witnessed it, in what dirt, what rags, what misery, the really poor Polish Jews are sunk, and this in spite of the many monopolies they enjoy. Though the Jews are the only great capitalists of the country, and though without them no one can obtain the loan of a single ducat, while with them 100,000 ducats are as easily obtained as one, yet their poor are sunk in want and misery far deeper than that of the Polish peasants, which is the more remarkable, as the Jews are no drunkards, gamblers, or spendthrifts, but, on the contrary, are always prudent, parsimonious, and industrious. The want, the disease, the hunger, the squalid misery and wretchedness contained in the damp, pestilential dwellings of the poor Jews of Warsaw, Cracow, Mitau, Lemberg, Vilna, and Odessa, where half-a-dozen families, all abundantly provided with children, though with nothing else, pig together in one filthy cellar, with bad food, and scanty light—all this cannot be equalled in wretchedness either among the Esquimaux, or the New Hollanders, or the inhabitants of Terra del Fuego. The cattle of Switzerland are far better accommodated than the poor Jews of Poland; and any one who wishes to learn how small a quantity of nourishment will suffice to keep life in a human body, how ragged a garment may become before it drops off, how pestilential the atmosphere of a human dwelling may be made without causing suffocation, how children may be *dragged* up (not brought up) without clothes, washing, or warmth, without brush, comb, or soap and water, without care, medicine, or education, has only to come and study the condition of the poor Polish Jews.

The statistical accounts estimate the Jewish population, throughout Poland, at only three millions. This appears very little, for the traveller may travel two or three hundred miles in the country, and at every place he comes to, the Jews appear to swarm. It seems almost inconceivable that all these swarms put together, should only amount to one hundred for each square mile.

Travelling from central Germany towards the east, the number of Jews increases more and more from its minimum in Thuringia. In Saxony, Leipzig, and Dresden, there are little colonies of them; in Silesia, Breslau and Posen they are abundant. At Cracow and Warsaw they appear to reach their maximum. In Galicia there are 450,000 Jews, and the total population of the country is four millions. There is, therefore, one Jew to every nine inhabitants, and three hundred to every square mile. As far as the Dniester their proportion remains nearly the same. Beyond the Dniester they gradually decrease, and at the eastern end of the old Polish kingdom they entirely cease. Their condition is the best in Prussian, the next best in Austrian, and the worst in Russian Poland.

THE GERMANIZATION OF GALICIA.

In a former chapter I remarked on the influence which the Poles have had upon the Rusniaks, and spoke of the Polonization of the Lithuanian, Rusniak, and other races. At Lemberg, where I lodged with a German host, ordered new boots of a German bootmaker, and had my coat mended by a German tailor, where a German waiter brought me my coffee, and the Polish hackney-coachman who drove me about the town spoke German, every thing reminded me of the influence of Germany on Galicia.

Of all the different fragments of the old Polish kingdom, the *Podgorski*

Voyevodstvi, or dukedoms of the promontory, now known as the kingdom of Galicia, have got on best, and, under their new rulers, have least cause to mourn the loss of their former independence. Prussian Poland (although indeed some classes derive much benefit from the political order introduced by Prussia) feels very acutely the difference in religion between herself and her new masters. The Baltic provinces of East and West Prussia, which harmonize in so many things with their new masters, suffer from the very unfavourable commercial position in which the division of Poland has placed her. Russian Poland suffers in a thousand ways; for to the differences in race and in religion between Poland and Russia, are here added the hardships of an iron despotism, and an almost total want of the corresponding advantages which in other parts of Poland atone in some measure for the loss of independence.

Austrian Poland shares with the above-named countries the one great evil of loss of independence: she mourns with them for the decline of the old kingdom, and is disinclined towards her new rulers; but she possesses many advantages denied to them. She has the advantage over the Prussian provinces of an uniformity of religion with her new rulers. The Austrians are Catholics like the Poles, and consequently all the clergy of the country are favourable to the government.

The benefits which Galicia has received from Austria are so numerous and evident, that an impartial traveller, whether entering the country from Russia or Hungary, must be struck by them. I believe that many a Pole, who finds it hard to forget the one great injury which Austria has done his country, yet feels himself compelled gratefully to acknowledge the beneficent influence of the Austrian government.

It gives one a feeling of security to enter the Galician territory, for one is there under the protection of a regular and orderly system of jurisdiction. The former state of justice in Poland was as rude and anarchical as the whole constitution of the country. In comparison with the past, the order and security of the present is truly wonderful. Formerly, whoever was not a nobleman, and could not make himself feared, whoever could not arm himself with gold, power, or cunning, was sure to be defeated by a more powerful antagonist. Austria has bestowed upon these four millions of subject nobles, clergy, citizens, and peasants, the mighty blessing of a security of rights to each. The traveller in Galicia has ample opportunities of seeing that this is no empty form. On the other side of the Russian frontier, the phrases here so common, "I will have justice," "I will complain to the magistrates," are scarcely ever heard.

In the old kingdom of Poland it was not uncommon for a noble who had undertaken a lawsuit with his neighbour, and been defeated, to collect a swarm of friends and retainers, and make war upon his antagonist. When a nobleman killed one who was not a nobleman, his only punishment was a fine of 200 marks; but when one not a noble denied the nobility of a genuine patrician, the law pronounced the penalty of death on the offender. The Jew and the peasant might almost be said to have no rights at all. Many of these abuses would no doubt have gradually been done away with, had Poland remained independent, yet it cannot be denied that, under the government of Austria, they have been more rapidly and thoroughly uprooted. The peasants, Jews, and other oppressed classes of society, moreover, would probably never have obtained the degree of security and freedom which Austria has bestowed upon them, and which, though far from being all that it should be, is yet admirable, compared with that of ancient or Russian Poland. In consequence of the improvements in the condition of the peasantry, the whole system of agriculture has been reformed, and Galicia, in comparison with other Polish lands, is extremely well cultivated.

The police regulations which Austria has introduced throughout the country, and particularly into the cities, are also numerous and excellent. Under the care of the Austrian functionaries, the towns of Galicia have entirely lost their old Polish appearance, and undergone a complete change. They are better built than in any other part of Poland, are by no means ill lighted, are paved throughout, are provided with handsome public buildings, and have civil officers, who watch over the health of the inhabitants, and the peace and order of the town.

The whole country is intersected by one great road, from which diverge smaller roads, extremely serviceable for internal transport and travelling. A history of the great Galician road, and of all the hinderances and obstacles it met with, would sufficiently prove that but for Austria, Poland might for centuries have wanted such a road.

The activity of Austria in disseminating the German language and German literature, must however be more particularly noticed. Galicia owes to the government not only the University founded at Lemberg in 1817, but a Gymnasium in every considerable town, and in even the very smallest towns, a large number of schools for girls and boys, for both Jews and Christians. In all these schools German is taught, and the German language is now so generally spread throughout Galicia, that every well-educated Pole speaks it, and, even among the lower orders, the knowledge of German is taken as a test of a good education. In Russian Poland this can never be the case, because the Pole places the language and literature of his own country higher than that of Russia. In Prussian Poland, also, the aversion of the people to every thing German is far greater than in Galicia. In the latter country many a pretty little Polish peasant girl can chatter her Austrian German like a native of Vienna; in Posen a Polish lady will deny her knowledge of German, even if she has any, and will converse with a German only through an interpreter. The popularity of the Germans among the Polish Galicians may be partly owing to the cordiality and *Bonhommie* of the Austrian nobility, with whom the Poles and Hungarians can assimilate better than with the more cold and reserved grandees of Prussia.

The number of German magistrates and civil officers is very great. In the year 1831, there were eight thousand men employed in the different branches of civil government in Galicia and Lodomiria. Two thousand six hundred of these were Germans. About one-third therefore of all the civil functionaries of this country are Germans. According to a moderate estimate, each of these civil officers has, on an average, at least four persons in his family, including children, wife, brothers, sisters, and other relatives; Galicia, therefore, contains 40,000 persons of this class, 12,000 of whom are Germans. One in every hundred of the inhabitants is therefore a civic functionary, and one in every three of these is a German.

Of the professors of the University of Lemberg two-thirds are Germans, and only one-third Poles. The theological faculties are almost entirely filled by Germans. All the directors of the Galician gymnasiums are

Germans, but the majority of the teachers are Poles. The teachers in the common schools, generally Poles, must always understand German.

The great increase of offices, public functionaries, and courts of law, which Austria has introduced into the government of Galicia, is one of those innovations most complained of by the Poles; but the fact is, the Poles had quite as many formerly, though many of the old ones were extremely useless; and even were it otherwise, the better order now prevailing, could not be kept up without this increase. The same may be said of the high taxation of Galicia, which the Poles so much complain of. Galicia is, no doubt, taxed twice or three times as much as Russian Poland, but if these taxes come back to the inhabitants in the shape of roads, canals, lights, public walks, and courts of justice, the people are amply recompensed for the outlay of their capital. These lamentations about high taxes are a great folly, unless they are badly levied or badly expended. Those countries in which the people live best, namely Holland and England, and some parts of Germany and France, are the highest taxed, and the wild Hottentots and Esquimaux are among the nations whose fiscal burdens are the lightest.

The Polish nobles form the most discontented class, partly because they suffer most from the loss of that independence of which they possessed the largest share, and partly because it is they who feel most disagreeably the effects of the social order introduced by Austria. The anarchy sanctioned by the laws of the old Polish kingdom was so great, that the strongest and boldest was always master, and society was but a fraternity of lawless despots, who, though themselves free in the widest sense of the term, were utterly unmindful of the rule—" touch not the rights of others," without which no social liberty can properly exist. As all those laws of the Austrian government, which protect the rights of the oppressed classes, must attack this anarchy and limit this despotism, they are of course opposed to the interest of the nobles. There is therefore scarcely any measure of the government which they do not consider a violation of their privileges.

With the Polish clergy, who always governed mildly, the case is different. They stand a step nearer to the government, and the more so as they agree with the latter in resisting the too great encroachments of the papal power. The burgesses of the towns are generally on the side of government, although there are among them not merely Poles, but even Germans, who are such Polish patriots that they sigh for the return of the old republic, although they do not desire the return of its abuses. The Jews are the most ungrateful towards Austria, for notwithstanding the protection she affords them against the tyranny of the nobles, they are always lamenting and complaining of the few limitations she has put on their usurious dealings.

The peasants have the most cause to be contented with the present order of things, for in the old Polish republic, in which the king was only the first noble, they had no protector, and their masters oppressed them at will, because there was none to speak for or defend them. The Austrian emperor, whose interest it is to preserve the smallest as the greatest of the forces at his command, is the protector and father of the peasants, and has proved himself to be so, more in Galicia than in any other part of his empire. But the Galician peasants are as yet too little advanced in knowledge and cultivation, to feel and acknowledge the benefits they have received, and it would not be much to be wondered at, if in case of an insurrection in Galicia, the infatuated peasantry were again to make common cause with the nobles, against the Austrian government.

THE GALICIAN NOBLES.

It is well known that, in the prosperous days of Poland, the nobles considered themselves as all perfectly equal, so that those various titles indicating different degrees of rank, which are used in England, France, and Germany, were unknown among them. Only nine native families bore the title of *Ksowze* (Prince), and they founded no particular claims on this title. All other titles were German or Russian, and were so sparingly used, that till the 18th century, Poland had but two counts, (Tentschin and Olenski,) two "Knäse," (Oginski and Massalski,) and one Marquis, (Vielopolski). All the others were simple "*Nobiles possessionati,*" the rulers of the country.

This state of things has very much changed under the Austrian government, which is by no means sparing in titles and orders. There are indeed only two princely families in Galicia, those of Lubomirski and Yablonovski, and they are of modern origin, and belonging to the old princely families of Poland. There are, however, no less than seventy-nine Galician counts, and nine barons.

The well-known professor *Schulze*, who has written an excellent work on Warsaw and the state of Poland, reckons the number of families who have divided among themselves the greater part of the country, and the places of honour in the state, at about one hundred, and among these hundred he names thirty, who by their great wealth and importance, exercise a marked influence over the government of the country. Among these are the Czartoriski, Potocki, Brannicki, Tshetvertinski, Radzivill, Czacki, Lubomirski, Massalski, Soltyk, and Rzevuski families, all of old Polish descent, whose names have always shone in the annals of their country. These families have spread over all parts of Poland, and there are many of them who are at the same time subject to the Emperor of Austria, the King of Prussia, and the Emperor of Russia. Originally, however, these great families belonged only to one part of Poland, so that they may be divided into Lithuanian, Podolian, and Galician families. In Galicia there are no Brannickis, Czartoriskis, Czackis, Dluskis, Gotskis, Malachovskis, Oginskis, Ossolinskis, Radzivills, Sapiehas, Soltyks, Sulkovskis, Massalskis, or Mostovskis; but the Stadtnickis, Zaluskis, Krassinskis, Yablonovskis, Lubomirskis, Skarbieks, Potockis, and Levickis, on the other hand, are the greatest families of Galicia, and the principal subjects of the Emperor of Austria. In addition to the foregoing we may mention the following names as belonging to noble families distinguished for their wealth or social position in Galicia : Ankvitz, Bilinski, Bobrovski, Brokovski, Bikovski, Dembrovski, Dziedushicki, Yastrebski, Illassivitsch, Ilnicki, Kepalski, Klossovski, Kurkovski, Lenkivitsh, Lobarzevski, Lozinski, Midovitsh, Podocki, Poziolovski, Volski, and Vshelatshinski. These names are familiar to every child in Galicia ; they are the names of men who never drive but with four horses, possess castles and houses abounding in all the luxuries of life, and are absolute masters of thousands of human beings. Their pride is boundless, and they never lose sight of the recollection that their illustrious races are rooted in the history of the world, like so many oaks that have braved the storms of a thousand years. Some of them live at

Vienna, Petersburg, and Paris, endeavouring in the tumult of the gay world, to forget the downfall of Poland; others live in gloomy retirement on their estates, to mourn that downfall in solitude.

Austria, very differently from Russia and Prussia, has left to these nobles many of the brilliant titles and dignities of the old republic, as harmless playthings. She has raised Galicia to the rank of a kingdom; the Emperor of Austria bears the title of King of Galicia; there, as in Hungary, Bohemia, the Tyrol, &c., he is seldom spoken of by any other name. With this title the high-sounding dignities and titles of the old republic of Poland, have been extended to Galicia. There is a Galician colonel of the Country kitchen, (*Oberst land küchenmeister*,) an Upper Land Marshal, a High Falconer of the country, an Hereditary Grand Carver, a Grand Country Carver, a Silver Chamberlain, a Swordbearer, &c.; titles with which the Polish nobles are as fond of decorating themselves as with diamonds and pearls. The Archbishop of Lemberg bears the title of Primate of Galicia. These dignities are always carefully set apart for genuine old Polish families, and are never filled by Germans. The Galician noblemen cling to them with great pertinacity, for in spite of their fiction about equality among noblemen, there is probably no nobility in the world so fond of titles, or so eager for distinctions, as that of Poland.

Not only is every body in Poland always addressed by his title, as "Pan Truchsess," "Pan Bishop," "Pan Voyevode," not only is this title, as in Germany, always bestowed upon the wife, also as "Panna Landhofmeisterinn," "Panna Truchsess," &c., but the official dignity of the father is inherited by his son. For instance the son of a marshal so long as he has no title of his own, is called Sir Marshalson, *Pan Marshallikovitsh*. Even a grandson will borrow his grandfather's title if he has none of his own, and call himself *Pan Marshallikovitshovitsh*, Sir Marshall's son's son; or if his grandfather has been a Grand Carver, the grandson will call himself *Pan Stolnikovitshovitsh*, or Sir Carver's son's son. There have been, however, at all times some very high lords and ladies in Poland as well known throughout the kingdom as the princes of the reigning family are in a little German principality, and who are never spoken of by their titles or their family names, but simply by their Christian names. Every one in Poland, knew formerly who was meant by Prince Adam, and Prince Joseph, or by Panna Maria, Panna Anna, and Panna Elizabeth. There are still in Galicia such Josephs, Adams, and Marias, who are as well known to all the world, as the saints of the calender, and who, purified in the vulgar eye of all the earthly dross of titles and surnames, are spoken of, like the apostles, only by their baptismal denominations. A similar custom prevails in Moldavia and Russia.

There are in all 2500 estates in the possession of the Galician nobles, of which on an average each must contain two thirds of a German square mile, seeing that the whole country contains 1500; many of them, however, are from twenty to thirty miles in circumference. Some families possess from ten to twenty such estates, and there are many which rule over not less than one hundred square miles. Very few estates have been taken from their old possessors, for during the sixty years in which Austria has ruled over the country, amid all the changes and disturbances in the rest of Poland, the Galician nobility have remained tolerably faithful to Austria, and have given little occasion for the confiscation of estates.

GRUDEK, MOSHISKA, AND YAROSLAV.

To our sorrow, the hour of our departure from Lemberg at last arrived. We would willingly have spent a few days more in observing the peculiarities of the city, and enjoying the comforts of our hotel, where we dined every day with eight Polish counts, and from ten to twenty Galician nobles; but the driver we had hired would leave us no peace. "His "*Gloswogen*" was already packed; his "*Scheckerl*," a little white poodle-dog, who was to be our future travelling companion, was already barking from behind the carriage; the lean, infirm, old horses were scratching the earth with their feet as though from impatience, so that nothing remained for us, but to take up our position on the two very inconvenient seats inside.

Had our coachman been a Russian Yamtshik, his conversation and behaviour during our eight days' journey, would have furnished us materials for a whole novel, but our charioteer was a dull-headed, prosaic German hackney-coachman, of the ancient city of Brünn, and never whistled a tune or hummed a song, but sat on the coach-block wrapped in his mantle, silent, reserved, and sullen, save when he dismounted to get a *schnapps* at a roadside inn, on which occasions he would storm and swear most furiously if not served to his satisfaction. He flew continually into a rage with his horses, and beat them unmerifully; demanded extra payment for the slightest deviation from the road, not stipulated for beforehand, and at last threatened us with a lawsuit at Vienna, because we resisted his exorbitant demands.

We drove away over the hills round Lemberg, along the road leading to Yaroslav and Cracow, and looked down for the last time on the forsaken city. At its gates we met the Catholic Archbishop of Lemberg. He was elegantly dressed in black, and his air and carriage were those of a nobleman, as he walked along by the side of his stately four-horsed equipage. Two young priests, also elegantly dressed in black, followed him. Every one stopped in the streets and saluted him respectfully, and he returned their salutations in a simple, dignified, and condescending manner. Formerly the Archbishop of Gnesen was the first, and the Archbishop of Lemberg the second clerical dignitary in Poland. He of Lemberg is now the first in the little kingdom of Galicia, and ought, according to Cæsar's rule, that it is better to be first in Marseilles than second in Rome, to be very well satisfied with the change; but there is no doubt that on the contrary, he would be very glad to exchange his present primacy, for his former secondary importance.

The principal commercial road, the "Cisarsky Doroga" or Imperial road, is as bad beyond Lemberg as throughout the whole of this soft chalky table-land, where the traveller is continually sticking fast in one hole or another, so that we did not arrive at Grudek, till the moon was already shining brightly in the heavens. A piercing cold, which covered all the lakes and ponds with thin crusts of ice, announced to us that we had entered the district of the Vistula, in Northern Galicia. It seemed to be already winter, but we afterwards arrived at Moravia and Vienna in a mild and cheerful autumn. This high land of Galicia which is protected by no mountains towards the north, is even colder than the plains of the Vistula.

The average temperature of Moravia is two or three degrees higher than that of Galicia.

At Grudek we heard the same old story, which is continually repeated to the traveller from the banks of the Oder till far into Asia: "This is a noble town, sir; it belongs to the nobleman —prtzkovski; a great lord, a very rich man, who possesses six towns and twenty villages. The peasants are poor people, who eat the bread of their master, and receive the blows of his servants. The towns folk are Jews, mingled with a few Poles and Germans."

At the inn we found some Polish women sorting feathers. The mountaineers here, are called *Huzzulen* as in Bukovina. We found two of them sitting by the fire at the inn, leaning upon their hatchets. They told us that they were never without their hatchets, that they travelled with them, danced with them, and wore them as a part of their Sunday finery. They went to church with their hatchets, but did not take them into the church. They hung them upon wooden posts outside, from which each on coming out took down his own again.

It was singular, that, however much we questioned the people, we never could learn what they called the Carpathians. They generally answered *Gori* (mountains), and sometimes *Byeskid* (chain of mountains), from which comes the geographical name of *Beskiden*, for the central part of the Carpathian mountains. The name Carpathians seemed to be quite unknown to them, except where a peasant here and there had learned it of some German schoolmaster. This is natural enough. It will always be found, that the common geographical names of mountains are not used by those who inhabit them, for where only the difference between the plain and the mountains is noticed, and not the difference between one set of mountains and another, the mountains are only called mountains. As we recede into the plain, and arrive at some distance from the mountains, where the view is not hemmed in, and two or three masses are seen at a time, particular names are used for the different groups. It is only the geographer, who, in drawing and surveying maps, surveys many great chains at once, and gives names to them, and to their subdivisions. With rivers the case is quite the contrary. They isolate and individualize themselves far more than mountains, and their currents offer a much more striking contrast to the dry land, than the mountains do to the plains. Their course is far more easily overlooked than the range of a mountain chain, and thus the name of a river is the same at its mouth and at its source, the same to those at a distance, and to those residing on its banks. The name by which the Poles call the Carpathians, is "*Khrovatsky Gori*."

Though now in the midst of the Carpathians, we seemed to be quite losing sight of them; and our investigations fared much the same respecting a kingdom, on whose very borders we knew ourselves to be, and after which, nevertheless, we inquired in vain. Nobody here knew any thing about the kingdom of Lodomeria, nay, nobody so much as knew its name. Some officers of Lemberg thought that Bukovina had once been called so, and others imagined it to signify Cracow; and yet the two kingdoms of Galicia and Lodomeria, are so closely connected, that their names are scarcely ever mentioned in any geographical class-book, but they are coupled together like twins. We ourselves were, of course, not so ignorant as the Galicians. We had long ago read the two thick volumes, entitled the

"History of Halitsh and Vladimir, with an examination and defence of the Austro-Hungarian claims in that kingdom, by Christian Engel." We could not therefore be ignorant that Vladimir the Great, the first Christian Grand Duke of Russia had a son, Yaroslav, who was likewise afterwards Grand Duke of all Russia, and that the latter had also a son, Vsevolod, Grand Duke of Kieff, who detached from his own principality the miniature principality of Vladimir with a capital called Vladimir, and bestowed the said miniature upon his nephew Yaropolk. This principality of Vladimir, or rather Volodimir, which was afterwards, by a slight corruption of the name, changed into Lodomeria, contained the present districts of Luck and Chelen in Volhynia. The boundaries of the little state were not very accurately defined, even at the period of its first formation. It was also several times subdivided among various princes. Sometimes it belonged to the princes of Halitsh. The greater part of the northernmost circle of Galicia belonged to this principality, and when the Emperor of Austria became master of Galicia, at the first division of Poland, in the year 1772, he availed himself of the opportunity to add the stately title of King of Lodomeria to his other denominations; which title is not the less fine sounding, that no creature in Austria knows in what region of the globe this fabulous kingdom lies. Besides it is not Austria but Russia, to which the greater part of the old principality, with its former capital of Vladimirz really belongs.

The next day we breakfasted at Sadova-Vishnia, and dined at Moshiska. At dinner we were waited upon by a blooming young Polish girl, of mean origin, but fair and graceful as a princess. Many writers have contended that the far-famed beauty of the Polish women was confined to the upper classes. I think they are mistaken. The lower classes appear less beautiful, only because toil, care, and want, too often imprint their marks upon the features, and because they are entirely without those advantages of dress enjoyed by the favoured children of fortune. Wherever Polish women are seen in comfortable situations, clean and neat, well fed, and clothed, the natural beauty of high and low, displays itself in their slender, graceful forms, their sparkling, dark eyes, the tasteful arrangement of their abundant ringlets, and their lively, sportive, charming manners.

The horse often makes a peculiar haughty motion, arching his neck and tossing his proud head. This he only does when particularly excited. No other animal, neither the ox nor the stag, makes a similar movement. Peculiarities of this kind may be noticed among different races of mankind, as of animals. For instance, we noticed in the Polish women, a certain pretty sportive waving motion of the head and neck, which was common alike to high and low in every part of the country. I cannot describe this gesture more minutely, for such delicate peculiarities are lost in description, and yet I should immediately know a Polish girl by it, in any part of the world. Neither the Germans, the Russians, nor the French, have any thing like it. When a Polish girl is dancing or talking sportively with another, this movement is particularly striking. It is one of those delicate traits of national character, of which it is almost impossible to give any one an idea who has not seen it.

The Polish girls are fresh and blooming as roses, and graceful in every gesture as sylphs; any one who undertakes to describe their numberless charms, in detail, can never cease admiring the abundance of beauty and grace, which Nature has so lavishly bestowed upon them. We needed neither flowers, nor sugar, nor wine, nor music, at our banquet, for our lovely Polish Hebe was all this at once to us.

How—music?—Yes music—whoever doubts it, and fancies the Polish language harsh and unmusical, let him come to Poland and hear it. It is curious, that on account of the manner in which it is written, this language has been considered as of a very barbarous sound, whereas every ingenuous traveller will confess, that it is not merely on account of their own pretty faces, that the native tones sound as sweetly from the lips of Polish damsels, as from those of a Roman or Tuscan lady. There is nothing harsh or grating in the Polish language; on the contrary, it is particularly soft and harmonious. The few harsh sounds that occur, are always softened by the intermixture of liquid syllables, and the hiatus of the vowels is mostly obviated by the introduction of the j, (pronounced like an English y). The softness of the Polish language, when spoken by the vulgar, sometimes becomes unpleasant. It is as if their flexible words had as little strength and dignity as their eternally bowing and twisting spines. The Germans have something monotonous and unbending in their language; the Russians something hollow, and at the same time shrill and squeaking, as if they were *screaming into a pot*. The Poles, on the contrary, speak very quickly and flexibly. They often rise into a faint treble, which when exaggerated, becomes squeaking and disagreeable. It is singular to observe, in what a miserable whining manner the Polish and Lithuanian peasants speak, particularly when addressing their masters. It is so peculiar a tone, that if once heard it will never be forgotten.

The variously modulated liquid tones, intermingled gracefully with slippery *l*'s and soft faint *r*'s, which sound roughly only from our clumsy German tongues, give to the Polish language something that to my ear resembles the twittering of birds. The abundant repetition of *brz, prz, scze, sdcz*, &c., look dreadful to us, and in our ignorance we exclaim, "What a barbarous language!" without reflecting that one should hear a language spoken, as well as see it written, before one can decide upon its merits. Let any one hear the words Zebrdzedowski, Peczyniscni, Rzeszow, Brzczani, Przemysl, Szczebrzeszyn, Strzyzew, Pomdzamczeprzytymce, Brzozw, Jastrzebski, Wrzepicki, Krzecynski, Wszelaczynski, &c., from the mouth of a young Polish girl, and he will confess that the words grace the mouth quite as much as the mouth the words. Bechmann has written a book about singing birds, in which he expresses the song of the nightingale, by the syllables *zizizi, zuizuizui, tirwizvoll, zvoll, zvoll*, &c. Now any one reading this without having ever heard the nightingale sing, might well imagine its song to be a very ugly and disagreeable one. It would be just as reasonable to decide thus, as to judge of the Polish language from its written appearance. The Polish women, it is true, add a grace to the language, by their own sweet, lively, charming manner of speaking it. Every word lives between their lips; every thing is soft, piquant, and expressive. A comic anecdote, related with all the beautiful modulations of voice, in which they are so skilful, or a tragic story interrupted by their spontaneous sighs and tears, is irresistible from their lips. The Russian tongue compared to that of Poland, is as the rough dialect of mountaineers, to the soft language of the plains. It sounds harsher, shriller, and hollower, and wants many of the liquid Polish tones, the want of which it supplies with hissing and grating syllables. Many Russian words sound more like inarticulate noises than articulate sounds. I once witnessed a ludicrous instance of this. An acquaintance of mine in Odessa, who was standing with me in a balcony before his house, sneezed rather loud just as a Russian Isvoshtshik was driving past in his droshky looking out for custom. He took my friend's sneeze for the usual summons, "*Sluishi Isvoshtshik*," and taking off his hat, he replied, "I hear you, sir. Where am I to go to?"

The Germans of Galicia, however long they may live there, never learn to speak Polish correctly. There are difficulties in it which they never get over. They therefore take the matter easily, and pronounce the words in their own way. They have Germanized the names of most of the Polish cities. Przemysl for instance in which the "z" is pronounced like the French *j*, while the *r* glides faintly along between the *p* and the *z*, they generally call *Pshemysl;* and Rzeszow *Reshov*, which has a particularly absurd sound to a Polish ear.

We descended from the chalky hills round Lemberg, and entered a new district, the scene of different manners and customs, and different historical events. The Greek churches, which before had alternated with the Catholic in the towns and villages, now entirely ceased, and we entered the land of the *Mazovians*. Leaving the great road which leads through Przemysl and Yaroslav,—our driver played us this trick while we were taking a short siesta,—we drove into the country of Mazovia, being thus deprived of a view of the fine town of Przemysl, whose towers in vain rose up in the distance behind us. Instead of the far-famed and beautiful episcopal town, with its shops, gymnasiums, and churches, we saw only a few peasants' huts and *Gehöfte*, which, with their sledges and beehives, reminded us of the north of Poland. Instead of the four-horsed equipages of the Przemysl grandees, we saw only little carts, with their two diminutive horses each, and instead of the solid new bridge built over the San at Przemysl, only a miserable raft, upon which our carriage was floated over, and a boat made of the hollowed trunk of a tree, in which we ourselves were rowed across.

The inhabitants of the country watered by the San have been little influenced by modern improvements. In their domestic arrangements and accommodations, there is scarcely a trace of any reform. On the contrary, the shape and material of every thing, proves how ancient are all their usages. They hollow their boats, and cut their beehives, carts, and ploughs, in the same way probably as their forefathers did more than a thousand years ago. Every thing, down to the smallest piece of harness on their horses, to the most trifling hem and border on their clothes, has remained for ages unchanged. Even in the most civilized countries of Europe, however, some traits of this kind are to be found; even in the middle of cultivated England, for instance, the same primitive method of crossing a river may sometimes be witnessed as was used in the days of Queen Boadicea. Everywhere, beneath the restless and tumultuous surface of the upper classes, there remain masses of the population which are as little moved by the stormy revolutions of centuries that pass over them, as in the fathomless depths of the ocean, the compact mass of water below is agitated by the turbulence of the upper waves.

The San, at whose source lies the town of Sanok, and at whose mouth that of Sandomir, is here tolerably broad, though not deep, like all the streams that rush down from the Carpathians. At its union with the Vistula, the courses of the two rivers are equal in length, so that the great river which flows to the Baltic from their junction, might as well have been called the San as the Vistula. The Vistula, however, does contribute a larger mass of waters than the San.

The Vistula in its course previous to its junction with the San, forms with the mountains an angle of about 30 degrees, Galicia wedges itself into this angle, between the Carpathian range and the river. Within this space, several little tributary streams flow into the Vistula, and they become longer, the further the mountains and the river diverge, so that they lie between them like the strings of a harp. These rivers are the Sola, the Skava, the Raba, the Dunayez, the Visloka, and the San. In travelling onward towards Austrian Silesia, we passed successively through all the districts watered by these rivers, beginning with that of the San. At Radymno we passed the night in a very badly heated room. When we complained of this we were told that wood was very dear. The forests, it was true, were only four or five miles off, but there was no imperial road that led to them. This very frequent complaint of the dearness in wood, in a country where trees are so plentiful as in Galicia, has always remained an enigma to me.

The people of Radymno still cling with great enthusiasm to all recollections of the Holy Alliance. Everywhere, we saw the walls of the rooms decorated with pictures of the battle of Leipzig, and the entrance into Paris, just as was the case with us in 1820.

The people wore, of course, Mazovian costumes here. The *Krakusca* the well-known, high, red, four-cornered caps, edged with fur, and the *Kurtka* with its girdle, white trousers, short boots, and generally a plume of peacock's feathers, were worn by all. The manners and costumes of the peasantry are transmitted from father to son, and do not easily alter, so that if ever the higher classes of Poles were to return to the ways of their forefathers, they would find little or nothing of innovation among the lower orders of the people.

We should have been very well pleased with our host at Radymno, had his supper-table been as plentifully provided with salt, bread, and butter, as his German speeches with obsequious Polish civilities ; such as " *Panye Dobroti—Panye Laskovi—yevo Moshtsh* " (Your Honour— your gracious worship—your grace). It is strange how fond even the Germans here are, of these Polish phrases and titles, which they use even when speaking German, exclaiming with every breath, " May it please you, Panye Laskovi;" " With your leave, Panye Dobroti." When a person of distinction is present they add, like the Polish peasants, " *Zalye nogi*" (I kiss your feet), and to a lady, "*zalye rontshki*," (I kiss your hands): The genuine Poles repeat these phrases eight or ten times in a breath, and the greater their respect, the oftener they repeat their " *Zalye nogi! zalye nogi! zalye nogi!*" " *Padam do nog! padam do nog! padam do nog!*" Sometimes they act their own words, actually falling on their knees, and kissing the hands, feet, or garments, of the complimented party. Formerly the proud republicans of Poland did this to one another. Since they have lost their national independence, their manners have lost some of this slavish servility, probably because their nobles have lost some of that greatness and power that formerly called it forth.

In no country of the world is there more kissing than in Poland. When a lady and gentleman meet, he always kisses her hand, while she bends down, and touches his forehead with her lips. When two Polish gentlemen meet, they kiss each other on each cheek, in such a way that while one kisses the right cheek of his acquaintance, the other kisses his left cheek, and then the same ceremony reversed. A stranger has to practise this before he can get the knack of it, and perform the manœuvre accurately, quickly, and gracefully. When a guest enters a circle of friends, he has to kiss and be kissed all round. Where the relations between the parties are of a more tender or sentimental character, the salutation may be twice or thrice repeated, and then there is no end to the kissing.

The Germans are more blunt, plain, and straightforward than the Poles, in all their dealings, and appear, consequently, less obsequious and servile in their manners. The dirt and laziness of the Poles, often excite the indignation of their German fellow-citizens, and the words *Laitak* (lazy Pole), and *Galgane* (dirty Polish thief), are terms of reproach often used when a German quarrels with a Pole. These are often returned with interest by the Pole, cringing and servile as he may be on most occasions. "*Shwabska Dusha!*" (dull-souled Suabian,) and "*Bestia Shwab!*" are common expressions of theirs. The term *cobblers*, is often used by Polish noblemen for Germans of every rank, and the disgusting and not unfrequent phrase of *Niemeczka pshagrev sobatsha!* is another phrase invented by the nobles of the land, and is one of which I will leave it to my readers to obtain a translation from some of their Polish friends. These terms of abuse are in some measure illustrative of the national characters of the two races. The German, when he contemptuously terms the Russian noble a *gruel-eater*, prides himself, with justice, on his better style of living, the consequence of his superior industry and cleanliness, and derides the dirt, laziness, and poverty of the Pole. The Pole, however, considers himself as less plodding and mechanical, and scoffs at the petty industry and careful spirit of the German, by calling him *cobbler*. The contrast too of this German care, frugality, and industry, with his own proud and haughty laziness, which scorns every thing vulgar, namely law, morality, and industry, and loves only the noble prerogatives of idleness, wastefulness, and dissipation, is expressed in the disgusting manner above quoted.

German coins are now used throughout Galicia, where a florin is called *Renski zrebrom*, literally a silver Rhenish. A twenty kreuzer piece they call a *Zwanziger*, and a *Groshen* a *Dutka*. The coin principally used, however, throughout Galicia and Poland, is the Dutch ducat, or *Tshervonez*. These ducats are by no means all coined in Holland; many which are struck at St. Petersburg, are not the less called Dutch ducats.

It was still quite dark when early the next morning we passed through Yaroslav. The only things in the town which we saw were two or three dirty coffee-cups, illuminated by a little tallow candle which a Jewish servant girl lighted for our breakfast. The short time which we occupied in passing through it, however, sufficed to convince us that in size and importance it was not to be compared to its namesake in Russia.

The sun was shining brightly when we entered the little town of *Przevorsk*, which pleased us on account of the pretty castle and garden it contained. The place is the property of the Lubomirski family. The garden was large, and laid out like an English park, with trees, lakes, rivers, lawns, and groves. In the middle of a lawn was a bronze bust of the last great King of Poland, John Sobieski, who, being a native of Galicia, enjoys great veneration here. Sobieski wore his hair in the old Polish fashion, cut close all round, with a long pigtail behind, and thick mustaches and beard. The contrast must have been curious enough between this powerful barbaric figure, and that of the proud, petty, ceremonious Austrian emperor, Leopold, who, instead of warmly embracing and thanking the deliverer of Vienna on the battle-field, made his cold and formal acknowledgments at a mere chance meeting. Sobieski, probably incensed at this demeanour, cut short the long and formal speech of the emperor, with the words, "I am glad to have been able to render you this little service, my royal cousin," and taking a hasty leave, returned to Poland.

The castle is handsome, but not splendid. The halls are decorated with copies of antique statues in marble and plaster. In the greenhouses we found a German gardener, who sold camellias for a florin each. Many interesting facts might be recorded of the extraordinarily rapid spread of this new species of flower in Europe. "Ten years ago," said the gardener, "each specimen was worth twenty or thirty florins here."

After having seen the castle, we went to a convent of sisters of charity, founded by a Lubomirski, a *Castellanus Cracoviensis*, in the year 1730. The humane and excellent orders of charitable brothers and sisters are very widely spread throughout Galicia and Moravia, and we found a convent of them established in almost every town. In the Greek Russian church no such useful fraternities have ever been formed, and it is almost impossible to estimate the advantage which this fact alone must have given the Polish cities of the middle ages over those of Russia. The abbess of the little convent, which lay beneath the picturesque shade of lofty and venerable trees, was of an old and noble race; the nuns were mostly strong, blooming young girls, who made it their business to attend on the sick, with touching kindness, and exemplary skill and patience. We were told that no sick person, whether stranger or native, Christian or Jew, was denied admittance into this convent. When I inquired after the physician of the place, I was answered, "Sir, we help ourselves as well as we can without one." Women have, in their very nature, something soothing and healing to sickness and suffering. One of the nuns whom I saw employed in carrying phials, basins, medicines, &c., in and out of the sick rooms, appeared so beautiful and graceful in her humble occupations, that I think the very sight of her must have had a healing influence on the invalids she tended.

We met large herds of oxen on the road to Lanzut, a castle and village belonging to the Potockis, where a cattle-market was about to be held. The cattle consisted chiefly of the gray oxen of the steppes. Thousands of these patient animals have wandered through the Carpathians every year for centuries, to nourish with their flesh Vienna and the countries through which they pass. We traced them the whole way from Bukovina to the capital, in the regular and peculiar furrows which they have drawn across every road, by their uniform tread, each stepping in the footsteps of his predecessor. They are taken to the great cattle-markets of Moravia, where the butchers of Vienna and Prague purchase them for the consumption of those luxurious cities. Many are also brought straight to Vienna, by Rusniaks, Walachians, and Poles. Formerly some of them were even taken to Munich and Dresden, by the cattle-drivers of the Carpathians. The Bukovinian and Galician markets are visited by the way, where the weaker animals are disposed of, and in this way they feed all the countries through which they pass. The Germans call them Polish cattle, because they receive them from Poland; the Galicians Moldavian, because it is through Moldavia that they reach Galicia. At Warsaw they are called Podolian, because it is from Podolia that they are brought to Warsaw. The steppes of Podolia and the Ukraine, to the shores of the Black Sea and the sea of Asoph, are the vast magazines from which all Austria is supplied with meat.

Another great road traversed by these animated embryos of roast beef runs through Kharkov to Moscow and St. Petersburg, ending in the Baltic provinces. Small herds are also collected together in Bessarabia and Walachia, and in the neighbourhood of Odessa, and are driven across the Danube and the Balkans to Constantinople.

THE CASTLE AND TOWN OF LANZUT.

Wenzel flourished his whip; with increased speed our *Gloswogen* turned the corner of the road, and the little poodle barked for joy, for before us lay the place where we were to pass the night, the pretty little town of Landshut (Lanzut is the Polish name), with its beautiful and vast old princely castle, which rose majestically from the plain, shaded by stately trees, and illuminated by the rays of the setting sun. Lanzut, the Pulavy* of Galicia, has been so continually lauded and described by Polish historians and chroniclers, that now when Pulavy is fallen, and Lanzut is the most beautiful and interesting castle in Poland, a few words about it by a German may not be misplaced. We went over the castle the same evening, and the next morning spent some hours in its delightful gardens.

Lanzut now belongs to the Potocki family, which is divided into several branches, and possesses large estates and magnificent castles, scattered through the countries between Vienna and the Black Sea, among which are Severinovka near Odessa, Sophievka near Kiev, Niemirov in Podolia, Lanzut and others in Galicia. Lanzut, however, the Potockis have only obtained by marriage, for it belonged formerly to the Lubomirskis, who possess also a pretty chain of villages, castles, and towns, in the valleys of the Dniester and the Vistula. It was a Lubomirski who originally built Lanzut, and the Latin inscription over the castle gate runs thus:

" *Stanislaus, comes in Wisniez-Lubomirski, Palatinus Cracoviensis, Zatoriensis, Scepusiensis, Niepolumicensis, &c. Capitaneus exercituum regni contra Osmanorum imperatorem et Dzianumbet Gerei Chanum Tatarorum generalis præfectus, ut viribus curis publicis atque bello Livonico, Moscovitico, Prussico, Scythico, Turcico, ipsaque demum ætate fessis quietem pararet, ædes has condidit et ornavit, utque saluti communi prodesset, propugnaculum adjecit. Anno p. C. N.* 1641."

(Stanislaus, count Wisniez-Lubomirski, Voyevode of Crakow, of Zatory, of Scepusk, of Niepolomize, &c., Royal Grand General, and Commander of the armies against the emperor of the Turks, and the Khan of the Tar-

---

* For the information of some of our English readers, it may be necessary to add that Pulavy was the family seat of Prince Adam Czartoryiski, the Polish patriot. The village, or rather the little town of Pulavy, contained about 3000 inhabitants, and the Castle was particularly celebrated for its splendid library of 60,000 volumes, and its magnificent English park. During the campaign of 1831, the castle and all its dependencies were completely destroyed by the Russians.—*Tr.*

tars, built and adorned this palace as a retreat for his old age, weakened by application to state affairs, and by the Livonian, Moscovite, Prussian, Scythian, and Turkish, wars, and added to it a fortress for the use of the state. In the year of our Lord, 1641.)

Such relics of ancient Polish greatness become scarcer every day. Inscriptions like this, the living mementoes of the splendour of the old Polish nobility, will in time become almost as interesting as those on old Egyptian temples, and should always be carefully copied by travellers. The Lubomirskis did not become princes, till after the 17th century, though they were always a powerful and important family. Visniez is a little town near Cracow, and a branch of the Lubomirski family is named after it. Palatine, or Voyevode of Cracow, was one of the principal dignitaries of the kingdom. The title and office of Voyevode, is one of the most ancient in Poland. It signifies leader or duke; but corresponded more to our word governor. The Voyevode not only conducted the administration of the provinces over which he was appointed (*Woyewodschaften*), but also distributed justice there, and commanded the troops. Niepolomize, &c., are little towns in the land of the Mazovians, and, probably, formerly belonged to the Lubomirskis. There were always two grand generals in Poland, one for Lithuania, and one royal grand general for Crown Poland. The above inscription proves, that in the 17th century, the latter office was no sinecure. Against how many different nations had the old statesman led out his forces! Every Polish nobleman was allowed to build fortresses on his own estates, for each was regarded as a petty but undisputed sovereign, the welfare and safety of whose little state, were as entirely his own concern, as those of a kingdom are to its government. They also kept little standing armies at their castles.

The castle of Lanzut is very large, containing spacious inner courts, and surrounded by walls, ditches, and fortifications. In the back ground rise abruptly the heights of the Central Carpathians, and towards the north extend the wide and smiling Polish plains, with their pleasant villages and green meadows. Many alterations and additions have been made to the castle since the days of the Grand General of the Crown. The grandmother of the present possessor, a Princess Lubomirska, it was who arranged the castle in the manner in which it is now shown to the traveller by an old Silesian steward. The ramparts are decorated with beautiful double avenues of linden-trees, the moats form pretty canals and lakes, with gondolas, and the inner wall has been taken away, and its place supplied with groves of trees. The inner and outer courts, formerly occupied only by a barbarous soldiery, are now filled with beautiful flower-beds and shrubs. The arrangements of the interior, the size of the rooms, saloons, and corridors, the beauty of the pictures, statues, and conservatories, the splendour of the furniture, the rank of its possessors (the present owner is a Potocki, and the High Marshal of the kingdom, his wife and mother were Czartoriskas, and his grandmother a Lubomirska), the multitudes of serfs, towns, villages, and ducats belonging to them, all this forms such a picture of princely magnificence that the imagination can conceive no worldly pleasure or luxury wanting to the lords of Lanzut.

The corridors on the ground-floor of the castle are the most elegant things of the kind ever seen. They are richly carpeted, and one is called the statue, the other the picture corridor. The one is full of excellent old pictures, the other of fine statues, some genuine antiques, others by modern

Italian sculptors. Rows of glittering chandeliers run along the ceilings. Between every two or three statues or pictures stand large and beautiful vases of porcelain, jasper, or malachite, and here and there little divans are concealed among vases of flowers and orange-trees. It may be imagined that the rooms to which such corridors lead are not deficient in magnificence. Indeed I doubt whether there are many houses in Europe equal to Lanzut in the elegance, splendour, and abundance of its tables, chairs, carpets, candelabras, vases, lamps, chandeliers, silks, satins, and gold and silver plate. Many of the pictures in the dining-rooms and drawing-rooms are splendid. The ball-room is lighted by twenty large candelabras. The floors of the audience-chambers and sleeping-rooms are all covered with the richest carpets of London and Constantinople. The study of the count is as magnificent as the audience-chamber of a prince. The portraits of Sobieski, of his beloved Maria Lescinska, and of his good old mother, decorate the count's bedroom.

Separate suites of rooms are reserved for different members of the family, who occasionally reside here ; those of the Countess Brannicka, a cousin of the count's, are particularly splendid. Paris and Lyons have furnished the richest silks for the curtains, tapestry, and sofa covers ; and London has lately furnished twenty comfortable armchairs for the castle chapel, for the service of which the count retains six Jesuits. The pencils of Rubens, Snyder, and Wouvermann, have served to adorn the walls of the dining-room. Vandyck, Mieris, Guido Reni, and Titian, have contributed to embellish those of the drawing-rooms. The tables before the mirrors are covered with presents from princesses, queens, and empresses. Every thing we saw around us showed us that we had entered the house of nobles, whose illustrious line of ancestry dated from remote ages, and numbered among its branches many a king and emperor.*

There is indeed something stately and imposing connected with so old and powerful a race, which perhaps is but little felt in the present day by any but poetical minds. In Poland this spirit of veneration for ancestral greatness is still alive and unweakened, for here are still old patriarchal families and vast feudal domains ; here are still faithful vassals and independent nobles.

---

* The Potockis have always been distinguished among Polish nobles. From time immemorial, the highest dignitaries in Poland have been filled by Potockis. They have also been remarkable for learning, refinement, and talents ; and wherever they have ruled, they have always left behind them some useful or beautiful trace of their government ; some castle, gymnasium, church, or garden. Even in the Russian steppes, some agricultural improvements mark their temporary residence there. Without being deficient in patriotism, this family seems to possess a certain easy pliability, and to submit to circumstances with a good grace; for many of them serve under the Austrian and Russian governments. They are more prudent and careful, and less extravagant than most Polish nobles ; so that, numerous as they are, they are all rich. Many of them have been remarkable for beauty. Ignaz Potocki, who lived towards the end of the last century, was known through half Europe by the surname of " *Le beau* ;" and the young Polish countess whose story has been sung by Puschkin, and who was beloved by a Tartar Khan in the Crimea, and was murdered by a fair rival in a fit of jealousy, was also a Potocka. During the last two hundred years, there has not been a single important Polish confederation which was not headed by a Potocki. Four Potockis, of whom Ignaz Potocki was the most famous, headed the different political parties during the attempt at the regeneration of Poland made in 1790. The old Severin Potocki is also a celebrated man.

RZESZOV, PILSNO, AND TARNOV.

From Lanzut to Rzeszov the distance is three (German) miles. In Galicia this is the usual distance from one town to another; that is from what we should call a town to another like it, for what are here called towns occur oftener. The Polish noblemen were always very anxious to possess towns, and exerted themselves much, therefore, to obtain for the villages on their estates the name and privileges of towns. The Jews of these villages also, were very anxious to become citizens, and towns therefore are as plentiful here as in the most populous parts of Germany.

Rzeszov is a more considerable town than we expected to find here. We saw streets which might have graced a German city, and shops so well furnished, that though our trunks had been full of ducats, we should not have been in the slightest degree embarrassed how to dispose of them. Stately old churches and convents, prettily situated on the banks of the Vislok, formed a picturesque and animated spectacle; and I was pleased to think how many a pleasant city lies hid in odd corners of the world, of which the rest of mankind know nothing. We lodged at an inn kept by a German host. The solidity and elegance with which this man had furnished his house, and the order and neatness everywhere visible, left us nothing to desire. I spent a pleasant hour with this intelligent man, who had travelled over all parts of Germany, and was well acquainted with the manners and customs of its different inhabitants. Of the different races whom we should see on our way to Vienna, he gave us the following account: "The Rusniaks, who are more blunt and honest than the Poles, you have left behind you. Next come the Mazovians, who, like all the rest of the Poles, are as great rascals and cheats as if they were Jews. Then you will come to the Water Polaks, and the Silesian Germans, who live among them. The former are lazy and dirty, every soul of them, and the latter, though not quite so bad, share these qualities with them. Then come the *Khuländl*, inhabited by German herdsmen, plain, honest, and blunt, like most pastoral tribes. There you will find districts where you might leave your trunks and your money-box standing night and day in the open air, without lock, key, dog, or keeper, and yet you would lose nothing. Next you will get among the *Hannaken*, rough and sturdy, as if hewn of oak and soldered with iron; they are passionate, determined, and quarrelsome, but industrious and prosperous. Last of all come the light-hearted Austrians. They are not bright or clever to look at, but they are cheerful, gay, and loyal; keep turning their spits all day long, and enjoy the honour of crowning the Emperor."

At Rzeszov there is a great state prison, in which three hundred prisoners are kept. It contains only those who are condemned to five years' imprisonment. Those sentenced for ten years are sent to Lemberg, those for twenty years or for life, to Spielberg. Our host gave us but a bad account of the state of morals in the town. No year he said passed away, without witnessing two or three executions. This year, indeed, none had yet taken place, but a crime had been committed, which must bring its perpetrators to the gallows, whenever they were discovered.

While we were conversing with our host, we were interrupted by the entrance of his brother, and when I turned to him, and asked for his opinion concerning the Polish nation, he gave me the following reply: "Oh, the Poles have excellent and noble qualities, but on the whole they are a lazy, dirty, degraded set. They know neither the comforts nor the duties of life, and have no idea of respecting each other's rights. In Germany the people know how to value one another, but among the Poles it is difficult to keep a whole skin. They are two thousand years behind other nations, I might say twelve thousand years, and in twelve thousand years more they will be no better than they are now. They are too degraded to be improved. The moment the peasant has saved a little money, and perhaps buys himself a little cow, the nobleman takes it away from him, and the moment the nobleman plants a tree, the peasant chops it down. If any one plants any thing in his garden, his neighbour is sure to steal it or destroy it. And then there is the Jew, creeping about stealthily like a cat, seeking what he may devour. The worst of all is, that every body is bent upon advancing his own petty interests, and cares not what becomes of all the world besides, nor how many he ruins to advance his own ends. Life in this country is so miserable, that the sooner one gets away from it the better."

I asked the speaker how long he had endured this purgatory, and he answered that he had been living there for thirty years. The engravings, the fine muskets and pistols, the neat beds and furniture, the writing-tables and wardrobes which adorned his own and his brother's rooms, their pretty pianoforte, and the little guitar, upon which he and his wife played us several pleasing tunes, gave us secret assurance, that there was a good deal of exaggeration in his account of life in Poland.

We were particularly struck here, by the quantity of poplars, which shaded all the roads in the vicinity of towns and villages. The Poles seem to have a particular fancy for this tree; for it is found in great abundance throughout the old kingdom of Poland, as far as the Ukraine. In Russia and the Baltic provinces it is not much found, but throughout Poland, and even in Prussia it exists in great numbers.

The next day the temperature was five or six degrees below the freezing point, and we were very cold when we reached Sendzishov. Far colder, however, were some poor travellers, with whom we dined this day; a tobacco-officer and his wife and children. Austria puts very little trust in the officers employed in the tobacco monopoly, and therefore in order as much as possible to hinder cheating, the government is continually transplanting them, and making them change posts. These poor people had come from Iglau in Bohemia, and were on their way to Stanislavov in Galicia. They lamented their hard fate most piteously. They had been travelling for fourteen days, at the rate of five (German) miles a day, and expected to be ten more days on the journey. They asked us for information respecting the distant parts of Galicia, as of a gloomy region of frost and barbarism, assuring us that they shuddered at the thoughts of Stanislavov. Every day, they said, the inns grew worse and worse, the coffee, bread, and sugar, dearer and scarcer, and the inhabitants more and more savage and barbarous; and they expressed their conviction that the further they got, the worse every thing would be. At Iglau it was still warm and pleasant; and the grapes were still hanging on the vines; here they had cold and frost, with coughs, toothachs, and colds, and no wrapping up could keep them warm. They demanded our compassion, and envied us that we were on our way to the sunshine, the plenty, and the refinement, of Moravia and Bohemia. They were much surprised to hear that we had enjoyed our journey through Galicia; and when we spoke of Russia, they shuddered and crossed themselves, as though we spoke of the infernal regions. Travellers coming from the western and southern parts of Austria, towards its northern and eastern districts, are very apt to speak and think in this manner. What an absurd narrowness of mind to enclose all possible earthly felicity within one little corner of the world, and never to think of the wide fair earth without, where the sun shines, and there is room for all! These people were in despair at entering a district which they considered the land of gloom and barbarism, and our Wenzel complacently remarked every day, as he took his seat upon the box, "Now every thing is getting better and better. Soon we shall lodge every night at a German inn; the Jews will become scarcer, the food better, the beds cleaner, the people more industrious, the climate milder, and the country more beautiful." We ourselves at last began to fancy that we had emerged from regions of barbaric darkness, and were entering those of sunshine and refinement; an idea which rendered us as happy as the travellers above mentioned were made miserable by the contrary feeling. Iglau in Bohemia was their *ne plus ultra* of happiness, Stanislavov in Galicia, their Siberia and Inferno. To us the sun, whose distant rays had shed a light upon the Polish wilderness around us, was Vienna the Imperial capital.

It is a curious fact that in Galicia the density of the population increases, as the fertility of its soil decreases, and *vice versâ*. Bukovina and the eastern circles of Tarnopol, Tshortkov, and Brzezany, (Austrian Podolia, as they are called,) are the most fruitful parts of the kingdom, and are spoken of as the granaries of Galicia, and yet upon an average they maintain only from two thousand to two thousand five hundred human beings to every square (German) mile, and contain only sixteen towns. Towards the west, the Egyptian fruitfulness of the soil decreases, till we come to the barren sandy shores of the Vistula. These western circles, however, those of Yaslo, Bochnia, and Sendez, for instance, contain from three thousand five hundred to four thousand inhabitants to every square mile. The number of towns, and the state of manufactures and industry, is also much higher in these less fruitful districts. Bukovina in the east, and Vadovize in the west of Galicia, form the most striking contrast to each other. There a town on very fifty square (German) miles, here one on every ten; there one thousand five hundred, here four thousand eight hundred inhabitants to every square mile; there scarcely any manufactories, here whole towns full of them; there all the mountains and valleys inhabited by wild Huzzulen, here filled with smiling villages and smoking towns; there as here a beautiful country in appearance, but for the dark firs of the west, the oaks, limes, and beeches, of a more fertile country are seen there.

The regular officially installed and acknowledged patron saint of Galicia and Lodomeria, is St. Michael. In western Galicia, however, St. Nepomuk has also many votaries, and the further we went, the more statues did we see of him on the bridges, roads, and market-places. We also observed an increase in the number of beggars, who are naturally not so plentiful among the fertile hills of Bukovina. The loveliness of nature here in some measure made amends to us for this; for we were again approaching the Carpathians, and the landscape was full of beautiful scenery.

At Dembiza we drank our afternoon coffee with two Austrian captains of cavalry, and looked over Savada with them, a charming estate, formerly belonging to the Radzivills, and now to the Ratshinskis. Dembiza is a poor town mostly inhabited by Jews, and it was their sabbath-day. We had here an opportunity of learning something respecting those curious lines of rope, which are drawn along from roof to roof in all Jewish cities in Poland; and of which some travellers have given most incorrect accounts. For example, one writer informs us, that they are boundaries which the despotic Polish noblemen assign to the Jews, and beyond which they must not stir on Christian Sundays for fear of giving offence. Now knowing how little the Jews of Poland appear to give offence to any one, how they are tolerated alike in palaces and huts, and swarm about everywhere like flies, how they even farm of the Catholic priests the fees of their office, the baptismal fees for instance, which they collect in their name, this account always appeared to me a very absurd one.

These lines are called "Sabbath strings," and in Hebrew, *Aïreph*. They are either of iron wire or rope, and pass from roof to roof, wherever streets or passages intersect the Jewish roofs, so that these do not touch one another; thus they divide and set apart the Jewish quarter of the town. When, as is usually the case, the Jews all live together in one quarter of the town, there is only one such ring or *Aïreph;* but when, as is sometimes the case, they live in little clusters in different parts, there are often a great many Aïrephs. Where Jewish and Christian houses are mingled promiscuously, there can be no Aïreph at all. On the Sabbath-day, the Jews may carry about in their hands or pockets whatever they please, within this Aïreph, but outside of it nothing, not even a purse or a pocket-handkerchief. They may not even take off a glove and carry it; it is only allowable on the hands, as an article of dress. It is even forbidden to them to carry a pocket-handkerchief in the pocket; but they may tie one round the arm, and then it counts for an article of dress. A walkingstick is strictly prohibited. We saw many Jews on the sabbath, walking with handkerchiefs tied round their arms. Any Christian or Jew who wantonly breaks or tears this Aïreph, is severely punished. If it be torn by a natural accident, the occurrence is formally announced to the synagogue, and till its formal restoration, nothing may be carried about even within the Aïreph; not even food or medicine for the sick. Children under thirteen, however, are exempt from this law, and are therefore employed to carry about absolute necessaries. The restoration of the Aïreph is performed by the chief Rabbi, with many solemnities. If it is of wire, it is reunited with a hook and eye, for to solder the broken part together is forbidden. If it is of rope, the Rabbi may not tie it, but must have an entirely new one. Where no Aïreph is used, the Jews are not allowed upon the sabbath-day, to carry any thing about with them; for the Aïreph is a privilege granted only to large Jewish communities.

At Dembiza we heard for the first time of the beauty of the girls of Biela, a pretty little town on the borders of Galicia. Throughout the thirty miles between Dembiza and Biela, we constantly heard of their celebrated charms, until we reached the place itself.

Milestones now began to appear at the roadside, a decided proof of increasing civilization. At Pilsno we passed large and gloomy pine forests, which extend from the Carpathians in close succession into Russian Poland. We took up and gave a lift to a German Bohemian, who had worked in the great tobacco manufactory of Lemberg. This is the largest imperial tobacco manufactory in the whole Austrian Empire. There is twisted every cigar used throughout the kingdom of Lodomeria and Galicia; and every pinch of snuff taken by a subject of those kingdoms, is there cut and prepared. The workmen in this manufactory are all Austrians, with the exception of a few Nurembergers, in the snuff department. Our Bohemian also told us, that the gray Polish oxen, are playfully called Lemberg students, in Austria and Bohemia.

The Visloka which we reached near Pilsno, must not be confounded with the Vislok which we passed near Rzeszov. This district had a pleasing and picturesque look, even in the scanty dress of approaching winter. The town of Pilsno itself, is as insignificant as its river.

Towards evening we reached Tarnov, lying on the river Biala, in the valley of the Dunayez. It is one of the principal towns in this part of the country, and has a very pretty townhouse in its market-place. Its streets are well paved, and some of the houses are three or four stories high. We visited in this place two very excellent apothecaries' shops, and an elegant pastrycook's shop, to which the Jews—the only guides in Poland—showed us the way. We had scarcely sat down there for three minutes, before one ragged Jew after another entered the room till it was quite full. They scrutinized us closely all over, inquired if we wished to buy or sell any thing, and on our replying in the negative, they went out one after another. The people of the shop did not trouble themselves about them, but allowed them to go in and out incessantly, like flies or dogs. The shopkeepers and innkeepers of Poland are used to this. When a Polish nobleman goes in anywhere to take a glass of liqueur or a cup of coffee, he is always followed by twenty or thirty Jews, who begin to traffic with him. If he has no money, they buy of him the two or three bushels of wheat which he has brought with him to the town.

The evening was very calm, with a clear sky and bright moonlight, and we determined to go on foot to the Dunayez where we meant to sleep at Voinitz. In the streets of Tarnov, we found the whole Jewish population out of doors. They were singing, screaming, bowing, and praying to the full moon, and formed the most curious and interesting groups. Some fixed their eyes steadily upon the moon, murmuring prayers, and then bowing down to the ground. Others had brought out little wooden desks into the streets, upon which they laid their sacred books and little lanterns. Wrapped in long white robes, bordered with black, they stood around in groups of six or eight, now muttering devout sentences, now shrieking, and beating their foreheads. Such scenes are peculiar to the oriental Jews of Poland. They assured us that whoever joined in this ceremony would neither die nor fall sick in the course of the month.

We persuaded a young merchant of Prague, who had been for some time settled at Lemberg, and was now returning to his native city, to accompany us on our walk, and he remained our travelling companion into Moravia. He was a handsome young man, and according to his account, his two sisters must have had no slight charms to boast of. The night air, the calm serene moonlight, and our quiet pleasant walk, seemed to open his heart, and he entertained us on the way with the history of these two sisters, of which one had had a strange, the other a terrible fate. The eldest married a rich merchant in a Bohemian city; a brutal and barbarous man, who even during the very honeymoon, tormented his wife in the most unrelenting manner. During the four years of her marriage, she bore him three children, whom their inhuman father tormented as much as herself. She at last resolved to separate from her cruel husband. But to her dismay, she discovered that the barbarian to whom she was married, who was at the same time spendthrift, drunkard, and gambler, had squandered away her fortune as well as his own, and as the death of her father soon afterwards left her no place of refuge, she resolved to destroy herself and her children. One dark and stormy night, she seized her three little ones, flung them one after another into a deep well, and then flung herself in after them. The next morning the four bodies were found in the well. Two of the little ones had clasped their mother's bosom in the agony of death; the fourth had been caught by a projecting stone of the well, but all were dead. The husband was sent to the house of correction for five years.

The history of the other sister reminded us of the Jewess of Lemberg, and showed us what romantic situations Catholicism gives rise to here. She loved a young physician, who returned her love with equal warmth; but during the medical examination, the result of which was to have been the forerunner to the fulfilment of all his hopes, and to his advantageous establishment in life, he had the misfortune to go mad from sheer anxiety. His agitation had already led him to make many wrong answers, and when the question was put to him, " How would you cure any one bitten by a mad dog ?" the word " mad," seemed to strike him like an electric spark. " Mad dog?" he cried, striking his forehead, " I would brand him with red-hot irons—I would—I would bite him in the leg, gentlemen! Mad dog ? Oh, 'tis horrible—have pity on me! Yes, I am mad—I am mad!" He was taken to a lunatic asylum. His poor bride felt this blow so keenly, that she resolved to forsake the world, and take refuge in the convent of St. Elizabeth. Convents of this order are numerous throughout Bohemia, Moravia, and Galicia, and it is the strictest of all in its discipline. No prohibition—not even that of a parent, is allowed to prevent those who wish to enter it from fulfilling their intentions. The moment a nun enters this order she is subjected to the severest privations, and the most rigid austerities. She may not even see her father, mother, brother, or sister, except in the presence of the abbess, and through an iron grating. All the despair of the parents, all their endeavours to turn her from her purpose, were unavailing, and she was enrolled among the nuns of St. Elizabeth at Prague. Soon, however, she had ample reason to repent of this step. At first she held out, but after three years of solitary sufferings in the monotonous loneliness of the cell, she found an opportunity of acquainting her father, through the grating, with her earnest desire to leave the convent. For some time her friends revolved all possible means of getting her out; but it seemed impracticable, except by means of the convent chimneysweeper. The father was a rich man, and promised him 1000 florins, if he brought him back his daughter. The chimneysweeper agreed, and one night went to the convent, clad in a double black suit, and descended the chimney of the cell pointed out to him. He then dressed up the nun as his assistant, covering her face and hands with soot. Money animated him, and despair sustained her, to carry out the deception; they escaped, and she returned to her father's house. In the mean time the happiest changes had occurred there. The young doctor, her lover, had completely recovered from his temporary insanity, and awaited his bride in an elegant travelling carriage. This event had been kept secret from her while at the convent, in order not to make her stay there yet more bitter. The couple hastened over the frontiers to Silesia, married, and then returned to Prague. The father's money bribed the priests to silence, who indeed could do nothing now, as the holy sacrament of marriage was a tie even stronger than that of the convent vow. The poor chimneysweeper, indeed, suffered three years' imprisonment for his share in the business, at the end of which time the money of the lady's father obtained his release.

The moon was still shining brightly, when we reached the banks of the Dunayez, which, next to the San, is the most important of the tributaries of the Vistula, rising in the Carpathians. It is more than thirty (German) miles long, and the valley of the Dunayez occupies a surface of 150 square miles. Its sources are on the highest points of the Tatra mountains, whence they flow down, strangely enough, on both the northern and southern side. Humboldt and Wahlenberg have already noticed this phenomenon. The Black and White Dunayez both flow in a northerly direction, but the Paprad, one of its principal feeders, flows first directly southward, as if to join the Danube. Afterwards it makes a bend eastward, and after flowing in this way for some time, turns off in a north-westerly direction, and breaking through the Carpathians, reaches the valley of the Vistula.

Forty square miles of the valley of the Dunayez is Hungarian territory. The river is large and deep throughout the year, and even its tributary the Paprad is navigable. By the commerce carried on upon it, the Hungarian towns of Käsmark, Felka, and Lublo, are connected with Warsaw, Dantzig, and the Baltic. Hungarian wines and fruits,—we saw ships laden with the wine of Erlau and Nessmüll, and others whose whole cargo consisted of jars of plums,—together with firewood, timber, and planks, are the principal goods sent down the river; at present, however, the political division of the Dunayez, its mouth being Russian, its source Hungarian, and the middle part Galician, has much injured its commerce, which was far more important, in the prosperous days of the old Polish republic.

A long wooden bridge crosses the Dunayez at Voinitz. We saw the clear, broad, beautiful river, tumbling its tiny waves beneath, in the full moonlight, and the opening of the mountain glen, from which it flows down into the Voinitz plain, lay right before us; but we were obliged to relinquish the sight of all those romantic waterfalls, lovely little mountain lakes, wild glens and valleys, gloomy caverns, snowy glaciers, and towering pinnacles, of which we had so often heard, and which the murmuring waves of the Dunayez at our feet, brought vividly back to our minds; for it was near midnight, and we had to seek our night's lodging. This was a true Polish one; for a few planks covered with straw formed our bed, our cloaks our coverlets, and a wooden box our pillow. We were, however, accommodated with a place by a fire, and with a cup of warm egged beer, by way of refreshment. Our entertainers were Polish nobles. They invited us to share their humble accommodations with great politeness, arranged our straw with a graceful dignity of demeanour, and presented us our beer with formal courtesy. They were very busy this night, for they were preparing cabbage for their winter subsistence.

I lay awake on my straw-covered plank, to observe the operations of these Polish picklers of cabbage. They were goodnatured, dirty old fellows, whom the master of the house encouraged to work, now with a dram and now with an oath. The whole floor was covered with leaves and heads of cabbage, among which lay boots, clothes, tallow candles, shovels, knives, and other household utensils, scattered in the wildest confusion. Some were employed round the long table, in chopping and cutting up the cabbage with choppers and knives. The pieces were then thrown into a large jar, in which stood one of the party, who was busy stamping and pounding the leaves together with his bare feet. The scene was extremely curious and picturesque. The last-named operator was full of wit and humour, making so many jokes, and cutting such odd capers, as he danced in his jar, that his comrades were ready to die with laughter. He sometimes snatched up his little skshibka, or violin, and played a merry tune, beating time with his feet among the cabbages. A second stood in a jar in another corner, smoking a pipe in silence, beating with his feet, and swaying to and fro with mechanical monotony and regularity. Occasionally he went out for a few minutes, but soon returned, and jumping into his jar again went on with his pounding, rising higher and higher as the jar filled, till he was lost among the smoke and mist which filled the upper part of the room.

I asked my host whether the cabbage did not lose some of its agreeable flavour by this manner of treatment. He did not think it did; grapes were treated in the same way, and the wine was none the worse. He forgot, however, that the cabbage was not strained and filtered afterwards, like the wine.

The quantity of cabbage eaten in Poland, must be immense. This household was a small one, and yet when six great jars had been packed full in this manner, three were still to be filled. Besides cabbage, a favourite diet with all Slavonic nations, potatoes and barley grits are the principal food of the country.

The next morning, when we had paid as highly for our fire, our beds, our beer, and our *tableau vivant* of cabbage-packing Mazovians, as if the fire had been of cedarwood, the beds of eider down, the beer champagne, and the tableau painted by Ostade, our Wenzel consoled us with the assurance that we had done with Polish accommodations, and should meet with nothing but good inns for the rest of the way to Vienna. We were sorry however that the improvement which had begun some time previously, did not continue more regularly, instead of allowing of such relapses.

One of the most important branches of commerce passing through Galicia consists of the numbers of carriages and equipages made at Vienna, for Poland, Russia, and Moldavia. Whenever the wealthy Poles, or Moldavians, or the rich Russians of Odessa, Kharkov, and South Russia, want any thing really good in this way, they send to Vienna for it. We saw some of them pass us every day, packed carefully in wax-cloth and matting. Almost every waggon drew after it an empty carriage; sometimes we counted twelve or fifteen in one day. Many are sent to Lemberg, but the greater number to Brody for Russia, or to Tshernovitze for Moldavia and Bessarabia.

The "*Neititshenken*" are a very peculiar kind of carriages, made in Austrian Silesia, in the little town of Neutitschein, and are used exclusively in Galicia. They are light, strong, cheap, and handsome; uncovered, and always coloured white, green, and black. In Galicia they are used by all who cannot afford a coach, and who yet will not drive in a common peasant's cart; the citizens and soldiers always use them, as does the nobleman when he is only going a little way, and does not wish to use particular ceremony, and the peasant when he wishes to cut a figure. Every tolerably prosperous family in the kingdom has a light swift little "*Neititshenka,*" and it is the prettiest, most suitable little carriage possible, for common occasions. Yet its use seems to be confined to Galicia; for it is never seen either in Russia or in its native land Moravia. Whoever wants a genuine Neititshenka, has to send to Moravia for it, for it is only there that the beech and birchwood are good enough, and the workmen sufficiently skilful.

The Carpathians on their whole northern side, are bordered, as many of my readers are probably aware, by enormous strata of salt. Unfortunately, however, immense masses of other earths have formed over these strata, so that their treasures remain deeply buried under the earth. Only here and there, small portions of these inexhaustible masses of salt are dug up, for only here and there are there spots where the salt is near enough to the surface, to be reached by man. One of these spots is at Bochnia, another at Vieliczka.

The town of Bochnia owes its existence entirely to its salt-mines, the shaft leading down to which, is in the middle of the town. As it was Sunday when we reached Bochnia, we could only visit the mines in imagination; for all the shafts were closed. From 300,000 to 400,000 hundred-weight of salt, are annually drawn from the earth at Bochnia; Vieliczka furnishes double this quantity. At Bochnia four hundred labourers work in the mines; at Vieliczka from seven to eight hundred. The salt of Bochnia is generally whiter and finer than that of Vieliczka. The Bochnians, with whom we dined, and from whom we learnt these particulars, also assured us that their works were deeper than those of Vieliczka.

We earnestly endeavoured to learn something respecting the well-known Polish disorder, the *Plica Polonica*, a subject as interesting to the inquiring traveller, as disgusting to the eye and the imagination. We found, however, that this disease was not seen nearly so often in the mountainous districts of the south, as in the cold plains of the north. We were told that among the Rusniaks, the hair sometimes grew into a clotted entangled mass, as is sometimes the case with badly-groomed horses, but that the disease never fully developed itself among them.

The little town of Gdov, lies in the valley of the Rabbat, between Bochnia and Vieliczka, the way to which passes through a beautiful district, with the plains of the Vistula to the right, and the Carpathians to the left. In all the inns by the wayside, we found on Sunday music and dancing. I shall never forget the pretty sprightly *Shenkerka* (barmaid) at Gdov, nor the grace with which she led us, her two evening guests, to the dance, a gay Mazurka, played by two Slovaks. Nothing can be more pretty or graceful than Polish girls when dancing. They appear all motion and animation, and while with us Germans only the feet dance, with them every muscle vibrates, and the eyes sparkle with delight. This was the first *Shenkerka* we had seen; for till now men had filled this office at all the inns at which we had stopped.

THE SALT-WORKS OF VIELICZKA.

Towards seven o'clock in the evening our carriage rolled over the heads of the salt-miners of Vieliczka, which have undermined the ground all round the town. We soon reached the free town of Vieliczka itself, with its towers, its old castle, its irregular streets, nestling in the sides of the Carpathians, and its German colony, or, as the people here call it, the "Swabian village," whose neat, cheerful houses cluster around the old Polish city. We felt that we knew but little about the famous salt-mines themselves, and, therefore, hastened to obtain information of the salt inspectors, whom we found assembled at the Golden Angel, in order that the next day we might be ready to visit them. Among these inspectors we found two who were both willing and able to assist our inquiries, and from whom we received the following particulars.

Above all, we had wished to learn something respecting the extent of the enormous stratas of salt which border the Carpathians; but our questions on this point, led us into such labyrinths of doubt and bewilderment that we soon became aware how little was known respecting it. One thing is certain, namely, that the salt-mines all along the northern side of the Carpathians, prove the existence of immense masses of subterranean salt. These masses have been pierced at Bochnia and Vieliczka in the north, at some parts of Moravia and Transylvania in the south, and lately at Sambor and Halitsh in the middle of the chain.* In all these places the salt is of the same structure and kind, and the arrangement of the strata is also exactly the same. What riddles and questions are raised by these simple facts, which science in vain attempts to solve! It may be that originally an ocean covered the whole of Russia and Poland, as far as the foot of the Carpathians, which, forming its shore, received its deposits of salt. But the south-side of the Carpathians also contains salt-mines and they extend even into Transylvania and Hungary. It would seem, then, that the enormous mass extended far around the Carpathians, and that these mountains were a later formation upon the salt strata. If this be the case, did the mountains form gradually upon that basis, or did they rise from beneath, piercing the crust of salt? Is the first theory possible? And if the last be correct, where are the fragments and pieces of salt thrown off? Was the salt formed suddenly, or slowly and gradually? In the latter case, how is it that enormous beds of salt are found perfectly pure and white, without the admixture of a single foreign particle? How far do the great salt masses extend? Does the whole kingdom of Galicia, with all its forests, rivers, towns, and provinces, rest upon one enormous bed of salt? Or do the strata only occur in particular places? How deep do they extend into the bowels of the earth? Where do they lie furthest from, and where nearest to the surface? Perhaps in many places they are close under the surface, and their discovery is only hindered by chance? The answers to these questions lie hidden from us,

---

* The mines of Sambor and Halitsh have not been followed up. In Moldavia, however, rock-salt has long been an article of commerce. Throughout South Russia and the Ukraine, the greenish rock-salt of Moldavia is often preferred to that of the lakes in the steppes. The Transylvanian rock-salt also extends on the other side into Hungary.

as in the bottomless depths of ocean. Like mice gnawing a cheese, the inhabitants pick a little here and there at the top of the salt masses, without seeing farther than the light of their lanterns reaches.

The Sarmatians of Herodotus, the Dacians, the Goths, and many other nations, wandered for centuries over these countries, without ever dreaming of the treasures that lay buried beneath them. They fetched from distant shores the scanty portions which they needed of a mineral of which inexhaustible stores lay scarcely one hundred feet beneath them. Six hundred years ago, in 1251, the discovery was first made, and then it was that the mines of Bochnia and Vieliczka were first worked. It is said that St. Kunigunda, the consort of Duke Bolislaus V., was the first discoverer. The manner of working, however, was at first very primitive, but afterwards miners were brought from Hungary and Germany, and the work was more regularly carried on. This was in the year 1442, but during the whole period of Polish domination, all the arrangements were very imperfect. The mines were let to Jews, who worked them very carelessly and improvidently, only intent upon a momentary profit. Not till the year 1772, when the mines became the property of the Emperor of Austria, was a prudent and rational system of management adopted. Since then regular accounts have been kept of the produce of the salt-mines, but only for the eye of the Austrian government, for towards a stranger so mysterious a silence is observed, that he can scarcely learn any thing respecting the increase or decrease of production, and the price of salt, of the gradual extension of the mines, of the improvement in the methods of working, and other such interesting particulars. There is no connected history of the mines before 1772 to be had, but only single and fragmentary documents.

The higher offices about the mines are now all filled by cultivated Germans, and all possible improvements which art or science can suggest are adopted, partly to remedy the defects of the old system, and partly to make the future more productive. Bochnia and Vieliczka taken together furnish about 900,000 hundredweight. That more might be obtained there can be no doubt; but the quantity taken is in some measure regulated by the demand. Of the 900,000 hundredweight, 200,000 are sent to Prussia, and 150,000 to Russia, at such prices as will just remunerate the Austrian government for the cost of production. The other 550,000 are sold by the government at arbitrary prices, in virtue of the salt monopoly which it possesses. They are consumed partly in Poland, partly in Silesia, Moravia, and the valleys of the Carpathians. The cost price for which the salt is sold to Russia and Prussia is a state mystery, though the common selling price is of course known. We were told at Vieliczka that the former could not be over one florin the hundredweight, including all the expenses of the works, while the government sells the salt at five florins the hundredweight to its own subjects. It makes, therefore, a profit of four florins per hundredweight, and the whole of the salt-works must furnish a revenue of 2,200,000 florins to the crown, so that Austria does not from all the rest of the kingdom of Galicia derive as much revenue as from those few salt-mines.

The higher functionaries are about eighty-six in number; workmen and all included they amount to two hundred. The upper functionaries are headed by a governor, and divided into "subterranean" and "upper-air" inspectors, or, as they are often called, gentlemen of the leather and gentlemen of the pen. The latter, councillors, governors, secretaries, and guardians, included, are all only employed in the administrative department; the subterranean functionaries in the inspection of the workmen and the superintendence of new works. These officers are well paid, and we were convinced of the easy circumstances in which they lived by the preparations for a ball which they gave during our stay at Vieliczka.

Shemnitz, in Hungary, is the principal academy for the instruction of these inspectors The workmen are of two classes, those who are paid by the year, and those who work by the piece; the number of the latter increases or diminishes with the demand for salt. There are 800 superannuated workmen and inspectors in the receipt of pensions, of whom most have been employed here for 40 or 45 years.

There are four great magazines for salt, where it is heaped up in huge storehouses to which the merchants come to buy it. Smaller stores are kept at Brünn, Teschen, and Bilitz.

The salt-works now cover a space of 35,000 square fathoms. The length of the mines with all their passages and alleys amounts to $7\frac{1}{4}$ (German) miles. Ten shafts connect this subterranean labyrinth with the upper world. One of them is used for draining away the water, two for the descent of workmen, and the rest for the raising of the salt, and the descent of the straw, wood, horses, and other things.

The whole works are divided into three departments, technically called *fields*; the Old field, the Yanina field, and the New field. The Old field goes in a southward direction from the town into the mountains; the Yanina field goes eastward, and the New field westward. The Old field consists of the irregular works of oldest date. The Yanina field, named after King John Sobieski, was dug upon an improved plan. The New field is of Austrian foundation, and has been always worked according to the best principles of art.

Each of these mines consists of five stories or *Contignations*, one above another, and each of these stories again is made up of numerous chambers, cells, and caverns, connected by horizontal passages. The different stories are connected by perpendicular shafts, or winding stairs. The descent to the uppermost story is thirty-four fathoms deep. Between each of the different stories an interval is always left of fifteen or twenty fathoms. The depth, which has been rendered convenient for descent by shafts and staircases, is a hundred and twenty-five fathoms; the entire depth amounts to a hundred and forty-five fathoms. Therefore, although Vieliczka itself is a hundred and fifty feet above the Vistula, and six hundred and ninety-nine feet above the surface of the sea, yet the mines descend five hundred and eighty feet below the bed of the Vistula, and three hundred feet below the surface of the sea.

The best kind of salt is the crystal salt, as it is called, which is of a snowy whiteness, and transparent as glass. It is found only in little masses or veins running through the other salt. Formerly this kind used always to be sent to the King of Poland, who made presents of small portions of it to the nobility, and also had it fashioned into various ornamental shapes for the decoration of his palaces. It was also used for presents to other sovereigns. The King of Prussia still receives annually two hundred-weight of this finest salt; the Emperor of Russia two and a half, as such, and two as King of Poland, and the Emperor of Austria three, as emperor, and one as King of Hungary. The statue of King John Sigismund, which formerly stood at Warsaw, and now stands at the salt-works, is made of the largest block which has ever been found of this finest crystal salt. The workmen make all sorts of pretty trifles of this salt for strangers; such as books, needlecases, crucifixes, billiard-balls, necklaces, rosaries, saltcellars, knives, inkstands, &c., which they sell at high prices. We were told that the year before, an English lord had bought up three hundredweight of these trinkets. Pieces are sometimes found which are as transparent and pure as the finest plate-glass. The attempt has even been made to manufacture mirrors of this salt.

Besides this best salt, which, as we have said, is found only in small quantities, there is the *Blotnik* or earth salt, the green salt, and the *Shibik* salt. The first named is found in the upper strata, and is called so because it is often mixed with earth and clay. No trouble is taken to obtain it, but it is necessary to get rid of it, in order to come at the better kinds, and it is either used up in the mines, for the building of props, vaults, and steps, or sold at the mouth of the mine for cattle.

The green salt lies in immense and dense masses, under the earth salt, and is the principal object of attention. It consists of small crystals, which adhere closely together. It is as hard as glass, and is of about the same greenish colour and transparency, as common bottle-glass. This class has many subdivisions, according to the quality and density of the masses.

The lower we descend, the whiter, finer, and better, the salt becomes. After the above-mentioned crystal salt, the best sort is the *Shibik* salt, which lies under the green salt. It is less green and more dense than the latter.

The earth salt is sold in such pieces as it happens to be broken into, to the inhabitants of the surrounding district, and is not used in commerce. The differences between the various kinds of green salt, are also too insignificant to be noted by the government, which only takes cognizance of three distinctions. There is,

Firstly, the Crystal salt;
Secondly, the Shibik salt;
And thirdly, the Green salt.

The crystal salt is brought up in as large quantities as possible, and is immediately formed into the required shapes by the chisel of the sculptor, or the knife of the workman. The shapes of the Green and Shibik salts, therefore, alone remain to be considered.

The salt at Vieliczka is commonly cut into either cylindrical or parallelopipedic shapes; the former are called "*Balvans*," and the latter *formal pieces*. The cylindrical form is the most common. We were told that Balvan was an old idol of the Sarmatians, and that from him the shape and name were derived. Perfectly cylindrical these *Balvanen* are not, but rather bulging out in the middle. They are cut into this shape by the workmen while still in the mine. They are rolled about by the workmen in the mines on wheelbarrows. Löllner and Sydov estimate the weight of a *Balvan* at from five to ten hundredweight; but we were told that they were never made smaller than two, and never larger than three hundredweight. This seems much more likely to be the truth; for how could a mass of ten hundredweight be rolled about in a wheelbarrow by a single man! The parallelopipeds are from two to three hundredweight. Those pieces which break off during the loosening of the blocks of salt, and which though of a good size, are not large enough to make into *balvans* and parallelopipeds, are called "natural pieces." They are sold singly and according to weight; the little fragments and pieces which are of small size, and not worth selling singly, are packed into jars and sold by measure. Each of these kinds has its particular customers. The natural pieces generally remain in the neighbourhood; the *balvans* are sent away by land carriage, and the parallelopipeds by water. The small broken fragments are bought by the neighbouring peasants.

Descending into the mine, the first upper crust through which we pass, is of clay, mould, and sand. At a depth of fifteen fathoms are found the first traces of salt, consisting of a few little crystals scattered in the clay. Here and there also the clay appears intersected by thin veins of salt, or impregnated with numerous particles of it; but at Vieliczka, these little pieces are overlooked in the rich abundance of the stores beneath. If the story is true that a shepherd named Vielicz, was the first discoverer of these stores of salt, it must probably have been originally found near the surface, for it is not likely that a shepherd should have dug to such a depth to get at a spring, or for any other purpose.

The deeper we descend into the salted clay, the larger become the masses which it contains; their size increases from five, ten, or fifteen feet in diameter to fifty or one hundred feet. In the upper parts these pieces are dirty and mixed with earth; but further down, they become clear, dense, and pure. These great fragments lie about in all directions, positions, and shapes; they seem to have once formed huge firm connected masses, which have been broken asunder by some great natural convulsion.

Under the old system the salt was taken wherever it was found, in as great quantities as possible, and no one was thoughtful enough to inquire whether the neighbouring strata of earth were firm enough to bear this undermining and scooping away. Wherever any thing was built, it was done in a bad and unsolid a manner. A penurious system prevailed in the building of passages, props, and shafts, as well as in the draining and ventilating of the mines. They were sometimes altogether neglected, and sometimes the passages were made so small, that it was necessary to creep through on all fours. Besides perpetual inconvenience, this niggardly system occasioned many accidents, such as the falling in of roofs and passages, the death of workmen, and occasionally when the upper crust fell in, whole streets of the town of Vieliczka were destroyed as by an earthquake. Of late, neither time nor money has been spared in remedying these ancient errors. The passages have been strengthened and widened, and under the roofs, props have been placed, mostly taken from the forests of Niepolomize. A great part of these forests lies at present beneath the earth, in the shape of props and beams.

In the new mine every thing is in the very best of order. The passages and staircases are broad and convenient; and wherever the pits and shafts pass through earth and clay, their sides are strengthened either with wood, or with masses of salt; where they pass through salt, this is unnecessary. The building with salt is carried on in this manner; the blocks of salt are simply laid upon one another, and then water is poured over them. The water impregnates itself with salt, and fills the smallest interstices; gradually the water evaporates, and the salt thus deposited in every interstice, forms a kind of cement, which binds the whole mass and renders it extremely strong. In this way, walls and ceilings of the greatest solidity are built of salt and water. When the salt is scooped out and taken away, columns of salt are left at regular intervals to support the arched roof; these columns give the appearance of long aisles in a Gothic cathedral to some parts of the mines. The number of all the chambers and vaults in the mines is uncertain; there are nearly a hundred of them which are distinguished by particular names. The entire labyrinth of rooms, vaults, ladders, pits, passages, staircases, stories, aisles, mines, and shafts, in this gigantic subterranean building, has become so enormous during the six hundred years of its constant growth, that there is not one of the superintendents at Vieliczka who now knows every part of it. Each knows his own district; but if he ventures into unknown regions, he requires a guide as if he were a stranger. There are even parts of the works which have not for years been entered by any human being. This may easily be imagined, when we consider that this concealed labyrinth would, if exposed to the light of day, present a surface of double the extent of the old town of Vienna, and of three times the perpendicular height of the church and spire of St. Stephen's in that city.

The next morning I descended into the mines, furnished with the knowledge of the above particulars, and with a ticket of admission from the governor. I wore a white linen blouse for the protection of my clothes. We almost regretted that we were not hung to long sticks, and wound down like so many bunches of grapes, in the manner old travellers have described; instead of this, we quietly walked down long convenient staircases. These steps, some of which are of wood and some of salt, were mostly built for the convenience of royal visitors. There is one grand staircase which was built for Augustus II., and another, the imperial stairs, which was built for the late emperor and some members of his family; common visiters descend by side steps. These, however, are very convenient and safe; indeed at times I wished for a few difficulties to conquer, for at the salt-mines of Vieliczka, one may ascend and descend as leisurely as on the staircase of a palace.

The Austrians are, as I have said, very mysterious and reserved with respect to their salt-mines. This secrecy is not merely observed in the administrative department, regarding the cost, the prices, the quantities taken, &c., but also with respect to the mining arrangements, the extent of the works, and other circumstances of the kind, for which it is not easy to account; strangers therefore, are never allowed to remain long in the mines, and are seldom permitted to repeat their visits. The system at Vieliczka is something like that of the Dutch spice establishments in India. For instance, it would be easy to obtain twice or thrice as much salt as at present, but the government will not do this for fear of lowering the price. Whenever the workmen leave the shafts, they are searched in a suspicious and insulting manner, as if it was a gold or diamond mine in which they had been working. This inquisitorial proceeding is far more likely to destroy than to preserve honesty; a liberal system, and a simple prohibition against the taking away of salt, would be quite as effectual. The workmen are otherwise well provided with salt, receiving besides their wages, a regular allowance of fifteen pounds of it annually for each member of their families. Another most offensively grasping proceeding is the care which is taken that none shall use the water impregnated with salt which flows from the mine, and cannot be used there. This water is conducted through subterranean canals into the Vistula, where, mixing with the river water, it soon becomes useless. In this way, six hundred *eimer* of the finest brine, for which in some countries it would be thought worth while to establish separate salt-works, are wasted every day.

The salt-mines of Vieliczka are certainly the most beautiful and upon the greatest scale of any in the world. Nowhere is dirt or disorder to be seen, but every thing shines and glitters with the purest brilliancy. Springs of water nowhere occur throughout the mines, and consequently the air is very dry.* This is proved by the excellent preservation of the salt statues erected here and there, which would soon decay in damp air. The human inhabitants appear in as good preservation as the statues; they all seemed very healthy, and most of them must be old, many having worked in the mines for forty or fifty years. The air seems also to agree very well with the horses, who soon grow fat in the mines, if they have been ever so thin before. Through all the passages flows a strong current of air, which at certain corners blows with astonishing violence. An extraordinary subterranean whirlwind took place here in 1745, when a great internal vault fell in. The condensed air shot up through the rafts and passages leading from the vault, upsetting the workmen and their tools in the upper stories, tearing down beams and opening doors, and finally throwing down all the buildings which stood over the pit.

Noxious gases and bad vapours, so common in coal, copper, and silver mines, are never experienced at Vieliczka. The masses generally cohere so closely as to leave no room for the formation of such gases. Occasionally there arises a combustible hydrogen gas, called *Saleter* by the Poles, which floats up quietly through the atmosphere, and burns away without causing the slightest damage. On these accounts labour in these mines is not nearly so dangerous or unwholesome as in others; and the dreadful accidents which sometimes occur in coal-mines are quite unknown here. Sometimes the fine particles of salt inhaled with the air render the miners consumptive; but for the most part they live long and enjoy good health. The air itself is preservative to animal and vegetable matter. The meat brought down into the mines, becomes naturally salted, and keeps for a comparatively long time. Dead horses have sometimes been thrown into unused chambers, because the workmen were too lazy to bring them up; and after years have passed away, both skin and flesh have been found perfect and entire.

We soon went down the upper flights of steps, passing through three fathoms of mould, sixteen ells of clay, and thirty feet of sand. Anxious to reach the salt-mines beneath, we paid little attention to these appearances, which otherwise might have been fertile in interesting suggestions and speculations.

At length we reached the upper story, and were shown masses and veins of salt in the walls of the pass. The mere tints along the walls sufficed to show us that we had passed into a stratum of a different kind. The first chamber we entered was the Upper St. Ursula's chamber, the next the Under St. Ursula's chamber, then the Michaelovitsh, the Drosdovitsh, the Emperor Francis, the St. Mary, the Rosetta, and the Pishtek chambers, &c. &c. These

---

* After digging below the strata of salt, the workmen come to springs, and on several occasions the mines have been placed in great peril by attempts to go beyond the prescribed depth. This is now carefully avoided. Fresh water has to be conveyed into the mines from above by means of pipes.

chambers have been named after Saints, distinguished mining inspectors, Polish kings, and Austrian emperors. On an average each of these is 100 or 150 feet high, and 80 or 100 long and wide. In some the works were still going on. Others were used as storehouses for the salt. They had the appearance of huge subterranean vaults of Gothic architecture. Wooden steps leading from gallery to gallery were fastened to the walls. Workmen stood in each of these galleries, holding torches and lanterns, which lit up the dark walls. One who stood in the highest gallery, lighted a large bunch of oakum, and threw it down the shaft. It burnt up in a moment, and the flame towered high into the air, as it floated away through the caverns, lighting up the glittering vault to its highest summits, and revealing fresh and unknown depths below. The old mines are very picturesque, particularly where the roofs dividing the stories have fallen in, and thus opened abysses to the view, at which the spectator shudders. The new mines, with their regular beams and props, strong, even walls, and strong neat chambers, were far more prosaic in appearance. In some caverns, immense chandeliers cut out of the salt have been hung up. In one which was called the "Great Hall," hung such a chandelier, thirty-five feet in height, and sixty in circumference. In another, the Lentov chamber, were six of them.

Some of the old salt caverns have been turned into stables, others into chapels and churches. The largest chapel is that of St. Anthony of Padua. It was built in 1698, and formerly mass was performed there every morning to the miners; this, I am sorry to say, Joseph II. abolished. Every year, however, on the 3d of July, service is performed there, followed by a grand festival. All the inspectors and workmen are dressed in gala costume, and dine at long tables spread out in the salt caverns. In the chapel every thing is made of cut salt, altar, walls, ceiling, doors, crucifixes, niches, pedestals, and the statues upon them, of St. Anthony, St. Paul, St. Dominic, St. Francis, St. Mary, St. Kunigunda, and the Bishops Stanislaus and Casimir. The light of a torch held behind one of these statues, pierces through its thickest part. It is wonderful how little some of these statues have suffered, though they have remained here more than a century. The sharpness of their features alone seems a little to have worn down. When we were there, an old workman was busy sharpening them up again, with a hammer and chisel. As he could only raise the nose by cutting at the cheeks, and the lips by cutting at the chin, he certainly did not improve their physiognomies. It would have been a hundred times better to have left them untouched.

Toys of this kind are very plentiful in the mines; for instance, salt obelisks as memorials of royal visits, and salt monuments of different festivals. Besides the St. Anthony's chapel, there is the Corporis-Christi chapel, in which every year, on the 3d of September, service is performed in memory of the visit of the late emperor Francis. The oldest salt statue is that of the Polish queen, Kunigunda, the founder of the mine. Around it hang also old lamps of cut salt. The most interesting trophy is a great Austrian eagle, surrounded by all the tools and instruments used in the mines. This trophy is in the Old Dancing Hall. In this saloon, whose walls are resplendent as with the gleam of thousands of diamonds, the subterranean fêtes are given; and the illumination on these occasions surpasses our most magnificent ball-rooms in splendour. The saloon must resemble a fairy palace when completely lighted up.

The stables, stalls, and troughs of the horses kept below, are also of salt. There are generally from sixteen to twenty pair of these horses; they are the only creatures who, when once brought down, never see the light of day again. It is extraordinary that so unnatural a way of life seems to agree so well with them. Though deprived of sunshine and daylight, of the cool fresh grass, and the pleasant air of morning, they are not only fat and strong, but live to a good old age. They are made use of to keep the machinery in motion, and for the transport of large masses of salt. The grooms who attend them, are often down in the mines for weeks together, without seeing the light of day. All the other workmen leave the mines after eight hours' work. When horses are to be taken down, they are fastened into a long basket, and let down by a rope. At first they resist this, but lie quite still the moment they get down into the dark part.

The most wonderful of all the wonderful spectacles which these caverns and vaults present, are the subterranean ponds or lakes. There are nearly twenty such, on which a few small boats are kept. We were rowed over two, which are connected by a canal. Each was several hundred feet long, and about twenty feet deep; and far above them arched the huge salt rocks. Never had a breath of wind troubled the surface of these Stygian waters; never had a swallow fluttered over them, or a lily bathed its petals in their still waves. Moved as if by an invisible hand, the silent boat floated over the smooth, tranquil surface. We seemed as if in another world, for even the sounds which broke the silence were strange and unfamiliar. We had taken some pieces of salt with us, which we dropped into the middle of the water, and the sound was as if we had struck the deepest bass chord of a harp. The echo lasted for several seconds, but did not seem to come from the rocks around, but to be reverberated from the depths of the water.

In one of the subterranean chambers a little museum has been collected, containing all the varieties of salt and other substances found in the mines. There are to be seen shells imbedded in salt—a proof that the salt was deposited by an ocean; petrified and salted wood; masses of salt with stones in them; pieces of clay containing particles of salt, and salt crystals in various curious and fantastic shapes. Some are remarkable for their smell, which is sometimes like that of truffles, at others, like that of phosphorus, and sometimes again like that of sulphuretted hydrogen gas, &c.

Four hundred cubic fathoms of the salt rocks yield 5000 tons of salt. Since annually, therefore, 35,000 tons of salt are obtained, the mines must be enlarged every year to the amount of 2800 cubic fathoms, which is equal to a space eighty feet in length, height, and breadth. It would be easy, therefore, to calculate about how much salt has been thus taken from the bowels of the earth, since first the mines were established. The hundred great vaults which the mines contain, have always yielded the principal part of the produce. On an average each of these vaults contained 2000 cubic fathoms of pure salt, and the aggregate amount of their contents would be 200,000 cubic fathoms, or 2,500,000 tons of salt. In this computation is not included the quantity gained from the shafts, passages, stairs, &c., which would double the amount. The total would be five millions of tons, which would probably be near the truth; for this would give for each year an average of between twelve and thirteen thousand tons of salt. If the price of a hundredweight of salt has on an average been three florins, these mines have, during the 400 years of their duration, set a capital of three hundred millions of florins in circulation; and, estimating the average annual consumption of every man, woman, and child, at ten pounds, have furnished three hundred millions of human beings with salt.

CRACOW.

In all Poland, there is no city whose first appearance can compare with that of Cracow. The valley of the Vistula here forms a deep, hollow, even basin, surrounded by hills, in the midst of which lies the stately old city, with its palaces, huts, and castles, and numberless spires and steeples. It is surrounded by pretty villas and convents, nestling among fertile meadows and blooming gardens, and the arms of the Vistula flow round and embrace it. Towards the north, the horizon is crowned by low wooded hills, and towards the south by the distant summits of the lofty Carpathians. Podgorze is separated from Cracow by the Vistula, and was formerly one of its suburbs. The people always call it by its old name, but the official Austrian name is inscribed on a great board over the gates, and runs thus: "Josephstadt, an Imperial free manufacturing city."

Zöllner tells a story of an old Polish gentleman living at Cracow, who never could look across the Vistula to Podgorze, without shedding tears. A town must certainly suffer much, when so important a limb is severed from its body, for towns are not like some reptiles, of which when cut into several pieces, each separate fragment grows fresh limbs, and becomes a new and complete being. On the contrary, the different parts of a town are so closely connected together, by so many ties, that it cannot be partitioned, without much suffering to all its parts. Podgorze, however, has not suffered from this amputation so much as Cracow; for it has prospered at the cost of the latter. The inns of Podgorze were far more suited to the dignity of Cracow than to the insignificance of its former suburb. Most of the tradespeople of Cracow have likewise establishments in Podgorze; some of them have even emigrated entirely to the Austrian side, so that the whole place presents a picture of rising prosperity, forming a striking contrast to the fallen state of Cracow. We took up our quarters at Podgorze, intending from thence to visit the old city on the opposite side of the Vistula. We presented our passports at the Austrian passport-office, and received permission to visit Cracow for six hours, upon our solemn promise to return within that time; the young merchant with whom we were travelling, a born Austrian subject, was not allowed to go at all. The reason of this was, that a Russian spy had been murdered in Cracow a few days before, on account of which the town was filled with Austrian soldiers, and was in the greatest alarm and confusion. A barrier was set up at the bridge, where some Austrian officers with sticks in their hands were marching up and down, not allowing any one to cross without a ticket of permission. The peasants and peasantwomen who understood nothing of the meaning of these obstructions and ceremonies, presented their tickets in puzzled silence as they passed through with their eggs, butter, charcoal, and other things for market. At the turnpike we left our poor young merchant, whose government kept such a strict surveillance over his proceedings. He looked sorrowfully across the bridge at the free city of Cracow, which remained to him a tantalizing *terra incognita*.

The fame of Cracow is connected with the oldest events of Polish history, and down to modern days the energetic race which inhabits this town and its neighbourhood, have always been among the bravest and best Polish patriots. Here Kosciusko celebrated his greatest triumphs. After the second and third partitions of Poland, and after the vain exertions made to avert that catastrophe, in which Cracow heartily joined, this city, which in the middle of the last century had numbered one hundred thousand inhabitants, sank to its minimum of importance, and at the end of the century, numbered only sixteen thousand inhabitants. The tranquillity which prevailed in Poland till 1830, caused it to recover a little, and from 1820 to 1830, its population rose to twenty thousand and twenty-four thousand; but since the end of the Polish revolution in 1831, Cracow has been sinking more and more. The Austrians of the three great powers that protect Cracow, are the least hated by the Poles, and it appeared to us to be the general feeling of the inhabitants, that the best thing for Cracow would be its speedy union with the Austrian Empire. Such an union with Austria seemed universally to be desired, and that with Russia to be dreaded; and the report prevailed at the time, that Austria would give up to Russia the circle of Tarnopol, and take Cracow in exchange. This favourable feeling towards Austria is the more natural, that half the inhabitants of Cracow are either Germans or Germanized Poles.

Six hours only were allowed me for this interesting and curious republic, so that I determined to use my senses to the utmost, and let nothing escape me, and I may truly say that I carried off from my brief visit, more information and more impressions than I shall here be able to record.

We reached the middle of the low old bridge, where the territory of Austria ceases, and that of the free republic, surrounded and protected by three powerful autocrats, begins. The Vistula here flows in many arms through a projecting rocky formation, which formerly connected the Carpathian mountains with the hills on the opposite side of the river. The Vistula, however, has now broken through this bank, and as this change must first have rendered the river navigable; it probably gave the first occasion to the building of Cracow, and to its subsequent prosperity. Hungary, Silesia, Galicia, and Poland, are countries which find in Cracow a natural place of exchange for their wares; and though recent unfortunate political events have greatly injured her commerce, yet Hungarian wine, Silesian manufactures, Vieliczka salt, and Galician honey and wax, still pass through Cracow along the Vistula. This city also carries on a trade with Warsaw and Danzig, furnishing them with spices and eastern commodities, and also with Carpathian stone, chalk, and gypsum. The little ships, called *Strusen* and *Pletten*, supply Cracow with wood, hay, butter, and vegetables, from the Austrian, Russian, and Cracovian dominions; and above all with coals from Prussian and Austrian Silesia. Among the minor branches of trade, is that of eggs, which is carried on through Cracow between Galicia and Warsaw; these eggs are principally the harvest of the poultry-yards of the Galician peasants, who are bound to send their lords a stipulated number of eggs at certain seasons of the year, particularly at Michaelmas.

It is a peculiarity in Cracow that all its quarters have distinct and different names; each of its parts forming, indeed, a separate little town, once governed by a constitution of its own, and still partially divided by walls from the rest of the city. They are the towns of Stradom, Kasimierz, and Cracow, and the suburbs of Clepardia, Smolensk, Vessola, Visna, Piasek, &c. We first entered Stradom, which lies upon an island in the Vistula, between Kasimierz and Podgorze; the two Cracovian sentinels who usually keep watch there, had been supplanted by Austrian soldiers. We found the principal street of Stradom lifeless and uninteresting, with small insignificant houses. As it was very winding and crooked, we had some difficulty in finding our way, but after a little while we had guides enough, for passing over an arm of the Vistula, we reached the Jewish quarter, the old town of Kasimierz. Here the streets were busy, crowded, and noisy as a beehive; and as all the inhabitants were Jews, they were all our servants for a small remuneration. We sent one for a fiacre, and engaged another to be our guide. The number of Jews who crowded the streets, doors, and thresholds of Kasimierz, was almost incredible, and though it was the sabbath, they did not seem the less busy and active. Many were working in different ways in the streets. This custom of living in the open air, seems to be transplanted by the Polish Jews from their native east. They were most of them very ragged, dirty, and miserable-looking, but through the windows we saw many a pretty face pertaining to the softer sex. We were struck with many peculiarities in their dress and appearance, such as the absence of the hood ornamented with beads which decorated the heads of all the Jewish women between Odessa and Lemberg. The girls had all of them their heads uncovered, and the ringlets of many were beautifully luxuriant. The married women wore gilt caps, edged with fur.

While waiting for our fiacre we entered the ground-floor of one of the most miserable Jewish houses, and the following was the picture that presented itself: The cellar, from which rose a pestilential vapour, was filled a foot high with water. The Vistula had overflowed in the autumn, and it had rained much, so that the water came through the broken walls which the landlord refused to mend; neither would he have the water pumped out, saying that it was not his business. The poor people had laid stones and boards across the flood, as bridges to their tables and beds. As we entered, a couple of naked lads came splashing through the water, whining and asking alms. In this hole lived no fewer than three families, all plentifully provided with children. They inhabited separate corners, and told us that in general they marked out their separate territories with chalk upon the floor, but that the water had now obliterated all such traces. The bedsteads, covered with straw, were almost buried in the water; and upon the highest of them sat a young mother, with her feet resting on a stone, suckling her child. Her rags covered but one leg; the skin of the other was tender and delicate. The water was splashing in the cradle of a young infant, and an old Jew, blind, decrepit, and diseased, sat by with the cold indifference of a statue, insensible to all around him. We beheld this picture of misery with shuddering horror, and having distributed a few trifling gifts and words of consolation, we hastened out, as we heard our fiacre drive up.

The rest of the Jewish quarter of Kasimierz was soon passed, and crossing the pretty stone bridge which leads over another arm of the Vistula, we entered the real town of Cracow. In the days when the Bishop of Cracow, who, with his spiritual dignity enjoyed the title of Duke in Severia, had still an annual income of 50,000 ducats, when the Voyevode of

Cracow ruled southward to the Tatra mountains, and when the Castellan of Cracow, not only the first Castellan in Poland, but in rank superior even to the Voyevodes, was a senator of the republic, and dispensed justice in the sight of all men in the public market-place; when those old houses which now look so black and ruinous, were inhabited by magnates, and overflowed with pomp and luxury; or coming down to later times, in the days when Kosciusko, the idol of Cracow, first raised the banner of freedom for his native land, then indeed this old capital must have been beautiful and interesting in the highest degree. Or when a newly-chosen monarch entered his capital in state, from the election field of the Vola; or when deceased royalty entered the city in all the pomp and pageantry of death, to lay his bones among those of his predecessors, amid the rocks of the Necropolis, how must the streets and houses have been crowded then with guests and strangers, how must the bells of the seventy-two churches of Cracow have rung in triumph or tolled in requiem! But those days of prosperity and independence found few to describe them, while the petty present, where every thing is levelled or effaced, is searched in every corner for topics and themes of interest.

We noticed a great many ruinous and falling buildings; and others which had been stopped in the building, and whose unfinished fragments were already becoming ruins. The streets were filled with Austrian soldiers, Jews, German mechanics, Polish peasants, and here and there a quiet Polish nobleman. Of the senators and presidents of the republic we saw nothing, but it would not have been easy to overlook the handsome stately building in which the Russian consul resides. We drove through several streets—many of them rich in interesting buildings—and at length passing through the *Grehsky Ulitza* (Greek-street), we reached the market-place or "Ring" of the city. It is one of the most interesting market-places possible, and but for the absence of the sea, might remind the spectator of St. Mark's place at Venice. It is a large open space, surrounded partly by handsome new, and partly by interesting old buildings, among which stands the *Sukonitza*, an old house, built in the Gothic style. It is a long hall, whose wide interior is intersected by two arcades, which cross one another in the centre. Our Jewish guide was very fluent in relating to us how this building was formerly called the Volnitza, or Hall of Election, and that for some time the kings of Poland were here chosen. The nobles assembled in the great hall, and the numerous side chambers were devoted to different minor purposes. Around this building is concentrated the chief bustle and noise of the town. The peasants sell the wares which they bring to market in their little carts, and then creep stealthily round the *Sukonitza*, wrapped in their sheepskins, to purchase the trifles of which they stand in need. The Jews follow them incessantly, to chaffer with and cheat them; even the little Jewish children begin early to practise these occupations, and hawk about with noisy importunity little baskets full of useless knickknackeries. Another prominent figure in the crowd is that of the priest, which is as frequently seen in Cracow as in Moscow, Benares, or Babylon. In the centre of the *Sukonitza*, where the four arcades meet, are the three great eagles of the three protecting powers perching together with brotherly unanimity. The castle and the market-place of Cracow have been the scenes of all its great historical events, the last of which was the triumph of Kosciusko, and his elevation as generalissimo of the rising republic. The whole market-place is now covered with booths, which are scattered about in picturesque disorder.

Upon the south-eastern side, lies the imposing and beautiful church of the "Holy Mother of God." It is built in the Gothic style, and its windows are stained with beautiful paintings on glass. Like most Polish churches, it has three organs, one large one opposite the altar, and two small ones on each side of the choir. The sound of these organs during service time, now repeating each other like echoes, now answering, and now joining in full chorus, must have a particularly beautiful effect, the discovery of which appears to be confined to the Poles, for out of Poland, as far as I know, this plurality of organs is quite unknown, whereas in Poland some churches have as many as five. Like all the churches of Cracow, for which the Polish nobility always did more than for any others in the kingdom, St. Mary's church is rich in monuments of Polish greatness. St. Anne's church offers but little historical interest. The only thing about it that is likely to attract a stranger is the tomb of Copernicus.

Cracow contains thirty convents, of one of which, that of St. Elizabeth, our Jewish guide related to us the following story. Three weeks ago a fire broke out in this convent, of which the nuns are subjected to very strict rules of discipline. Some of them, in this emergency, left their cells without further ceremony, and took refuge in the neighbouring houses; but others, shrinking with horror from the idea of violating a vow which binds them under no circumstances ever to leave the convent, preferred to remain and meet their fate. They would have perished in the flames, had not the Jewish firemen rushed in and saved them by sheer force. Throughout Galicia the Jews are the only firemen, and the numerous fires which are constantly breaking out in Cracow give them plenty to do there. They must even help the Christians to save their convents and churches, though, except in the hour of danger, the pollution of their presence would not be allowed there.

We had now already spent a good quarter of the time allowed us by the Austrian police, and had not seen the greatest lion of Cracow, the capital or Acropolis of the city, called the Vavel, with the old Königsburg, and the cathedral. We accordingly, after a hasty view of the churches of St. Anne and St. Peter, the Franciscan convent, and the episcopal palace, proceeded towards the Vavel.

The hill upon which stand these old buildings, the most sacred and highly-valued remains of Polish antiquity, is, upon one side very steep, and towers with gigantic majesty upon its frowning rocks, from among the petty web of streets at its feet. Its excellent fortifications must have been of some importance when it was the citadel of the metropolis of Poland. During their occupation the French strengthened these fortifications, which, however, seem now to be falling into ruins. A broad and handsome road leads up to the Vavel, resembling that which leads to the castle at Edinburgh, and commands, in every part, a beautiful view of the town, the landscape, and the Carpathian mountains beyond. Up this road the fifty or sixty kings of Poland passed, each of them twice, surrounded by all the pomp and magnificence of their station; once on horseback, in the prime of manhood and the zenith of glory, surrounded by the magnates of the kingdom, in order to be invested by the primate, in the cathedral, with the thorny diadem of Poland; and a second time, likewise in all the pomp of royalty, and surrounded by nobles and grandees, but pale, motionless, and unconscious, to join the departed sovereigns in their silent abode on the Vavel.

It is curious to read with what ceremony, pomp, and magnificence, the coronations and funerals of the Polish kings were conducted, a deference and veneration for the royal office being then manifested by the nobles, which afforded a striking contrast to their conduct towards reigning and living sovereigns. Kings, who exercised, while living, scarcely the shadow of real power, were buried after death, with a state which the most powerful autocrats have rarely equalled. The body of the deceased king was first taken with great ceremony to Warsaw, where it was embalmed, and lay in state in the principal church, till a new king was chosen. Next it was brought to Cracow in grand procession, followed by the new king and the greatest nobles of the country, and laid in the church of St. Stanislaus, where the Primate of Poland and the Bishop of Cracow performed the funeral obsequies, assisted by the assembled clergy; and finally, after numerous further ceremonies, the body was deposited in the vaults of the cathedral. The newly-chosen king was obliged to be present at all these solemnities, in order that he might remember the vanity of earthly greatness.

At the entrance of the cathedral, to which we first directed our steps, our Jew gave us up to the guidance of the sexton. I never remember to have seen a church so rich as this in interesting monuments and royal tombs. The cathedral itself is a splendid and majestic building, built in the Gothic style. The body of the church is large and lofty, surrounded by numbers of small chapels. The pillars are marble, and their ornaments, as well as the decorations of the twenty-four chapels, with their sculptures, pictures, statues, and carvings, astonished us by their beauty and variety. On entering, the eye is first caught by the splendid monument of St. Stanislaus, consisting of a catafalk and coffin, with the statue of the sainted bishop, and a number of figures of angels and others, all of pure and shining silver. This Stanislaus is one of the many priests, who, during the struggle in the middle ages between the spiritual and the temporal power, received death from the latter, and the crown of martyrdom from the former. He and King Boleslaus played here in Cracow, parts nearly identical with those of Nepomucene and King Venceslaus in Prague.

Stanislaus Shtshepovski was a native of Kenty, a small Polish city, where his parents died in indigent circumstances shortly after his birth. A wealthy noble adopted him, and educated him for the church, where his talents soon distinguished him so much, that while yet a young man, he obtained the dignity of Bishop of Cracow. Here, according to the narrative handed down to us by contemporary churchmen, he led so exemplary a life, that his very virtues became a thorn in the eyes of the wicked, vicious, and godless King Boleslaus II., whose natural aversion to the bishop, was inflamed to the most inveterate animosity, when the good man ventured to reproach him with his licentiousness, cruelty, and irregular way of life. All the bishop's remonstrances were of no avail, and he found it necessary to proceed to more serious measures. The king persisted in his wicked course, and the bishop forbade his entrance to the church. Boleslaus, in defiance of the prohibition, forced his way in, Stanislaus immediately interrupted the course of divine service, and was about to pronounce a curse on the sacrilegious monarch, when the latter and his attendants rushed upon him, hacked his body to pieces, and threw these into the Vistula.

An important part of the story is usually omitted by the reverend historians. The time of the tragedy was the papacy of Gregory VII., and the bishop had his private grounds for quarrel with the king. The foster-father of Stanislaus had bequeathed his estates to his adopted son; but the king refused to recognise the will, though the bishop, in proof of its validity, performed a multitude of miracles, calling the old knight, for instance, from the grave, to give his hand to his foster son, and attest the will anew. The king enforced his claim, nevertheless, though the tribunals decided against him. *Hinc lacrimæ! hinc iræ!* No doubt, the king behaved with great injustice to the bishop, but it was the partial judgment of the priests that made the one an angel and the other a devil. Boleslaus, however, was soon overtaken by divine, or rather by priestly, vengeance. Gregory VII. excommunicated him, and declared him to have forfeited the throne. He fled into Hungary, where he died by his own hand, in 1081, and is one of the few kings of Poland whose remains have not been interred on the Vavel. Stanislaus, meanwhile, was canonized. Doves and ravens brought together the fragments of his body, and some were respectfully collected in the river by the fishes. The limbs joined themselves together of their own accord, and the reunited body was buried with great pomp in the cathedral, where it became an object of worship to the multitude, and for nearly eight centuries, candles have not ceased to burn night and day before his grave, nor prayers to be offered up to him for intercession.

With few exceptions all the Polish kings lie buried here. Those of the dynasty of the Piasts, who reigned for 500 years, those of the race of the Yagellons, who flourished for three centuries, and lastly the elective monarchs, the Bathorys, the Sobieskis, &c. The first Piasts lie together in a plain antique unornamented chapel, and simple tablets of marble mark their graves. But these are not wanting in expressive inscriptions. Thus, on the tablet of Vladislaus Loketer, the first of the Polish kings, we read the words : " *Ubi Nodus Gordius, ibi ille Macedo et ensis.*"

The monuments of the later kings of Poland are far more splendid and various, the titles longer, and the inscriptions more pompous. In the older chapels, sixteen or twenty royal personages often repose together, while the modern kings have each a separate chapel. The monuments of some are not in a chapel at all ; that of Casimir the Great, for instance, one of the most ancient and simple of all, stands against a column in the body of the church. In the middle of the church before the altar, lies the metal plate which covers the grave of Queen Hedviga, the daughter of King Louis of Hungary and Poland.

One of the most beautiful chapels, is that of the two Sigismunds, containing their statues fashioned out of that flesh-coloured marble used here for all statues and pillars. The art and skill manifested in these statues, cannot be too much admired, and is a proof of the high state of art in Poland at the time. In one side of the chapel hangs a silver plate, on which the warlike deeds of John Sigismund are represented in bas-relief by the hand of the artist warrior himself.

That heart must be made of stone which is not powerfully affected by this vast collection of royal graves and monuments, this history of Poland in stone. How thankful we felt to the old priests, whose care and devotion had preserved to posterity such valuable relics of antiquity! The grave of the noble and courageous Stephen Bathory " *pacis bellique artibus magno,*" particularly attracted our respectful attention. He is buried in a chapel, in which the later Polish kings often heard mass. Above him are the royal arms of Poland, and at his feet those of his family.

Close to the chapel of Stephen Bathory is that of a kindred mind, John Sobieski, " *electione Polonicus, Lithuanicus, Prussicus et liberatione Austriacus, Pannonicus, profligatione Ottomannicus, Thrasicus, Scythicus, cui regnum gloriam sempiternam peperit.*" Neither so long and pompous an inscription, nor such an overloading of ornament, were necessary for the monument of so truly great a man as Sobieski, whose simple name and statue would have been imposing enough. From the columns of the body of the church, droop like banners, six large and splendid pieces of tapestry, which were taken from the tent of the Grand Vizier, by the Poles under Sobieski. They represent the history of Jacob and Joseph, and were probably the work of Grecian artists. Many private persons, generals, bishops, &c., have had the honour of monuments in this Polish Westminster Abbey. The famous Bishop Soltyk of Cracow, who was captured and taken to Siberia by Cossacks, has a marble statue here, with the inscription " *Patriæ libertatis intrepido adsertori, non tam ob suam, quam republicæ calamitatem ægritudine oppresso,* 1788." There is also a beautiful white marble statue by Thorwaldsen of Count Vladimir Potocki. The erection of monuments to Polish greatness in this cathedral has been continued even to the present day, for while we were there, the workmen were still occupied in the decoration of a chapel in honour of Count Arthur Potocki. It will not be excelled by the royal chapels around in splendour and magnificence. The Countess Brannicka, the widow of the Count Potocki, has laid out 20,000 ducats upon it.

The church seemed full of living countenances on every side; here rose the Bishops Lipski and Matshiovski, there the thick nose of the Castellan Dembinski, there the jolly countenance of Bishop Gamrod stared us in the face; endless varieties of royal, martial, and episcopal physiognomies. " To see them all," says Zöllner, " we had neither time nor inclination." I cannot conceive how he could say so. Time indeed we had not, for the fourth hour was just ended, but inclination! How it would have delighted us to learn by heart all that we saw before us, and to engrave those countenances indelibly on the tablet of our memories. But our Jew stood at the door and shouted to us to make haste, for we had still a great deal to see; the priests and sextons kept jabbering over their phrases learnt by rote; the peasants and citizens were going in and out continually; the maids and servants were bustling about with brooms and dusters, in preparation of the next day's festival. How amid such accompaniments could the mind raise itself to feelings worthy of the place? Ah, if we had had the graves of the kings all to ourselves, amid the silence of the night, with the tranquil moon and stars peeping down through the stained oriel windows, we might have felt and written something worthy of the theme!

In spite of these interruptions, however, we would not leave the cathedral without visiting the subterranean vaults which contain the bodies of Poniatovski, Sobieski, and Kosciusko. The coffin of the latter bears for its inscription only the name Kusciusko, and at his head the red Krakuska or cap worn by him, when he was raised in Cracow to be the Natshelnik of the Polish nation. We were willing enough to dispense with seeing the jewels, gold, and relics preserved in other parts of the cathedral, and accordingly, leaving the graves of the Polish monarchs, we proceeded towards the palace which they occupied during life, and which, at the period of our visit, had been converted into a barrack for the accommodation of Austrian soldiers.

In the handsome courtyard Austrian soldiers were parading to the sound of the drum. Some parts of the palace were desolate and ruinous.

"In old Afrasiab's consecrated halls,
The hooting night-owl to his brethren calls,
And o'er the palace's majestic gate,
The spider hangs his canopy of state."

An old Polish seneschal showed us over the rooms. In the state bedroom of Queen Hedviga, Austrian soldiers were rolling on their straw beds. In the study of King Sigismund Augustus, they had hung out their shirts and stockings to air at the windows. In the middle of the great audience chamber, they had made a fire, and were frying sausages!

The more melancholy and desolate every thing around appeared, the more the old seneschal exerted his eloquence to give us an idea of its former magnificence. The windows had once been of the finest kind, and painted in the most splendid manner; but they had been broken and supplied with the common glass we now saw. The borders and cornices had once been of silver, but they had been taken down and melted. The bronze of the magnificent doors and doorways of the throne-rooms and dining-saloons, and the beautiful bas-reliefs illustrative of memorable events in Polish history, had been converted into Austrian cannons. The finely-woven tapestry had been torn down and cut up by the soldiers for bedding. All the marble and mosaic had been covered with chalk, but here and there the destroyers had done their work in a slovenly manner, and a few unchalked statues, a few pieces of tapestry left hanging, and a few places where the mosaic of the ceilings had been too high to be conveniently reached, was all that remained to tell us of the former splendour of this magnificent palace.

In one of the rooms we found some paintings thrown together in a corner, which represented the principal events of the life of Kusciusko in America, Poland, and Switzerland. The soldiers had turned the royal chapel into a store-room, and the only beauty of the place which they had been unable to injure, was the lovely view it commanded of the city, of the fertile plains of Cracow, and of the distant Carpathians.

As we left the Vavel, there arose between us a dispute, as to whom the great bones, which hang in chains over the cathedral gates, could have belonged to. This is generally the case with all travellers who arrive here. Some said they were the jaw-bones and ribs of a whale, and others that they were mammoth's bones found near Cracow. Our Jew declared that they were the shoulder-bones of a giant, who formerly lived here, and our coachman denied this, affirming them to be the remains of a monster who once raged in the neighbourhood of Cracow, and who was killed by some valiant knights.

Of the University of Cracow we saw only the Botanical Garden and the Observatory. We used the telescope of the latter to examine the beautiful panorama at our feet, and above all the peaks of the Tatra mountains, which, with the help of the telescope, and of the delightful autumn weather, we saw as distinctly as we did the houses of Cracow.

Our Jew did not fail to tell us several interesting circumstances respecting these mountains. He assured us that on the top of the Lomnitz mountain, lay a lake, so high that no one had ever yet reached it. Upon its surface floated one of the boards of Noah's ark. At the day of judgment, this board would become a ship, in which all the Jews of Cracow would securely sail to the Land of Promise. We appeared incredulous, but he assured us that this story was believed by all the Jews of Cracow, and that a brother Israelite of Hungary, whom he had lately consulted on the subject, had expressed his belief in it. Of the Käsmark mountain he related to us a more credible story, namely, that there are three villages there, whose inhabitants distinguished themselves in some old Polish war, and received in reward, the privilege of wearing swords like noblemen; a right of which they still continue to make use.

We spent the last hour of our stay at Cracow, in visiting the public promenades of the city, which were formerly ramparts and ditches. The botanical garden was in good order, and was peculiarly rich in marsh and aquatic plants.

It is surprising how much may be seen and done in six times sixty minutes. Upon the whole we had used our time well, and had seen and heard much that was new and interesting; and yet we were conscious that some of our minutes had been wasted, and that we had even once or twice felt something like ennui; but upon the whole, we crossed the Vistula well contented with our six hours' amusement, and arriving at our "*civitas regia et libera, Podgorze*," we presented ourselves at the Austrian passport-office, scarcely five minutes after the appointed time.

PODGORZE.

We determined to remain the rest of the day at Podgorze, in order to enjoy the prospect of the old city opposite, at our leisure. The place from whence the best view of Cracow is obtained, is the "Krakus-hill." This hill is the work of human hands. It is a complete cone, rounded off at the top, two hundred and eighty paces in circumference, and about ninety feet high. It is an old custom of the Poles to raise hills of this kind as monuments to their great men; besides the Krakus-hill there are two similar mounds near Cracow, one in honour of the Princess Vanda, and another of Kosciusko. Every year on the first of May, the citizens of Cracow pour forth to these hills to celebrate their May-day festivals. On the third day of Easter they also flock thither in great numbers, and even the inhabitants of the Carpathians descend from their mountains, to share in the festival.

Krakus was the founder of Cracow, and the great Polish chieftain. With the exception of him, and of Vanda, his daughter, no Polish hero had been thought worthy of the honour of having a mountain erected to his memory near Cracow, until the days of the great Kosciusko. If, as the people say, Polish history really began with Krakus, and if the dying prophecy of Kosciusko on the battle-field prove true, these hills may serve as monuments of Poland's birth and death, of the beginning and the end of an eventful thousand years.

Probably no modern hero has ever been honoured with so peculiar and interesting a monument, as that of Kosciusko. He enjoyed such universal esteem and affection in his own country, such high veneration from all strangers, and such respect even from his political enemies, that not only all Poland, but also foreigners, lent assistance to the raising of a monument to his honour. Even the Russian Emperor Alexander was not behindhand. Not only hired labourers, but volunteers of the highest rank, worked at the raising of the hill, in the erection of which two years were spent. Citizens, nobles, and councillors of Cracow, as well as noble ladies of the highest birth, cast earth with their own hands on the mausoleum of their noble *Natskelnik*. Every Pole who passed through Cracow at the time, claimed the honour of throwing a barrowful of earth on the hill of Kosciusko. The hill is 120 feet high, and 300 paces in circumference. Winding walks, bordered with flowers, lead up to its summit, which is shaded by linden-trees. With the surplus of the subscription a piece of ground was bought, upon which were settled a few old veterans, whose business it is to watch and take care of the monument.

Other nations, besides the Poles, have had the custom of raising hills in honour of distinguished heroes; indeed it is extraordinary that this habit has not become universal, for such a monument is the most durable of any. No enemy would find it worth his while to carry away the worthless mould at a great expense of labour, and the powers of Nature would pass as harmlessly as those of man over the smooth round surface. By this means also, a monument is raised which forms a striking object in the whole surrounding landscape. The fertile hill of Kosciusko is a prominent point in the view to every one on entering Galicia, from this side of the Vistula, and it is the first object seen by every citizen as he passes out of the city gates. If, indeed, it were placed between the walls of a city, it would be hidden, and have to be sought for.

On the morning of our arrival in Podgorze, we had been met by a great wedding procession. The bridegroom was led by two girls, the bride by two lads, and these were followed by a promiscuous train of men and women. The whole was preceded by music, and by two jesters, who played all sorts of comic tricks and grimaces. When we returned from the Krakus-hill in the evening, we found the whole company dancing at the hotel. They had already got to their national dances, a sign that the wedding cheer had already begun to affect the guests. "For, contrary to the German practice," observed one of the dancers afterwards to me, "which is to begin with our Polonaise, and afterwards to go on to the German dances, we begin with the quiet, orderly, and decorous dances of Germany and France. Afterwards, when the wines of Nessmull and Erlau have made us lively, we fly to the Mazurka, and there is no end to the swinging and twisting and twirling about. Hurrah! Merrily, merrily! trallala, trallala!" and with these exclamations he sprang into the dance. It was the Krakoviak, a Cracusian variation of the Mazurka. This is the most wild, stormy, and passionate dance I ever beheld. Sometimes the whole group of dancers flew round in a wild circle, sometimes the ring broke up into single pairs, who whirled round and swung backwards and forwards with the maddest fury, and sometimes the dancers would all cross hands and dance about, in what appeared complete confusion. The wild and passionate action of the men, their noisy songs, and stamping feet, formed a striking contrast to the quiet, passive manner of the female dancers, as they passively allowed themselves to be twirled about by their active partners. Not merely the dancers, but all the spectators joined in the chorus, including a couple of shoemakers' apprentices and two old beggars, who stood at the door. The guests were all of the lower orders, and this dance alone appeared to me to refute the notion, that in Poland the nobility alone are national and patriotic. "Ah! the Poles," said our German host, when we retired for supper, "the Poles have all, from the prince to the beggar, more patriotism, more spirit, and yet more carelessness and indolence, than any other nation in the world. They are a wonderful people, full of contradictions and anomalies. They have such talents, such intellect, and withal so much generosity and magnanimity, that after living fifty years among them, I sometimes feel a love, an actual admiration for them, although at other times I feel so heartily disgusted with them, that I should like to see them all soundly flogged: yes, I should like to horsewhip them all myself. I am certain, if the gold that is hidden in the Polish character was cleansed from the rubbish with which it is encumbered, that this people might become the first in the world. Yet they will never come to any good, for they are eaten up with laziness, have no perseverance, are treacherous, and deceitful, never agree among themselves, and the noble tramples on the rights of the Jew and the citizen, and the Jew and citizen on those of the peasant. Poland is like a cedar devoured by insects, like a lion crushed by snakes."

Our host we afterwards discovered to be a very important man in the city. He had built a new church in Podgorze, and a manufactory in Cracow. His appearance was that of a blacksmith, his thoughts those of a philosopher, and his language that of a member of parliament. I never heard any one reason more correctly and acutely concerning the state of Poland.

"The worst of it is," he continued, "that the peasant has too few, and the noble too many rights. The peasants are the first and most important class in the world, and all the rest, citizens, nobles, artists, merchants, and men of letters, are nothing to them, nothing I say. The Polish nobility are a mere rabble, I wouldn't trust 'em with any thing. They are the most artful rascals in the world. It is not to be denied that there are many estimable exceptions; I have known some Polish nobles whom I would have died to serve. Oh! sir, I knew the great Kosciusko well; and have shouted hurrah at his approach in the market-place of Cracow, while yet a mere boy, when all the people cheered him, and a thousand red Krakuskas flew upward to greet their beloved Natshelnik, who, advancing from among them, raised his right hand to Heaven, and cried, 'I swear fealty unto death, to you, to our cause, and to our country.' The Russians had already left the place, for they had got wind of a conspiracy to murder them all. Kosciusko set out after them, with three or four small cannons, and with a continually increasing army, and took them all prisoners. Three months afterwards he was himself taken prisoner by the Cossacks. Good Heavens! what revolutions have I not witnessed here during fifty years! When I came here, Cracow was still the capital of the kingdom of Poland, then it became the property of Russia, then of Ducal Saxony, then of Austria; next the Vienna Congress made it a free republic, and now the Austrians again occupy it, and will perhaps annex it to Galicia. Characters like Kosciusko's show the height to which their good qualities might yet raise the Polish nobility; but they are at present,—not merely those whom you meet riding a dozen together in a little Matshenka, their common property, but also those who drive about with four horses to their showy equipages,—they are all, at present, a very worthless set. They torment and flog their poor peasants, and squander away what they have robbed from the poor, in drinking and gambling. They have, however, somewhat improved, and the condition of the peasantry is no longer what it was. The Poles have certainly gained in order and civilization, what they have lost in political independence. Forty years ago I was in Lemberg; there were then scarcely a dozen storehouses in the city, and the town was regularly burnt down every ten years. Now Lemberg is almost as stately as Warsaw, and more pleasant and beautiful than Cracow."

The sons of my host, who had been born in Poland, and were in consequence completely Polonized, as the Germans in France become Frenchified, those in St. Petersburg Russified, and those in London Anglicized, sat silently in opposite corners of the room, without joining in our conversation, and appeared to laugh at us for the attention we paid to their father's remarks.

LANDSKORONA AND BIALA.

The next morning we turned our backs upon Cracow and Podgorze, and proceeded through the easternmost circle of Galicia, the Vadovize circle, which is embellished by the Tatra mountains and their pretty mountain streams, and has a fertile soil and an abundant population. This circle contains 5000 inhabitants to every square mile, and it is the most beautiful and prosperous part of Galicia.

After passing the lovely fields of Mogilany and Isdebnik, we came to Kalvaria and Landskon, or Landskorona, as the people of the country call it. Kalvaria is an estate formerly owned by the Zebrzedovski family, but lately purchased by a German of the name of Brandis; Landskorona, formerly the property of the Krasinskis, belongs now to the duchess of Carignan, the mother of the king of Sardinia, and herself, by birth, a Krasinska. Landskorona contains thirty villages, and 40,000 inhabitants. A picturesque convent is perched upon a projection of the mountain, which overhangs these pretty villages. This convent possesses a miraculous picture of the Holy Virgin, which is the object of a great many pilgrimages. The festival which assembles the greatest number of pilgrims here, is that of the Ascension of the Virgin, when the number sometimes amounts to 100,000 peasants, nobles, and citizens, from Moravia, Silesia, Galicia, Cracow, Poland, and Hungary. We were not a little eager to see this famous place of pilgrimage, so widely honoured, and so much frequented in Poland.

The foot of the mountain is clothed with fertile cornfields, and its summit loses itself in pine forests, which in this part of the Carpathians are particularly beautiful, with the tall, straight, smooth, white stems, and dark green foliage. The first projection is occupied by ruins of an old castle. On the top is situated the convent itself, which, with all its churches, towers, and minor buildings, forms a most picturesque object. The path up to it is marked out by numerous small chapels and crosses.

The castle offers little attraction to the traveller, while the convent, with its courtyards, handsome gates, iron gratings, and sculptured figures in front, looks as imposing from the outside, as its stately halls and beautiful chapels do within. The whole path up was trodden into steps by the feet of the thousands of pious devotees of every rank, who have ascended it for centuries. The monastery is very rich in statues and pictures, many of which are works of very superior merit. A few poor cripples and beggars perpetually hover round it, to beg alms of the pilgrims.

At Kenty, which we reached the next day, begins the manufacturing district, which extends from Galicia through Austrian Silesia, into Prussia, almost to the Giant Mountains, and which produces an immense quantity of linens, woollens, calicoes, &c. There are a hundred and forty weavers at Kenty, but the cloth manufactured there is coarse, and only intended for the Galician peasants. That of Biala is much finer. In Biala there are some houses in which a hundred looms are constantly kept going; that of the seven brothers Bartelt, for instance, whose father is now dead. They are all married, and all have children, so that if the children stick to the business as their fathers have done, the company will consist of at least thirty cousins. One of the brothers is established as an agent at Pesth, another at Brünn, a third at Breslau, and a fourth at Cracow.

Biala and Bielitz form one town, and contain together 10,000 inhabitants. It is quite a modern place, and most of the inhabitants can remember the time when field and forest covered the ground now occupied by crowded streets.

The principal market for the wares of Biala and Bielitz, is Pesth. Some of the manufactories annually send thither from four thousand to five thousand pieces of cloth. Some of the larger ones have their own agents at Pesth. The Jews, however, contract for the produce of the other manufactories, and buy the cloth while it is yet unwoven. The best and finest wool comes from Bohemia and Austria, the worst from Hungary, and that of middling quality from Galicia. The colours used are chiefly English.

Much as the prosperity of these districts has upon the whole increased of late years, yet many complaints are made by the smaller spinners, weavers, fullers, dyers, &c., that they are oppressed and crushed by the great capitalists and manufacturers. They all date the beginning of their misfortunes from the year 1825, though on what account I know not.

A walk among the houses in the charming little town of Biala, possesses many features of great interest. The state of the manufacture is different in every house, and in each the work is at a different stage of its progress. In one the inhabitants are spinning, in another weaving, in another fulling, in another roughing, in another dying; but everywhere all is activity, bustling, and industry. Every one has introduced little improvements into his machinery, as far as his means allow. One moves his machine with water, another with horses, another with only his own hands and feet. One works with ten apprentices, another only with the members of his own family. Here a poor old widow spins a few threads to earn herself a scanty subsistence, there a great capitalist keeps his thousand spinning-wheels going at once. In one place we find the Jews busied with the bales of wool which they have received from Pesth, in another filling their magazines with the produce of the German looms, in another chaffering with the manufacturers about cards and colours. All these sights and sounds apprize the traveller from Russia, that he has left the agricultural districts of the east, for the manufacturing countries of the west.

I mentioned above a very interesting class of productions, for which Biala and Bielitz are not less famous throughout Galicia than for their

AUSTRIAN SILESIA.

...nufactories, I mean the pretty girls of Biala. They appeared to ...ectly deserving of their reputation, and not only graceful and ... to look on, but, moreover, intelligent, industrious, and well ... . They are sought after very much in Galicia, as teachers, ...ses, housekeepers, and upper servants. Their beauty and superior ...n make them everywhere welcome; "a Biala servant-girl is often ...lucated than a Polish noble's wife," said a Biala patriot to me once. ...f them go to Russia, and their serving career often terminates in a ...tch with some Russian officer or Polish noble. Almost in every ...e entered in Biala, we heard of some daughter who was a comfort-...sewife in Warsaw, Breslau, Cracow, or Lemberg. The dress of ...a women is gay and becoming, and at the same time neat and un-...ng. They wear blue aprons, black gowns, white handkerchiefs, ...w-white hoods, from which hang down behind two long pieces of ... striped linen.

...erly Biala and its neighbourhood, including all the pretty girls ...ced, belonged to the family of Prince Shulkovski. Now this noble ...as only the monopoly of all the brandy and beer sold at Biala.

AUSTRIAN SILESIA.

... we drove over the bridge from Biala to Bielitz, we reflected with ...easure that after a long separation, we were now again re-enter-...; wide extent of variously peopled countries, which is termed the ...'s fatherland.

...iece of Germany which we were now about to traverse, is thorough-...an only in its town life. In the open country, the Germanic and ...an races are mixed. The nobility are, indeed, all of German ...n, and many villages are entirely German, but the Poles have ... predominance. Many German villages have Polish masters, and ...a. How long the races have been thus mixed, cannot be precisely ...d, but Tacitus speaks of "Germans inhabiting the countries near ...ces of the Vistula, who are closely connected and intermixed, ... Sarmatians; it is strange that having been so long intermixed, ...ie two races has not by this time absorbed or expelled the other."

... market-day at Skotshau, and the peasants were pouring in from ...ntains and plains around, to buy the produce of the iron and ...anufactories; for at Skotshau weaving is as busily carried on, ...ala and Bielitz, and a new branch of industry is also followed, ...the smelting of iron.

...curious to observe how uniformly the wolf disappears with the ...ace. Galicia is full of wolves, particularly the eastern part, but ...a, particularly in Western Silesia, which contains more Germans ...Poles, the wolf disappears almost entirely. In the villages of the ...a mountains, it is the custom for the killer of a wolf to take the ...ound from house to house, and receive at each a little present, of ...l of flour, or a piece of bacon, or a little loaf. He afterwards ...he head, and receives a ducat for it from the government.

... was formerly governed by almost as many separate and inde-... sovereigns, as it now contains great nobles. Skotshau was the ...f one of these petty monarchs, who were called dukes, and a ... of traditions are still preserved respecting a certain Duchess

Lucretia of Skotshau. These dukes, however, although sovereign princes, were so little respected, that a Silesian town once took the liberty of apprehending one of these potentates for sundry acts of roguery of which he had been guilty, and the result was that his highness was executed by the sturdy burghers as a common criminal. It is strange how completely all these princely families have died away, to make room for the enlargement of the houses of Austria and Russia.

The Vistula (*Weichsel*), whose sources lie about four miles from Skotshau, consists at its source of two separate rivers, the Black and White Vistulas, which unite at the village of Weichsel. Between Skotshau rises a little chain of hills, which separates the valley of the Vistula from that of the Oder.

Teschen, like the whole country round it, is pleasing and indeed beautiful in appearance. Its old castle rises abruptly from a projecting rock on the banks of the Olsa, and the cheerful little city lies grouped around it, on both sides of the river. It is partly Polish and partly German in architecture. This town is said to be a thousand years old. The history of its origin runs briefly thus: Three Silesian dukes lost their way hunting in the wild forests of the Beskids, which then covered these now smiling and prosperous lands. Exhausted with fatigue, and almost dying of hunger and thirst, they at length were all found again by their retinues, at a spring in the forest. In grateful recollection of this fortunate termination of their sufferings, they determined at this spring to build a "cheerful city for contented men, and to call it Tieszem, 'we rejoice.'" This spring is still pointed out to the curious at Teschen.

We visited the old castle by moonlight, on the evening of our arrival. Part of this castle is new, but of a portion the antiquity ascends far beyond any existing record. On one side stands a sexagonal tower, said to date from heathen times, and once to have been a heathen temple. From this point we enjoyed a beautiful view of the moonlit landscape, the quiet town, and the gently splashing waves of the Olsa at our feet. The castle is the property of one of the archdukes, and it is said that his steward, who has *carte blanche* as to its entire management, means to raze the castle to the ground, and to convert the hill into a promenade for the inhabitants of Teschen. He has already begun the operation, in spite of the remonstrances of many lovers of antiquarian relics.

The most remarkable thing in Teschen is its Protestant church and congregation. The greater part of the population of Silesia, as of other parts of Austria is Catholic, but the Reformation had many zealous adherents here from the first, and Teschen and its neighbourhood contains no fewer than 10,000 Protestants. The lofty steeple of their church forms a prominent feature in the view of Teschen, from whatever point it is seen. In the whole Austrian empire this is the only Protestant house of prayer which is dignified with the name of a church, and is allowed a steeple and the use of bells. The inhabitants of Teschen received this privilege, on which they set no little value, from Joseph II. When the great bell rings on Sunday morning, the Protestants of all the neighbouring country come pouring in, red stocking'd and gaily attired, winding in long processions towards their church.

Among the nobility of Austrian Silesia, the two most numerous families are those of Haugwitz and Martinglott. So much so, that if you meet a nobleman, you may almost lay an even wager that he is usually known by one or other of these two names. Larich, Arko, and Bäss are also great names in this part of the world. A Count Larich is the greatest landowner in Austrian Silesia; his income is estimated at 400,000 florins. He is an active, benevolent, enterprising man, universally loved and respected. His estates are the best managed in Silesia, and his wool stands in high repute in the fairs of Breslau and Brünn, while the spirit from his distilleries is famed far and wide in Moravia for its purity and strength. He has founded many cloth, calico, and other manufactories, and has opened large coalmines on his land. Happy the country whose rich men thus employ their capital!

The next day we crossed the remainder of Silesia and entered Moravia. It was All Saints' Day, and the pretty country was sprinkled all over with white mantled women, hastening to church. Although it was the 1st of November, the landscape was so smiling and beautiful, that we could well understand how Austrian Silesia should be a land of promise to the Breslau students, who are as fond of it, as those of Göttingen are of the Harz mountains, those of Heidelberg of the Odenwald, those of Munich of the Tyrol, and those of Leipzig of Saxon Switzerland.

MORAVIA.

THE KUHLANDL.

MORAVIA has certainly extended itself on this side beyond its proper boundaries, and appropriated to itself a portion of the Oder valley, whereas that of the Morava alone rightfully belongs to it. It stretches out a long arm between the old duchies of Troppau and Teschen, severing them from one another, and touching on the Prussian territory. The sources of the Oder, therefore, rise on Moravian ground.

In this district of Moravia, the Archduke Charles is the great lord of the soil. To him belongs Mistek, the frontier town between Moravia and Silesia, as well as many other towns and villages near; for him the huge beams and planks of the Moravian forests move down the Straponiza to the Oder; to him the peasants far around pay their tribute or Robbot of unrewarded labour.

In the church at Freiberg, the town which we reached after leaving Mistek, we saw an altar picture which, coming from the East, struck us with a pleasant sense of having entered a land of humanity and Christian charity. An old peasant was represented as being conveyed to heaven by seraphs, while other friendly angels were taking from him his spade and rake, and winged genii were drawing the plough in his stead. In Poland and Russia, no one ever thinks of picturing to the oppressed peasant the consoling hope of a land of repose in the vista of futurity.

Towards evening we reached the town of Neutitschein, or Novy Gitshin, as the Moravians call it, far-famed throughout Galicia for its excellent little carriages or Neutitshenken, which I have already endeavoured to describe. Neutitschein contains 7000 inhabitants, and lies in the so-called Kuhländl (cowland), a country inhabited entirely by thriving Germans, and flowing, if not with honey, at least with milk. It is the only part of Moravia rich enough in cattle to export butter and cheese. The inhabitants of this district have so improved their breed of cattle, by crossing it with those of Tyrol and Switzerland, that the Kuhländl now carries on a considerable trade with Poland and Russia in cows and oxen.

But it is not by means of this trade in cattle that the natives of the Kuhländl have exercised their chief influence on the world beyond their valleys. Kuhländl was the cradle of the wide-spread sect of the Moravian brothers, in whom the Herrnhuters and Quakers of other lands had their origin. Fulnek, a small town in the Kuhländl, was the principal stronghold of this sect, who, driven from their native land, afterwards founded a second Fulnek near Leeds, in England.

The whole central part of Moravia, a fertile country inhabited by the Slavonian race, is called the Hanna. Strictly speaking, this term originally included only the land on each side of the little river Hanna, but it is now used for all the wide district around Weisskirch, Prossnitz, Olmütz, Kremsier, and Wishau. It is a very fertile and perfectly flat piece of country. Throughout Moravia, the inhabitants of the plains are of Slavonian, those of the hills and mountains of German race. Simple as this at first seems, it is astonishing how complicated is the classification and distribution of the Moravian population; how various are the different subdivisions of the Slavonian and German races, and how irregularly these are intermixed, without ever being blended together, for however inextricably entangled the different threads of the variegated texture may be, they always remain distinct and separate.

The country round Weisskirchen, is beautiful and fertile; producing an abundance of wheat, hops, and wine, and fifteenfold of grain. "The people here," said our host at Weisskirchen, "are rough and barbarous like all the *Hannaken*. The richness of their land does not inspire them with that gratitude to God, and that benevolence and charity to man, which ought to be its effect. Neither do they endeavour to bring up their children with care, and they are unwilling to have schools in their villages. Their prosperity only increases their natural pride and obstinacy, and their strength is oftenest shown in fighting and quarrelling; indeed I think the very twigs in the Hanna fields, make better rods than those of any other country!"

The town of Weisskirchen is built in the same way as all the other Moravian towns. The houses are of tolerably equal height, and in the inner part of the town, each house is fronted by a projecting piazza, which joins that of its neighbour, so that they form long arcades edging the streets. These broad and beautiful covered walks, are called "*die Lauben,*" or "*Loben.*" This mode of building is quite Moravian, and is used throughout the country.

Our way from Weisskirchen to Leipnik, lay through a lovely country. Before us, stretched far into the horizon, the broad, open, fertile, plain, sown with smiling villages, and through it wound along the pleasant little stream of the Betsha. Behind us lay the hills of the Kuhländl, and on the horizon rose the nearest summits of the Carpathians, crowned with picturesque ruins. A white thick morning vapour yet covered the valley, above which arose majestically the stately pile of Helphinstein.

The race of the Helphinsteins has long been extinct, and their castle and estates belong now to the Dietrichsteins, who, with the Lichtensteins, the Hartensteins, and two or three other Steins, are the greatest people of Moravia, and own nearly half its soil. The serfs in this part of Moravia, usually work one or two days *Robbot*, in the week, for their masters. "The master may flog his serf to the amount of twelve blows," said one of my informants, "but he must first state his reasons to the nearest magistrate, and it may cost a man a deal of trouble if he punish his peasant unjustly, for here the serf is protected by the law as well as the master."

In this respect Moravia appears to be a kind of land of transition between Russia and Germany. The farther west we proceed, the more circumscribed becomes the dominion of the rod. In Russia the peasant is continually flogged, without so much as knowing why. In Moravia it costs the master some trouble to flog him. In Austria the peasant is not flogged unless he has positively broken the law. In Bavaria and Wurtemberg, he is not flogged at all.

The Emperor Joseph II. wished to make the Moravian peasants entirely free, and he caused contracts to be drawn up between the lords and the serfs of different estates; but his death prevented the fulfilment of his beneficent designs.

OLMUTZ.

The great central road which traverses Moravia from east to west, would doubtless have been drawn right through the centre of the country, had not peculiar circumstances rendered Olmütz the central point of the commerce and population of Moravia. In order to pass through this town, the road rises out of the valley, up a barren range of hills, crowned with fir and pine forests. The view from these hills has little that is pleasing. The villages are built of pine wood, and, as we ascended on our way, a cold November wind was blowing round the heights, and snow already covered the valleys here and there. We seemed to have left the cheerful valleys of Moravia, for the barren and dreary plains of Poland. But it did not last long; towards noon we again descended the hills, and the forests were now and then lit up by sunshine. Here and there glimpses were displayed of the verdant meadows and smiling plains beyond, and at length the broad and beautiful valley of the March lay spread out before us, in the midst of which rose the picturesque town of Olmütz. The view was here pleasing and interesting. The town is divided into three parts, the convent of Raab, with the houses round it, on the right hand side, the old town on the left, and the cathedral with all the handsomest buildings in the middle. The rocks upon which the town is built, here and there reveal themselves in their bare and rugged nakedness; for in some quarters of the town, this rocky basis forms the foundation of the houses, and the pavement of the streets. The cellars of the Olmütz citizens are all hollowed out of the rock, and are, therefore, particularly cool and dry. The situation of the town is safe from attack, for, in case of danger, the whole surrounding country could be laid under water, while Olmütz would remain high and dry upon its rocky basis.

We paid our friendly host of the Eagle, in the market-place at Olmütz, a sincere compliment upon the beauty of his native city. "Yes, yes," he replied, as he set down before us a bottle of good Carlovitz wine, with a plateful of Klobank nuts and Reschner pears; "yes, our *Holomutz* is a stately place. The Emperor Maximus, its founder, would be delighted if he could see how the town has prospered and improved since his time. The streets are clean and well paved, the houses solid and airy; and though the town is built in the Gothic style, it is not dark and dirty like so many old towns, and though regular and handsome, it is not monotonous and unvaried like so many new ones. The people, too, are handsome, lively, and good-humoured. You come from Russia, gentlemen? I see it by your furs and caps. I have been in Russia and Poland too; I know the countries well, but I am glad to have returned hither. The people there are not fond of the Germans; every thing there is so gray, so dull, so rough, so unvaried. Here in Moravia we have sunshine and cheerfulness, bright ribbons to our hats, and red cheeks to our faces. Come here, Hannah! Look at my wife, gentlemen. Is she not a pretty specimen of Moravian physiognomy? And there are plenty like her here."

The hostess of the Eagle was, indeed, the very beau ideal of Moravian beauty. The grace, freshness, warmth, and naïveté of the women of this country have an irresistible charm to the traveller from the cold north. Olmütz seemed to have a plentiful supply of pretty girls and women, for every moment a pair of bright blue eyes and rosy lips, and a slender graceful figure tripped past our window.

The prince bishop of Olmütz is the wealthiest, grandest, and most powerful lord in Moravia, and one of the most richly-endowed prelates in the Austrian empire. His yearly income nearly amounts to half a million of florins. He lives in great splendour, and keeps open house to a great number of guests. When we saw his palace, the prince bishop, attended by many other prelates, was just taking a drive in a carriage drawn by four magnificent horses, preceded by haiducks in splendid liveries running on before. The palace of the prince bishop, where he keeps up a truly regal state, is in the middle of the town. He maintains a body-guard of twenty-four picked men, who wear black and red uniforms and high bearskin caps. In summer he resides in the beautiful little town of Kremsier, in the middle of the fertile Hanna, seven miles from Olmütz. He possesses a magnificent palace there, with choice libraries, a fine cabinet of natural history and mathematics, the most beautiful gardens and parks, and a splendid orangery. He keeps up another smaller body-guard of eighteen men at Kremsier. This prelate seldom visits Vienna; his journeys are chiefly confined to the road between Olmütz and Kremsier; in May he sets out to the beautiful shades of Kremsier, in October he returns to the regal splendour of Olmütz. Thus it has been for centuries that these holy men have passed their luxurious and uneventful lives, beloved and revered by their vassals, screened from all worldly cares and troubles by a revenue of half a million, welcomed with fêtes and balls by the Austrian officers of the Olmütz garrison in autumn, and greeted with flowers and music by the inhabitants of the Hanna in spring. Truly an enviable position! Austria is the only country, whose government allows of such regal state in her subjects. The sons and brothers of the emperors, are often brought up to the church in the hope of catching some of these rich clerical prizes. The last archbishop of Olmütz was the Archduke Rudolph. He did not, however, live as comfortable a life as the present prelate. He was, on the contrary, the complete slave of his attendants, who enriched and enjoyed themselves, while he ventured to do nothing without their leave. He was a weak and sickly hypochondriac, did not dare take an extra spoonful of soup without his physician's permission, and lived in continual fear of death, and " sure enough" the result justified his apprehensions, for death carried him off at last in spite of all his precautions. The good heart of this weakminded prelate, for he was good-hearted at bottom, is preserved in a silver vase in the subterranean vaults of the Olmütz cathedral, and over it is placed his red cardinal's hat. In death as in life, the head is wanting between the worthy bishop's hat and his heart.

One of the most curious public buildings of Olmütz is the Trinity Column, in the middle of the upper market-place. It is a monument "erected to the honour of the Divine Trinity" (*deo triune veroque*), and is so strange a building that it is difficult to give a good idea of it on paper. Eight rows of steps, containing eight steps each, lead up to eight doors, opening into a small eight-sided chapel. This chapel is surrounded with a grating, to which cling stone angels holding lanterns. Above the chapel rises a sort of obelisk or pyramid, to the height of 114 feet. Groups of stone figures of bishops, saints, and angels, are clustered in astonishing abundance on the insides of this pyramid. At the top is a large simple three-cornered stone, upon which stands an angel who holds up a cross, surmounting a large golden ball. The whole is beautifully sculptured, and most elaborately carved and ornamented, but the style has such a fantastic Chinese quaintness about it, that it is strange how any one could ever think it suitable to the noble simplicity of Christianity. Such obelisks are, however, common in all the towns of Moravia, and are all built in the same elaborate and fantastic style. They are erected upon different occasions of rejoicing, such as the visit of an emperor, or the termination of some epidemic disease, plague, or cholera.

The open places of Olmütz are large and cheerful, and the numerous springs and fountains of the town are very tastefully built, and are a great ornament to it. The worst of it is that they give very bad water; and in order to get a better supply, it has been found necessary to bore an Artesian well. A hundred and sixty thousand florins, and six years' labour, have been expended without leading to any result; and though the well is now carried to a depth of eighty fathoms, nothing but dry barren rocks have yet been found. The undertaking, however, is still persevered in.

We drank tea on the last evening of our stay at Olmütz with a Russian family, who were anxious to make our acquaintance, because they heard that we were just come from Russia. They had left their native country for the first time, and intended to spend the winter in Italy, for the benefit of the lady's health, and in the spring to have a consultation of physicians at Vienna, to determine what watering-place should be visited in the summer. They were full of wonder and admiration of the many cultivated, well-educated people, neat dwellings, and cheerful pleasant towns, which they found in the country. I assured them that although a German, I was myself surprised, for I had never heard any description of Moravia half so favourable as it appeared to me to deserve. My Russian gentleman could not get over the indignation he felt at seeing so many pretty, tidy, well-taught girls, working so hard as they appeared to do. " Why these are all young ladies," said he, " and yet what heavy burthens they carry; what hard work they endure. In my country a horse would not be so hardworked as one of these pretty girls is here. I think the Germans must be a hard-hearted nation." " An industrious one, you should rather say," I replied. " In Germany, labour extends higher and cultivation lower than with you, and those girls, who, if Russians, would sit with their hands before them all day, are here obliged to use them. That is no hardship."

" I would allow you to be in the right, if it were only a question of men, but to use girls, and pretty, tidy girls, in this way, is really shameful. I saw a number of young laundresses standing together in the market-place to-day, and every one was so slender, so graceful, so pretty—but, good Heavens! what loads they had to carry! I only wonder they do not all grow crooked and crabbed, instead of continuing so straight, so cheerful, and so merry, in spite of what they endure."

"Labour," I replied, "is here no disgrace. It is partly a necessity, for there are here no enslaved working-classes, upon whose shoulders all hardship and all labour may be thrust; it is partly the nature of Germans to be industrious. Even the wealthy and great among us are not idle; therefore those below them have no example of luxurious do-nothingness before them, to render toil distasteful."

"Ah, if these pretty girls were to come to Russia, we would soon relieve them of their burdens. I wonder they do not all emigrate."

"Yes, if the whole population of Olmütz, all its talented men and beautiful women, were suddenly put down in the middle of Russia, there would be a great change in their condition. Many powers, which in the superabundance of talent are here overlooked, would there find plenty of occupation. Even those who are here reckoned second-rate men, would there be eagerly sought after. The men of most intelligence would rise to the administration of provinces; the prosperous citizens would become nobles; all would advance in rank. The pretty, industrious young washerwomen, servant-girls, and sempstresses, would become the wives of captains and colonels, and would have plenty of servants to do all their work."

"Ah, how happy we would make them in Russia."

"Well, Cathrinel, what do you think of the Russian general's remarks?" said I to the chambermaid of the inn, later in the evening. She was a fresh, handsome girl, neatly dressed, with gold earrings in her ears, and the manners of a lady, and yet was active and bustling in her vocation. "Why really I don't know," she replied carelessly, in her Austrian dialect, which lent an indescribable comic humour to her words. "I'm quite satisfied. One may be satisfied if one has but bread to eat. I live well, I sleep soundly, I'm always in good health, I get up early, and work every day in the week and all day long. Strangers give me a *batzerl* now and then, and of a Sunday one rests and spends one's money. Good night, gentlemen; to-morrow I'll remember the coffee and the fresh fruit. Good night."

THE HANNA.

We would willingly have spent some time among the cheerful and contented citizens of Olmütz, but the next morning we were again driven onwards by our inexorable Wenzel. The largest town between Olmütz and Brünn, is Prossnitz, but it has not the pleasant, handsome, and animated appearance of the first-named town. We noticed a peculiar species of hollow ostentation at Prossnitz, which was quite new to us. Those houses, namely, which were only one story or two stories in height, had another false story added, in the shape of a front wall, with nothing behind it. So far was this carried, that these false walls had not only windows, but even false painted blinds. This ridiculous kind of ostentation seemed to be universally prevalent at Prossnitz.

We determined to spend the night in a little village called Dreisitz, in the midst of the Hanna plains, and if possible to obtain some knowledge of the country and its inhabitants, from what we might see there. Accordingly we drove up to the village inn, and entered the large parlour, where twenty or thirty *Hannaken*, all stout, sturdy, strong built men, sat at different tables; they were almost all drest in red and white caps, yellow trousers, and short fur jackets. Two of them seemed to be quarrelling desperately; they were scolding and swearing at each other, I could not well make out why. One of them sat still at his table the whole time, while the other went storming about the room, beating the walls and doors with his fists. None of the bystanders meddled in the noisy discussion, but all appeared to await a personal combat with a kind of grave satisfaction. I wished the landlord to interfere and stop the row, but he said that would be an impertinence which he dared not venture upon. Their language was very abusive, but yet they appeared to avoid giving any decisive word. "They often abuse one another for whole days together, before they come to blows," said the host; "but when any insulting term is used, which can only be answered with blows, the fight, if it once begins, is as lasting and as furious as the wordy strife which preceded it. They often quarrel for weeks, before it comes to a crisis, but when they do fight, one of the two is often left dead on the field."

We were glad to escape from the noise and confusion of the common parlour, to our host's comfortable room, where over some hot egged beer, he favoured us with his remarks upon the Hanna and its inhabitants.

The real Hanna, in which we now were, is only five (German) miles long, and extends from Wishau to Kremsier. The villages here are large and numerous, and the population abundant. As the law of primogeniture is scrupulously observed among the peasantry, the younger sons generally emigrate in great numbers, and the Hannaken may be found scattered about as tradesmen, mechanics, and labourers, all over the Austrian and Russian empires. In autumn they go into the Archduchy of Austria, to work at the harvest. They traverse Hungary in great numbers, as smiths and masons, and may be found in all parts of Germany selling leather and wooden wares, knitted and woven garments, and dried fruits. Those among them who vend medicines for men and animals, often travel into Siberia with their goods.

The country of the Hannaken is one of the most fertile in the world, corn yielding easily ten, twelve, or fifteen fold. The chief article of cultivation is wheat, but their mills are so good, that even their rye bread is among the whitest and most pleasant kinds eaten anywhere. They have excellent horses, of which they take great care. They are all free owners of their land, but they are obliged to work one or two days Robbot in the week, for their lords. Every peasant is obliged to use a cart, two horses, and a man, and maid servant, in the landlord's service, while he works for him. A thriving peasant of the Hanna, has generally about 120 bushels of seed, six or eight horses, eight or ten cows, no oxen, from 100 to 150 sheep, and a good herd of "bristly beasts," as they call their pigs. The Hannaken are divided into the different classes of whole peasants (such as I have just described), three-quarter peasants, and half-peasants; the latter are of course proportionably less wealthy.

The greatest landowner in the Hanna is Prince Metternich, and next to him comes the Prince of Lichtenstein, who is master of ninety-nine great estates in the Austrian Empire, thirty-three of which are in Moravia.

The Hannaken are passionately fond of music and dancing, like most Slavonian races. Their national songs and melodies, which are for the most part very old, are almost all in the minor key, the prevailing characteristic of all Slavonian music. Most of the writers who have described Moravia, agree with Hanke and Lichtenfeld, in calling the *Hannaken* " upon the whole good men, faithful subjects, and devout Christians." This, however, is somewhat unmeaning, and leaves but a vague and often an untrue impression, and might be applied with equal correctness to half the nations of Europe. As being the wealthiest owners of the best land, the Hannaken are at once the proudest and most hospitable among the inhabitants of Moravia.

The next morning we pursued our journey through the Hanna. The young corn rose green, fresh, and flourishing on every side of us, and the whole country looked like one unbroken cornfield. The luxuriant growth of the wheat, had scarcely left room for a single tree.

It is curious to observe how the most trifling customs of Vienna are aped throughout the Austrian provinces. The sausage dealers, for instance, seem all over the empire, to be cut out after the pattern of those of the capital. They are all little lads of ten or twelve years old, and carry their sausages in little boxes strung to wooden sticks. They also carry a metal vessel full of hot water, which they keep boiling in the same way that the Russians do their tea-water. When a customer wants a sausage, they immediately heat it for him in this hot water. All the nations ruled by the Austrian sceptre have accustomed themselves to delight in these Vienna sausages, which are now to be met with in every little town till you reach the Russian or Turkish frontier. The sausage may not inaptly be considered the savoury bond that unites the heterogeneous parts of the great monarchy.

AUSTERLITZ.

Behind Wischau, the country rises into a low chain of hills, which forms the boundary of the real Hanna. After crossing these hills, we reached those plains rendered for ever memorable in history, by the events of December, 1805. Neu Rausnitz is the first place which trembled beneath the thunder of the cannon of Austerlitz. It was plundered by the Cossacks, and burnt by the French.

The town of Austerlitz had in fact nothing to do with the battle named after it. It lies more than a (German) mile from the scene of conflict, and its church towers cannot even be seen from the battle-field. The people of Rausnitz declare that the battle was only named after Austerlitz, to please Prince Kaunitz, to whom the place belonged, and who had built a fine castle there. It would have been better to have named the conflict after the more important city of Brünn. We hoped to have found some of the old veterans of Austerlitz at Rausnitz, but the last of them had died the year before. An old man at Brünn informed us, that some months before the battle, an extraordinary omen had been observed. The whole neighbourhood, namely, had been covered with a shower of hailstones, that lay half an ell deep on the ground, and the little river Ponawka, generally an insignificant brook, had risen so high as to threaten Brünn with an inundation. He had said at the time that this portended some great event, although he did not exactly foresee that the hail was to be the forerunner of cannon-balls, or that the deluge was to consist of French soldiers. Another assured us, pointing to a little chapel upon a neighbouring hill, that the effigy of the Virgin Mary which it contained, had been seen to weep bitterly after the battle. This chapel had before been wooden, but it was now rebuilt of stone, and was the scene of many pilgrimages. On the road near Rausnitz, we noticed two old trees, splintered and crippled by the bullets and cannon-balls of the great battle. These trees are, however, covered with fresh vegetation, and are the only things which bear any traces of the conflict. Every thing else has returned to its old condition. Those hills of which, on the battle day, every thicket, every mound, and every bush was a matter of life and death, have now returned to their old insignificance. The field is covered with luxuriant corn; the graves of the warriors have been given over again to the plough. No monument of any kind has been erected on the field of battle. Not far from the field of Austerlitz, however, a monument has been erected to commemorate an event of a very different nature from that of the great carnage of December, 1805. That most paternally beneficent of emperors, Joseph II., while riding through the country on the 19th of August, 1769, saw a poor peasant who was leaning exhausted on his plough, unable to continue his labour. The emperor dismounted, and taking the plough in hand, finished the man's day's task for him. A monument has been erected upon this spot, consisting of a large iron pedestal, upon which is perched an Austrian eagle. On that side of the pedestal which is turned towards the road, the emperor is represented driving the plough; beside him stands the old peasant, and on the other side the emperor's servant, holding his horse.—Beneath is the inscription: "*Josephus II. Semp. Aug. agriculturæ generis humani nutrici honorem deferens hoc in agro sulcum duxit. Die XIX. Augusti, 1769, memoriæ principis incomparabilis ordines Moraviæ hoc monumentum posteris sacrum esse voluerunt,* 1835."

BRUNN.

The city of Brünn, superior now in population and commerce to any other town in Moravia, owe its prosperity, partly no doubt to the activity, industry, and spirit of enterprise, which distinguish its citizens, but partly also to its geographical position. It lies at the southern point of a range of hills, which run out from the Bohemian and Moravian mountains, and at the juncture of two rivers, the Schwarza and the Zwittava. On the south, west, and east, the town is surrounded with a level plain, a position particularly calculated to favour the extension of the city.

The appearance of Brünn is very picturesque and imposing. As we drove towards it from the field of Austerlitz, and beheld the fine old city, lying before us so peacefully and gaily, surrounded with beautiful gardens and cornfields, with its background of distant hills and dark forests, and its centre group of stately spires clustering round the old cathedral; as we saw it thus spread out at our feet, in the midst of a wide and beautiful plain, dotted over with smiling villages, and nestling far away in the woody hills beyond, and stretching its pretty suburbs down to the river banks, our hearts beat with patriotic emotions, and we felt that we were indeed really and truly once more in our own fair native land!

The inns and hotels of Brünn leave the traveller nothing to desire. They would satisfy an Englishman in point of comfort, a Dutchman in point of cleanliness, and a Russian in the variety and abundance of their eatables. As half Russians, and as hungry travellers, we were particularly interested in the latter item, and after doing ample justice to the well-supplied table of our hotel at Brünn, we had only just time for an evening's walk. The city did not appear to us so clean and neat as Olmütz, although by no means a dirty place; and though it has many narrow streets, it contains no fewer than seven large open squares.

The capital of Moravia is of course not wanting in great numbers of those architectural toys to which the Moravians are so partial; springs, fountains, Trinity columns, &c. All the open spaces are decorated with monuments, strange rather than beautiful. In one stands a marble column, " erected, in honour of the Holy Mother of God, the Patroness of the sick, the Consoler of the suffering, the Protectress of the Dead, on the occasion of the great plague in 1680, and renewed in the year 1831, on the occasion of the great cholera." In another a column " erected in honour of the Holy Trinity," and decorated with hundreds of different stone statues like that of Olmütz. Fountains are common in all parts of the town, one of them is very handsome and curious, and is called the "Parnassus" by the inhabitants. It consists of artificial rocks, piled upon one another to the height of fifty feet, forming a large grotto, in the midst of which stands a colossal Hercules, struggling with a three-headed Cerberus. Outside, the rocks are covered with an abundant growth of fresh ivy, which clothes it all the year round in living green. From all the little rifts and niches of the rock, rise stone figures of serpents, lizards, mermaids, naiads, &c., who spout up water to a great height, which falls again into the large basin surrounding the grotto. The whole is surmounted with a female figure, with a crown and sword, representing "the Virgin Mary, the Queen of Nature."

The Franzensberg, the beautiful promenade of the citizens of Brünn, is a projecting eminence of the Petersberg, upon which is built a part of the town, including the Cathedral itself. The Franzensberg was formerly covered with fortifications, but these were razed to the ground by the energetic and popular Count Antony Frederick Mittrowski von Mittrovitz and Nemishl, then Governor of Moravia, and the rocks, after having been made level in several places, were covered with a thin stratum of mould, in which a number of beautiful flowers and shrubs were planted. The hill is now crowned, not with frowning towers, but with green thickets, blooming parterres, and verdant lawns. It commands a lovely prospect over the town and the sea, of waving cornfields and green meadows beyond; but on the north-western side this smiling landscape is broken by a painful object, which is alone sufficient to mingle a feeling of bitterness and melancholy with the pleasing sensations which the rest of the view inspires; this painful object is the Spielberg, with its frowning bastions and gloomy dungeon towers. Here are music, sunshine, gaiety; well-dressed citizens with their wives and children, drinking coffee under the trees, and wandering among the shady walks, enjoying the beauty of the evening:—there opposite are sighs and tears, fetters, and dreary cells; hard-hearted jailers, and suffering patriots; Gonfalonieris, Andryanes, and Pellicos. On the day in question, indeed, I could gaze upon the dark towers of Spielberg with somewhat a lighter heart than I could have done had my visit been less happily timed, for it was the very day on which Imperial clemency had enlarged the last of the Italian captives. With what feelings of delight must the unhappy prisoners have turned their backs upon the hateful house of bondage! With what rapture must they have gazed upon the sunny meadows and blooming gardens of Brünn! What would we have given to have had one of them beside us on the Franzensberg, enjoying with us the delightful scene! This indeed was not possible, for although released from their dungeons, they were still subjected to the strict superintendence of the police. They were to stay some days in Brünn, and then to be conducted to Italy under an escort of *gendarmes*. If even a foreigner never crosses the Alps without eager expectation and enthusiastic delight, with what words can we hope to describe the feelings of these unfortunates, when they behold once more the sunny blue sky of Italy!

A permission to see the interior of the Spielberg is not obtained without some difficulty, and the short time I was likely to remain did not allow of my going through the required formalities. I contented myself, therefore, in the evening, before going to bed, with reading a tolerably full history of the noted fortress, which is supposed to be of greater antiquity than any other part of Brünn. In the earliest chronicles of the city, the Spielberg is spoken of as the *Brünner Burg*, or citadel of Brünn, but it was only in the fourteenth century that the old citadel received the name of the Spielberg or *Mons Lusorius*. What the circumstance was which led to this change of name, is altogether unknown. During the thirteenth, fourteenth, and fifteenth centuries, the Spielberg was the residence of the Margraves of Moravia, and the diets of the country were frequently held within its walls. Like all the castles of the middle ages, it had at all times its dungeons, but it was only in the year 1740 that the building was converted into a state prison, in consequence of its fortifications being deemed insufficient to resist the more formidable means of aggression which modern science has placed at the command of conquerors. The last remnant of the fortifications of the Spielberg were destroyed by the French in 1809.

The Spielberg is used not only for state prisoners, but for all criminals in the Austrian empire, who are condemned to more than ten years imprisonment. The name of Spielberg is as much dreaded in Austria, as that of Siberia in Russia, that of Botany Bay in England, and that of the Bagnes in France. It has lately derived a European notoriety from the memoirs of the Baron von Trenck, and *Le Mie Prigione* of Silvio Pellico. It contains on an average three hundred prisoners, a fourth of whom are women. If we allow an average duration of fifteen years, for the imprisonment of each, and estimate the population of the Austrian empire at 35,000,000, every 100,000 inhabitants furnishes once in every fifteen years, a criminal condemned to more than ten years imprisonment, and every 1,500,000 inhabitants, one annually. This certainly seems a very small proportion.

Great as is the horror which the name of Spielberg inspires in Galicia, Slavonia, Illyria, Bohemia, Bukovina, and Italy, this feeling is certainly not owing to any outrageous severity in the treatment of the prisoners. There are scarcely any subterranean dungeons now. Till 1791 indeed, things were very different there; till that time, the *carcere duro* consisted of deep, dark, underground holes, only four feet square, where the miserable prisoner was laden with chains, placed in solitary confinement, and fed on bread and water. The door to these wretched cells was only four feet high. Good God! with what agony of mind must the unfortunate doomed to such misery, have crept through the narrow opening! Truly the gulf which separates the nineteenth century from all preceding centuries, has never been done justice to by any historian. Such inhuman barbarity as this is happily almost inconceivable to us now, and yet it was only the last generation which abolished these horrors.

The Spielberg—the events which pass within the Spielberg—the prisoners just let out of the Spielberg—the criminals just taken into the Spielberg—this subject occupies two-thirds of all the conversation at Brünn. Even the women over their tea, and the children at play, talk of little else than the Spielberg. One might wish its gloomy towers removed, far from the lively little city, whose gaiety, sunshine, and cheerfulness, must embitter yet more the sufferings of the unhappy inmates, to some dreary desert suitable to the desolate cheerlessness of the odious pile.

The next day, a fine fresh November morning, we set out to see the Lions of Brünn, that is, those among them in which we felt interested. First among these was the convent of the Brothers of Charity. This order is certainly the best and most beneficent of all those which have ever sprung from the bosom of the Catholic church. Austria contains no less than twenty-three of these monasteries, which supply the want of hospitals and other benevolent institutions, to no inconsiderable extent.

The convent, we found, was large and spacious, and the wards for the sick lofty and airy. It is certainly pleasing to see these pious old monks, who were formerly occupied only with idle prayers and mortifications in their solitary cells, now usefully and actively employed as physicians, apothecaries, and nurses. They have renounced the pleasures of the world, but not its cares and labours.

The surgery of the convent was large and well arranged, and its walls and ceiling were decorated like those of a chapel, with pictures of saints and angels. The laboratory was like the cell of an alchymist: dried plants, stuffed crocodiles, snakes, fishes, and elephants' teeth were ranged round the walls. Every thing was, in the highest degree, neat, orderly, and well arranged.

The novices are educated in the monastery, and each monk studies medicine, surgery, or pharmacy, according to his inclination or talents. Many devote themselves to the household duties and management of the convent, and four of them are constantly travelling to collect the voluntary contributions, by which alone the convent is supported. The charitable gifts of the rich, could not easily be devoted to a better purpose. The invalids had all clean beds, and seemed to want for nothing. In one of the rooms we found a monk just performing an operation for the cancer. Not only are sick persons tended in the convent, but medicines and food are daily distributed gratis to the poor in the city.

Of the numerous churches in Brünn, the cathedral and the church of St. James (*die Jacobskirche*) are the most interesting. The latter is one of the finest remains of Gothic architecture we possess.

Brünn is the Manchester* of Austria, the principal seat of its woollen manufactories, and volumes of smoke issuing from lofty chimneys, in all parts of the town, announce the activity of the never resting steam-engines. The leather manufactories are of older date, but by no means of less importance, and among these, the largest and most famous is the Lettmayer manufactory. Its present possessor, who conducts every thing in the name

---

* Qy. Leeds ?

of his widowed mother, is a handsome, agreeable, intelligent young man, and gave us many interesting particulars respecting an article which serves at least half mankind to walk upon. His establishment uses up no less than 20,000 skins a year. In ten years, therefore, he tans the skins of no less than 200,000 oxen, that is four times as many as the whole margravate of Moravia contains. Almost all these skins are brought from Hungary, for the skins of the Polish and Russian oxen are thinner, weaker, and oftener spoilt by insects, than those of the great Hungarian cattle.

At the booksellers' shops of Brünn, we looked over the newest blossoms of Moravian and Tshekhian literature. Though the dialects spoken by the Bohemians and Moravians are different, yet their written language is entirely the same. The numerous elegant new publications in the Tshekhian language, which we saw at Brünn, some of them original productions, and others translations from the French and German, seemed to testify to the existence of a large literary public among the Tshekhs. It is a singular fact that half a dozen new languages and literatures are at present fast springing up and bearing fruit within the Austrian empire, and still more singular, that the government by no means restrains this movement.

We had occasion to rejoice, that the projected railroad from Brünn to Vienna was not yet completed, for if it had been, we should have flown along rapidly to the imperial city on the wings of the mighty magician, Steam, and have seen nothing of the interesting countries that lie between. As it was, we plodded on, the next day, at the same leisurely pace as before, along the good stone road which intersects the vineyards round Brünn. About half a million *Eimers* of wine are annually produced from the vines of Moravia, but this manufacture is only kept up by the high tax upon Hungarian wines. All the vineyards of Moravia would soon be destroyed, if the government were to take off the heavy duty which prevents the importation of the cheaper and better wines of Hungary ; yet I cannot help thinking the government would do well to open the floodgates that would let in the racy tide, for the many thousands who now employ themselves in the manufacture of a sour and detestable beverage, would turn their hands to other branches of industry, more beneficial to themselves and their country.

THE CASTLES OF THE GREAT AUSTRIAN NOBILITY.

The southern part of Moravia is not one of the most uninteresting portions of the Austrian empire. The castles, estates, and palaces of its most distinguished families, are there crowded together in great numbers. This district is now almost entirely German. The most interesting of its old family seats, are Nikolsburg, Eisgrub, and Falkenstein, the dwellings of the Dietrichsteins, the Lichtensteins, and the Bartensteins, which all lie close to one another. Of all the nobilities of Europe, that of Austria has lost least of its old feudal power and splendour, while in culture and refinement it is not behind that of any other country. Humane in his conduct, patriarchal in his habits, unostentatious in his luxury, magnificent in his undertakings, the kind protector of his peasantry, the judicious patron of arts, letters, and manufactures, such is the true old Austrian nobleman; and the castles and estates above mentioned, testify to the truth of the picture.

We were glad to be able to devote a day to the view of these three interesting places, of which Nikolsburg, the seat of the Dietrichsteins, was the first we reached.

The castle of Nikolsburg stands on a hill, at the foot of which lies the town of Nikolsburg, containing 10,000 inhabitants. This town is built in the usual old Moravian style, decorated with statues, fountains, Trinity columns, &c. The citizens of Nikolsburg were formerly subjects to the Dietrichstein family, but one of its heads gave them entire freedom, and endowed them with the right of choosing their own magistrates, saying, that he preferred having free and grateful citizens round him to obsequious and servile vassals. A handsome broad road leads up the hill to the castle, winding through the flower-gardens and orchards which adorn the terraces. The entrance to these gardens is a grand triumphal arch of cast-iron, forty feet high. The gates of the castle itself are massive gloomy old portals. Reaching the first courtyard, we entered a maze of flower-beds, vineyards, ruins, and dwelling-houses, ancient and modern, wild naked rocks, and dainty new buildings, old Gothic portals, and new cast-iron gratings, flung together in strange but not unpleasing confusion. The domestic offices were appropriately decorated, the stables with stone figures of horses, the cowhouses with those of cows, &c. We felt doubtful whether a warder would blow his bugle on the turrets, or a nymph glide from some neighbouring grotto, or a modern dandy usher us into an elegant drawing-room. No one, however, came, till we at length found our way to the *Schlosshauptman*, who politely gave us permission to see the castle, and referred us to the *Zimmerwärtel*. The Zimmerwärtel himself was ill in bed, but his wife brought out a great bunch of keys, and led us into the castle. We were glad to have a woman to show us the place, for women are more talkative, and are also generally better acquainted with the details of a family than men. The comfort and neatness of these insignificant servants of the family surprised and pleased us. They had all spent many years in their present service, the *Schlosshauptman* twenty years, the *Zimmerwärtel* thirty, and his wife forty years. It is the good old patriarchal custom of the Austrian nobles to choose their servants carefully, to keep them long, and to treat them well.

The old woman took us first into the dining-saloon, or as it was here called the eating-room. The floor is inlaid with oak, and the long dining-table is of the same wood, which is used but little in castles of a more recent date. The walls of the great saloon are adorned with animal and flower pieces by the best Dutch masters. Six doors lead out into the immense balcony, which is the largest in Germany, larger even than that of Heidelberg. There is room in this spacious balcony for a grand banquet to all the nobility of Moravia. It projects far beyond the outermost ridge of the castle hill, and commands a lovely view of the rich meadows and cornfields around, which are among the most fertile in Moravia, with here and there the ruins of an old knightly castle, perched upon a craggy eminence.

Leaving the eating-room, we came to the " great sitting-room, where the gentry sit after dinner," said the old woman; for the word grand drawing-room is not used here. Every thing here was being repainted and decorated. "The old Prince Dietrichstein feels himself dying," continued the old woman, "and he is having every thing done up, that at his death, which may God long avert! the next prince, his son, may receive the castle in good condition. Eleven young painters from Italy and Vienna have been working here all the summer."

The Dietrichsteins have always been one of the most distinguished families in Austria, and princes of this house have filled many of the highest offices in the government. Their castle therefore abounds in historical relics and trophies, and in presents from kings and emperors. The "great sitting-room" is decorated with portraits of almost all the Austrian Emperors, and distinguished generals; among the most conspicuous are those of the great Wallenstein, who married a lady of the house of Dietrichstein, and who is represented riding on a fiery bay; of Joseph II. as a boy, playing with his golden chain; and of Maria Theresa, first as a happy wife, then as a crowned empress, and lastly as a sorrowing widow. The portraits of the Dietrichsteins, some as cardinals, others as warriors, others as abbesses, &c., hang among the imperial portraits.

We next entered the Hall of Audience, in which the Princes Dietrichstein are accustomed to give audience to the inhabitants of their subject towns and villages. Few royal palaces contain more magnificent audience chambers. The walls are covered with the choicest Gobelin tapestries, representing the Judgment of Solomon, and scenes from the life of Moses. From the audience chamber we passed through the Spanish room, through a new-fashioned billiard-room, through a library, containing 20,000 volumes, through a museum of natural history, and finally through an armoury. The latter contains arms of every kind, from the most barbarous old weapon to the most complete new-fashioned percussion gun. The walls are covered with hunting pieces. Among the weapons are preserved all the swords which have ever conferred knighthood on the different Dietrichsteins; as well as the great sword with which criminals were executed, and which is kept here, as a sign of the judicial power of the family.

The walls of the castle are nine feet thick; the doors of all the rooms are of massive oak, and the furniture ponderous and old-fashioned. The firescreens are of plaited straw, but are, nevertheless, elegant and strong. The beds in the sleeping-rooms are as large as if they were intended for a whole family to sleep in. The commodes and toilet-cases, are little more than gaily-coloured boxes, stuck upon high pedestals.

The corridors of the house are decorated with the most interesting pictures. One of them represents the celebrated Dietrichstein wedding, and bears the inscription, "*Nuptiæ Dietrichsteinianæ trecentis dapibus affluentissime in ædibus Dietrichsteinianis Vindobonæ* 1515, *concelebratæ.*" At this wedding, at which the Emperor Maximilian, the bosom-friend of the bridegroom presided, the middle tables were occupied entirely by kings and queens, and the side tables by dukes and princes.

The family chapel contains the body of St. Donatus, before which a lamp has been constantly kept burning for two hundred and fifty years. The most magnificent part of the castle is the *Ahnensaal*, containing the portraits of all the Dietrichsteins, as large as life. Among the most interesting is that of the famous Cardinal Dietrichstein, a man of the most distinguished talents and character, the pride of his family. He was the builder of the cathedral of Olmütz, and was in his time one of the most powerful supporters of the Imperial family and of Catholicism in Austria. He solemnized the marriage of three emperors, viz., Matthias, Rudolph, and Ferdinand. He was taken prisoner during the Swedish invasion, and confined in the convent of Nikolsburg close by. While shut up there, he contrived to have an underground passage bored through the rock of the Ahnensaal of his own castle, in whose thick wall he scooped out a little chapel, where he came every morning, to pray for the preservation of his own and the Imperial family. This little chapel is still shown behind his own picture. He afterwards engaged and defeated the Swedes, at the battle of Kalisch. This battle, his subsequent interview with the Emperor Matthias at Kremsier, his triumphal entry into Milan as papal nunciate, his courageous conduct during a storm on the Adriatic Sea, and other prominent scenes of his life, are represented in fresco on the ceiling of the Ahnensaal.

Napoleon Buonaparte spent some time in the castle, just before the battle of Austerlitz. During our passage through the rooms, we had the honour of sitting down upon the same green sofa on which Buonaparte breakfasted on the morning before he set off for Austerlitz. The old woman told us that the emperor had, like ourselves, seen the castle in detail, but that it was "Old Haller" the former Zimmerwärtel, who had shown him the rooms.

We did not visit Falkenstein, the seat of the Bartensteins, for fear of having no time left for Eisgrub. The present Prince of Bartenstein lives entirely at Vienna, and has allowed his castle of Falkenstein to fall into decay. He possesses a better castle near Wagram; and his estates there have been finely manured by Napoleon, as those of Prince Kaunitz have been at Austerlitz.

The way to Eisgrub lies though a beautiful country, full of rich vineyards, cheerful villages, waving cornfields, and swelling hills and dales.

The Lichtensteins form one of the oldest and most distinguished families in Moravia, and the estate of Eisgrub, has been their own during an unbroken succession of two hundred and fifty years. They were, indeed, possessors of it as early as the fourteenth century, but it fell out of their hands afterwards, and was not regained till the reign of Rudolph II. Although Eisgrub is only one of their ninety-nine Austrian estates, it is the usual summer-residence of the head of the family, and its magnificence is worthy of the sovereign rank of the Lichtensteins.

The stairs, the corridors, the concert-rooms, eating-rooms, sitting-rooms, and conservatories, are among the most splendid in Germany. The magnificent orangery, five hundred feet long, contains a forest of nine hundred orange-trees, the largest collection of this beautiful plant, north of the Alps. Many of them have lived under the northern sun for two hundred years. There are also large greenhouses, containing all kinds of rare and curious plants, of different climates, among which are 1500 aloes.

The park of Eisgrub has no equal in Munich, Schwezingen, Worlitz, or Dresden. The river Thaya flows through it; the building of the aqueducts alone, to water the park, cost 200,000 florins. In order to have it well stocked with exotic American plants, the distinguished botanist Dr. Wanderschott, was sent to America, to bring over whatever specimens were likely to grow in this climate. The avenues of Canadian poplars, the groves of plantains, acacias, palm-trees, bananas, and hundreds of other rare and beautiful trees, are arranged in such a manner as to satisfy alike the scientific botanist and the lover of the picturesque. The *points de vue* are marked by beautiful buildings, of which each is a complete masterpiece of this kind. The mosque, for instance, with a minaret to which three hundred and two steps lead up, has been built of freestone, at an expense of a million of florins, a cost for which twenty Turkish villages might have been furnished with good mosques. The Chinese rotunde, the bathing-house, the fishing-hut, the Temple of the Muses, the Hansenburg, and other playthings of the kind, are here all built in the most solid and massive manner, with the most picturesque elegance, and the most elaborate propriety. To see, enjoy, and describe them all, was impossible. The Hansenburg particularly attracted our attention, being a real old knightly castle of the middle ages, of which every part is appropriate and consistent. It is built with towers and turrets like those of the fourteenth century, and the furniture is all genuine, being taken from sundry old knightly castles belonging to the Lichtensteins. This building is shaded by venerable oaks, four hundred years old, and surrounded by a menagerie containing large herds of deer and stags.

One of the lakes in the park forms the boundary between Austria and Moravia; and twenty-six years have already been employed in adorning it. Beautiful groves of trees have been planted on its once naked shores, and islands formed upon it with stately buildings upon them. We next entered a spacious rotunda, the antechamber of the cow-house, and passed through doors of the finest plate-glass, first to the palace inhabited by the cows and oxen, afterwards to that of the merino sheep, who are 1000 in number.

I doubt whether any Roman Grandee of the Augustan age, possessed parks of such regal magnificence as that of Eisgrub. The temple of Apollo and that of the Graces, are masterpieces of architecture. The latter is 150 feet long, supported on Ionic columns, and contains many fine marble statues of mythological and allegorical figures.

The building which marks the entrance into the park from the Austrian side, might well be taken by a stranger for the castle of Eisgrub itself. To describe its cupolas, halls, columns, porticoes, &c., took up three closely-printed pages of Walni's Chronicles of Eisgrub.

The Teimer forest adjoining the park, is surrounded by a wall three (German) miles long. The centre is marked by a building in the form of a Roman triumphal arch, with the inscription,

"Dianæ venatrici ejusque cultoribus
Has tibi, blanda soror Phœbi, sacravimus ædes
Intactus semper crescat tibi lucus honori."

It is intended for a rendezvous for hunting-parties, and is adorned with fine statues of Endymion, Diana, Actæon, Bacchus, &c.

The so-called "*Monument auf der Reisten*" is a good deal similar to the Ahnensaal at Nikolsburg, with this difference, that it is a separate building, standing alone in the park, and that the portraits of the Lichtensteins, which it contains, are statues, not pictures.

We spent the night at the village of Eisgrub. The next day, crossing the boundaries of Moravia, we entered the Archduchy of Austria, and came in sight of the snow-covered summits of the Eastern Alps. We traversed the *Marchfeld*, amid the hissing and screaming of the wild geese, which, since time immemorial, have never ceased upon this plain. Gradually the dark towers of St. Stephen's appeared in the distance, and we passed Jeddlersdorf and the Brigitten-Au. "Here we are!" cried Wenzel at length, as he opened the door, and we stepped out before the "White Lamb," in the Leopoldsvorstadt at Vienna.

In the twenty-five (German) miles of Moravian territory, which we had traversed, we had passed thirteen towns. Moravia and Bohemia contain more towns than all the rest of the Austrian Empire put together. Moravia has twice as many as all Hungary. In Bohemia and Moravia, there is one town to every four square miles, in Austria to every ten, in Galicia to every fifteen, and in Hungary to every seventy. Moravia contains 4000 inhabitants to every square mile; that is, twice as many as Hungary, three times as many as the Tyrol, and four times as many as Dalmatia.

THE END.

C. WHITING, BEAUFORT HOUSE, STRAND.